The Writers

The Writers

Portraits by Laura Wilson

Foreword
Charles McGrath

Introduction
Louise Erdrich

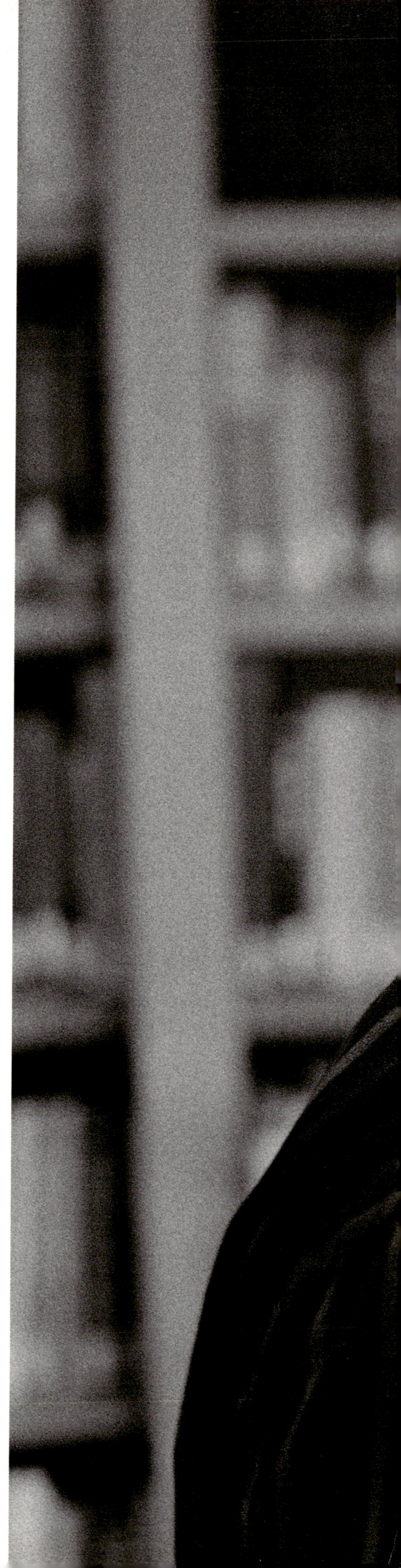

YALE UNIVERSITY PRESS

NEW HAVEN AND LONDON

IN ASSOCIATION WITH THE HARRY RANSOM CENTER
AT THE UNIVERSITY OF TEXAS AT AUSTIN

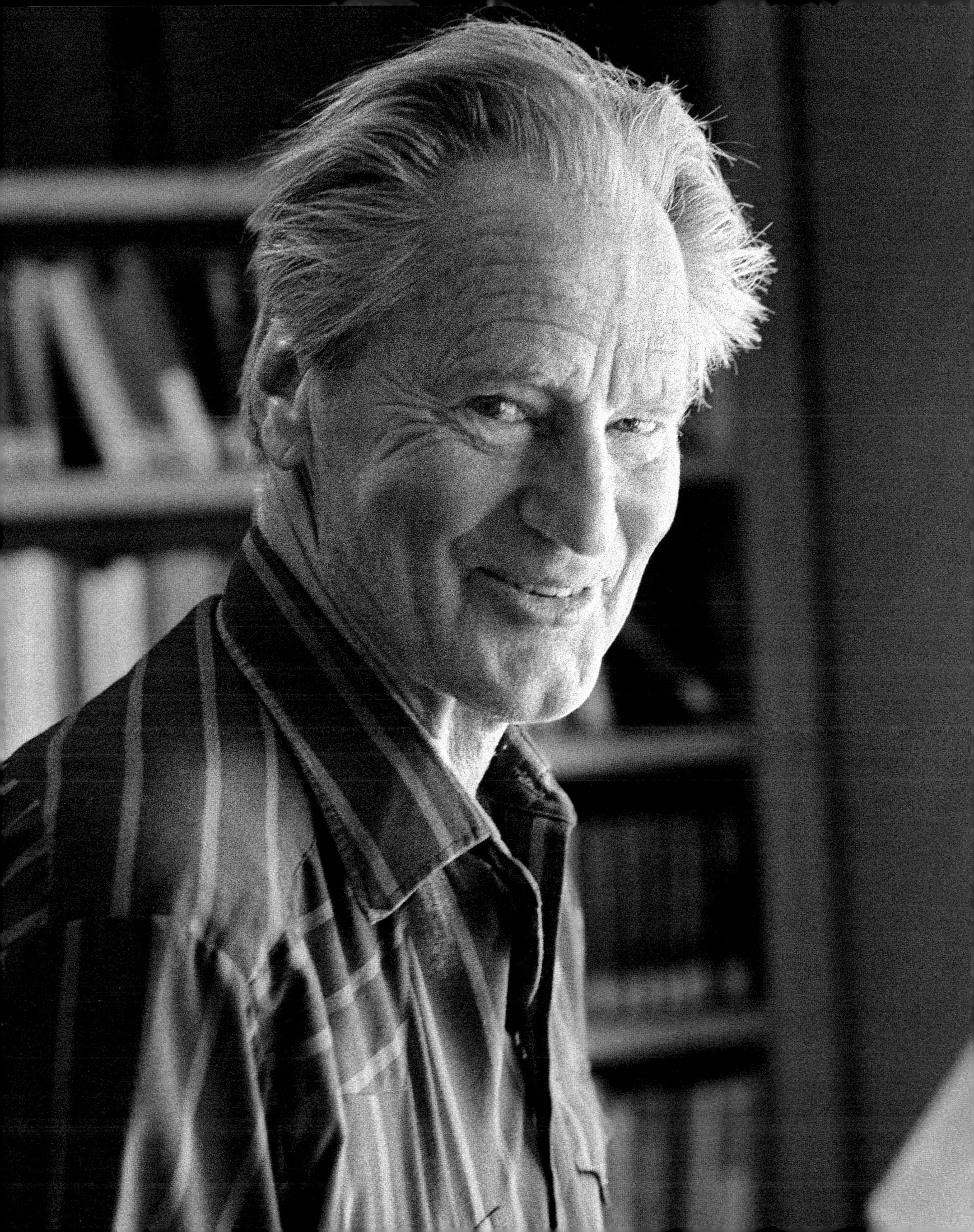

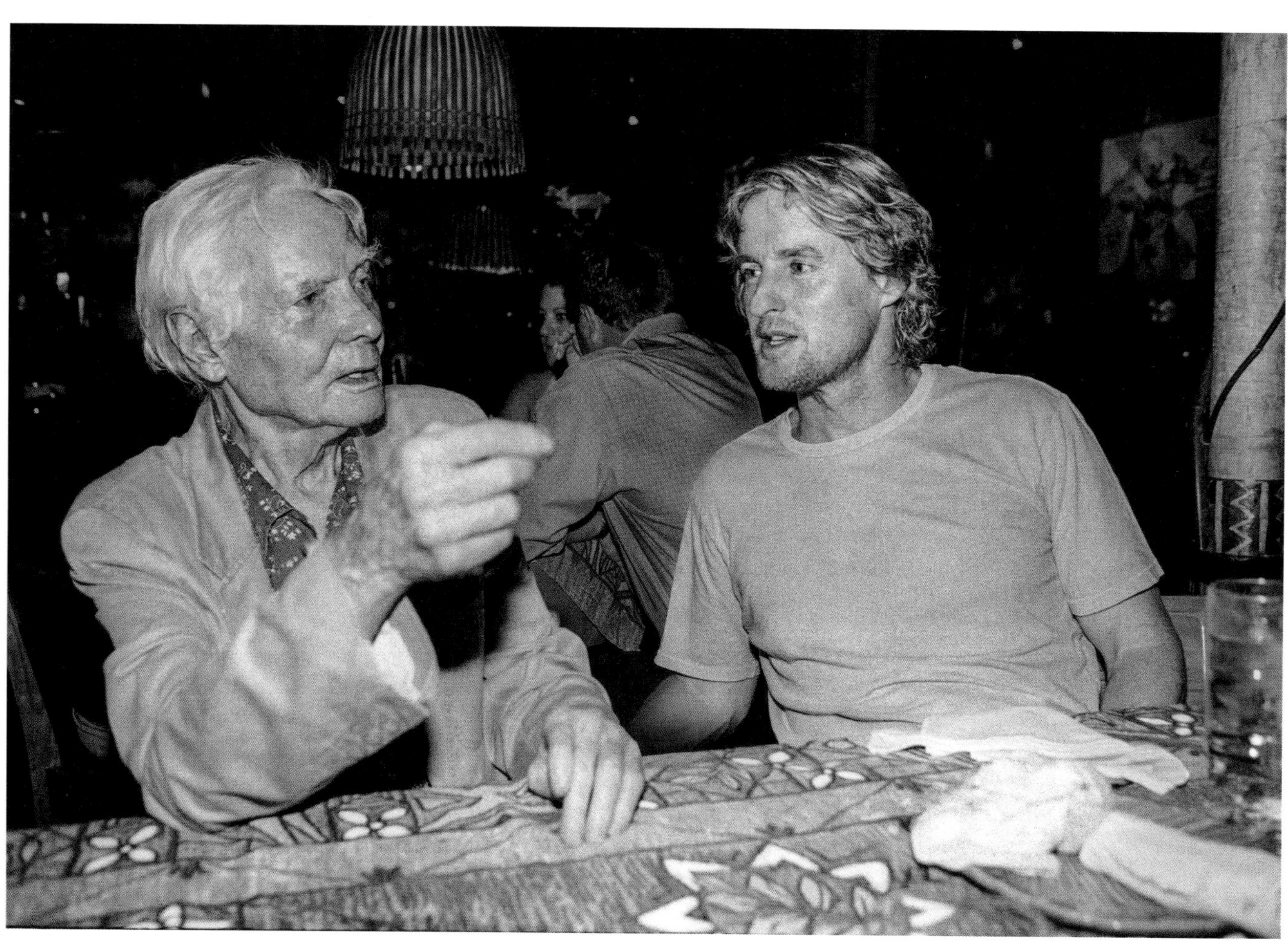

This book is for my son

OWEN CUNNINGHAM WILSON

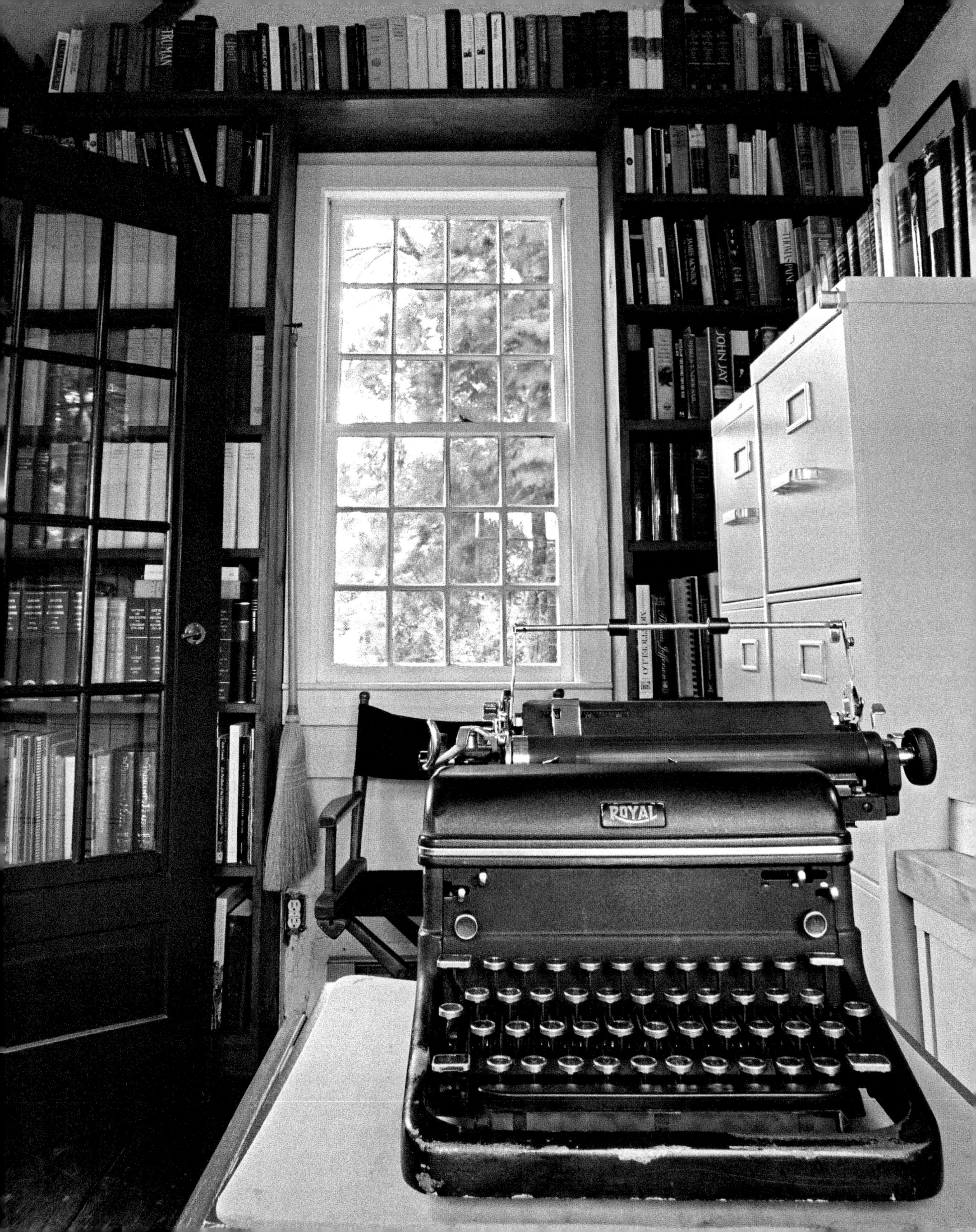

Contents

David McCullough's typewriter, West Tisbury,
Martha's Vineyard, Massachusetts, July 2010

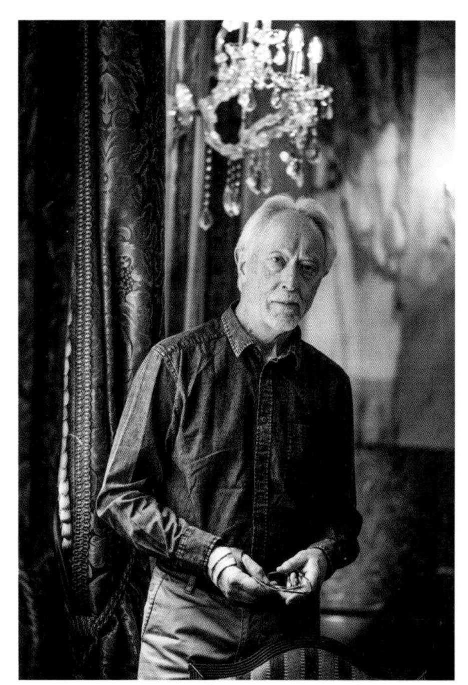
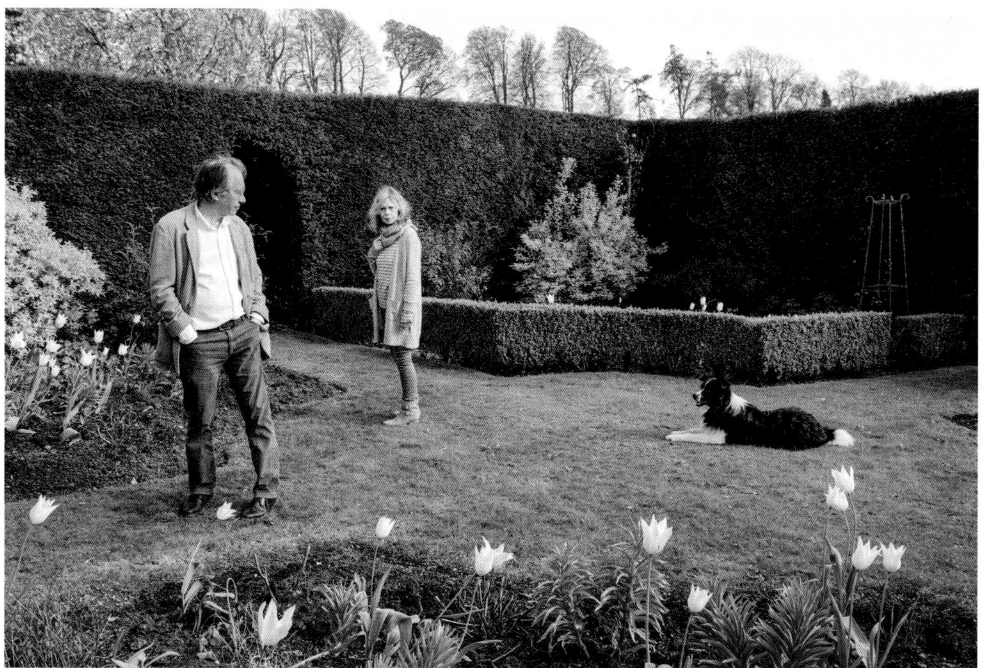
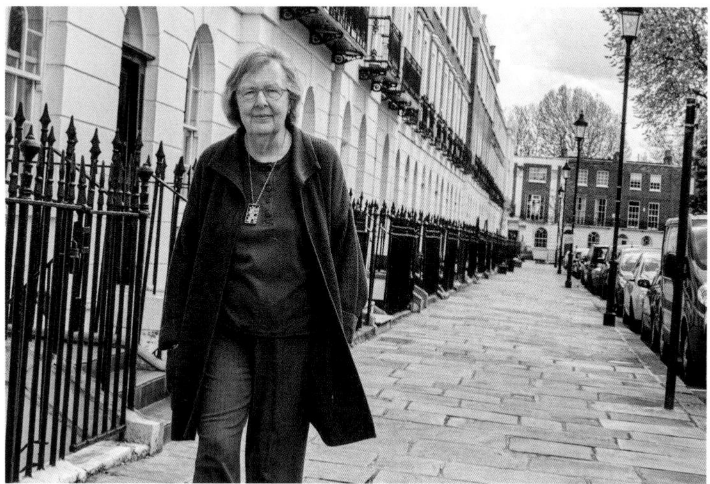
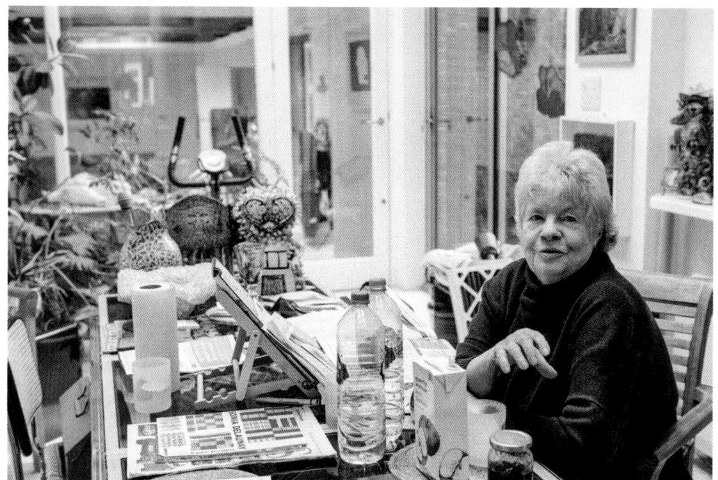
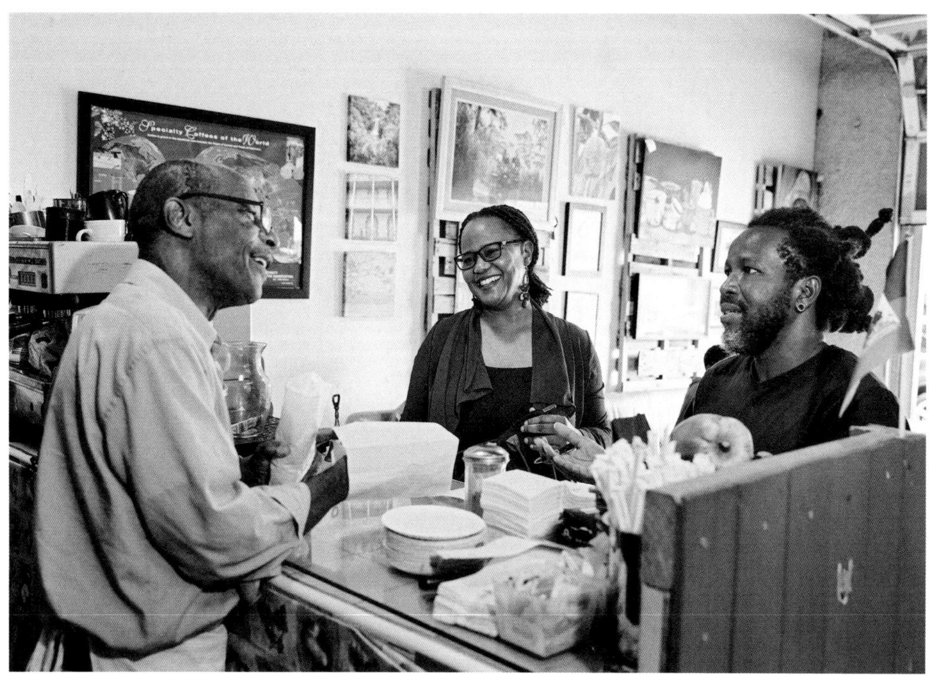
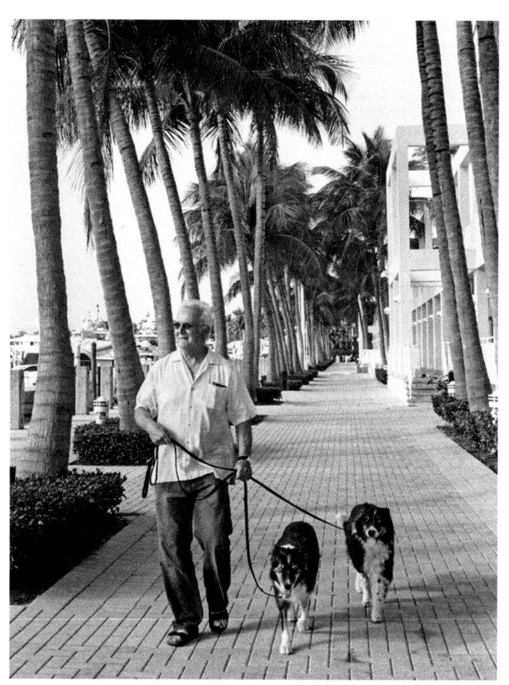

Director's Foreword

STEPHEN ENNISS

Betty Brumbalow Director, Harry Ransom Center

For more than a decade, Laura Wilson has been traveling the world to photograph some of our finest poets, playwrights, and novelists. In the early days of this project, I naively imagined she was photographing authors represented in the Harry Ransom Center's collections. Only later did I come to realize that I had it backward: the Ransom Center was collecting the archives of writers that Laura Wilson was photographing.

It was my good fortune to get to know Laura in the course of this work and to follow closely the project's progress over the years. Whenever I was in Dallas, Laura would spread out her latest work in her studio. Her warmth and openness no doubt served her well in gaining the trust of the writers themselves. Often, she photographed them in their own homes, and homemaking is a recurring theme of many of these photographs. Many of the writers appear with partners, family members, or dogs. Sometimes the settings seem an extension of the inner worlds they have so memorably created in their poems, novels, and plays.

Gabriel García Márquez chose to be photographed in a simple and coarse cloak that evokes his origins. We see the Haitian-born novelist Edwidge Danticat in Miami's Little Haiti, where she has made a home away from home. Laura captured Seamus Heaney, a poet of the hearth, in his kitchen, while Rachel Cusk, for whom home has sometimes been problematic, is on a salt marsh on the Norfolk coast, a setting that is Lear-like in its exposure to the elements.

It is in the portraits—of Colm Tóibín, Zadie Smith, Tom Stoppard, among others—that Laura shifts from the familial and the social to the solitary artist, and that she most powerfully evokes the rich inner lives of her subjects. She returns their intimate gaze to give us penetrating portraits of remarkable power.

It has been a pleasure to watch this body of work grow and it is gratifying to share these photographs with visitors to the Ransom Center in the exhibition *The Writers: Portraits by Laura Wilson* (August 26, 2022–January 1, 2023), and in this companion volume beautifully produced by Yale University Press.

I want to thank our generous sponsors who have made this exhibition and book possible: the Marlene Nathan Meyerson Family Foundation, Richard Groenendyke, and David and Ellen Berman.

LEFT TO RIGHT, FROM TOP: J. M. Coetzee, Vienna, Austria, March 2019; Ian McEwan and his wife, Annalena McAfee, Sudgrove, Gloucester, England, April 2015; Penelope Lively, London, England, April 2015; A. S. Byatt, London, England, May 2015; Edwidge Danticat in a café in Little Haiti, Miami, Florida, March 2019; and Russell Banks, Miami, Florida, February 2013

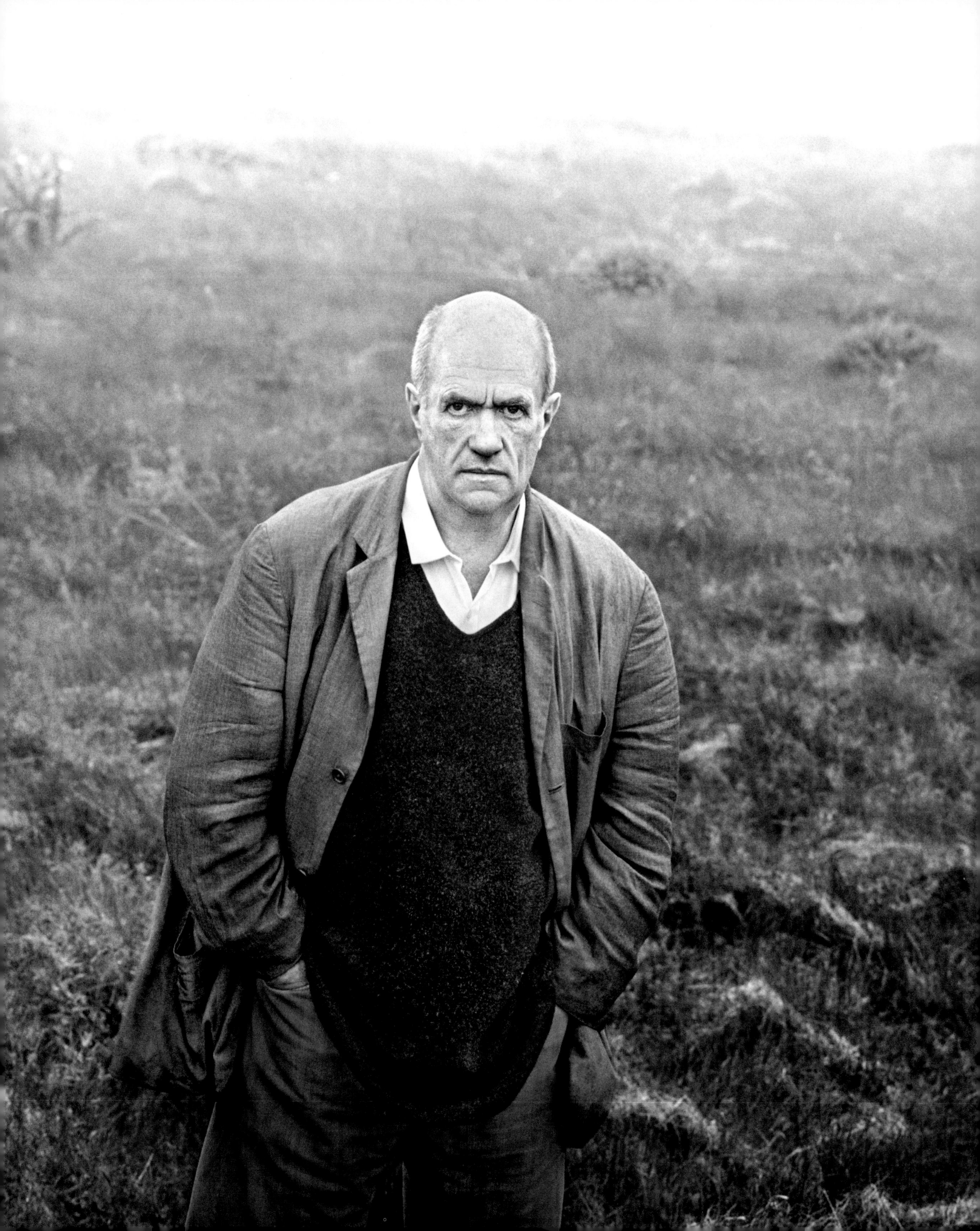

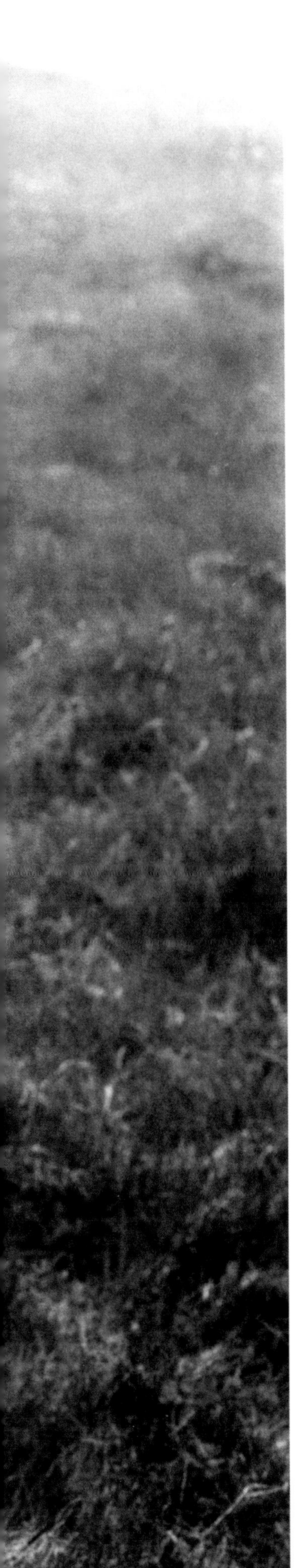

He could control her destiny now that she was dead, offer her the experiences she would have wanted, and provide drama for a life which had been so cruelly shortened. He wondered if this had happened to other writers who came before him, if Hawthorne or George Eliot had written to make the dead come back to life, had worked all day and all night, like a magician or an alchemist, defying fate and time and all the implacable elements to re-create a sacred life.

—Colm Tóibín, from *The Master*, 2004

PAGES 12–13: Marjane Satrapi, Paris, France, July 2021

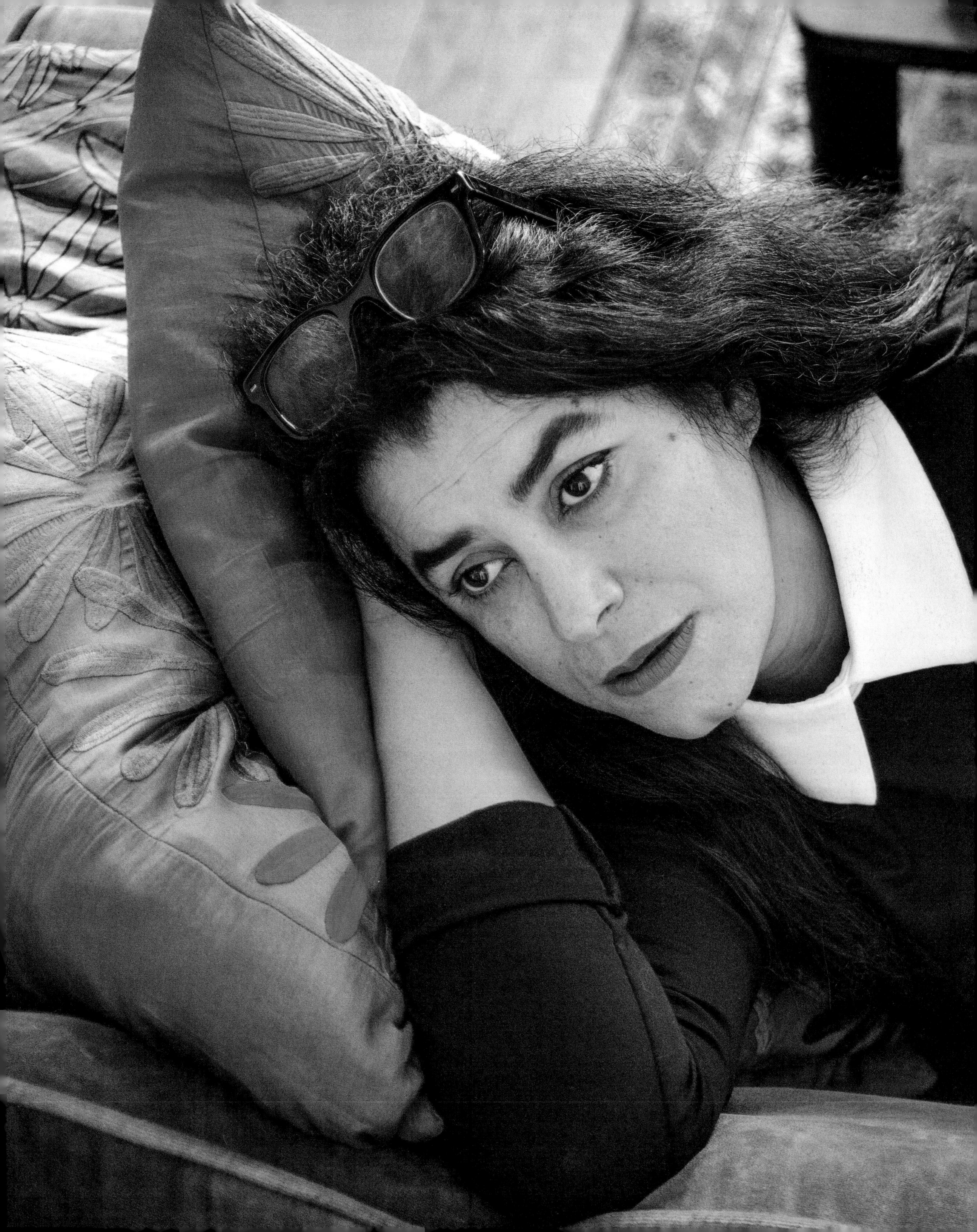

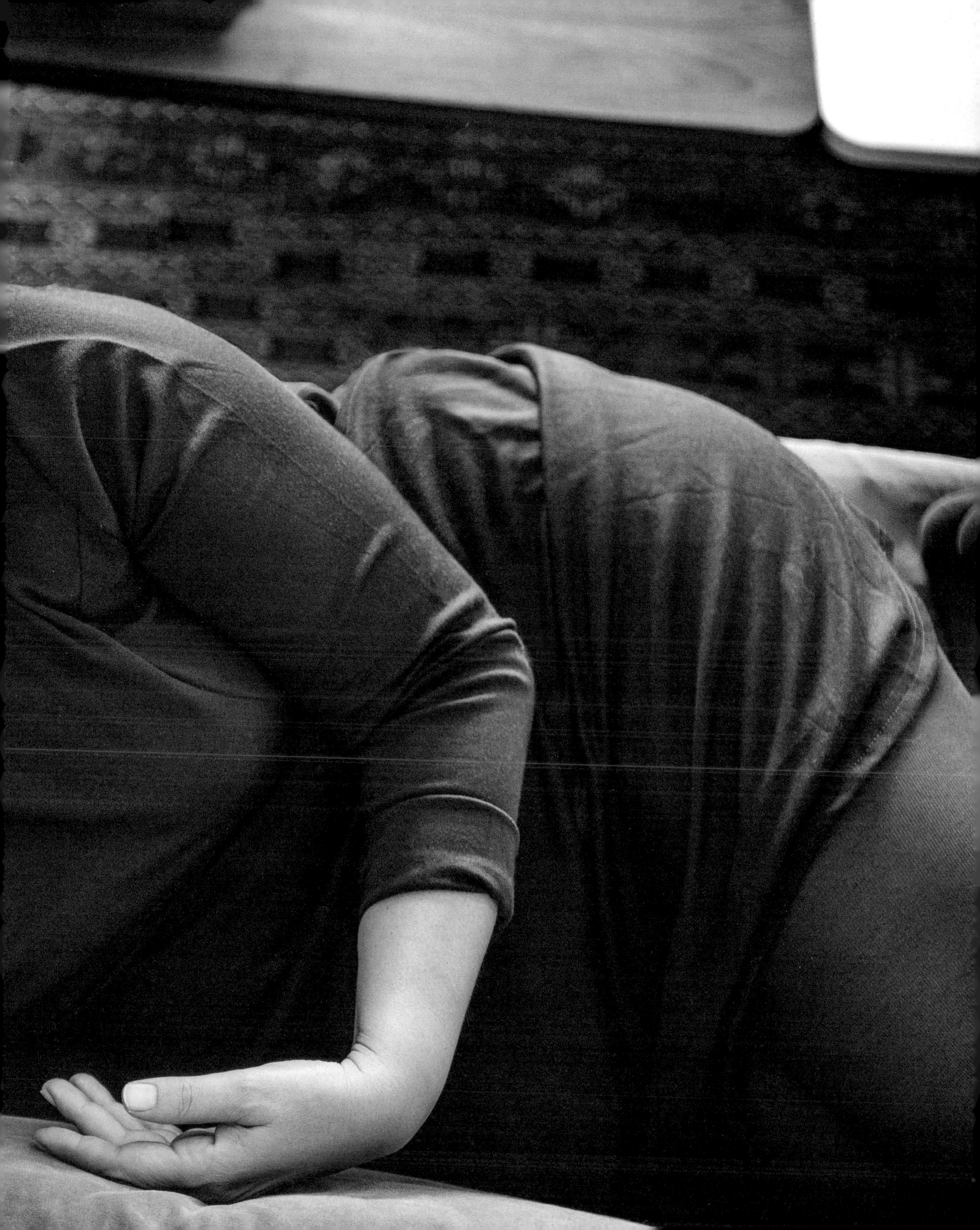

Foreword

CHARLES McGRATH

Many of us get our notions about writers—who they are, what they're like—just from those pictures on dust jackets. They've become a sort of art form in themselves, turning up all the time now on the back flap or, if the writer is a sufficiently big deal—at Grisham level, say—the whole back cover. They're called "author photos" in the trade, and writers, who are just as vain as the rest of us, have been known to spend staggering amounts of time primping for them. The problem such a photo presents is twofold. You want to look good, of course, and, if possible, maybe a little younger than your actual age. But you also want to look writerly. One way to signal this is by cupping your chin in your hands or by running your index finger up the side of your cheek—by striking a pose, in other words, that you'd normally be embarrassed by. Or maybe you tilt your head away from the camera—as if you didn't know anyone was there snapping your picture—and gaze thoughtfully into the distance. (There's a famous Cecil Beaton photo of the British novelist Henry Green in which he is completely turned around, so all we can see is the back of his head.) Dramatic lighting helps, and so does lots of contrast and brooding shadow. The great master of these effects is Marion Ettlinger, whose author photos are so dark and inky they almost look like etchings. Her portraits of writers like Raymond Carver and Truman Capote are so stark and dramatic that—even now, years later—they're impossible to erase from your head. That they don't actually look much like Carver and Capote is almost beside the point. They're meant to suggest something more profound than mere likeness.

But some of us, when we look at a photograph of a writer, especially one we particularly like or admire, want to think we're getting an idea of what that person looks like in real life, not on the flap of a jacket. And, as Laura Wilson has remarked, a lot of author photos fail in this basic task. Her disappointment is what got her started on this twelve-year project of taking pictures of writers—that and her love of their work. The writers included in this book amount to a kind of pantheon—they're among the best and most famous and influential of contemporary writers. There are three Nobel Prize winners, even more winners of the Pulitzer Prize, PEN Literary Award, or National Book Award, and at one time or another, practically everyone pictured here has perched atop the best-seller lists. These also happen to be writers whom Laura has read and reread. Her selection process had less to do with checking off an all-star list than with something closer to ordinary fandom—the same impulse that makes the rest

OPPOSITE: Cormac McCarthy, Santa Fe, New Mexico, July 2015

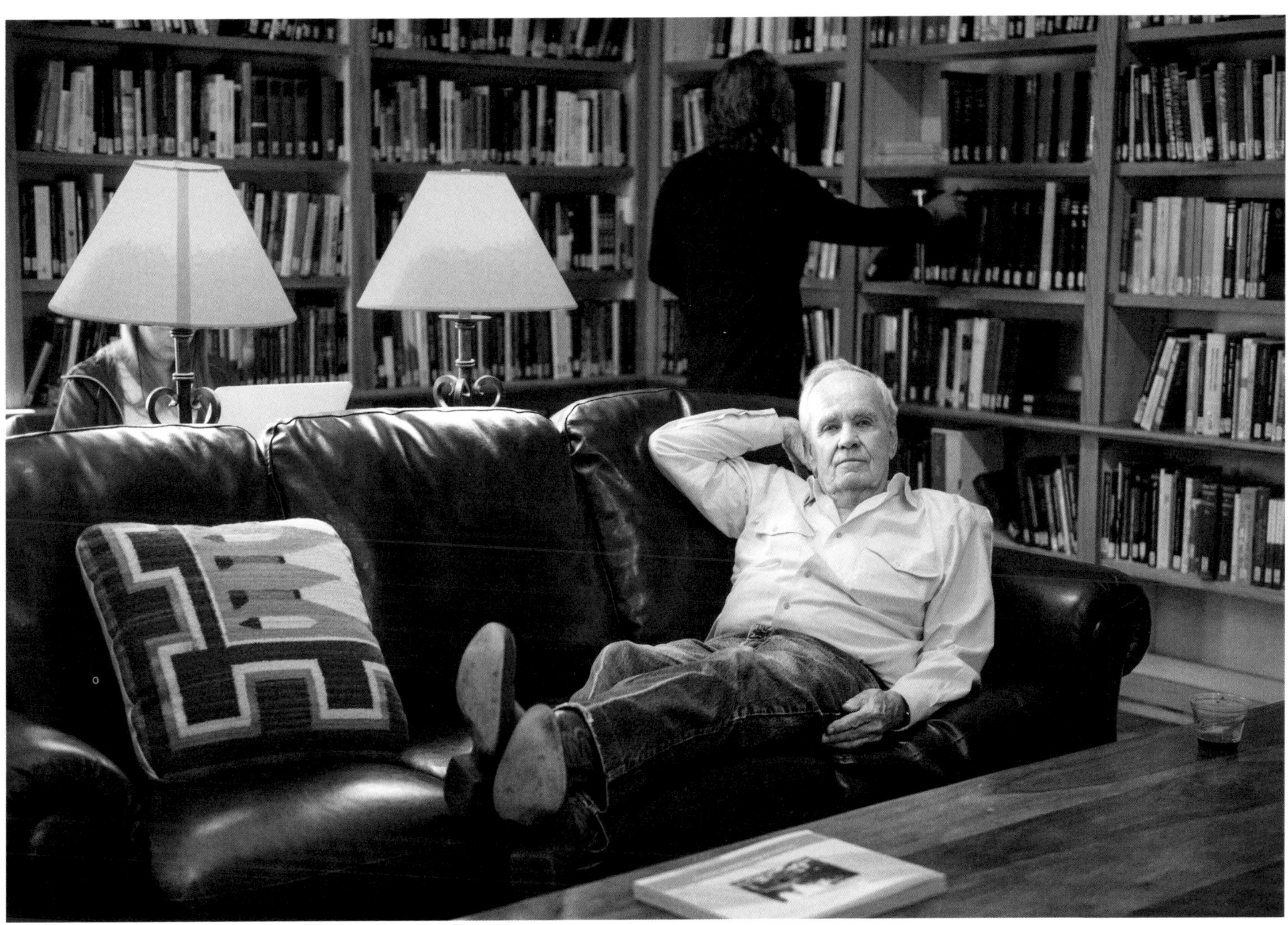

of us turn so hopefully to those dust jacket photos: We want to know more about the writers we love. In Laura's case, her talent and enterprise enabled her to actually spend time with these writers—the fan's greatest dream of all—and to take pictures that do more than show us what they look like when, as Laura has, you really look at them. Like all great portraits, they go beyond mere appearance and begin to suggest something about who these people really are.

I should probably mention that Laura is family: the widow of my sorely missed cousin Bob. I have admired her work for years, and have followed this project with particular interest, marveling at her patience and stamina, her ability to track down the far-flung, like Haruki Murakami and J. M. Coetzee, as well as writers, like Brit Bennett and Cormac McCarthy, who seldom pose for photographers. McCarthy, especially, is so famously elusive that finding him here is like suddenly coming upon Garbo or Salinger. There are also some faces in this book that, for one reason or another, we've seen a lot: Seamus Heaney, for example, and Tom Stoppard and Sam Shepard. But even with such familiar personalities, Laura has managed to capture something we haven't seen before and might otherwise have missed—Heaney's concentration, Stoppard's purposefulness, Shepard's wistfulness.

Laura's formal portraits seem to me to belong in the great tradition of Julia Margaret Cameron, with her famous pictures of Tennyson and Virginia Woolf (perhaps the most iconic and evocative author photo ever), and, later, of Berenice Abbott, whose photographs of James Joyce and Edna St. Vincent Millay are still so magisterial and compelling. They have the same steadiness and attentiveness, the same unmannered directness. That all three great photographers are women is probably no accident, and to the list of exceptionally good and sensitive photographers of writers we can also add two of Laura's contemporaries, Nancy Crampton and Jill Krementz. I suspect

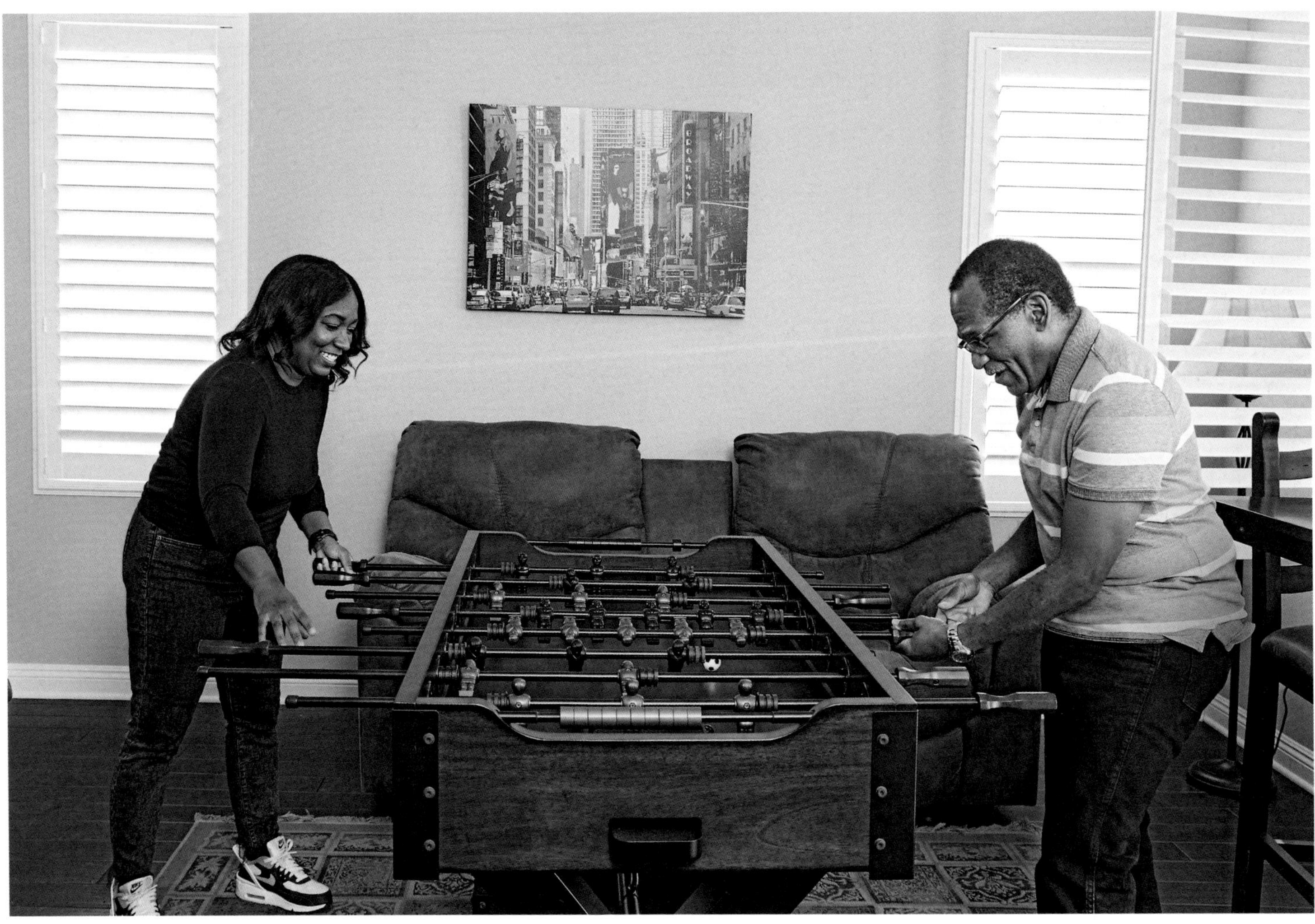

a key to their success is assuredness and lack of bristling ego. They know how good they are, and have no need to make themselves the subject, not the sitter. They appreciate writers as fellow artists trying just to get things right. Laura, I know from experience, is also passionately curious and an almost breathless listener, the kind of person who genuinely wants to know what you think. When you're with her, you can find yourself forgetting that you're having your picture taken.

That she has a great eye goes without saying, and in this book she has been particularly fortunate in her subjects. She chose them for their work, not their looks, and yet it's remarkable how striking they all are. We know, or think we know, that the genes for looks are distributed randomly and unfairly.

There are beauties who are vapid, geniuses who are plug-ugly. And yet, on the evidence of this book, you could conclude that great writerly talent confers on the bearer a certain physical distinction as well. Some of them are practically movie-star handsome—Richard Ford, Thomas McGuane, Zadie Smith, Rachel Cusk, Louise Erdrich, Sam Shepard (who really was a movie star, as well as a playwright and short-story writer). Others have faces that suggest rugged depths of character, lives lived full of intensity and purpose. My favorite in this vein is Jim Harrison, whose face is as monumental as W. H. Auden's, its every weather-beaten line and crease a testimony to a career, as he once told me, that did not exclude actresses, waitresses, drugs, and rock 'n' roll. He should have added epic feats of gastronomy. There are other photos like his. Colm Tóibín, for example, has the gravity and stolidness of an Easter Island statue; Annie Proulx reminds you of a Rodin sculpture. It may be an illusion, but we can't help feeling that these faces have been shaped by the same care and concentration that goes into

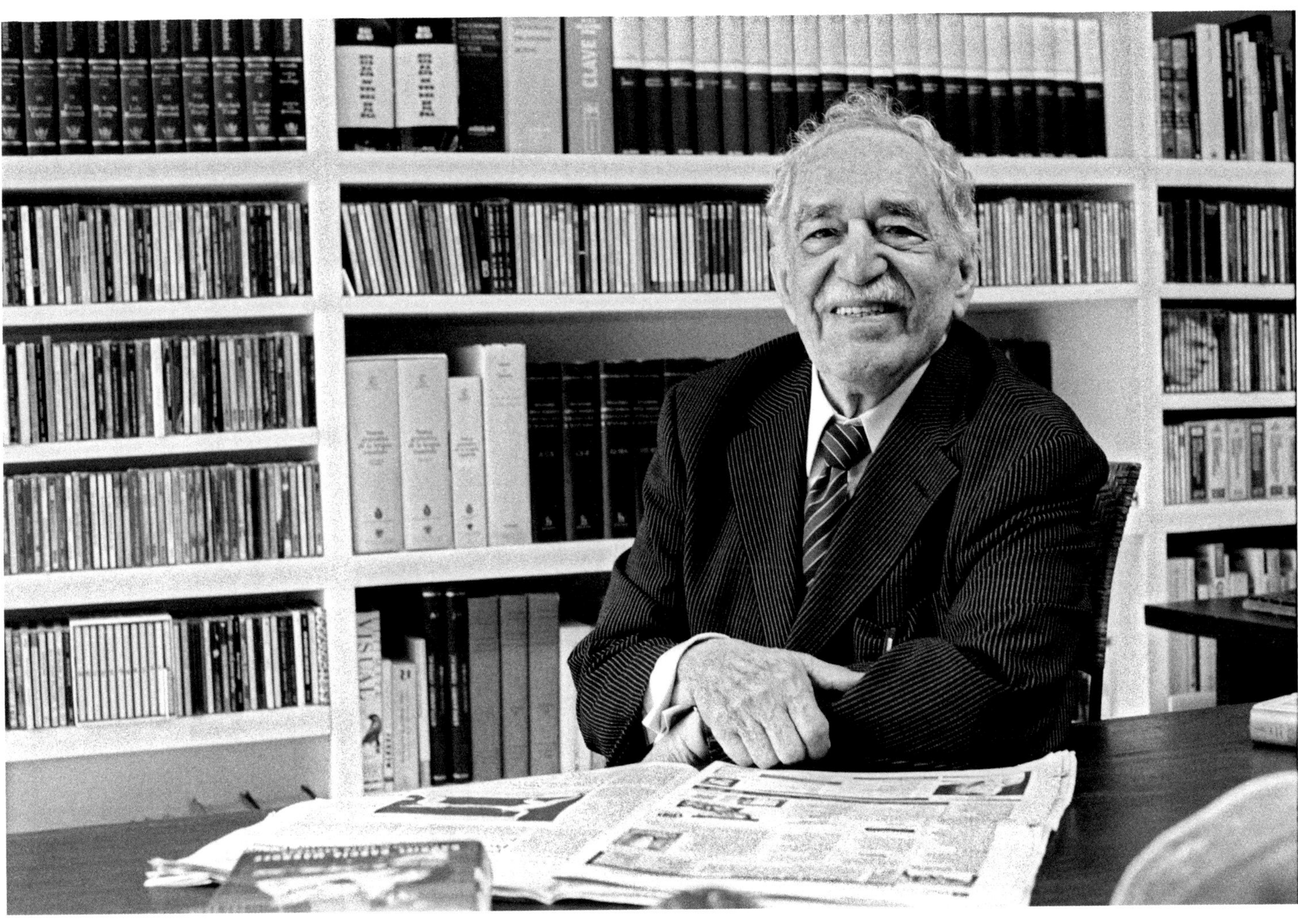

the shaping of a sentence or a chapter. They're faces that repay a second look.

Perhaps the most eloquent face here—and also the most touching—is that of Gabriel García Márquez, which has about it both a fierce dignity and a slight uncertainty (see p. 25). We know now, from his son's memoir, that in his final years García Márquez was struggling to keep it together, worried about losing his edge and his memory. So this is a photograph not just of genius and success but also of mortality, and a reminder that several of these writers are no longer with us: García Márquez, Carlos Fuentes, Jim Harrison, Larry McMurtry, W. S. Merwin, Sam Shepard. These portraits of Laura's are our last looks at these exceptional artists, and a chance to reflect once again on what made them so distinctive. This is the way, surely, that these writers would want to be remembered—for looking like who they were. I could be wrong, but I like to think that Carlos Fuentes would be particularly pleased at this glimpse he's left us—every bit as elegant in appearance as he was on the page.

The candid photographs here came as something of a surprise to me. When Laura first began working on the book, I saw only the formal, posed portraits. But the candids are just as remarkable in their own way, and a valuable, unexpected clue to the private lives of these writers. That Ian McEwan was an avid gardener I already knew—though until Laura's pictures I had no idea on how grand a scale. But that Tobias Wolff was a swimmer, Tim O'Brien an amateur magician, Brit Bennett a player of foosball and giant outdoor chess—this was all very welcome news to me. I was also pleased that there weren't too many pictures of writers actually writing. That's the one thing we already know they do. On the other hand, I was struck by how many of these photos show writers being sociable, hanging out with friends and loved ones, and by how often these writers are laughing. Good writers are very funny, we shouldn't need to be reminded—even the serious ones. That's why they're such good company—even vicariously, in the pages of this generous and revealing book.

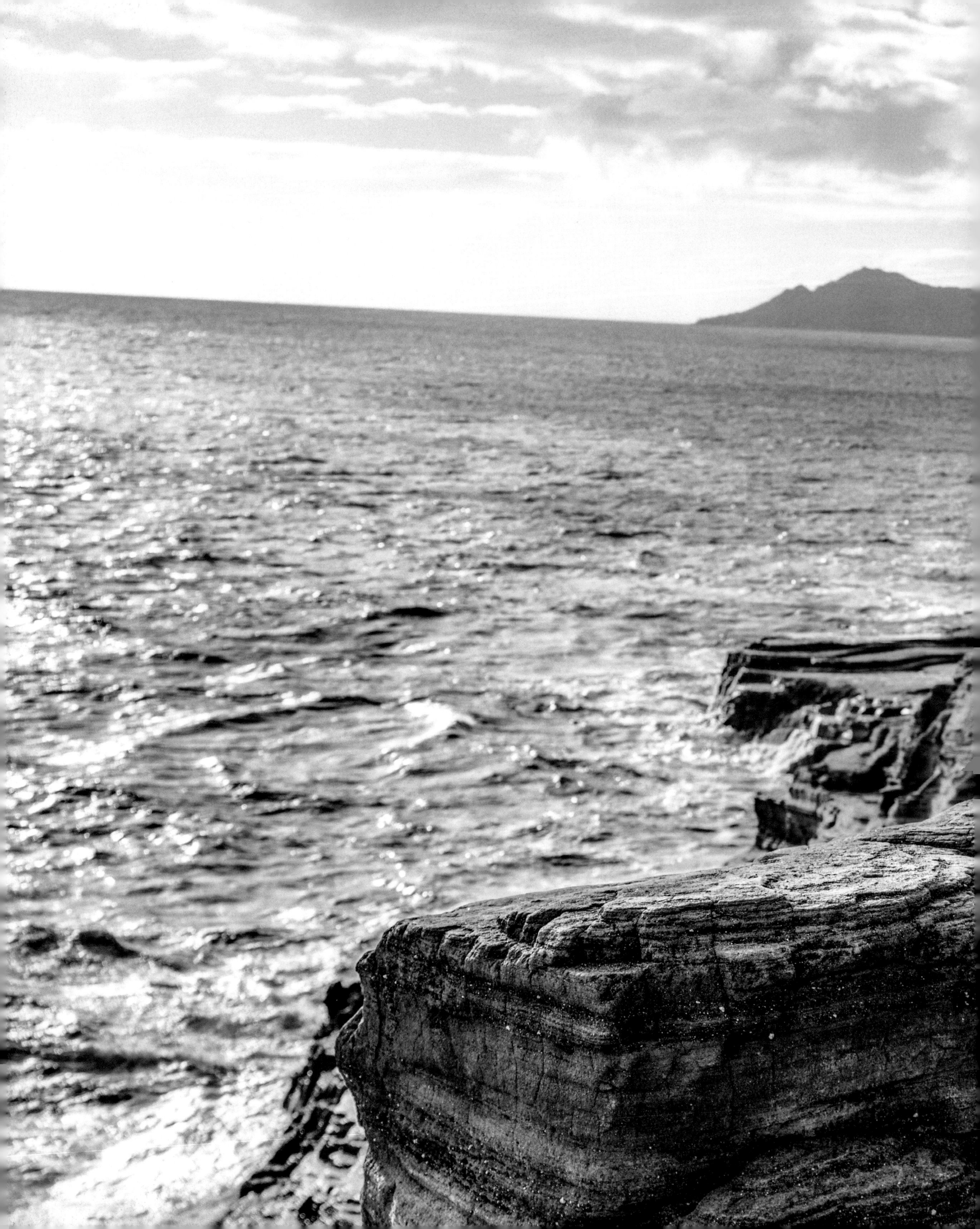

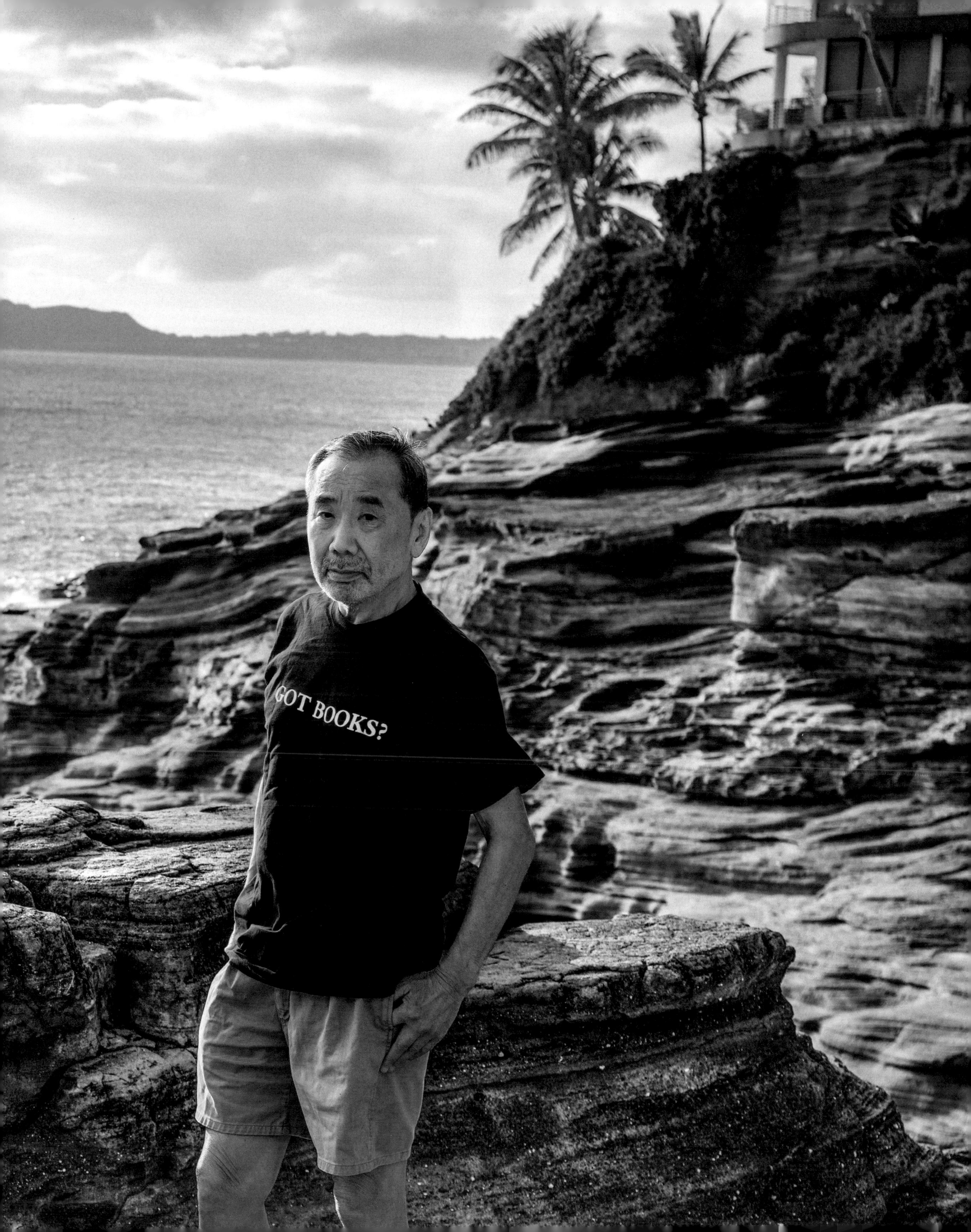
GOT BOOKS?

Introduction

LOUISE ERDRICH

Writers do not generally like to have their pictures taken. Most of us are reclusive by nature, as writing demands. Being photographed is intrusive, time-consuming, faintly ridiculous. So why do the writers in this engaging book of portraits seem to be having a good time? The secret is Laura Wilson. I speak as a subject who tried in vain to resist Laura Wilson. Many of my favorite people don't see the inside of my house, but when Laura appeared on my front steps and gave me a lovely, friendly, excited smile, I opened the door. Laura and her kind and efficient assistant entered. Soon I entered the spirit of the surprise collaboration. I pretended I didn't know that Laura was a yard away, her camera purring. I hugged my dog, brought her over to my family's Native-centric bookstore, Birchbark Books, and began sharing books with a customer. Walking home, I got smooched by my neighbor Jim Martin, who had just repaired a watering can I'd tried to throw out (he repairs everything). In short, things happened that I couldn't control, as occurs in life whenever I leave my writing desk.

Knowing from my own experience how this process of beguilement worked, I find these portraits especially layered. I can see writers thawing and beginning to enjoy themselves, becoming unexpectedly playful or just getting on with domestic tasks, which mostly take place in interesting kitchens and range from preparing food to conducting a move-in. The writers take Laura along as they walk beaches or step out beneath lichen-furred branches, as they visit neighborhood shops or cathedrals. These portraits are especially rich and often poignant. Laura's devotion to this project began long ago, so there is a sense of both joy and loss within these pages: Here is Gabriel García Márquez smiling, beaming, at once aged and youthful. Here is elegant and elegantly disquieted Carlos Fuentes, and my friend, exuberant and wildly humane Jim Harrison. Here is inimitable Sam Shepard, wise and kind Larry McMurtry, and one of my heroes, W. S. Merwin, what sorrow . . . and oh, here are the rest of us and here is Louise, still among the living. It is unnerving. In this book we are a page away

PAGES 22–23: Rachel Cusk with her husband, Siemon Scamell-Katz, Stiffkey, Norfolk, England, October 2018 from gone. Yet, in admitting Laura into our gardens, kitchens, studies, cabins, to our dinner tables and porches, bookstores, favorite plazas and colonnades, we appear in the thick of things, part of the quotidian orders and disorders of life.

A reader usually gets to see a writer from the shoulders up. At some point as I read a book, either a superlative or an awful moment, a "who the hell wrote this?" moment, I check the picture on the back flap. The picture never solves the mystery of the writing. None of these pictures can either, but there is much to solve in each composite portrait. If you are partial to a writer, their surroundings or favorite people are subjects of intrigue. For one thing, I enjoy knowing that the writers whose work I love probably lead lives with complications similar to mine. Perhaps it helps readers to know that writers don't operate in a rarified realm. It is reassuring to know that some of us can't buy a book or a coffee or a piece of fruit without falling into a conversation. That others occupy most happily soft chairs, and still others ride horses. Writers have dinners to make, food to gather, dogs to walk. Husbands, wives, children, friends, neighbors, shop owners, and customers appear. There is joy. Laughing people are hanging out around dinner tables or in living rooms enjoying company. Annie Proulx gestures with a spoon. The shadows of raptors fixed to her windows discourage songbirds from ramming into invisible barriers. I appreciate that. David McCullough leaps high and clicks his heels. One can't help but admire his well-tuned old-school Royal typewriter and try to read the page that he's revising by hand. There are also glimpses of the writing studios where we do our secret work—we write in comfortable clutter, mainly, but other studios are suspiciously neat. Some are charming cottages, others multileveled, be-postered, with totemic items on display. Most have dizzily shelved or piled heaps of books. There are beds or couches where a writer can dream, lounge, read, sleep.

A little stuffed monkey on the windowsill, a real dictionary, a thick sheepskin, a sleepy dog siphoning off the camera's attention. Laura Wilson has an eye for the compelling detail, for objects that simply make you wonder. What about pelts draped on a chair—badger? Skunk? Vases of flowers. For what occasion? A game of darts, a Santa Claus, a hanging bed, an enormous game of chess. And of course, more books, treated with special care, sometimes labeled. Organized on bookshelves that reach to ceilings or wind along walls below windows. I can't help smiling at Margaret Atwood's aslant copies of foreign editions of *The Handmaid's Tale*. It's a wonderful chance composition. In another of Atwood's portraits, there is also a huge rock. Margaret is lifting the rock. There is compost. She is stirring it, and shoveling it into flower beds, feeding beauty. She is living out metaphors for the writing process. As are many writers—I love that Edwidge Danticat is visiting around in her neighborhood, and is obviously well known to booksellers, shop owners, workers. While she's at it, Edwidge showcases the lively street art of Little Haiti. There's generosity and fun in what she's doing.

In these many interesting spaces, I wonder, were we being ourselves? Or were we self-consciously choosing settings in which we still could hide? Do these portraits contain truths writers ordinarily disguise? Or are we still in disguise? Maybe the animals in these portraits tell the true story. Wilson is adept at drawing out their feelings, too. A resolute pug dominates a kitchen. A Persian cat's regal pride sets off a writer's tenderness. Australian shepherds and hunting dogs lavish love on their humans and accompany us through life.

Do these photographs get at the question every writer is asked a thousand times within a life span—what makes you write these books? These photographs make writers seem suspiciously normal. Yet something happens when Laura Wilson goes back to her photography studio and we sit down to write. We tap into the ancient pleasures of storytelling and at the same time take on the human struggle against the obvious. Horseman, pass by.

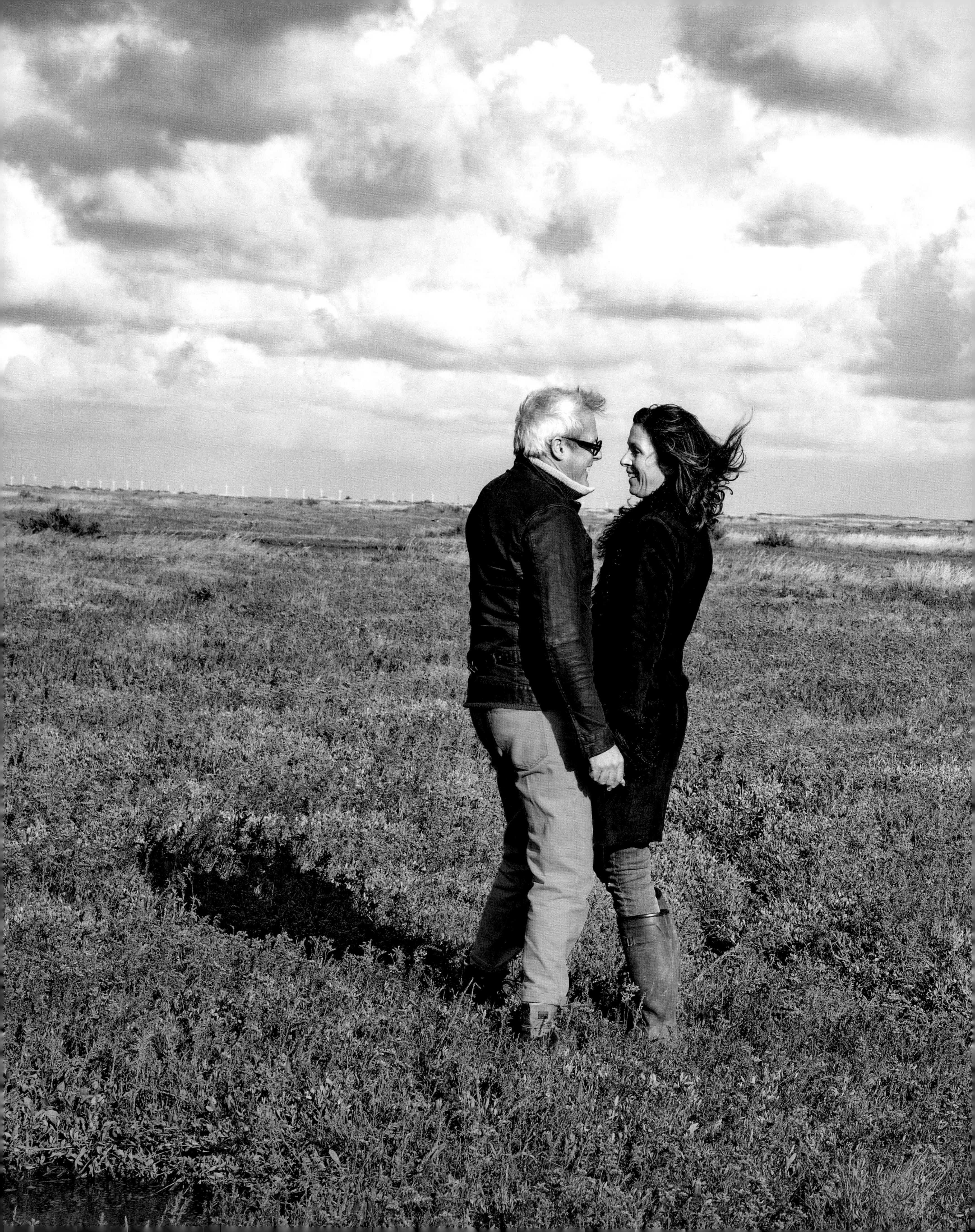

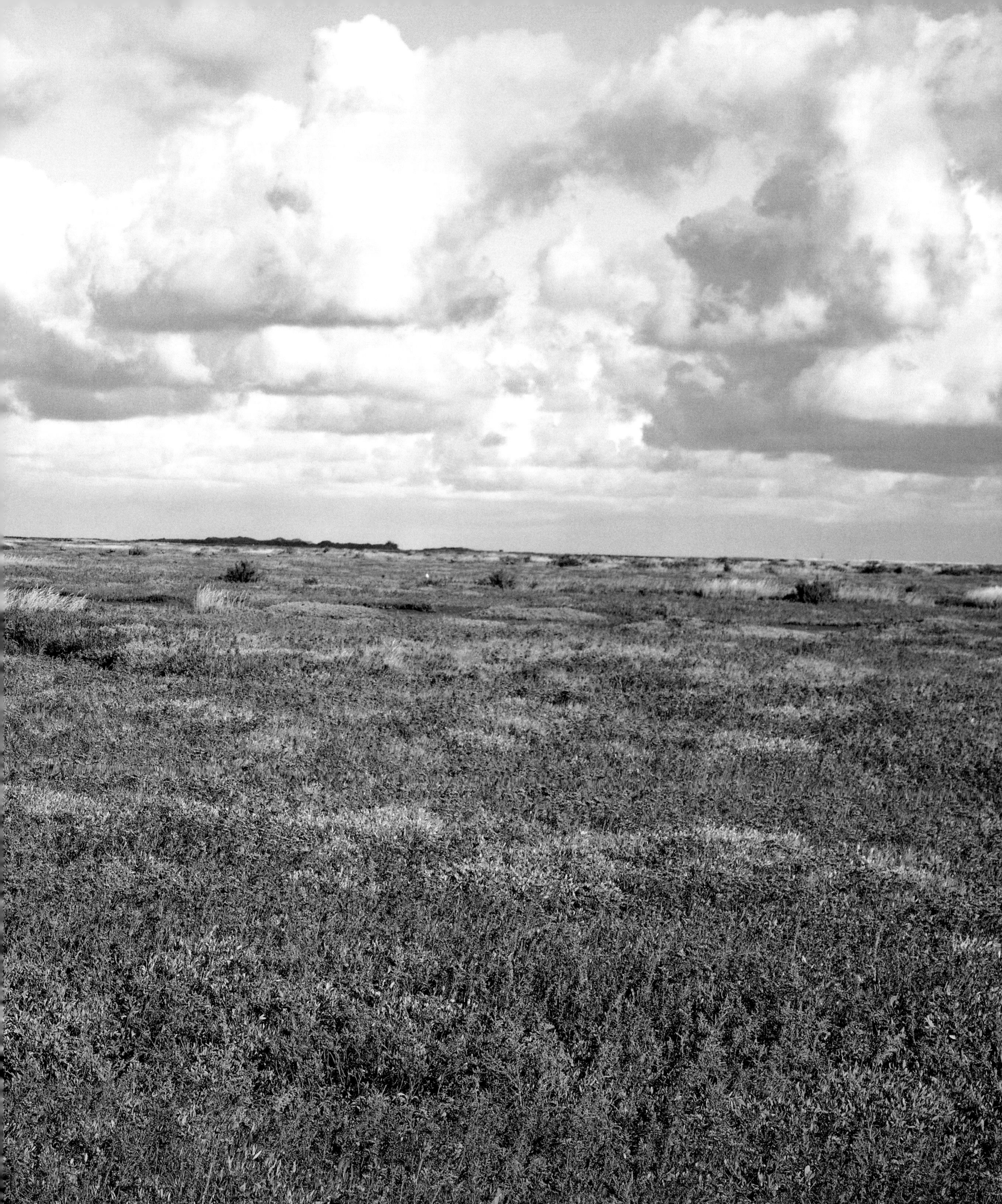

Gabriel García Márquez

Colombian (1927–2014)

Photographed in Mexico City, Mexico, April 2012

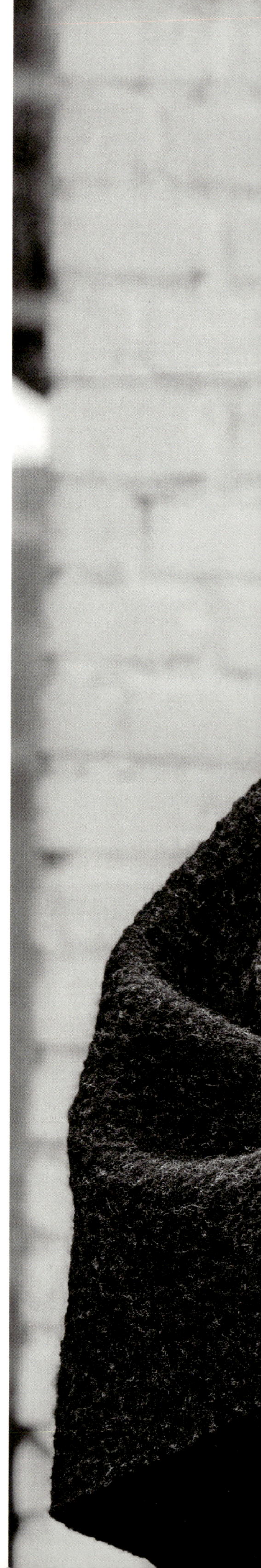

Gabriel García Márquez lived with his wife, Mercedes Barcha, in the Pedregal de San Angel of Mexico City. When I photographed him there, in the garden outside his library, the Nobel Laureate wore a ruana. This coarse, heavy wool poncho is traditional with the indigenous people of the Sabana de Bogotá, near the Andes Mountains in Colombia, with whom he felt a kinship.

He did not speak English and Matt Lankes, my assistant, and I did not speak Spanish. But curious and alert, García Márquez made clear to us that he wanted to hold Matt's old 1930s Voigtländer camera. He examined it with care, beaming like a boy who knows he is holding something special and fragile.

My friend from Mexico City, Pancha Reynaud, went with us on the second day to help translate and she was charmed by him—and he by her. Pancha asked him to inscribe a copy of *One Hundred Years of Solitude*. He immediately crossed out *Solitude* and wrote instead "felicidad para ti" (happiness for you).

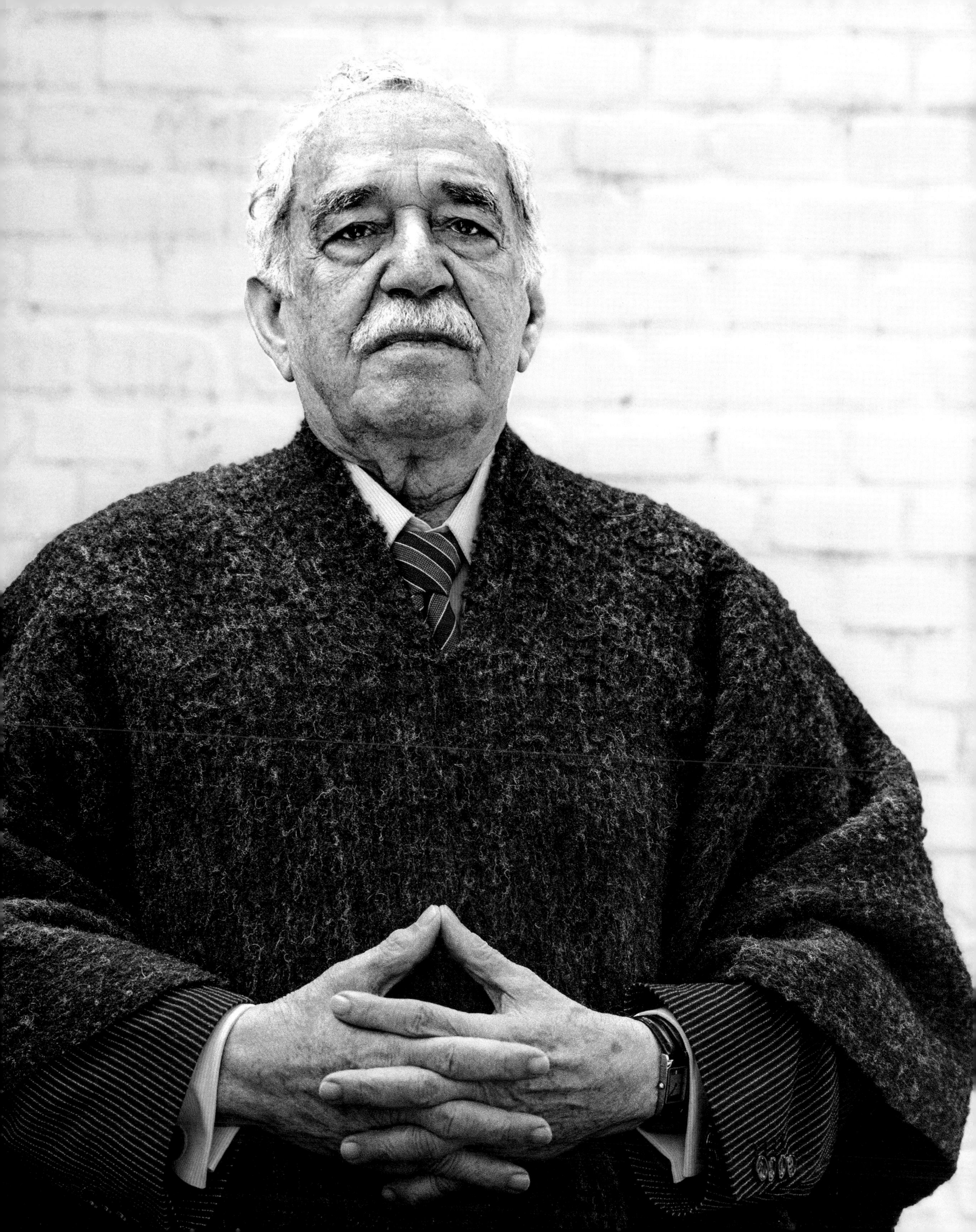

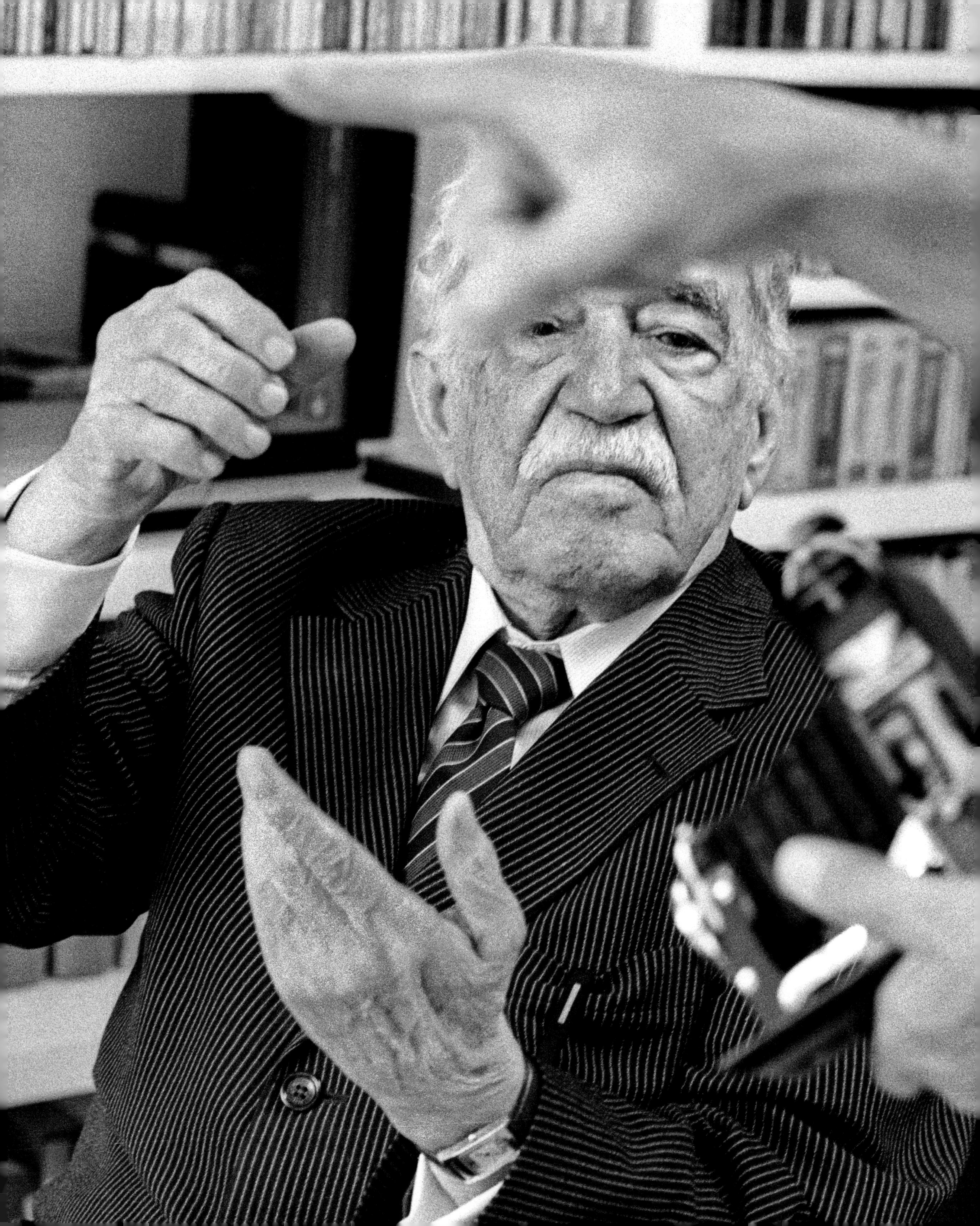

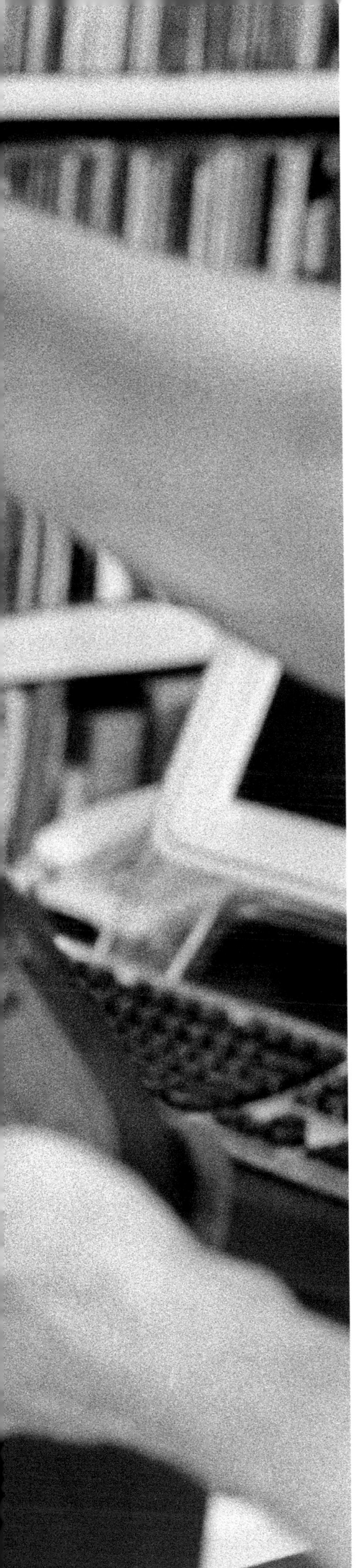

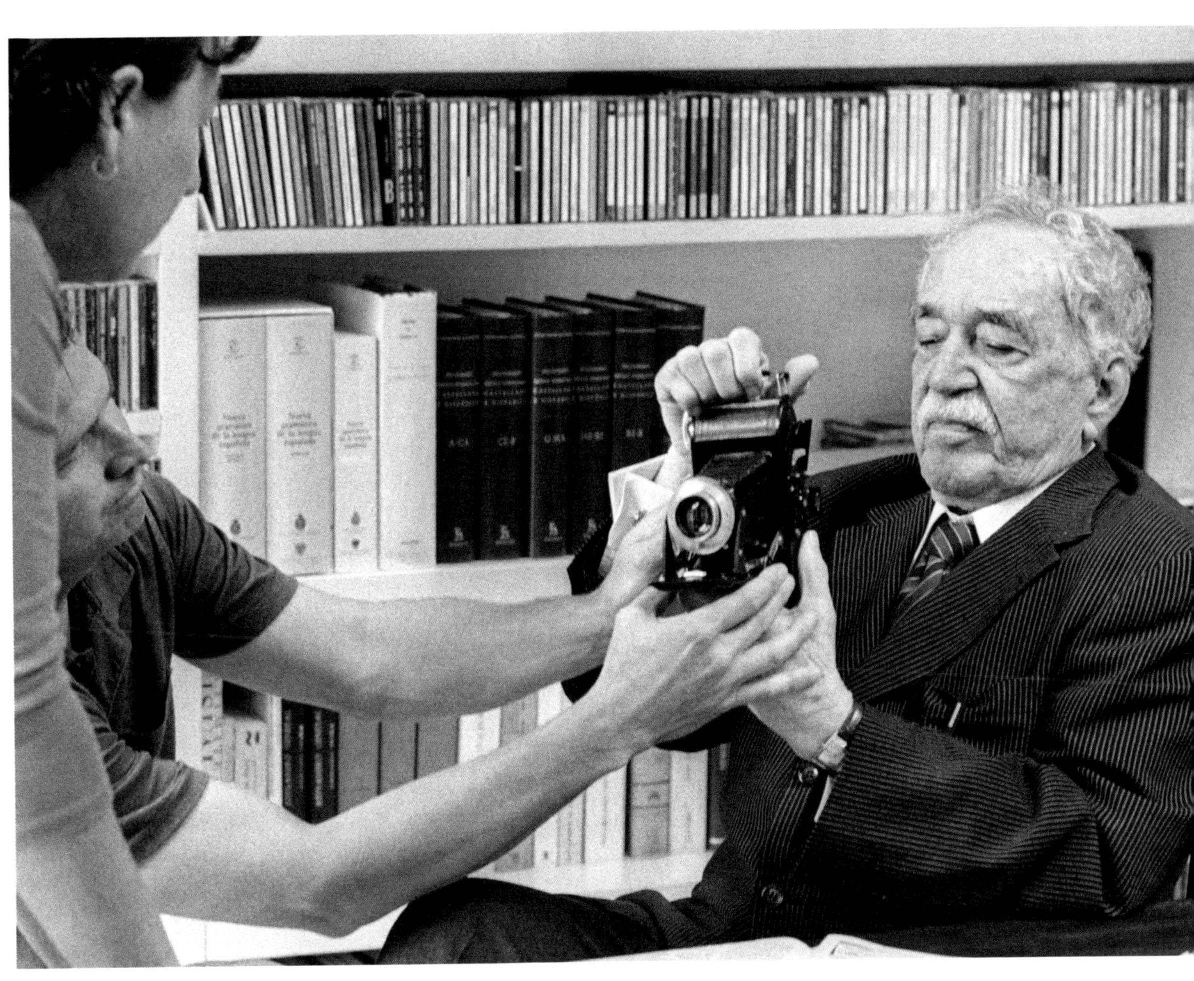

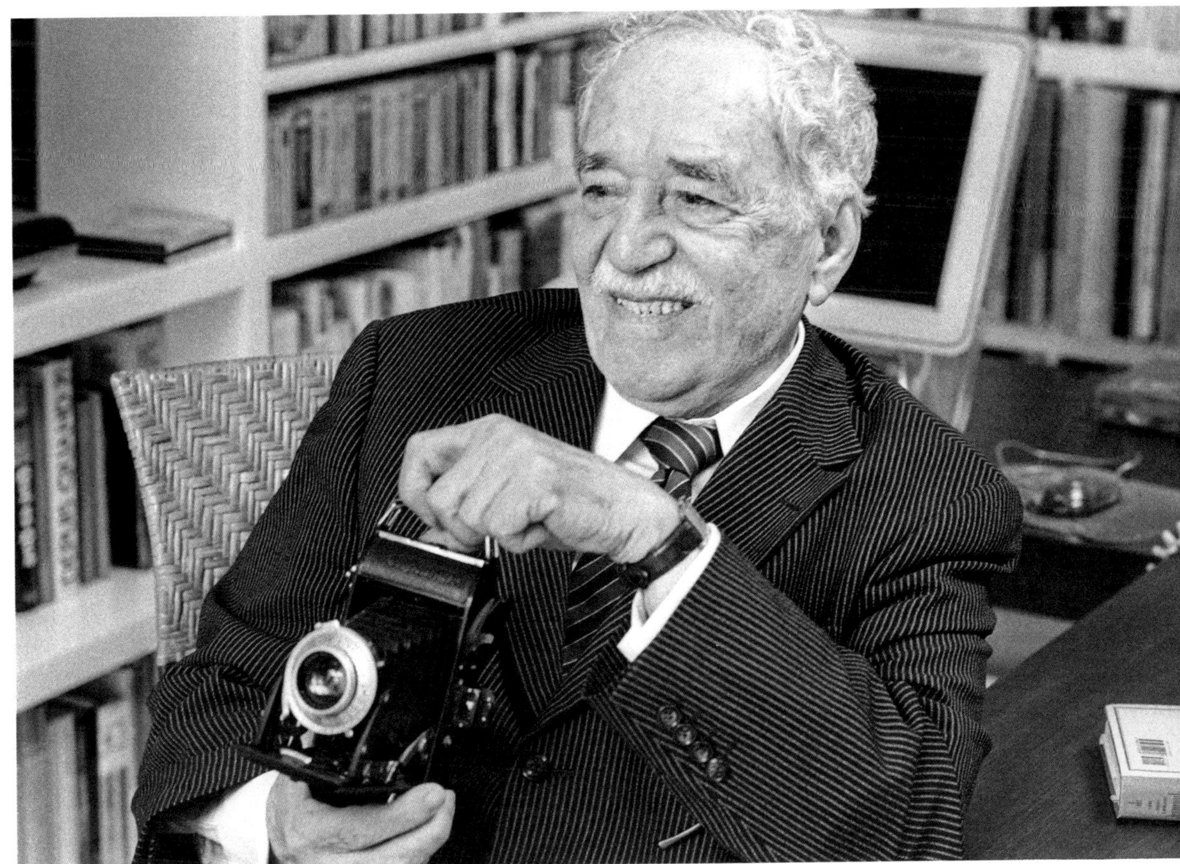

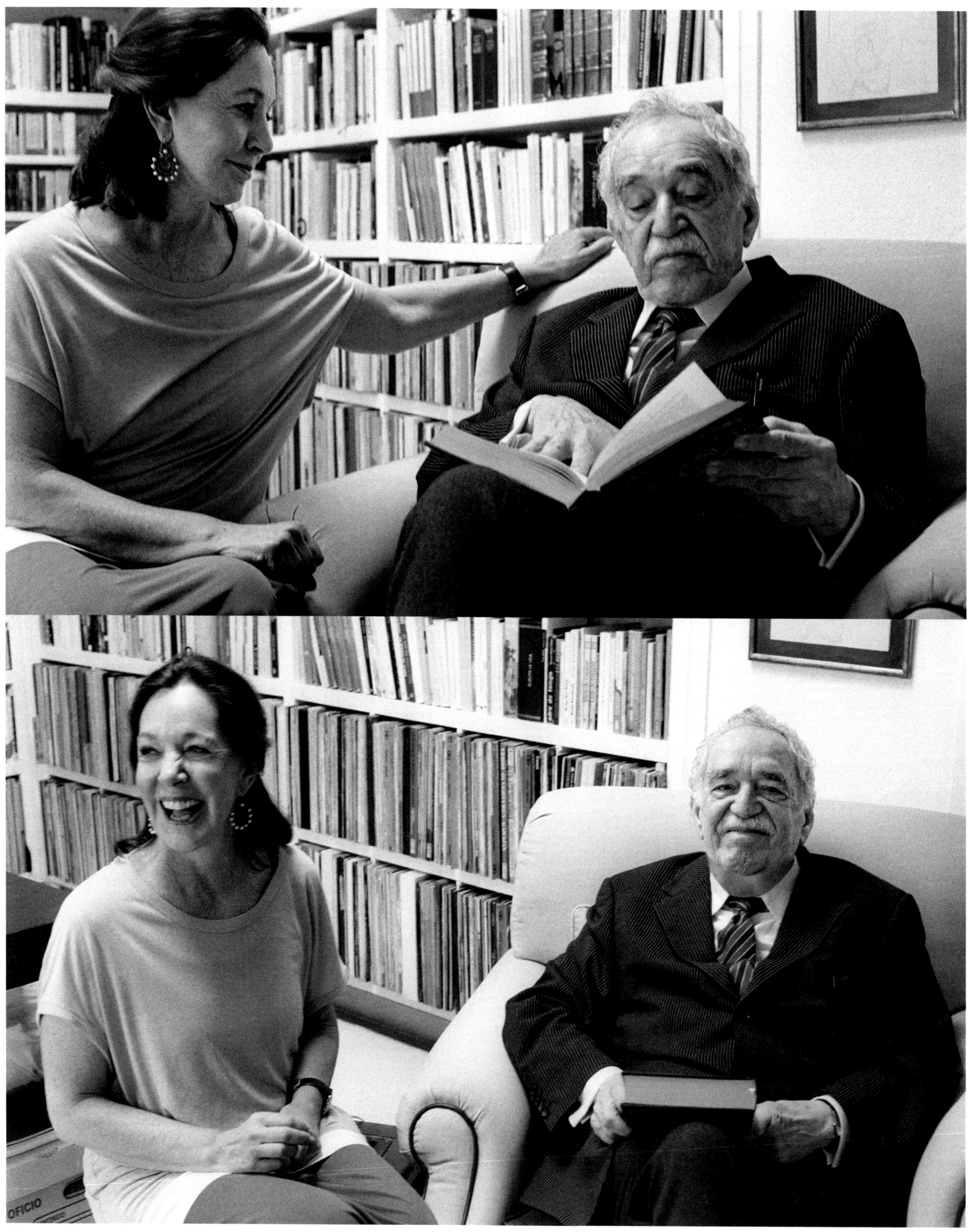

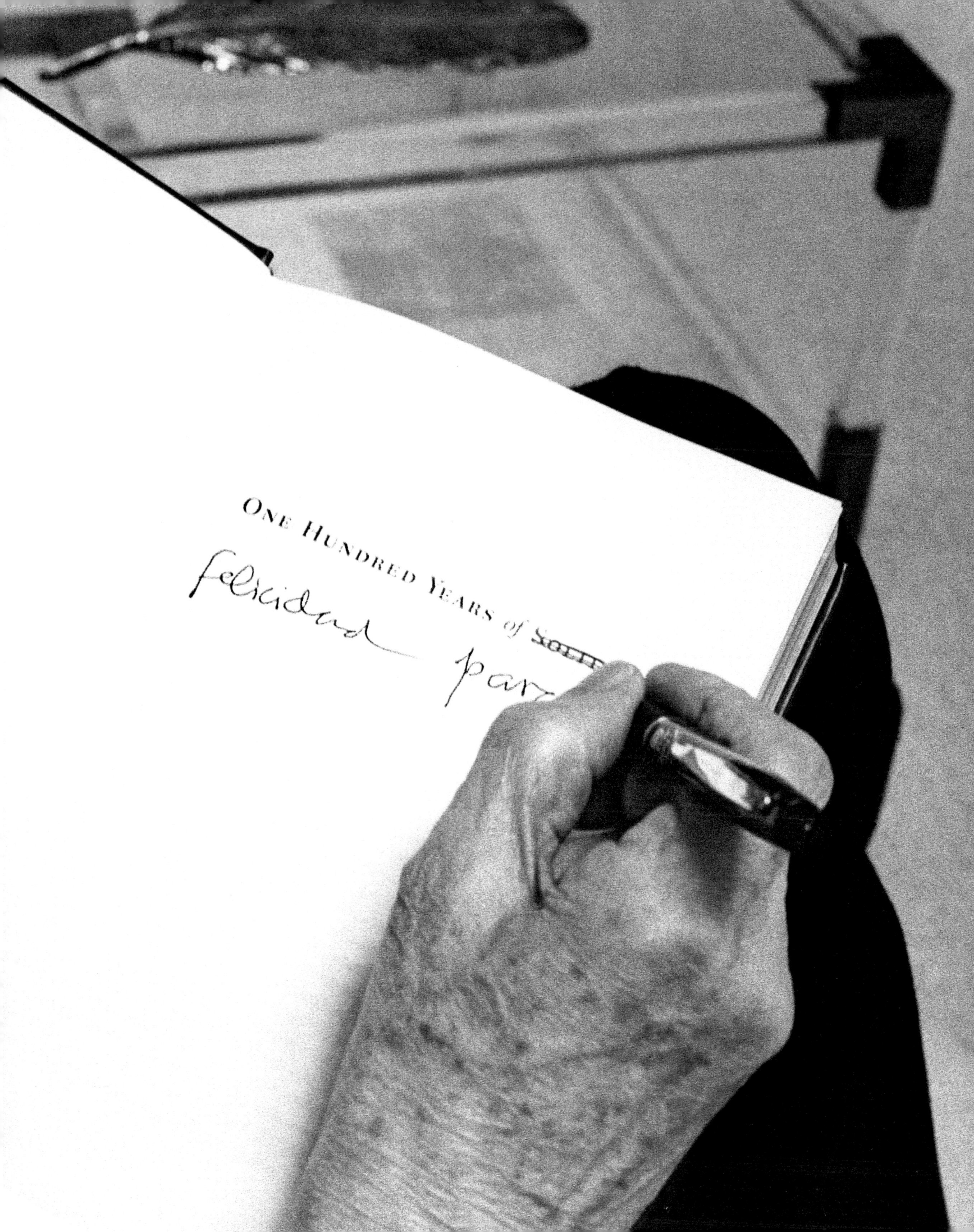

One Hundred Years of
felicidad
par

Louise Erdrich

American (b. 1954)

Photographed in Minneapolis, Minnesota, May 2018

Louise Erdrich owns a spirited independent bookstore in Minneapolis that sells carefully selected books of general interest as well as Native American literature and art objects. The place is tended by an experienced staff, but Erdrich can often be found there, which pleases customers, eager to meet this National Book Award– and Pulitzer Prize–winning writer. I watched one afternoon as she listened with remarkable patience to a Native man who brought her a book and then went on, and on, about various issues. I wondered if she was fusing the real with the imagined voice of a character in a future story.

The morning I was saying goodbye to Erdrich at her house, Jim Martin, a neighbor, stopped by to return a watering can he'd repaired for her. He began to tell a joke. Concentrating on f-stops and shutter speeds, I wasn't really listening, but the trajectory of the joke seemed to be heading in an alarming direction. Then, at the last moment, the watering-can repairman swerved with his story—to Erdrich's relief and amusement.

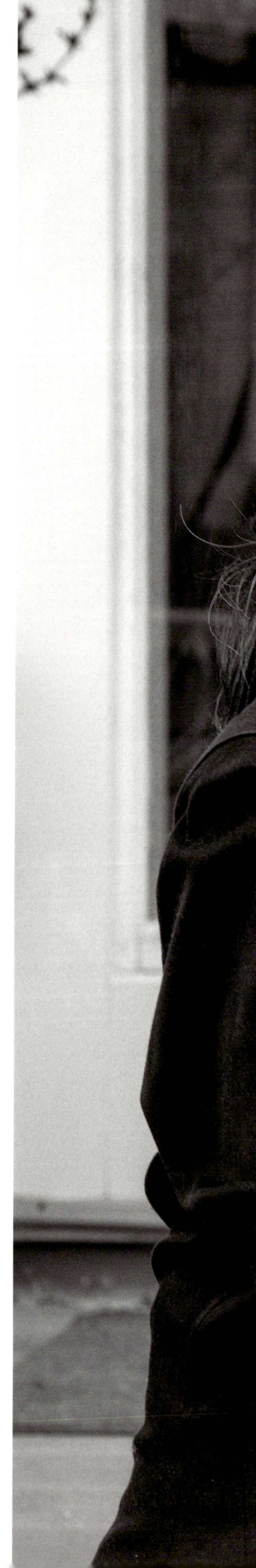

Louise Erdrich on the back porch of her house in Minneapolis, Minnesota, with her dog, Maki, Ojibwa for *wolf*

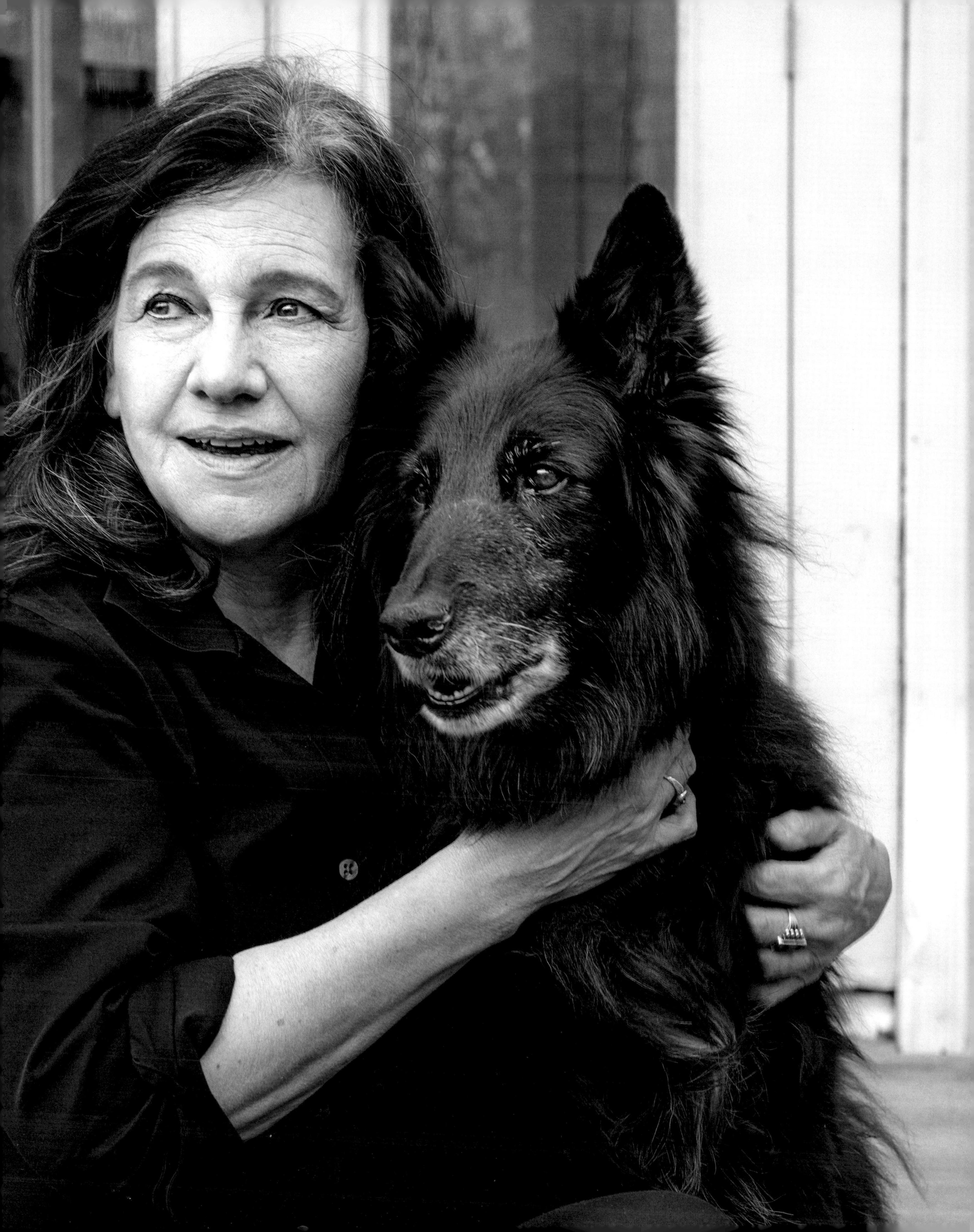

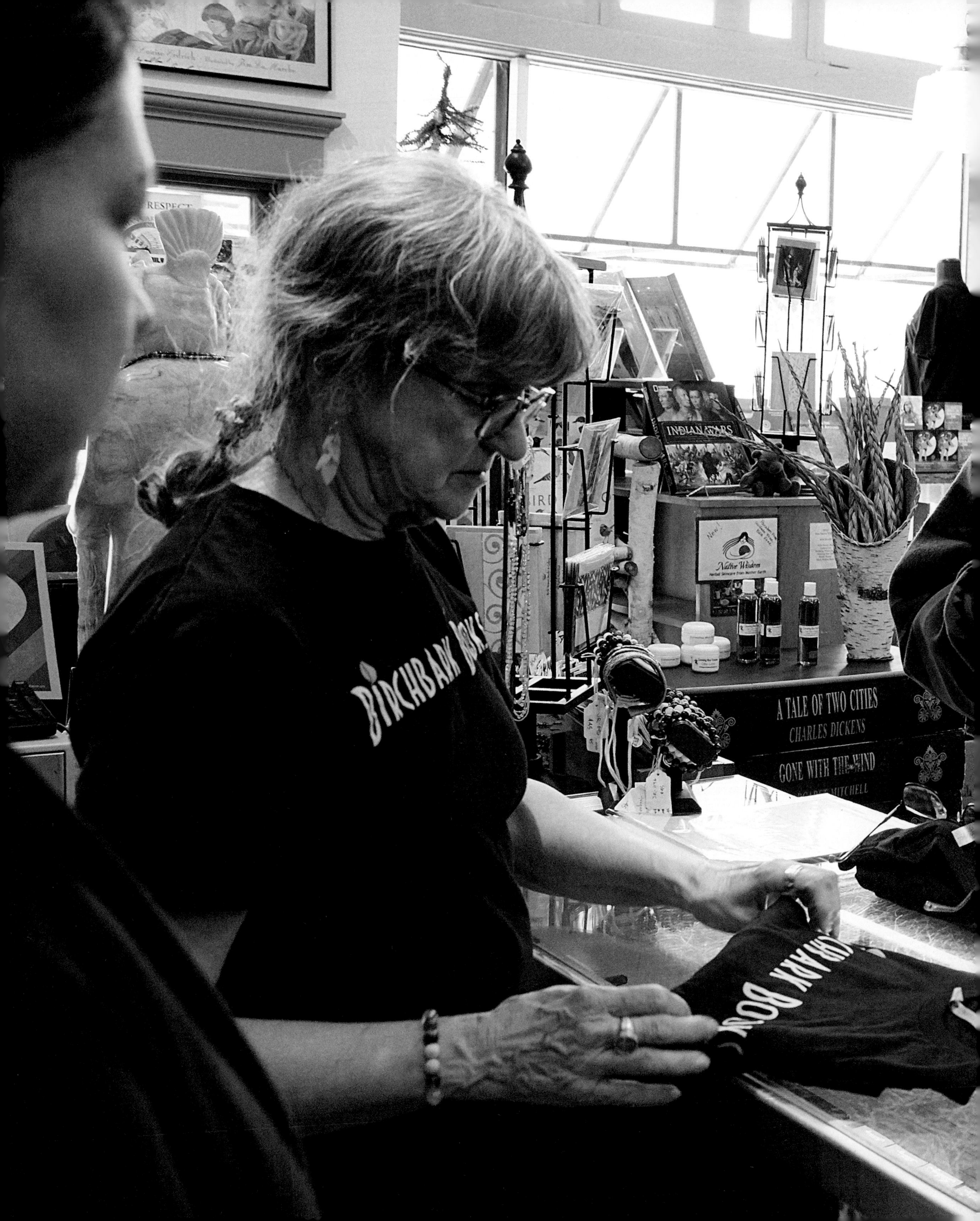
BIRCHBARK BOOKS
INDIAN WARS
Native Wisdom
Herbal Skincare from Mother Earth
A TALE OF TWO CITIES
CHARLES DICKENS
GONE WITH THE WIND
RESPECT

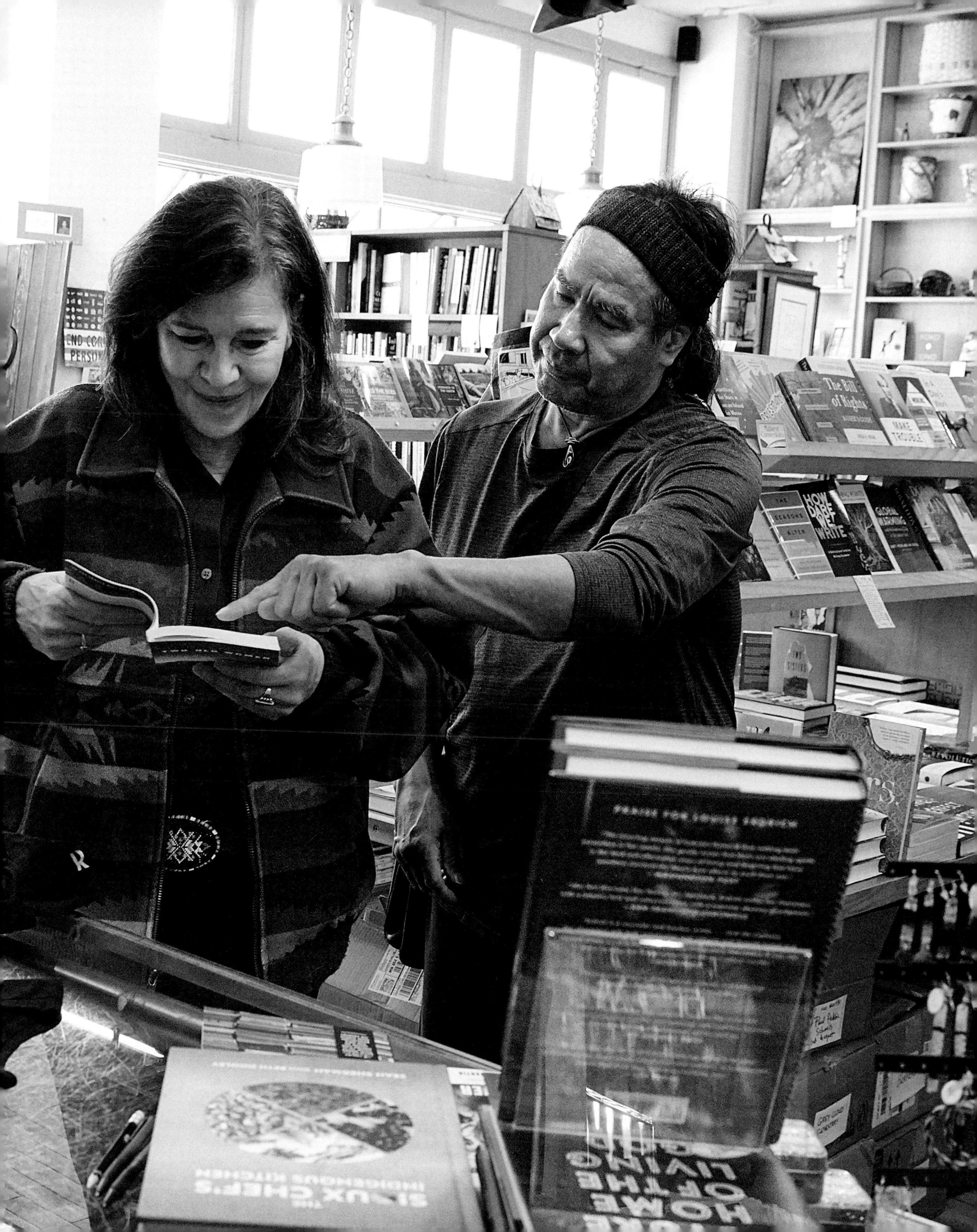

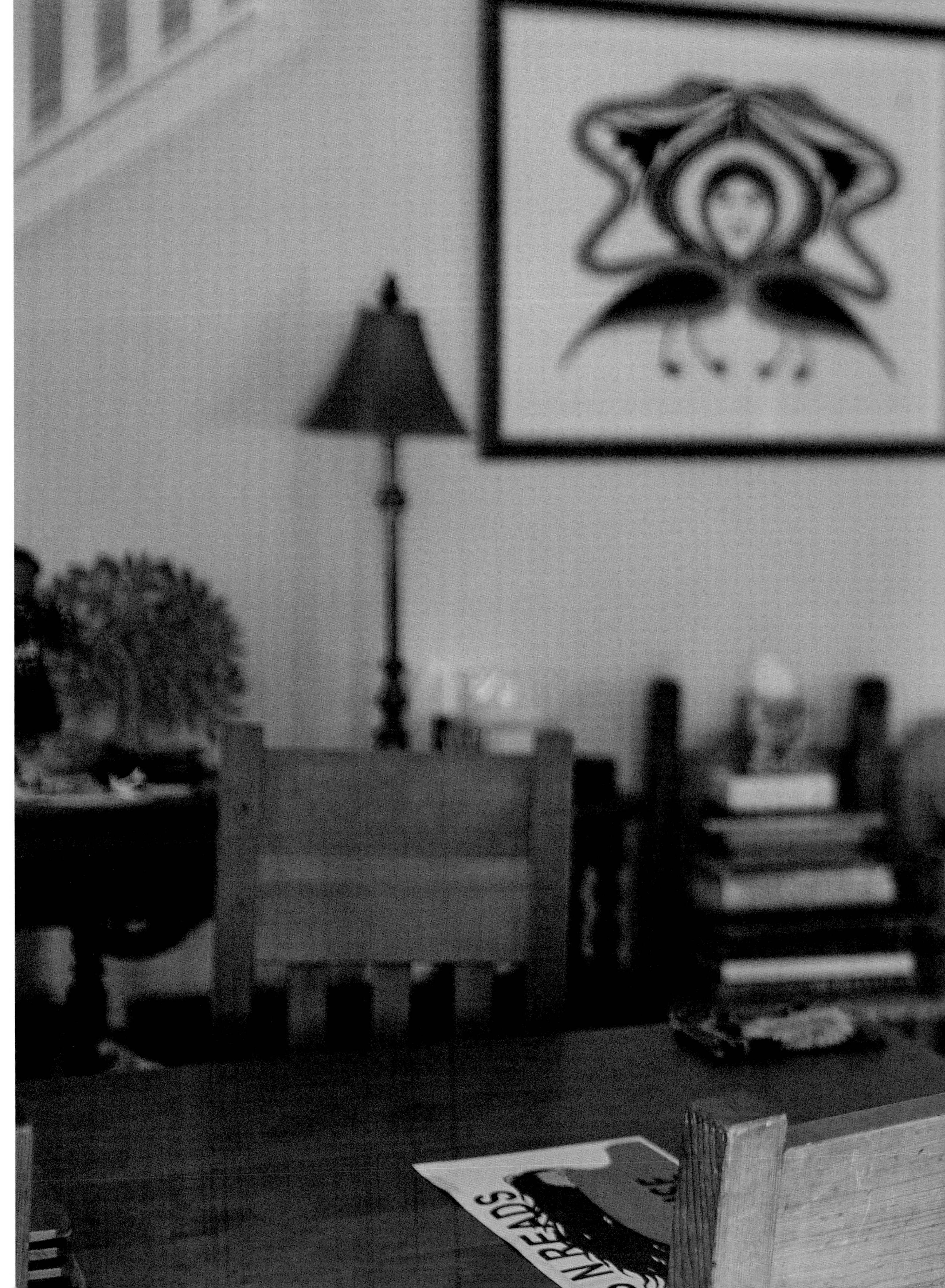

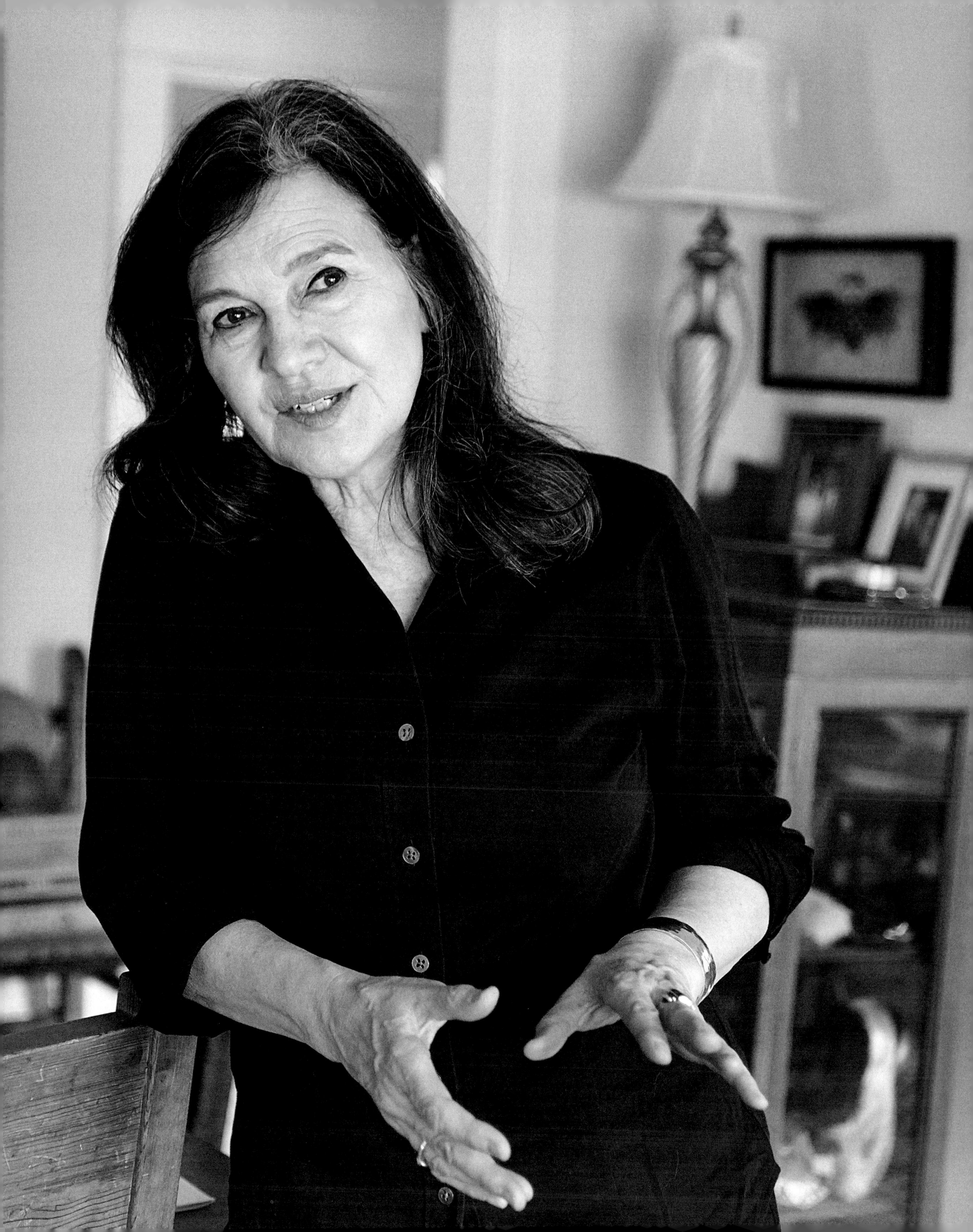

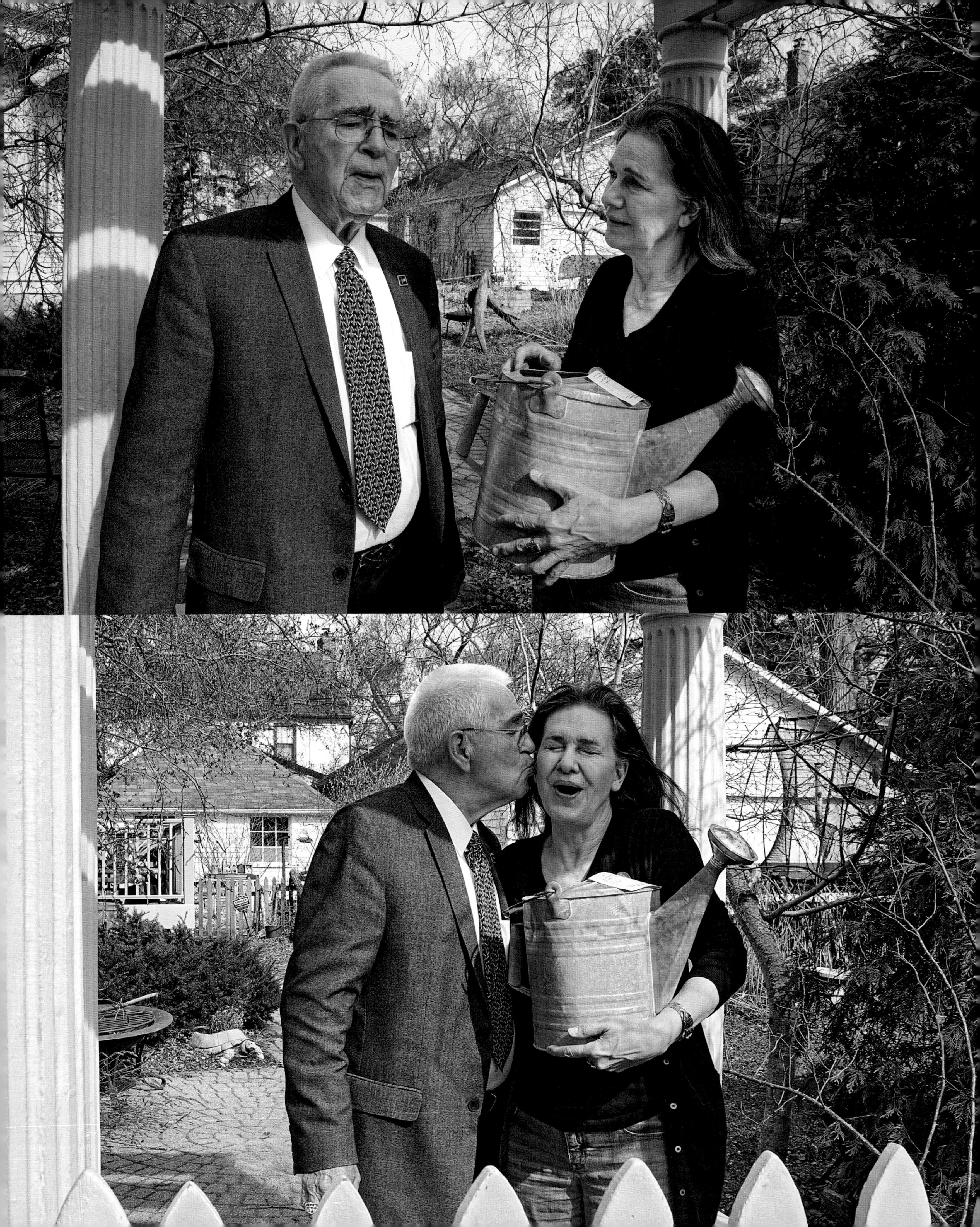

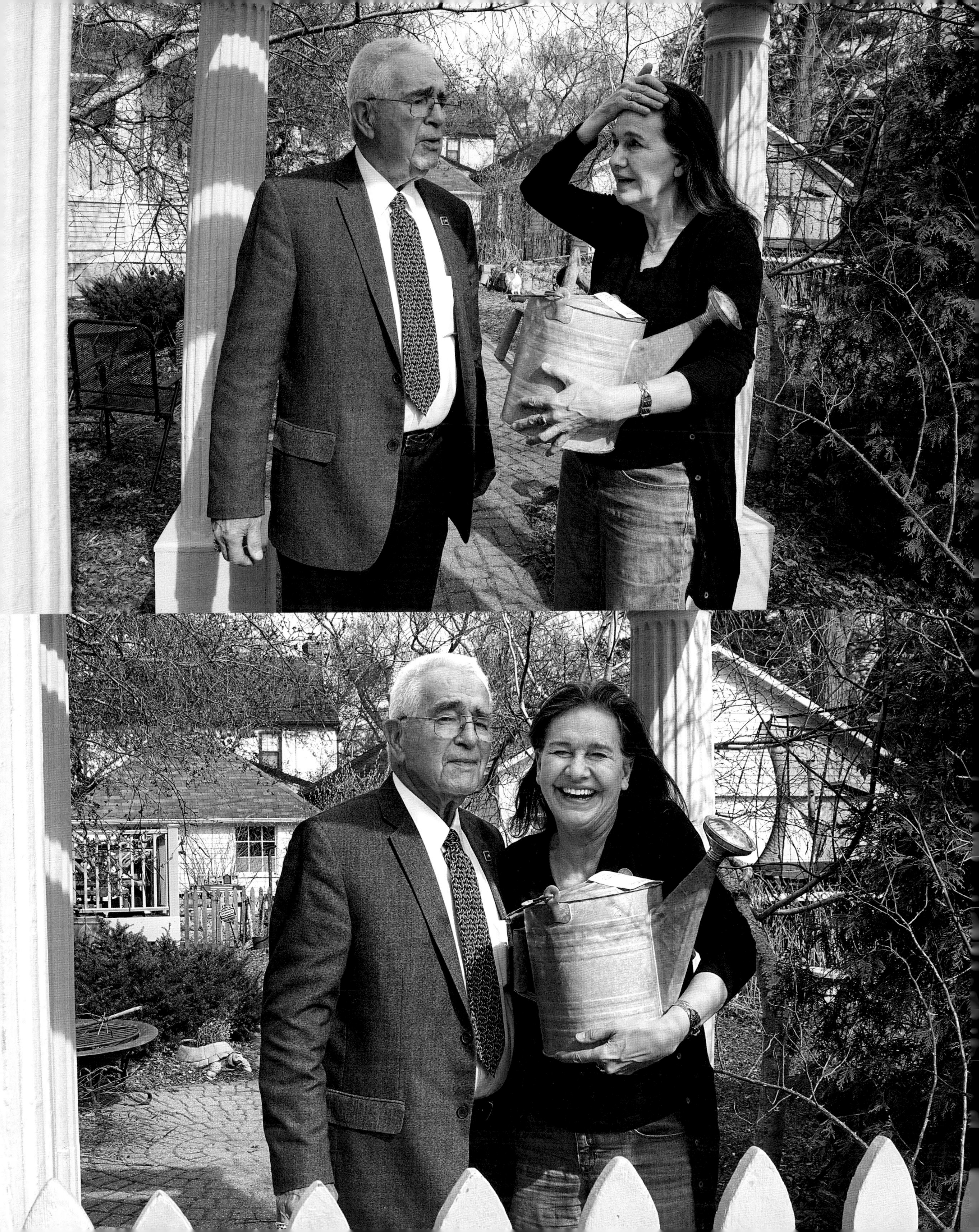

Michael Ondaatje

Canadian (b. 1943)

Photographed in Petaluma, California, March 2010

Michael Ondaatje was born in Sri Lanka of Dutch and Sinhalese (Indian) ancestry. He now lives in Toronto, but I met him in Northern California, a few miles south of Petaluma. During the winter months, Ondaatje usually works here in a cabin, enjoying the solitude of a friend's ranch on the great, open California hills, with live oak and bay trees nearby.

Ondaatje was at a critical stage in *The Cat's Table* and wrote me to say: "I am one of those people who finds it difficult to be photographed; and when I am in the middle of something it discombobulates me utterly, for a long time. This is unreasonable I know, but it is true."

Nevertheless, his natural kindness and generosity overcame his resistance and he set aside time to be photographed on a warm winter afternoon. He walked among the magnificent trees, and edited pages of his novel on a small table close to a suspended bed and a rocker softened by sheepskin. Some of his book *Divisadero* comes out of this landscape.

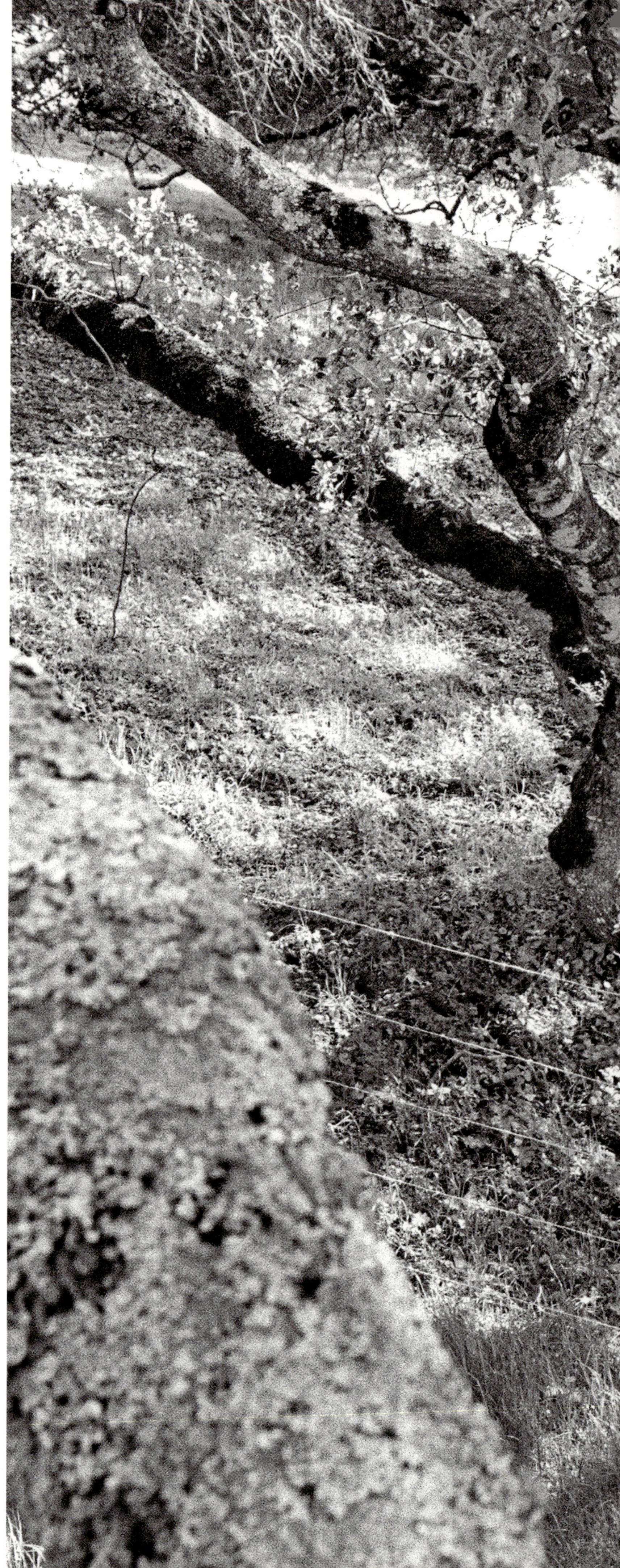

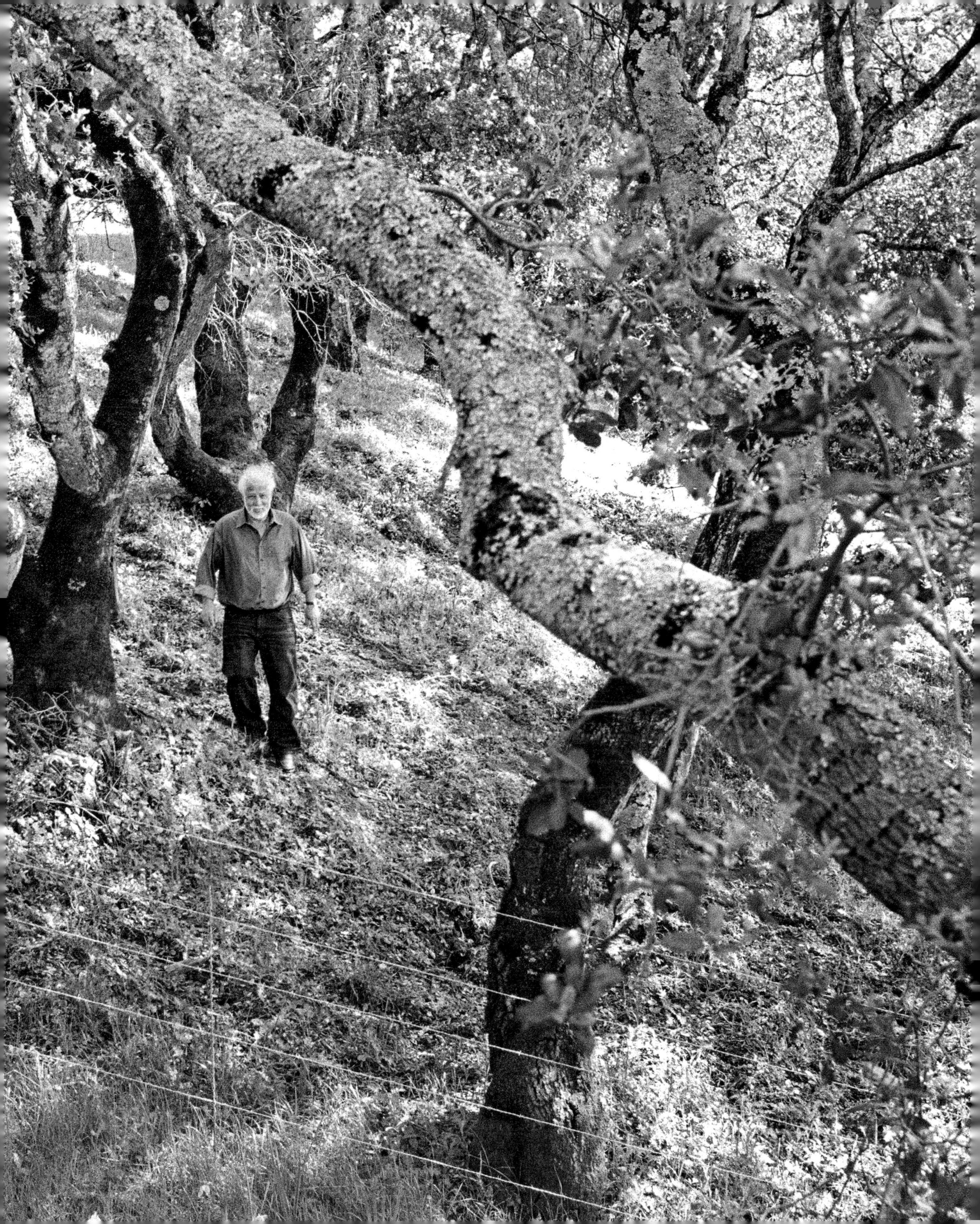

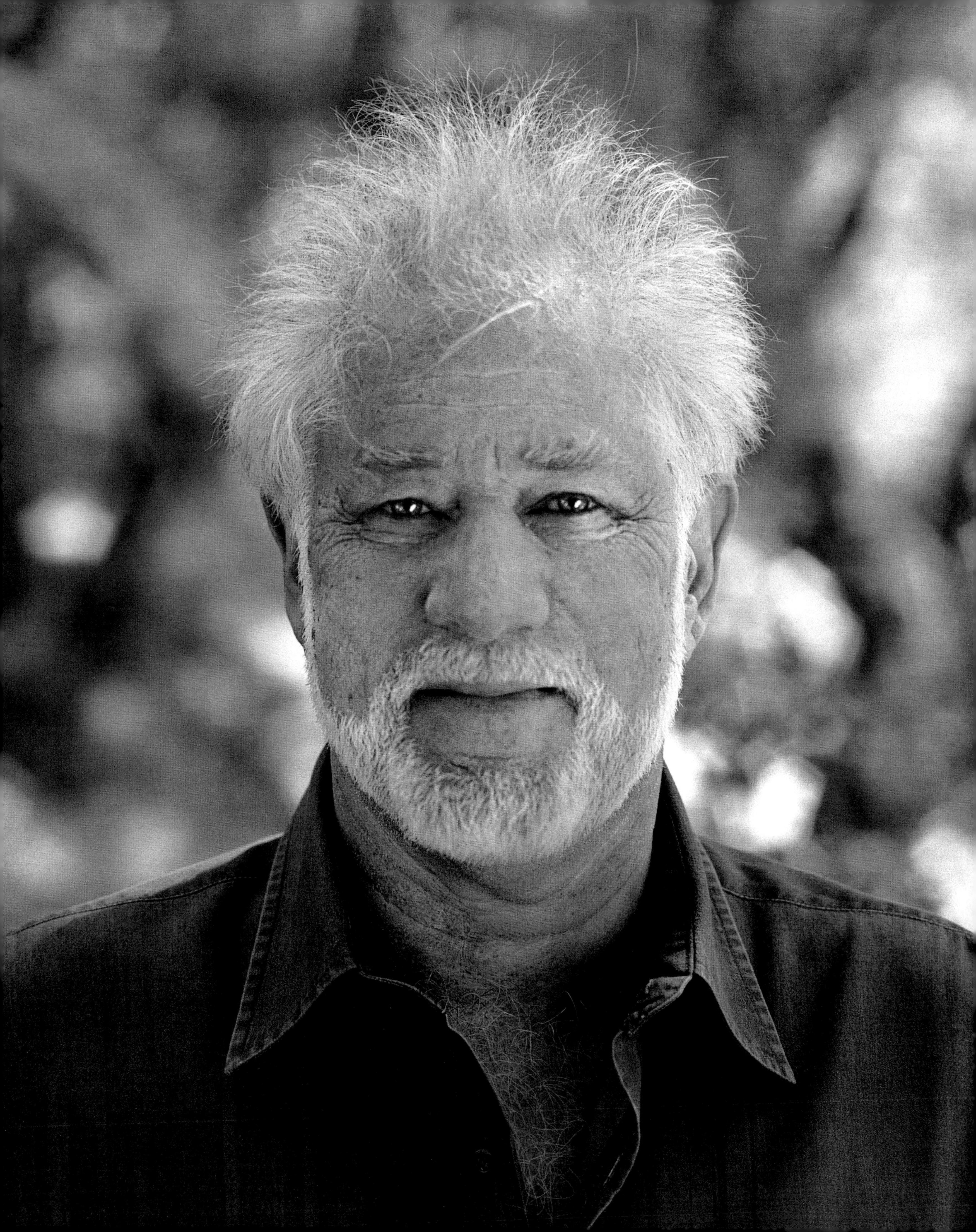

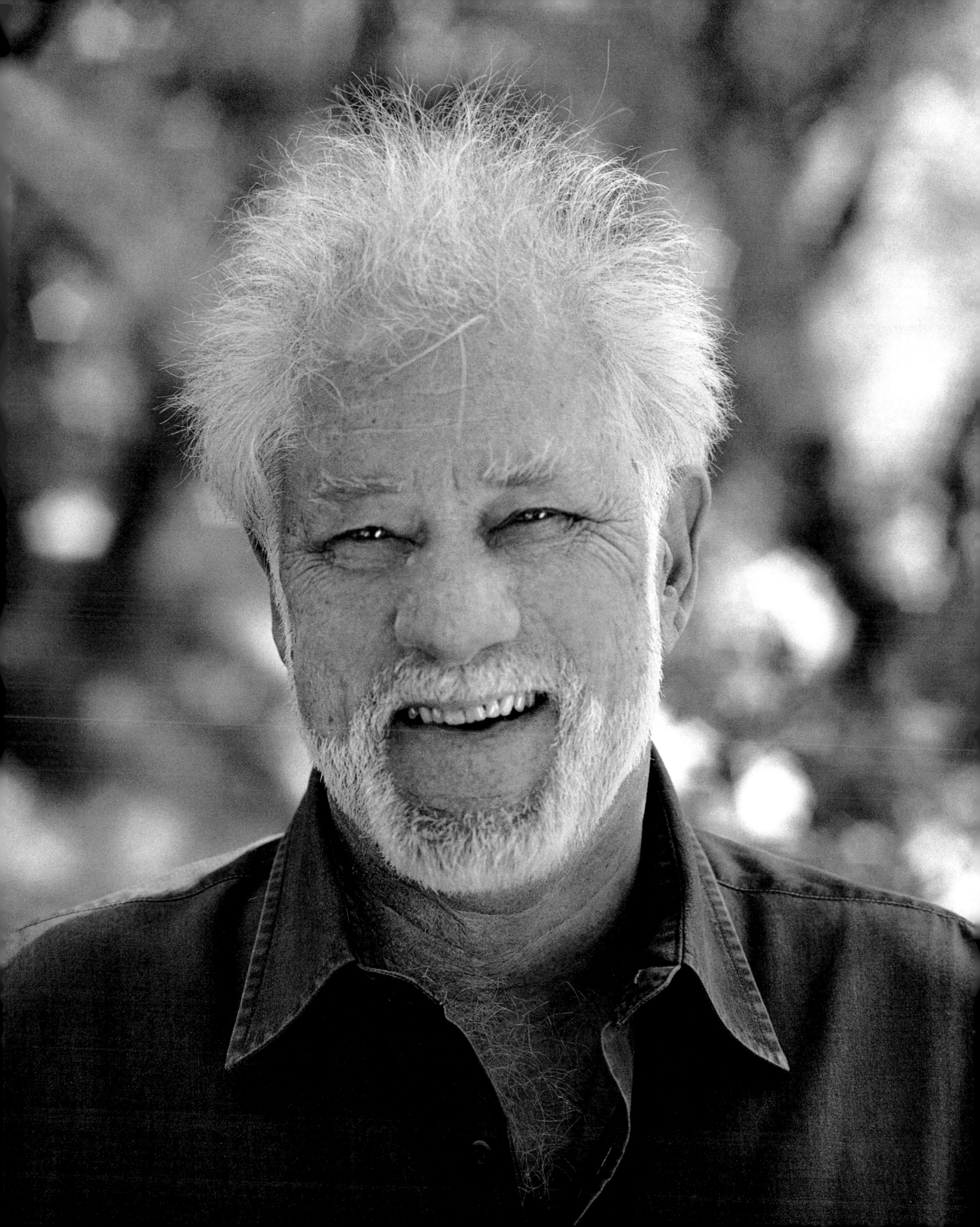

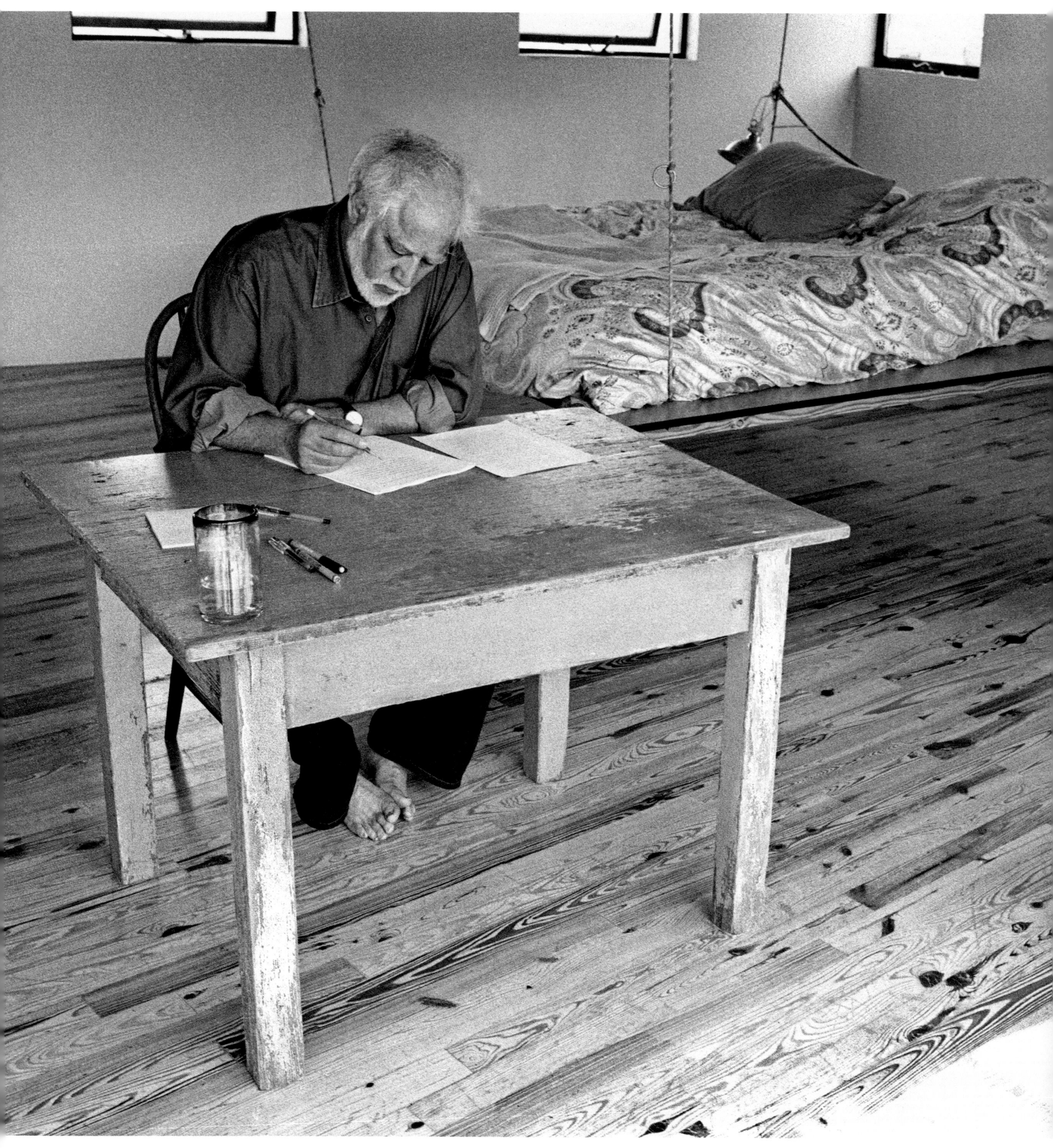

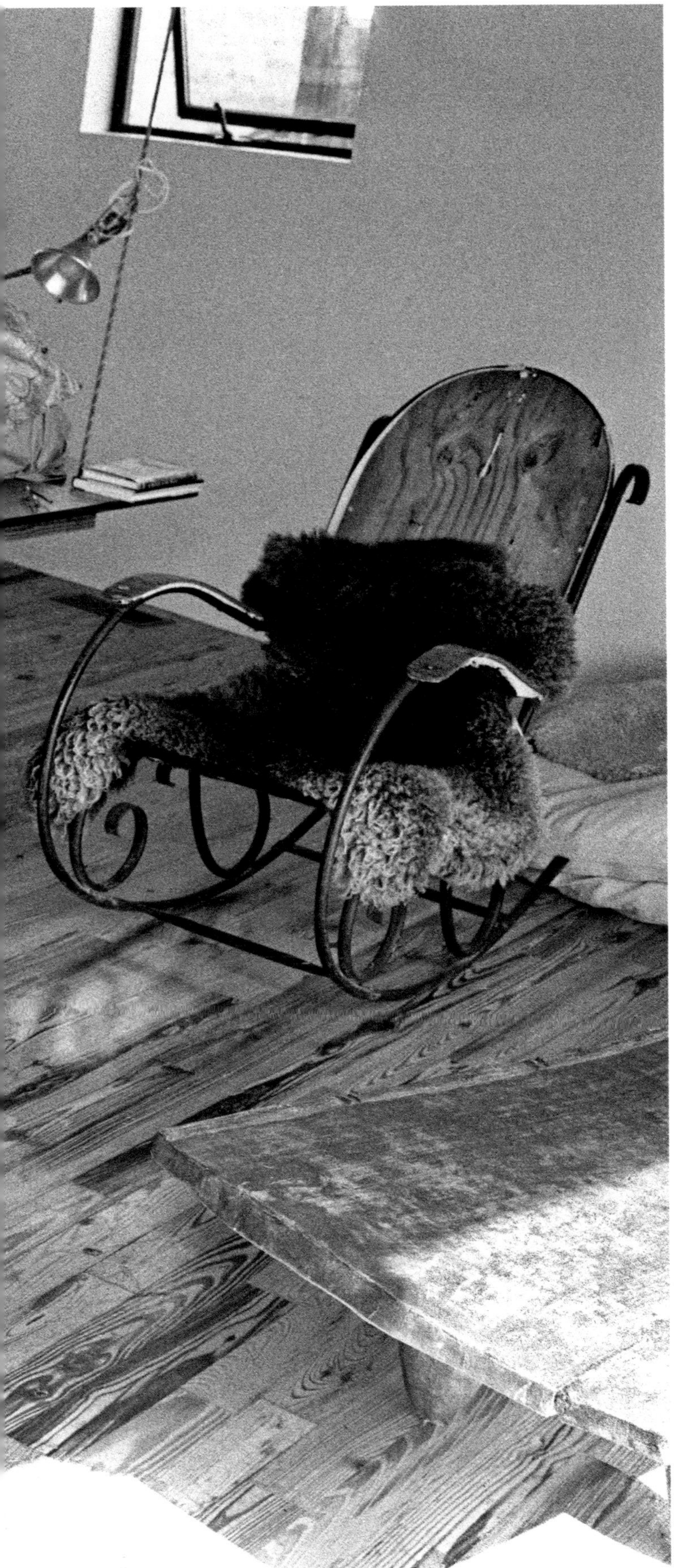

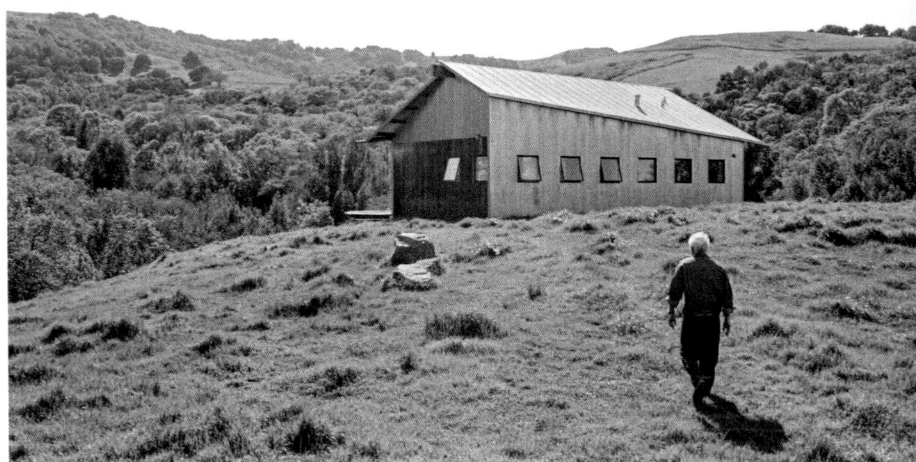

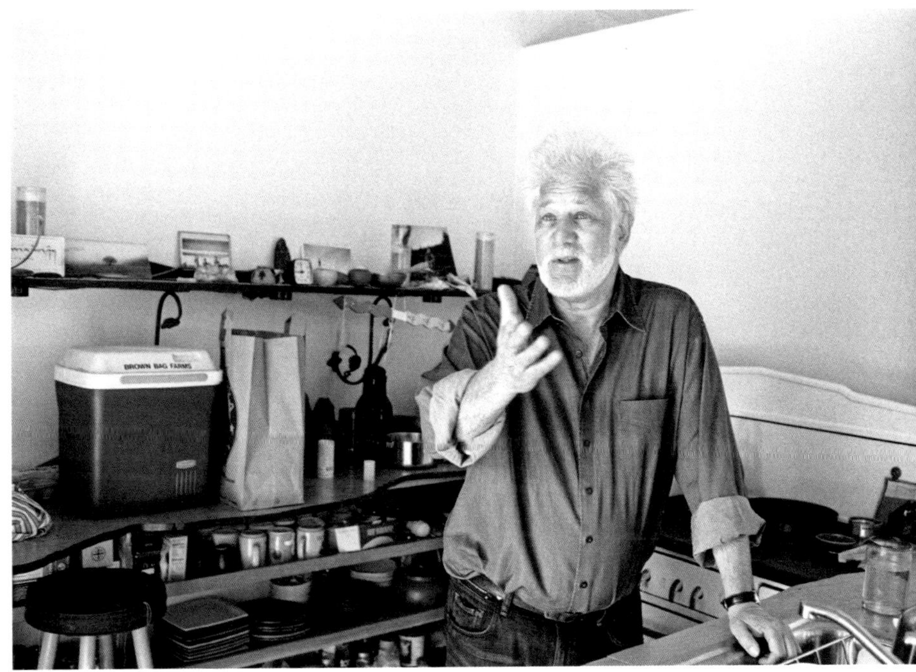

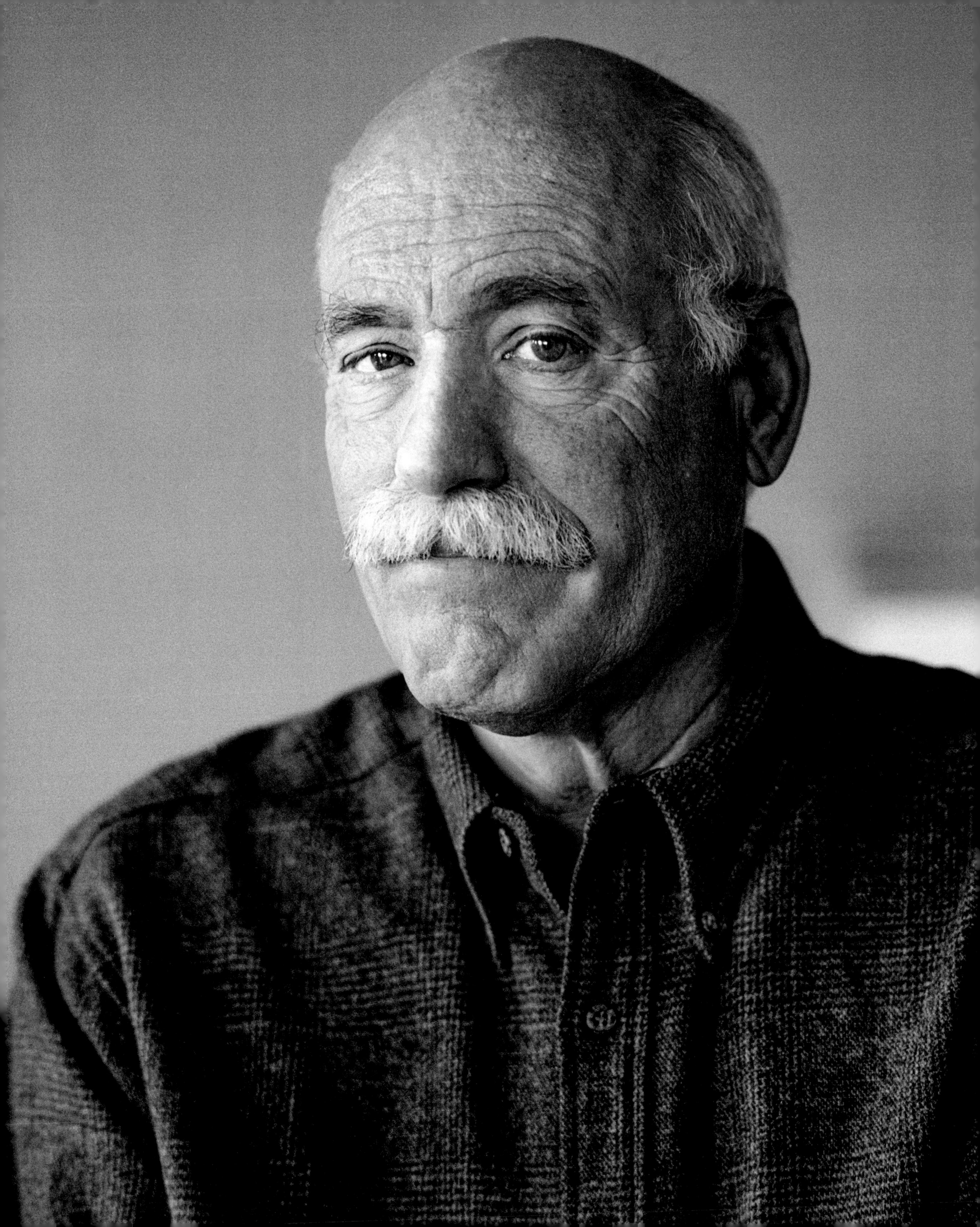

Tobias Wolff

American (b. 1945)

Photographed in Stanford, California, January 2010

Tobias Wolff taught at Stanford University for twenty-two years in the Creative Writing and English departments. Just as he must have been with his students, he was considerate and helpful to me while I photographed him at his house in Stanford. He spoke with admiration about a number of writers who interested me, and was thoughtful, without being harsh in his assessment of their work. I asked whom he'd like to see included in this book. He mentioned eight or so people, all of whom, I now realize, I've photographed.

When I asked Wolff about his interests beyond writing and teaching, he told me he swam each day at the university. I asked him if I might photograph him swimming. He pulled back, uncomfortable with even the thought. "Oh, I was afraid you'd want to do that."

But as a storyteller, a maker of pictures himself, he understood, and overcame his natural reticence. Eleven years later, when we spoke in 2021, he reflected: "At the time you took the photo, I swam for an hour each day. Now I'm happy with forty-five minutes."

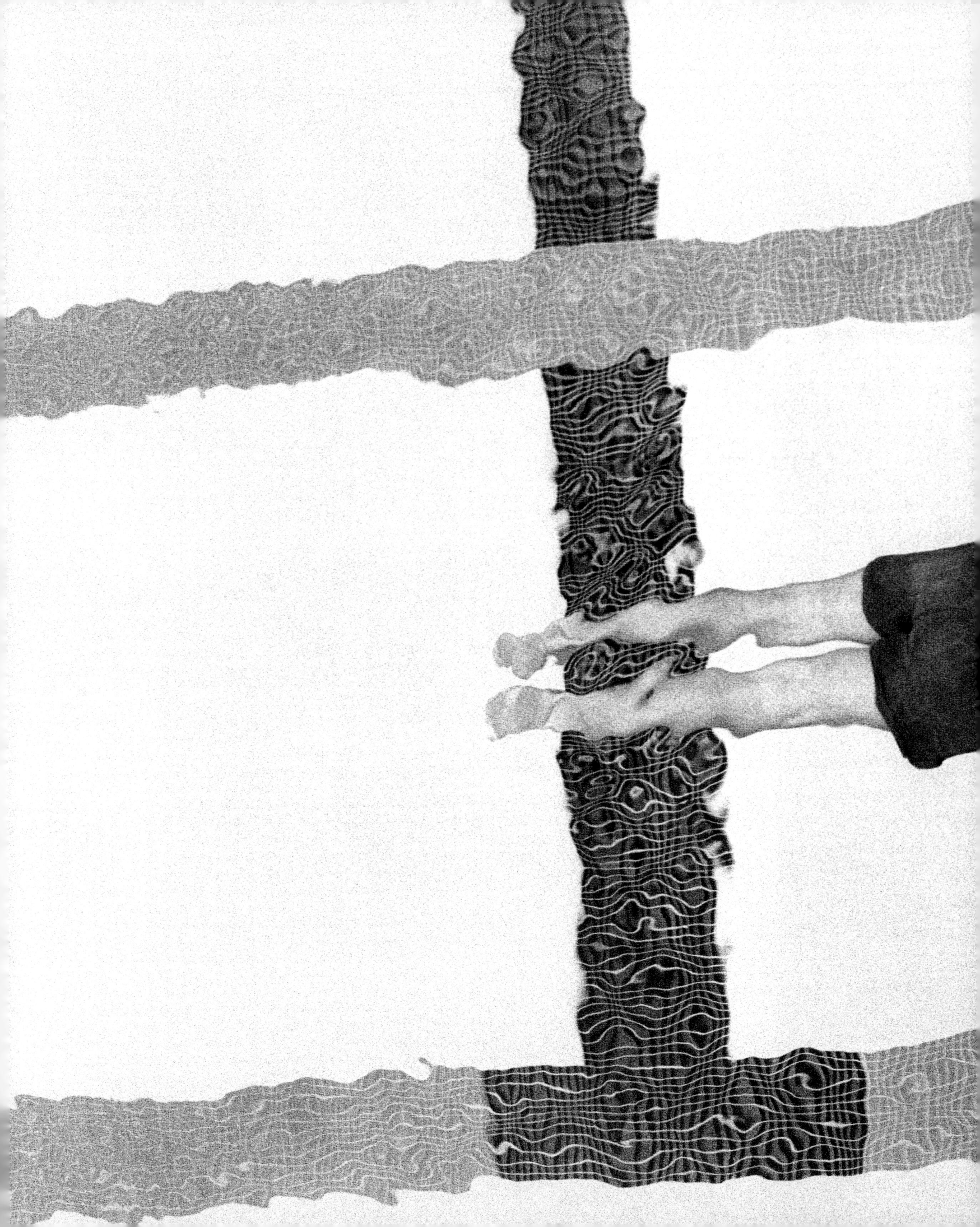

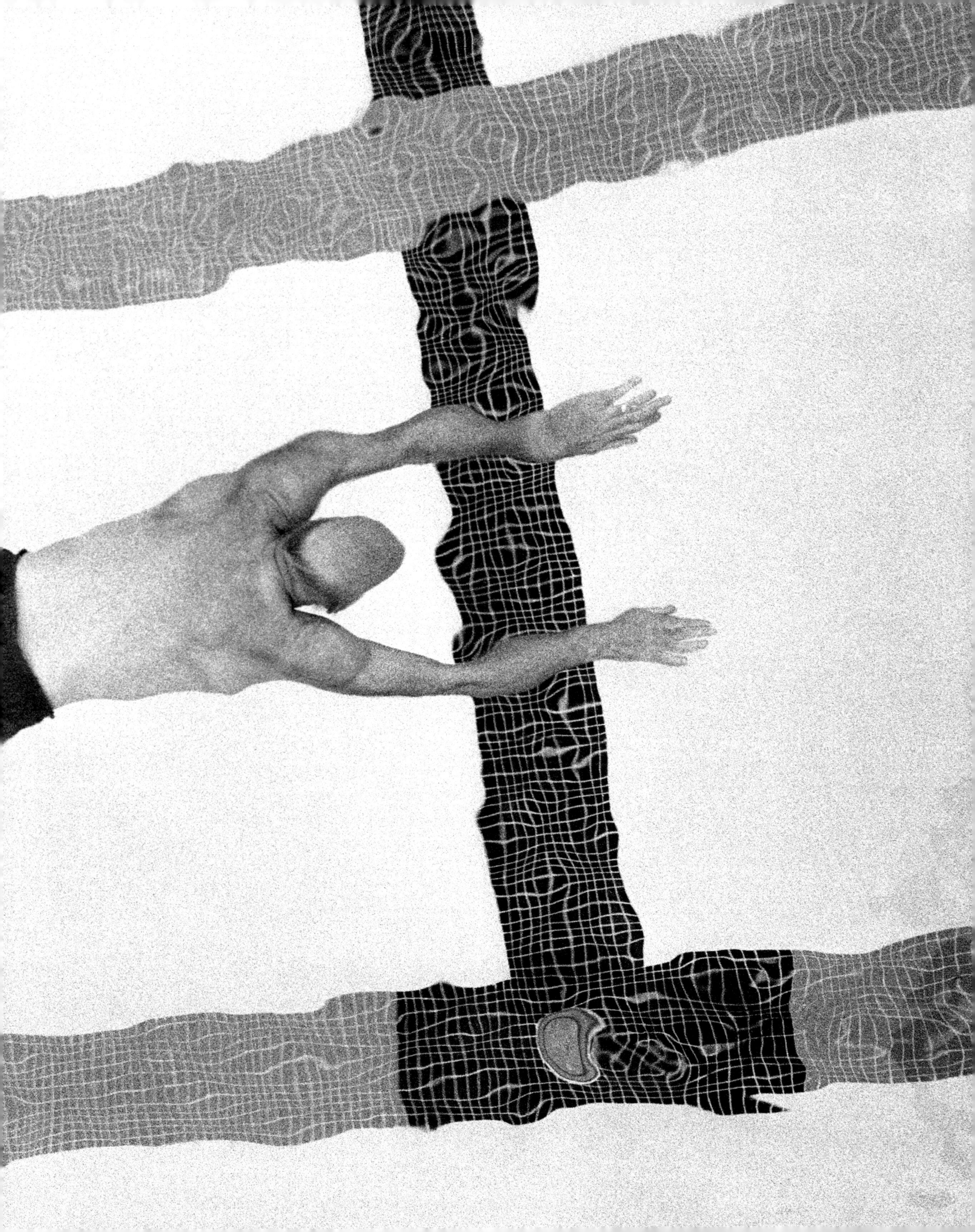

Zadie
Smith

English (b. 1975)

Photographed in New York, New York, November 2013

Zadie Smith, her husband, Nick Laird, and their two children were still in the process of settling into a new apartment near New York University when I arrived to photograph her. Smith, juggling her tenured position as a professor of creative writing and taking care of her young family, was putting all of their possessions in place. Her little dog seemed shell-shocked.

We removed ourselves from the hubbub and went out onto the porch to do the portrait. It was a brisk, November day and the light had such clarity that I could see myself reflected in Smith's eyes.

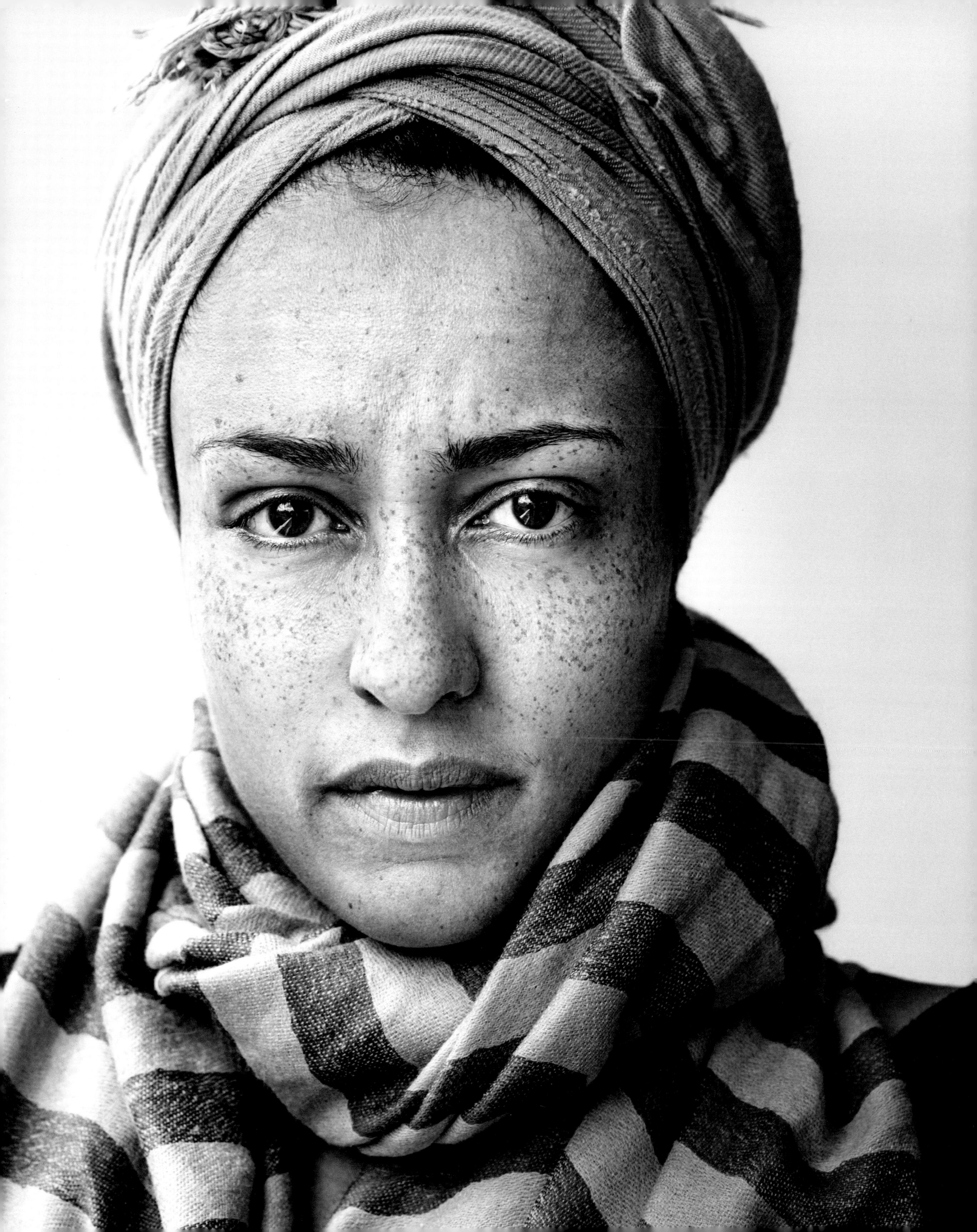

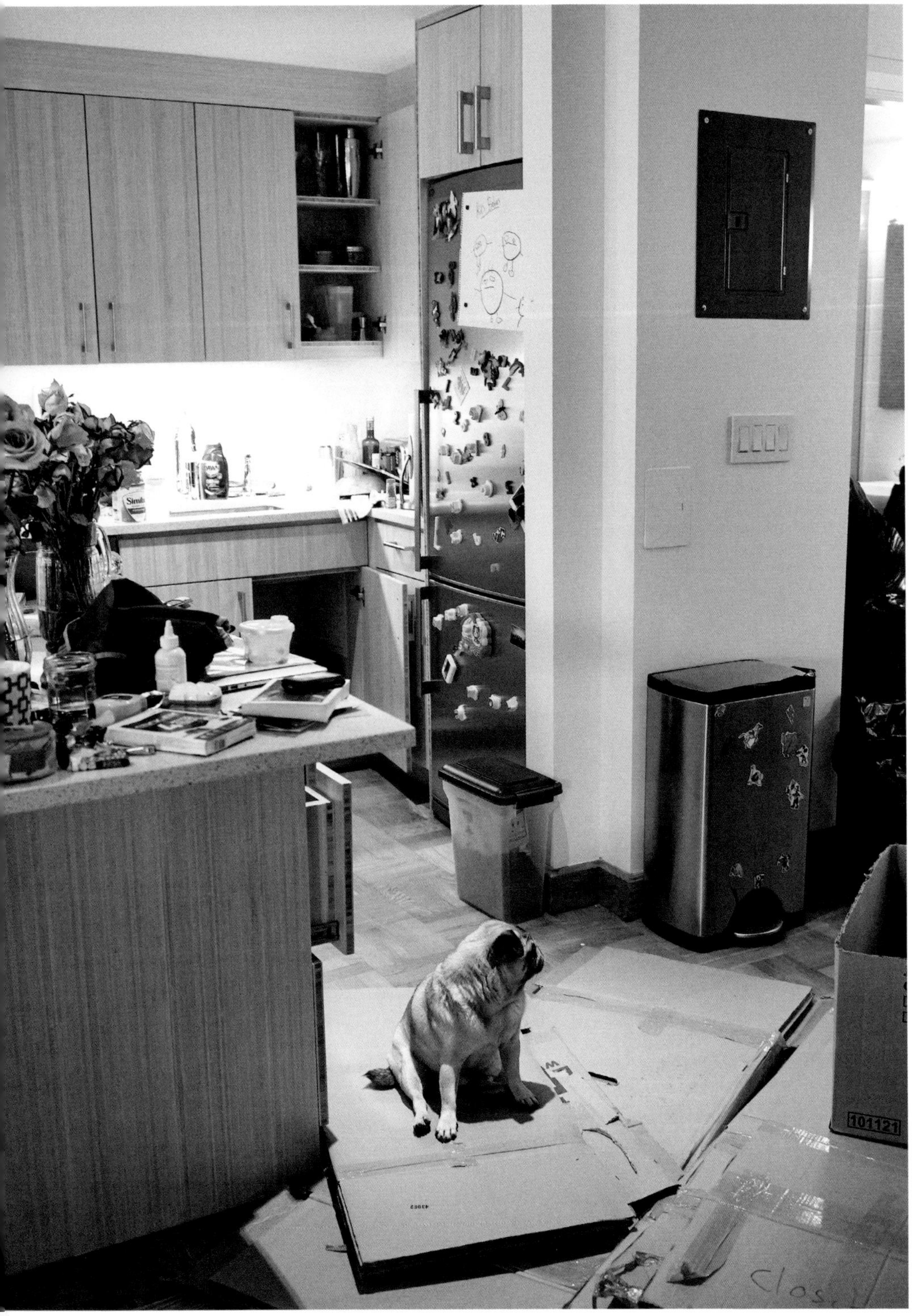

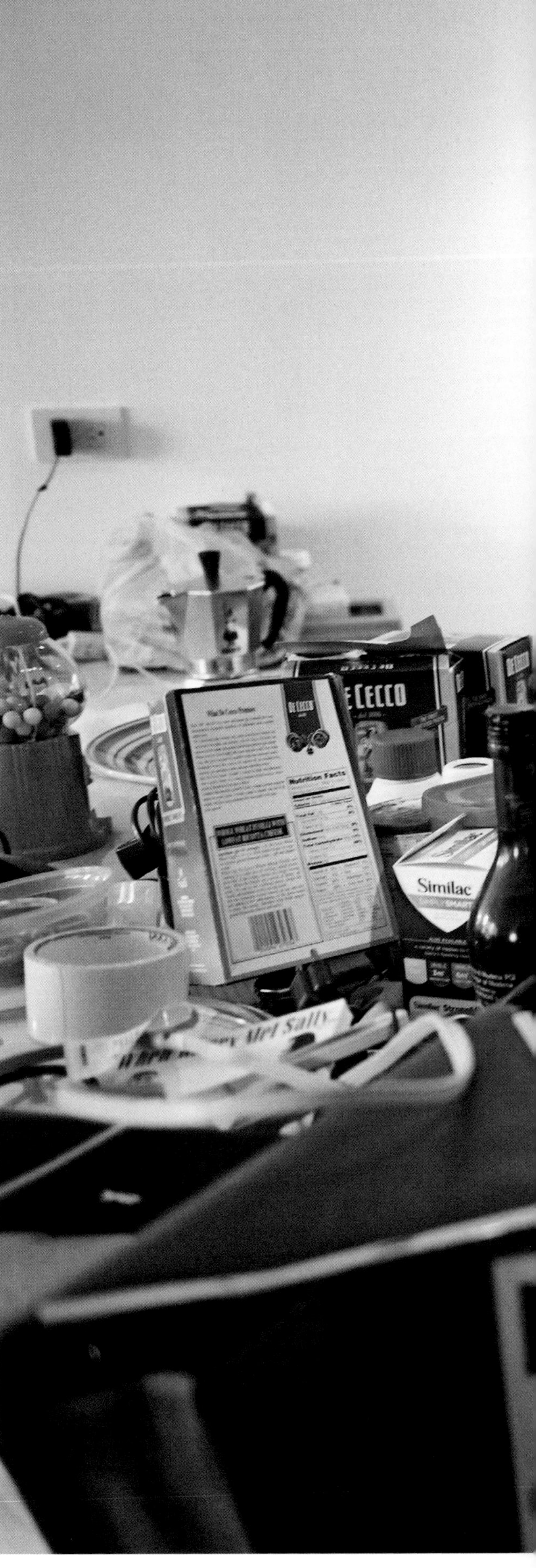

Later, Colm Tóibín, flipping from the portrait to the photos of Smith's chaotic kitchen, said, "Oh, this is what makes it interesting."

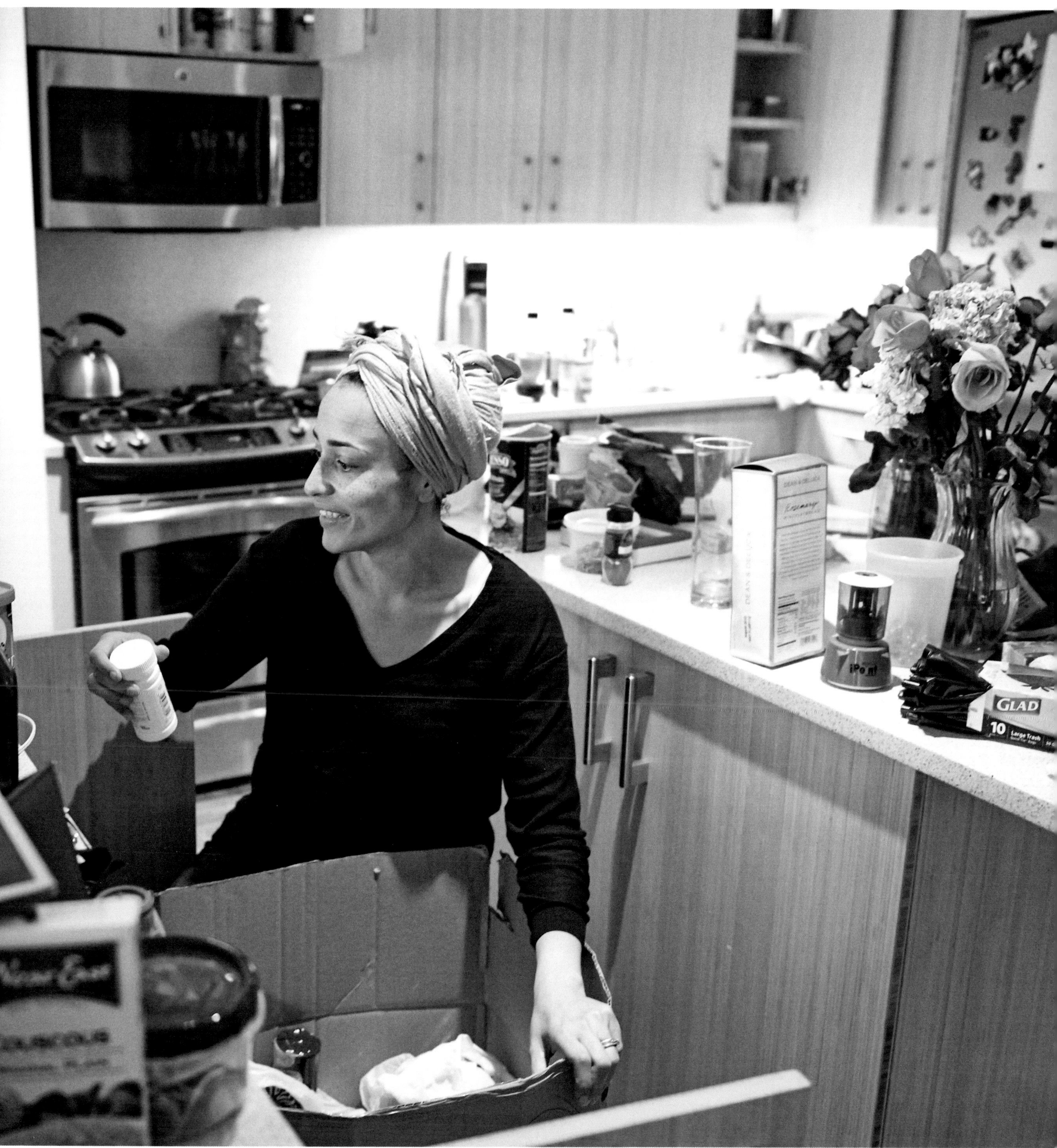

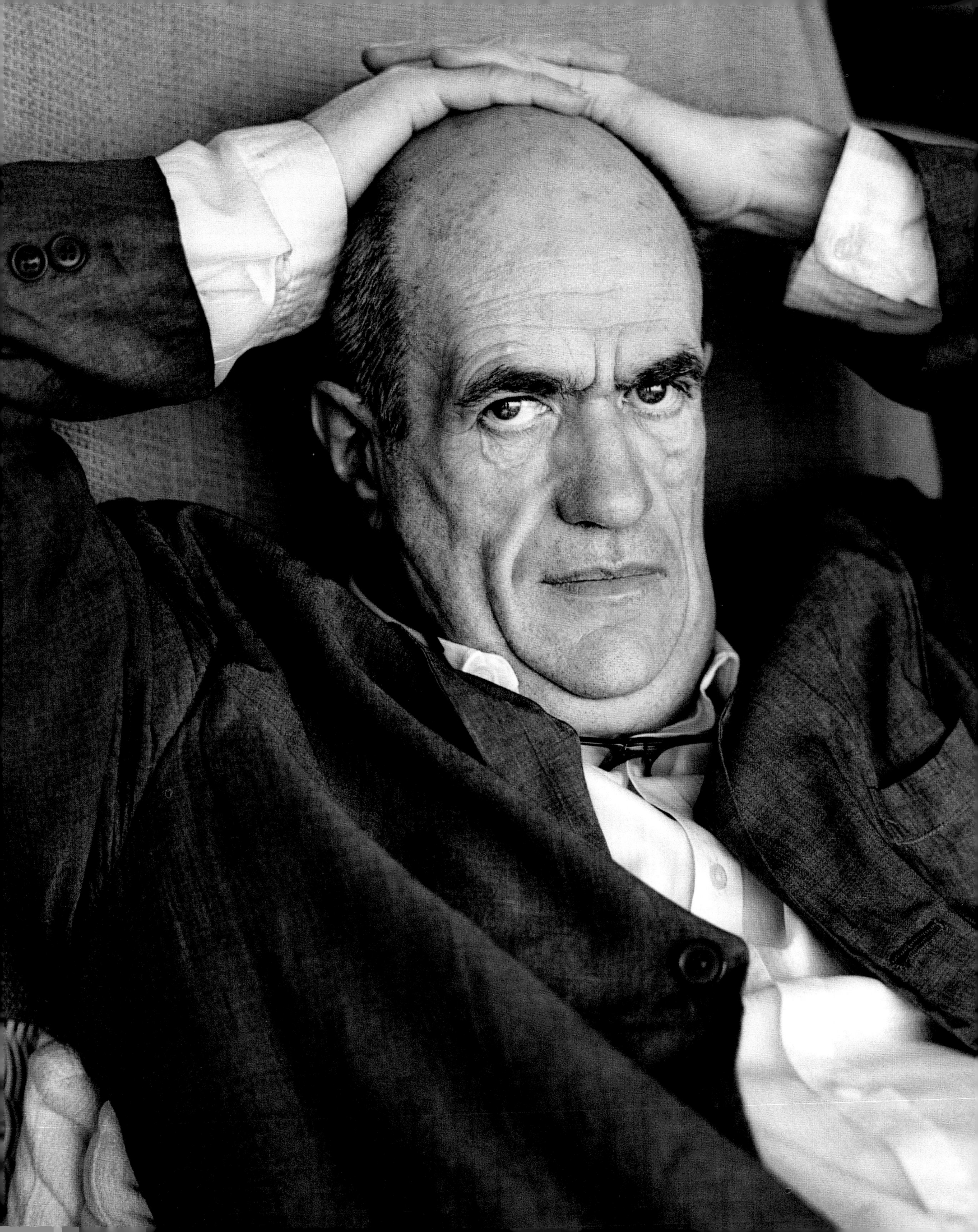

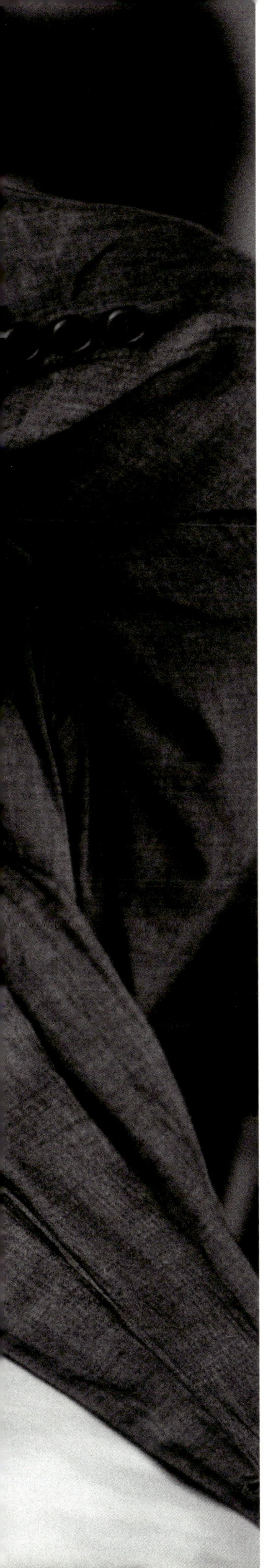

Colm Tóibín

Irish (b. 1955)

Photographed on Cush Gap, County Wexford, Ireland, May 2011

Colm Tóibín lives in a modern house on Cush Gap, in County Wexford, Ireland. The house sits on high cliffs overlooking the Irish Sea.

Tóibín took me to the Saturday farmers' market in Enniscorthy, where he shopped for fresh rhubarb, asparagus, potatoes, and lamb from his favorite vendor, a local farmer. He's a regular at the market and enjoyed chatting and joking with each stall-holder.

Tóibín is the essence of Irish—a great storyteller, opinionated, and quick to laugh. As we sat in the market having a morning coffee, he spoke to an old school chum, then in an aside, said to me, "I don't like him." When I asked why, he said, "Because he thinks he's English."

With the farmers' market provisions, Tóibín worked all afternoon preparing dinner. And, without the least trace of angst common to many cooks, he served the delicious lamb roast with condiments and wine on a multicolored textile from the Mexican state of Oaxaca.

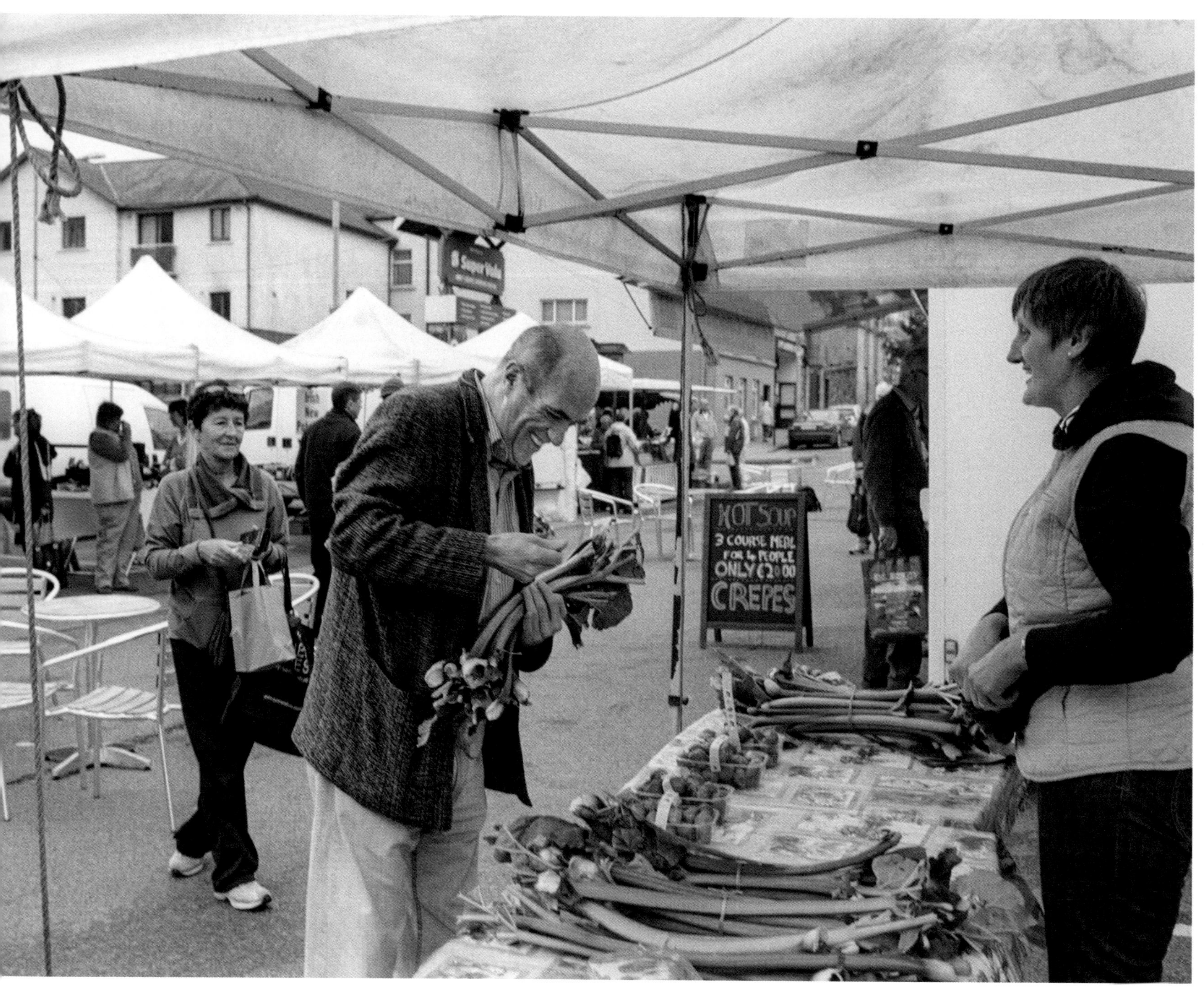

PAGES 56–57: Tóibín sat reading as fog rolled in from the Irish Sea, the unmown grasses on the high hill reflected in his living room window.

PAGES 58–59: Tóibín goes down off the cliffs for frequent walks along the strand of the Irish Sea. I asked him what he thought about on these walks. "I leave my head empty," he said.

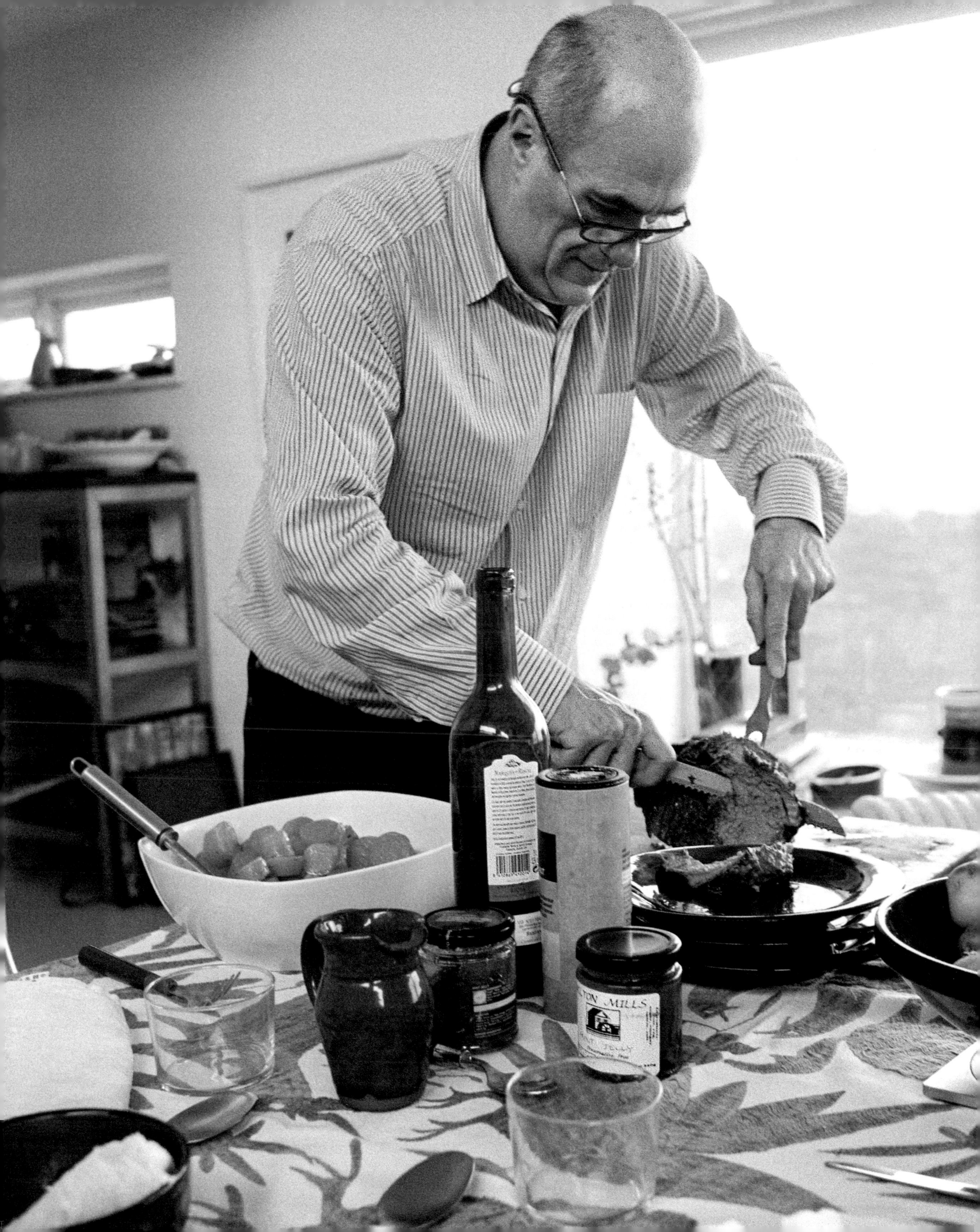

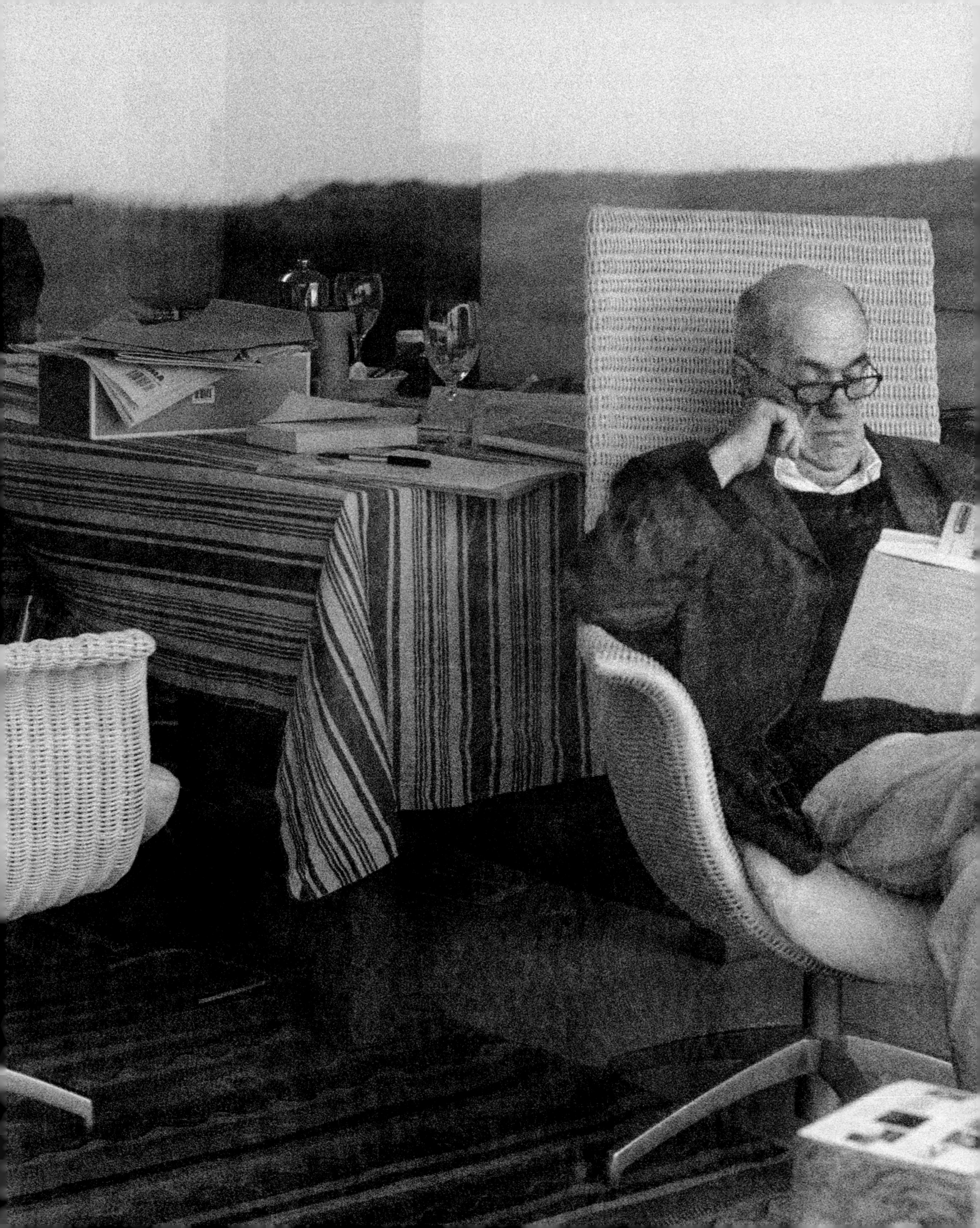

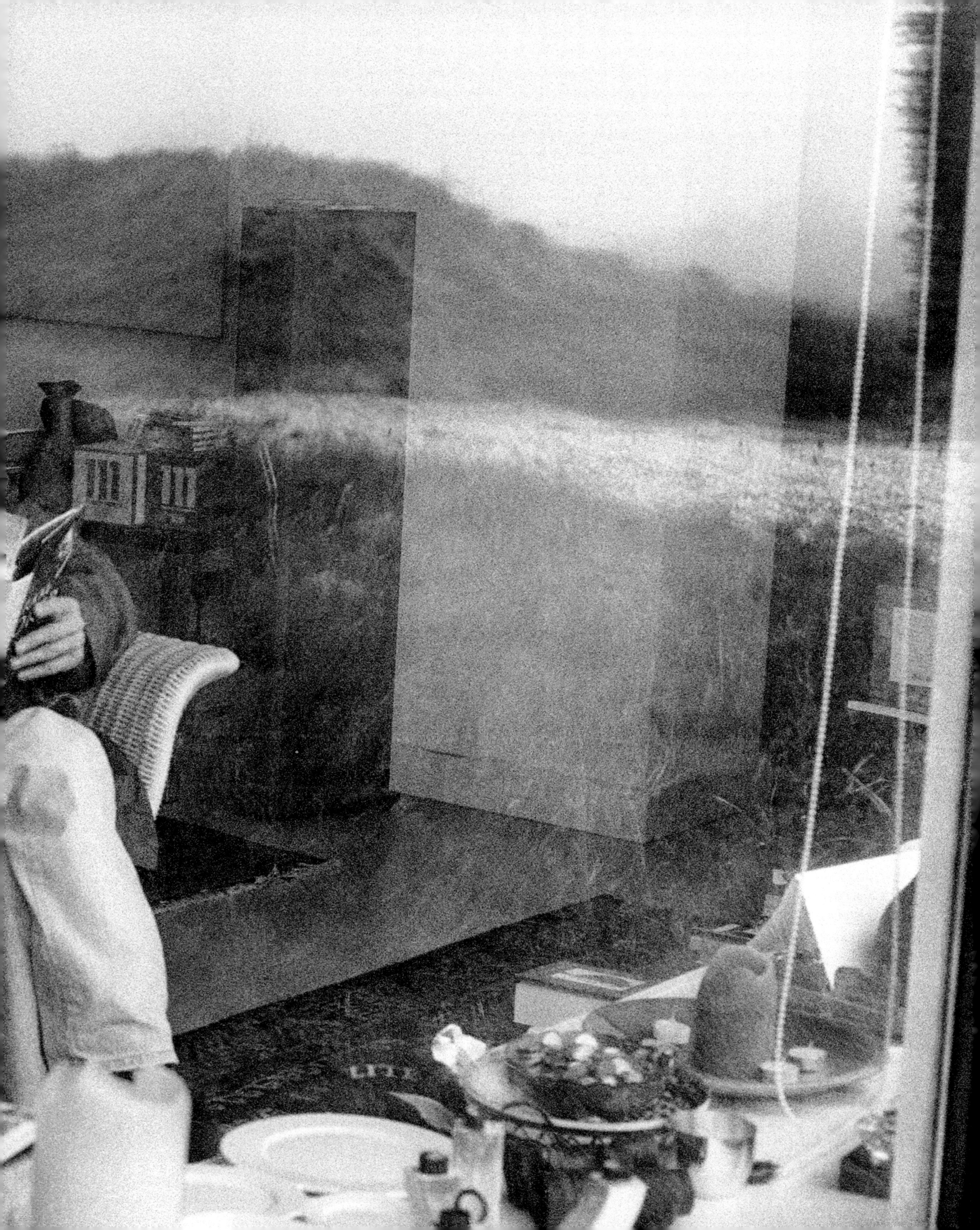

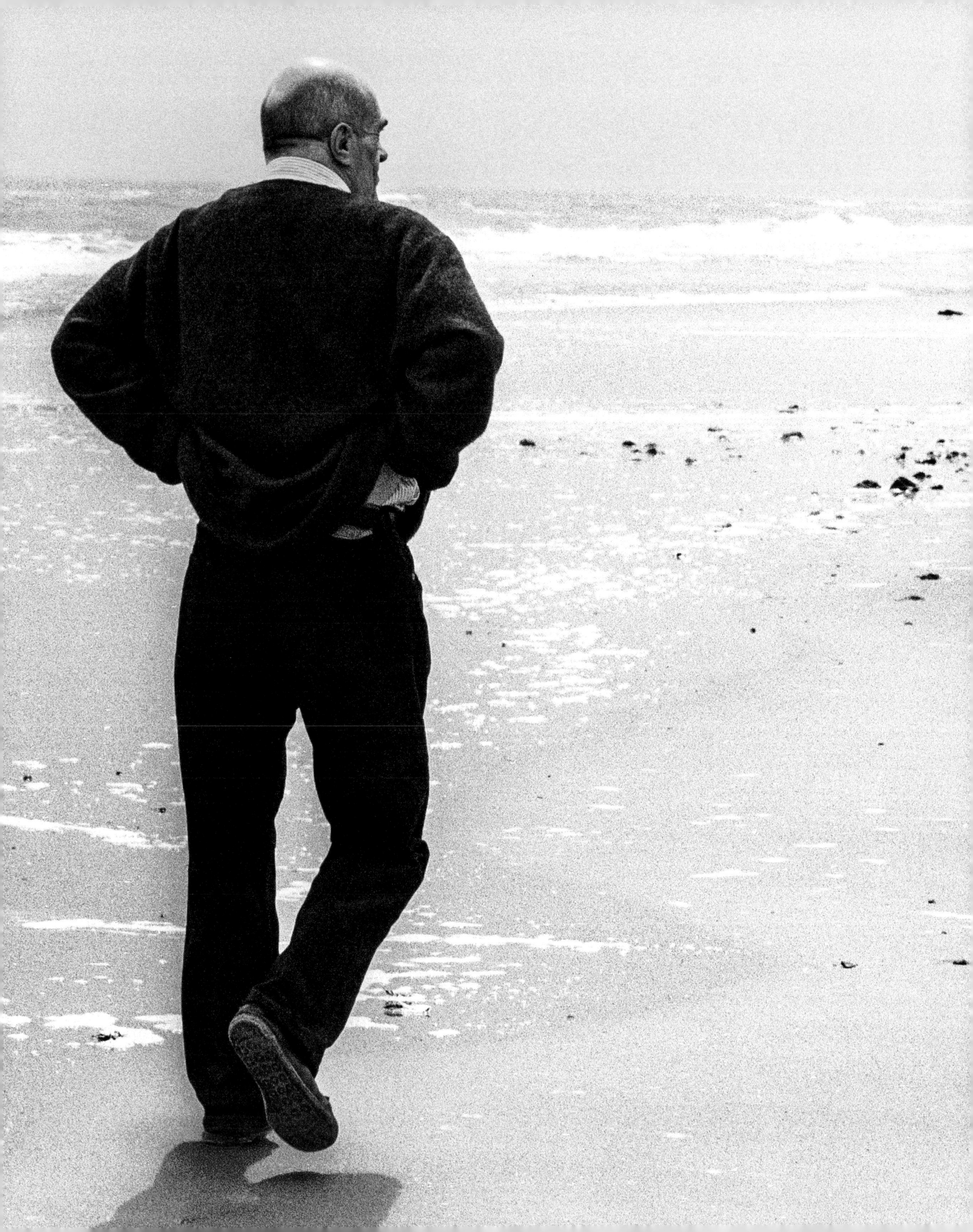

Rachel Cusk

Canadian (b. 1967)

Photographed in Stiffkey, Norfolk, England, October 2018

Rachel Cusk lived a few miles outside of Stiffkey in Norfolk, England, when I photographed her in the studio of her husband, Siemon Scamell-Katz. Together they had built a contemporary house, designed by Scamell-Katz, on the Norfolk coast. It sits above the salt marshes on the North Sea and the isolation suits them both. Paths through the marshes are ideal for walking, and the village of Blakeney is not far.

One night, while I stayed in the village, the River Glaven flooded its banks after a full moon and big rains. In the morning, the main road was completely under water. Good-sized boats appeared to be floating down the street warning cars to take higher ground.

Just about three miles from Rachel and Siemon's house sits Binham Priory, a stone church built in 1091 on land given by William the Conqueror.

A weekly ritual of the couple's country life, a life of homebodies essentially, was visiting with local friends at the Stiffkey Red Lion pub.

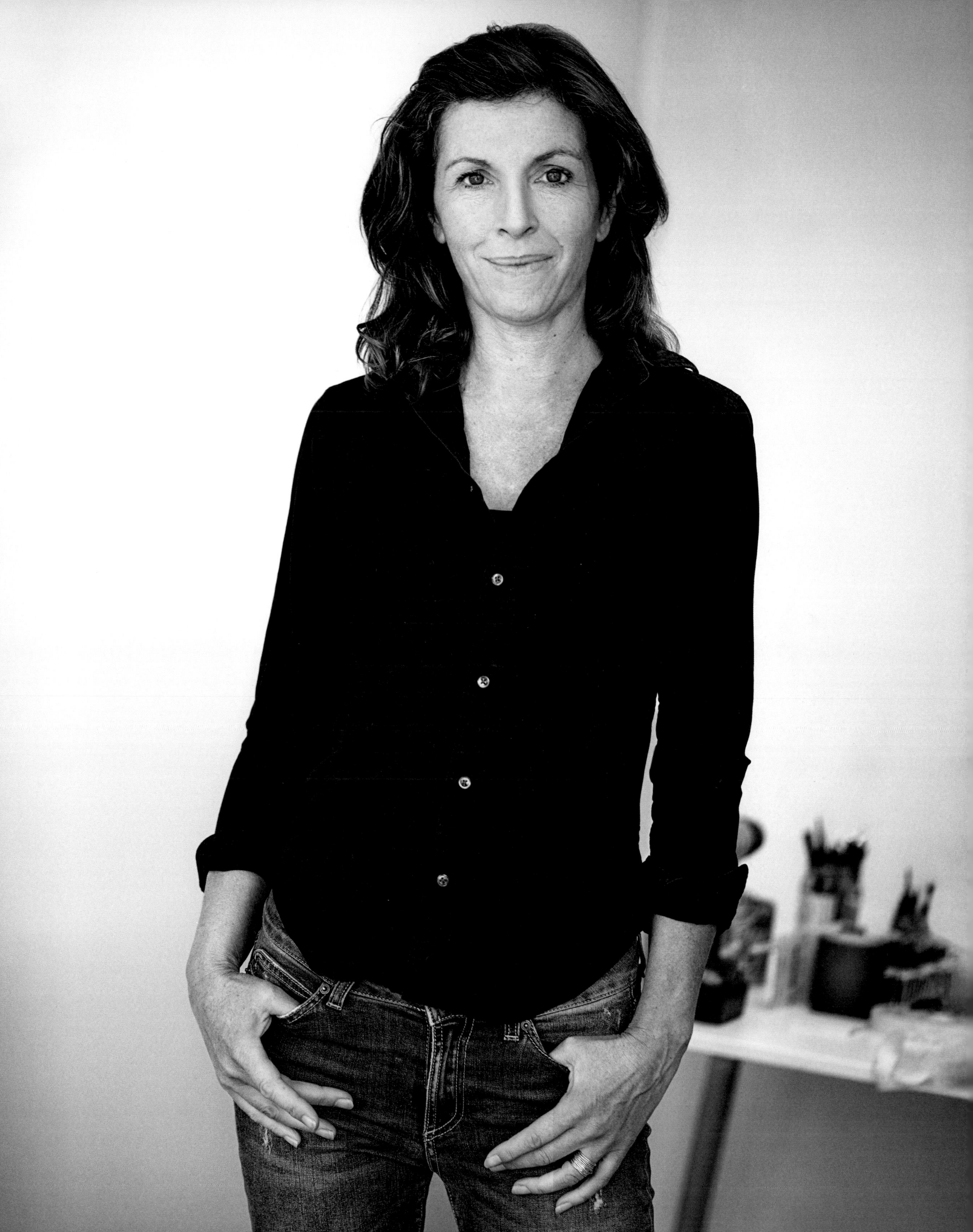

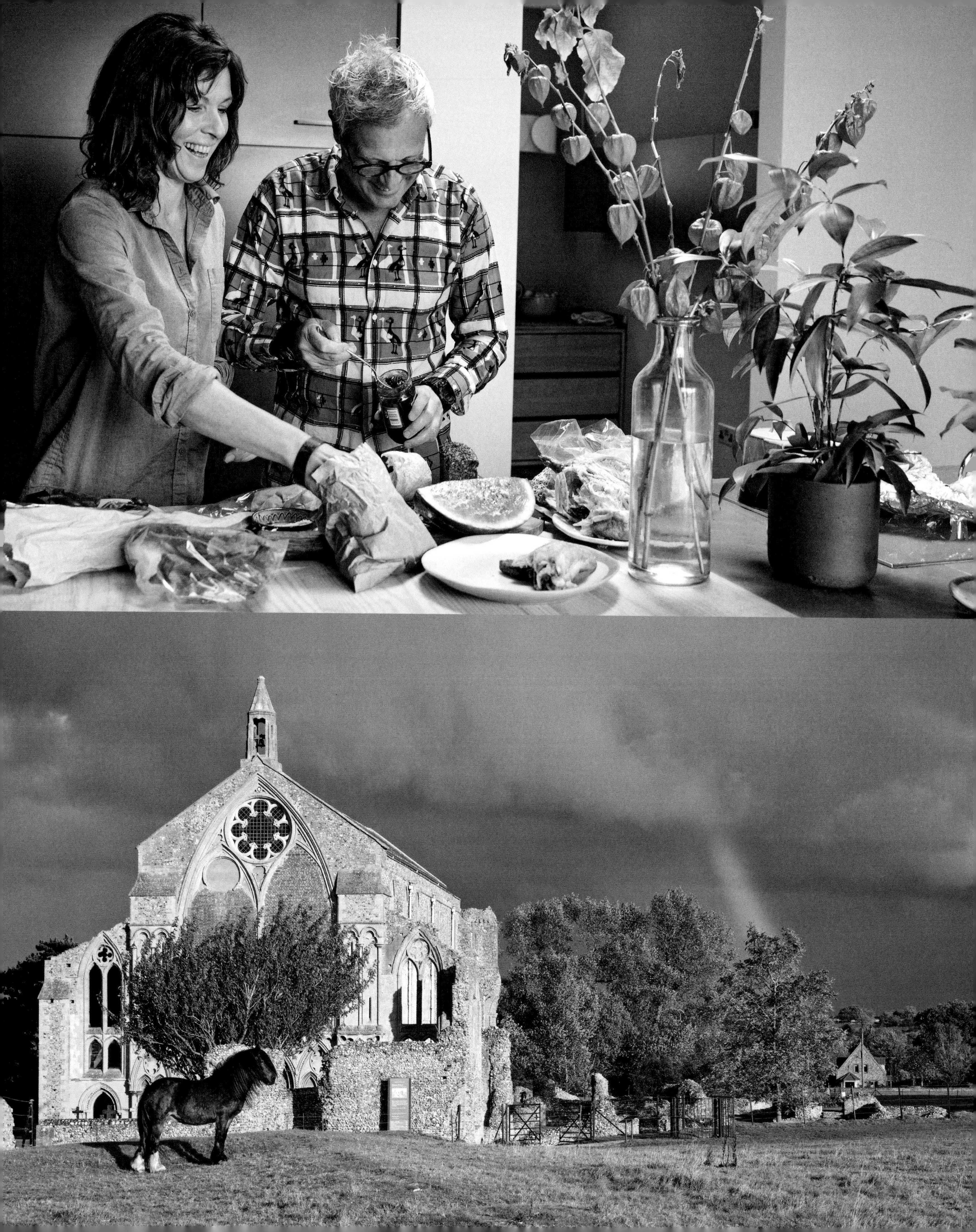

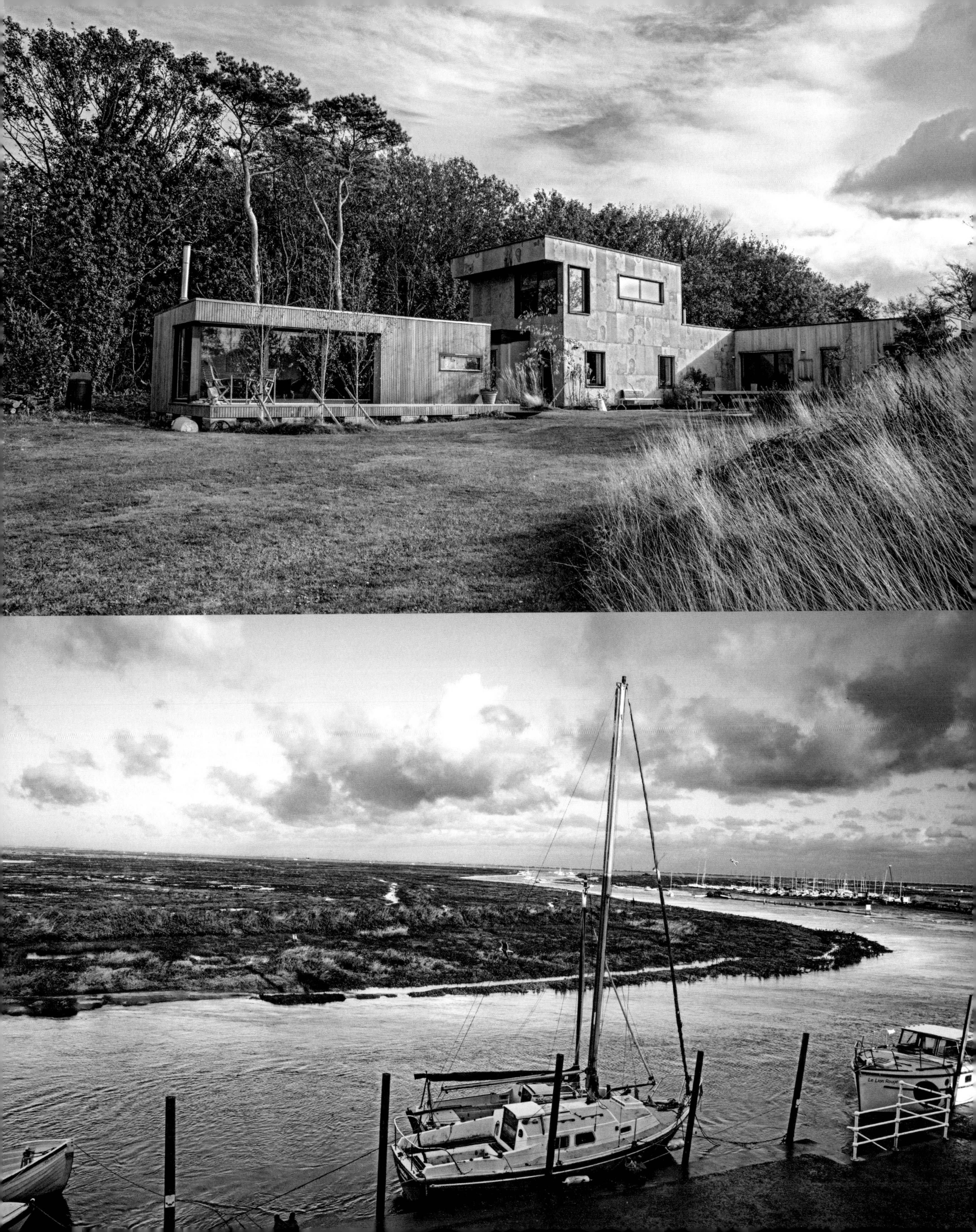

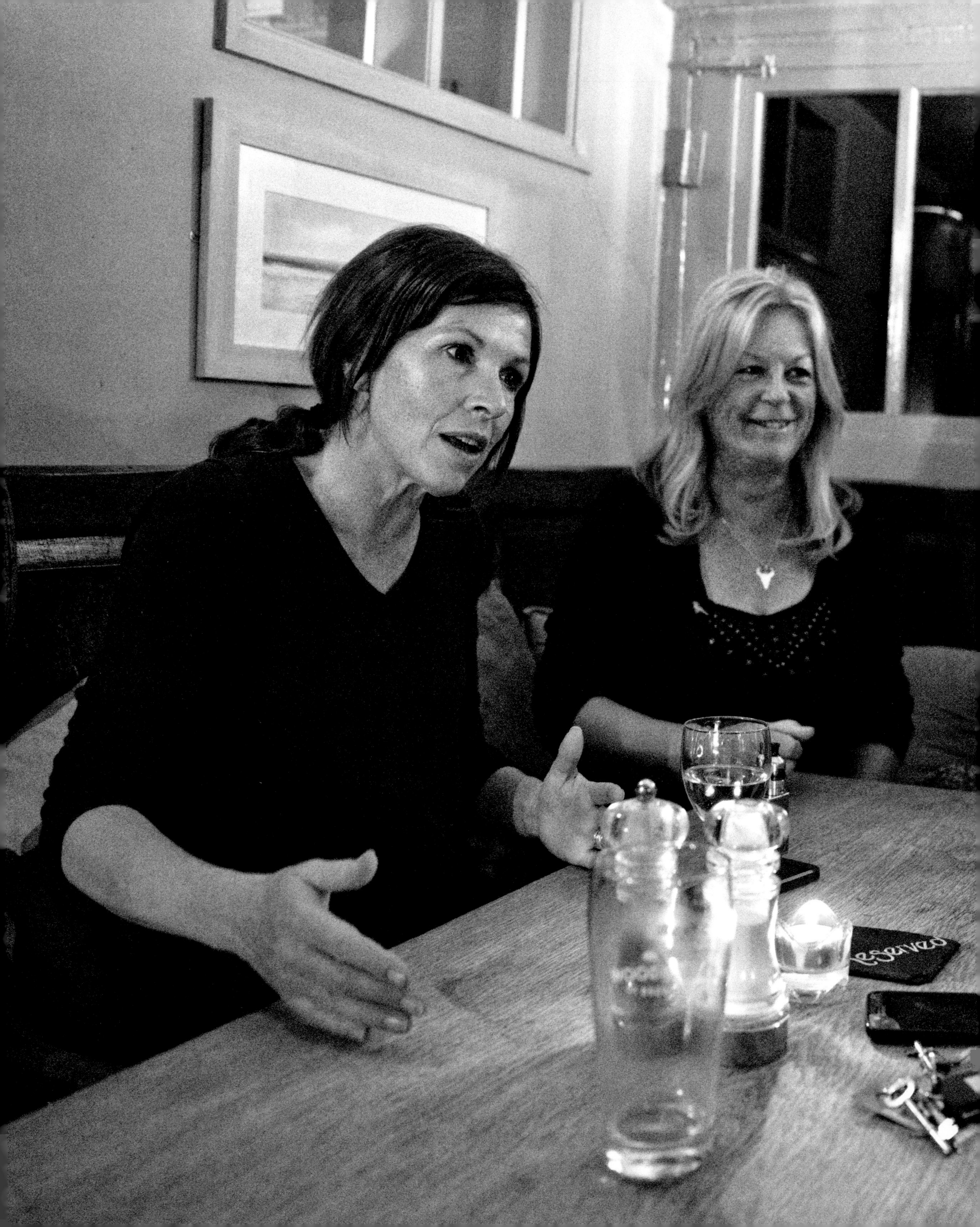

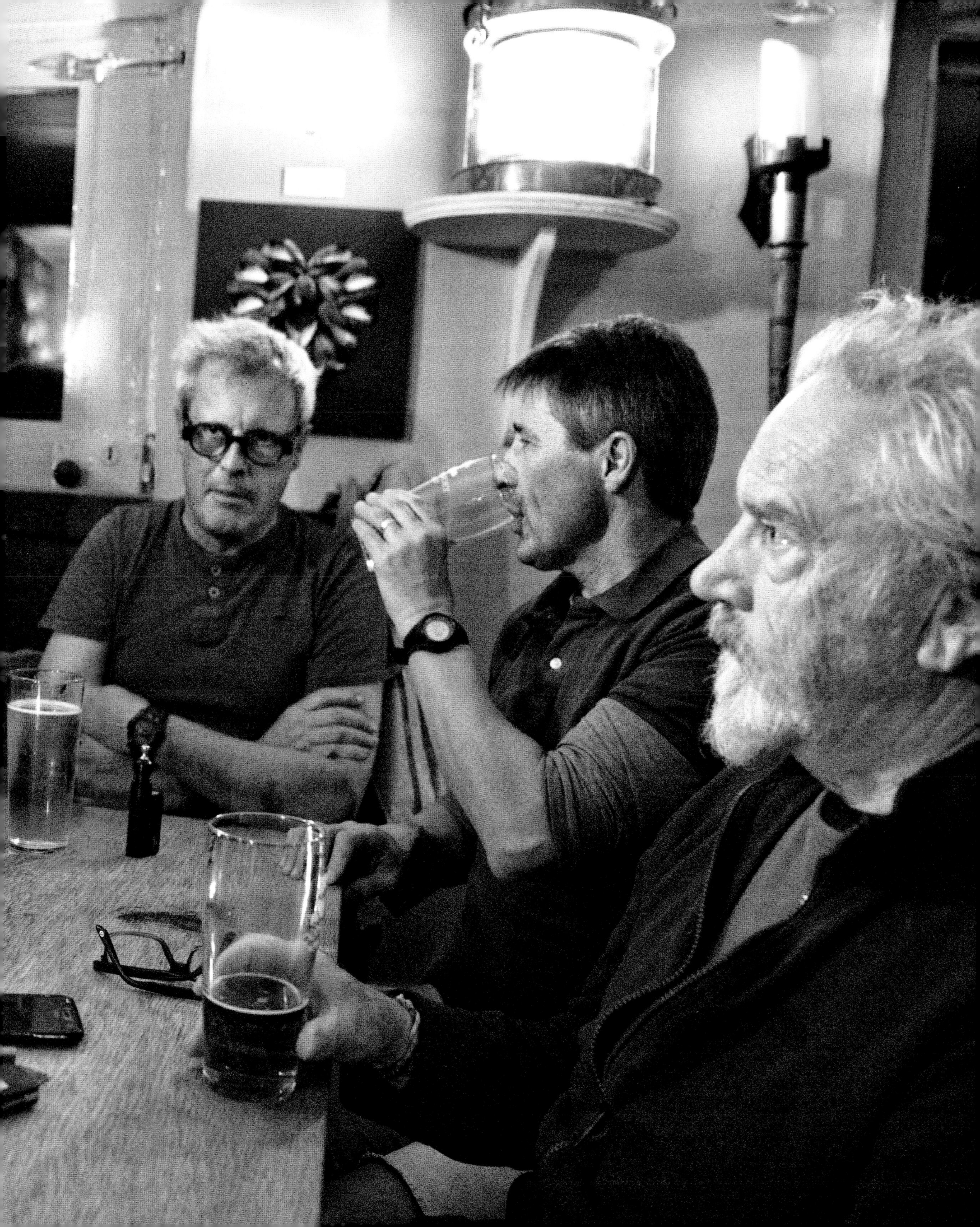

Richard Ford

American (b. 1944)

Photographed in East Boothbay, Maine, July 2010

Richard Ford came with his wife, Kristina, to live beside the ocean in East Boothbay, Maine, more than twenty years ago. And it is where they live now, beside Linekin Bay, which opens onto the Gulf of Maine and the Atlantic Ocean, in a classic New England Cape surrounded by flower gardens.

There is an old boathouse on the water previously owned by a lobsterman who stored his dory and traps and nets inside. Ford shored up and insulated the boathouse for year-round use as a writing refuge. It's silent here. Even on a bright day, the light inside is low and as I looked around, Ford said, "I manage to seclude myself here pretty ruthlessly, simply to get my work done." His Brittany, Scooter, played out from swimming after the kayak all morning, slept nearby. A little painting of a red brick house, propped up on a shelf, depicts where Ford grew up in Jackson, Mississippi. "The scene was painted by my dearest high school friend, Cleta Ellington, and it's treasured by me."

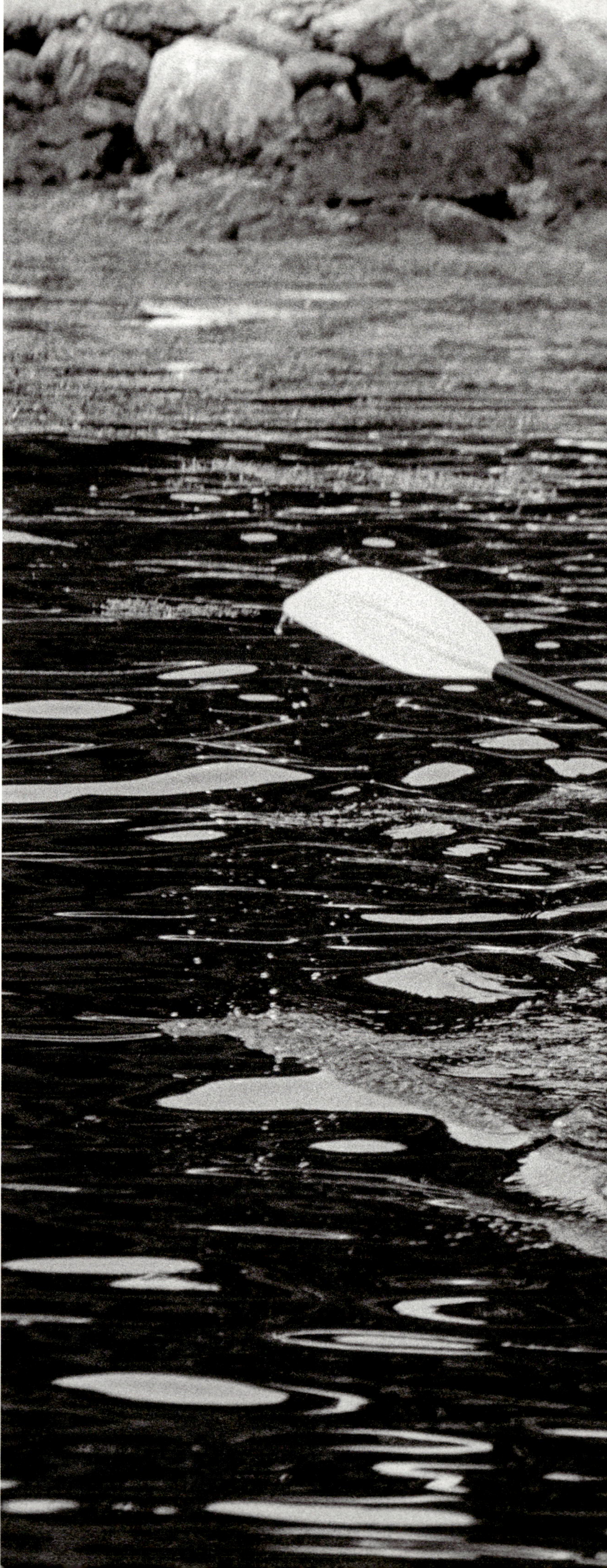

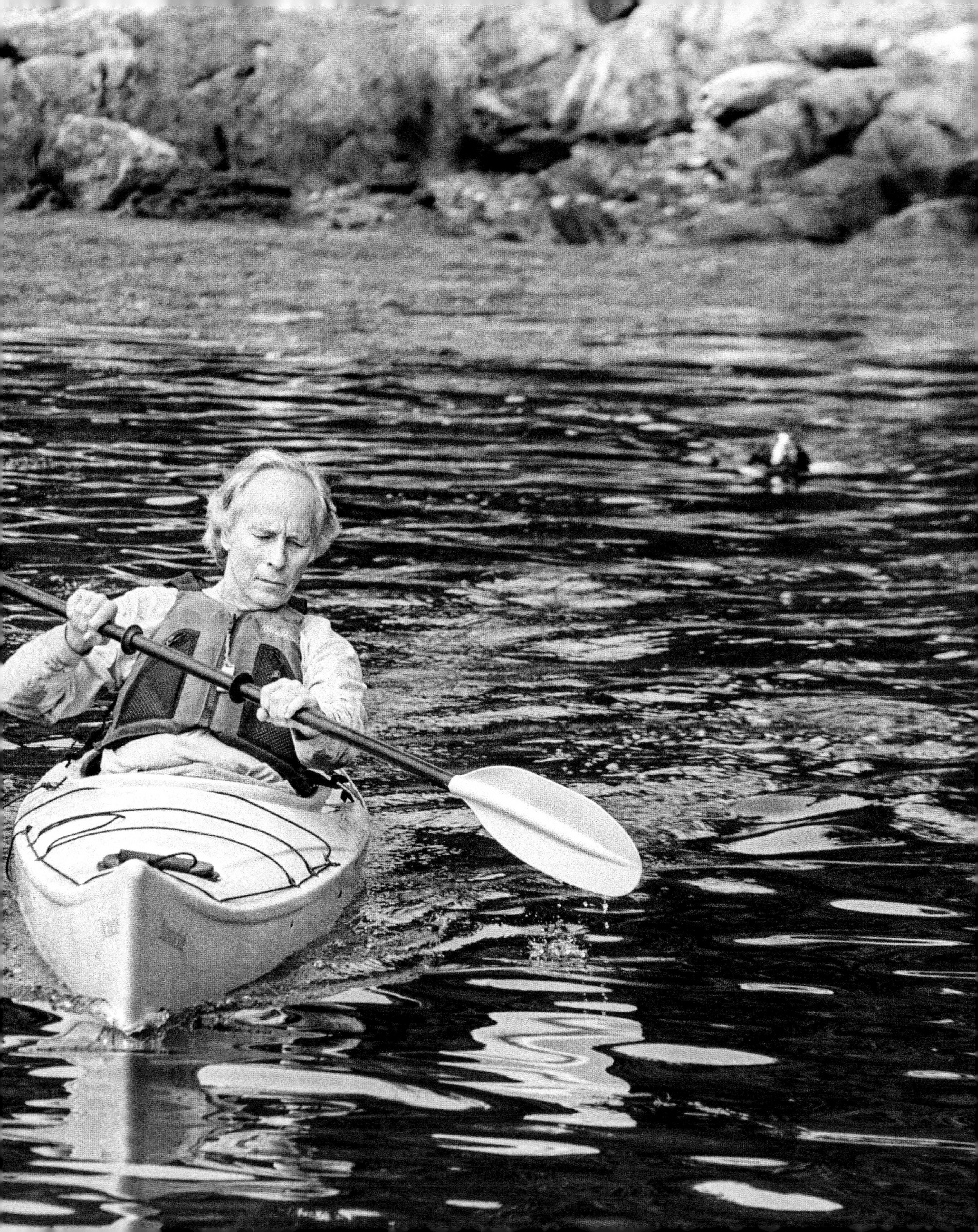

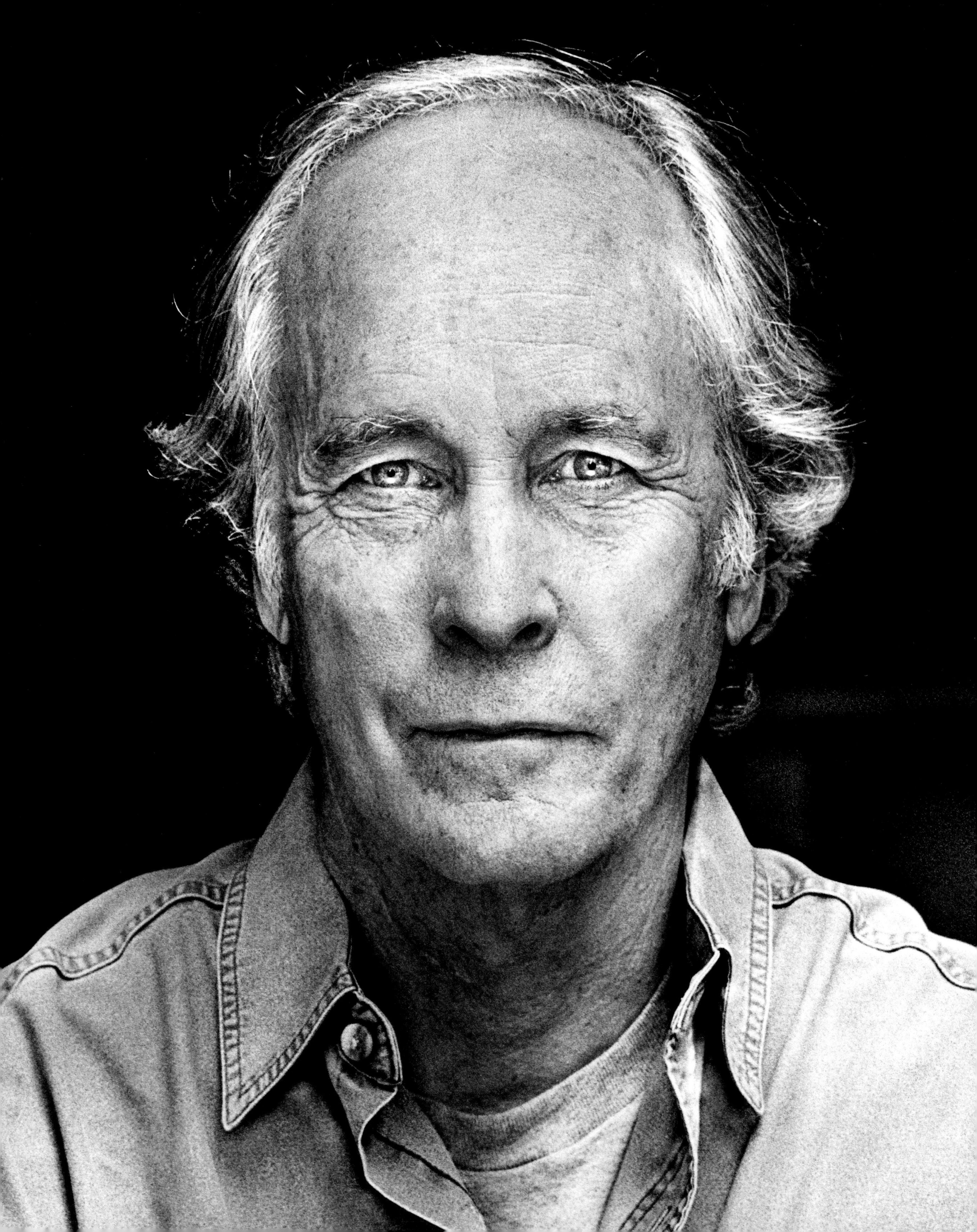

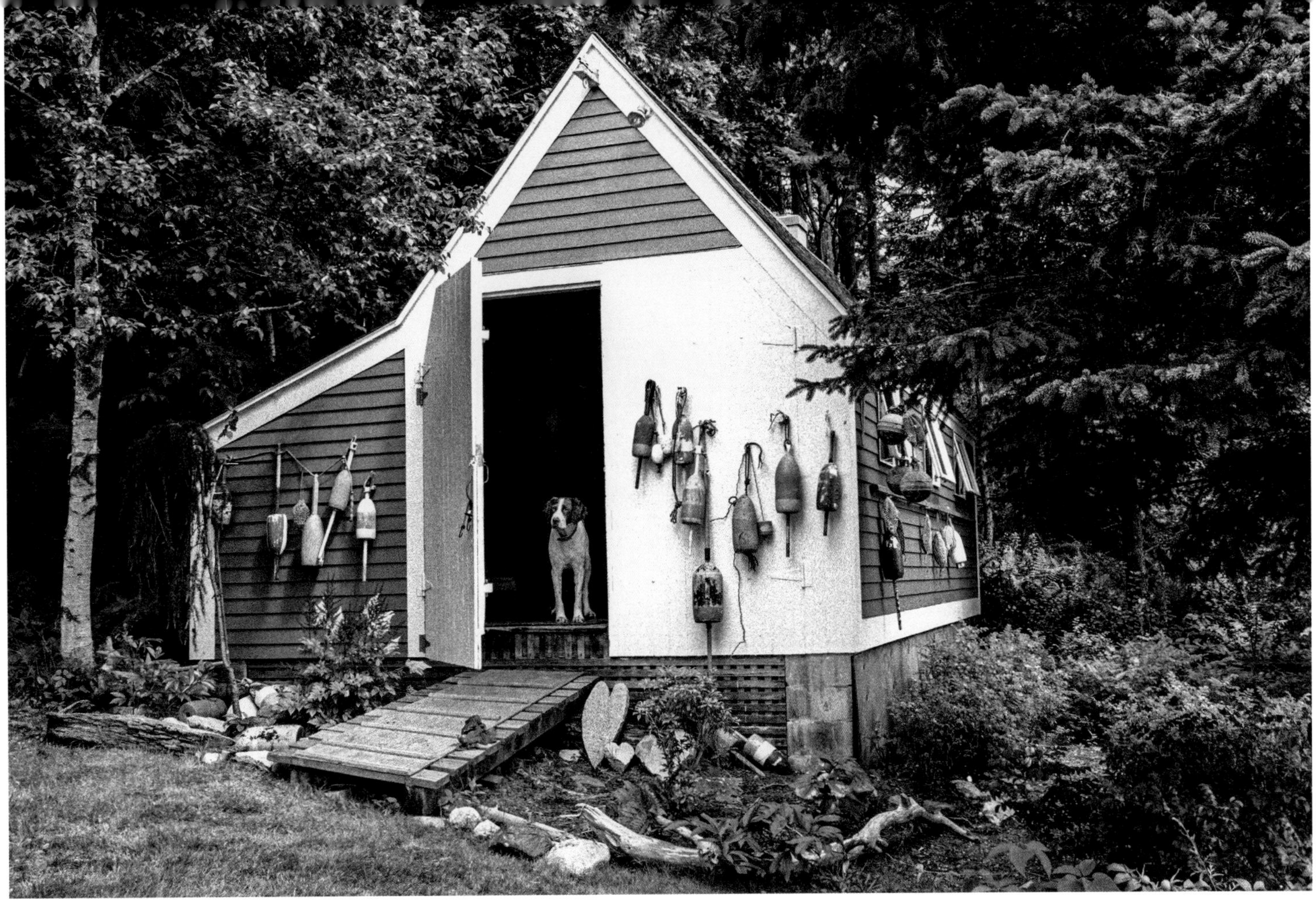

As idyllic as the house and grounds are, Ford claims he's never felt a strong sense of home anywhere. "It's mostly a matter of living where Kristina lives." He can write anyplace. "On buses and trains and ferryboats and airplancs, for surc. In borrowed apartments in Berlin and Paris. In rented houses in the west of Ireland. In Billings, Montana." Growing up in Mississippi in the 1950s, Ford longed to see the rest of America. He learned the necessity of functioning in all sorts of places.

People in Maine are known to be closely guarded and plainspoken to the point of being abrupt. But Ford sees them as a lot like people he's met elsewhere. Even as a young writer, he tried to blur regional differences, preferring to think of people in Egypt or Russia or Ireland as attuned to the same concerns as he. "Life concerns, you know, the large ones—love, death, place." This has allowed Ford, "a Mississippian, to think, I can write for anybody who can read, and make a difference."

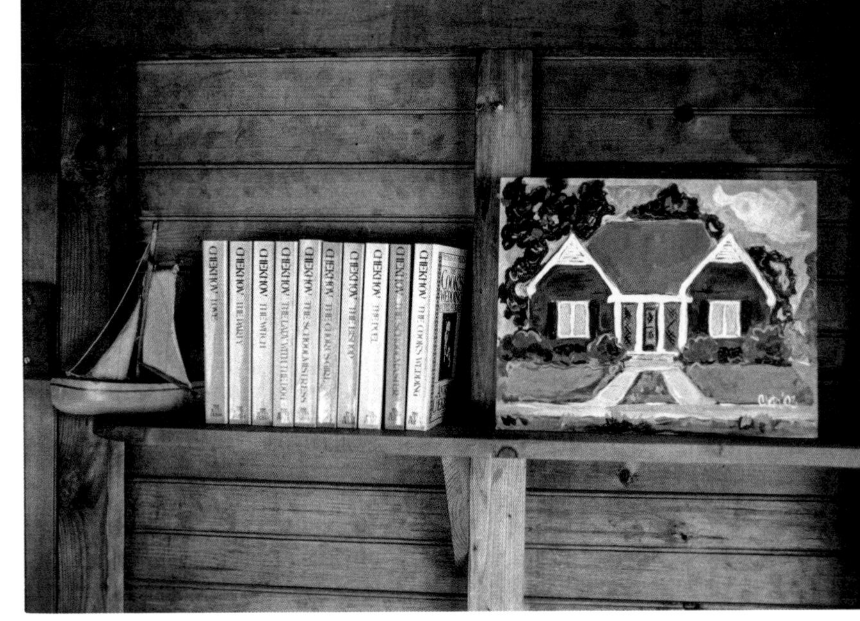

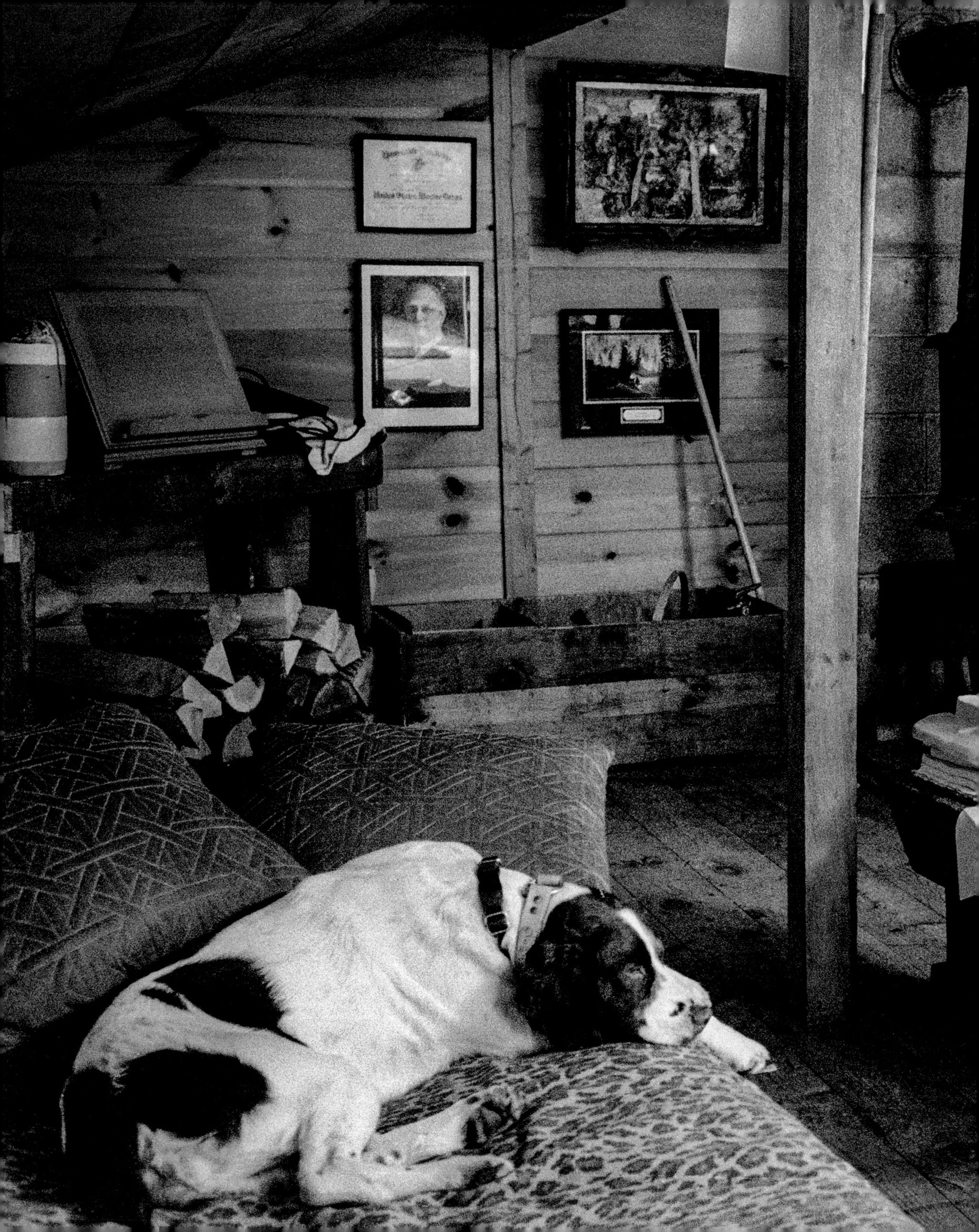

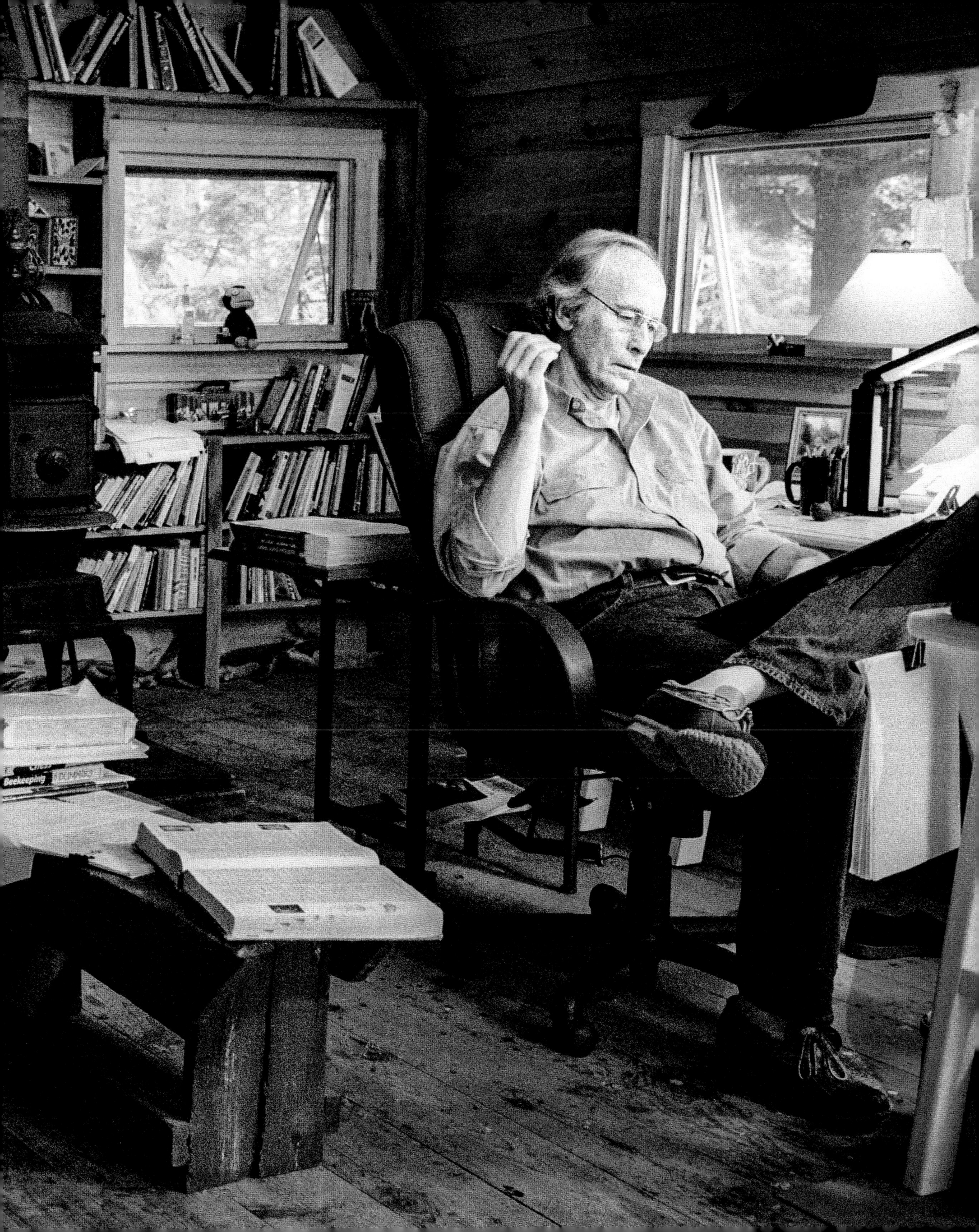

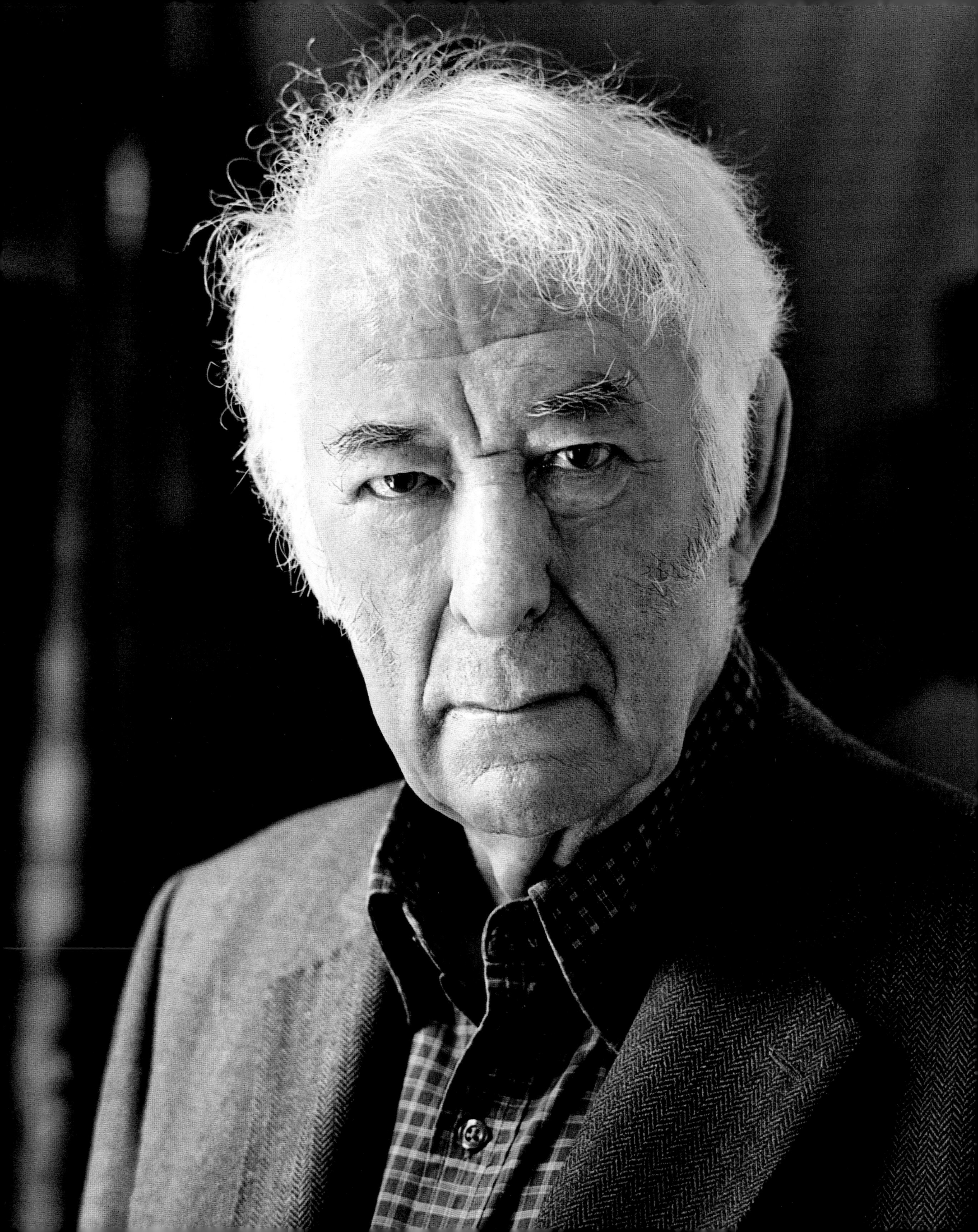

Seamus Heaney

Irish (1939–2013)

Photographed in Dublin, Ireland, May 2011

My assistant and I were standing on the steps of a Victorian house in Sandymount, a seaside neighborhood on the south side of Dublin, when the front door opened. A tall man with a shock of white hair said, "Welcome." Seamus Heaney, Nobel Prize winner and one of the world's most famous poets, warmly invited us in. He took the time to carefully go through the photos I had done of other writers, asking about a location, or commenting on a writer's interests. He called some writers by their nicknames. It felt as though we were looking through his family album.

Heaney then showed me two pelts on a chair in the living room, an otter and a skunk, gifts from Ted Hughes presumably referencing the two love poems, "The Skunk" and "The Otter," written by Heaney to Marie, his wife of forty-six years. Hughes and Heaney had become close friends and edited two anthologies together.

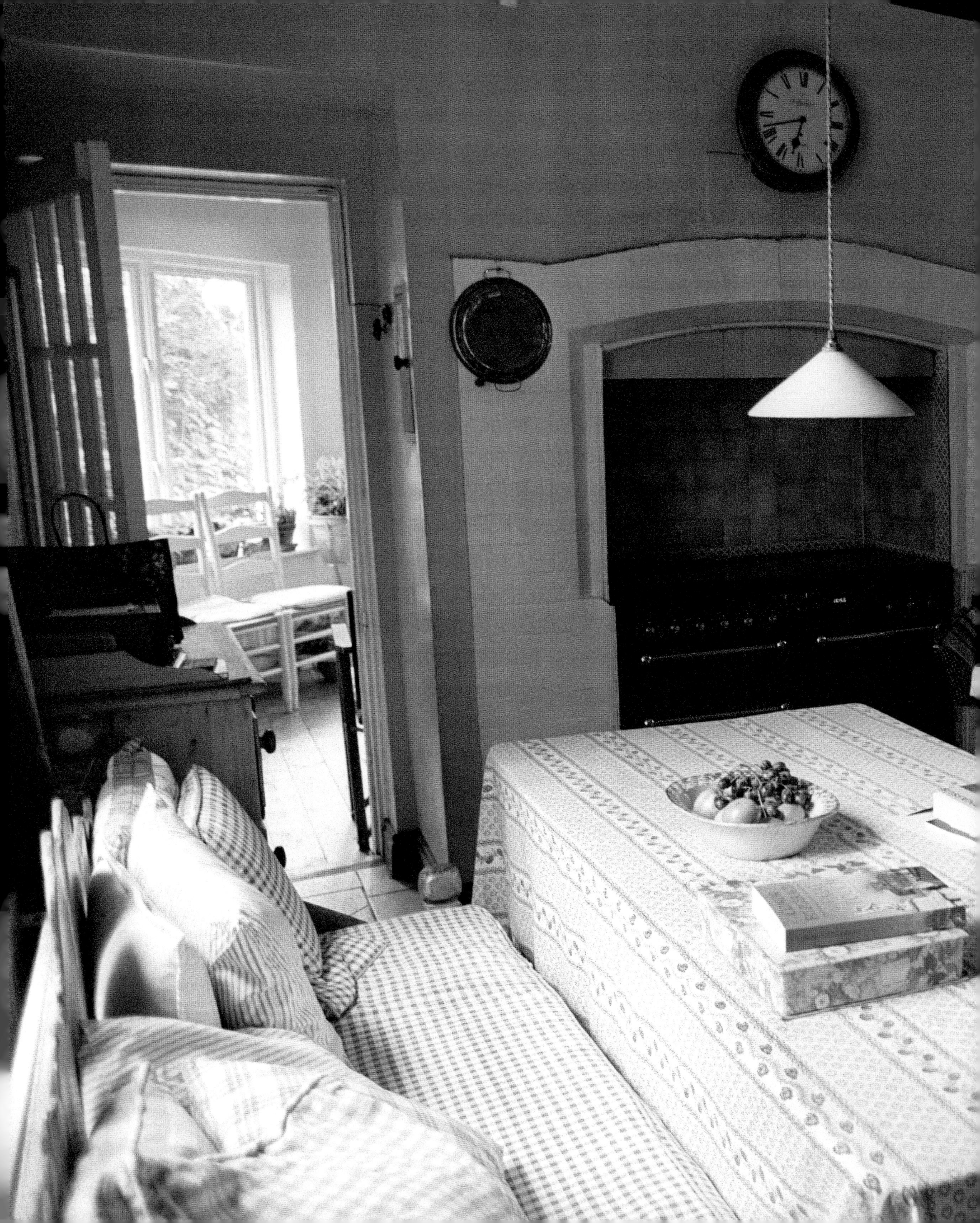

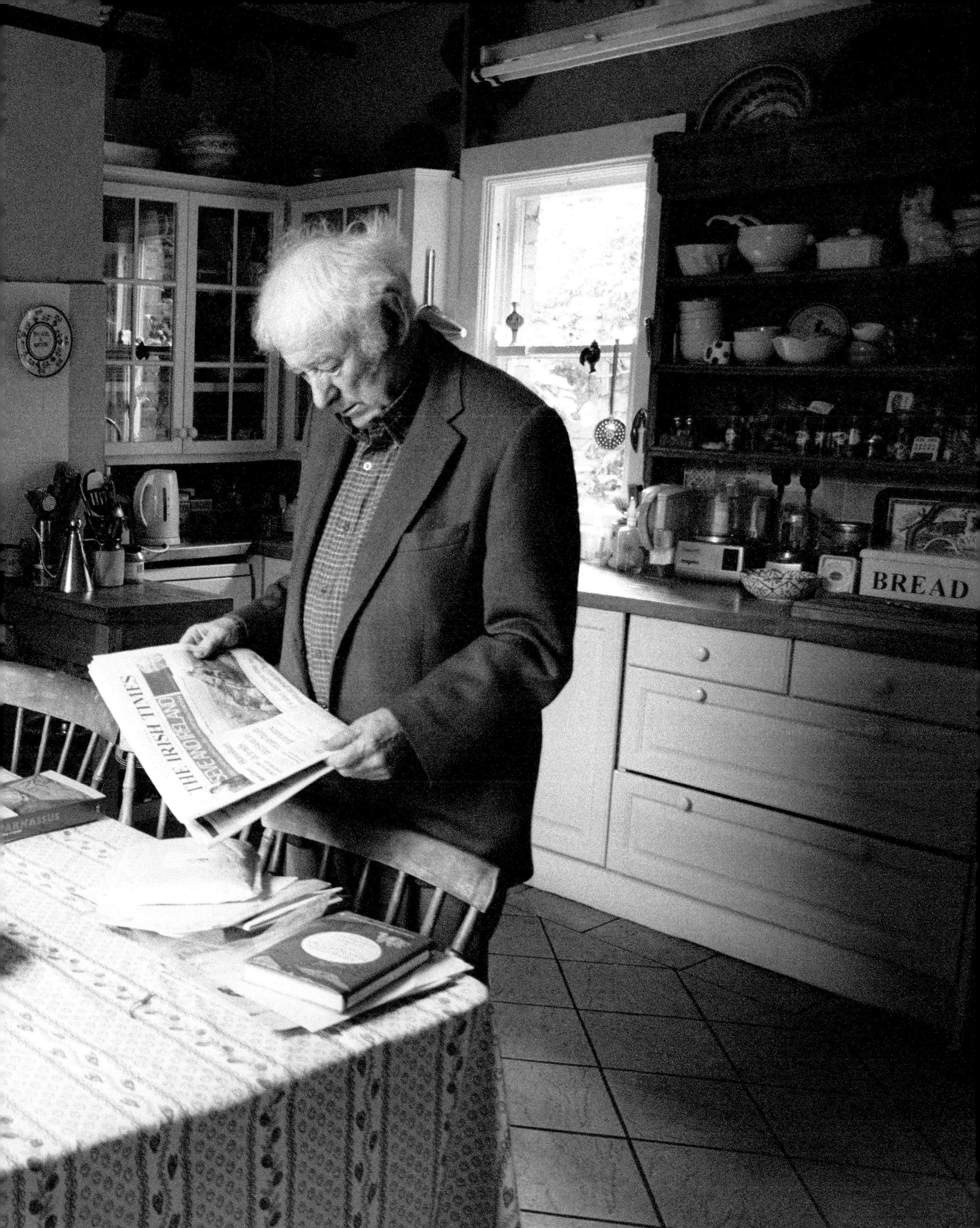

THE IRISH TIMES
IRELAND
BREAD

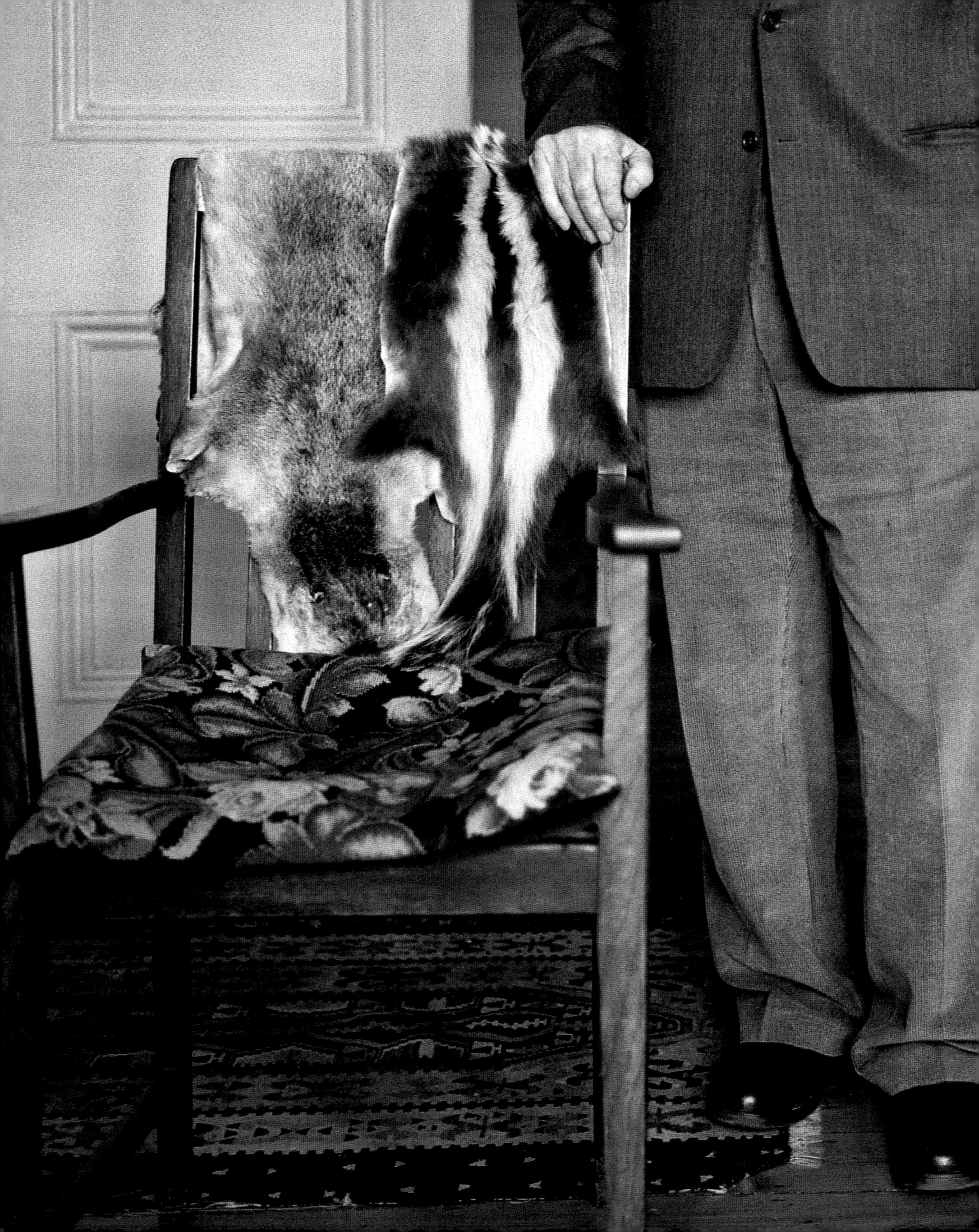

Throughout my visit, Heaney was attentive, his manner a template of how to lead with kindness. Colm Tóibín had told me he was beloved "on both sides of the Atlantic" for his decency and goodness. As our session came to an end, Heaney searched for a printed copy of his poem "A Drink of Water," and inscribed it:

> for Laura—
> to remember Strand Road—
> fondest wishes,
> Seamus Heaney
> May 9, 2011

After we had packed up our equipment and my visit with Seamus and Marie was over, I walked down the front steps. They had both come to the top of the stairs to say goodbye. They looked happy. I asked if I might take one last, quick snap. They were amused—and generous.

I took two.

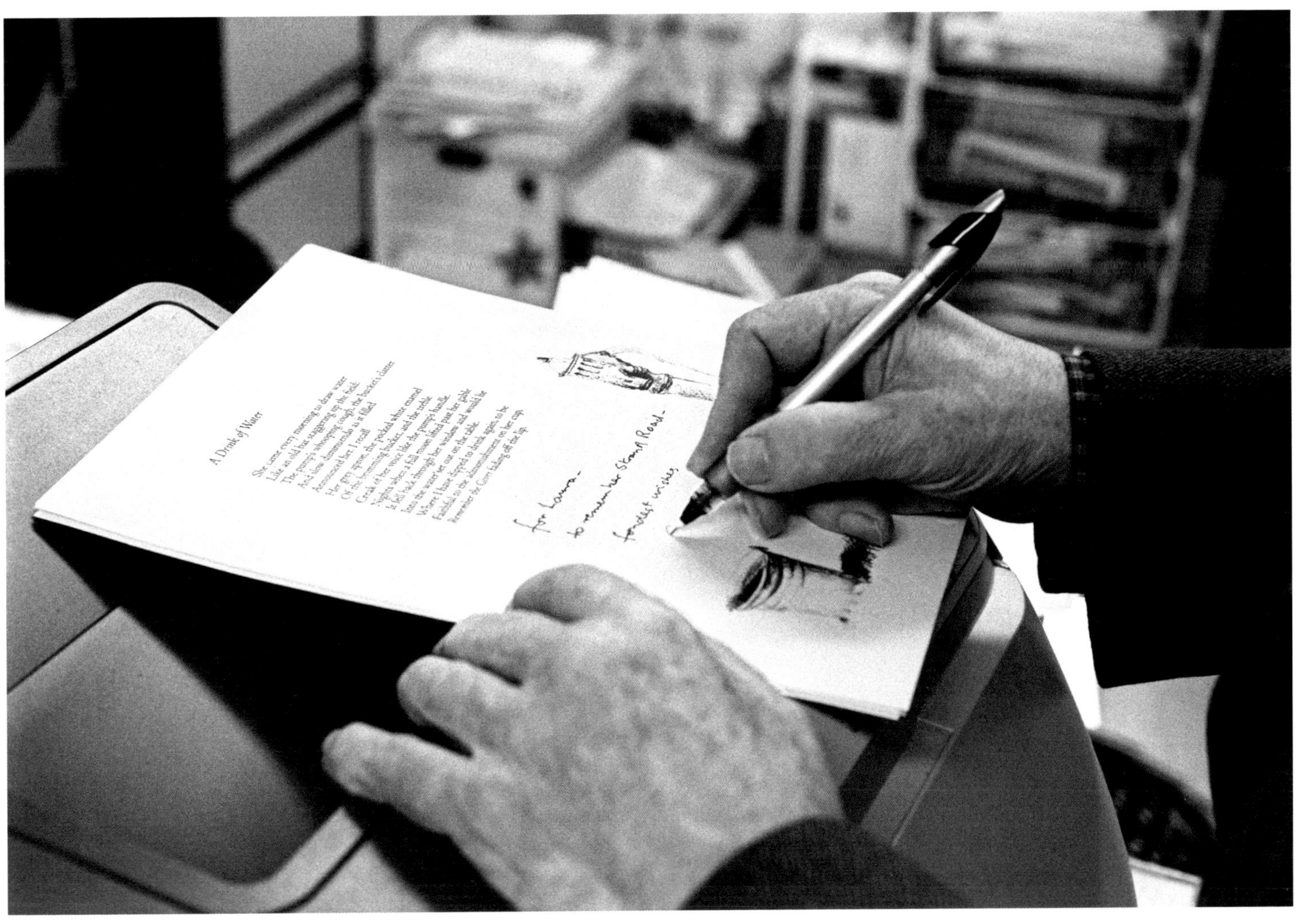

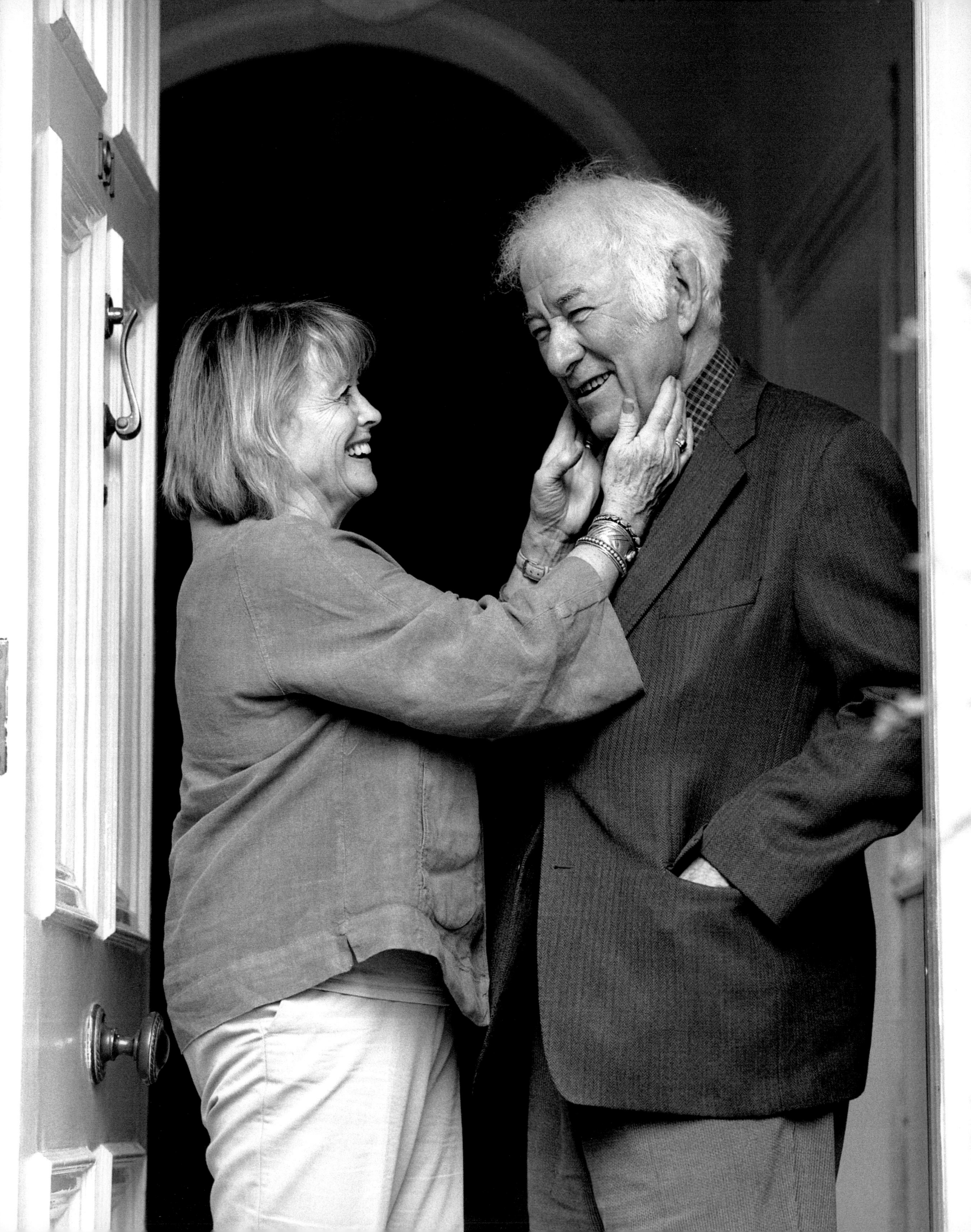

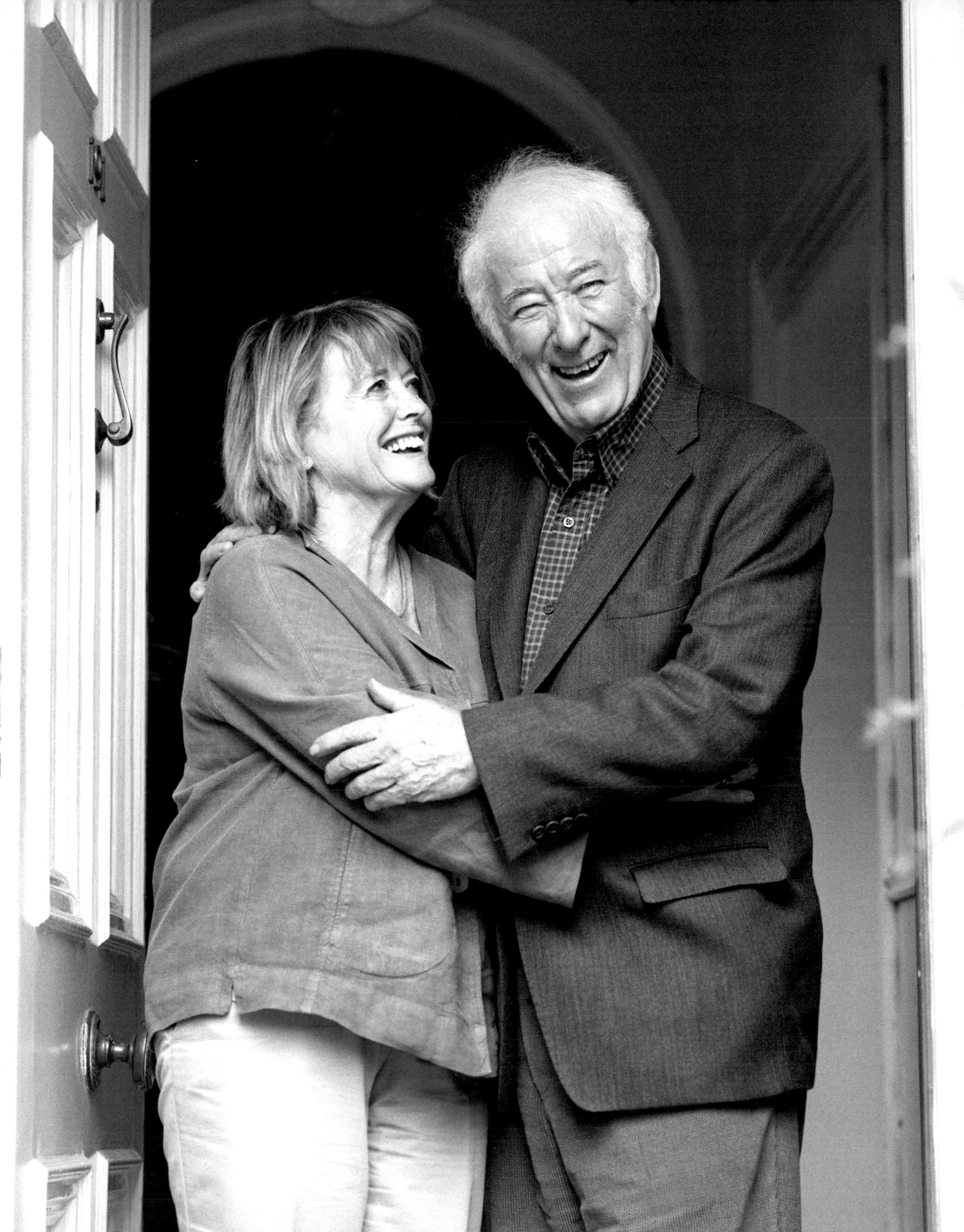

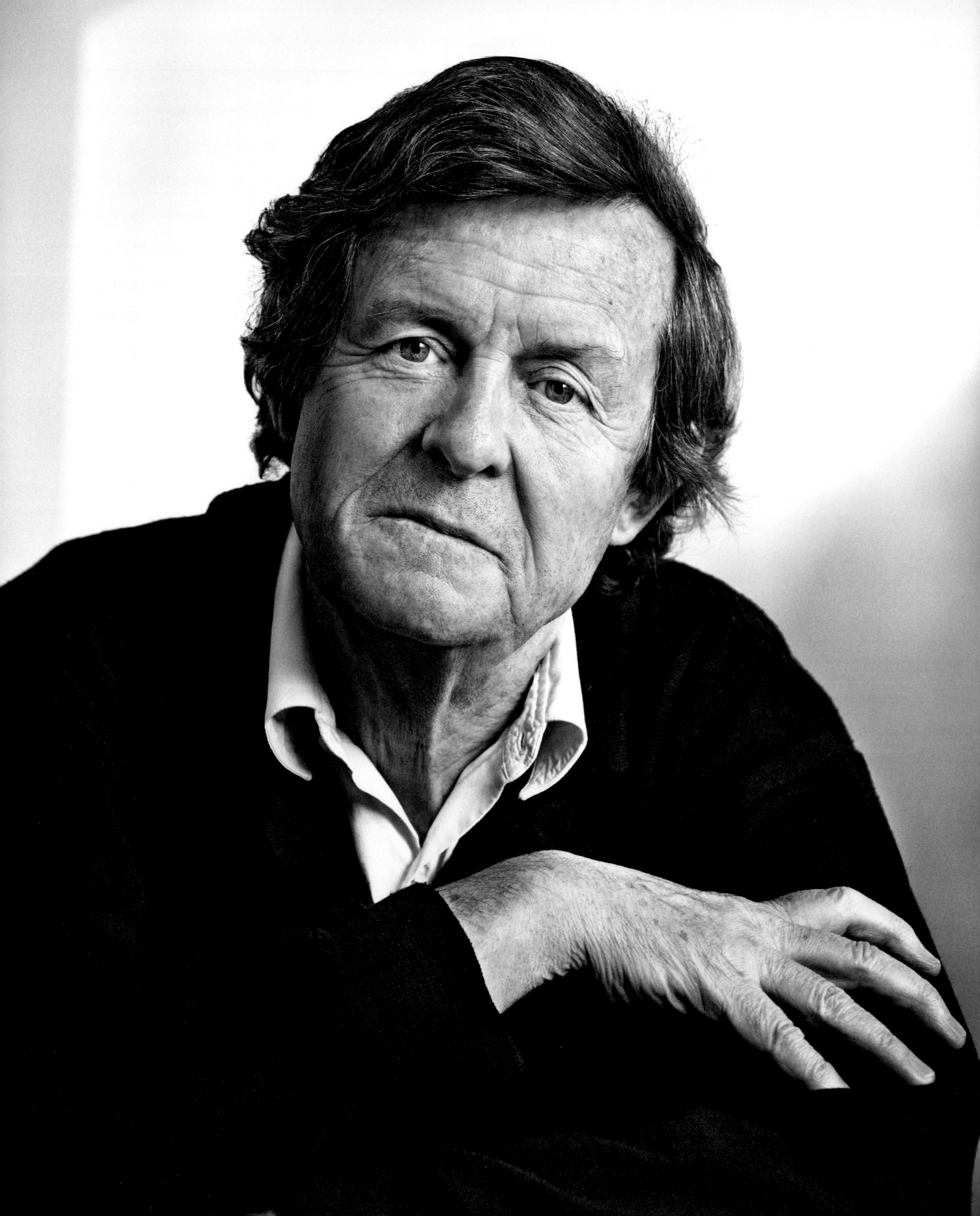

David Hare

English (b. 1947)

Photographed in London, England, May 2015

David Hare, knighted by Queen Elizabeth II in 1998, tends to be seen each day by the residents of the Hampstead section of London on the ten-minute walk from "The Old Mansion" on Frognal, where he lives, to his studio on Rudall Crescent.

He welcomed me into his studio, a charming space that in the 1800s had been a sculptor's loft with a half balcony. Now—with theater and movie posters on the walls, books and papers piled high on desks, tables, and the floor—the place announces itself as the work space of a major literary figure. All this material is the accumulation of a person who works extraordinarily hard. And like all hard-working people, Hare had no time for chitchat.

I rarely discussed their work with writers. They seemed more interested in photography or films or news of other writers. Hare never reads his own reviews. I was told that whenever someone tries to discuss a review, even if it's positive, he gets quite cross. But I found him cooperative and attentive, easy to photograph because of his respect for serious effort. When I asked him about his trip to Texas, where his archives are placed at the Harry Ransom Center, in Austin, he became animated. And he instinctively knew, without my saying anything, exactly what I needed. After all, a playwright and screenwriter understands performance.

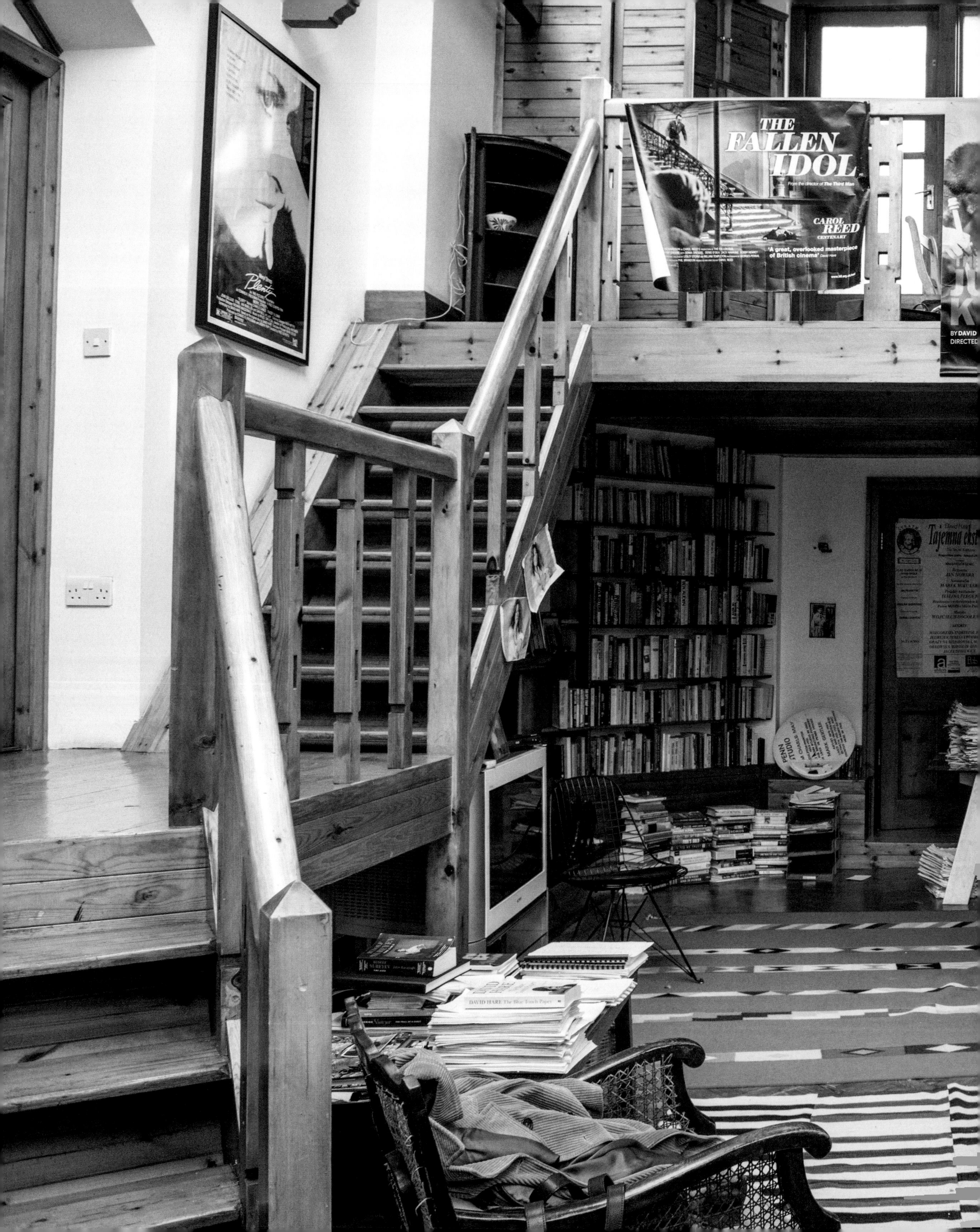

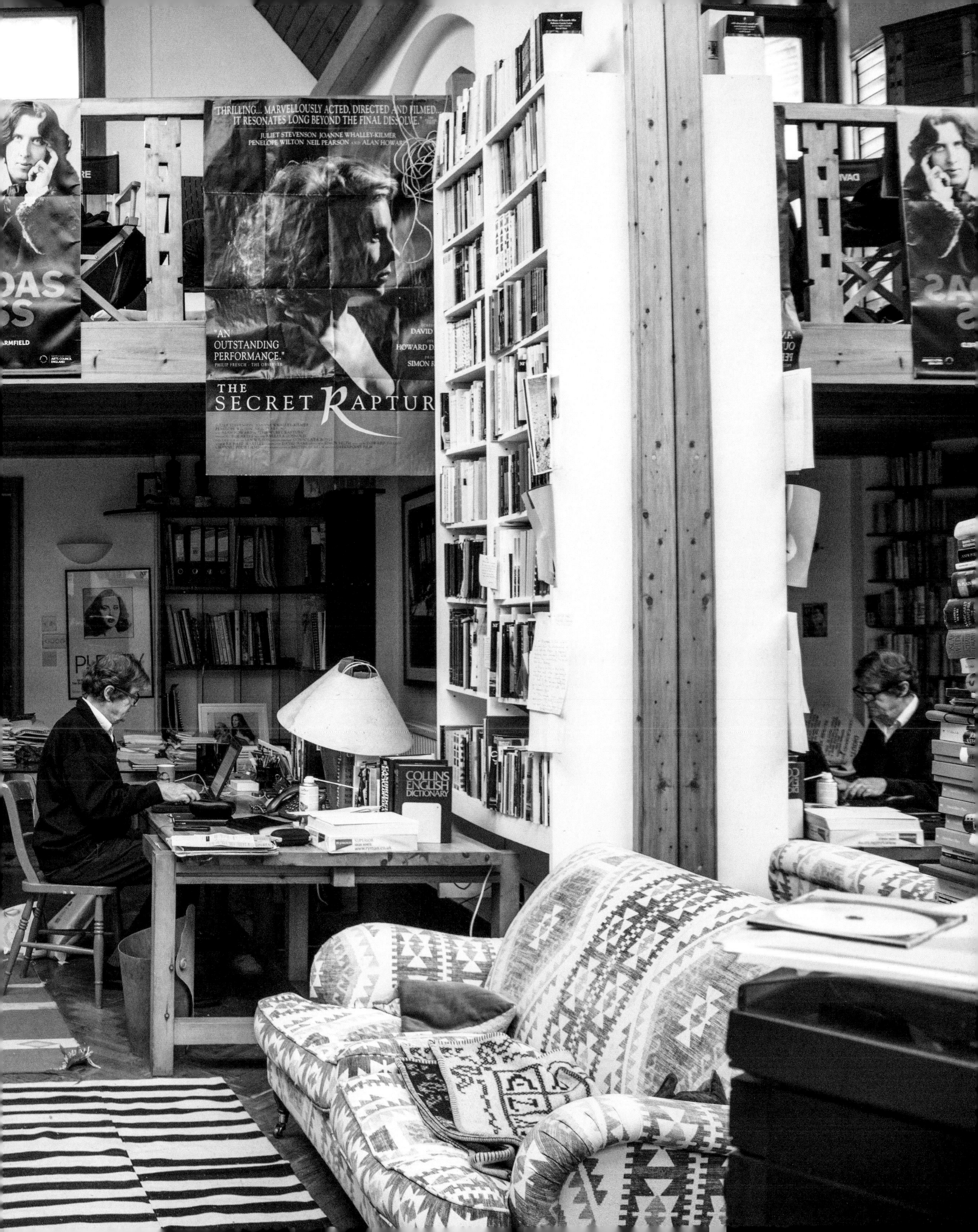

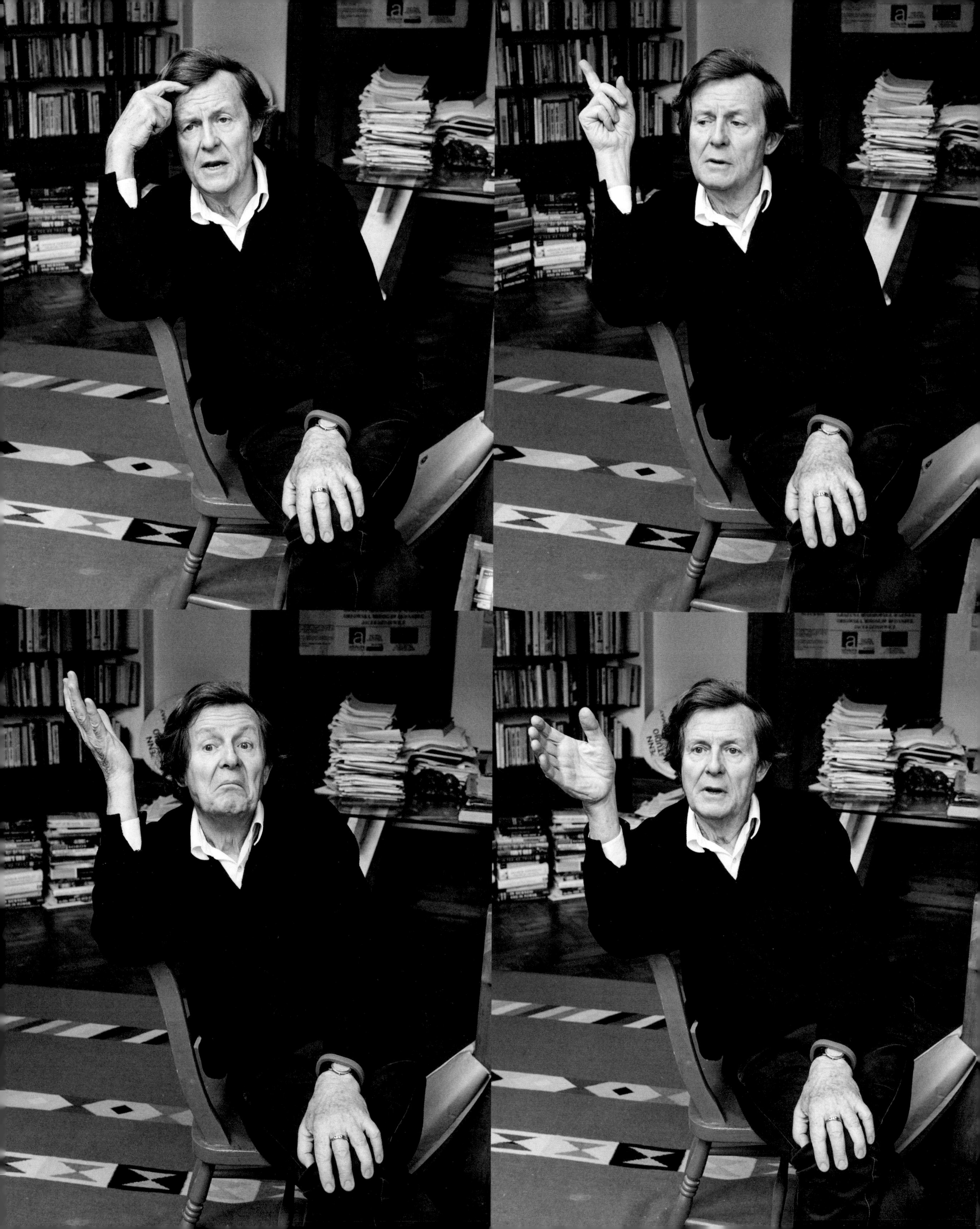

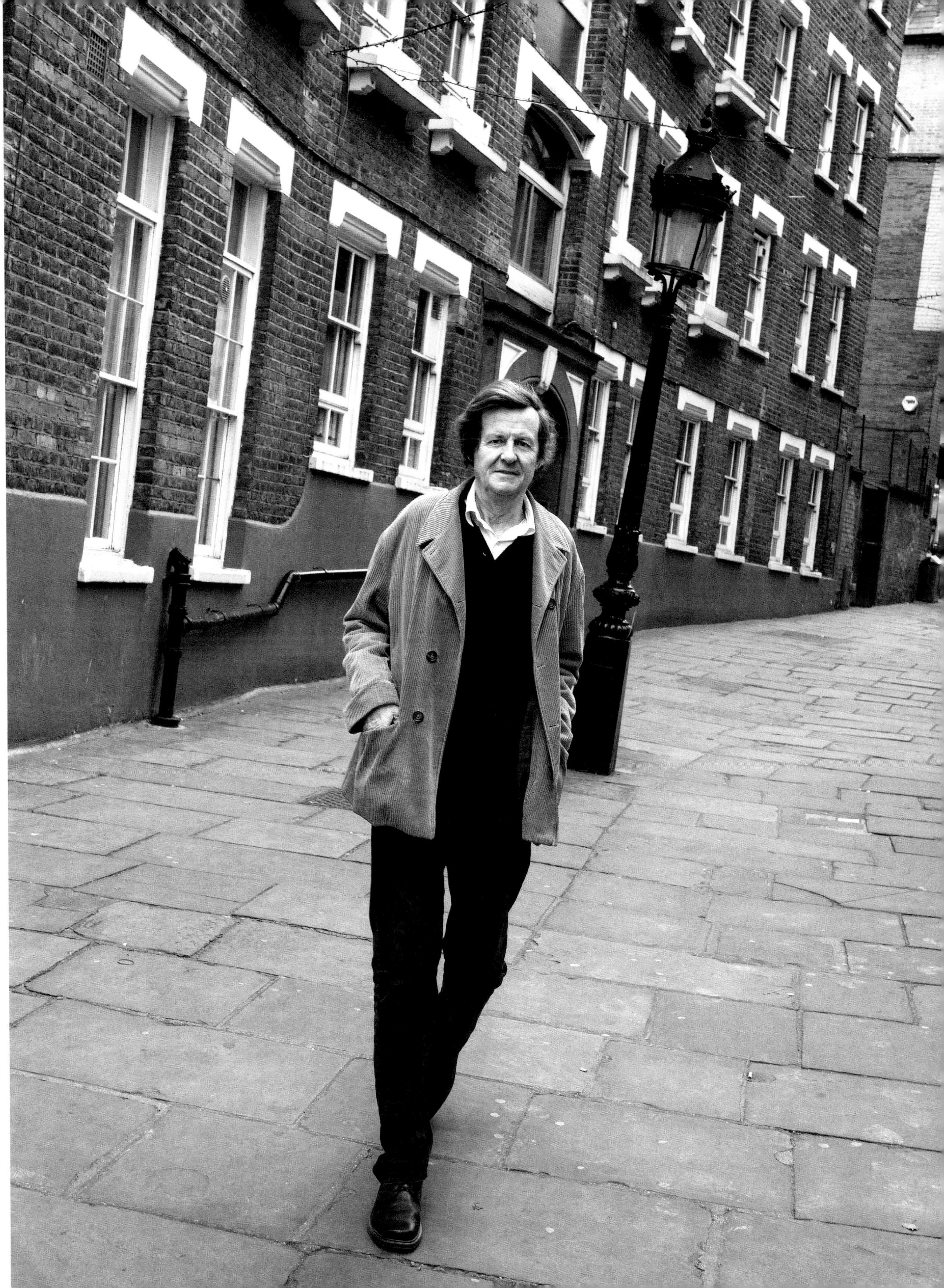

Margaret Atwood

Canadian (b. 1939)

Photographed in Toronto, Canada, April 2018

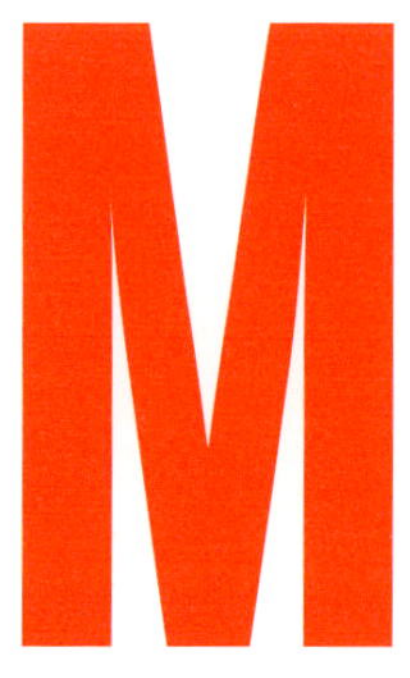

Margaret Atwood lives in a large Edwardian house in the Annex, known as the intellectual neighborhood of Toronto, far removed from the wilderness of northern Quebec, where she grew up. Her father was a forest entomologist, and Atwood's current prominence in Canada's environmental movement might well be traced back to her early exposure to the natural world. It was an immersive education. She was eleven years old before she attended a full year of school.

Even today, Atwood remains a determined gardener. She has an unfussy area behind her house—compost bins, water flowing over boulders, and daffodils in spring. On the first morning, my assistant, Andrew Mitchell, and I waited there for her. She came briskly from the house at the exact arranged time and, without a hello, said sternly, "You're standing on the ferns!"

We both looked down. I stood on flagstones. Andrew stood on dirt at the outer edge of the garden. We said, simultaneously, "There are no ferns here."

She pointed to Andrew. "They're under your feet!" Looking again, Andrew politely said, "No, not here."

Now, quite exasperated, Atwood said, "Under the ground!"

Andrew jumped to a walkway.

A few minutes later, as we were doing the portrait, Atwood sotto voce said, "You have your agenda, I have my agenda, and the ferns have their agenda."

Atwood suggested ideas for photographs, but was precise with her time. She is organized and highly focused. While signing her name on the title page of one thousand copies of *The Testaments*, she spoke with her assistant about the day's responsibilities. In her work area, I noticed a long wall of bookcases six feet high. Every book on every shelf for all twenty-five feet was "By Margaret Atwood"—various editions in various languages.

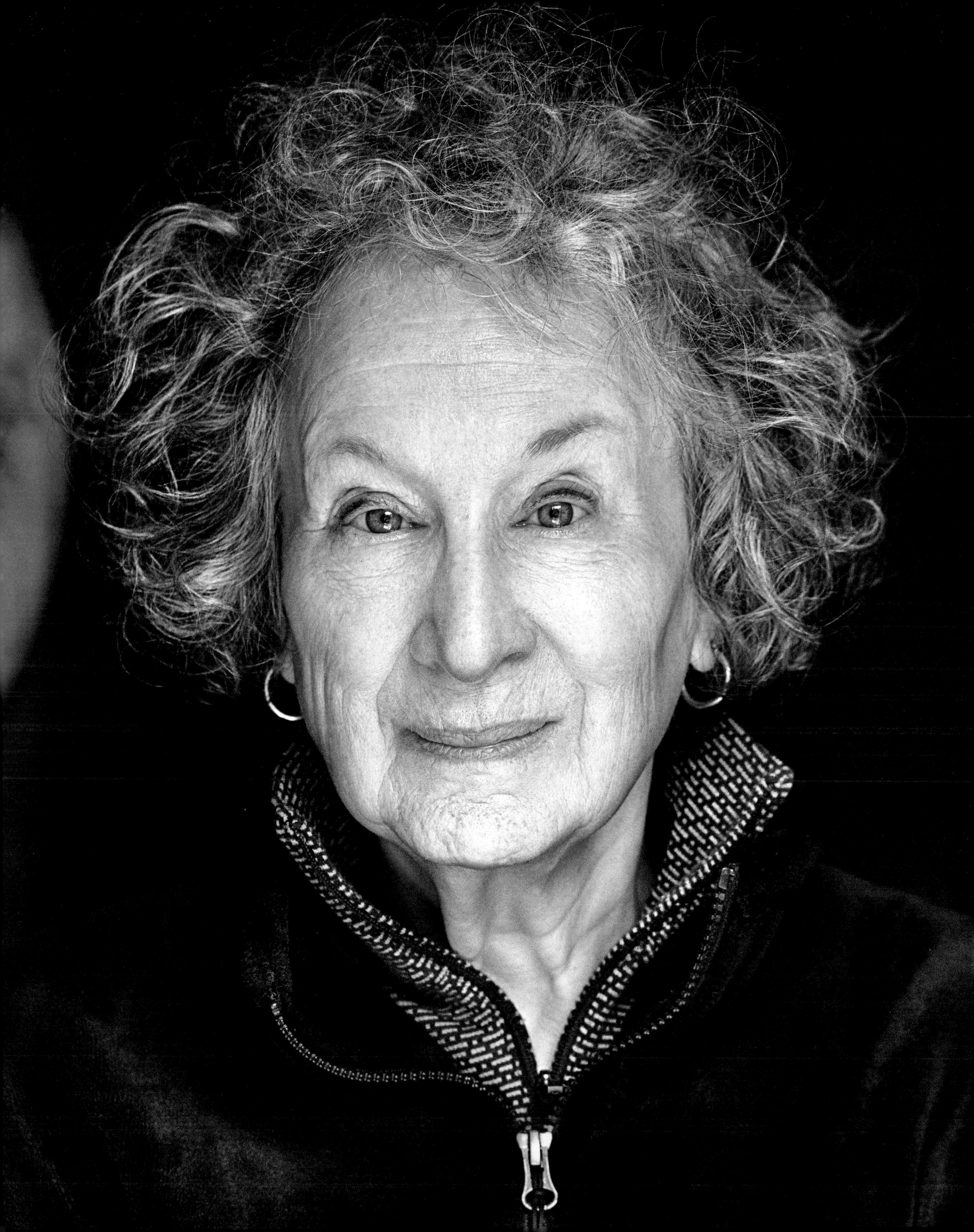

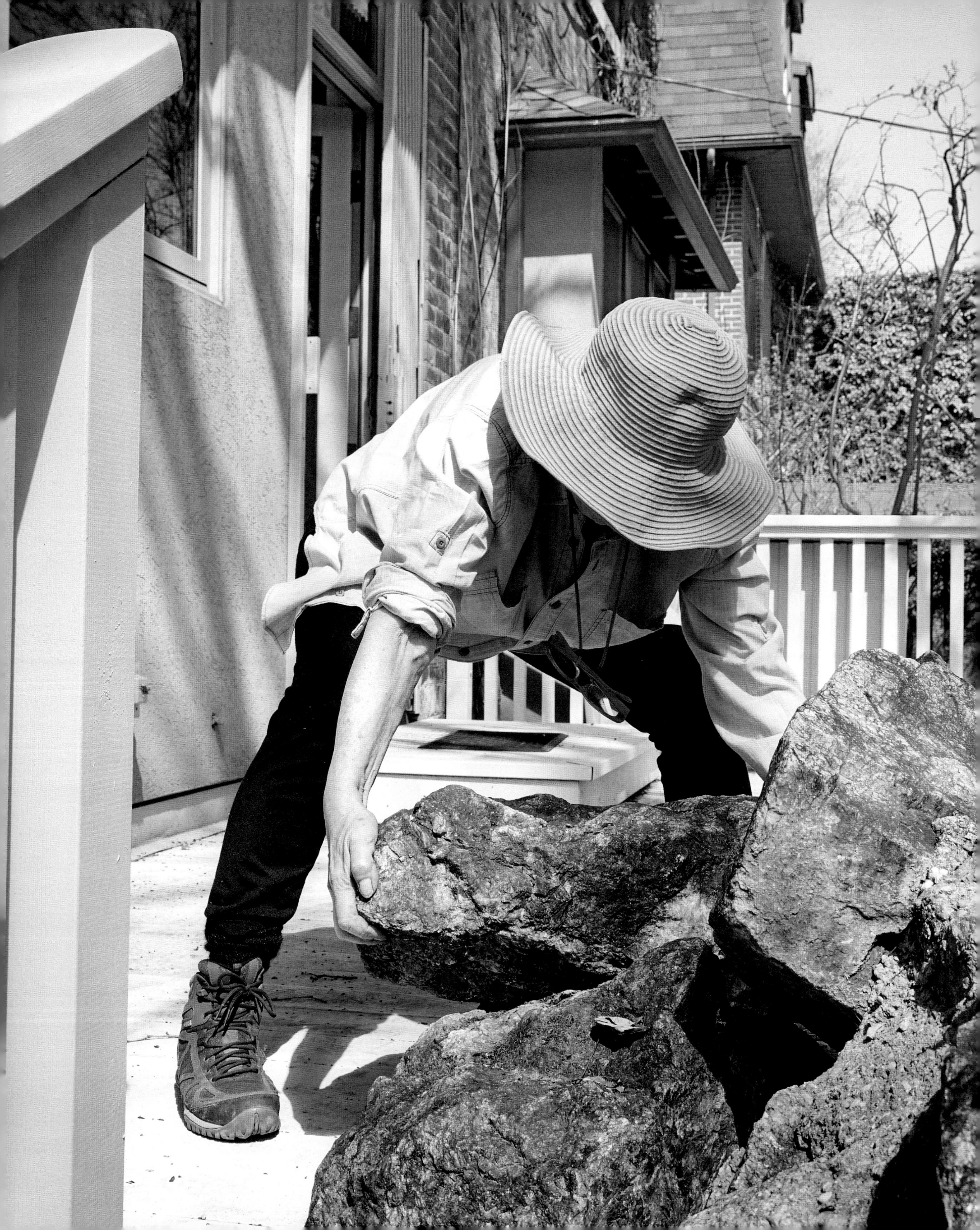

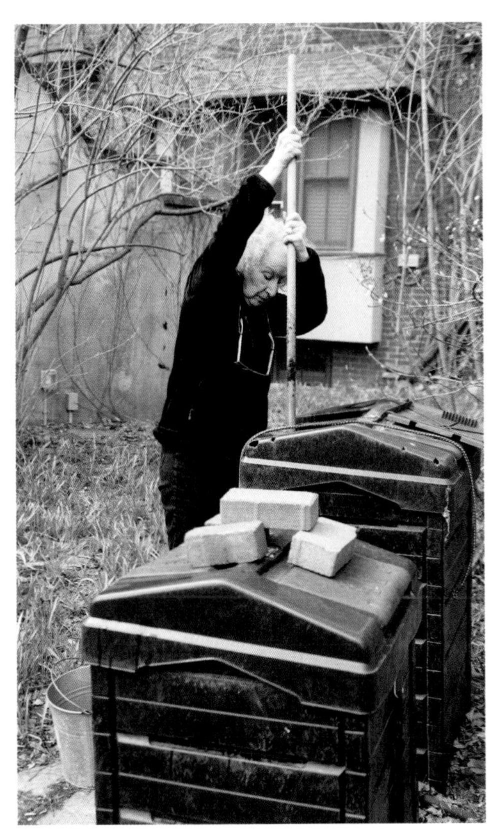
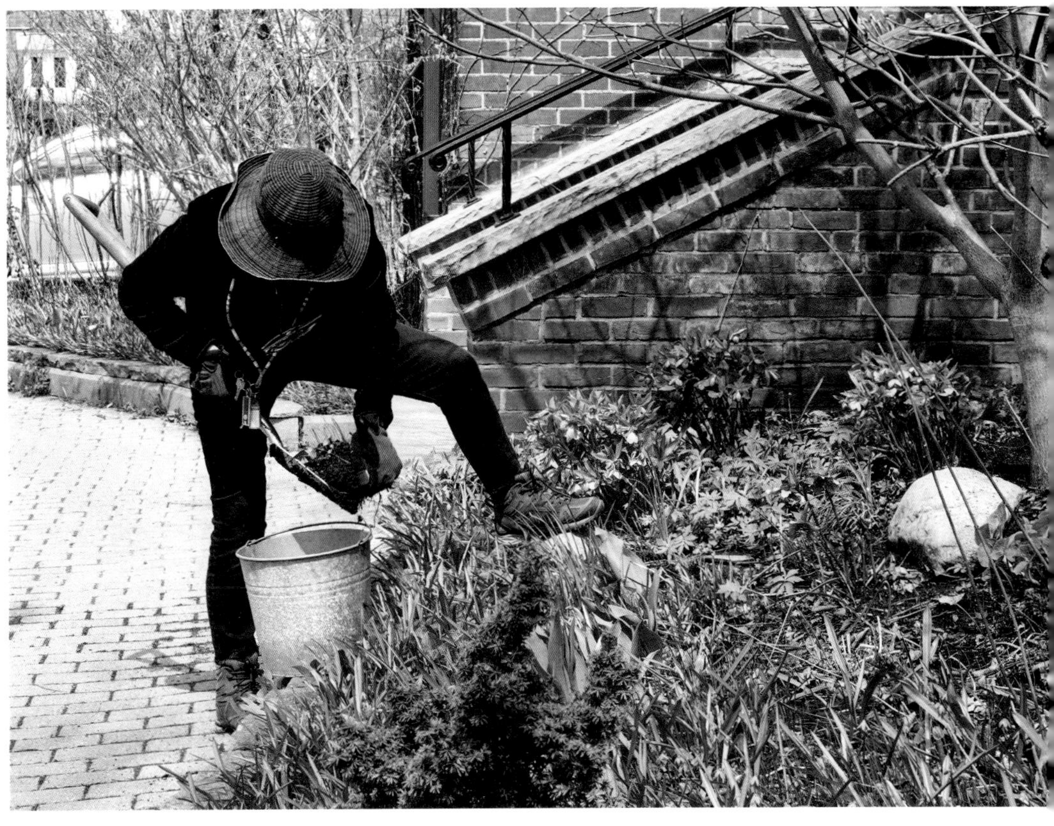

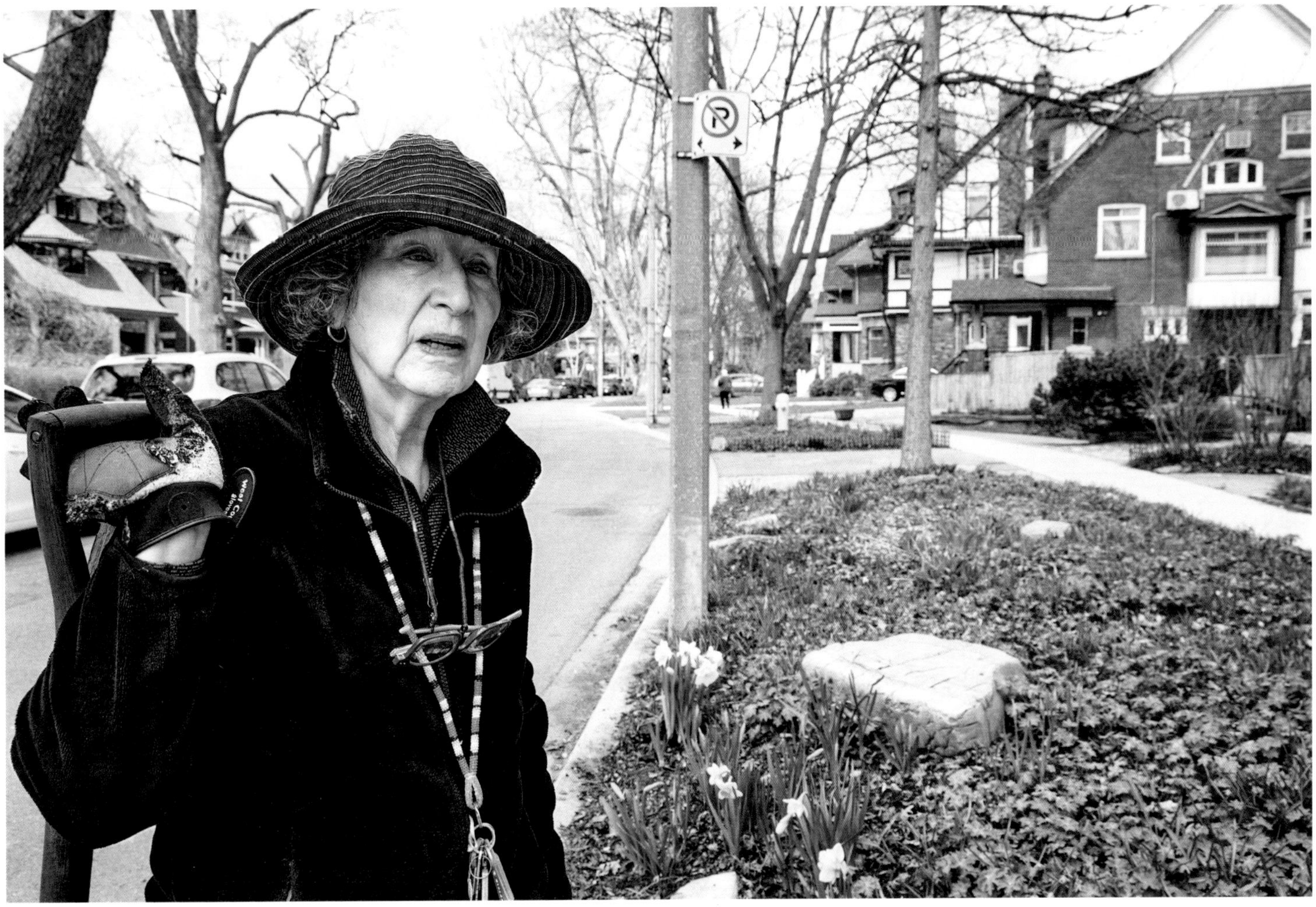

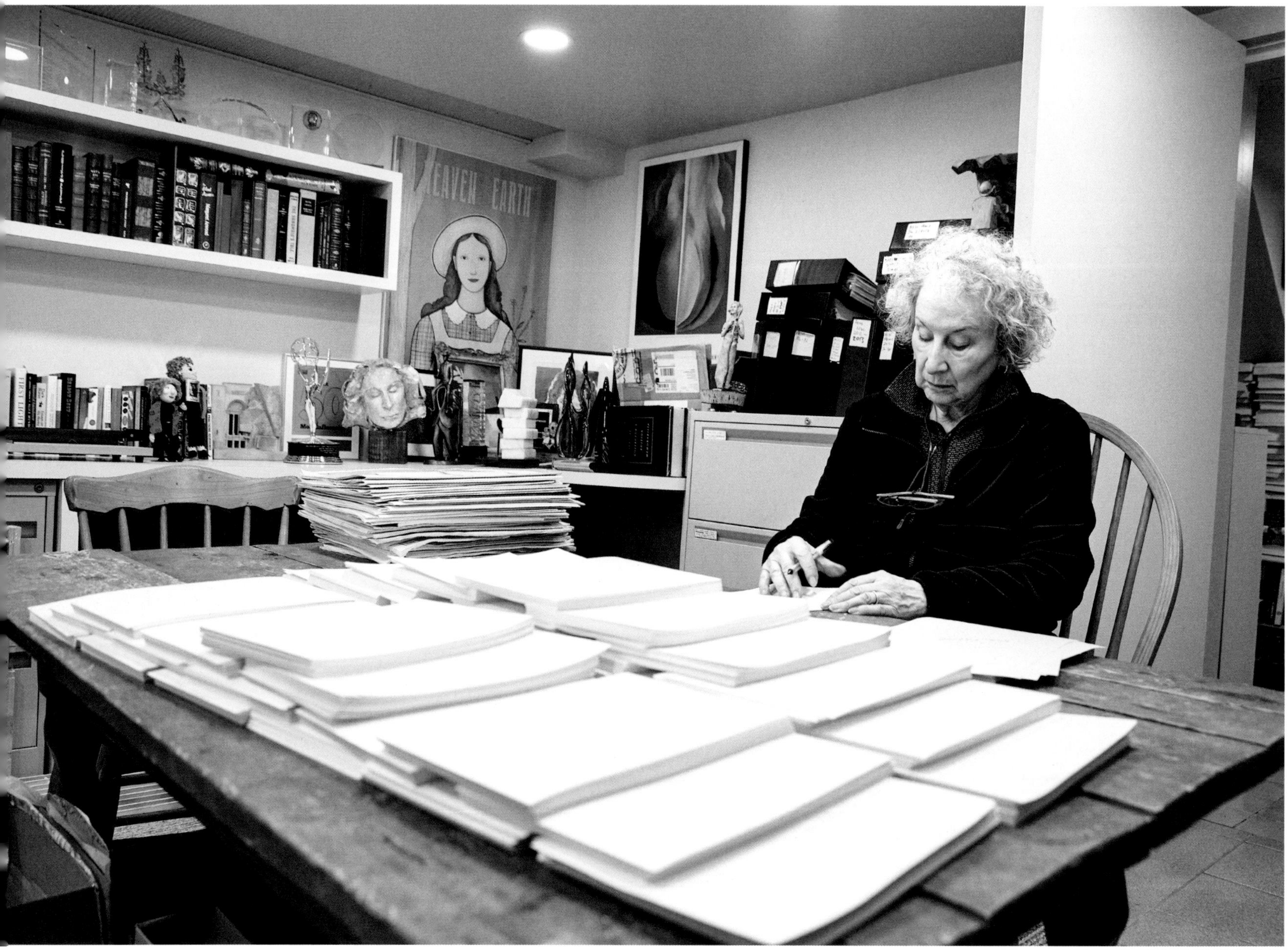

When we were nearly finished, I had one more thought: I wanted to photograph her with her longtime partner, the novelist Graeme Gibson. For years, she and Gibson shared interests in environmental and ornithological causes. Gibson now suffered from dementia, yet he still took pleasure in walking outside. Atwood stood tenderly next to him in the warm afternoon sun of a Canadian spring day as I photographed them.

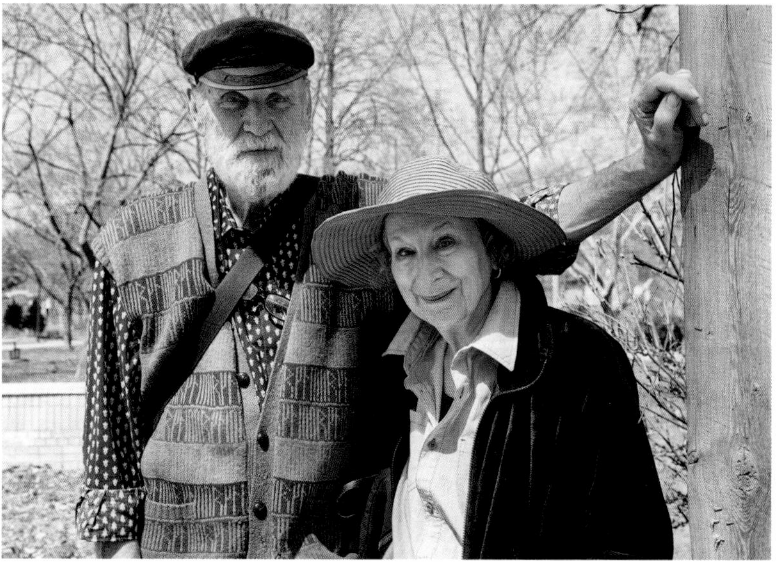

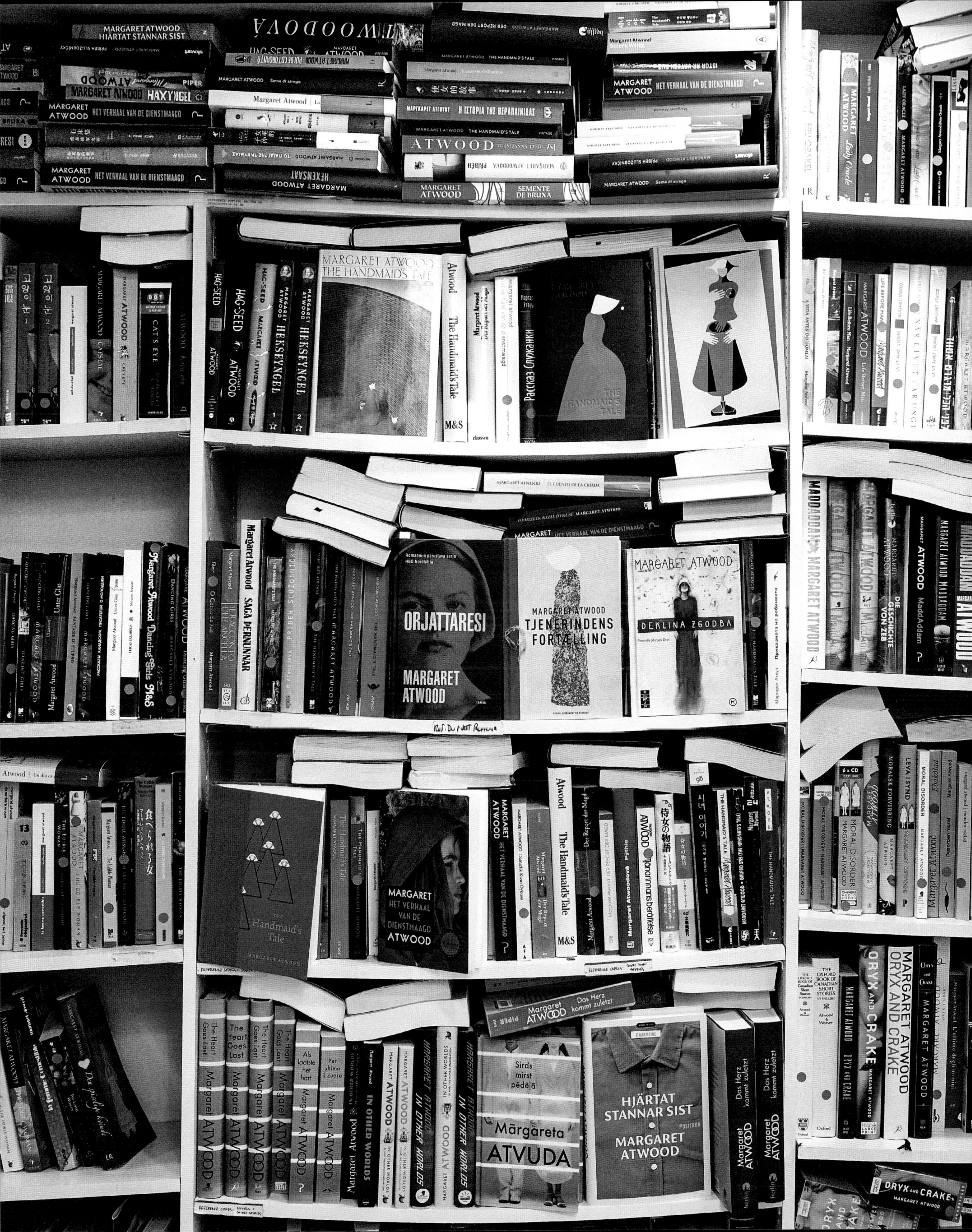

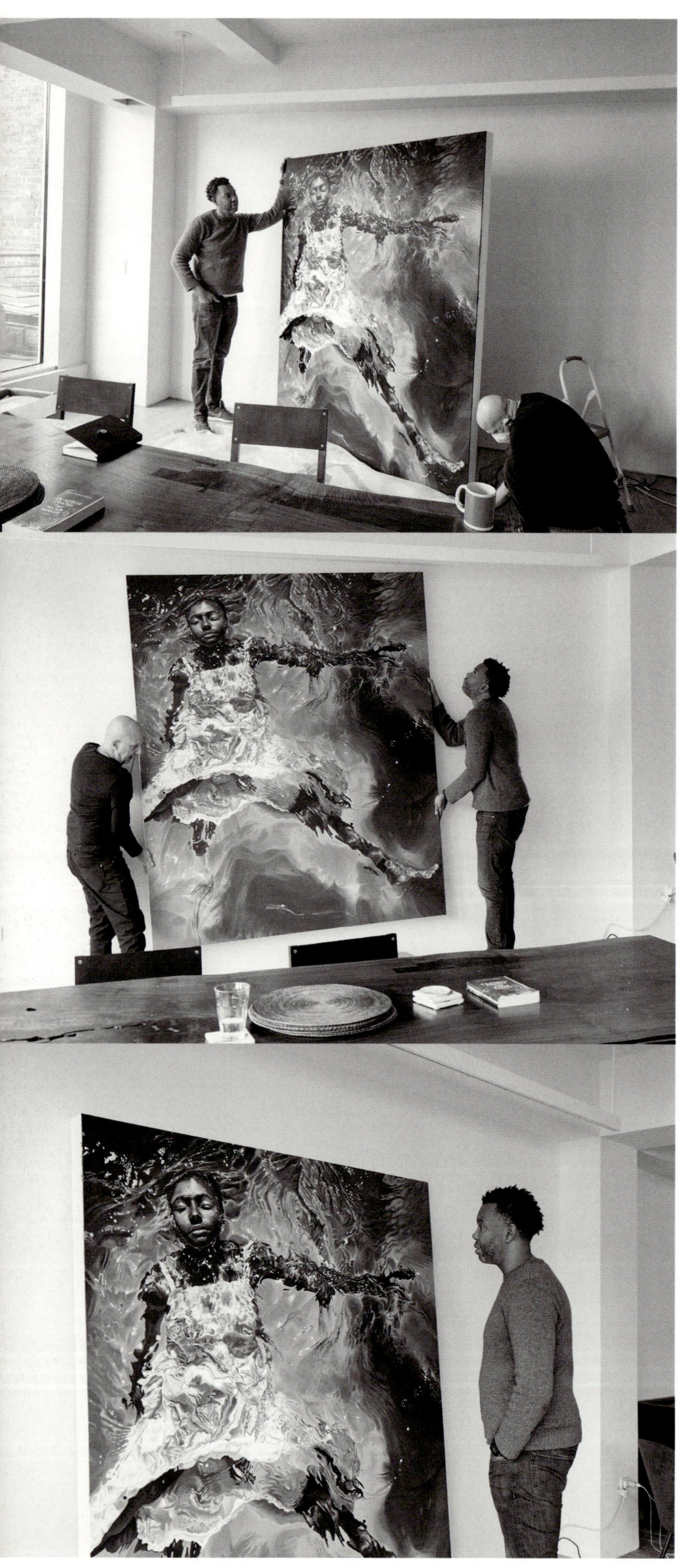

Ta-Nehisi Coates

American (b. 1975)

Photographed in New York, New York, January 2022

Ta-Nehisi Coates, like many writers, grew up reading. "I read like other people play video games," he told me. "But it's sad. You don't realize the time it takes to write actually takes away from reading."

When I visited Coates in Brooklyn, we made a trip across the East River to McNally Jackson in Soho, where Coates had fun talking with Sarah McNally, the bookstore's owner. He left with a bag full of books, but was wistful. "I'm always jealous," he said, "when I talk to my editors or even Sarah, who we just left, because they read so much more. They don't have to write." Coates, of course, does read but not the way he used to. He reads mainly in subject areas he feels he needs to know more about. He misses reading for pleasure. "I don't have time to be a hobbyist."

Coates is reserved, a careful listener, and, at 6 feet 4 inches, has the natural dignity of a man with height. He and his wife, Kenyatta Matthews, moved to New York more than twenty years ago. He was an aspiring magazine writer, and New York City was magazine central. But at this point in his career Coates could work anywhere. "I don't feel New York has any sort of monopoly on creativity," he said. "I don't feel it's any more inspirational than Baltimore where I grew up, or Chicago, where Kenyatta is from. We love New York but creatively, I don't need to be here. I work in a world of books. I can get that anywhere."

But what Coates does need in his life is peace. "All of my adventures are in my work," he explained. "I

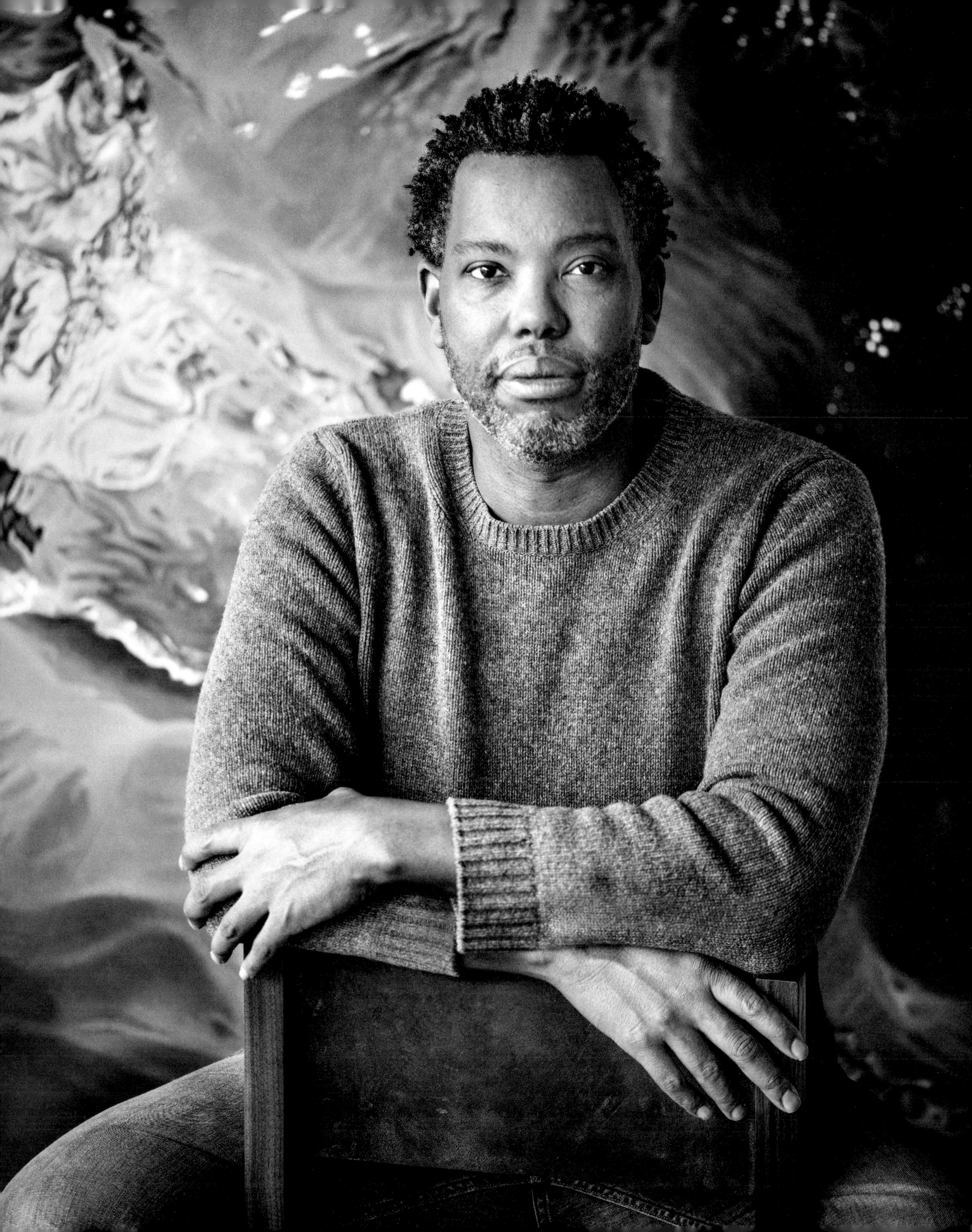

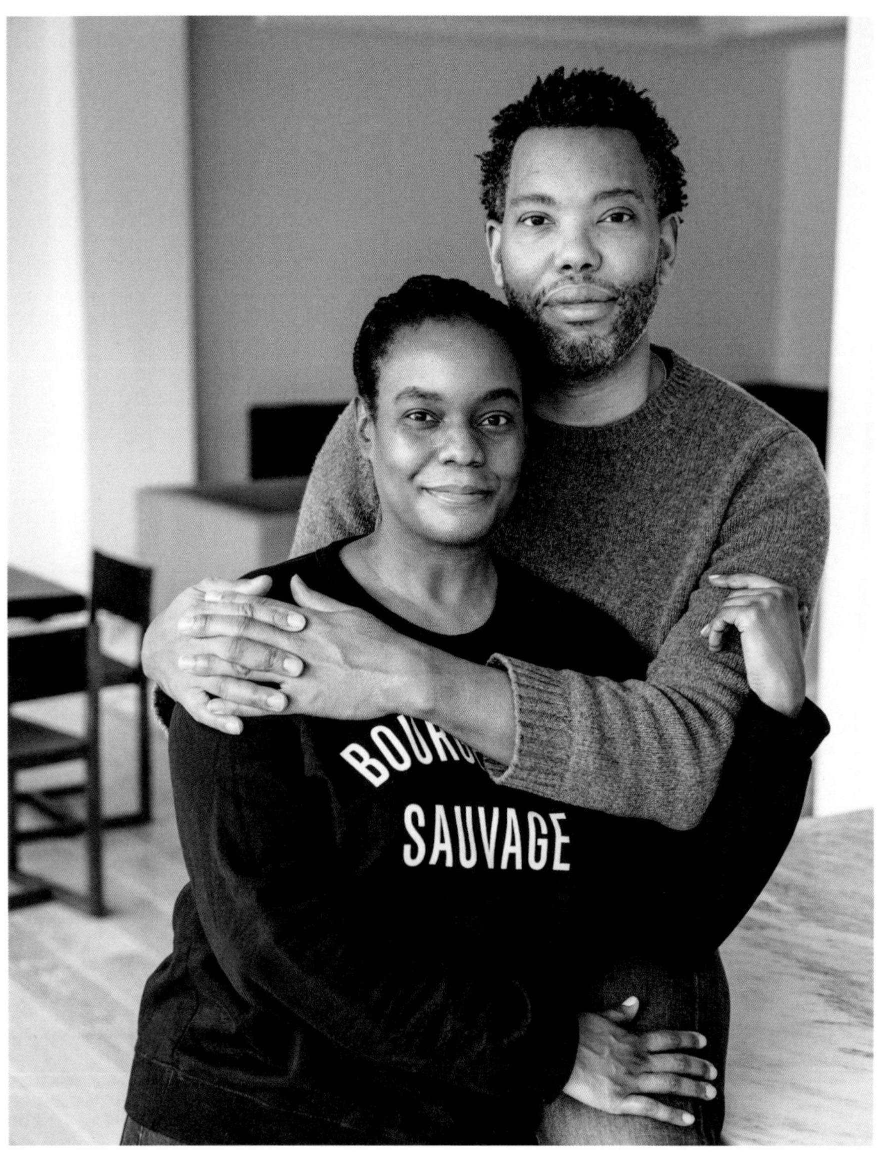

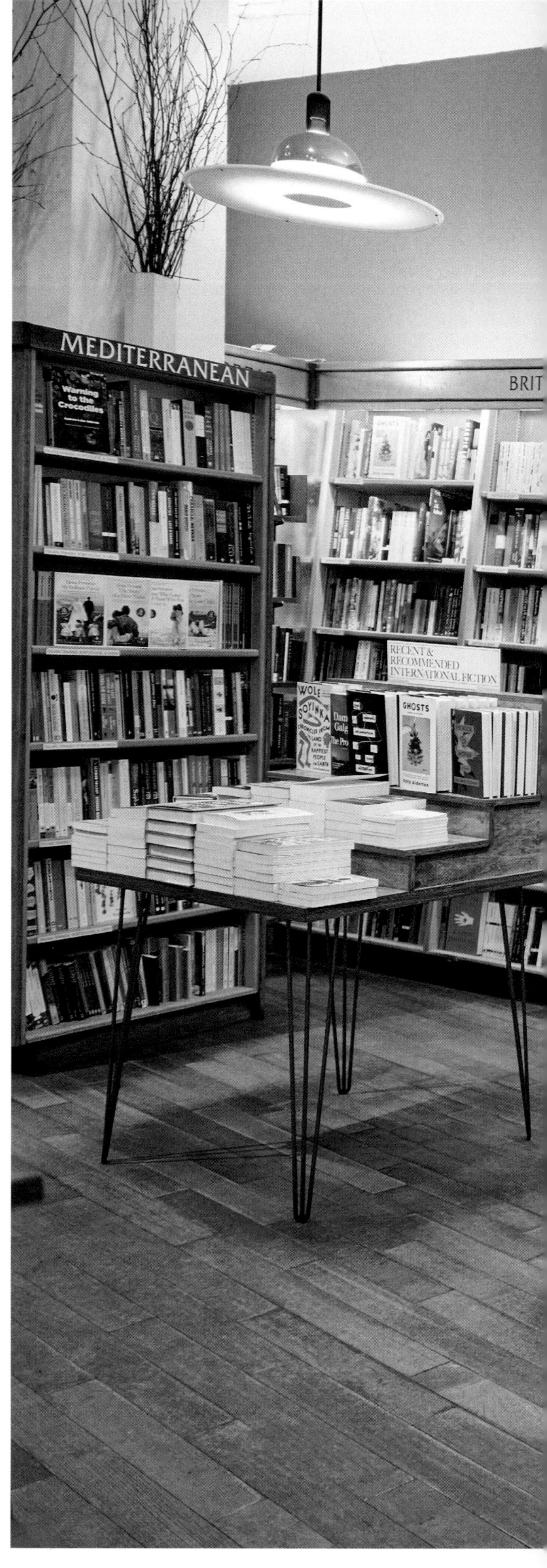

can't do what it takes to write, which is often chaotic, and then have a chaotic personal life." His home and marriage with Kenyatta are dependable and give his life the normalcy he needs. This doesn't mean it has to be boring or unromantic, he told me, but it can't be full of upheavals. "I can't go from crazy to crazy. I just can't."

The desire for peace may also have freed Coates from feeling he is in competition with other writers he admires. "I'm answering things that are deep inside me," Coates said. "Fiction is like we're all going to run, but we each invent our own race. My race is like a steeplechase. There are hurdles and water. For another writer, it's running ten miles straight, in another person's race there'll be a long jump and other obstacles. What we're trying to do is so darn different, it's just very hard to compare each other. What it comes down to is, I guess, recognition, which we all want."

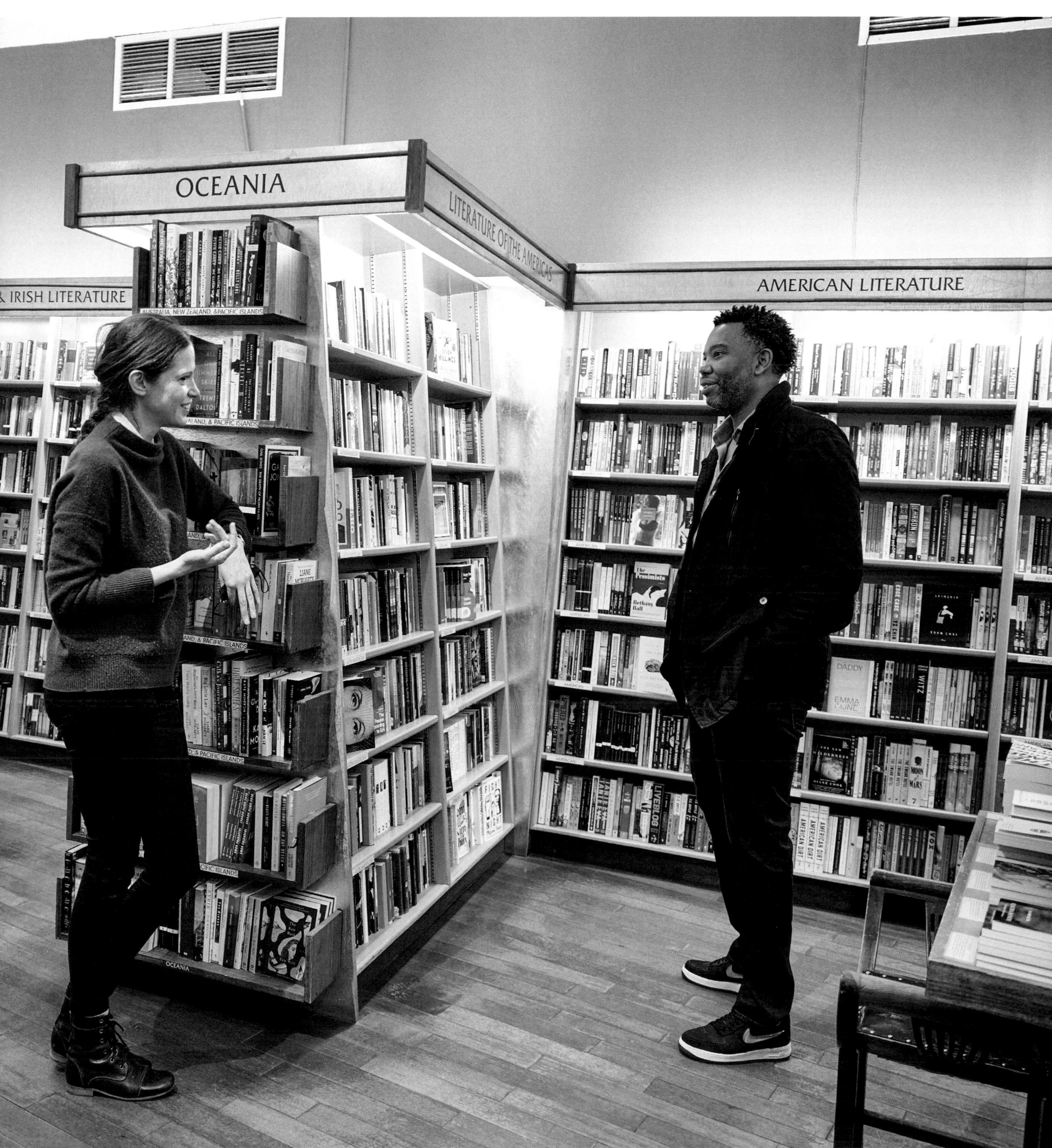

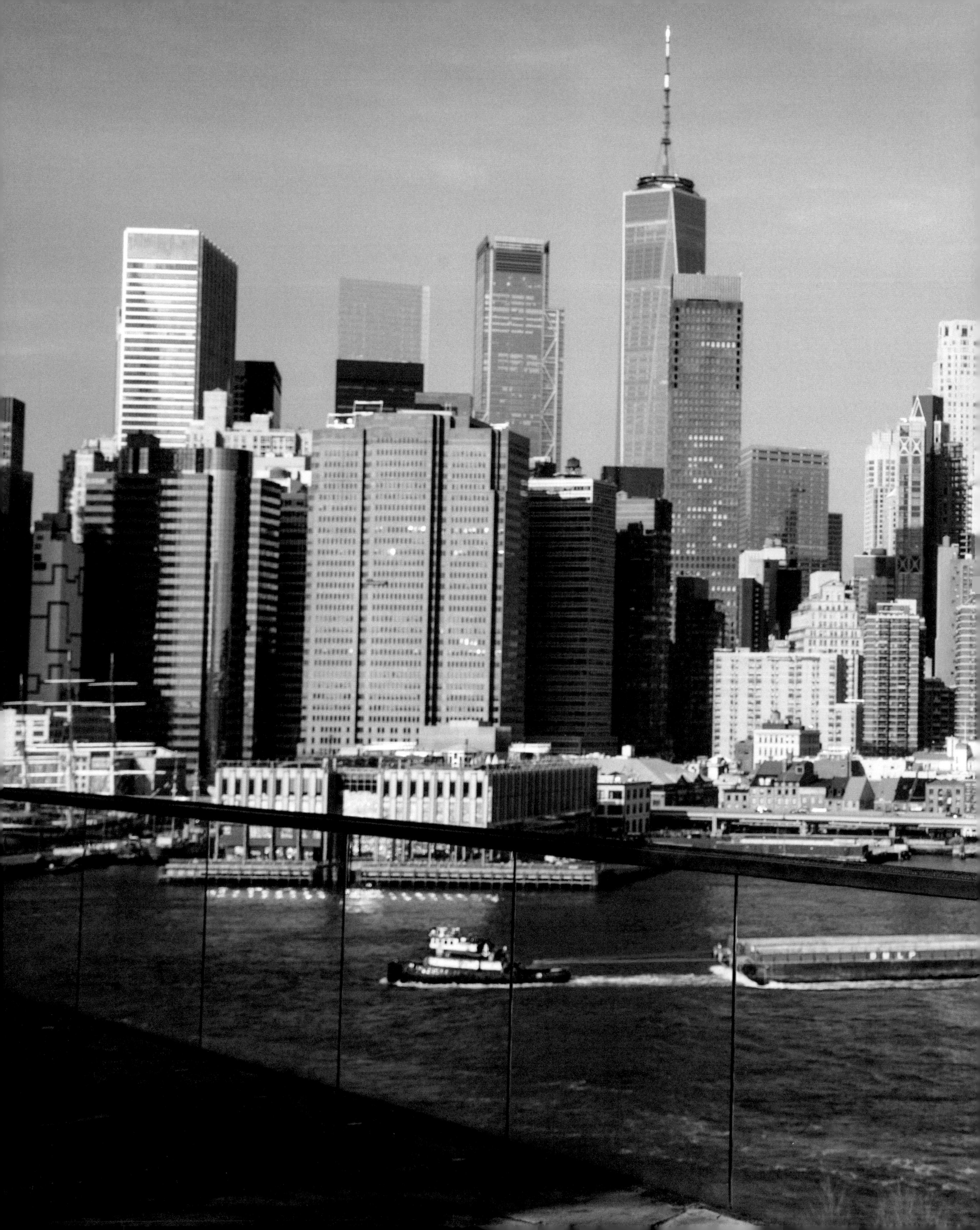

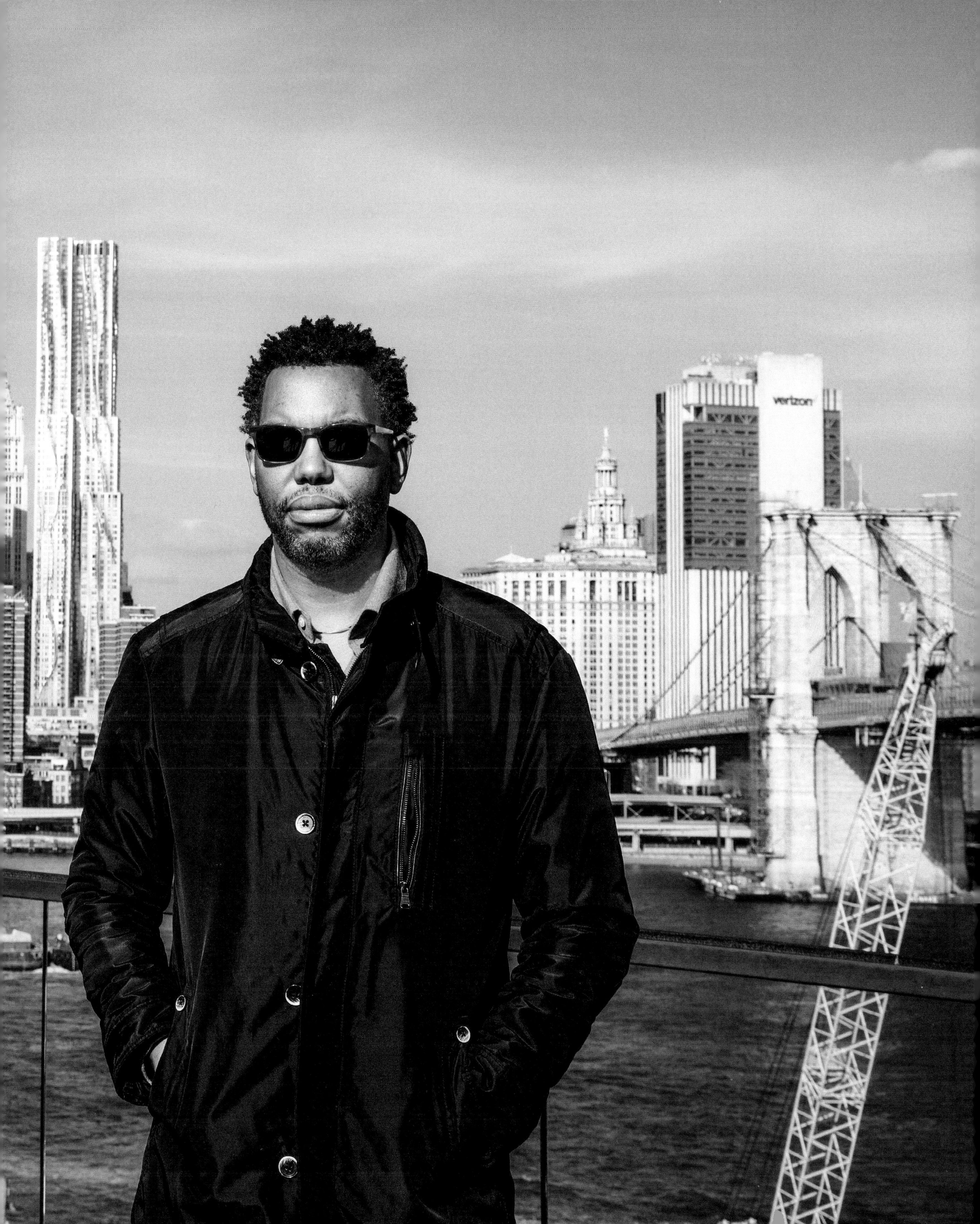

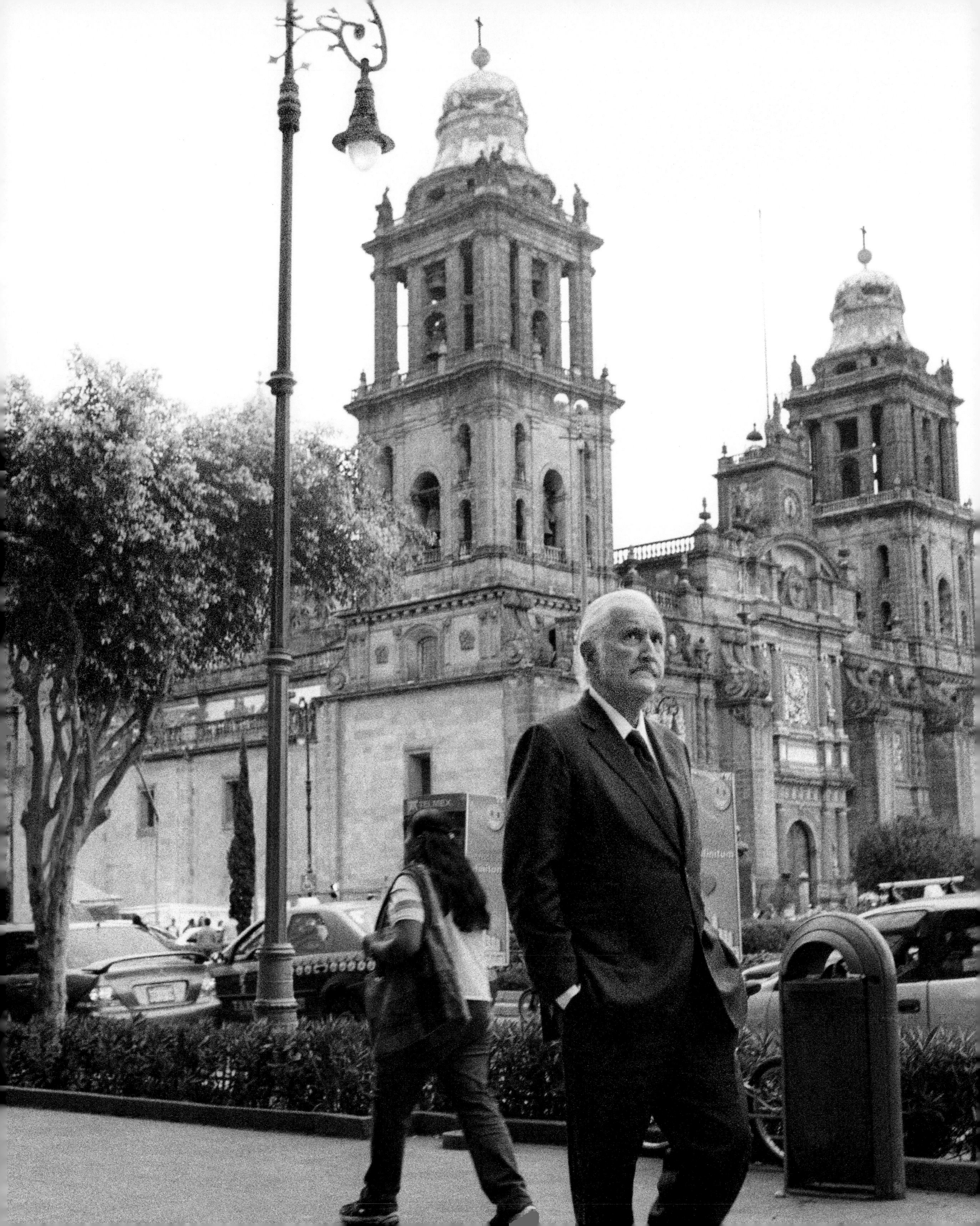

Carlos Fuentes

Mexican (1928–2012)

Photographed in Mexico City, Mexico, February 2012

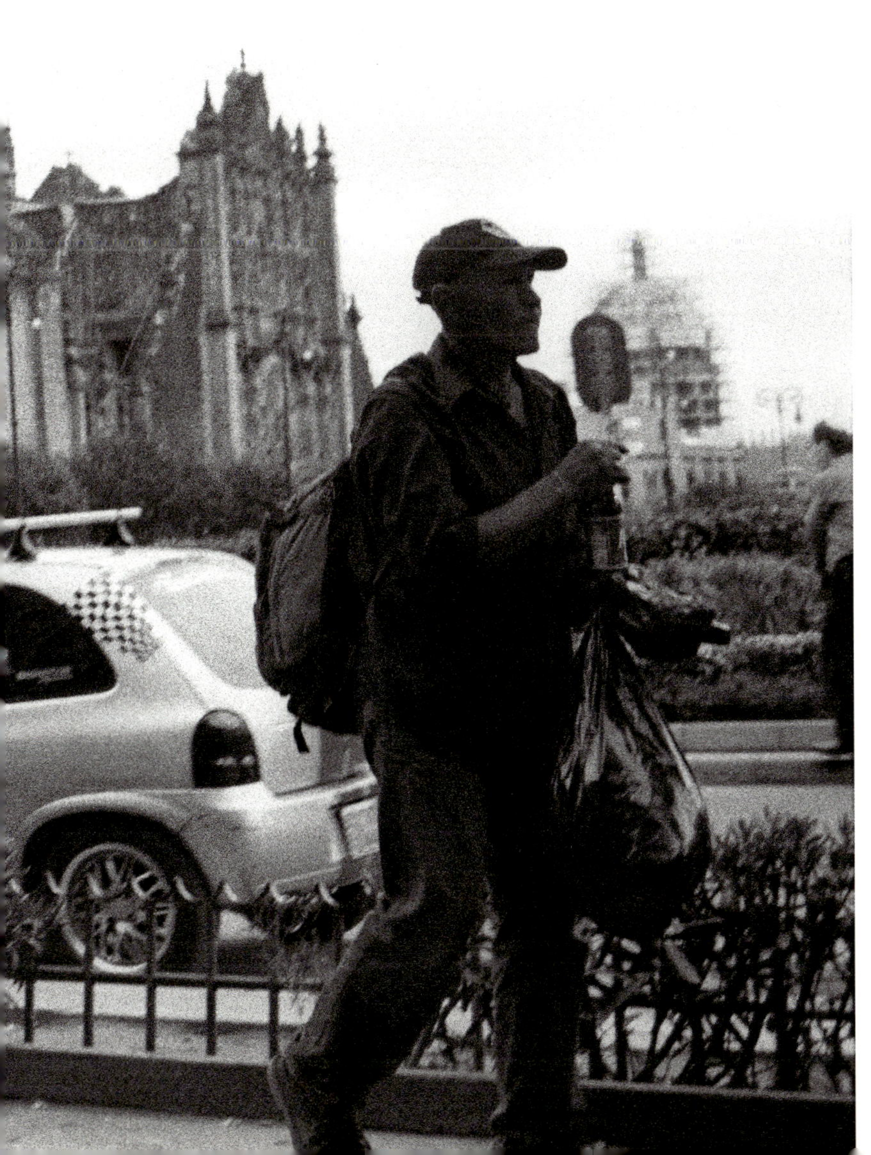

Carlos Fuentes wanted to go to Centro Histórico, the ancient heart of the Aztec Empire, in Mexico City. It was dusk as we walked in the Zócalo, past the Metropolitan Cathedral, the largest and oldest cathedral in the Western hemisphere.

We walked three blocks farther on to Plaza de Santo Domingo, his favorite square in this city of 22 million people. It was here where he first lived as a young law student when the population was only 1.5 million. To this day, men sit, as they have for centuries, at desks hand-writing legal documents and love letters for illiterate people.

Fuentes was so recognizable with his white hair, distinguished features, and elegant dress that people flocked around him. He had star power. A construction worker ran across the plaza with a Bible, asking him to inscribe it. Just as Fuentes was about to sign his name, he glanced at me with a little smile and said, "Maybe I shouldn't be doing this."

Fuentes was besieged by students. They called him "Maestro." With patience, he answered all their questions, unperturbed by the constant interruptions. Later, when we stopped for dinner at Sanborns, all the waitresses and kitchen workers gathered around him for cellphone snapshots. I asked him if he was ever annoyed by the ceaseless public attention. He said, "Not at all, these are my readers."

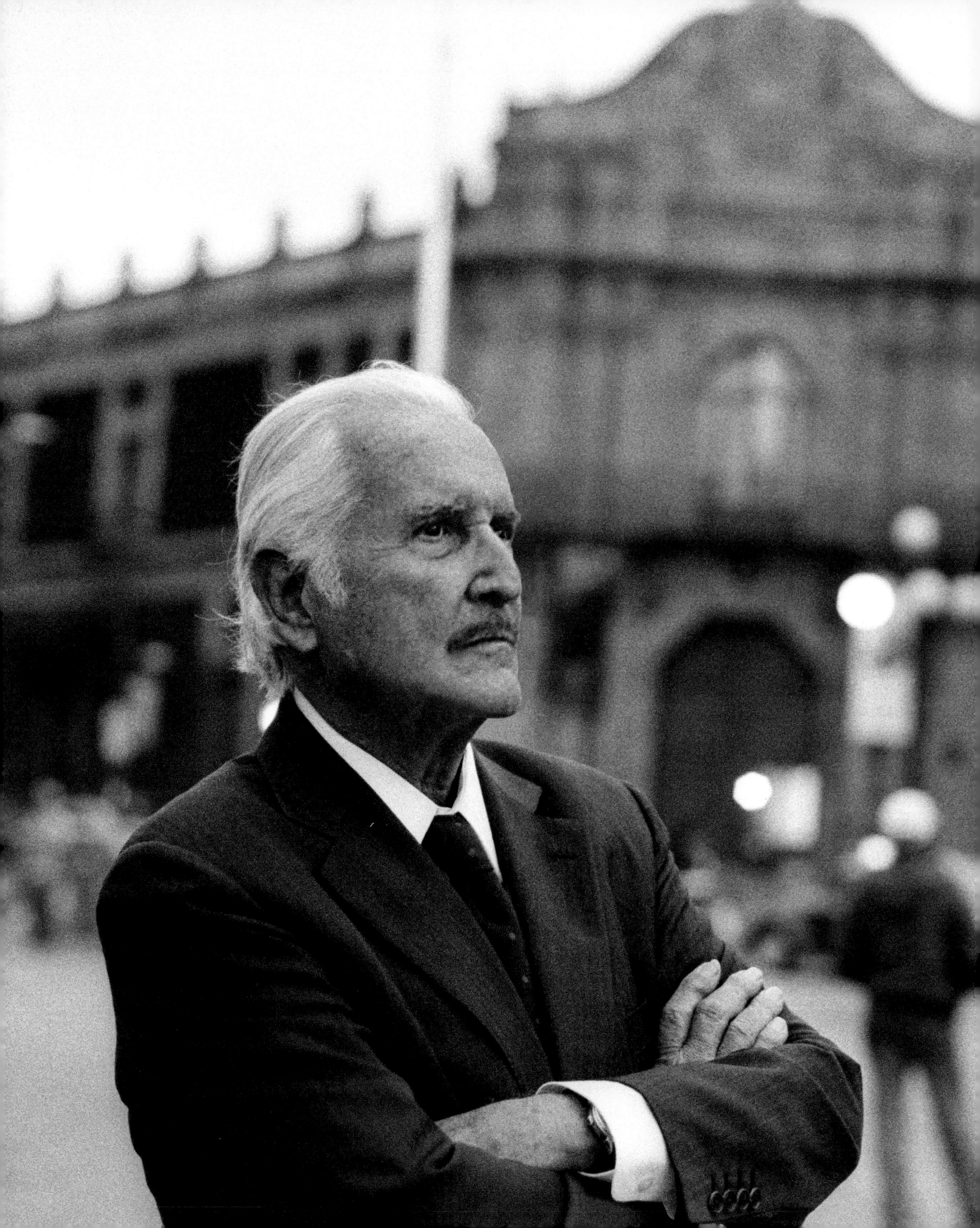

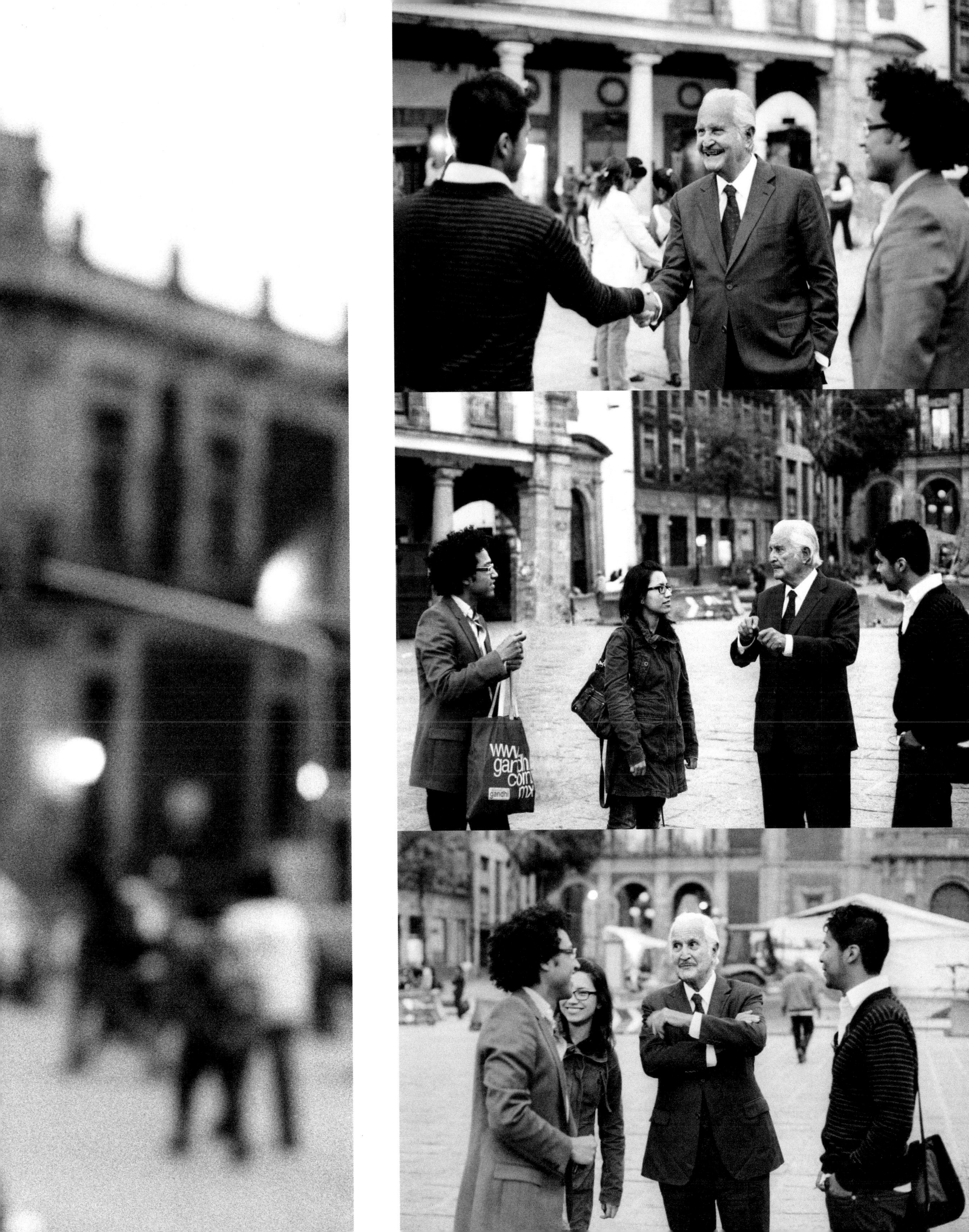

His family was from Veracruz, but Fuentes spent his childhood years from four to eleven in Washington, D.C., where his father was a diplomat. He learned to speak English fluently in public school and every weekend his father took him to the movies. "We saw triple features, not double. I liked Westerns best. We watched all of John Ford's movies and I fell in love with Maureen O'Hara."

Most people who are photographed frequently have a practiced look for the camera. Fuentes was no exception. Here, however, when I looked up from changing film in my camera, I saw a grave, heartbreaking expression on his face. Fuentes had a charmed life—as a writer, as a diplomat, as one of Mexico's most beloved public figures—but he grieved the loss of both of his children, one to suicide, the other to an overdose. Carlos Fuentes died on May 15, 2012, less than three months after I did this portrait.

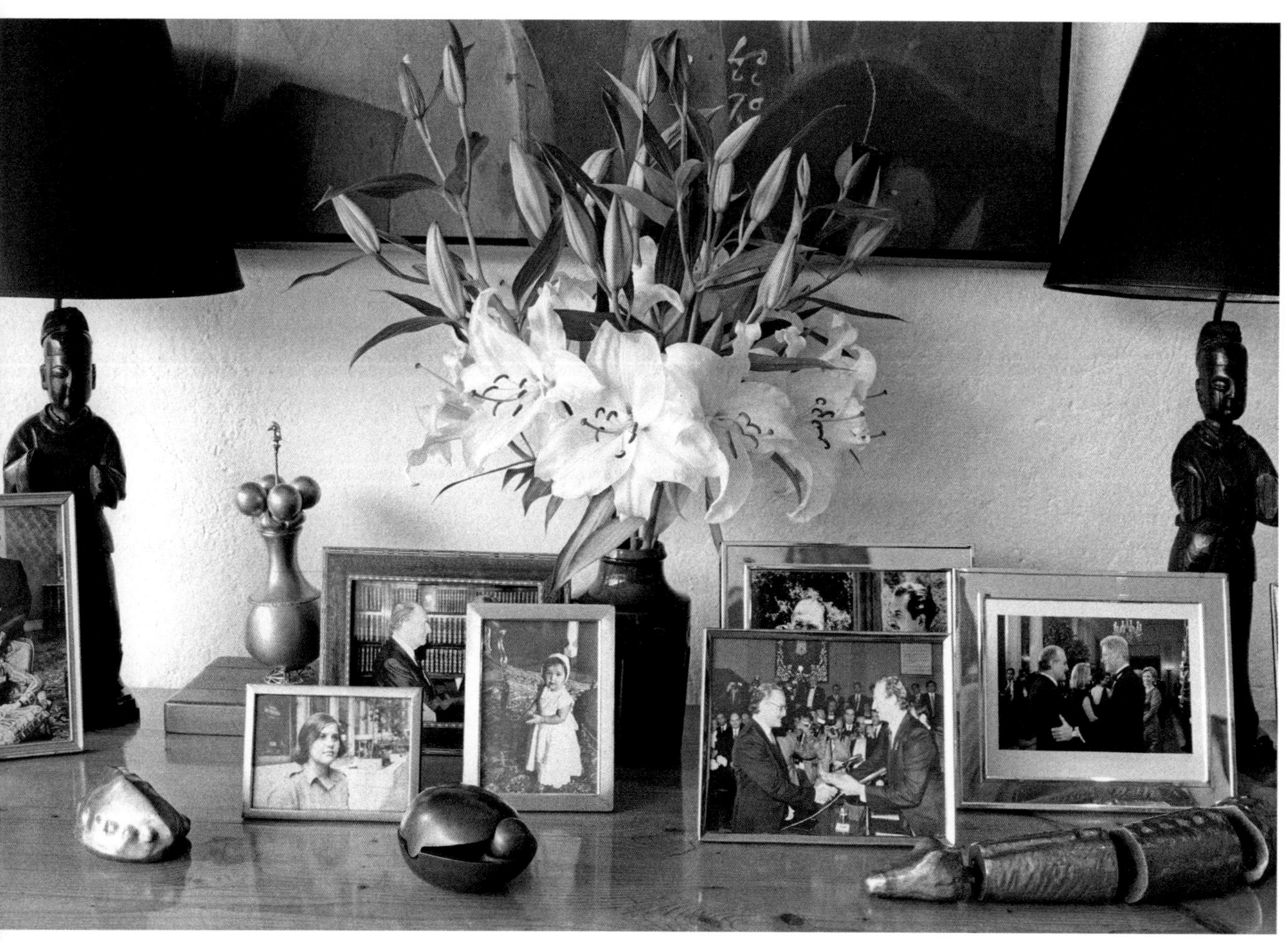

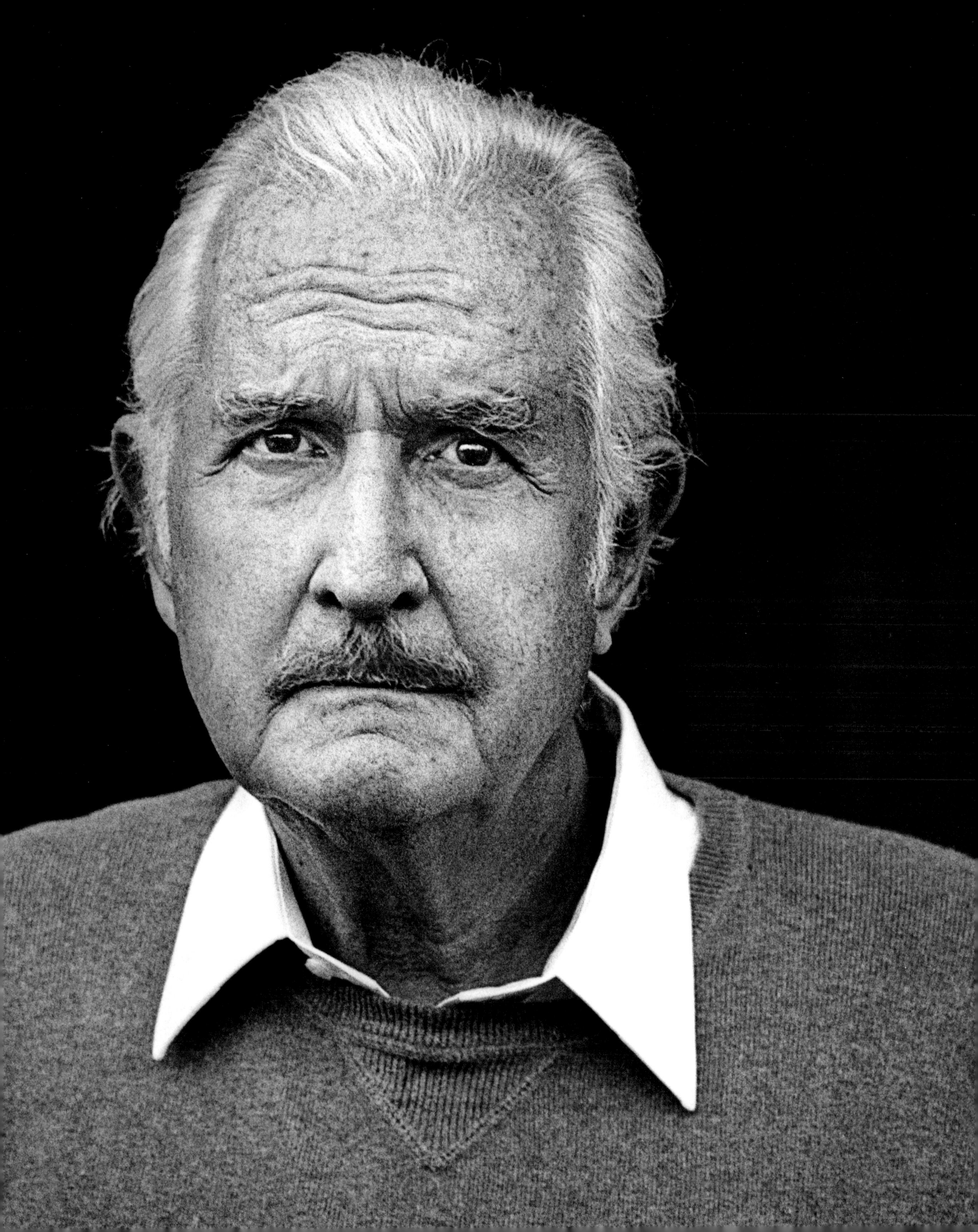

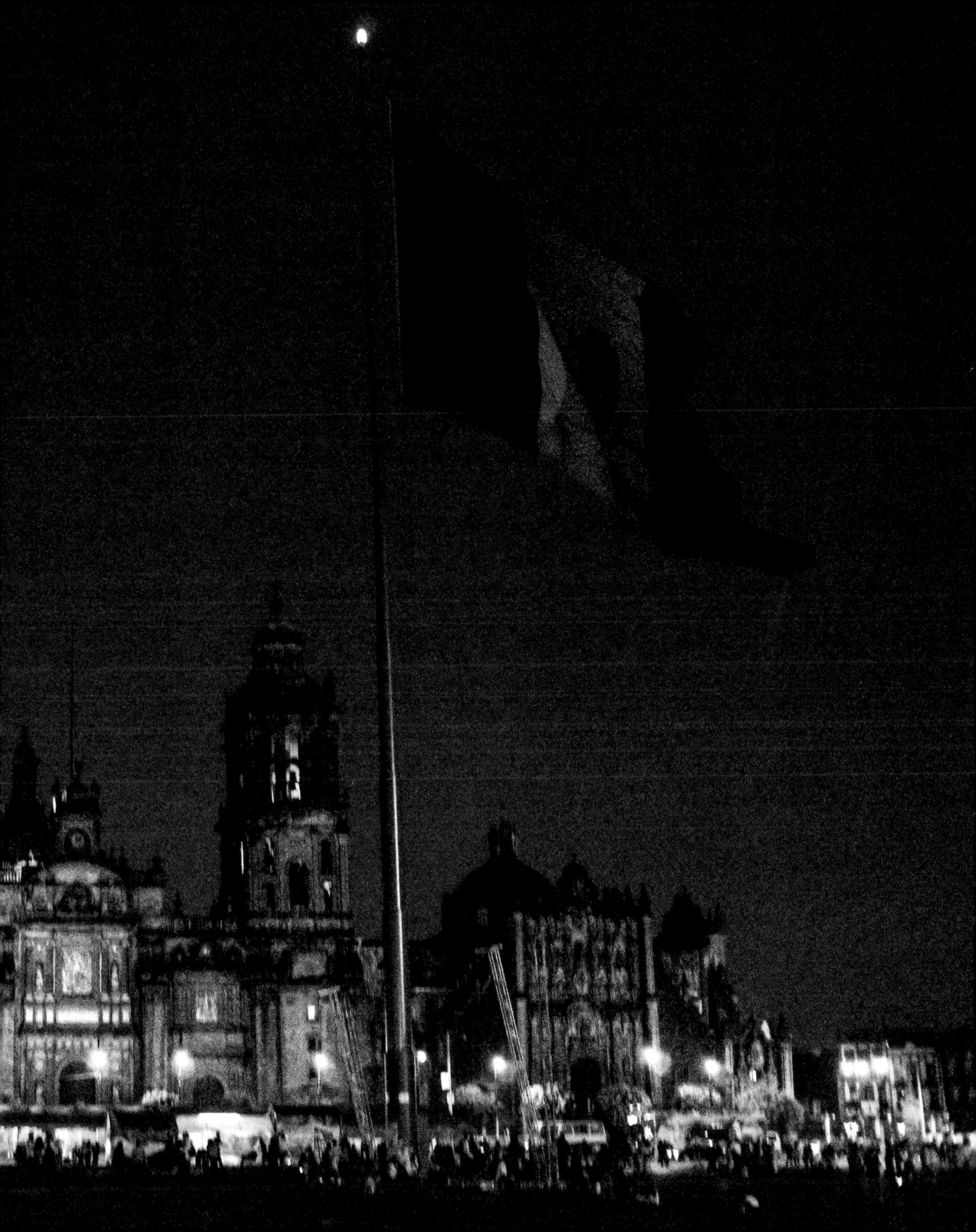

Marjane Satrapi

Iranian (b. 1969)

Photographed in Paris, France, July 2021

Marjane Satrapi, the acclaimed graphic novelist and filmmaker, prefers to be called a "comic novelist." She's the only comic novelist in this collection. When we first met, in the crowded Marais in Paris, I immediately recognized her. She looked exactly like the drawings of herself in *Persepolis.*

Satrapi is a force majeure, full of vigor and exuberance. Born in Iran, she grew up under a repressive fundamentalist regime. At fourteen, she was sent by her parents to study in Austria and ended up homeless, living on the streets of Vienna. She returned to Tehran at eighteen and suffered an early, debilitating marriage. At last, she found her bearings in the cultural and intellectual life of Paris. Now, successful and confident, she told me: "I am a sort of Iron Man mixed with Captain America."

Today, Satrapi lives in a spacious, light-filled apartment in the Marais with her husband, Mattias Ripa, and an immaculate white cat, Mitzi. The apartment is filled with an eclectic mix of antique and contemporary furniture. Vintage Batman and Clark Gable busts suggest a wide-ranging accumulator. But everything is perfectly ordered, neatly dusted. There's not a cat hair to be seen. When I commented on how tidy her house was, she said, "I'm a nineteen-fifties housewife."

Her studio is a ten-minute walk from the apartment. It is spare and open to the rooftops of her neighborhood at the Bastille. On her walks back and forth, she has an easy rapport with a small community of friends. She has coffee and a chat with a waitress from Laredo, Texas, who wants to be a dancer, she samples handmade chocolates at Alain Ducasse's Le Chocolat, and she regularly checks a few special bookshops in the Marais. "Since I am aware that I don't have a hundred other years to live, I read mostly the classics," she told me, "especially Russian literature."

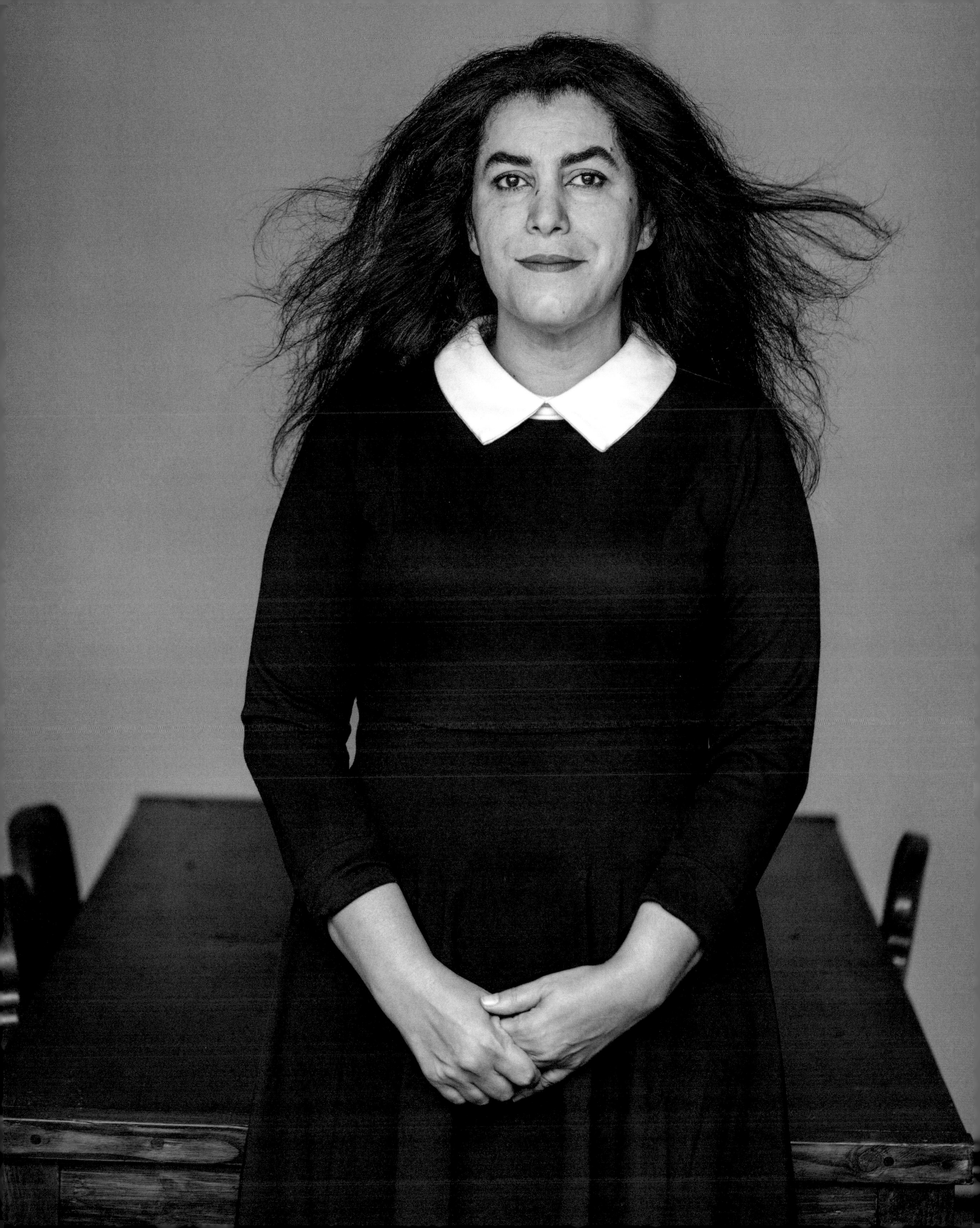

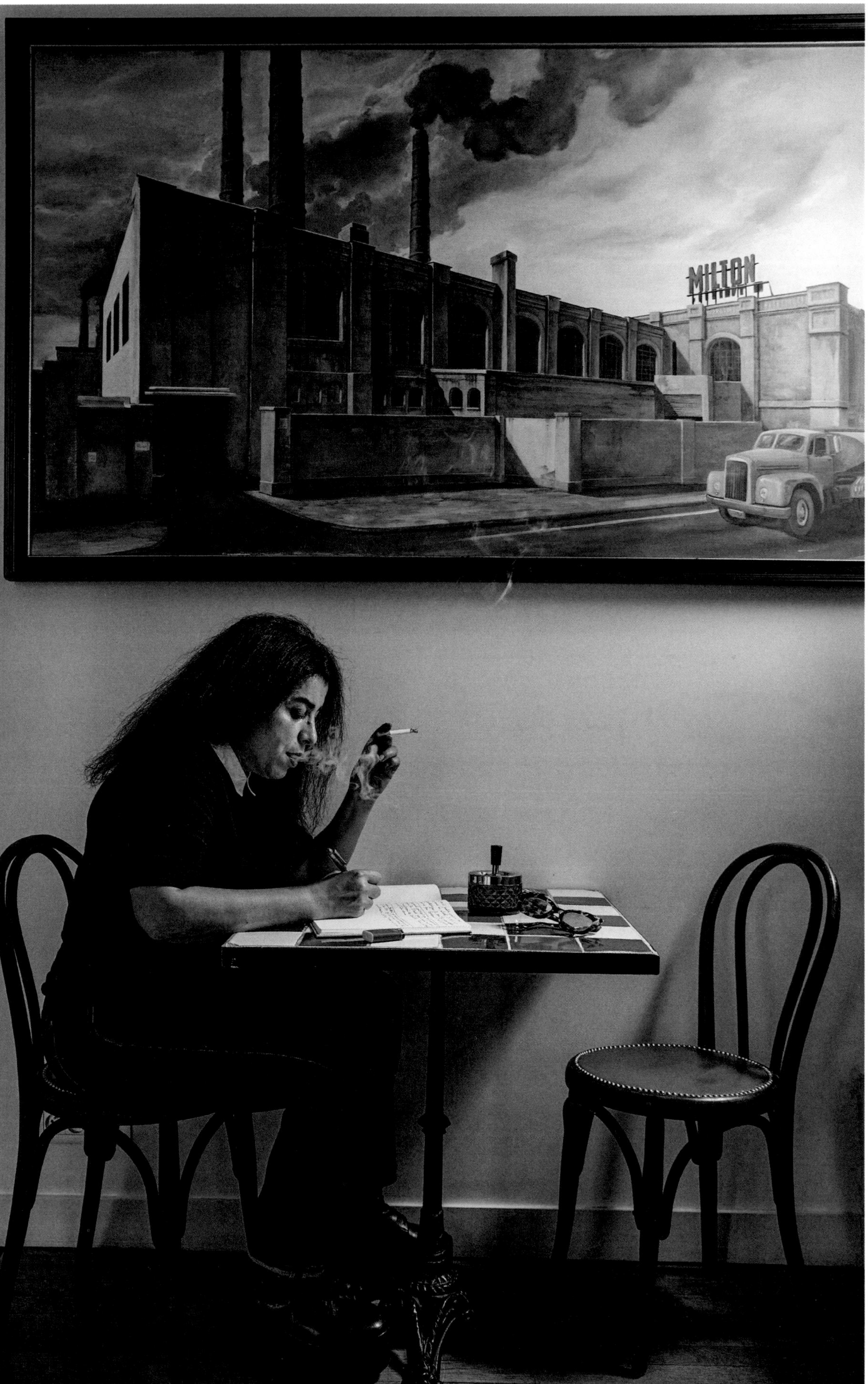

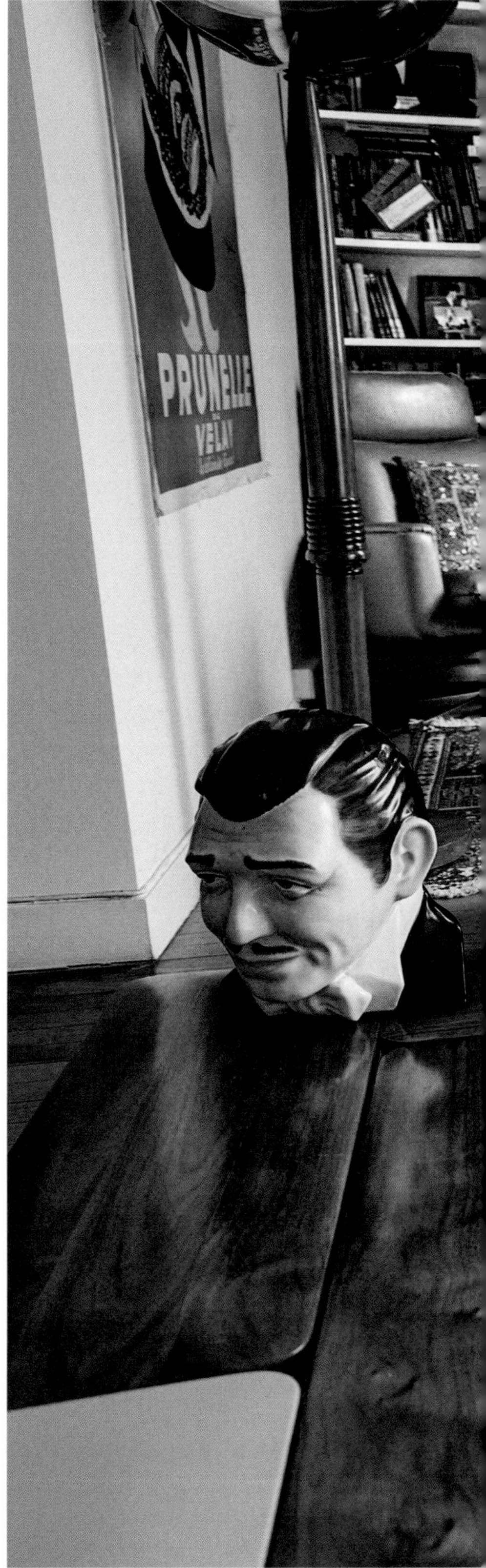

MILTON
PRUNELLE
du
VELAY

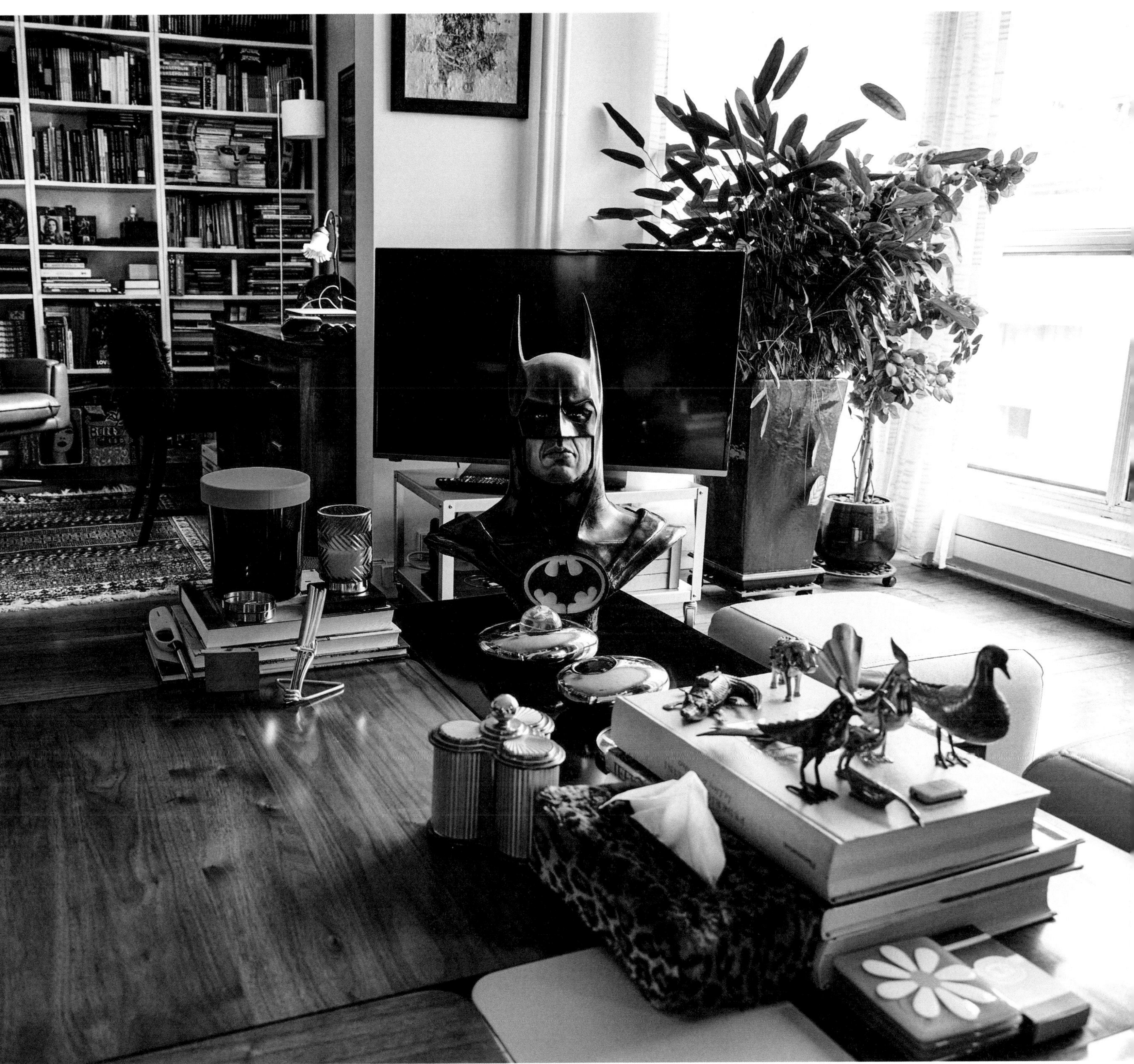

To relax, she plays darts, alone. And to simplify life, she wears a uniform—white collar, black sweater, black pants or skirt, and highly stylish chunky black shoes. But what could be interpreted as a demure, schoolgirlish look contrasts sharply with her surprising use of expletives—in all six of the languages she speaks so comfortably.

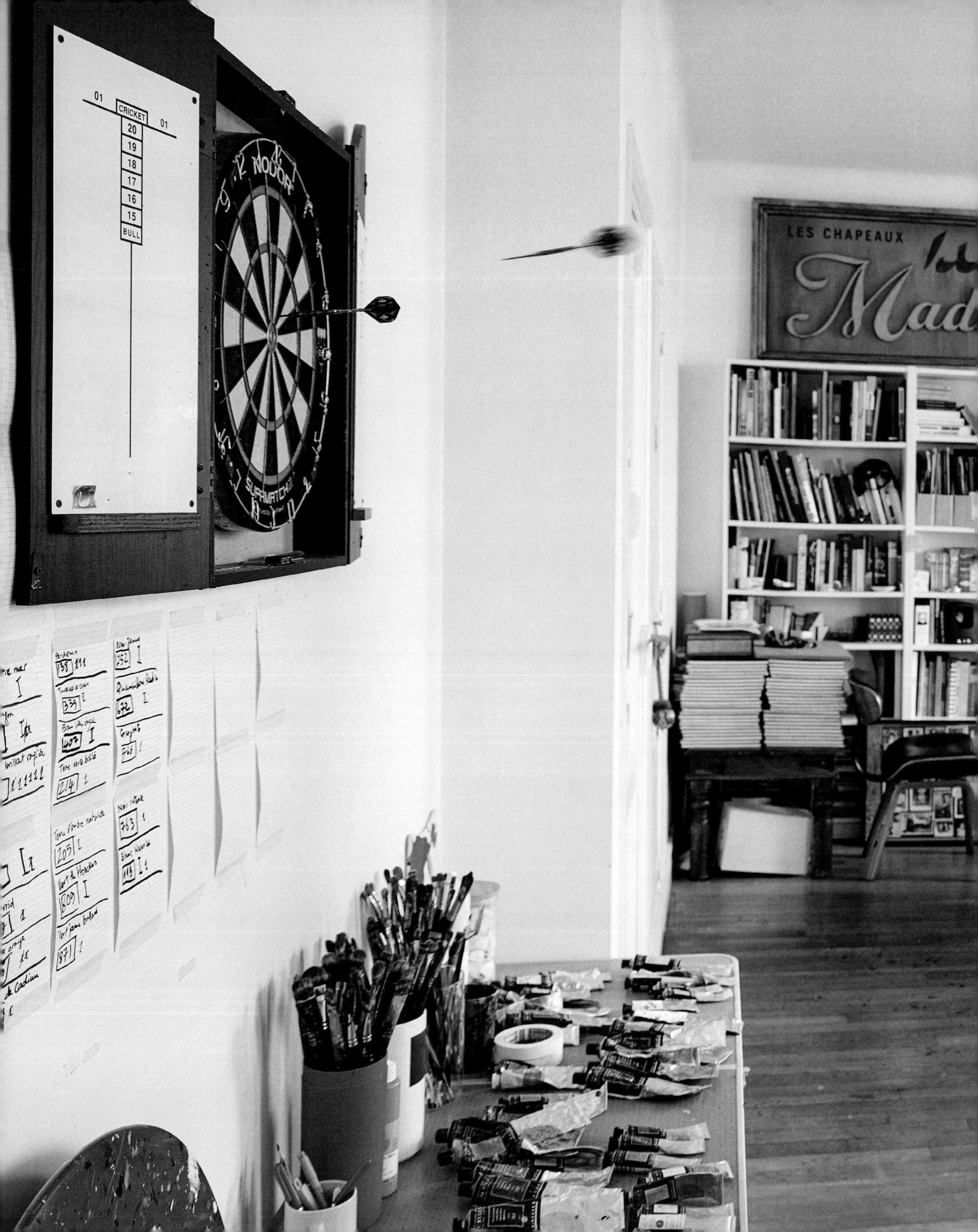

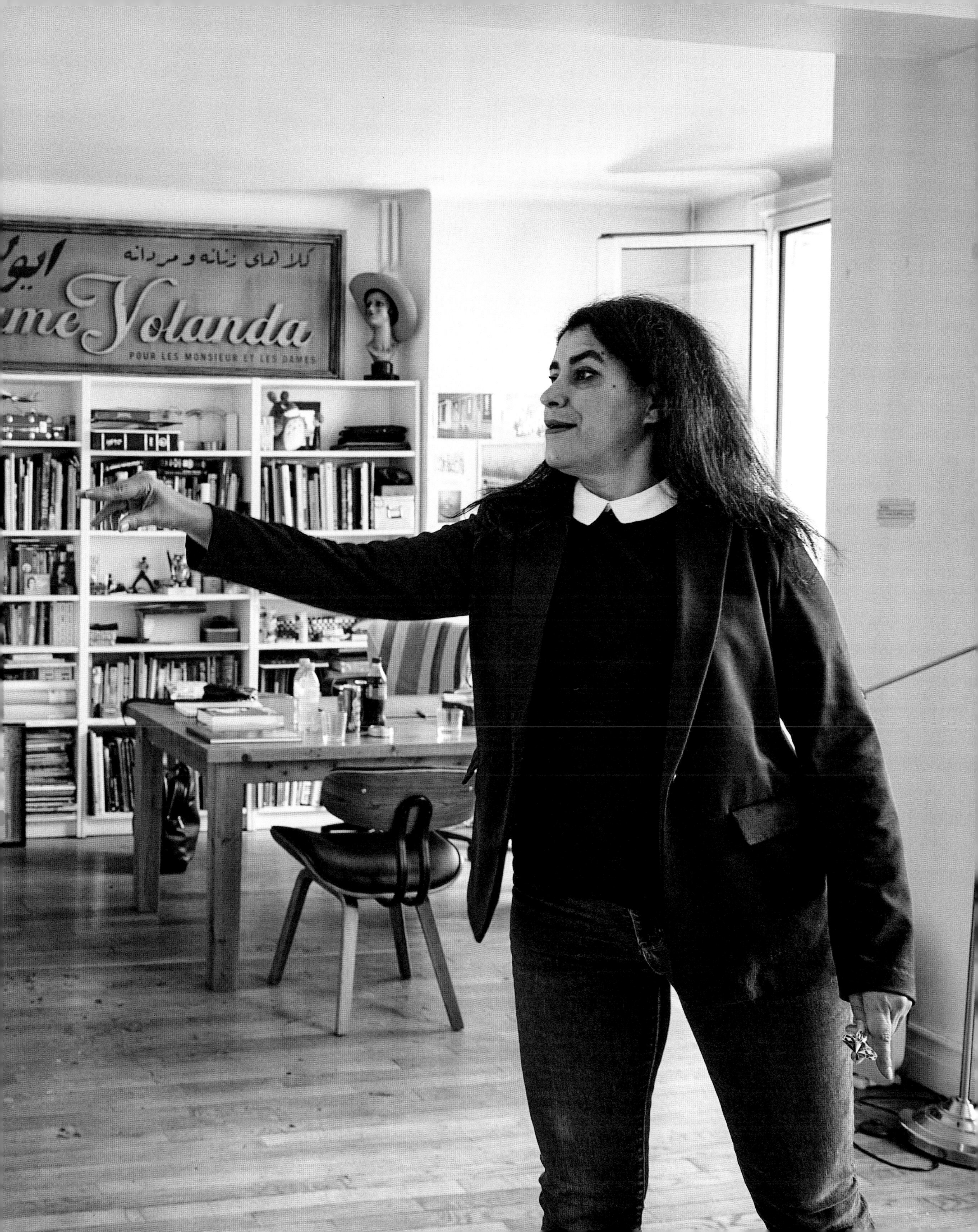
کلاه‌های زنانه و مردانه
ایو
me Yolanda
POUR LES MONSIEUR ET LES DAMES

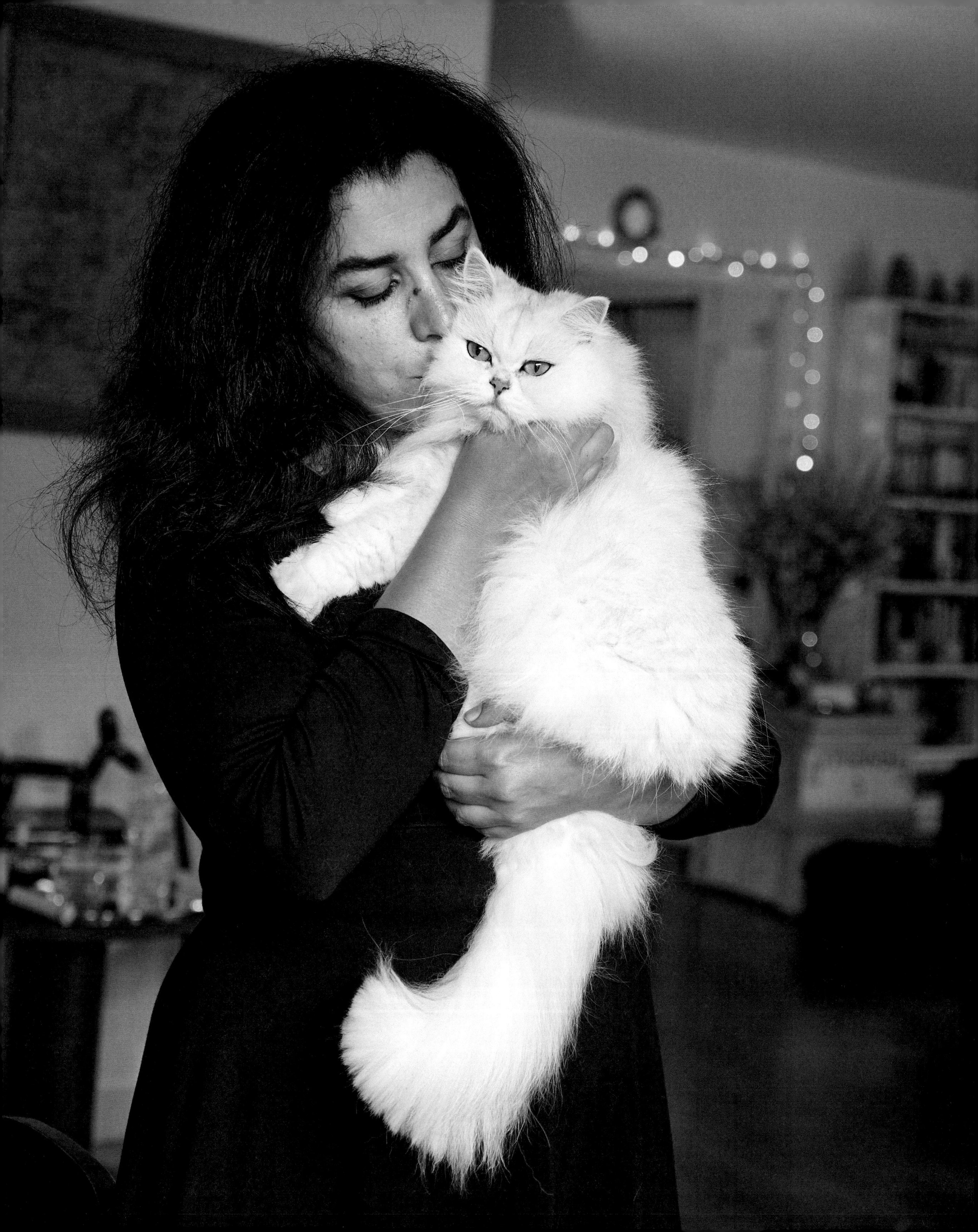

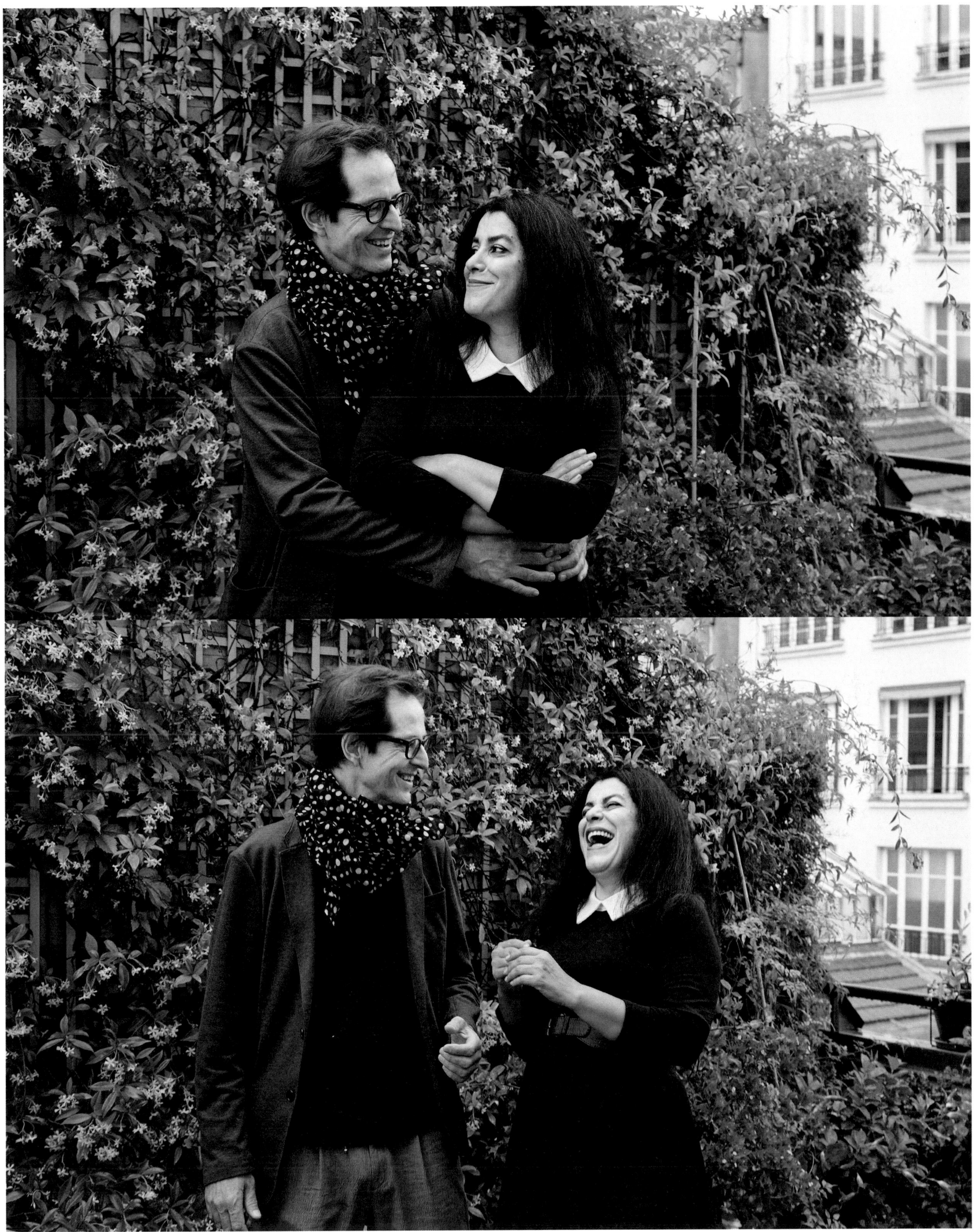

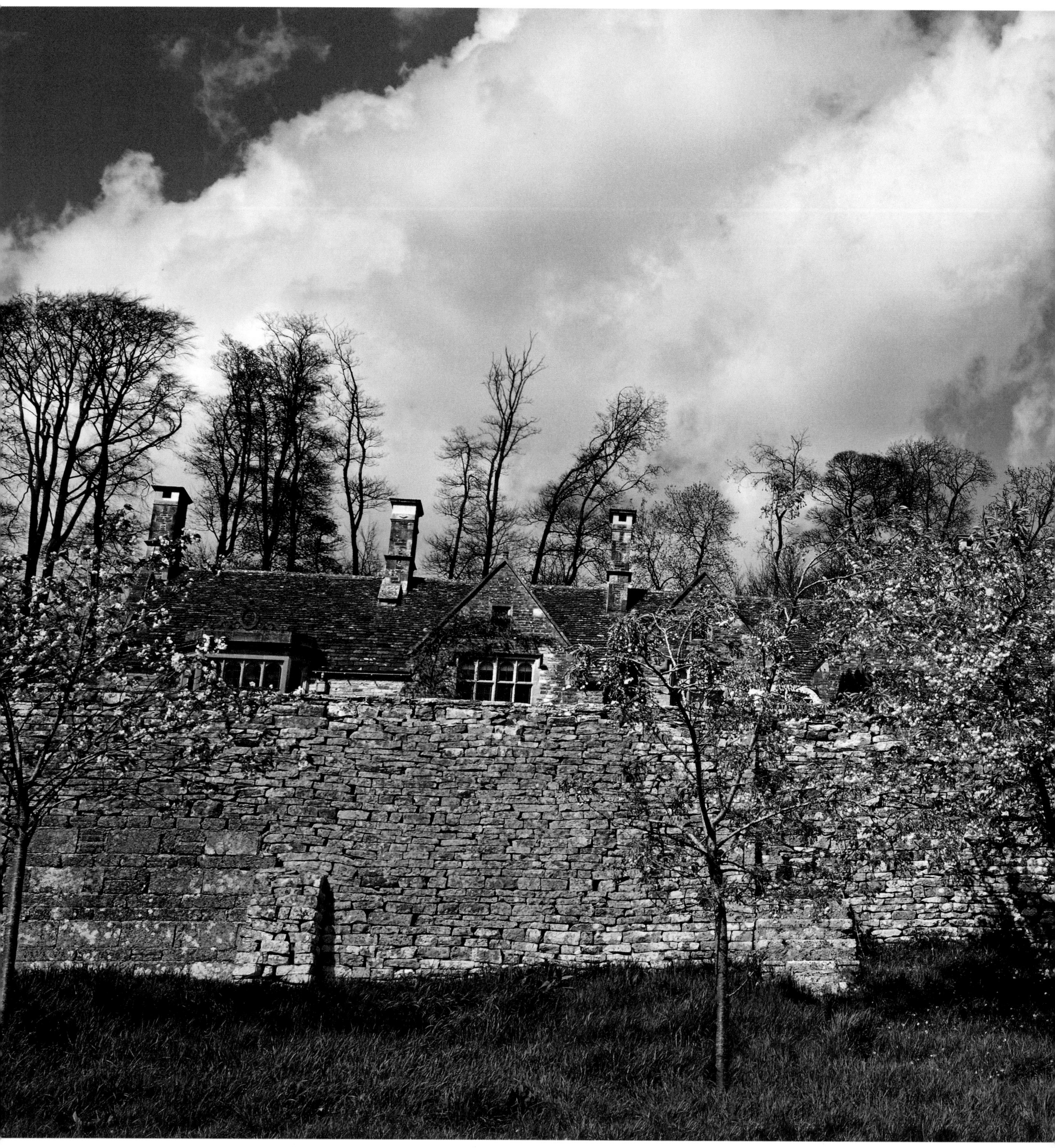

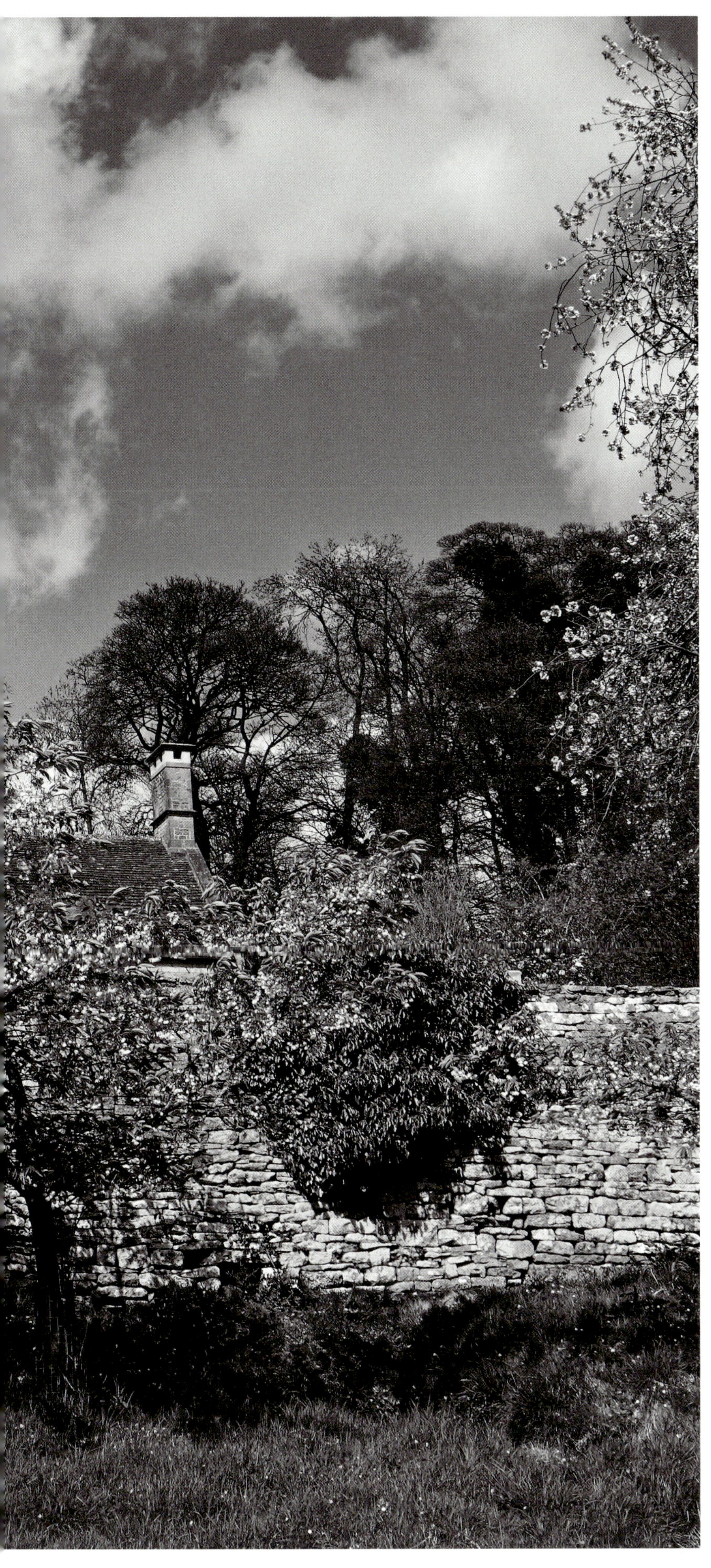

Ian McEwan

English (b. 1948)

Photographed in Sudgrove, Gloucester, England, April 2015

an McEwan lives with his wife, Annalena McAfee, a novelist, in the Cotswolds. This was the center of the English wool industry in the early part of the twentieth century, and wool merchants built large manor houses in the hills here. In 2012, the McEwans bought one of those splendid limestone houses and with adjustments and additions incorporated the styles of Gothic, Italianate, and Arts and Crafts. Their grand house today dominates the surrounding nine acres.

McEwan told me that neither he nor Annalena had grown up in such an imposing place and, wanting to be worthy of their good fortune, they continue to improve the gardens and meadows beyond. Sheep graze all around on neighboring hills (although they own none themselves).

McEwan is a dedicated walker. His writing schedule includes a daily tour over the estate with his border collie, Rab. A good summer's day walk, he told me, would be some twelve or fifteen miles into the surrounding hills, punctuated by a leisurely picnic. "However," he said, "when I'm working hard—as in the past twenty months—I don't walk every day. I stroll with the dog."

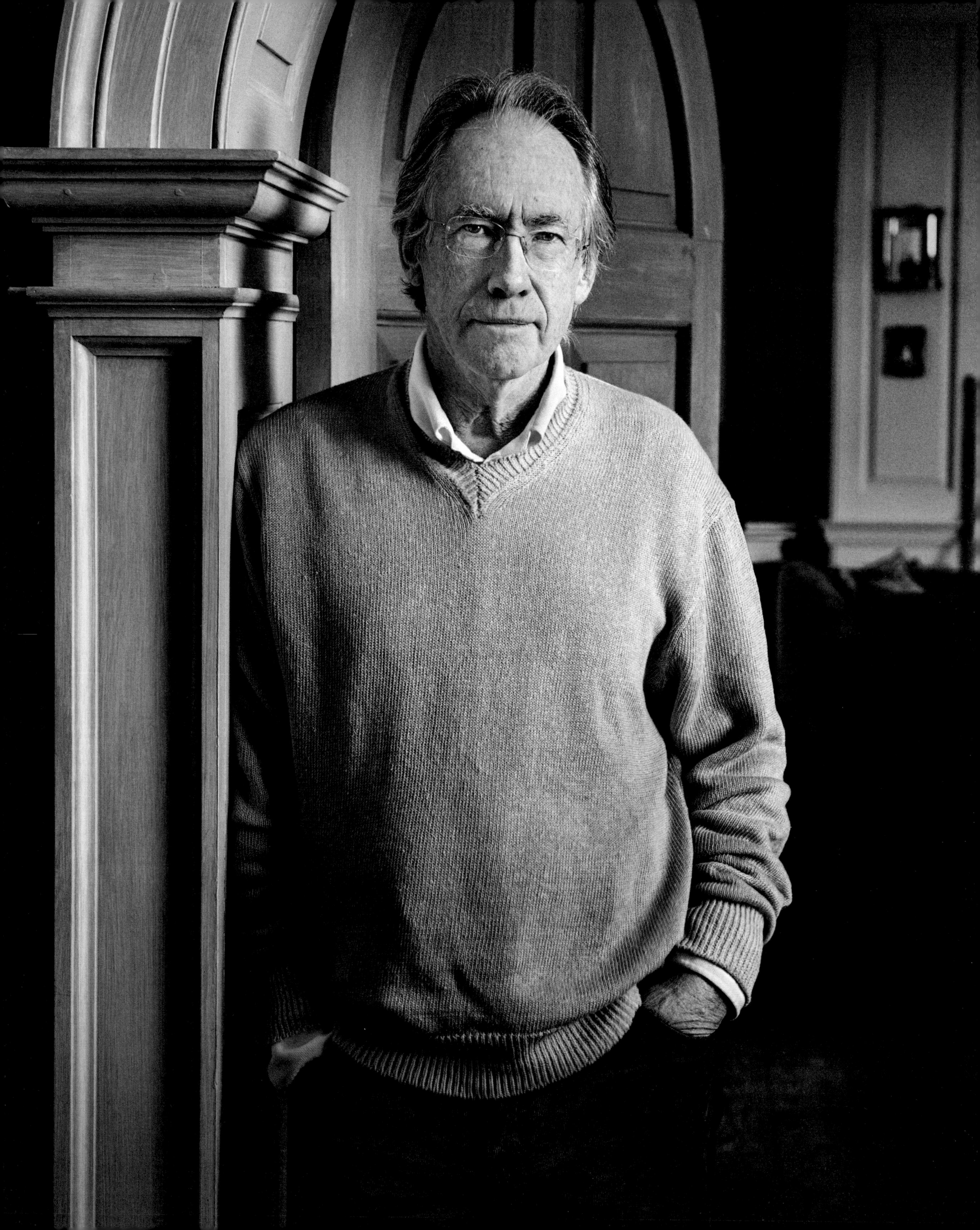

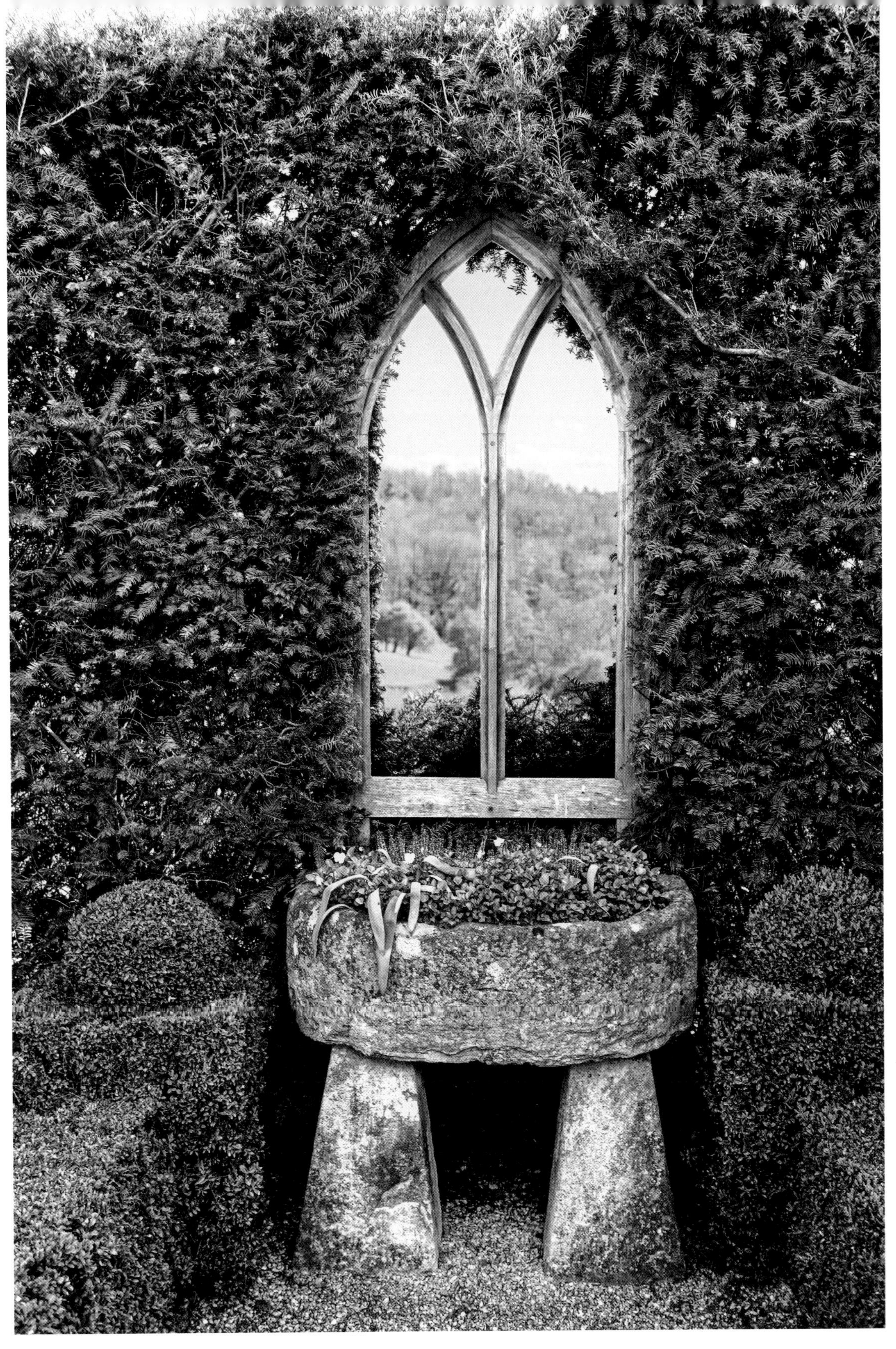

Both McEwan and Annalena have carefully restored the yew-hedge rooms of the formal garden, adding soft, unstuffy irises and geraniums, poppies and foxgloves, and have planted wildflowers in the meadows. "As for surrounding beauty," McEwan told me, "I suppose it creates an enhanced sense of mental space—good for work and general well-being. Also, to have ended up here is a piece of luck for which I am profoundly grateful."

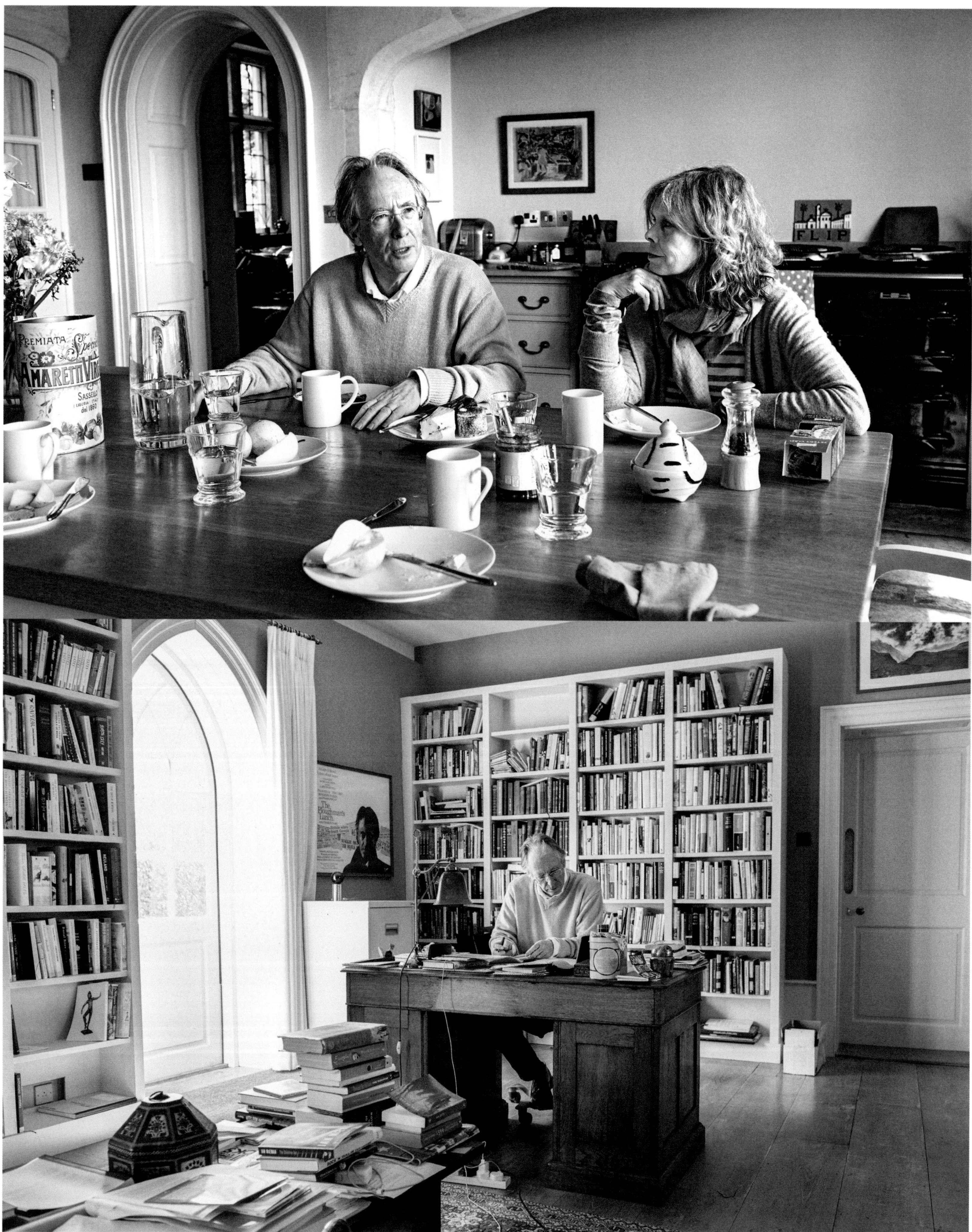

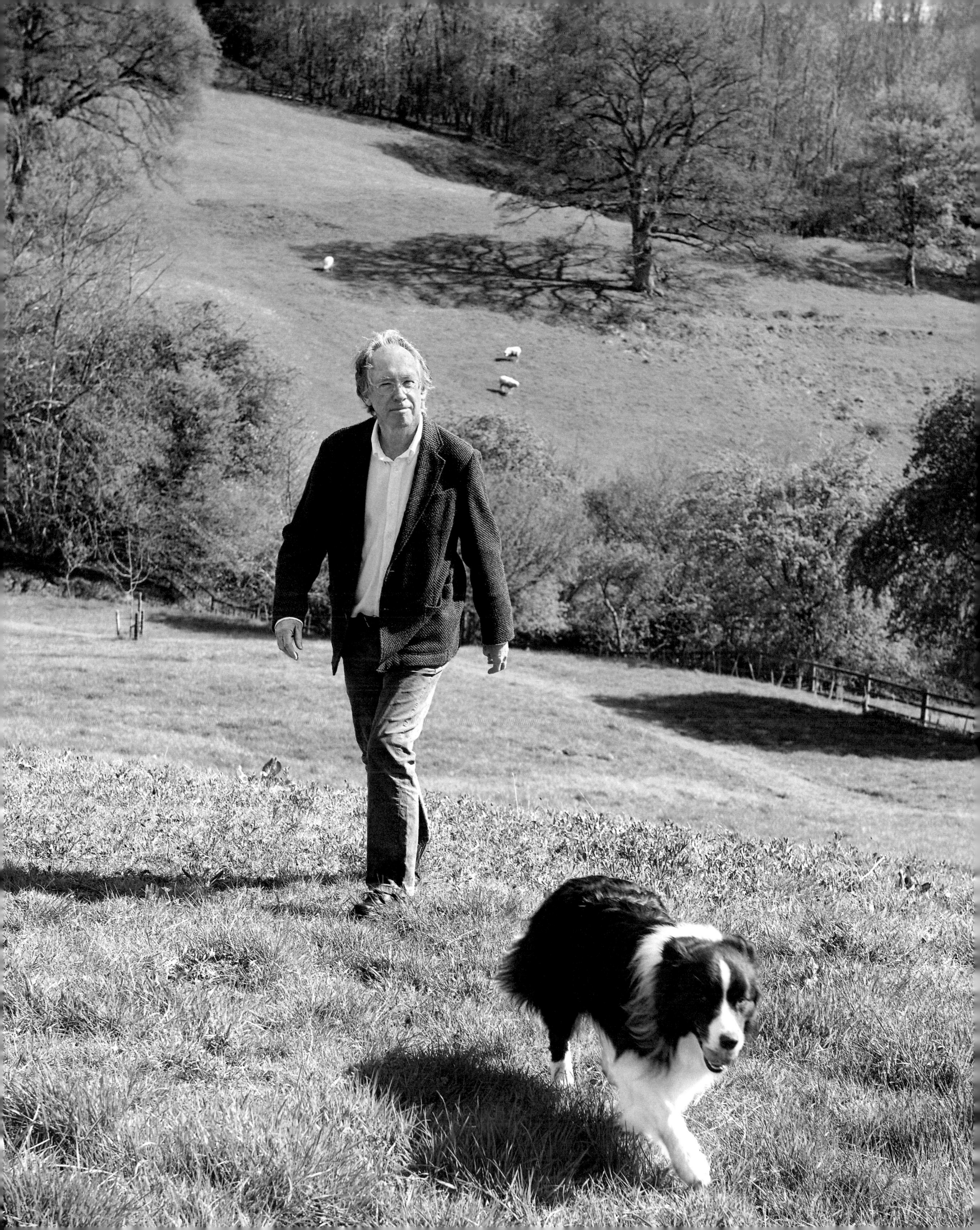

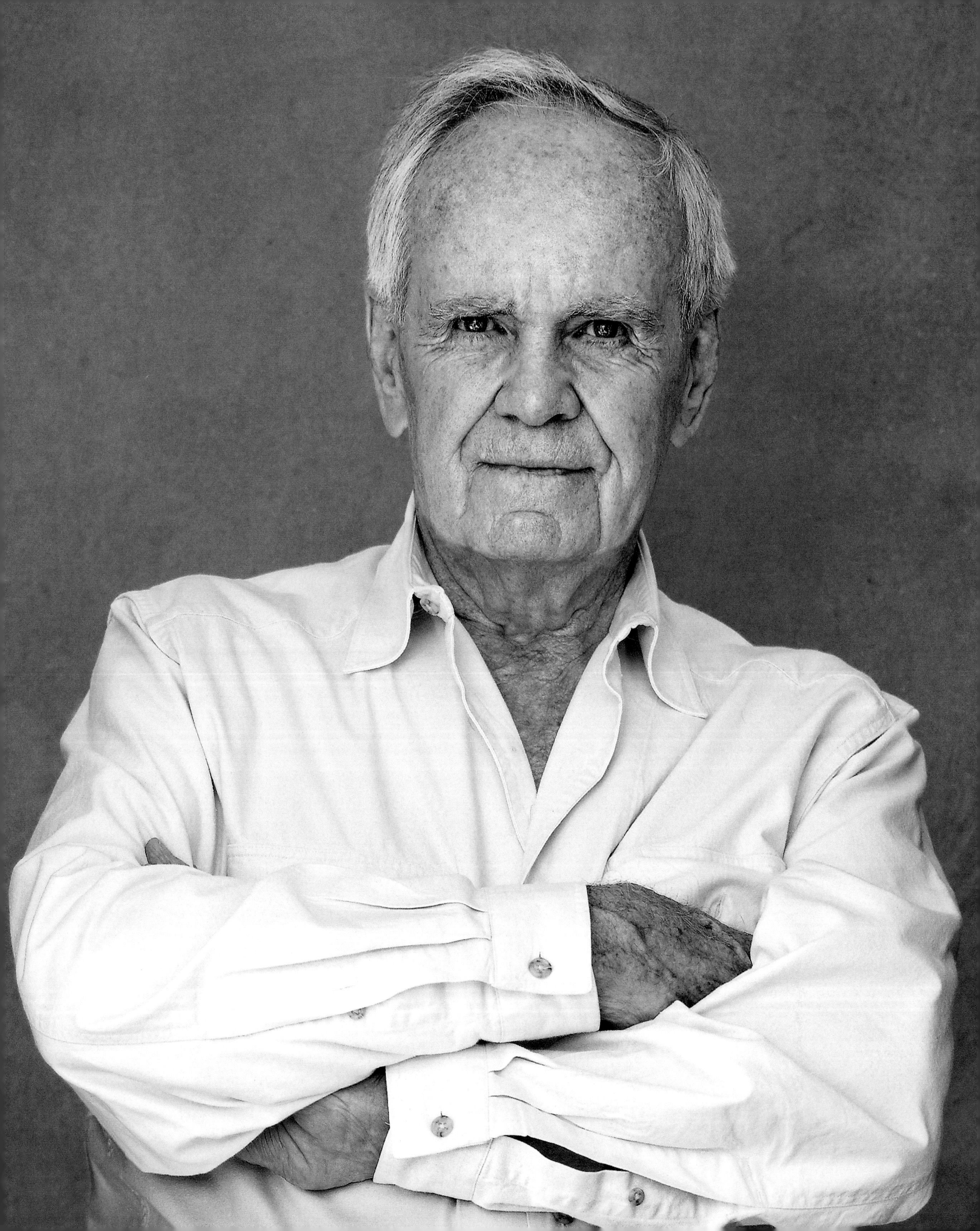

Cormac McCarthy

American (b. 1933)

Photographed in Santa Fe, New Mexico, July 2015

The Santa Fe Institute spans two idyllic adobe campuses situated in the foothills of the Sangre de Cristo Mountains, where top-level scientists try to make sense of this world as well as any other, possible worlds. And, as if that were not enough, the scientists share their home with one of the most admired, and most private writers in the world.

Cormac McCarthy was invited here in the 1990s, as one of two writers-in-residence, because the Institute believes that mingling science and art is a good way to understand humanity's place in the universe.

I went to photograph David Krakauer, the president of the Institute, with McCarthy, and their friend, James Drake, an artist. The three men formed their friendship years earlier over long discussions of shared interests—McCarthy's preoccupation with human suffering and violence, and Drake's exploration of the human figure within the geometry of the universe. Both McCarthy and Drake appreciate the company of scientists. And Krakauer, an evolutionary theorist, is widely read, and familiar with the work of contemporary artists.

The opportunity to photograph three good friends would produce, I knew, good pictures. At the time of my visit, they were working on a performance piece with music based in part on a novel by McCarthy and interspersed with conversation between Krakauer and Drake.

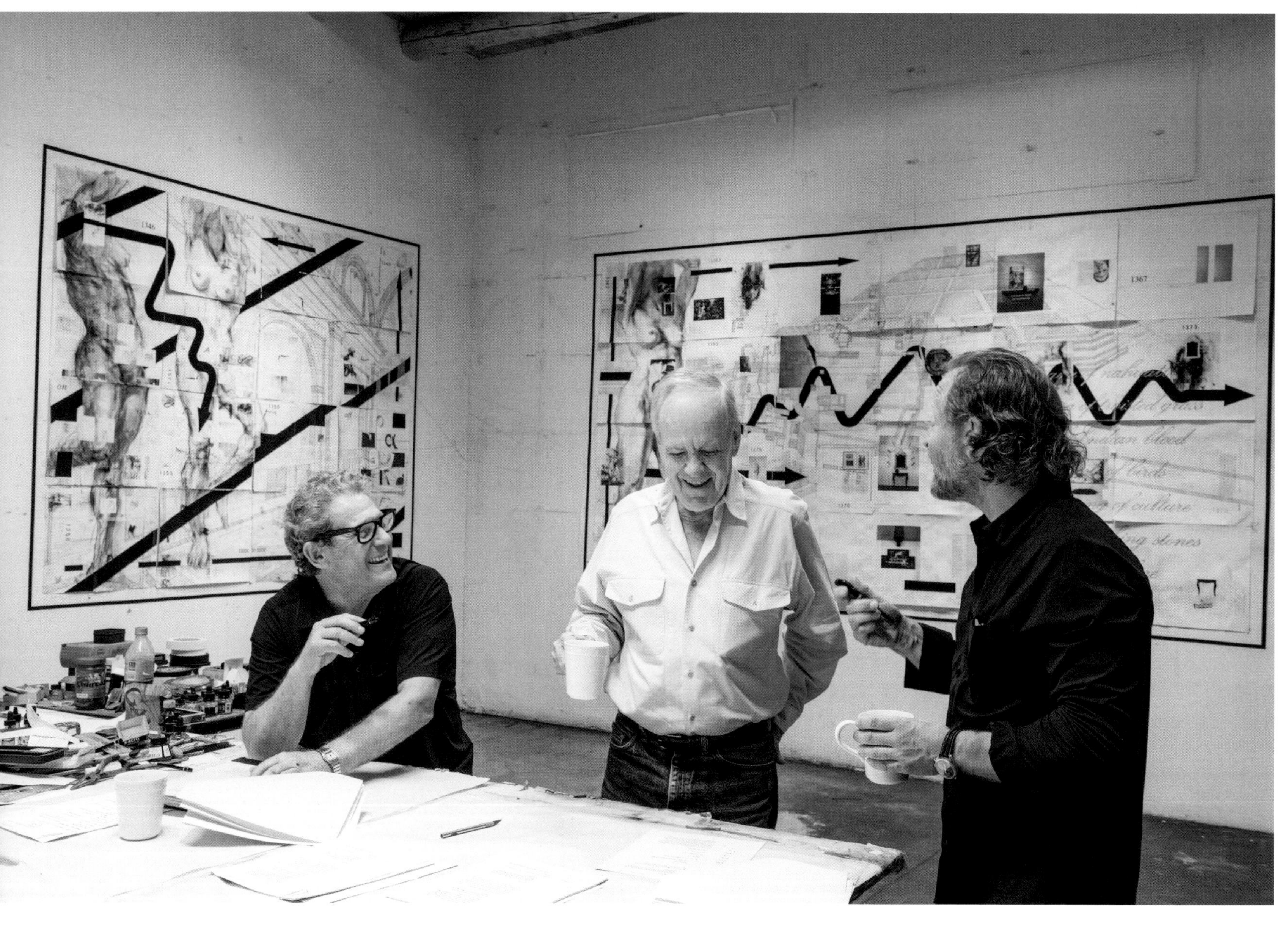

We began in Drake's studio, with the fresh desert air blowing in through open doors. Bold charcoal drawings dominated the high walls of the studio. The three friends were relaxed, having coffee as they talked. Their discussions were lively, punctuated by bursts of laughter.

After lunch in the garden at Drake's studio, we drove to the Institute, where Krakauer lives in the summer months with a hundred or so other scientists. McCarthy is a trustee. He was modest and self-effacing but willingly showed the library that he had redesigned with long stacks of books on one side of the room and big leather couches, paintings, and Navajo weavings on the other.

Soon enough, the three friends settled into another long discussion, talking about how science, like art, searches for patterns in the complexity of life and the universe.

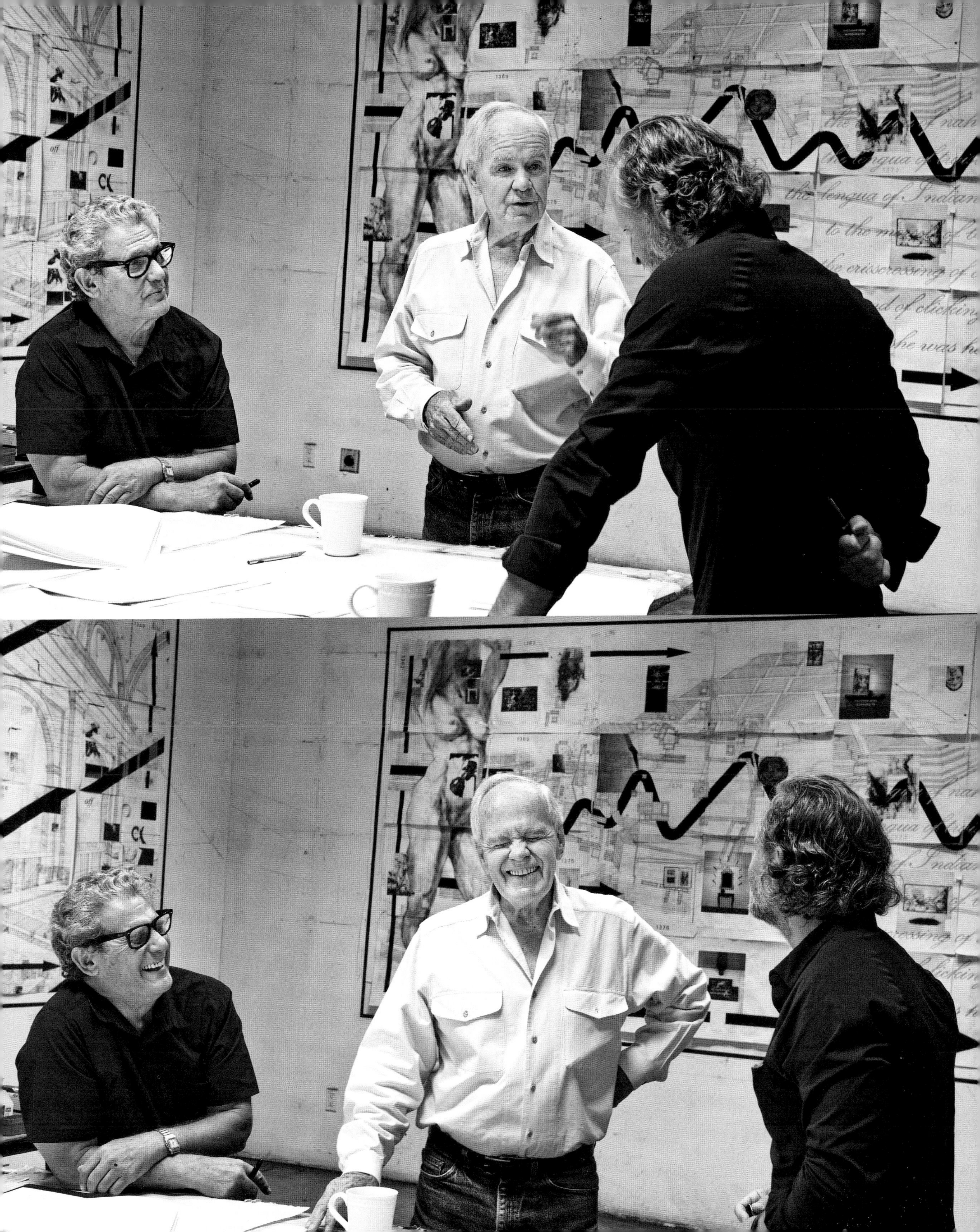

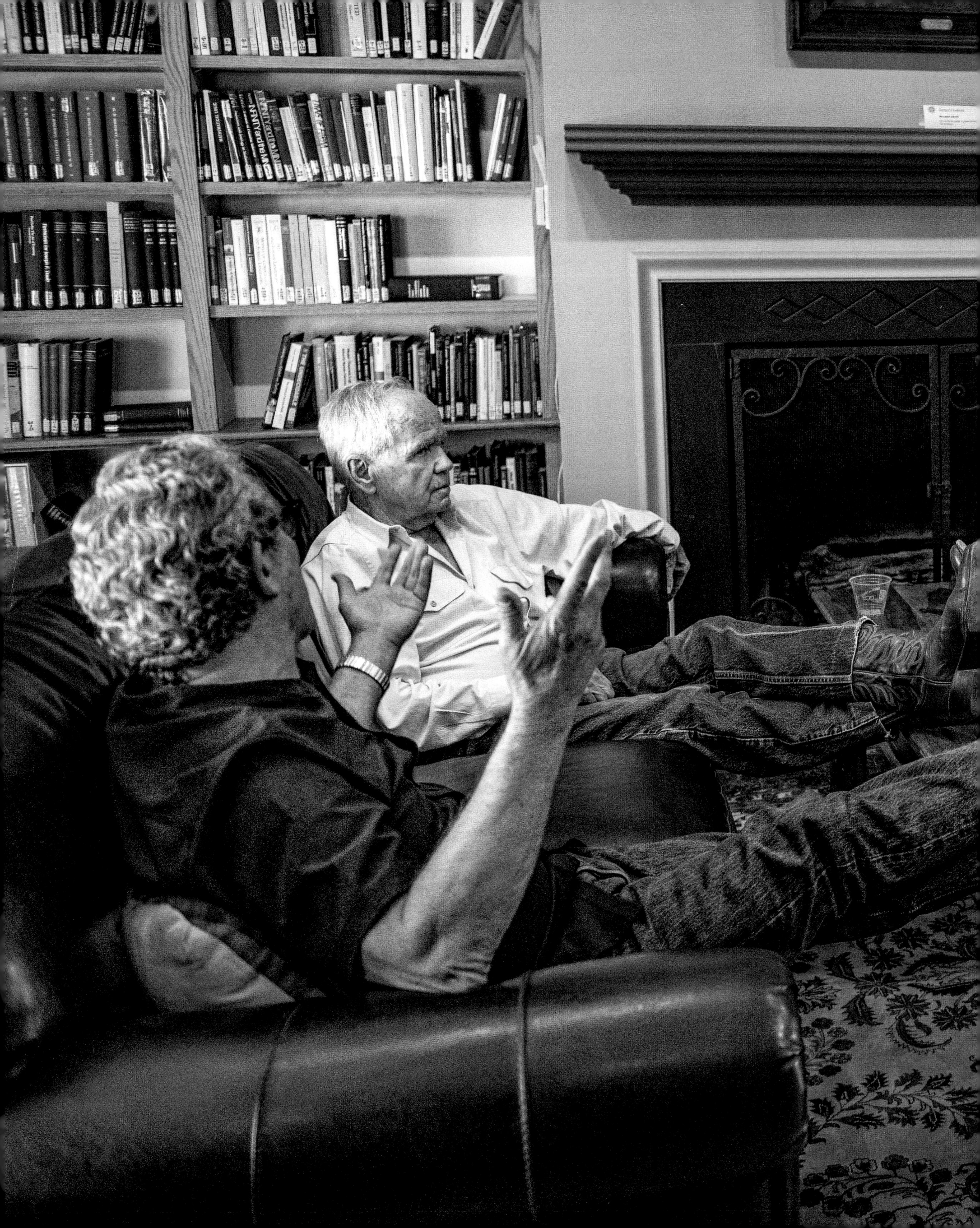

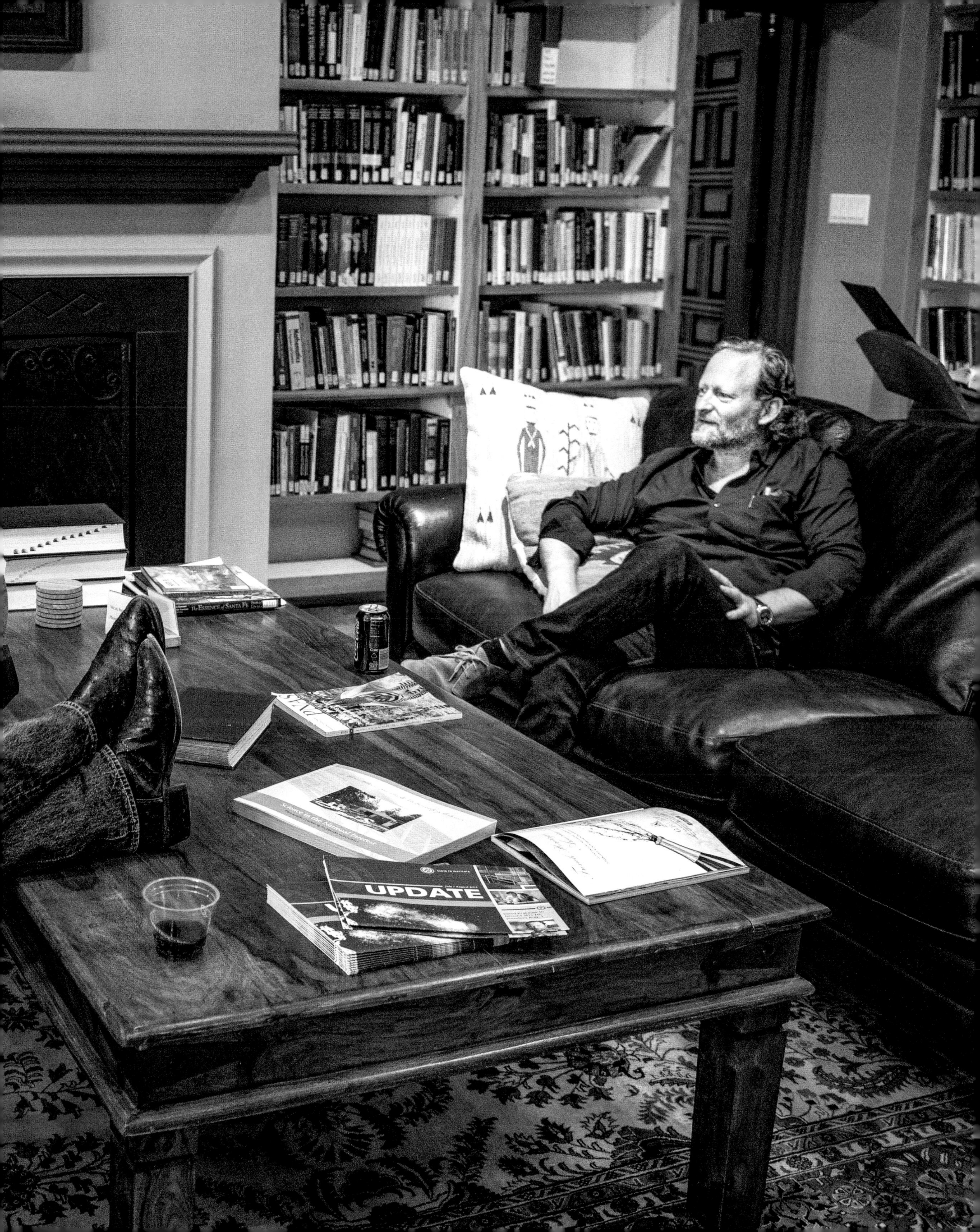

Michael
Chabon

American (b. 1963)

Photographed in Berkeley, California, March 2010

I t should be understood that each of the writers in this collection is busy—all the time. Their lives are arranged around their work. They are either starting a project, in the midst of a project, or recovering from a project. Michael Chabon was no exception.

And, like most people, Chabon doesn't enjoy being photographed. "A camera," John Steinbeck said, "is so much more sure than I am about everything."

I photographed Chabon in the garden of his large house in Berkeley, where he lives with Ayelet Waldman and their four children. He had generously set aside time for me because the director, Wes Anderson, a mutual friend, had encouraged his participation.

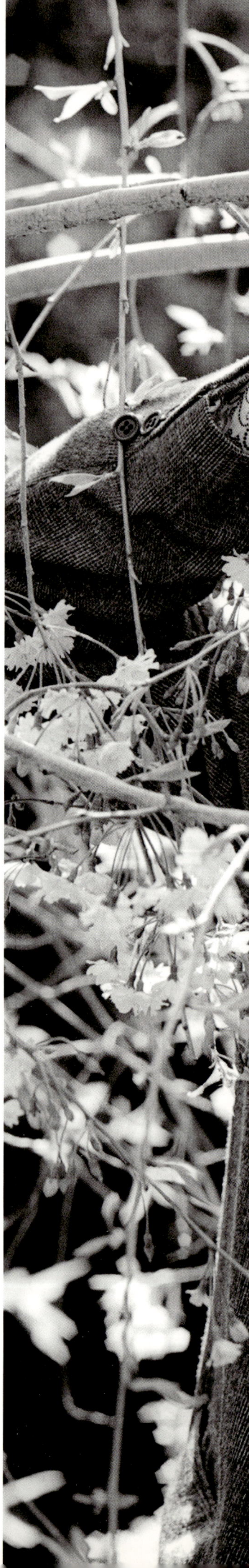

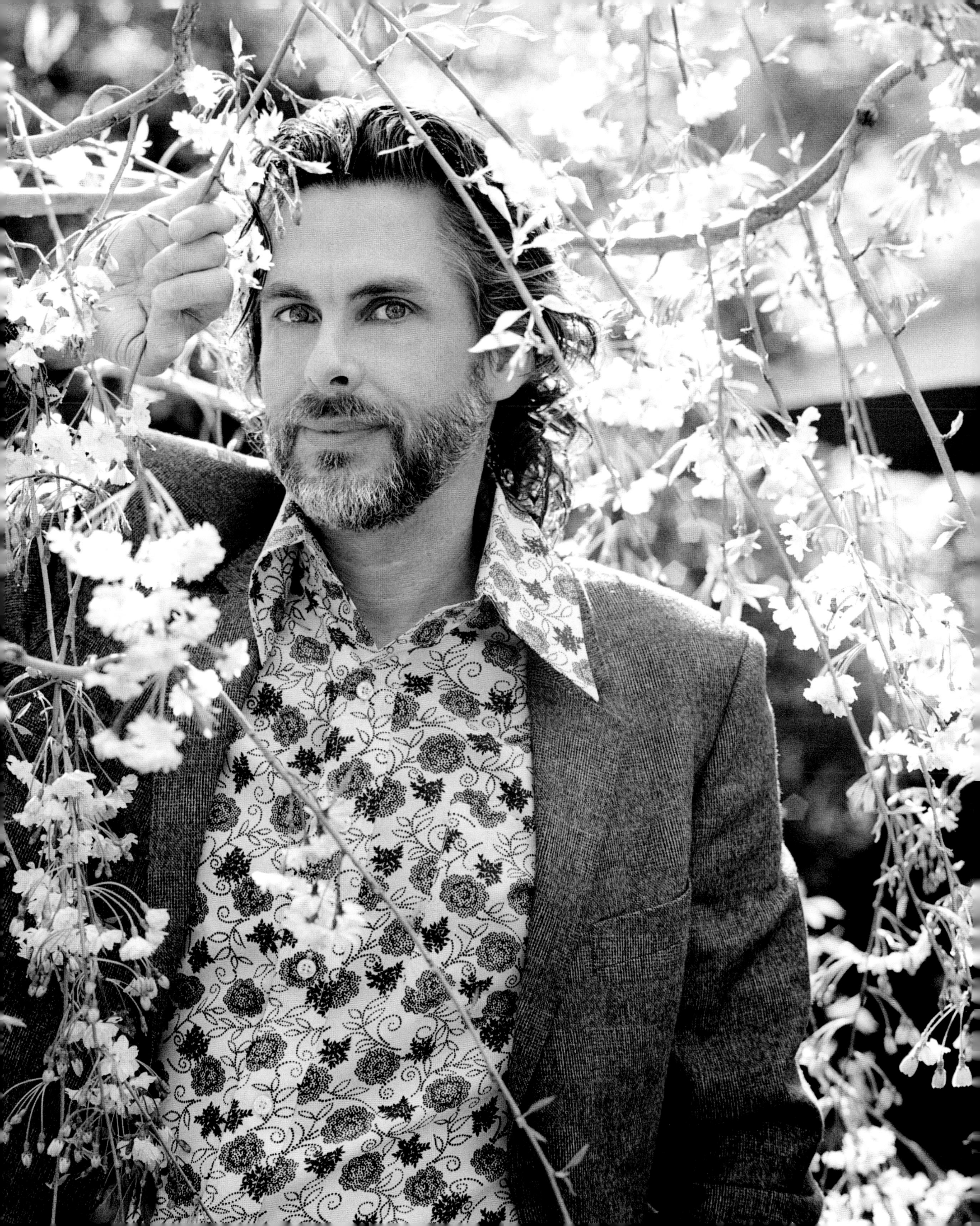

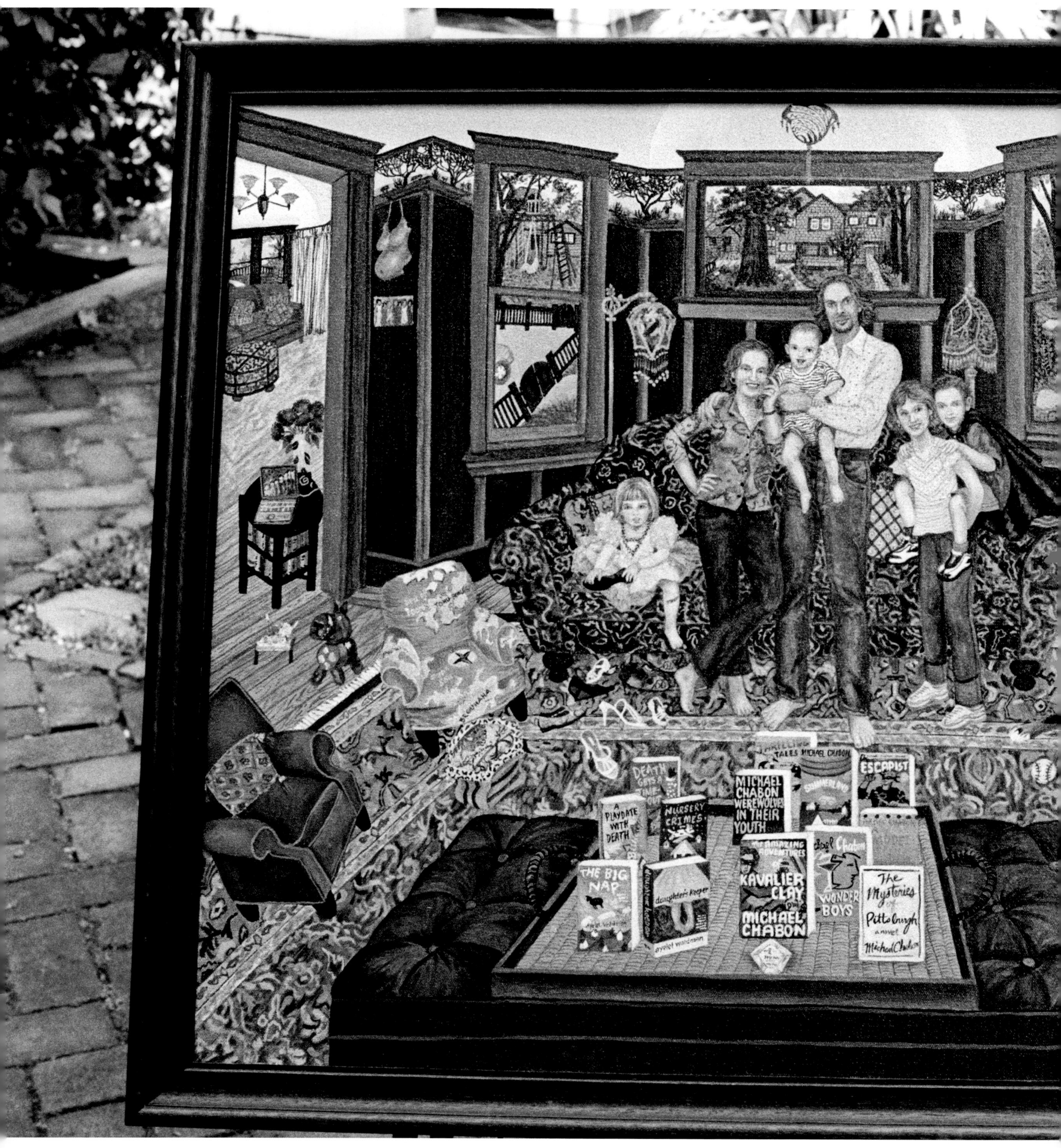

A PLAYDATE WITH DEATH
NURSERY CRIMES
DEATH GETS A TIME OUT
MICHAEL CHABON WEREWOLVES IN THEIR YOUTH
ESCAPIST
SUMMERLAND
THE BIG NAP
daughter's keeper
THE AMAZING ADVENTURES OF KAVALIER & CLAY MICHAEL CHABON
WONDER BOYS
The Mysteries of Pittsburgh a novel Michael Chabon

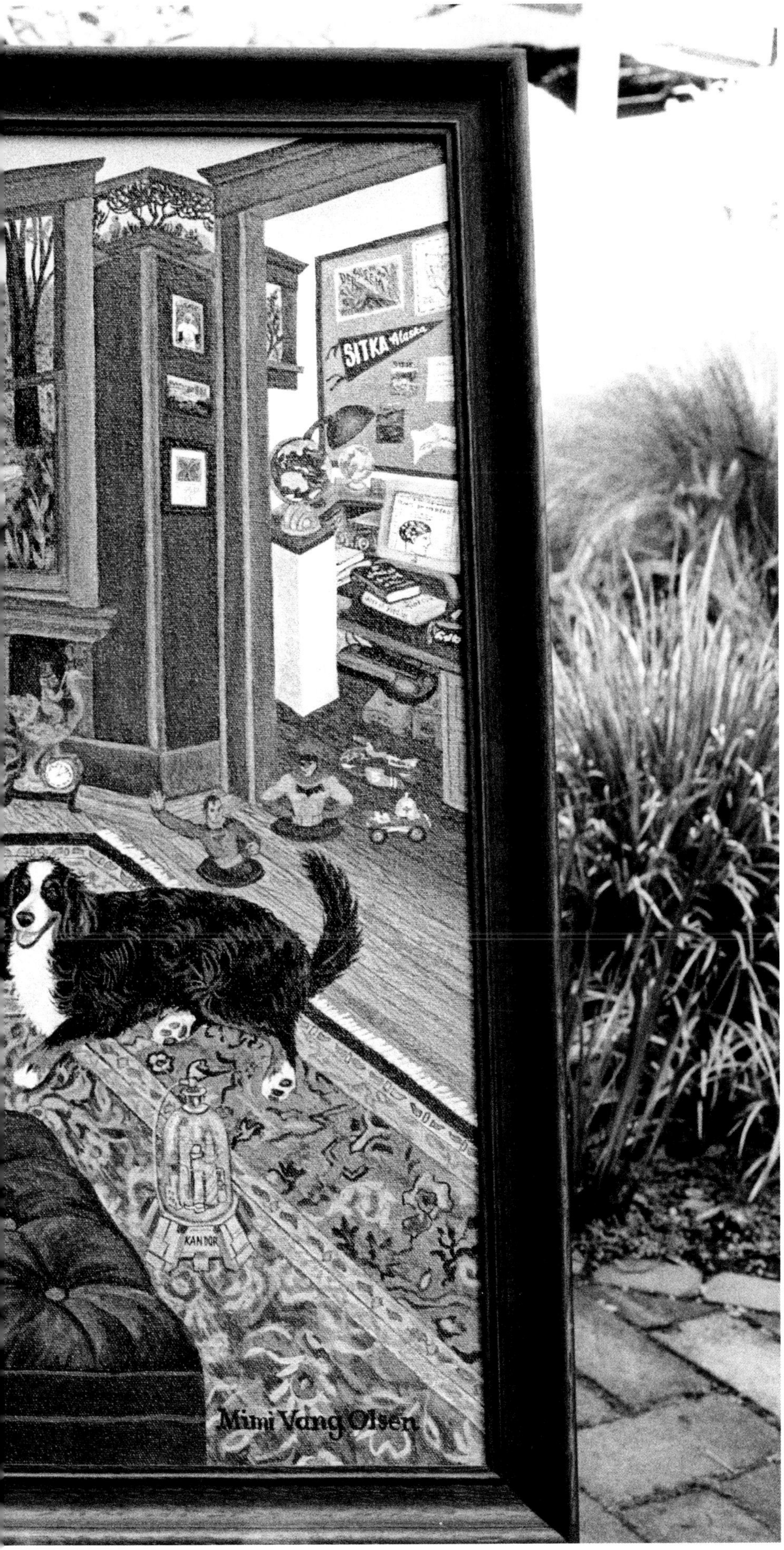

Chabon has said that, for him, the stable, structured life he and Ayelet have created is his best environment. A small, charming painting of the young Chabons by Mimi Vang Olsen gave me a sense of their family life. The pen-and-ink drawing by cartoonist Will Eisner of his best-known character was given to Chabon to celebrate the publication of *The Amazing Adventures of Kavalier and Clay*. Eisner had been among the first golden-age comics creators Chabon admired.

Mimi Vang Olsen

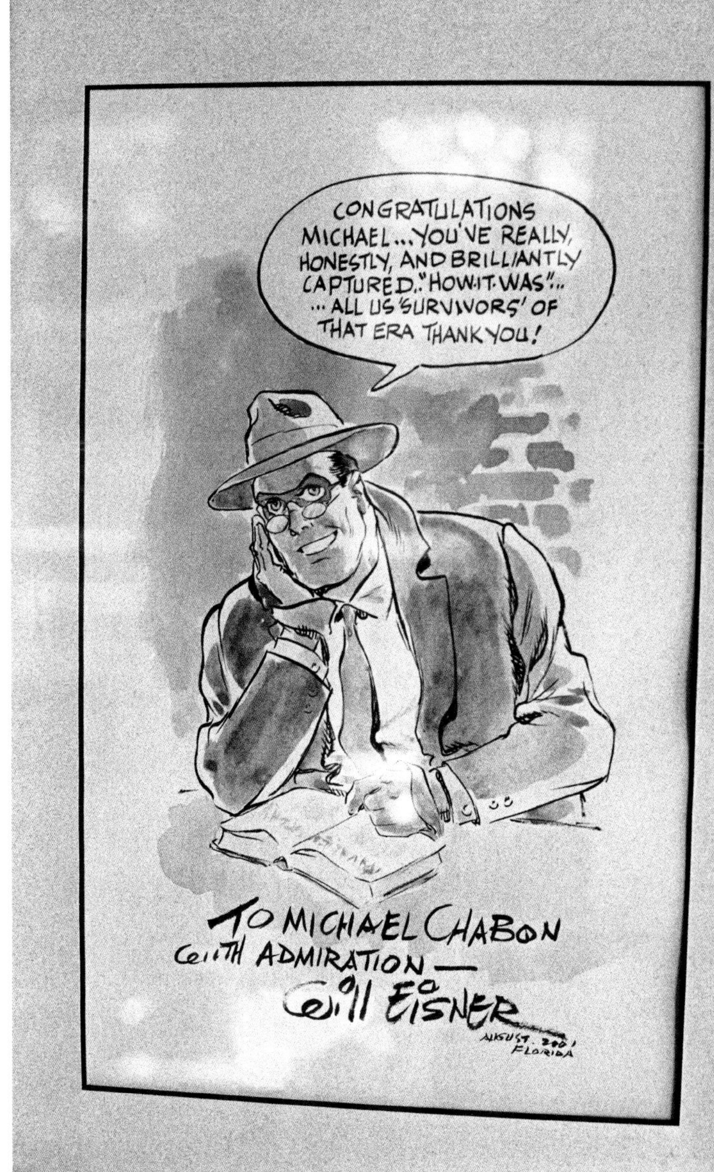

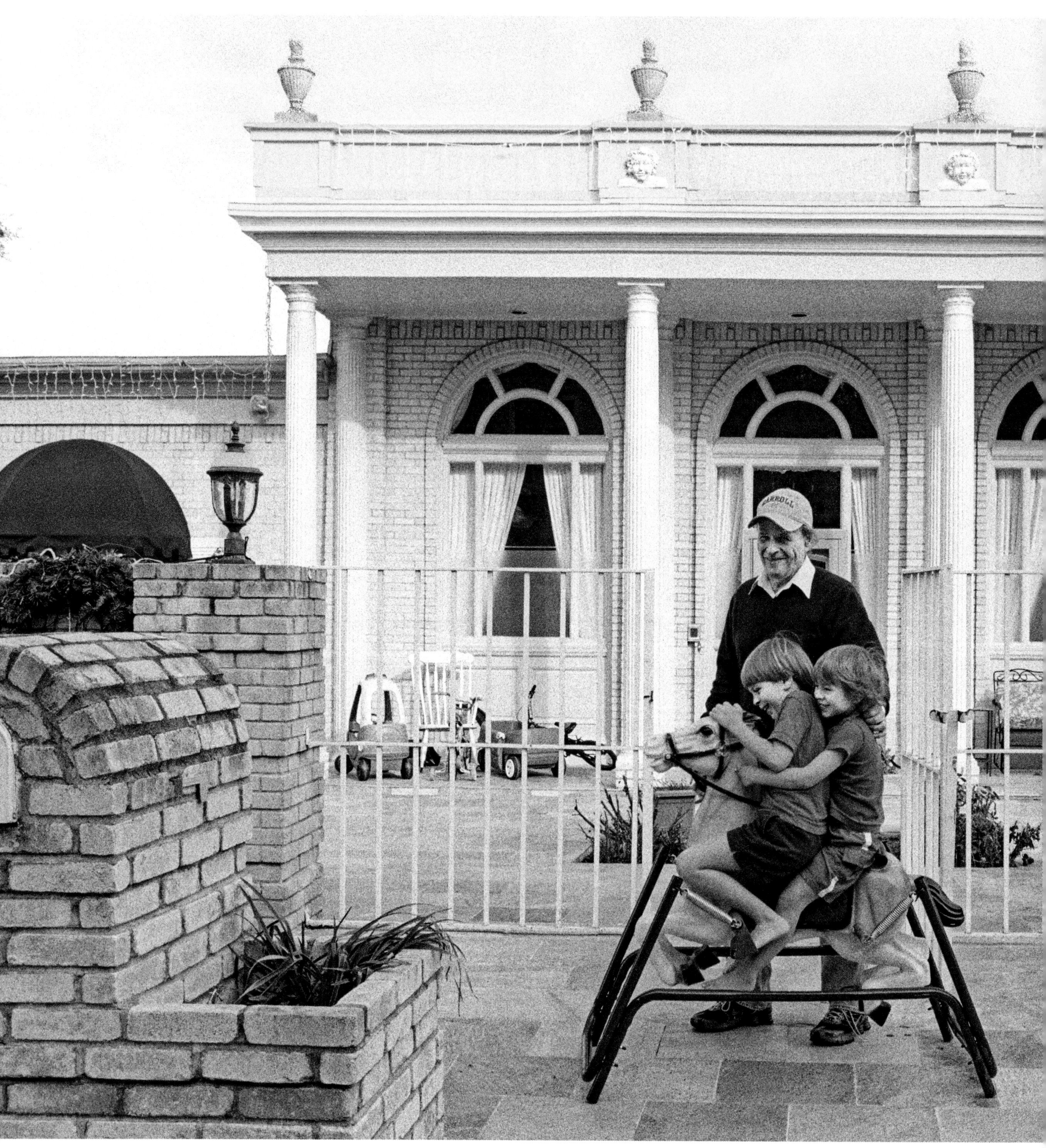

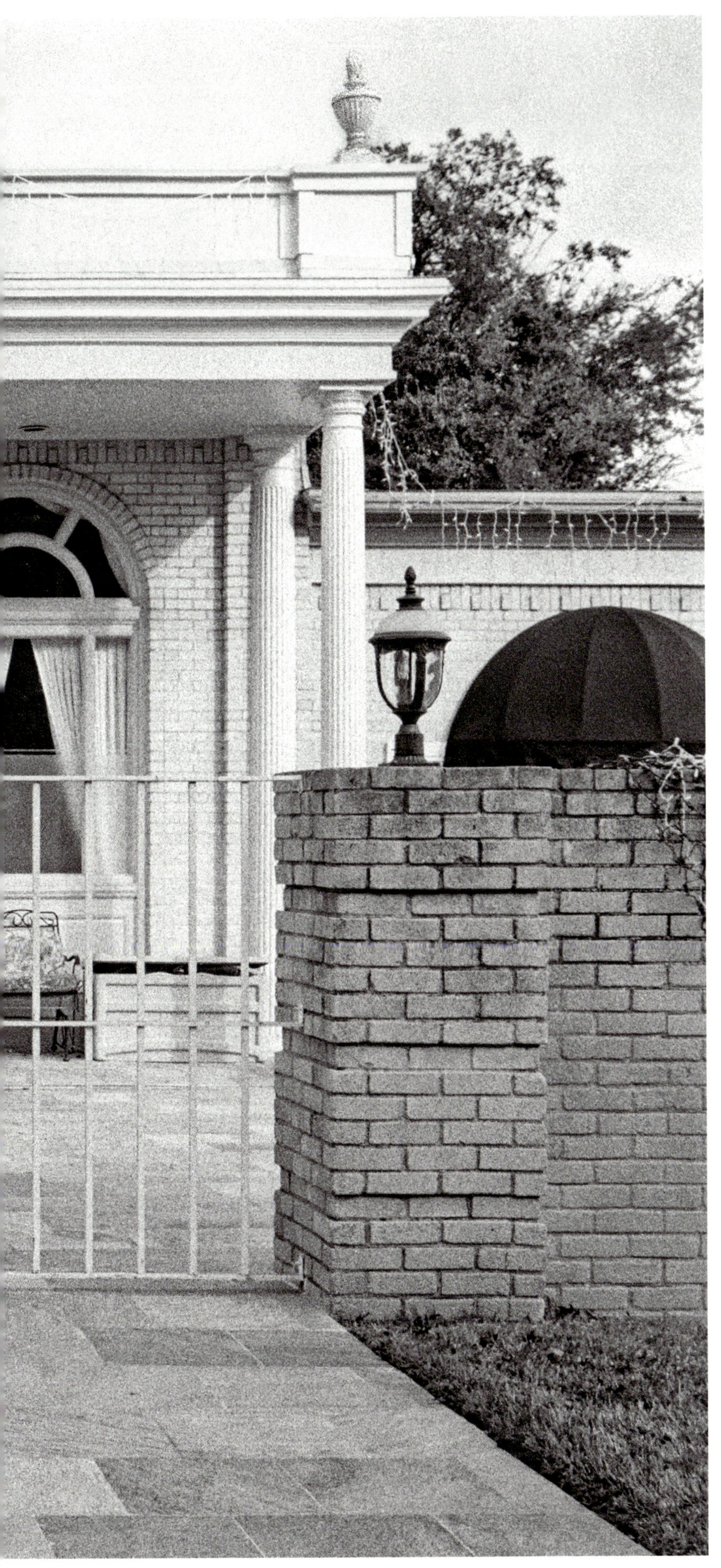

Tim O'Brien

American (b. 1946)

Photographed in Austin, Texas, December 2009

Tim O'Brien, his wife, Meredith Baker, and their two sons, Timmy and Tad, live in a white, neo-classical house outside Austin, Texas. Family means many things to O'Brien. "They are a wellspring of dramatic material," he told me, "an audience I hope to please, and a source of comfort when the writing goes badly—which is most of the time."

O'Brien has never tried writing away from his house, for fear an office might freeze him up, make him self-conscious, and cause the writing to seem obligatory in a going-to-a-job sort of way. "Mainly," he said, "the commute here at home from my bed to my desk is a much shorter one."

O'Brien is the only writer I photographed who is also a skilled magician. Magic and fiction are illusions of a sort to him—not real in any ordinary sense—and yet, both as a writer and as a magician, he hopes the audience will suspend its disbelief and enjoy the show. Meredith and the boys are insiders, but I, as an outsider, was dazzled by the tricks. For me, there was no illusion. He really did swallow a razor blade and pull a noose through his own neck.

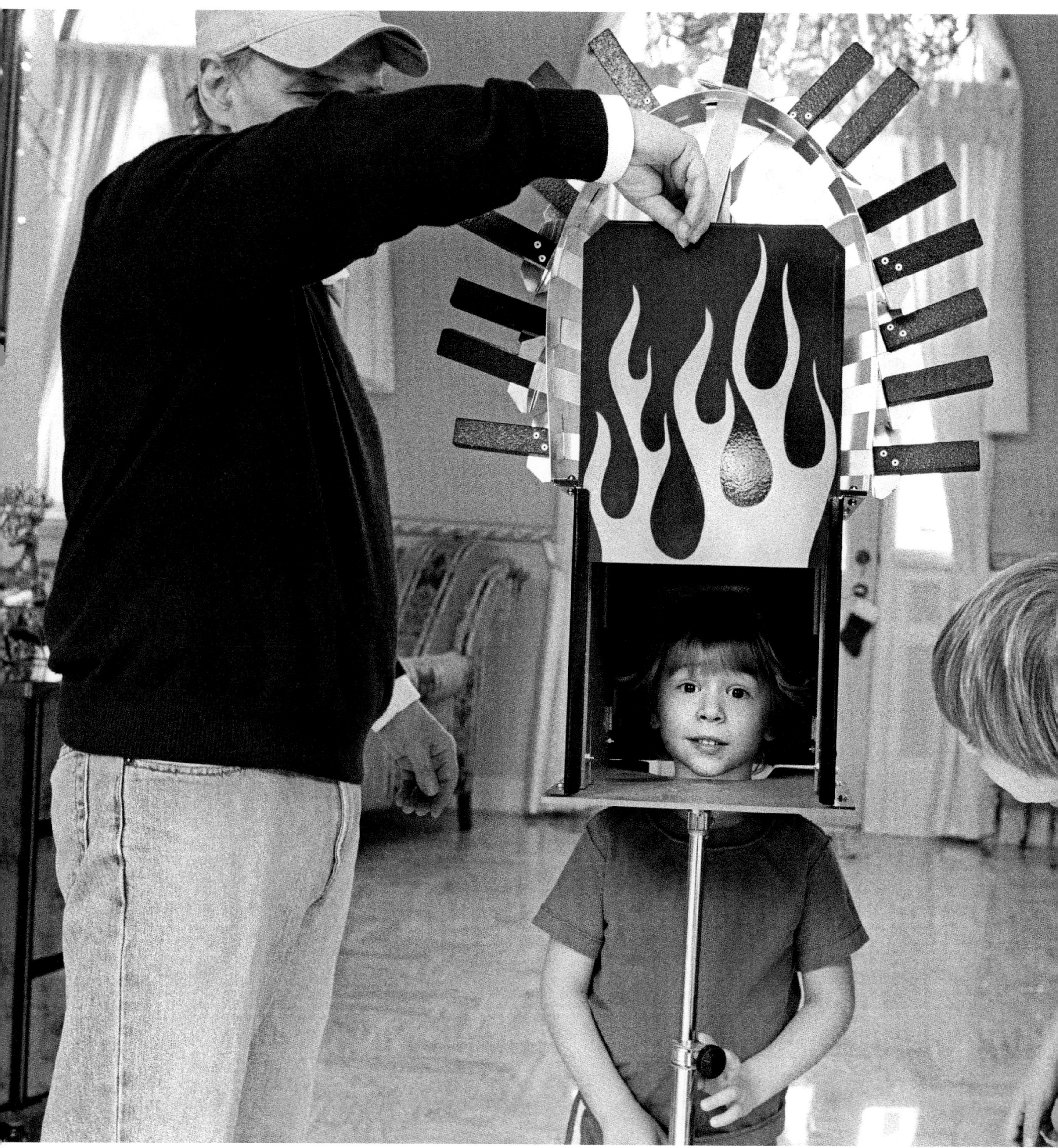

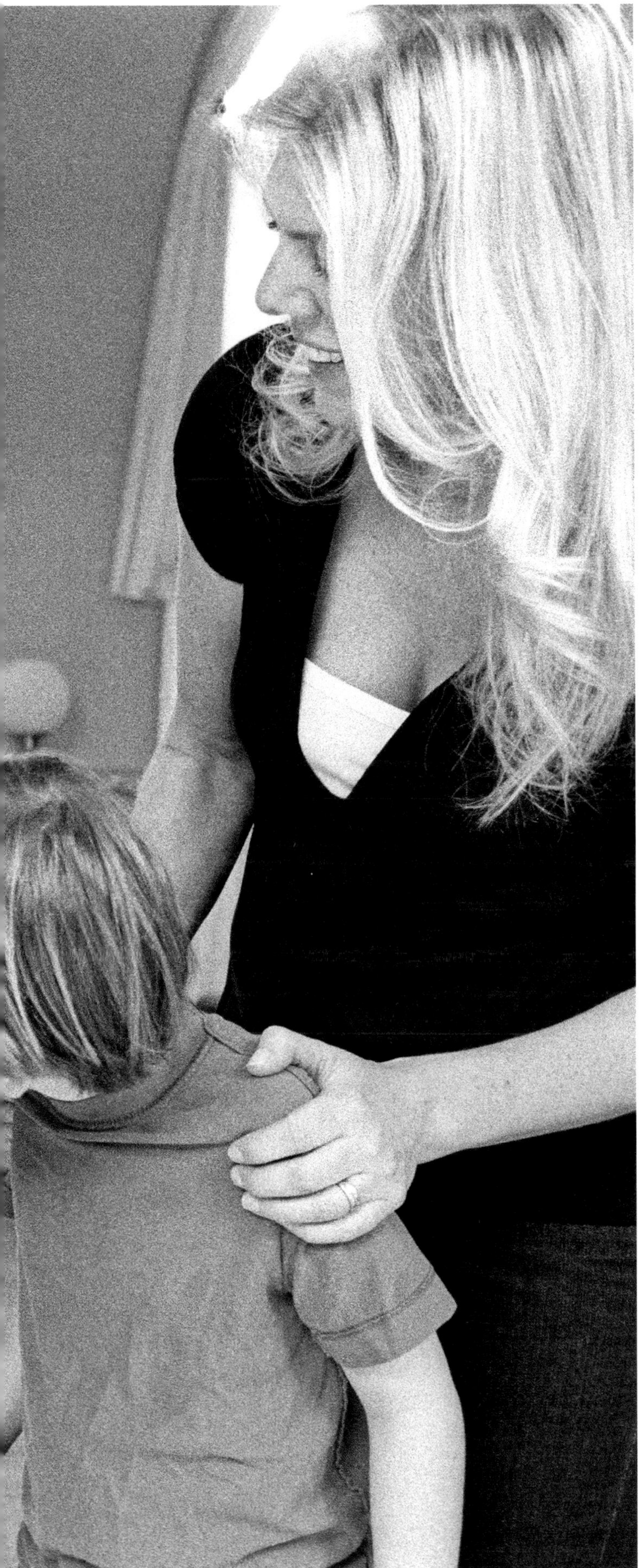

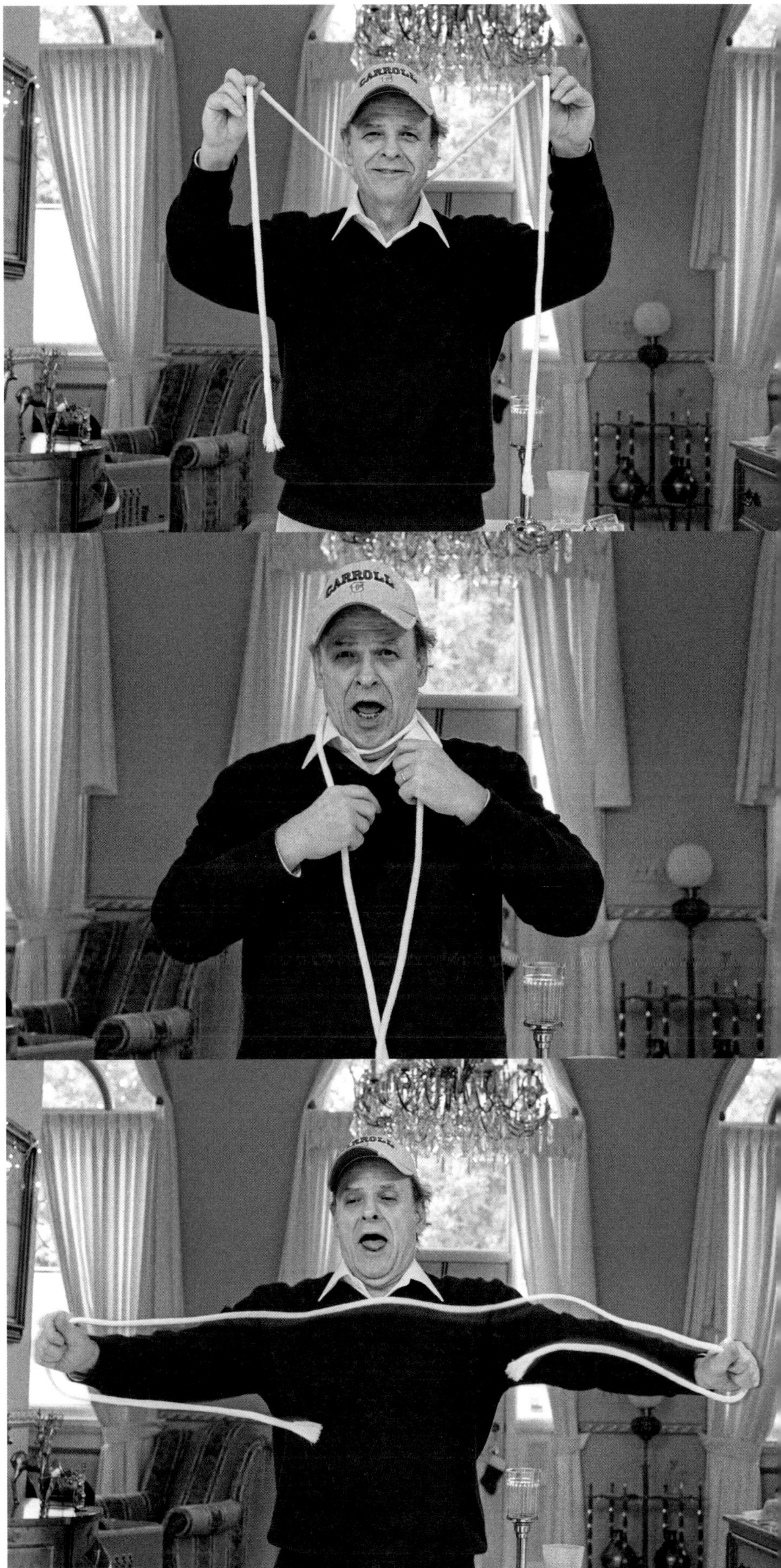

But O'Brien is better known as the creator of stories and novels revealing the barbarity of the Vietnam War, and on the last day of my visit, I asked him if we might do a portrait. He agreed, and without a word from me he looked straight into the lens with all the sensitivity and emotion of a man who has seen the savage and unforgivable.

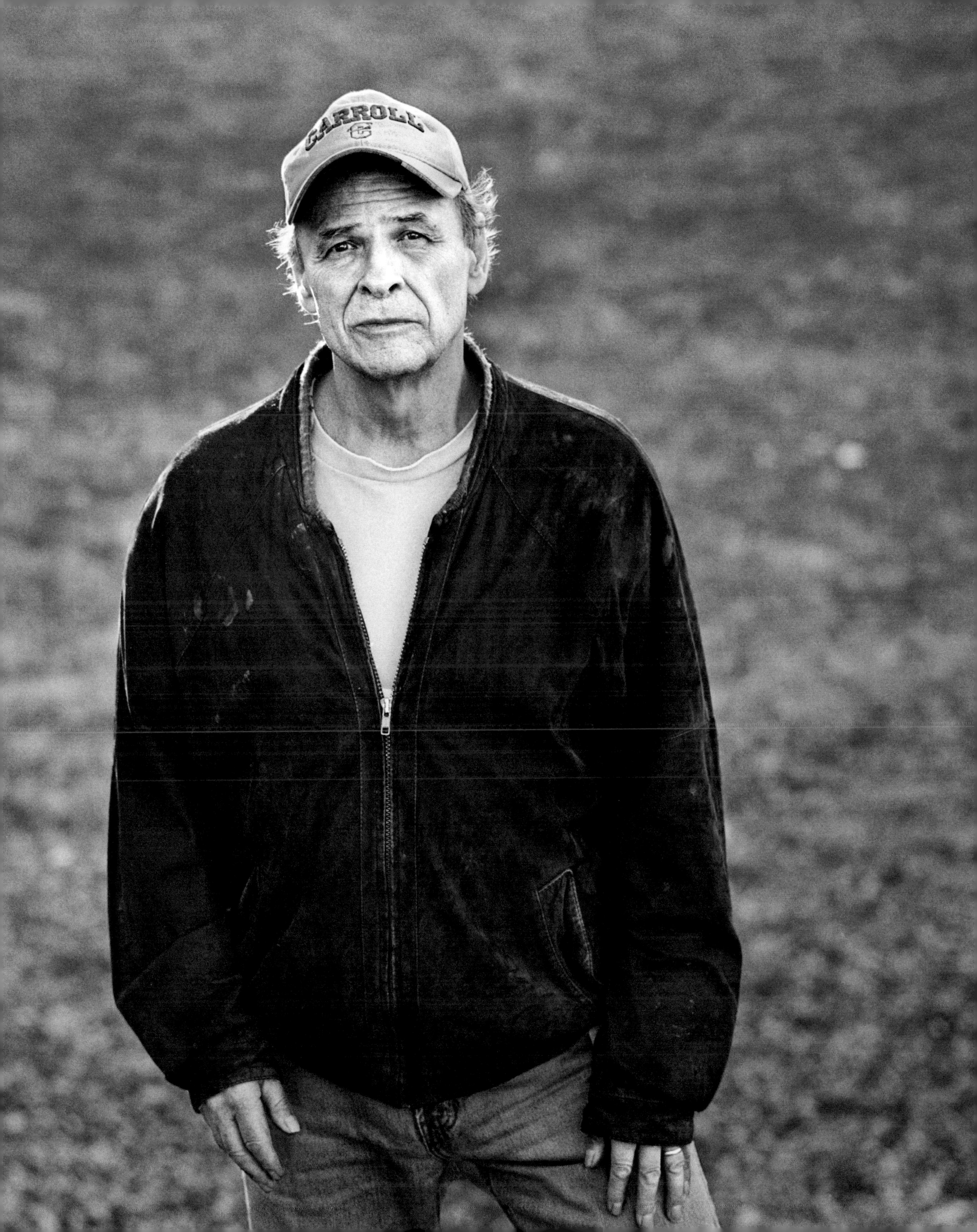

Jim
Harrison

American (1937–2016)

Photographed in Patagonia, Arizona, April 2012

To escape the bone-cold weather of the Upper Peninsula of Michigan, Jim Harrison spent many winters just this side of the Mexican border, in a small adobe house overlooking a creek on the edge of Patagonia, Arizona. He had various bird-hunting dogs as companions, but seemed to me to be especially fortunate to have such a kind and receptive person as Linda, his wife, with whom he shared his nontraditional existence.

Thunder, hard rain, and high winds subsided about the time I knocked on their front door. Linda welcomed me into the kitchen as Harrison emerged from a dark hallway, growling, "You're two minutes late." I said, "No, I'm three minutes early." With that exchange behind us, we settled into a good afternoon of photography.

I did a portrait of him on the back patio with the Hasselblad, then out into the mud for more pictures. A place down by the creek looked good—would have been good had Jim not worn his bedroom slippers. We stayed on high ground.

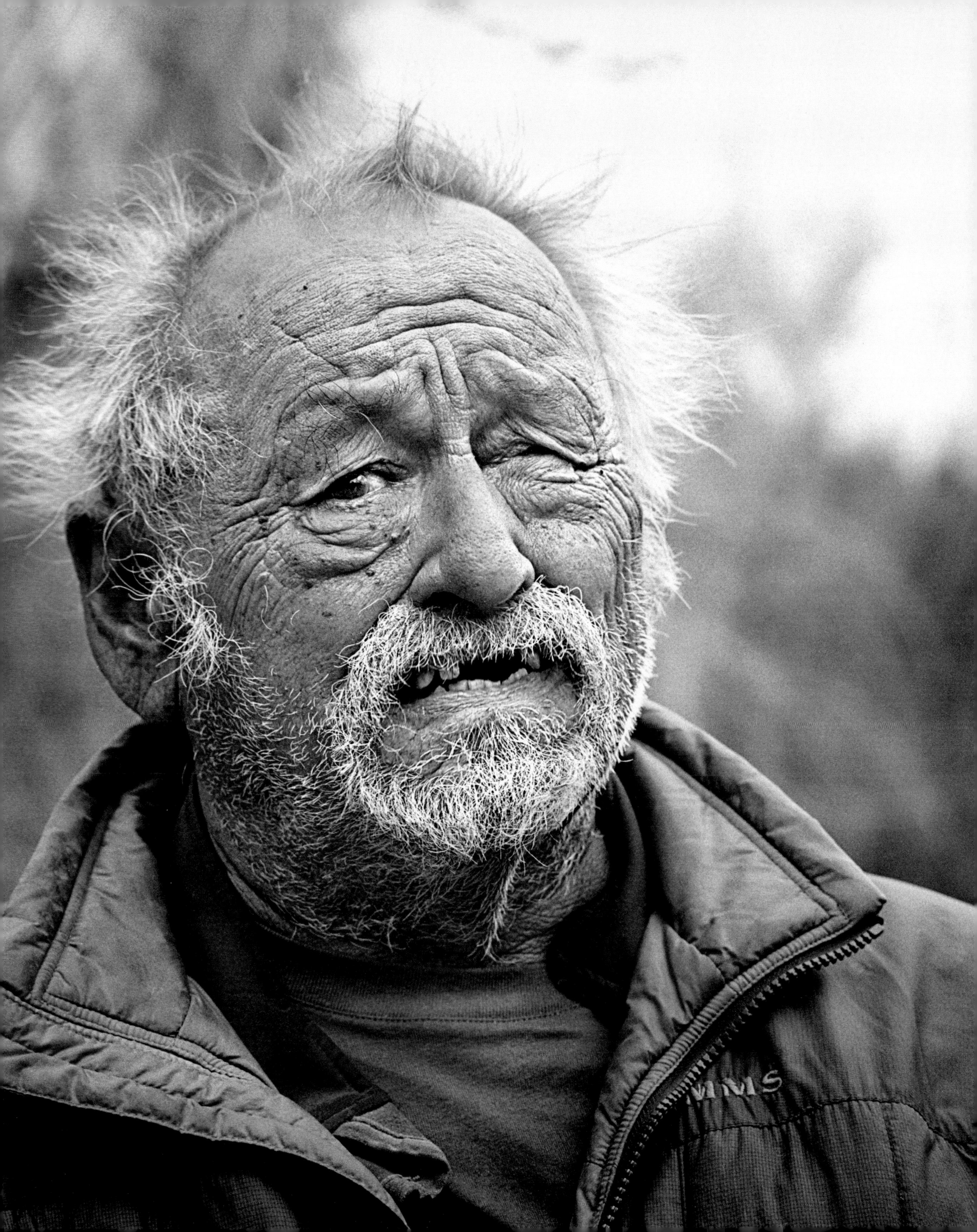

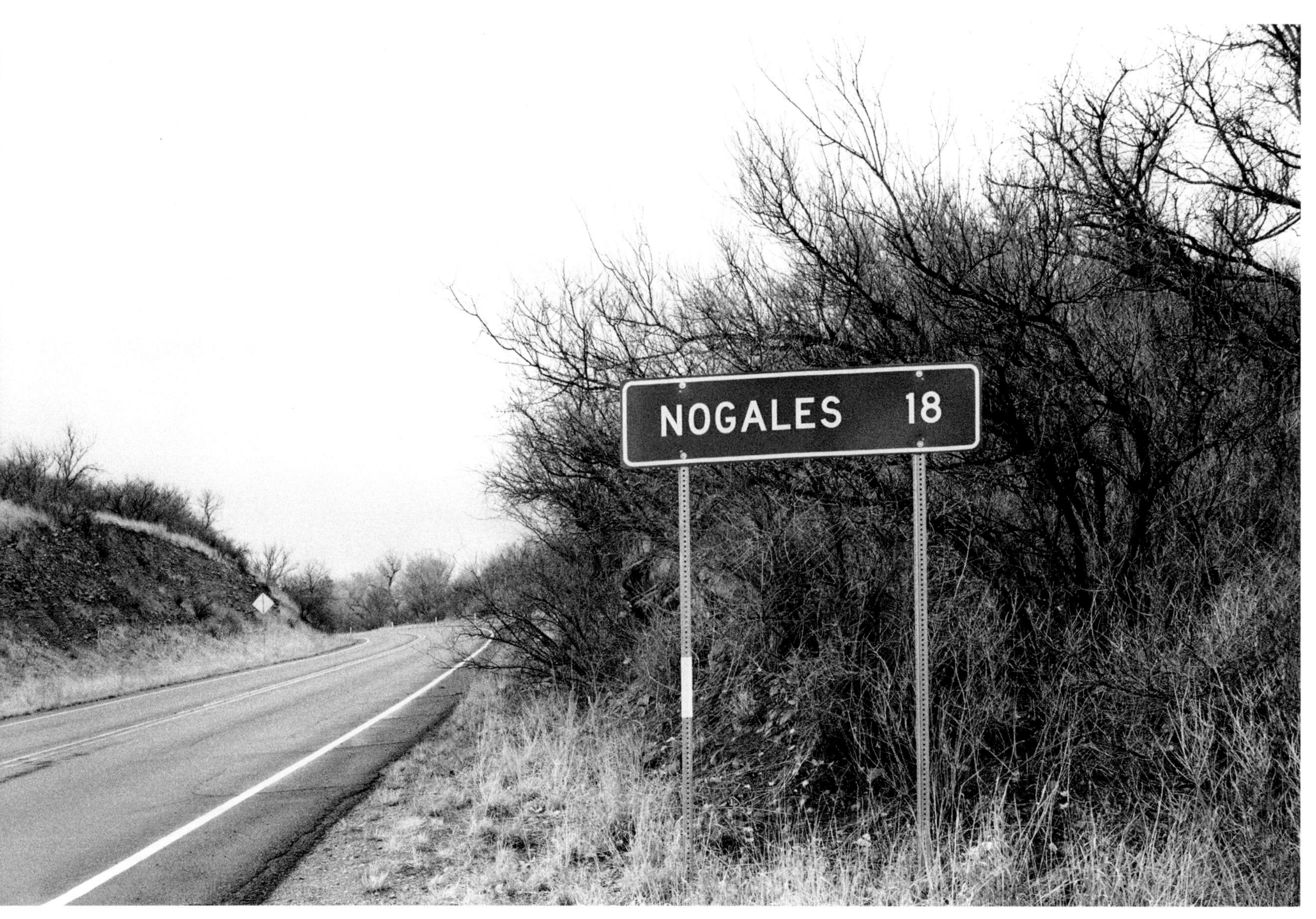

His conversation was charming and sly as he talked about writing poems for Jack Nicholson to read to Diana Vreeland on her deathbed, then quoted W. H. Auden. As I fumbled with what I thought was a malfunctioning camera, Harrison offered a suggestion: "Remove the lens cap."

In a part of the country most people would surely call remote, Harrison clearly had no trouble gathering bird-hunting friends. Over long lunches, Philip Caputo, Jim Fergus, Ross Humphreys, Guy de la Valdène, and Josiah Austin gathered for civilized meals with many glasses of wine, and for Jim, the double-barreled intake of cigarettes and alcohol, until it was too dark to hunt.

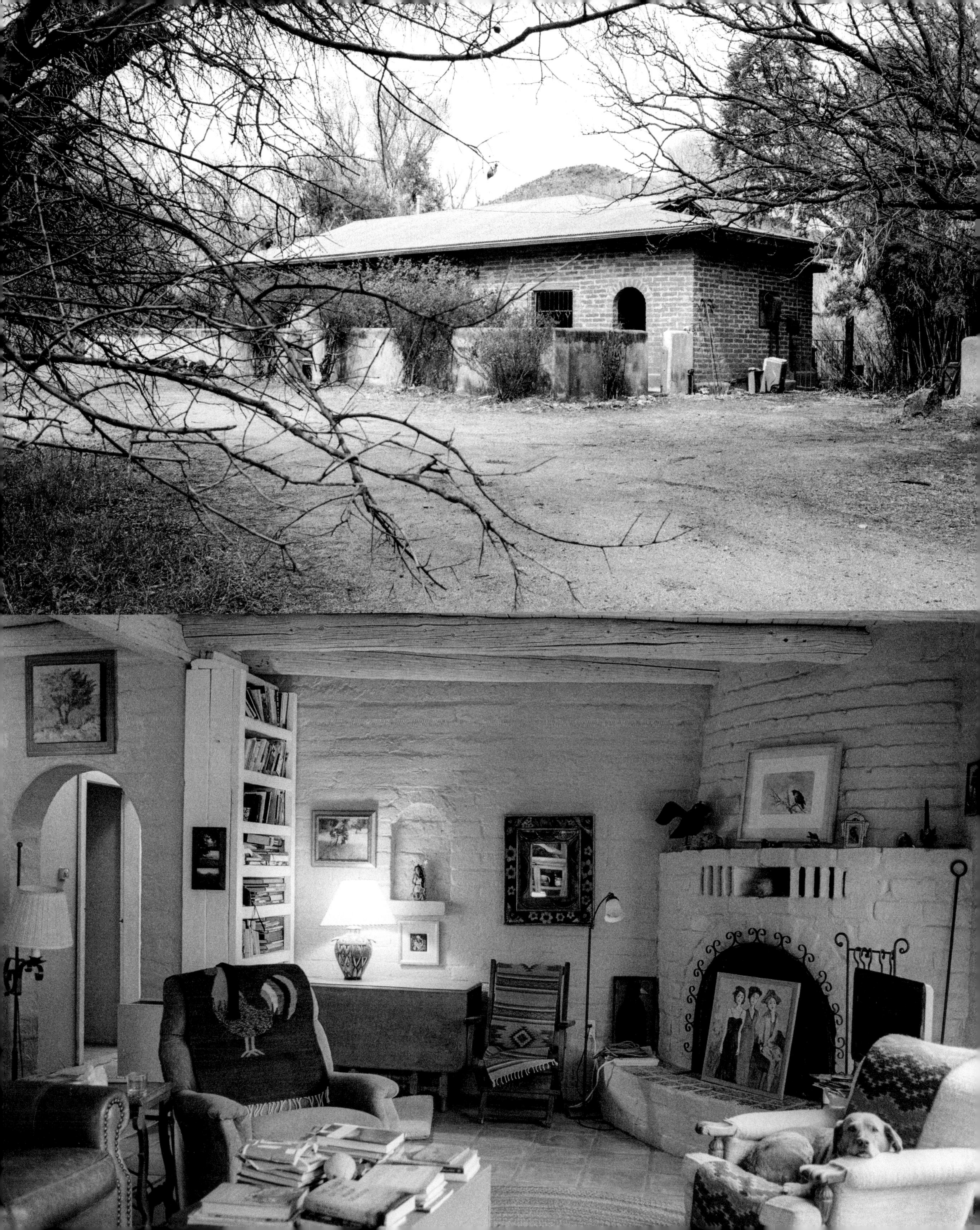

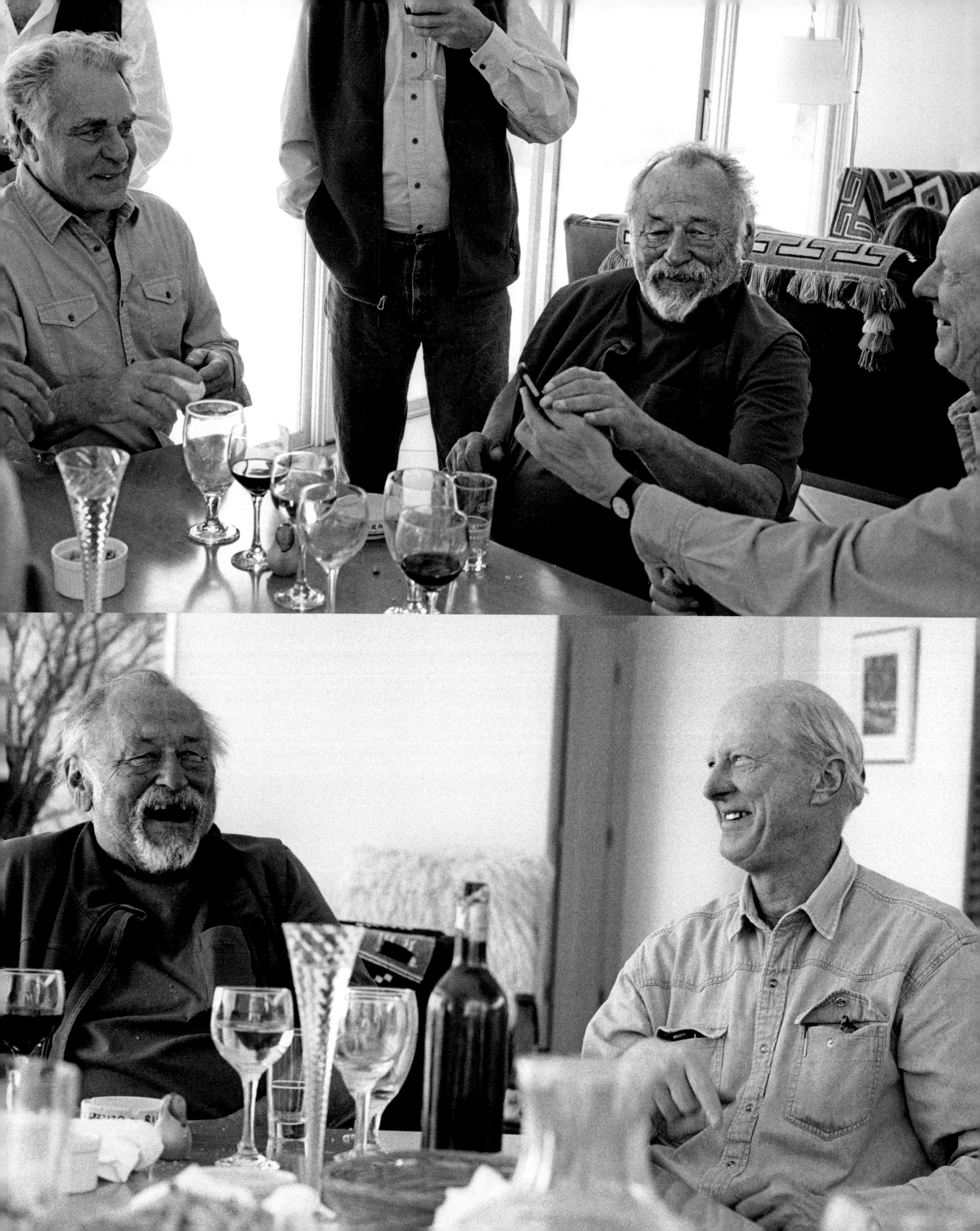

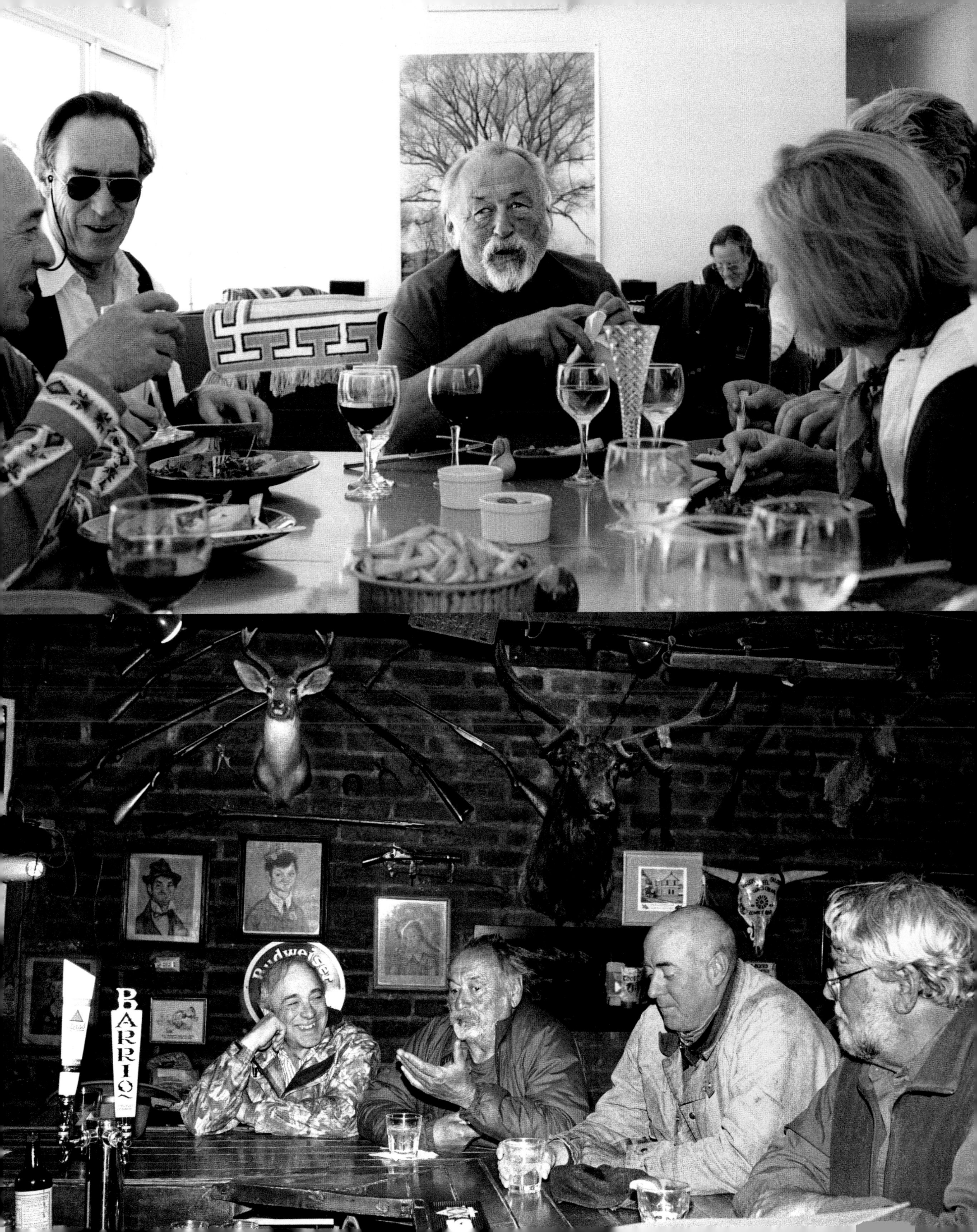

Brit Bennett

American (b. 1990)

Photographed in San Diego, California, December 2020

Brit Bennett, the youngest writer in this collection, was only thirty years old when I photographed her in San Diego. She had moved from Brooklyn to live there temporarily with her parents during the height of the Covid-19 pandemic in 2020.

On the first day, I wore a mask. After about ten minutes, Bennett asked if I would remove it. Every strong portrait is a collaboration. But for the first time, I realized that the need to watch my face, to read my expressions, could be as critical for my subject as my need to see her.

The Bennett family is especially close. Brit and her father, Duane, a retired lawyer, share competitive, outgoing personalities. Brit's mother, Lena, sensitive and observant, comes from a small Louisiana town. Lena's stories of growing up there, and Brit's visits with her back to that community, are a strong influence on Brit's writing. But Brit has never strained under a sense of familial obligation. She said simply, "I like being around my family. We love each other."

During my time with the Bennetts, President Obama announced his list of the most important books of the year. Bennett's *The Vanishing Half* was among them. Immediately, congratulatory messages from friends lit up Bennett's phone. Her father's response to the news, as he ran from his office with outstretched arms, was one of complete happiness.

Sitting with her family, Bennett amused us with this anecdote: "My friend Chris McCormick said to me once, 'Some writers are too smart to write fiction.' He meant that there are some aspects of writing fiction that can't be intellectualized. But I also thought it was funny, because the other implication is that good fiction is smart, but you might have to be a little stupid to write it well—which, I told him, was probably true of the both of us."

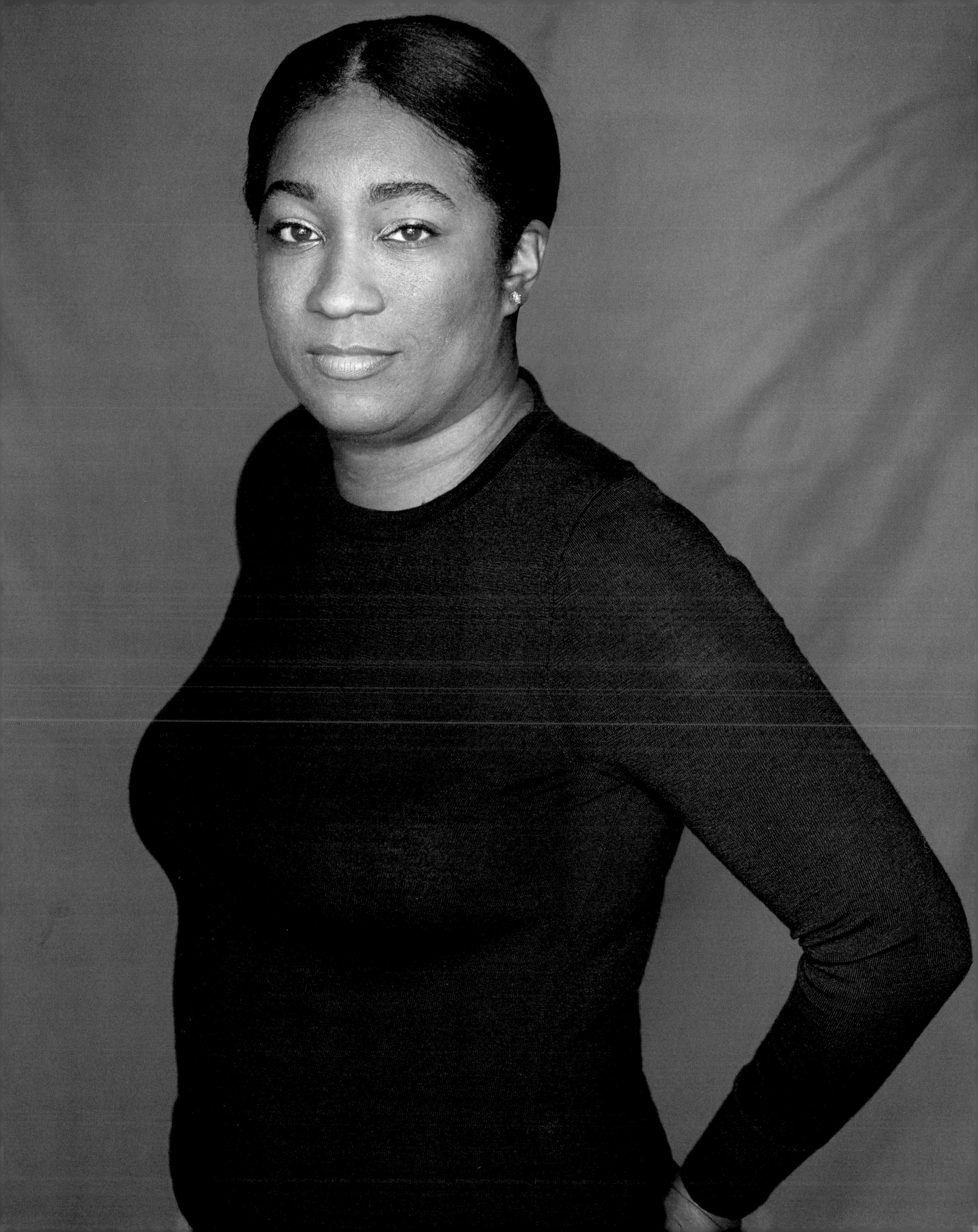

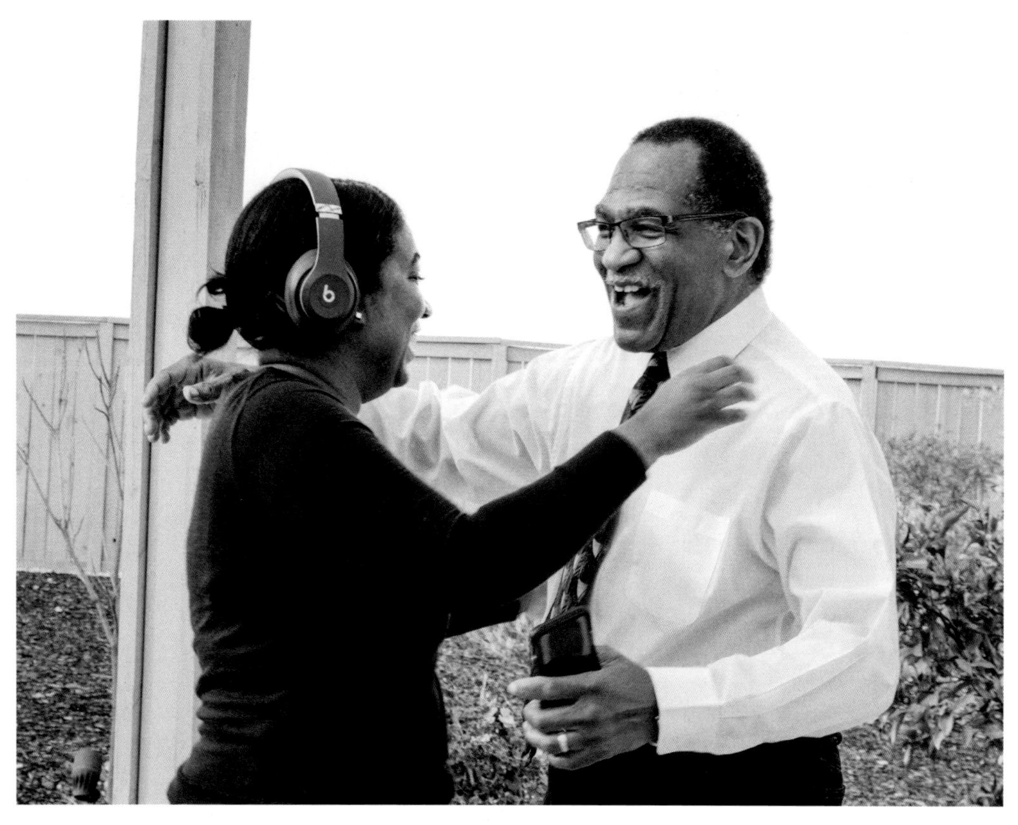

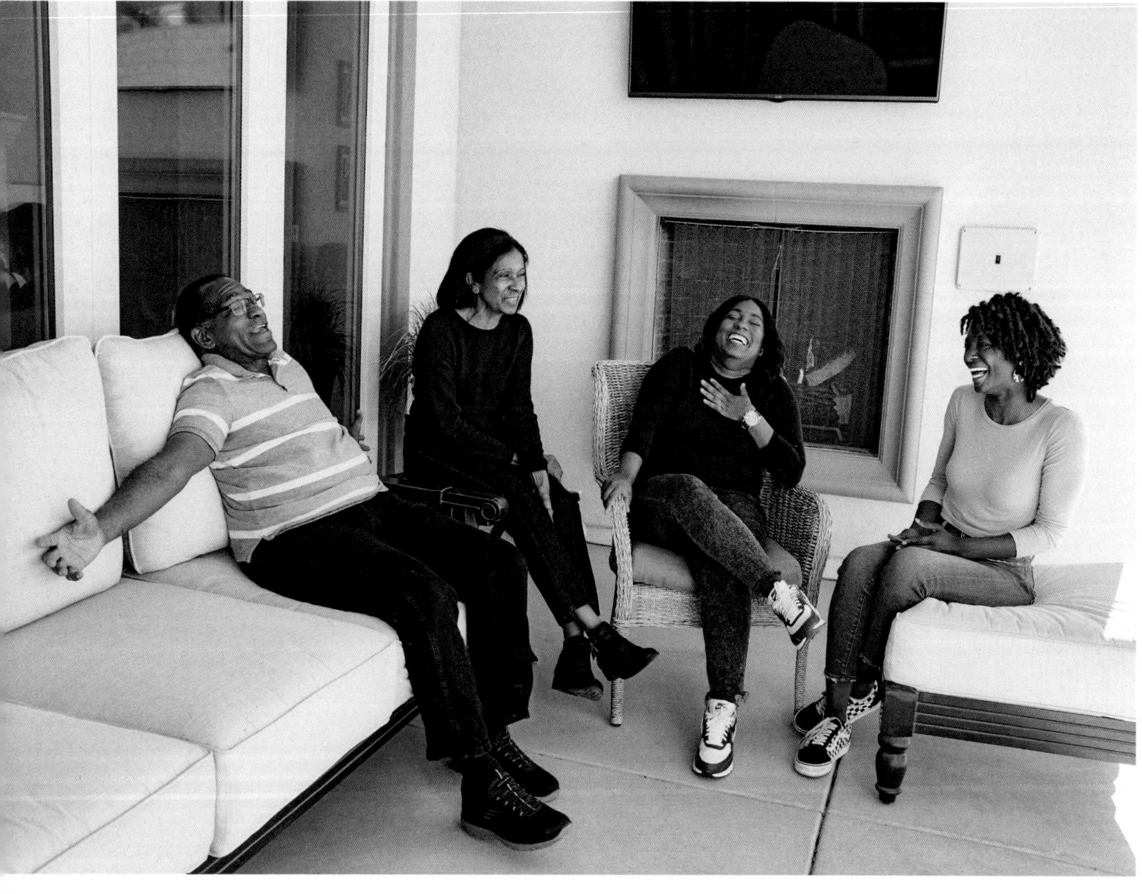

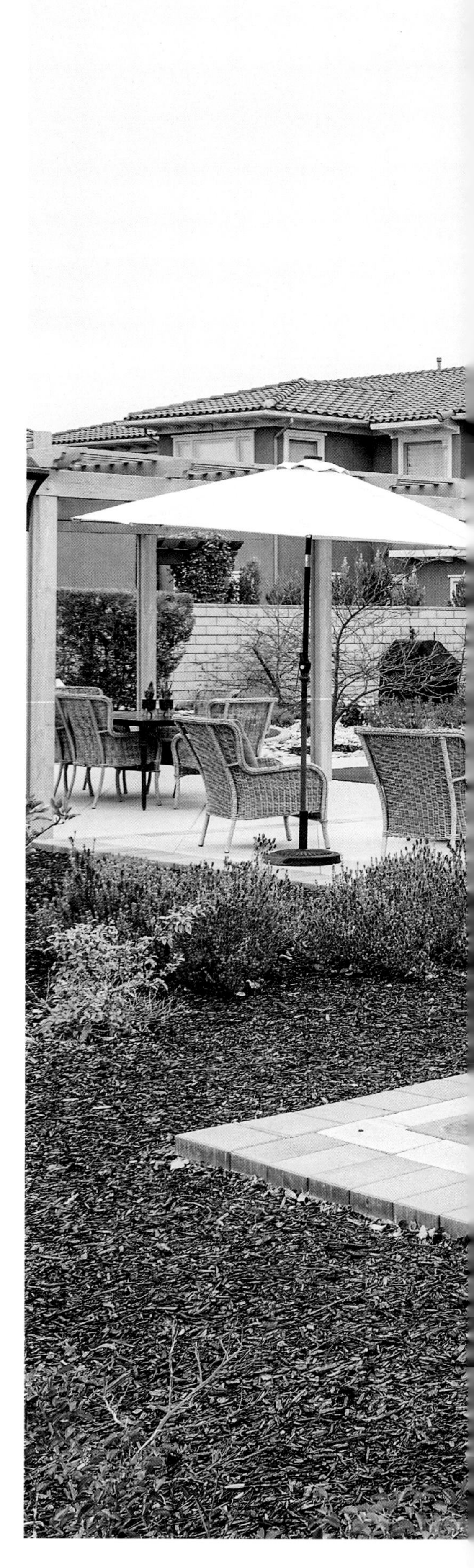

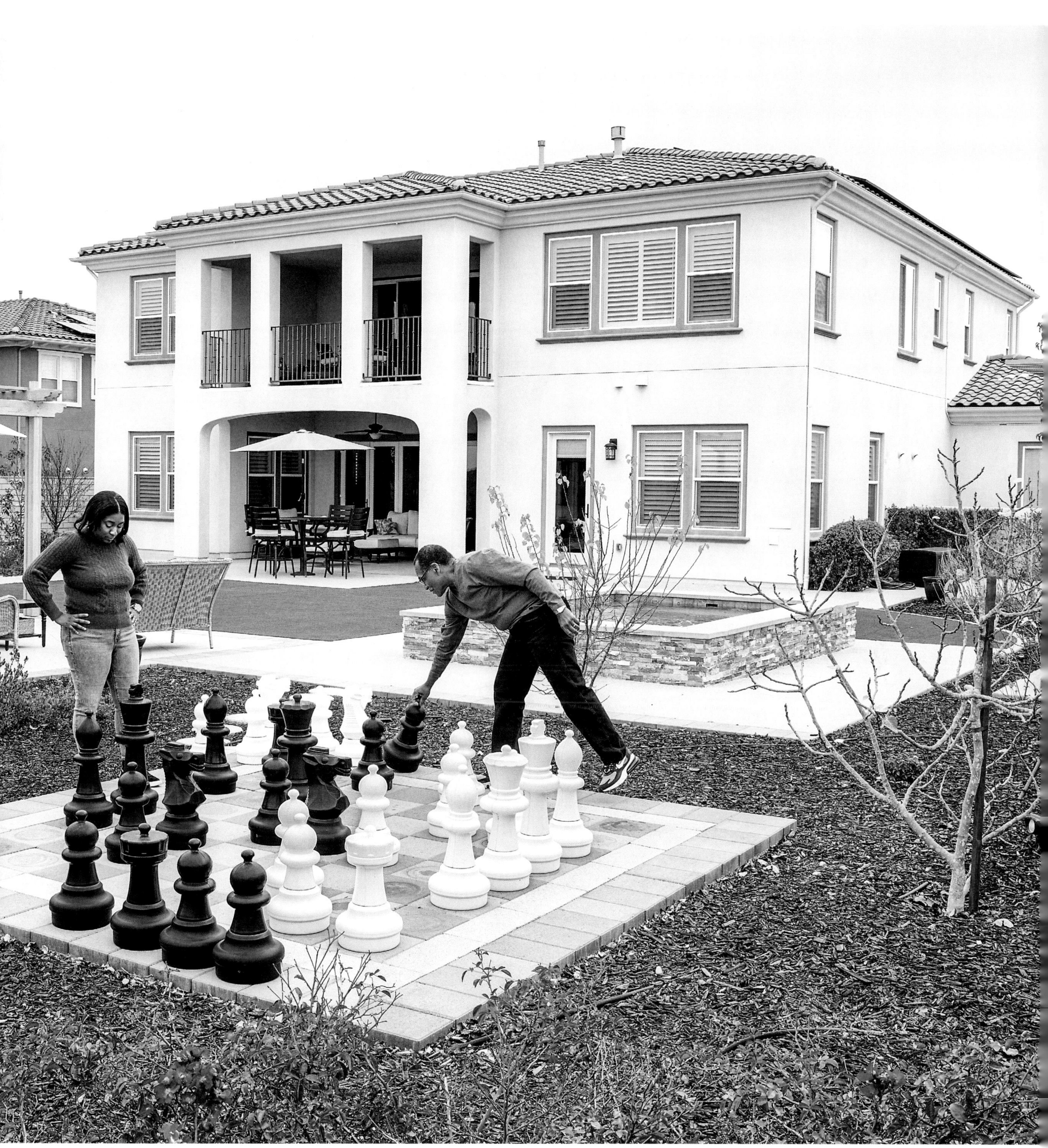

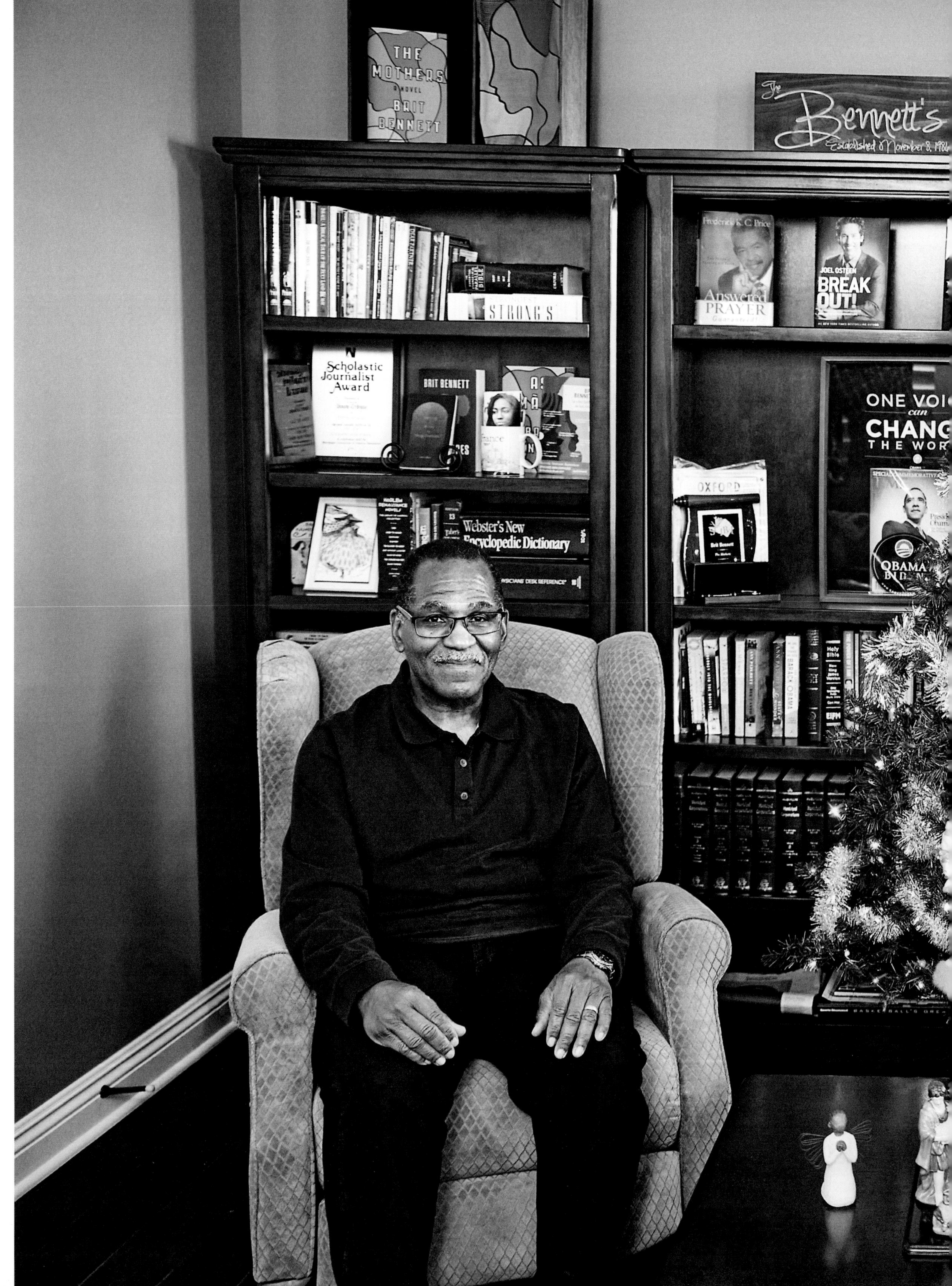

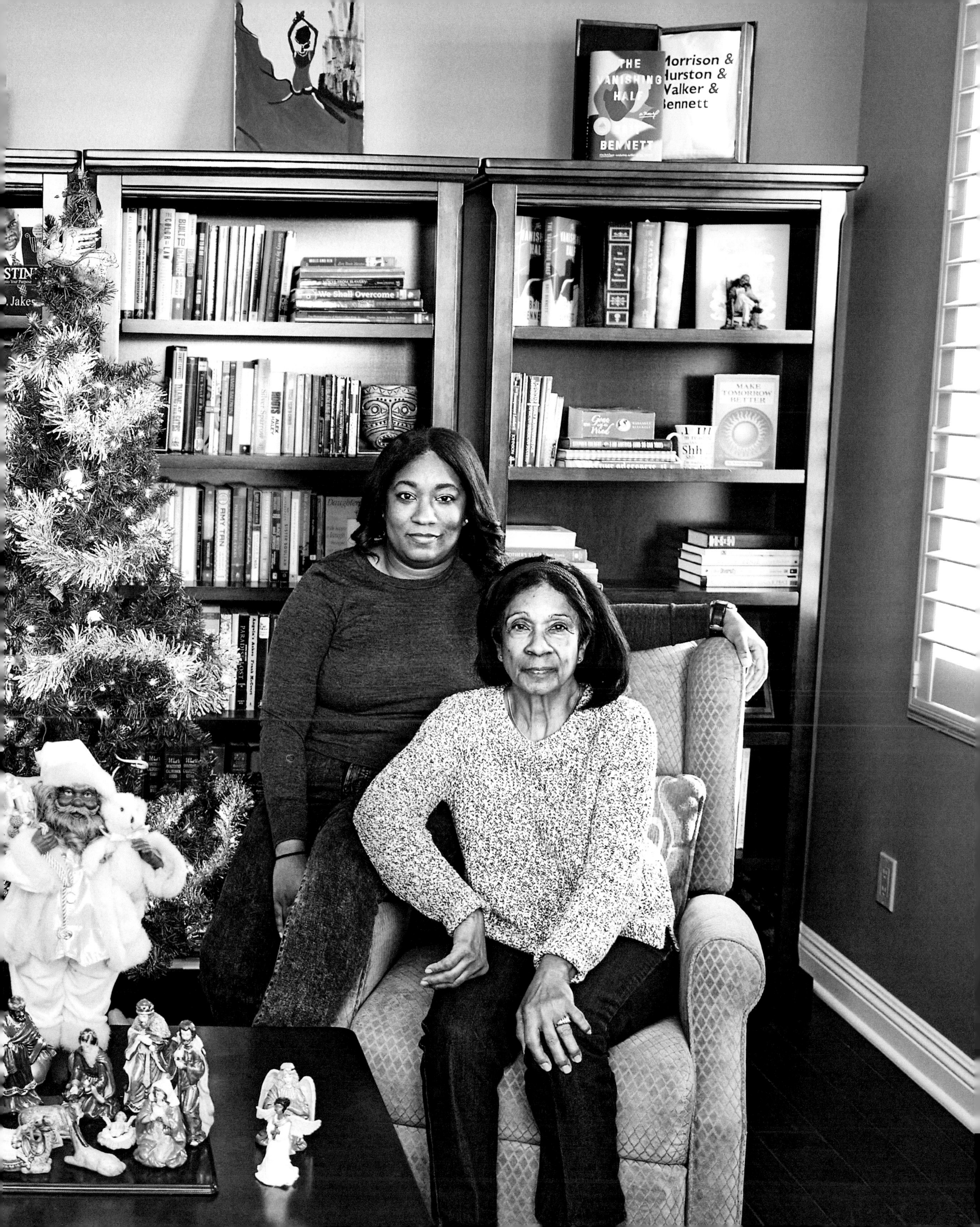

Thomas McGuane

American (b. 1939)

Photographed in McLeod, Montana, June 2011

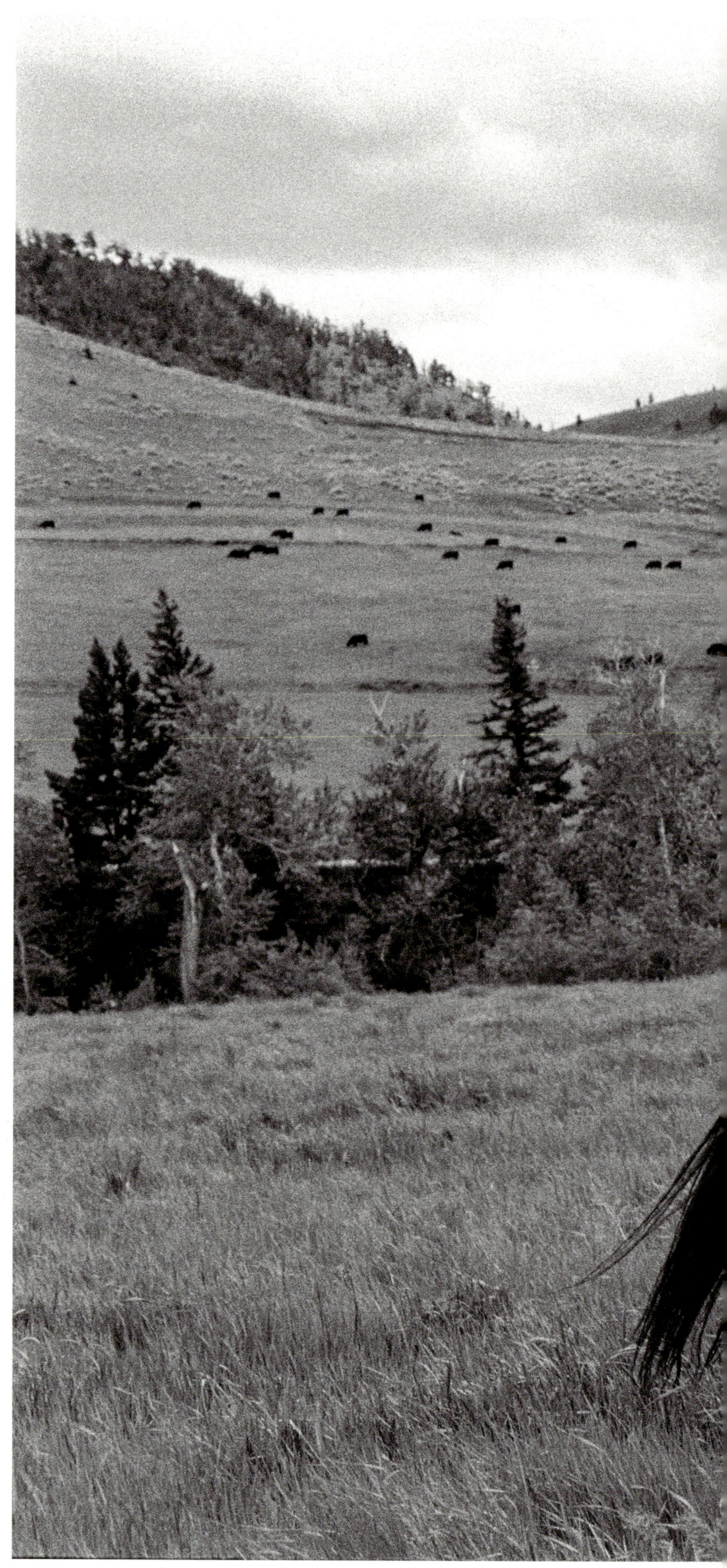

I f you were to imagine the perfect place to live in the American West, this would be it. In Sweet Grass County, Montana, about thirty minutes south of McLeod, the Boulder River Valley, lush with tall grass, lies between the snow-tipped peaks of the Absaroka Range.

It is here that Thomas McGuane and his wife, Laurie Buffett, live. Their house—built by hand in 1903 by the homesteader George Muncaster of logs felled in the wilderness, floated down the river, and hauled ashore by draft horses—sits in a bend of the river, sheltered from strong north winds by elevated cliffs. The ranch, with its authentic pioneer house, wood corrals, and mountain meadows, surely would have been chosen by the director John Ford as the ideal location to film a classic Western.

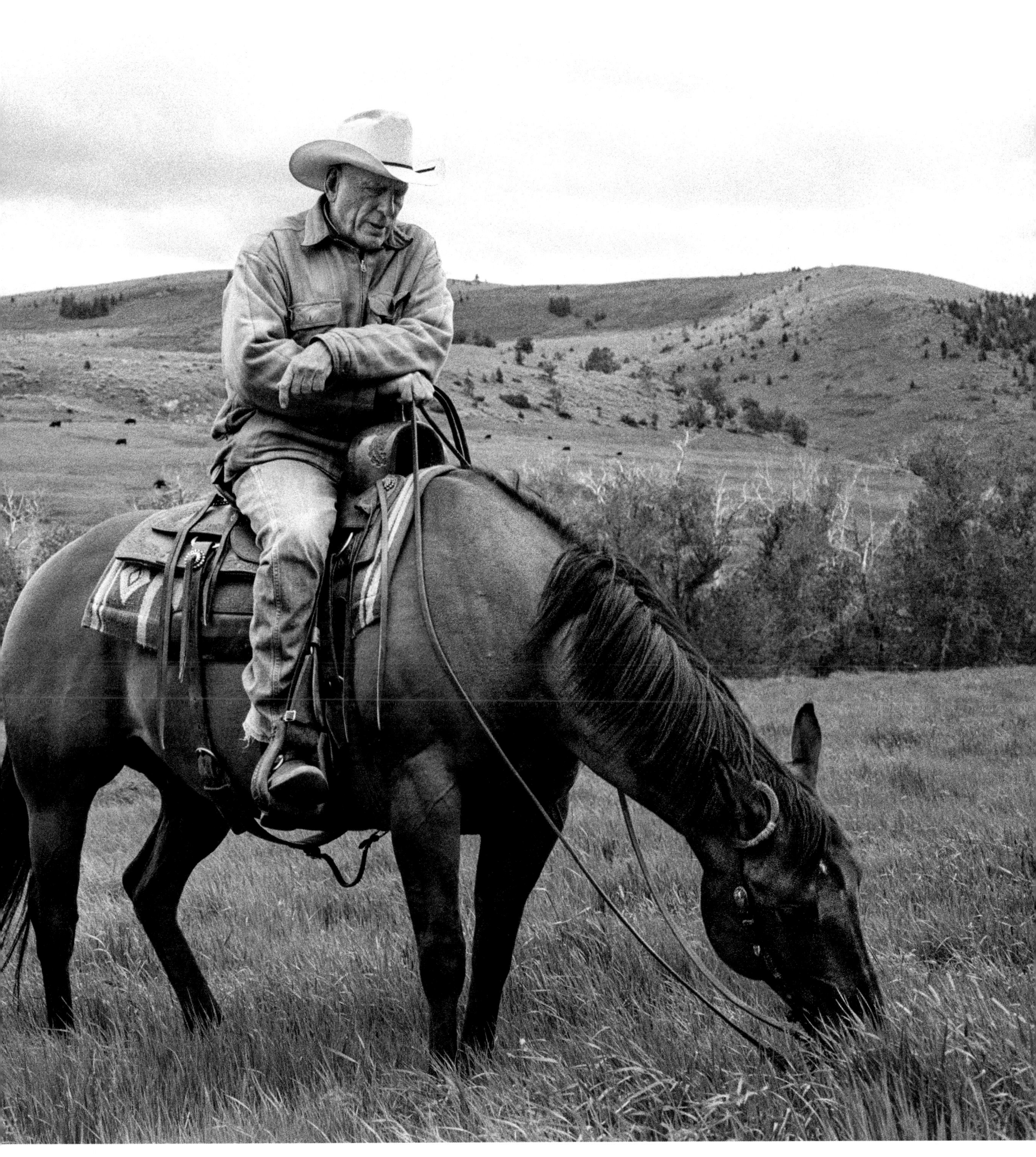

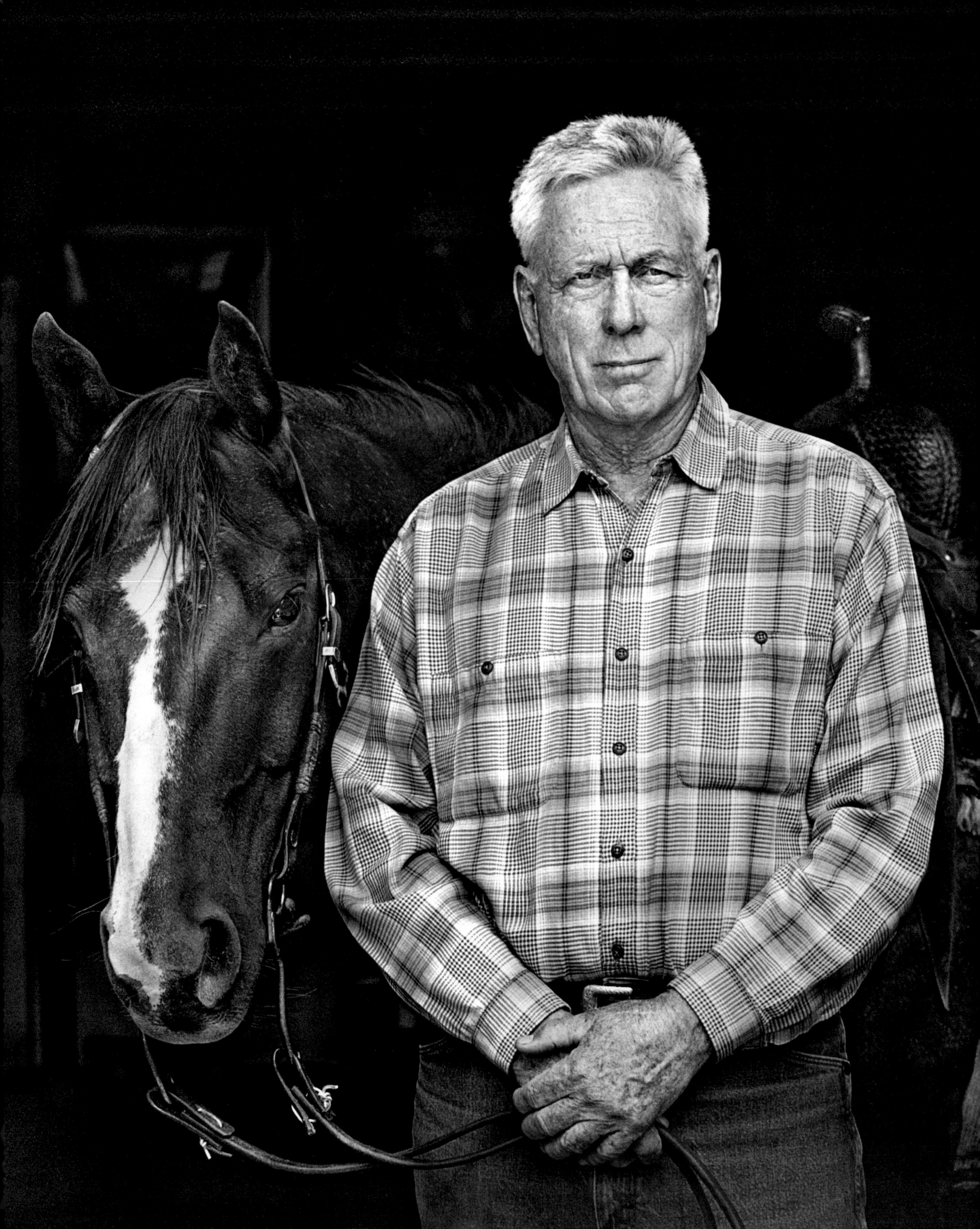

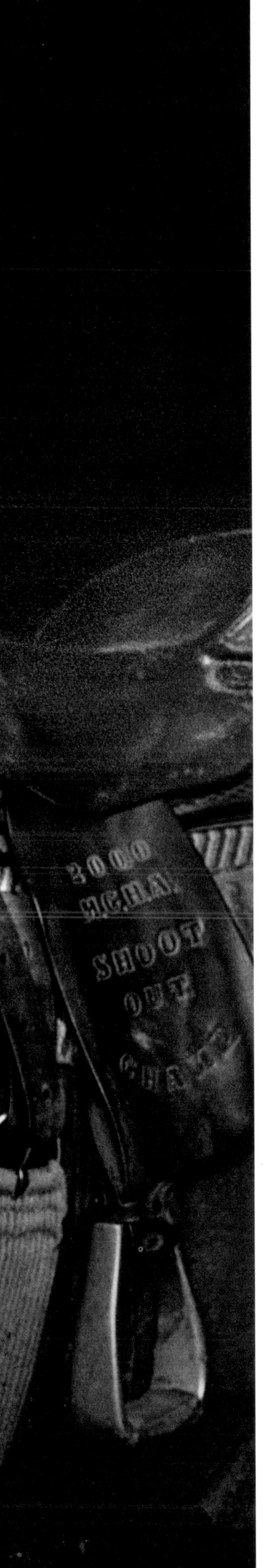

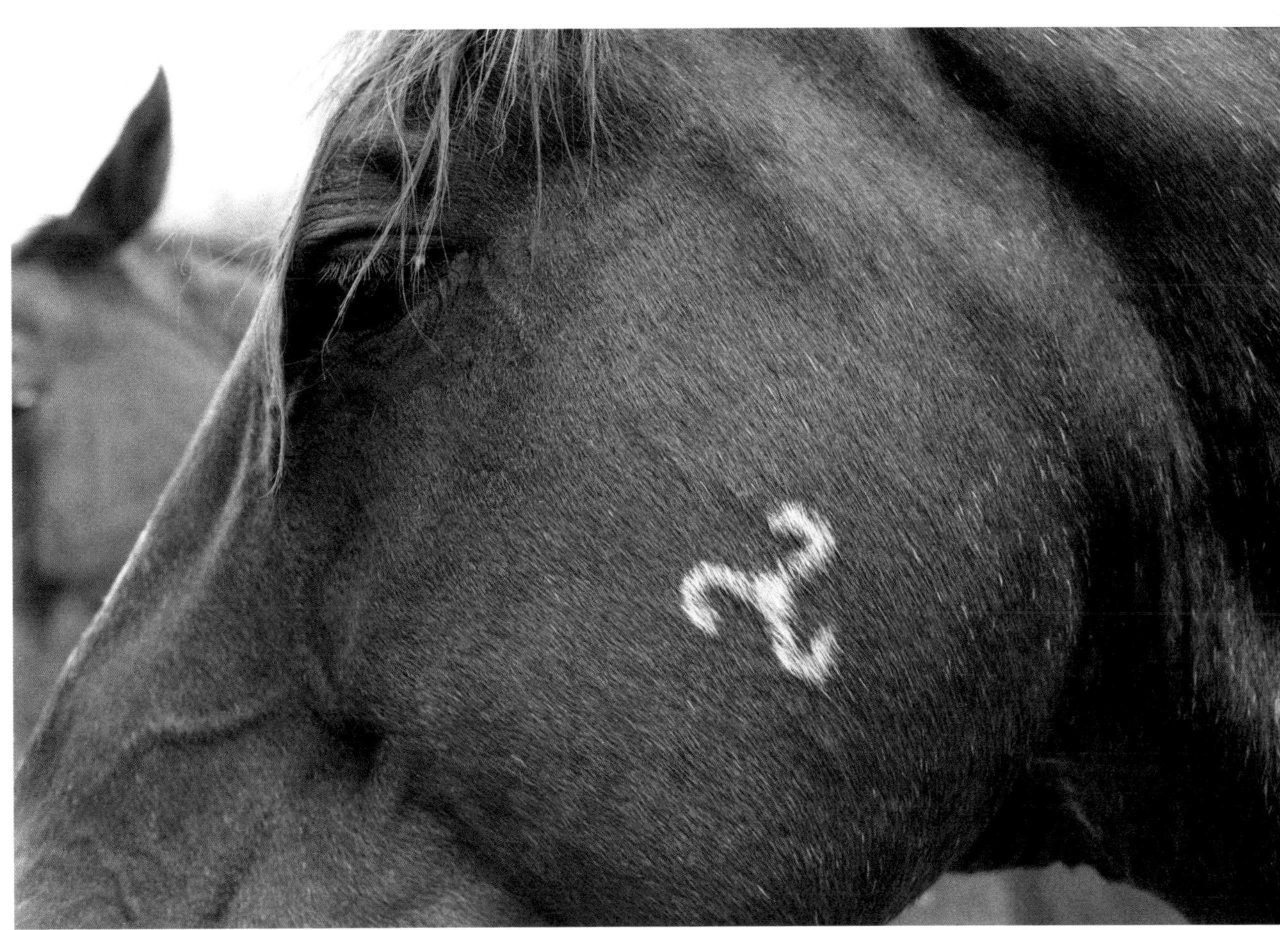

The ranch is a haven for Tom and Laurie. The tumult of Tom's time in Hollywood as a successful screenwriter in the 1970s, and the generally ruinous effects of an untethered life, came to an end when he and Laurie married. Here the McGuanes share the satisfying work of tending to their land and animals. And it is here where McGuane writes.

Starting at a young age, reading Mark Twain and Jack London, McGuane imagined a writer's life to be one of adventure. Now, as an industrious writer of novels and short fiction, he spends a good deal of time outdoors hunting and fishing and raising horses. He trains and competes on championship cutting horses. He marks them with a pinwheel symbol, an old Montana brand, much desired because of the simple, clean mark it leaves on an animal.

McGuane's office is in a small, detached building a short walk from the log house. Near a table where he ties flies for fishing, he has a daybed tucked next to his writing desk. When he's stretched out, he appears to be in a sunken chamber amid his books.

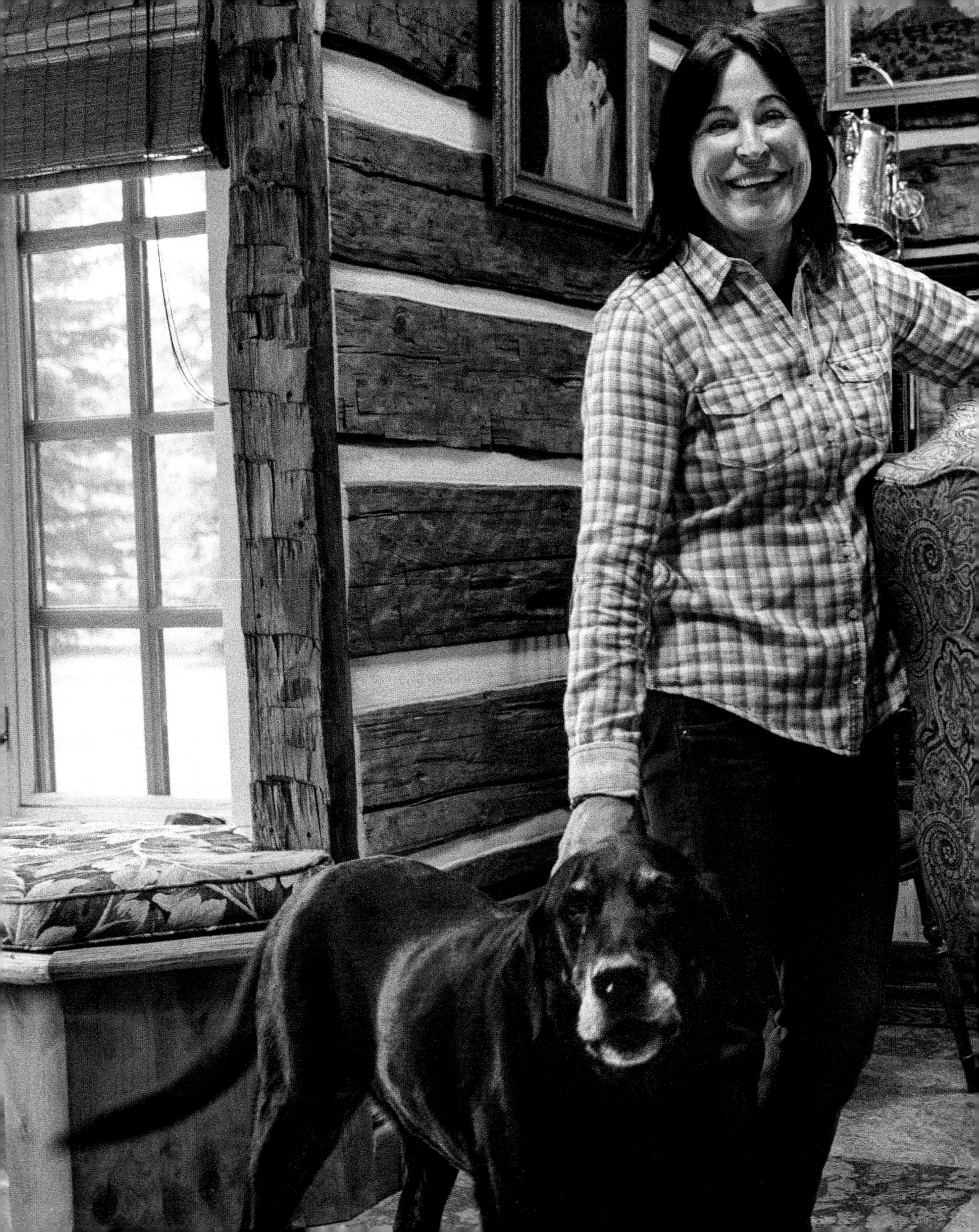

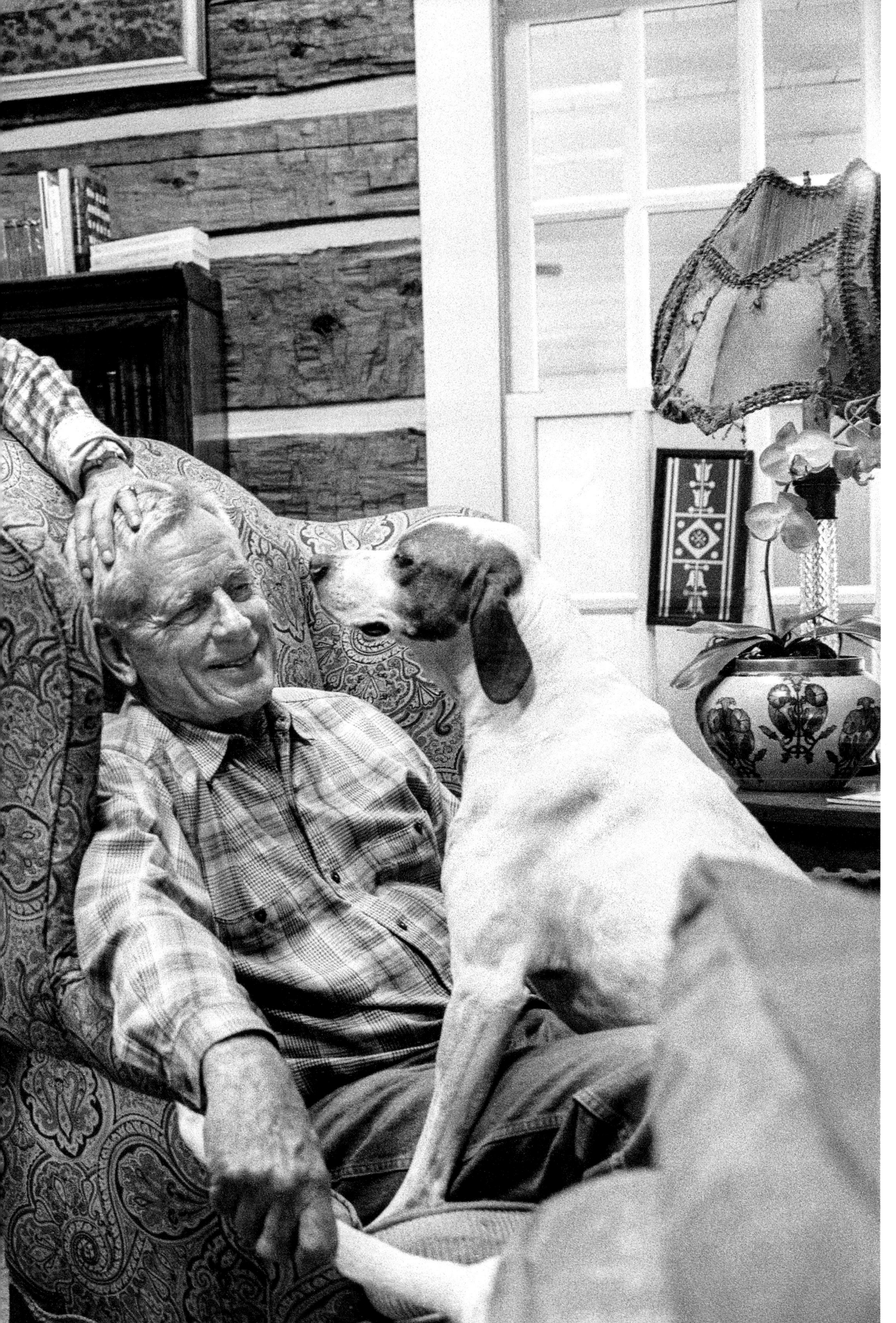

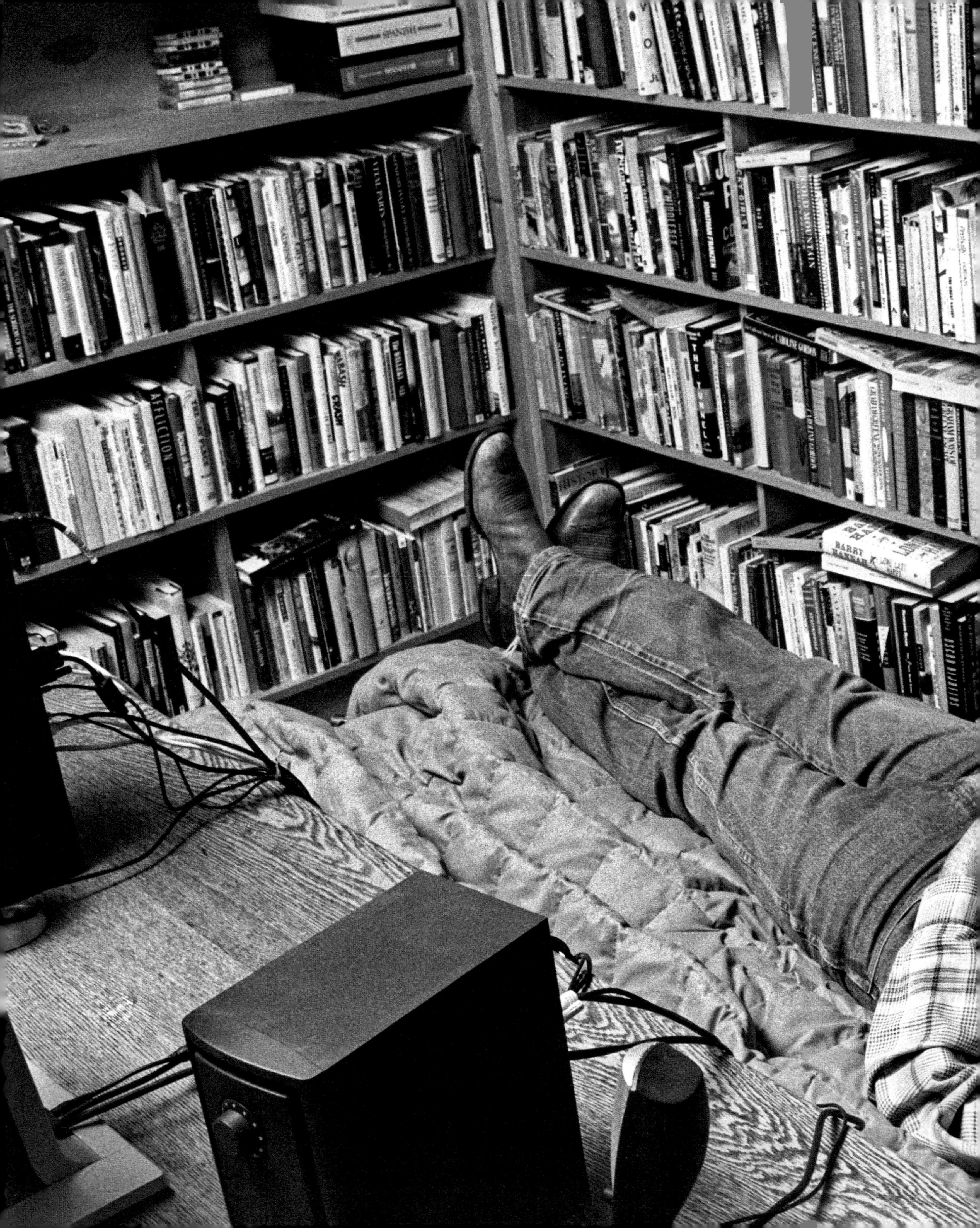

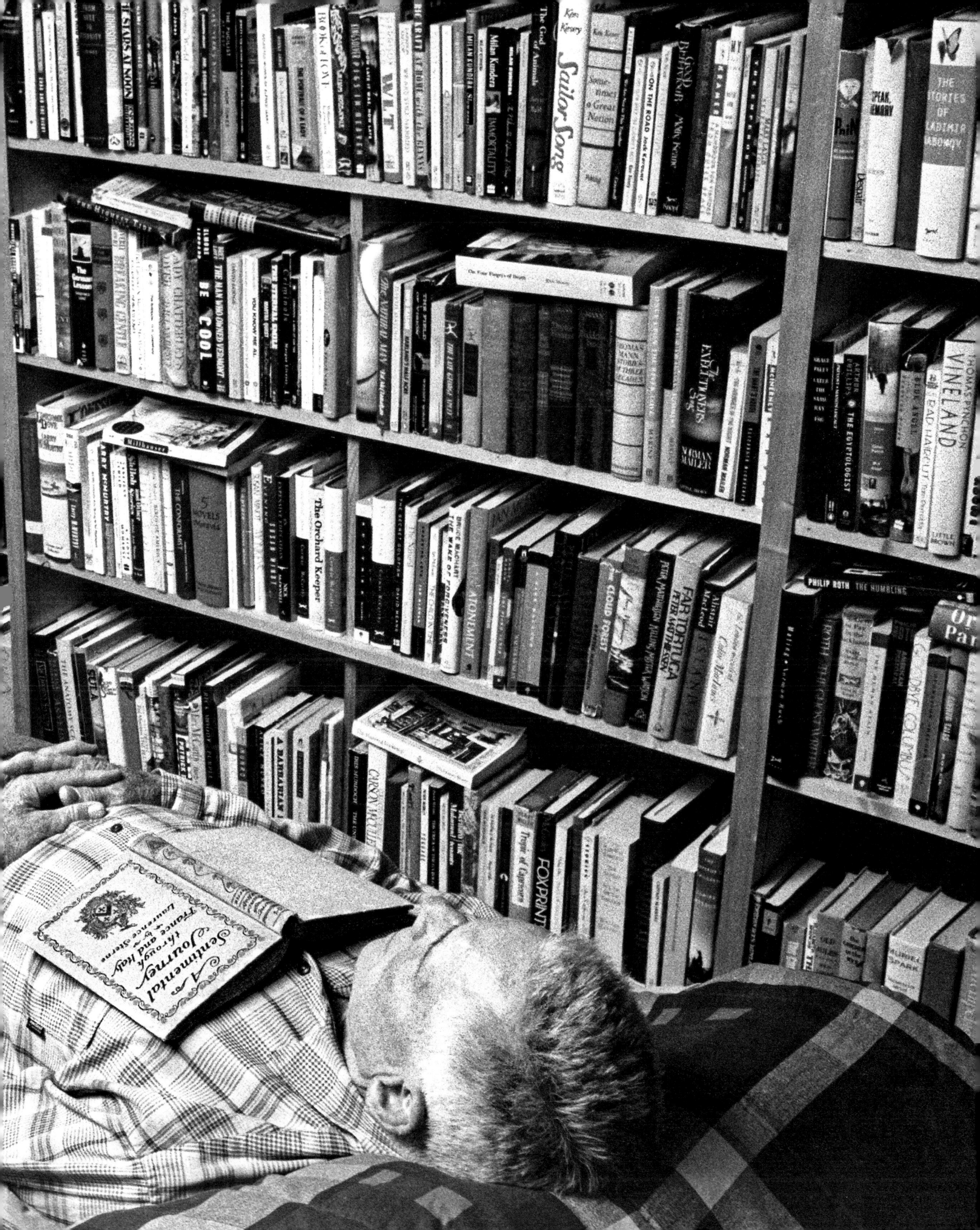

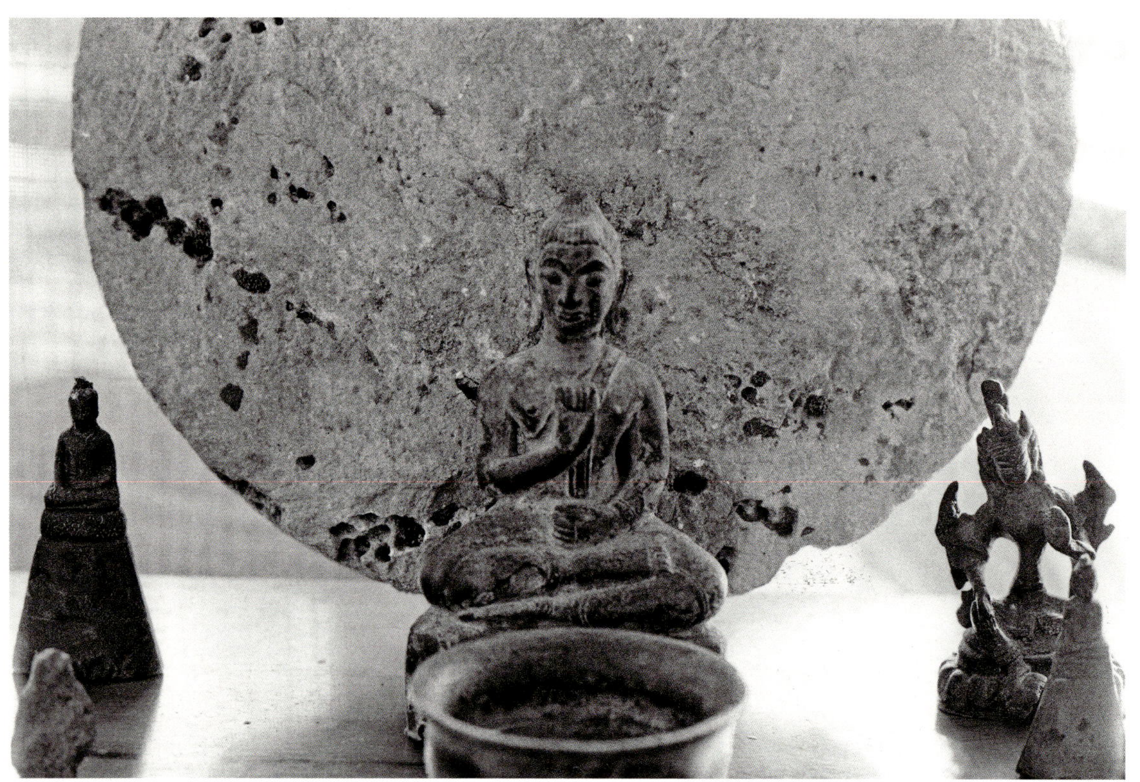

W. S.
Merwin

American (1927–2019)

Photographed on Maui, Hawaii, October 2012

On the island of Maui, off the coastal highway to Hana, I drove down a volcanic red dirt road to meet W. S. Merwin, one of the world's foremost poets. He and his wife, Paula, lived secluded in a handmade house engulfed by dense tropical forest. Forty years ago, their nineteen acres were barren, chemically damaged by pineapple growers. Merwin, who had come to Maui in 1976 to study Buddhism, thought, "Maybe I could save it." He set about planting, tree by tree—a tree a day during rainy season—almost 3,000 palms, representing 480 species from around the world.

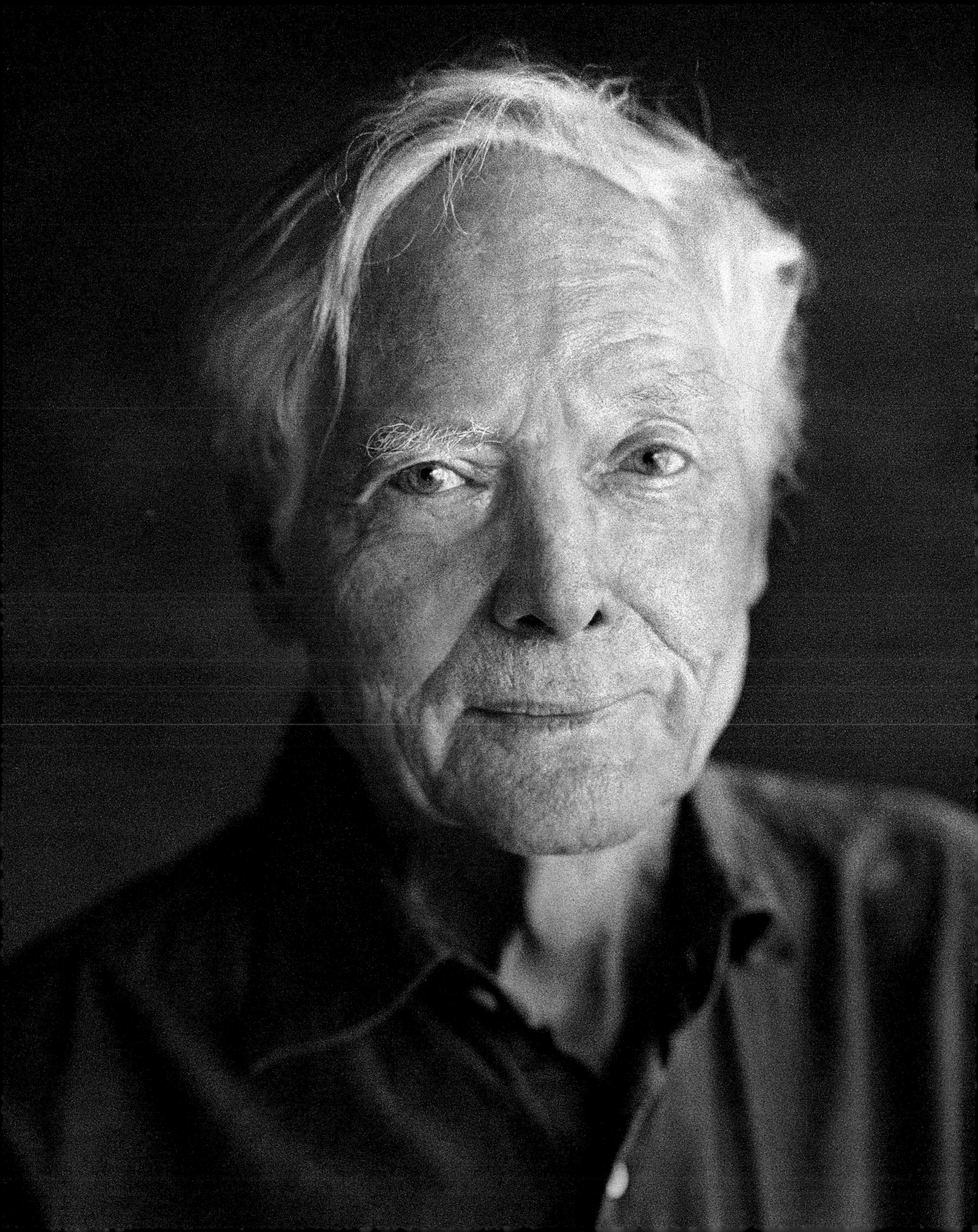

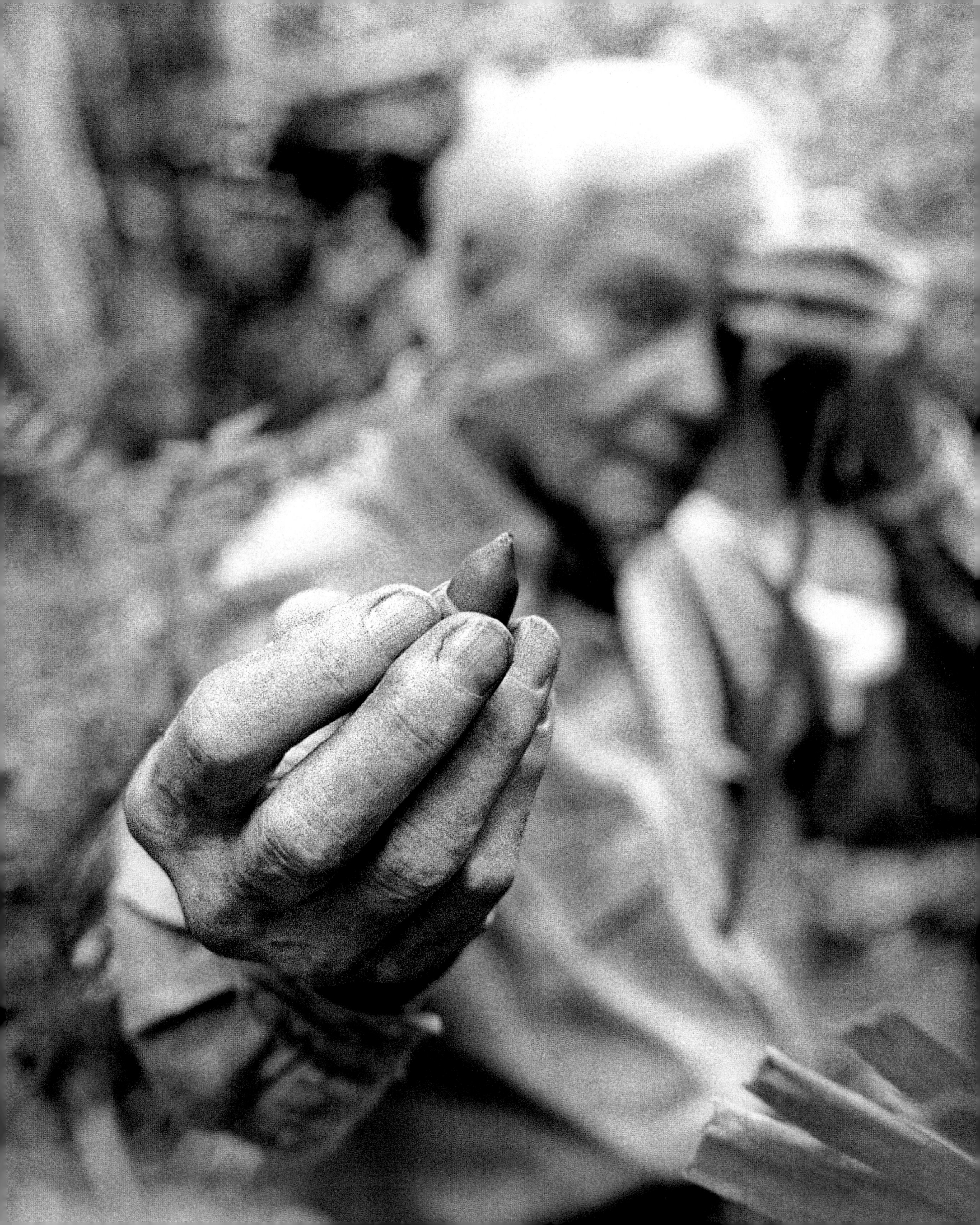

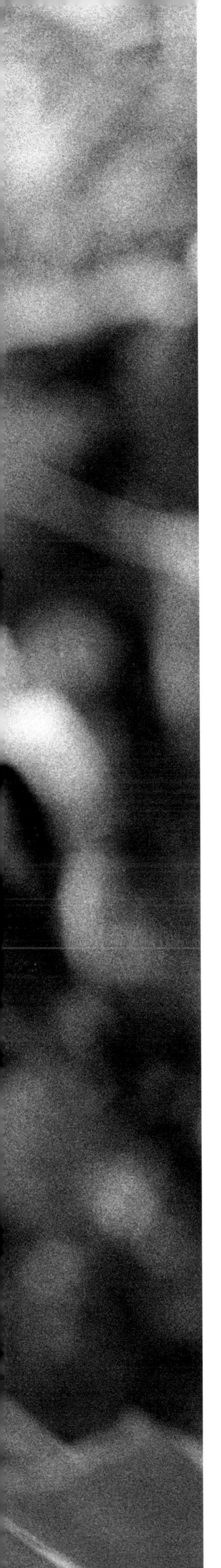

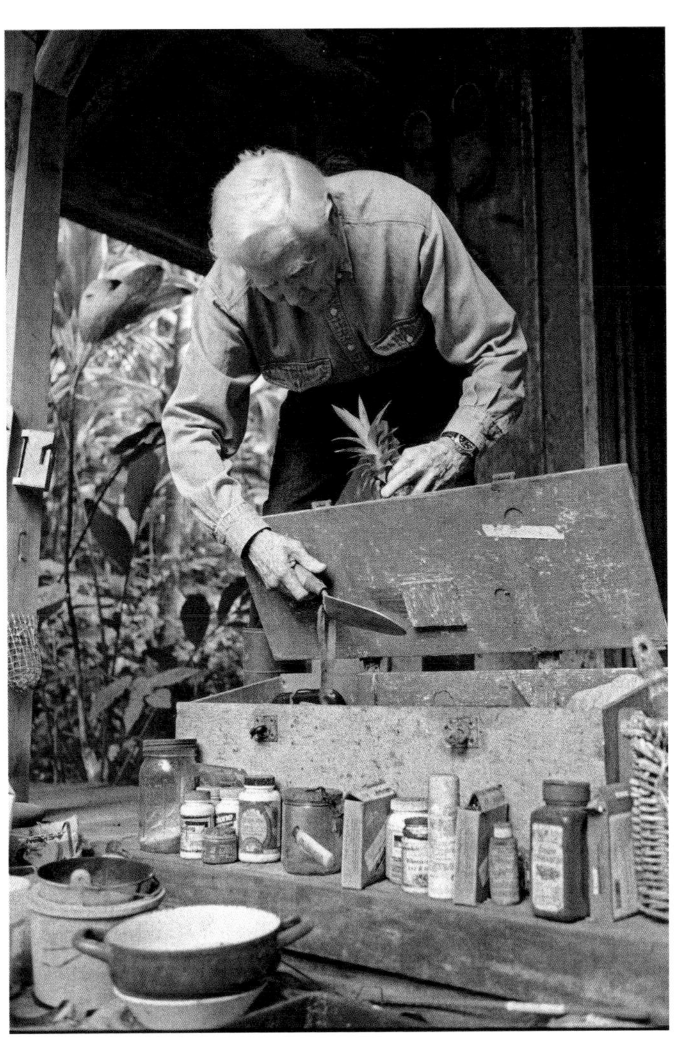

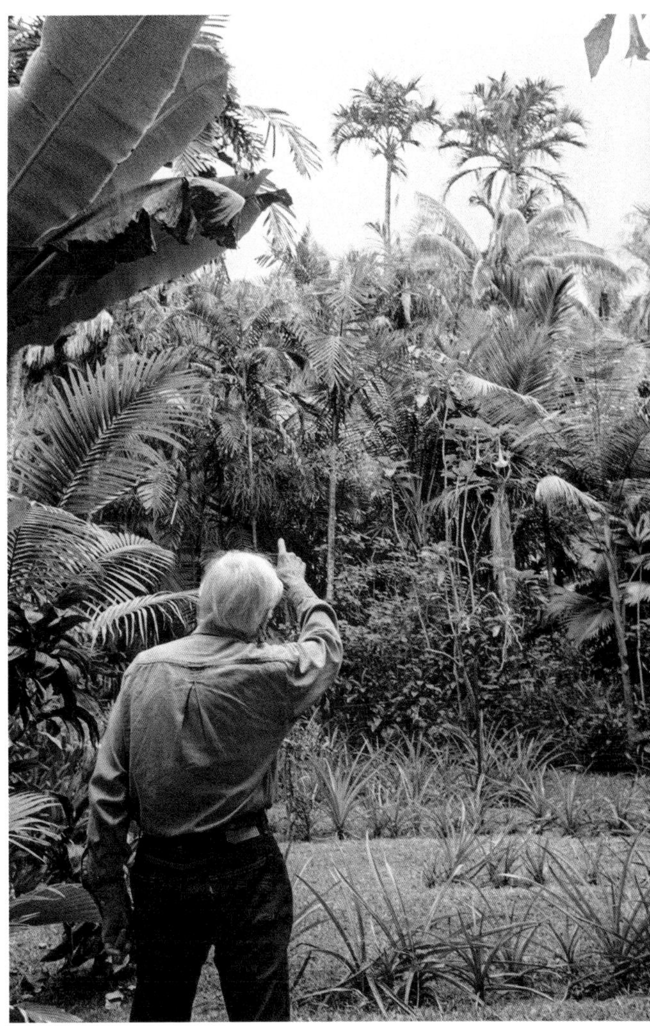

On our walks through the forest, he'd point to one tree, then another: "You see that tall palm? It came from an acorn sent from a friend in Madagascar." The palms seemed to astonish Merwin. They were never static, constantly in motion. By the time I met him, he had created a kind of Noah's Ark of rare palms. Botanists call his forest "a living treasure of rare palm DNA."

Merwin woke up each morning to practice Buddhism, alone, in a room off the living area. He wrote every day, even as his eyesight deteriorated, breaking only for lunch with Paula on a high, open porch. Often garden visitors came by later in the day, some staying for dinner.

During my visit, I could see how kind Merwin was, interested in the lives of his guests and sympathetic to my husband's struggle with Alzheimer's. At dinner one night, he talked with our son Owen about military history and Vladimir Nabokov's early memories.

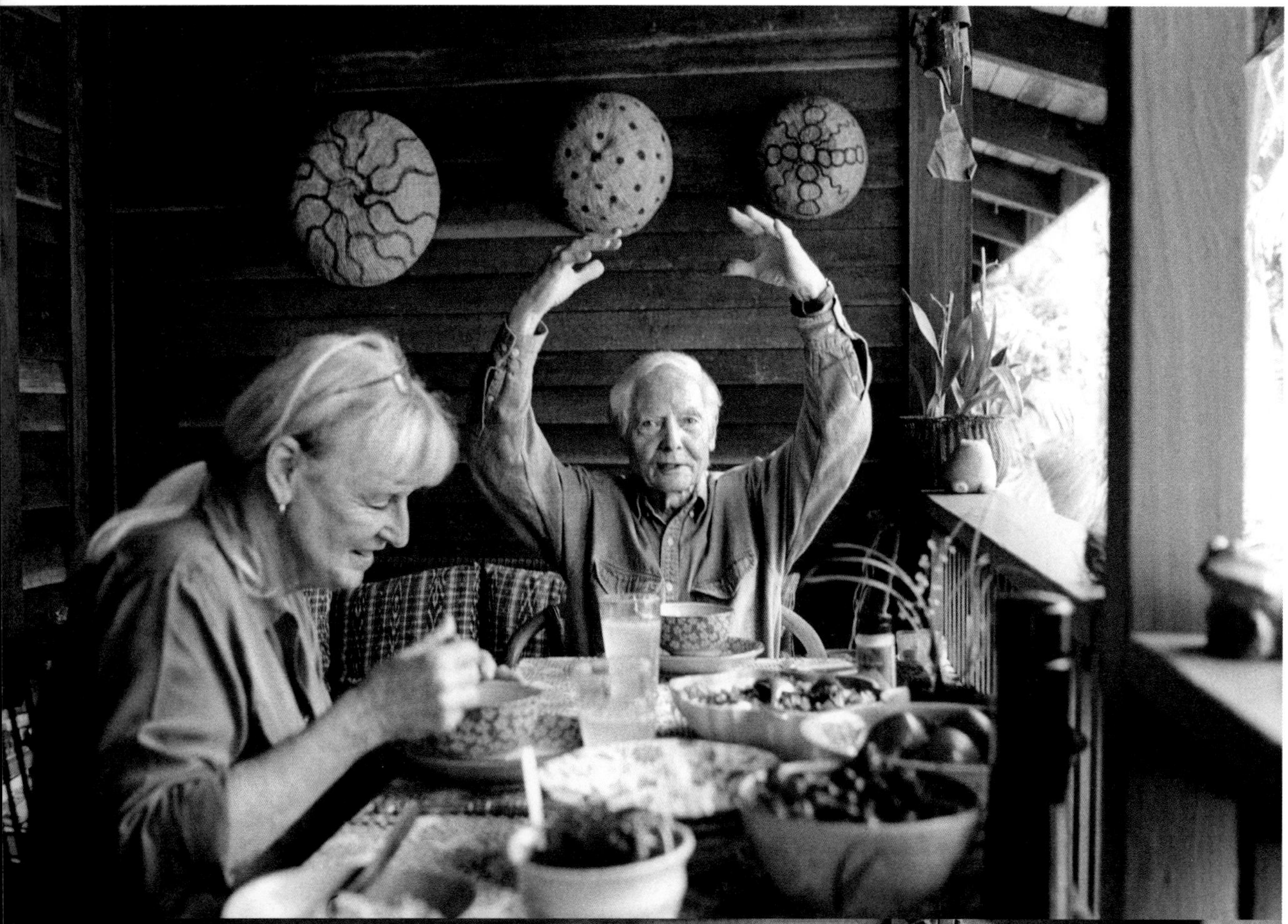

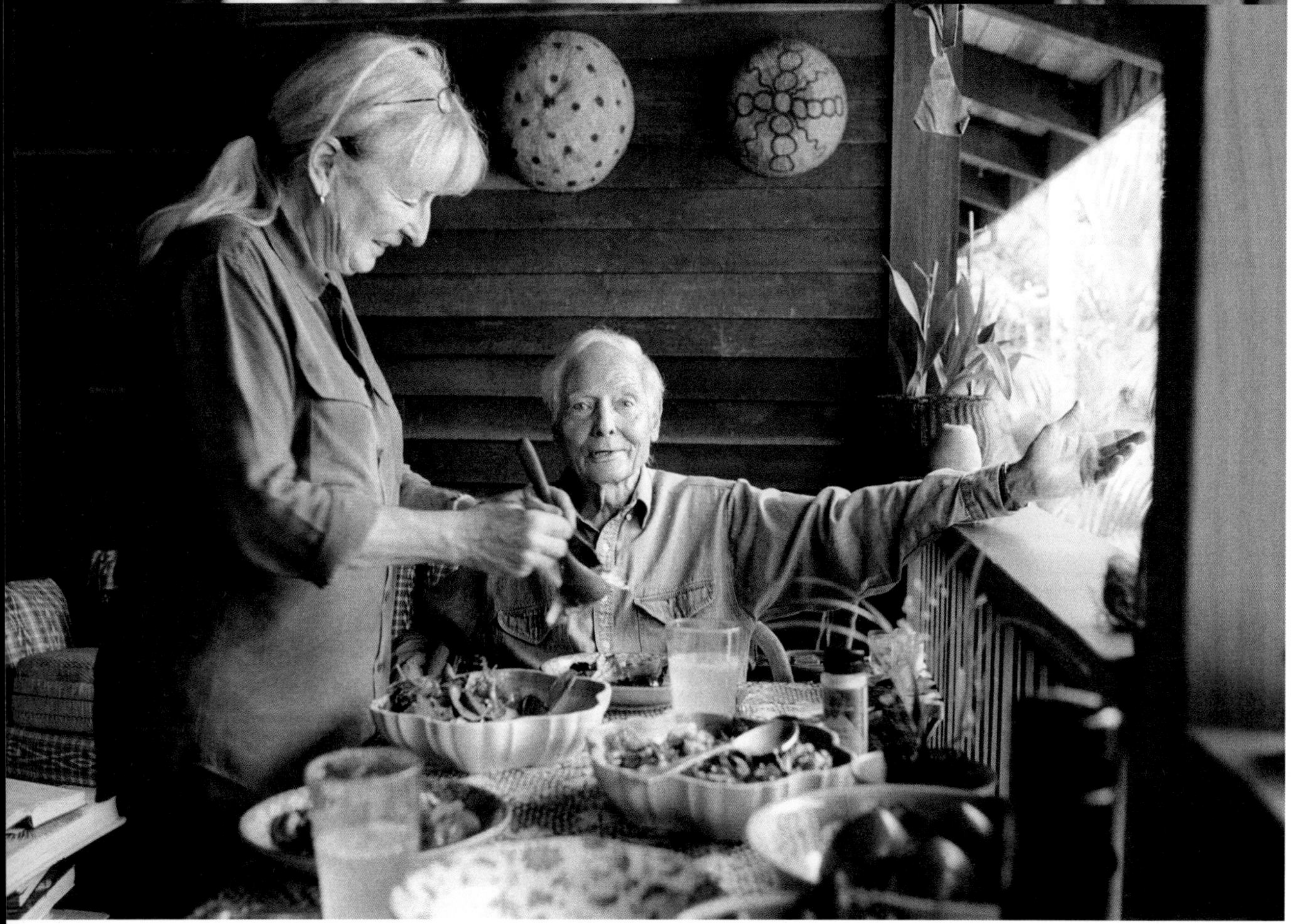

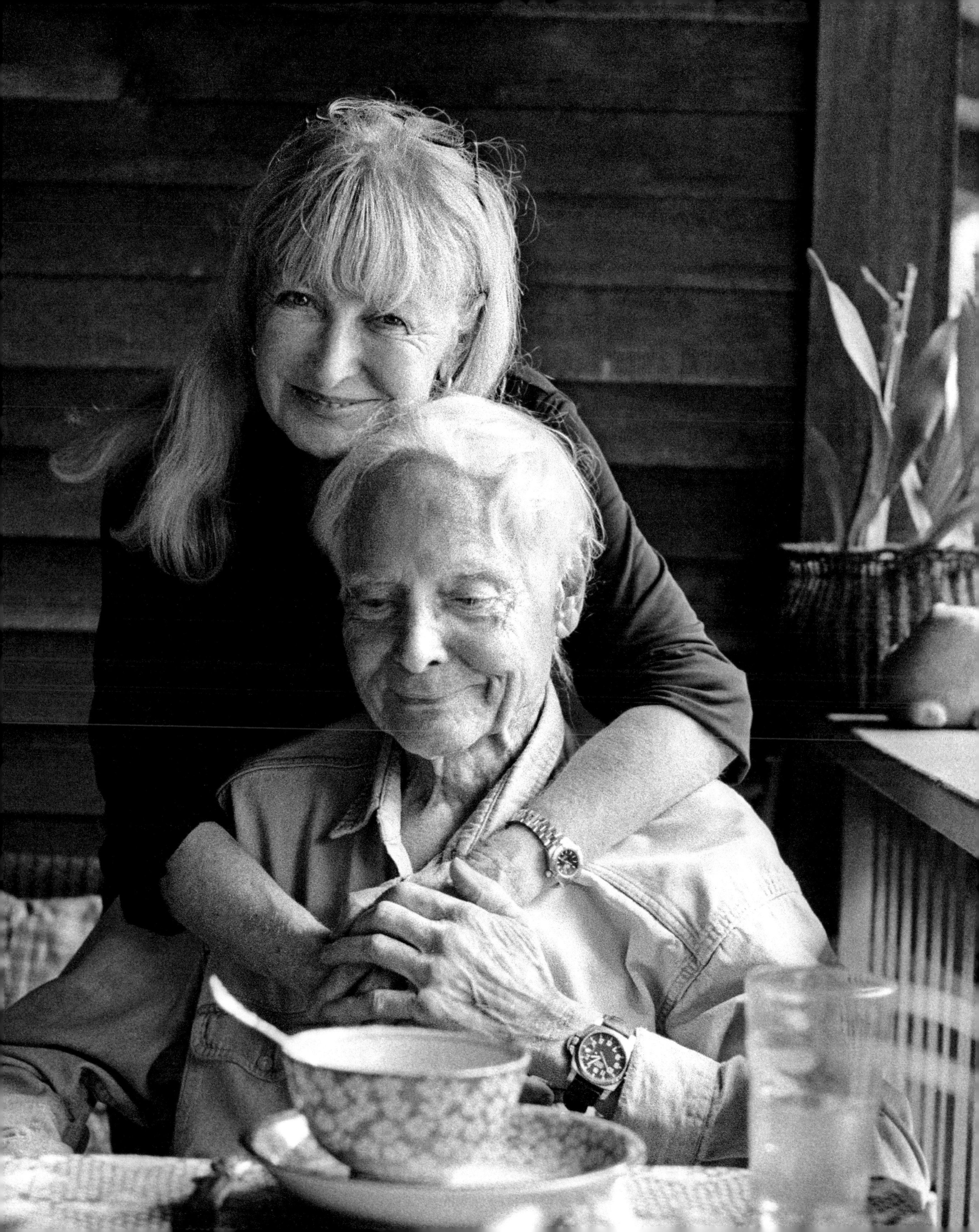

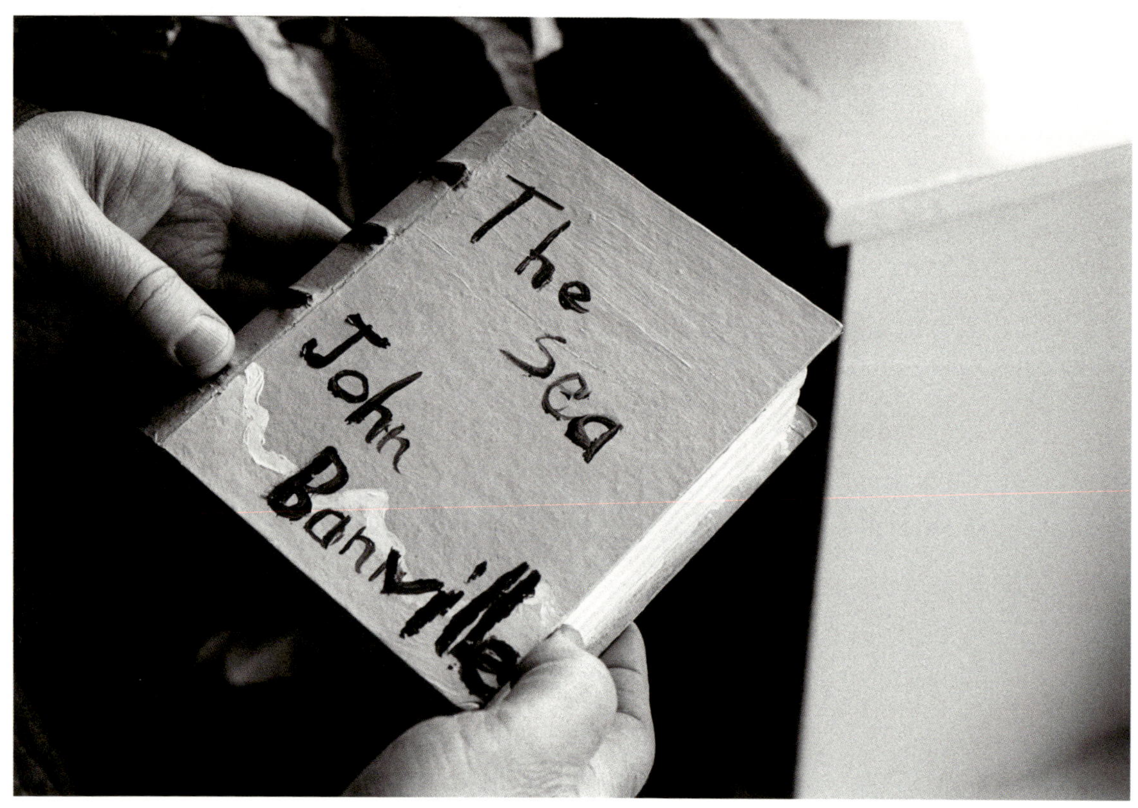

John Banville

Irish (b. 1945)

Photographed in Dublin, Ireland, December 2011

When John Banville won the Man Booker Prize, in 2005, his young daughter, Alice, eight years old at the time, made him a special celebratory edition. He keeps it in his office, in the center of Dublin, where he also writes popular crime fiction under the pseudonym Benjamin Black.

Banville lives in Howth Head, a village about ten miles outside the center of Dublin, where, from his desk, he can "look across the bay to the island of Ireland's Eye, the 'sleeping giant' in James Joyce's *Finnegans Wake*." He added: "And I walk my dog among the rhododendrons on Howth Head, where Leopold Bloom courted Molly. So, I like it here, despite many frustrations." When I asked him if he, like Joyce, would ever live in another city—Paris, for instance—he said simply, "Paris is for visiting."

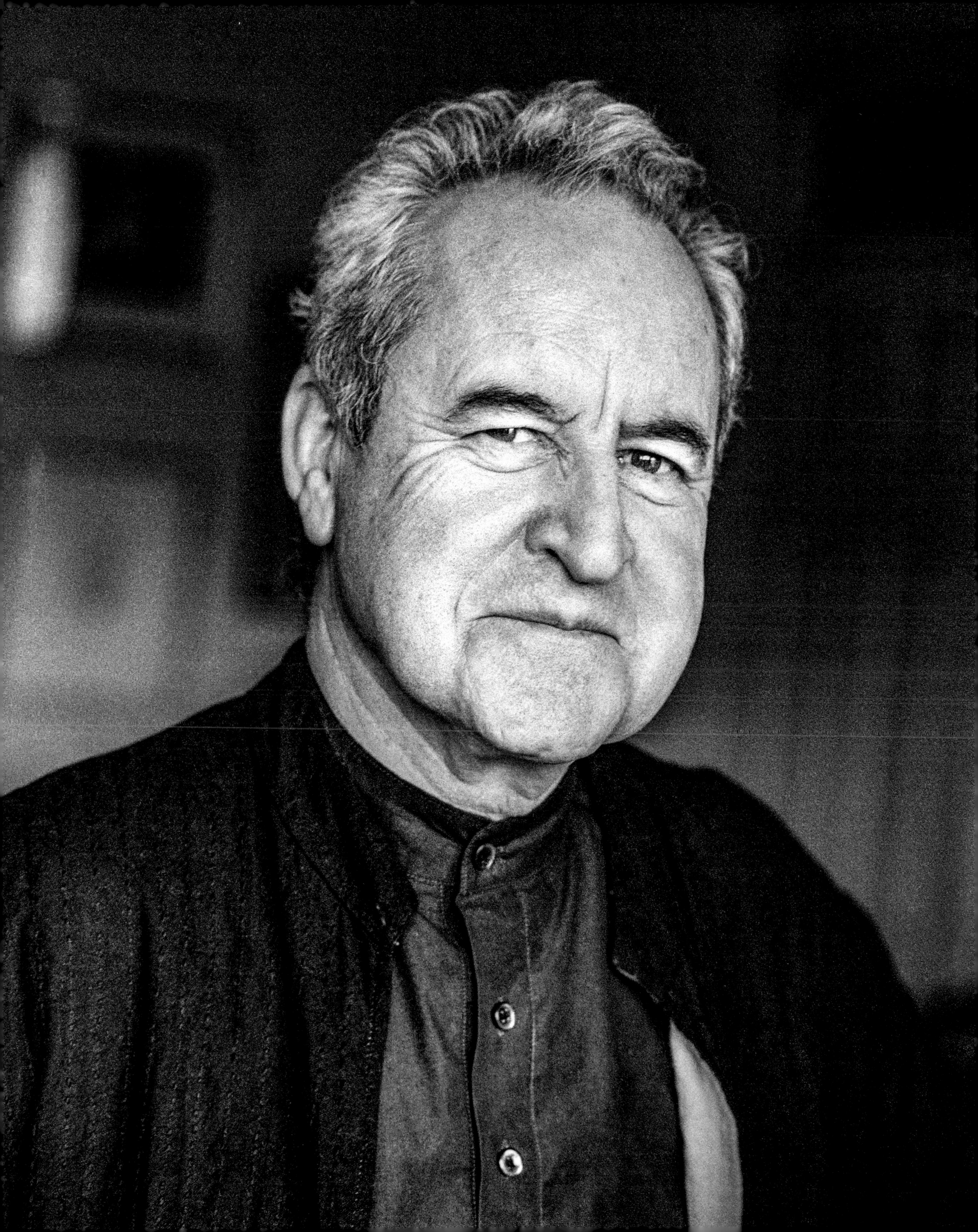

When he left Wexford in his late teens and settled in Dublin, he lived in the old Georgian part of the city, on Upper Mount Street, where I photographed him outside his flat at No. 39. "It's one of the loveliest streets I know anywhere," he said. "I had inherited the lease of a dilapidated flat from an aunt. W. B. Yeats's daughter, Anne Yeats, had her studio on the floor below mine. A nice woman. Life in Dublin in those days was poor, spiritually as well as financially, but it had a certain shabby elegance that is now largely gone."

During my time with Banville, we visited the master bookbinder Tony Cains in his shop nestled under the front stairs of his house in Dublin. Banville selected hand-marbled papers made in the last century by the English firm Cockerell and Son. Cains then bound the sheets into notebooks in which Banville was to handwrite, as he always had, his next novel.

"I handwrite because this gives me the ideal pace. Computers are much too fast. I like to craft a manuscript. My handwriting is vaguely italic. It used to be quite good. Now that I'm old, it's terrible. But I still plough on. I write with a fountain pen, then edit with a computer." (Benjamin Black, however, writes directly on a computer.)

After I left Dublin, I wrote asking Banville if he would order a book from Cains for me. He said, "It is an expensive little volume. Last time round I paid him around three hundred and thirty euros [$382] per book. Do you want to go ahead? It's a lot of money for a blank book . . ."

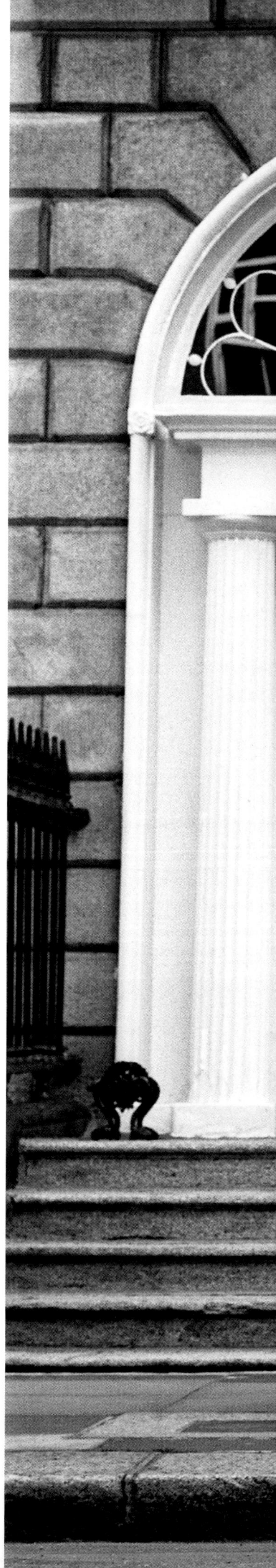

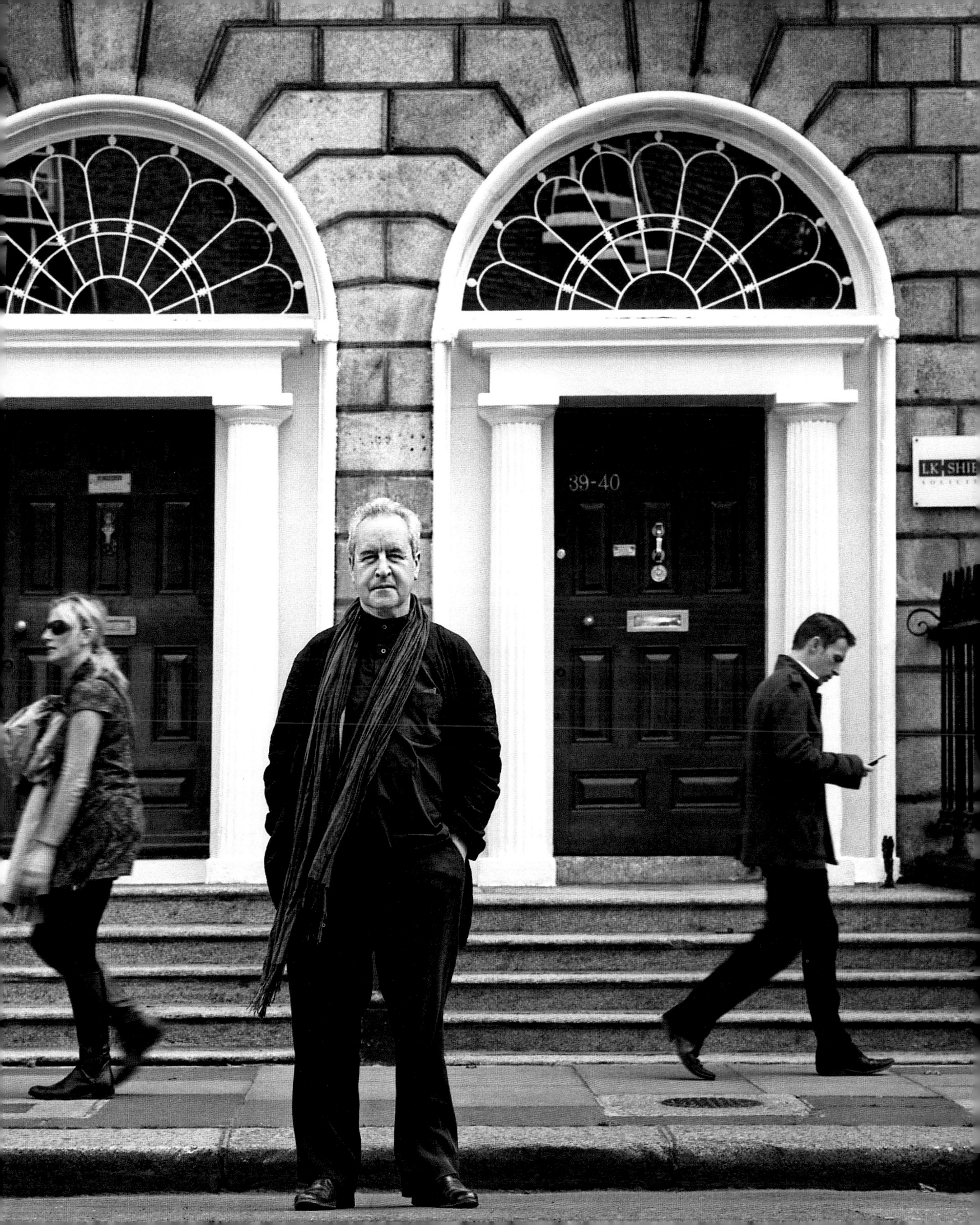
39-40
LK SHIE

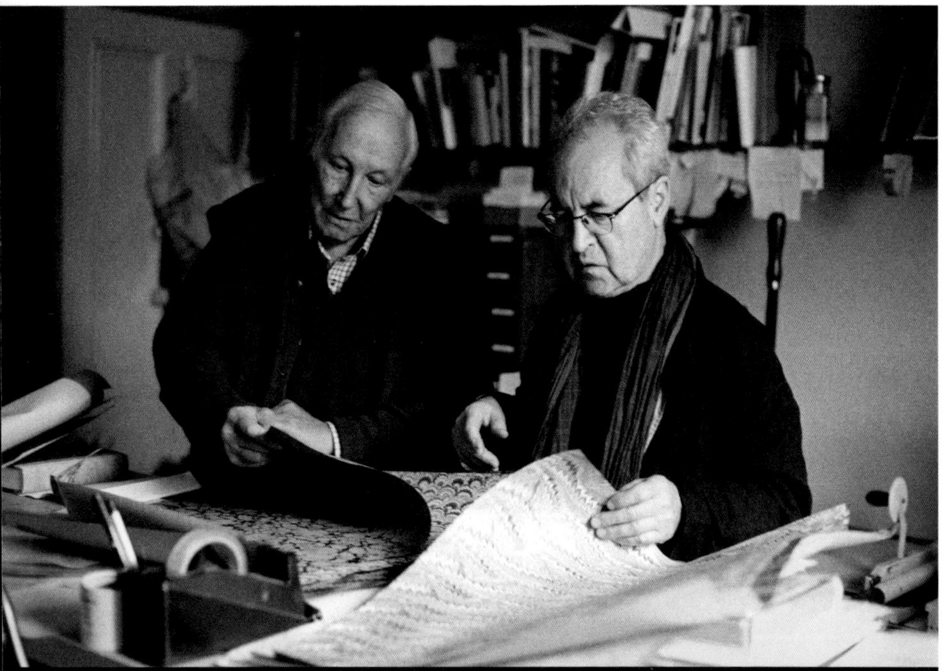

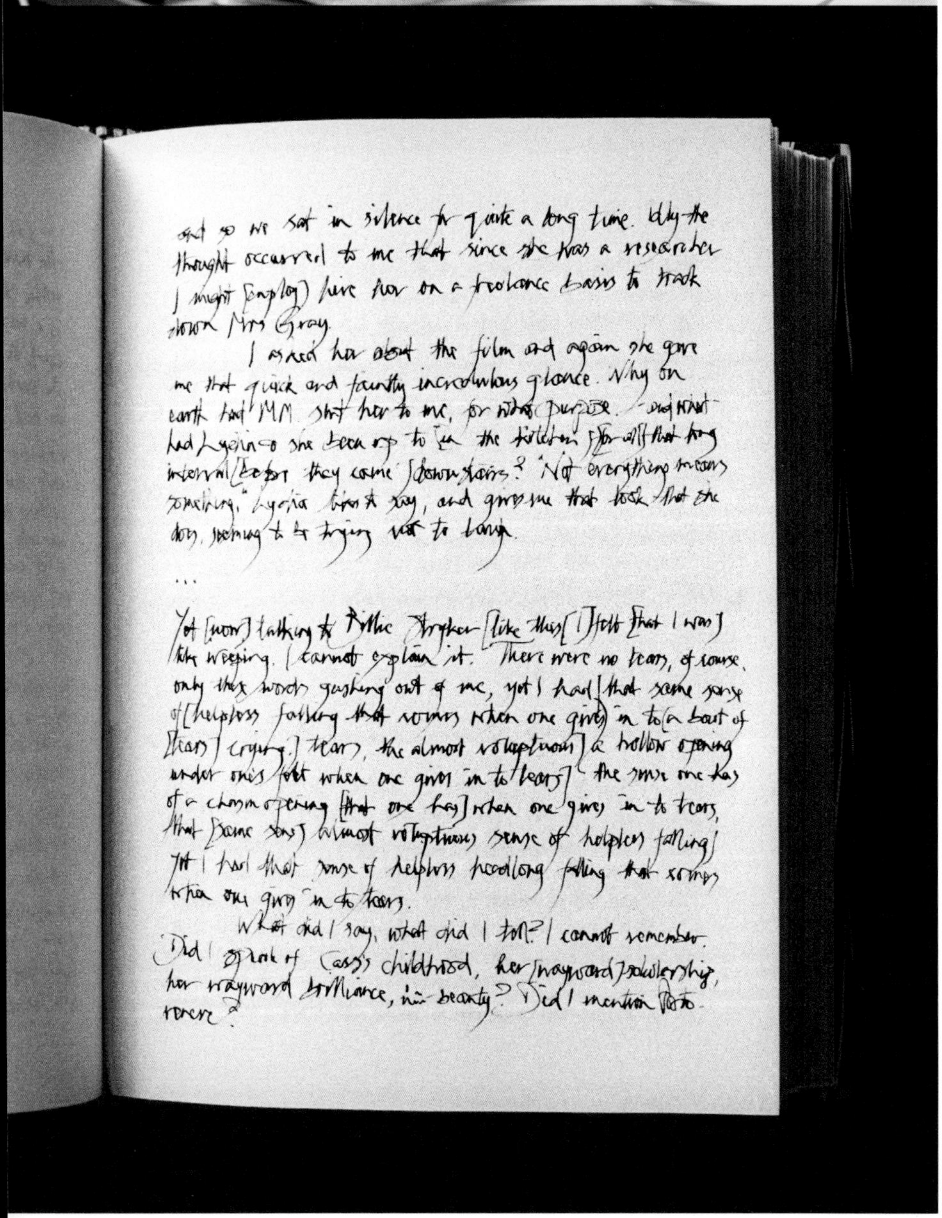

...and so we sat in silence for quite a long time. Idly the thought occurred to me that since she was a researcher I might [employ] hire her on a freelance basis to track down Mrs Gray.

I asked her about the film and again she gave me that quick and faintly incredulous glance. Why on earth had MM sent her to me, for what purpose. —and what had [going] so she been up to [in] the [kitchen] [for all that long interval before they came] downstairs? 'Not everything means something,' Lydia [burst] say, and gives me that look that she does, meaning to to trying not to laugh.

...

Yet [now] talking to [Billie Stryker] [like this] [I] felt [that I was] like weeping. I cannot explain it. There were no tears, of course, only these words gushing out of me, yet I had [that same sense of [helpless falling that comes when one gives in to [a bout of [tears] crying] tears, the almost voluptuous] a hollow opening under one's feet when one gives in to tears]—the sense one has of a chasm opening [that one has] when one gives in to tears, that [same sort] almost voluptuous sense of helpless falling] yet I had that sense of helpless headlong falling that comes when one gives in to tears.

What did I say, what did I tell? I cannot remember. Did I speak of Cass's childhood, her [wayward] scholarship, her wayward brilliance, her beauty? Did I mention Porto-venere?

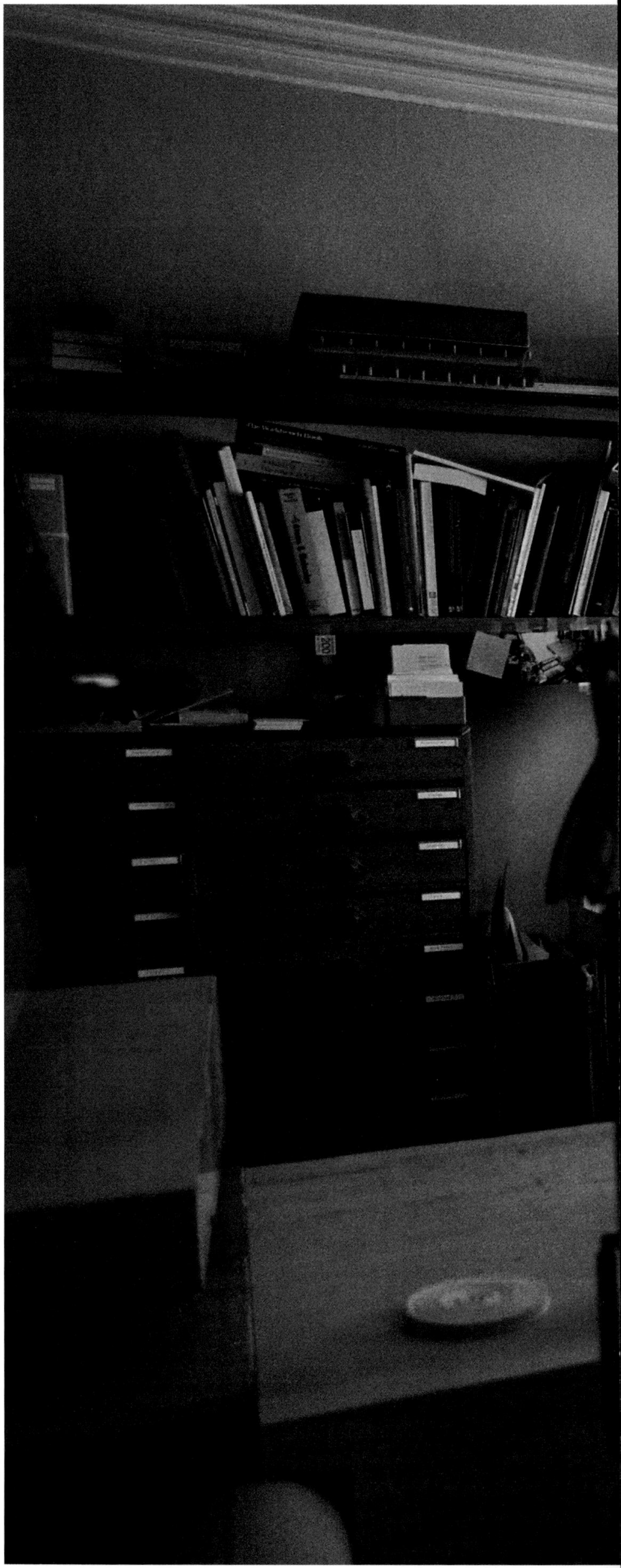

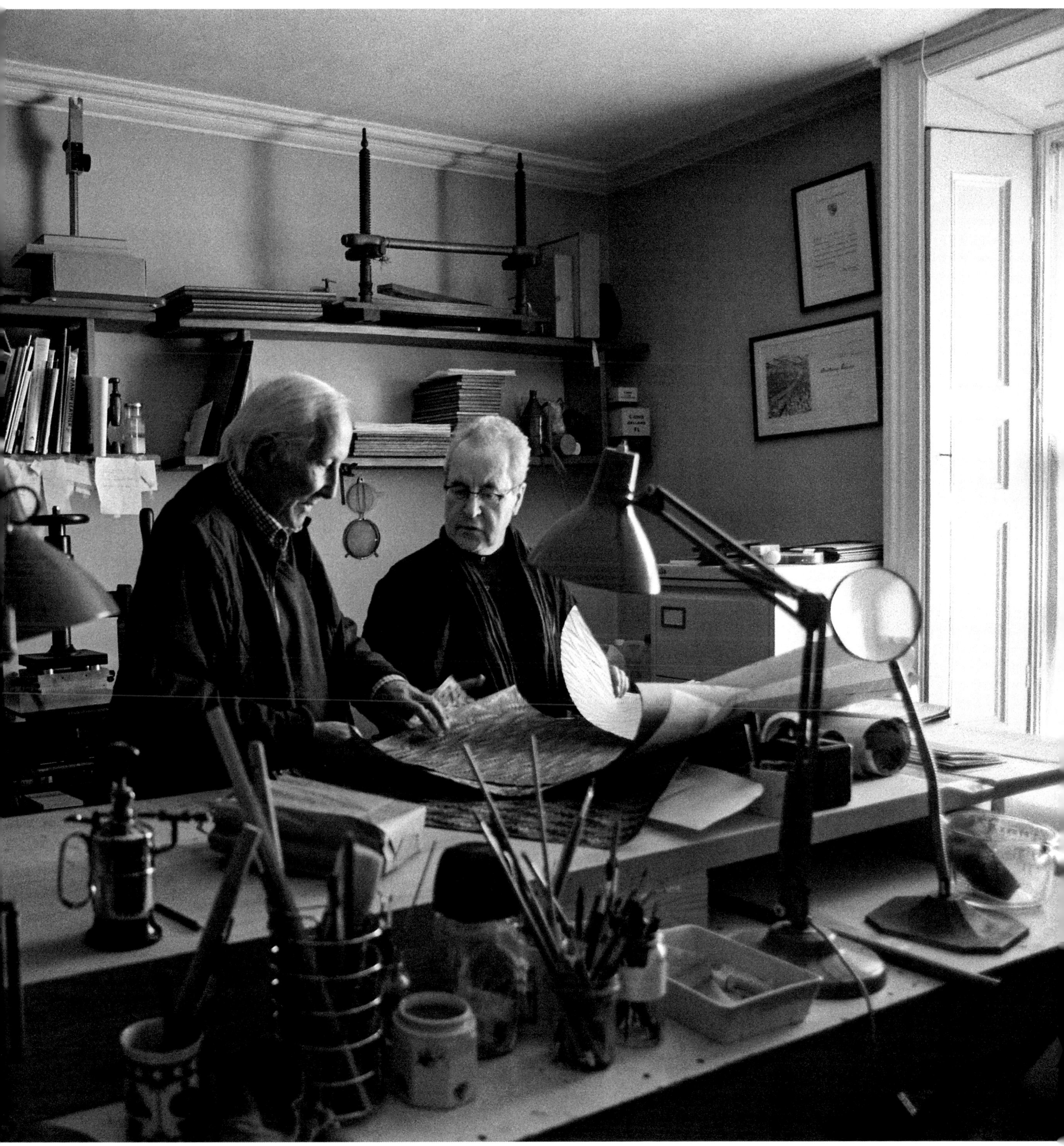

Penelope Lively

English (b. 1933)

Photographed in London, England, April 2015

Penelope Lively was born in Cairo and lived there with her English parents until she was twelve. When she was a young mother with a boy and a girl, she began writing for children. After several years, she switched to adult fiction. Impressively prolific, she has now been writing for over fifty years.

I met Lively at her elegant house on Gibson Square in the Islington neighborhood of London. When I asked her about several objects in the house, she pointed to a bronze Egyptian cat, and told me it was a copy of an ancient one in the British Museum. "It has special significance for me because it was collected by an English Orientalist known as Gayer-Anderson Pasha, who had been a friend of my grandmother's. Family legend has it that before donating it to the museum, he lent it to her and it sat for a while in the middle of her dining table."

Another childhood memory accompanied a mother-of-pearl Bible, "bought for me by Lucy, my nanny, in Jerusalem in 1942. We had gone from Egypt to Palestine (as it was then) when Erwin Rommel's army was seventy miles from Cairo." A fragment of twelfth-century Islamic pottery was given to Lively by an archeologist friend, who found it at Fustat, the first and earliest site in Cairo, now a rubbish tip.

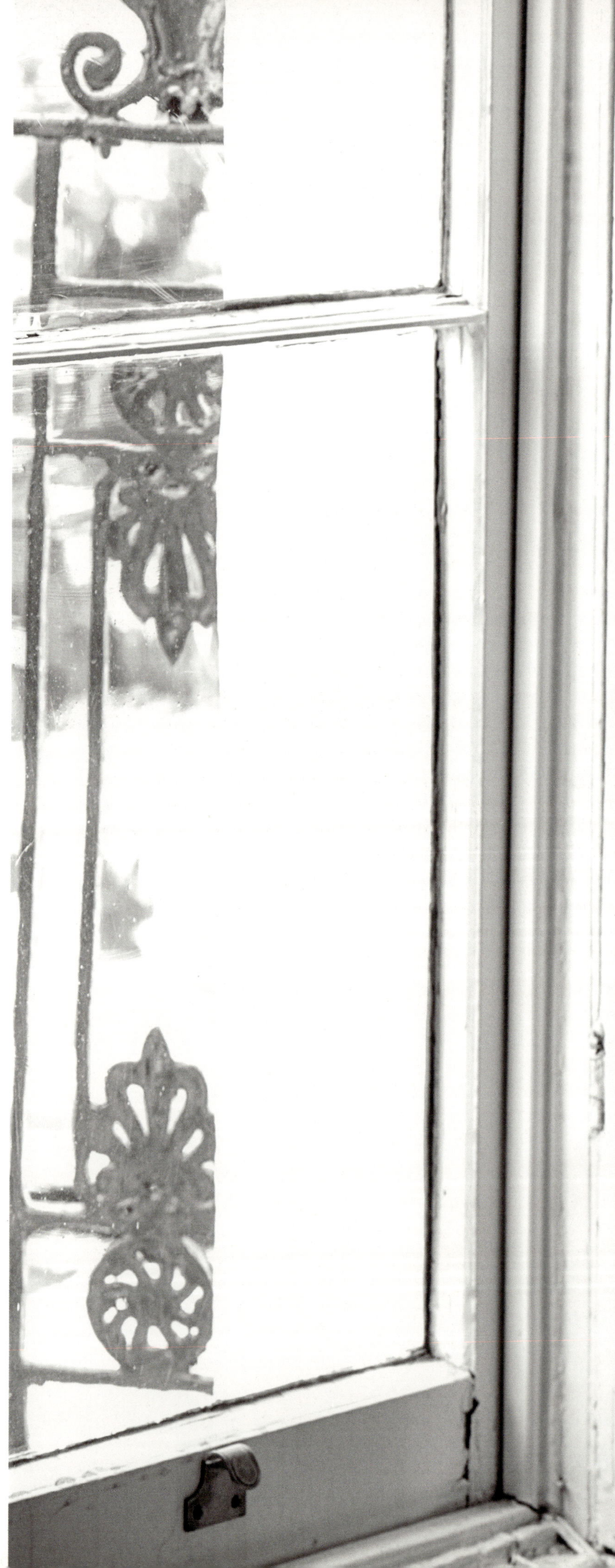

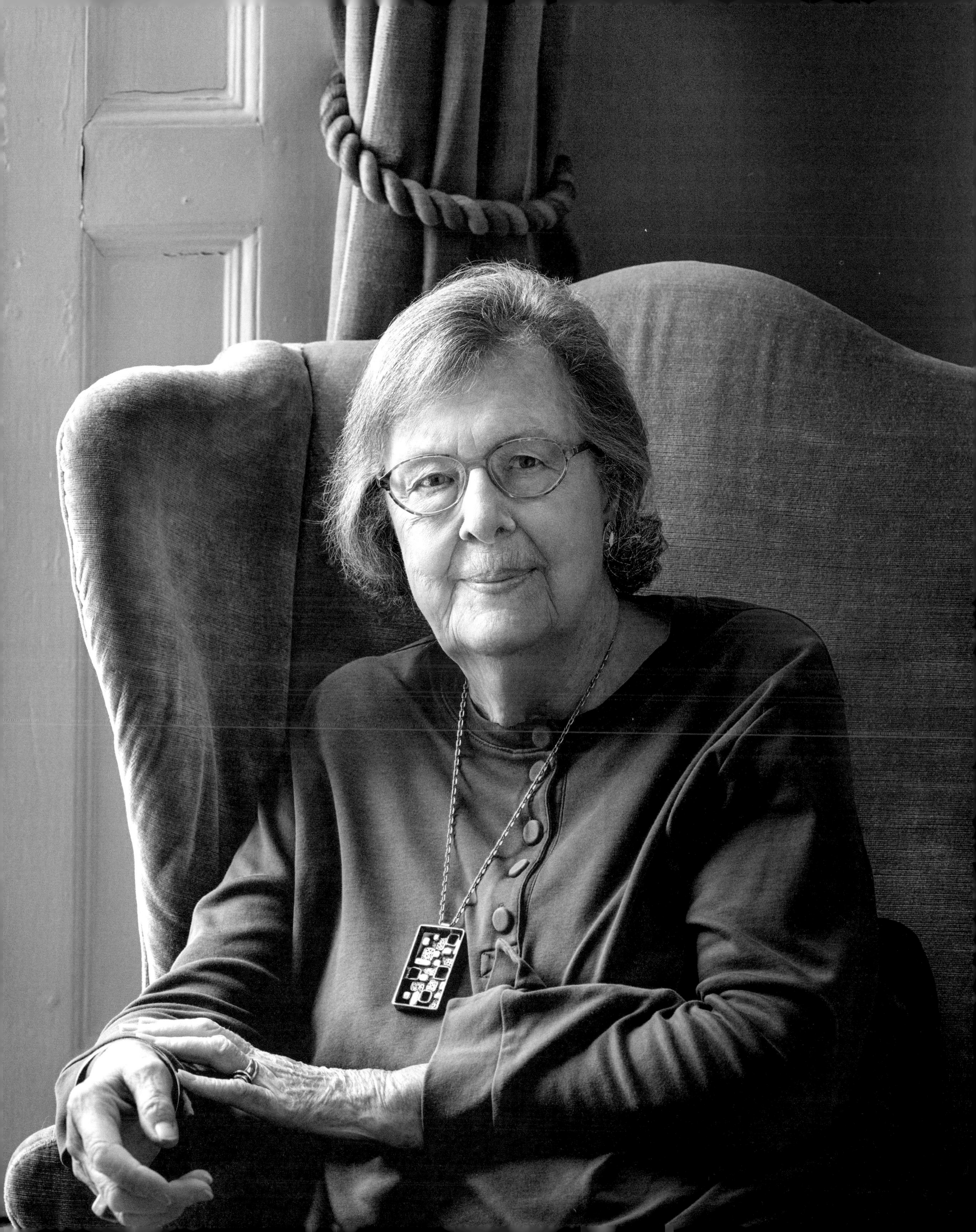

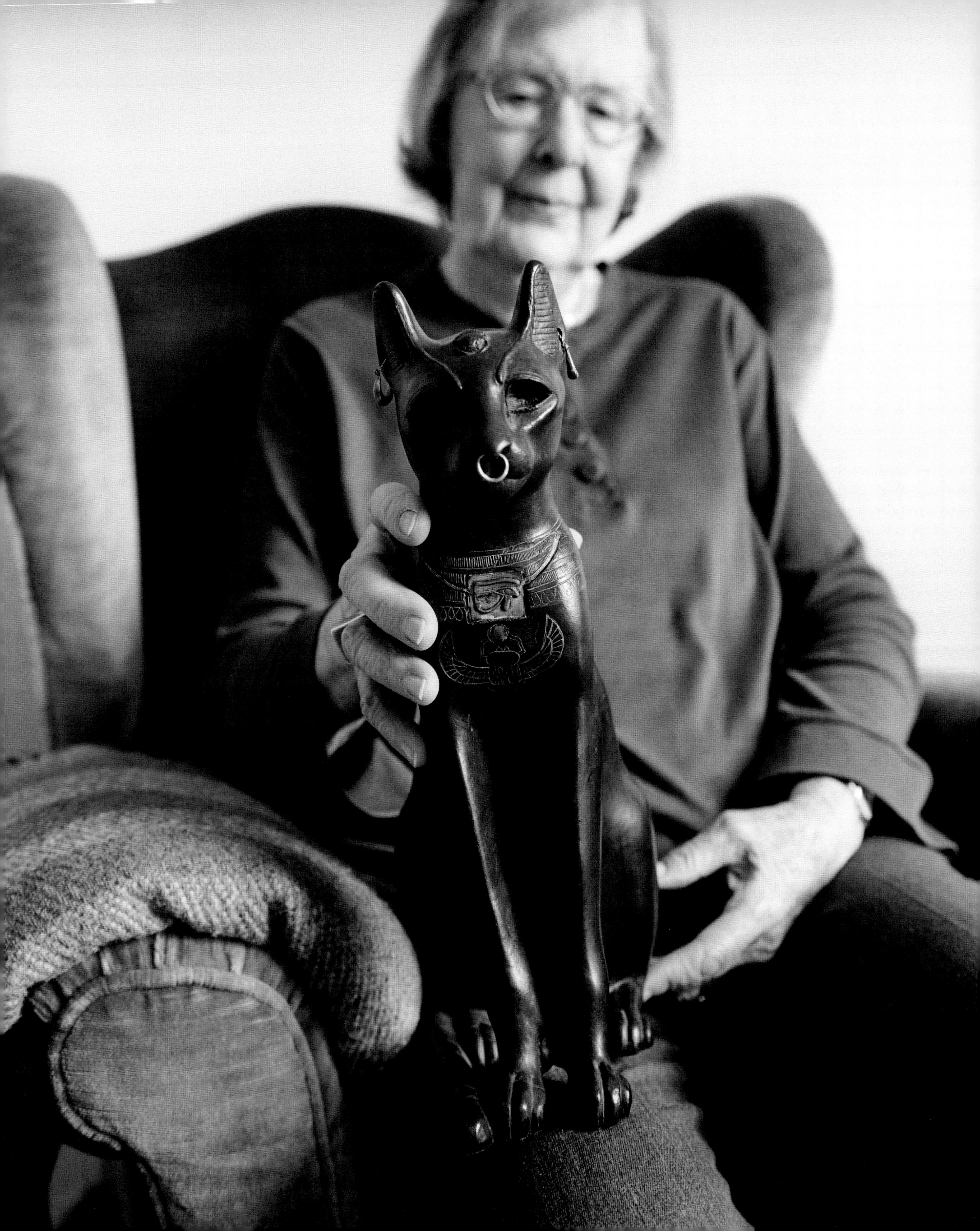

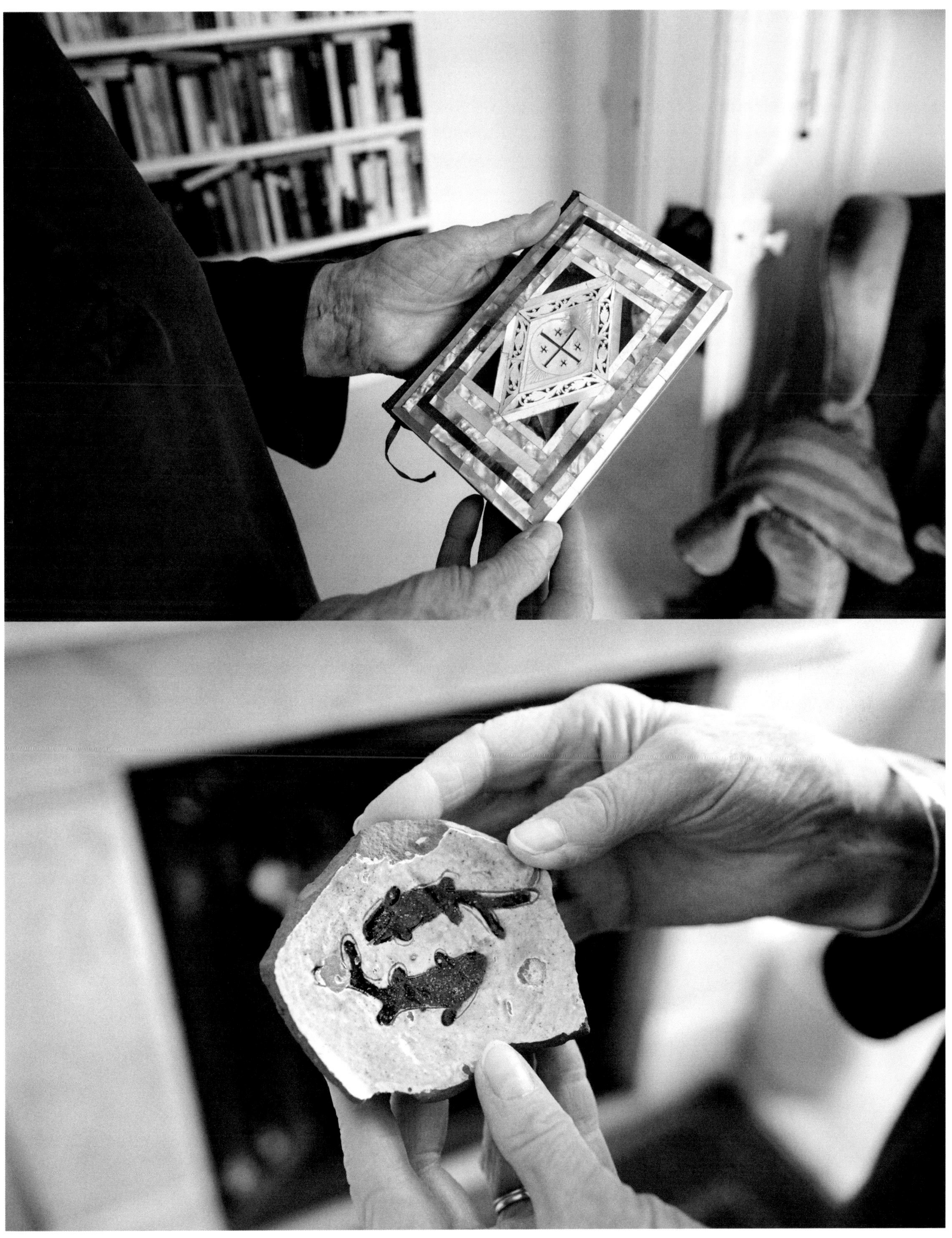

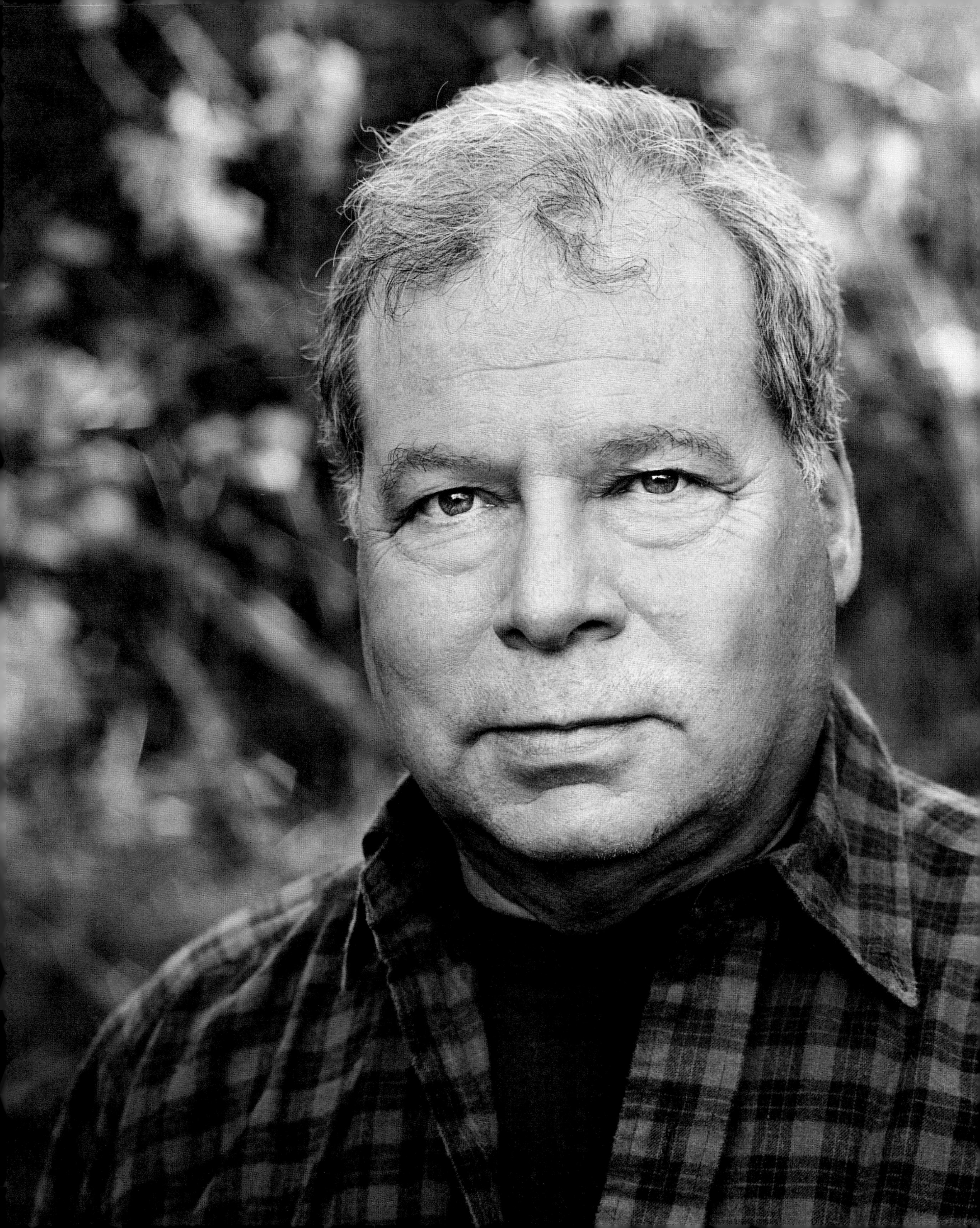

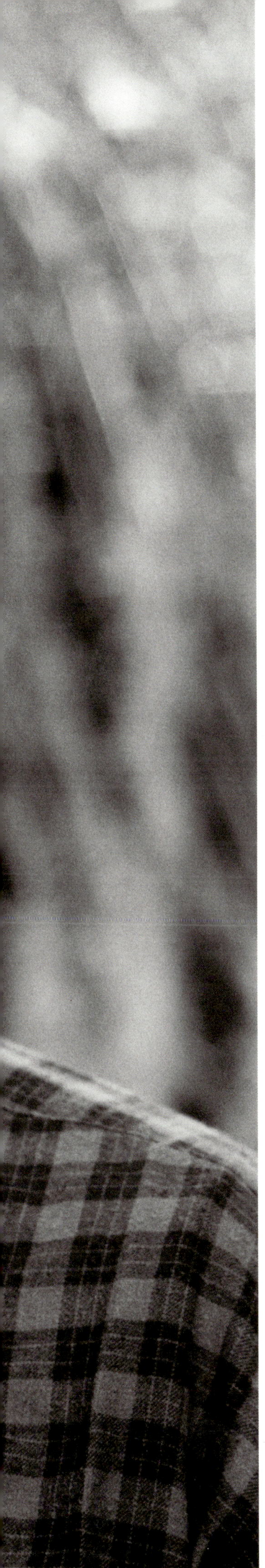

August Kleinzahler

American (b. 1949)

Photographed in San Francisco, California, January 2010

The poet August Kleinzahler lives in a modest, comfortably furnished apartment overlooking a loosely tended garden in San Francisco. "I am nothing if not a poet of place. I'm pretty much Velcroed here," he told me. One of these places is this quiet oasis on the edge of Haight-Ashbury; the other is room 1020 of a Sheraton in Weehawken, New Jersey, where Kleinzahler can look across the Hudson River at the Manhattan skyline. The view from this room is similar to the one from his childhood house on top of the Palisades in Fort Lee, where he grew up in the 1950s, when mobsters still lived there.

Kleinzahler is an easy, charming conversationalist, although he claims to be "an isolato." "I detest literary company," he told me. "I probably belong in a lighthouse by myself on the coast of Newfoundland." I caught him between marriages, which he said "is always an unstable place."

On the sofa in his living room in the Haight, Kleinzahler has tried to create an environment receptive to inspiration. "Poems come," he told me, "always in different ways, but unfailingly for the past fifty years or so, somewhat in the manner of a muse's invitation. It still seems to me a marvel, something quite beyond my will, like an unexpected romantic infatuation."

Amoeba Music has been one of the great boons of Kleinzahler's life in the Haight. He said an ex-wife once told him he'd have no life at all if it weren't for Amoeba, but he added, "I don't think my ardor for the place or my once almost daily attendance for the past twenty-five years has been my sole raison d'être."

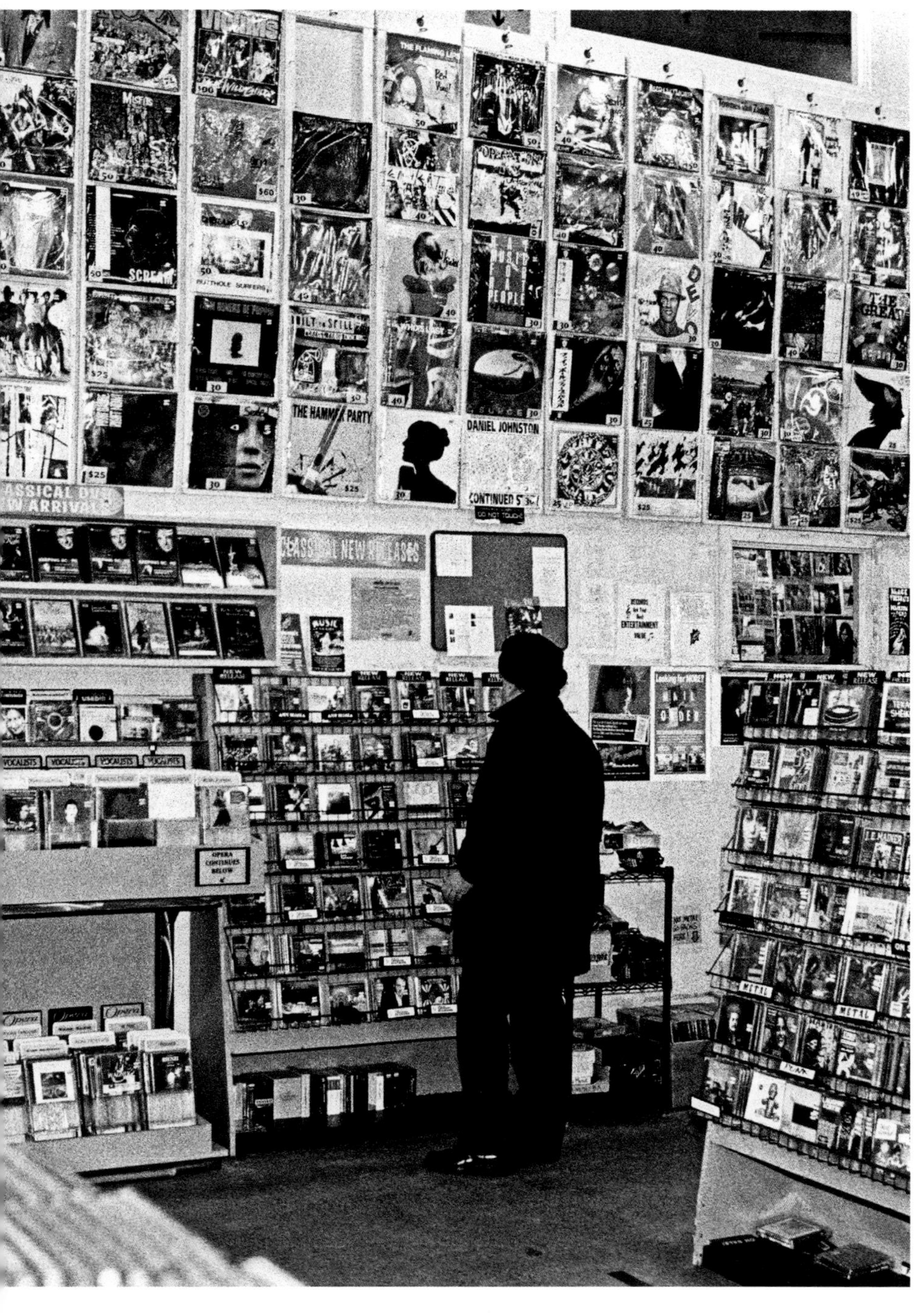

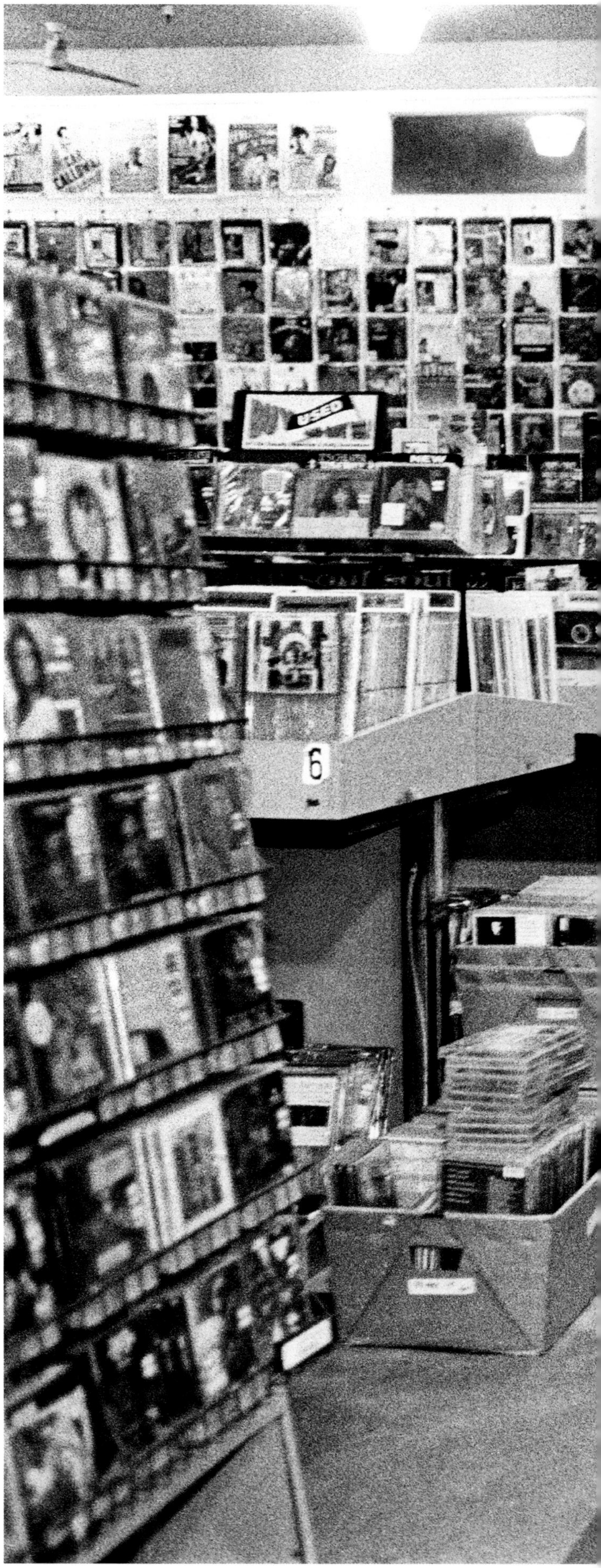

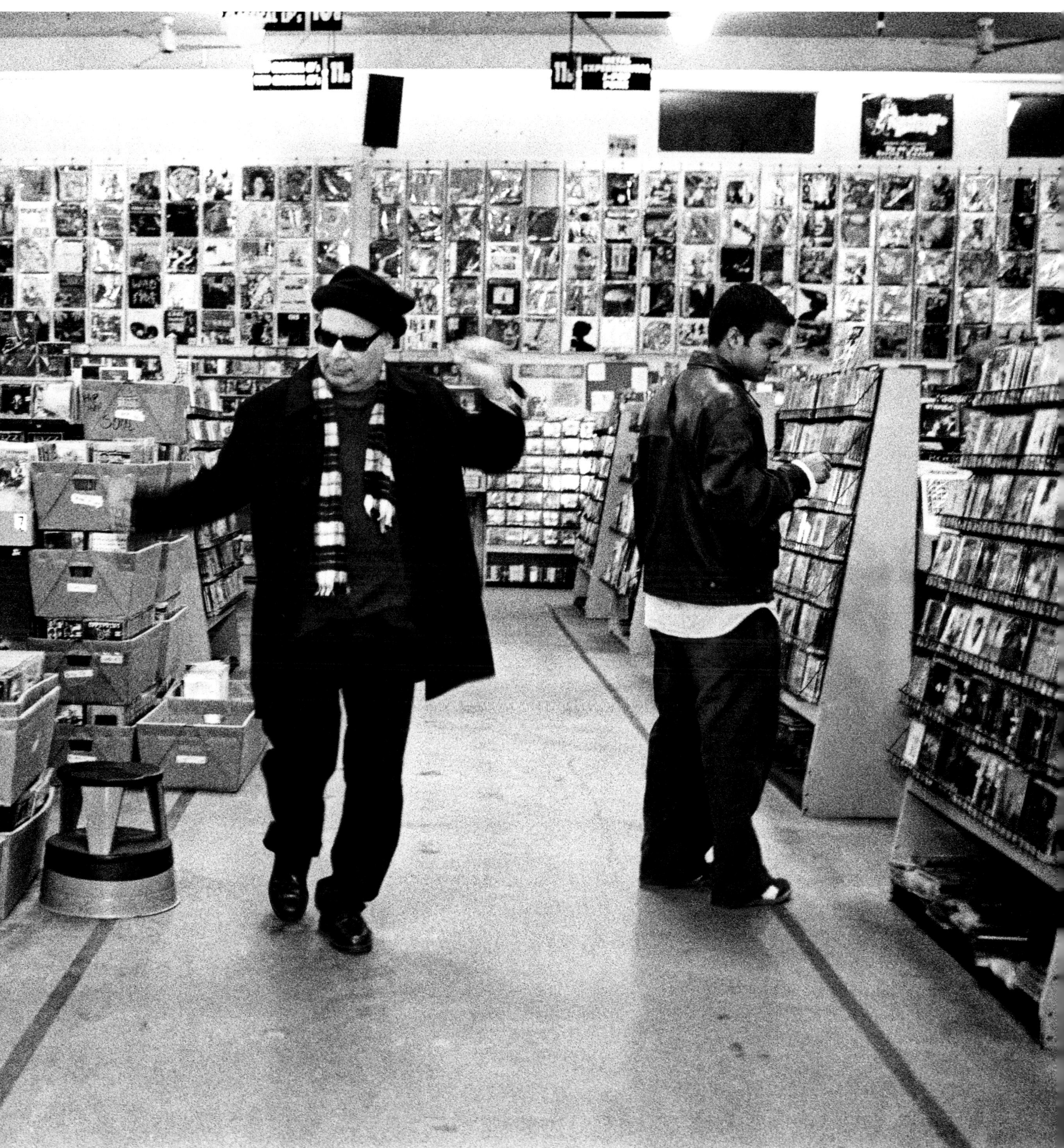

Tom Stoppard

English (b. 1937)

Photographed in London, England, April 2015

For various reasons, Tom Stoppard or I had postponed the shoot several times in the previous ten months. Finally, on a late afternoon in London, we met on the sidewalk in Covent Garden.

But Stoppard was short of time. He planned to meet his family for dinner at a restaurant nearby, and leave for New York early the next morning. "Can you do it in fifteen minutes?" I said that I could.

The streets were jammed with tourists and people leaving work. I suggested taking the pictures inside the restaurant, in a quiet corner. But Stoppard didn't want to cause a disturbance among the diners. My assistant, Andrew Mitchell, and I spent seven tense minutes on the streets searching for a calm spot. At the eighth minute, Andrew found an open arcade with shade and ideal late-afternoon light. Standing directly in front of the camera, Stoppard said, "How do you want me . . . serious, smiling, what?" I took one look through the lens. "You are perfect," I said.

And in four minutes we were done. A strong, unsparing portrait, with three minutes to spare.

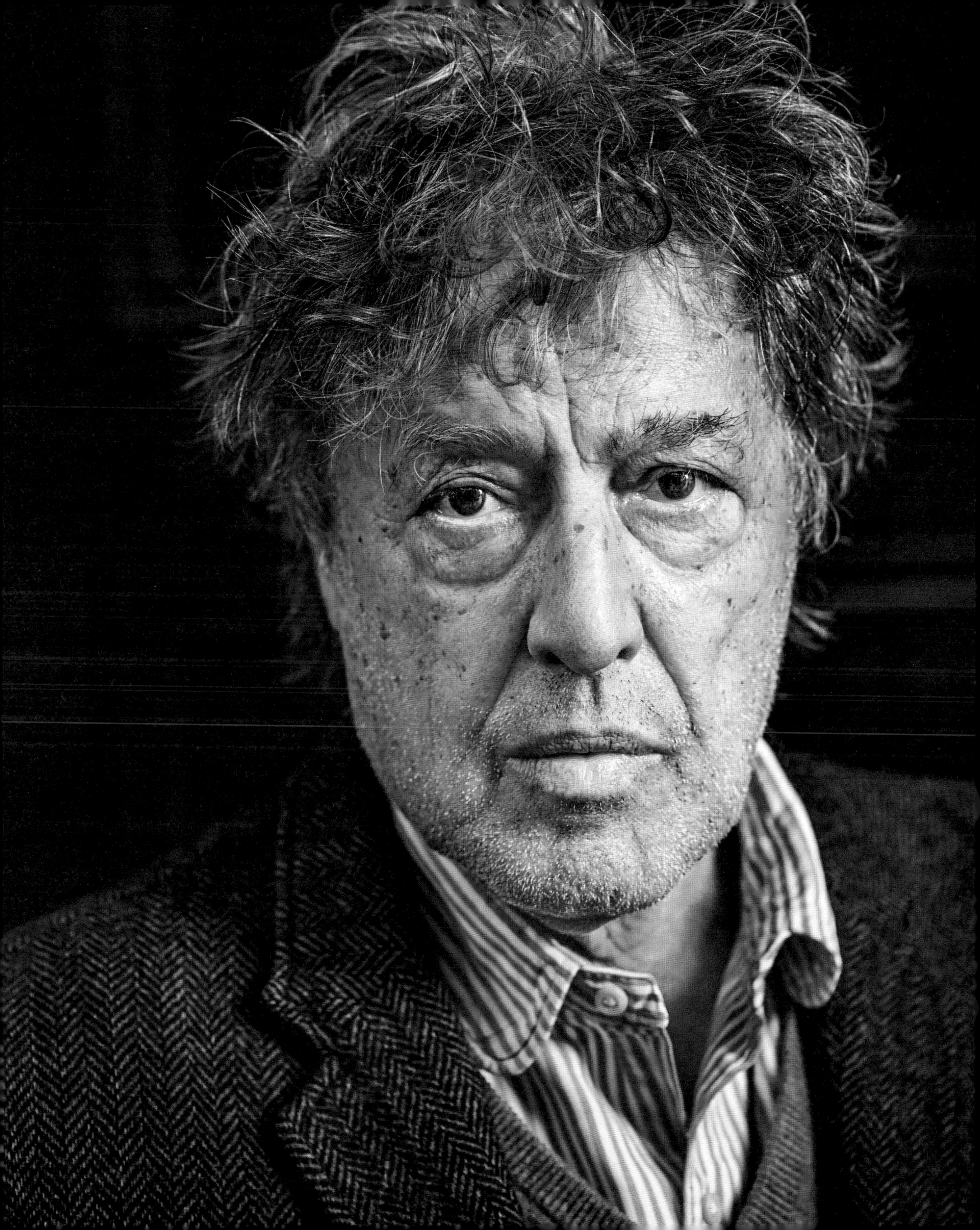

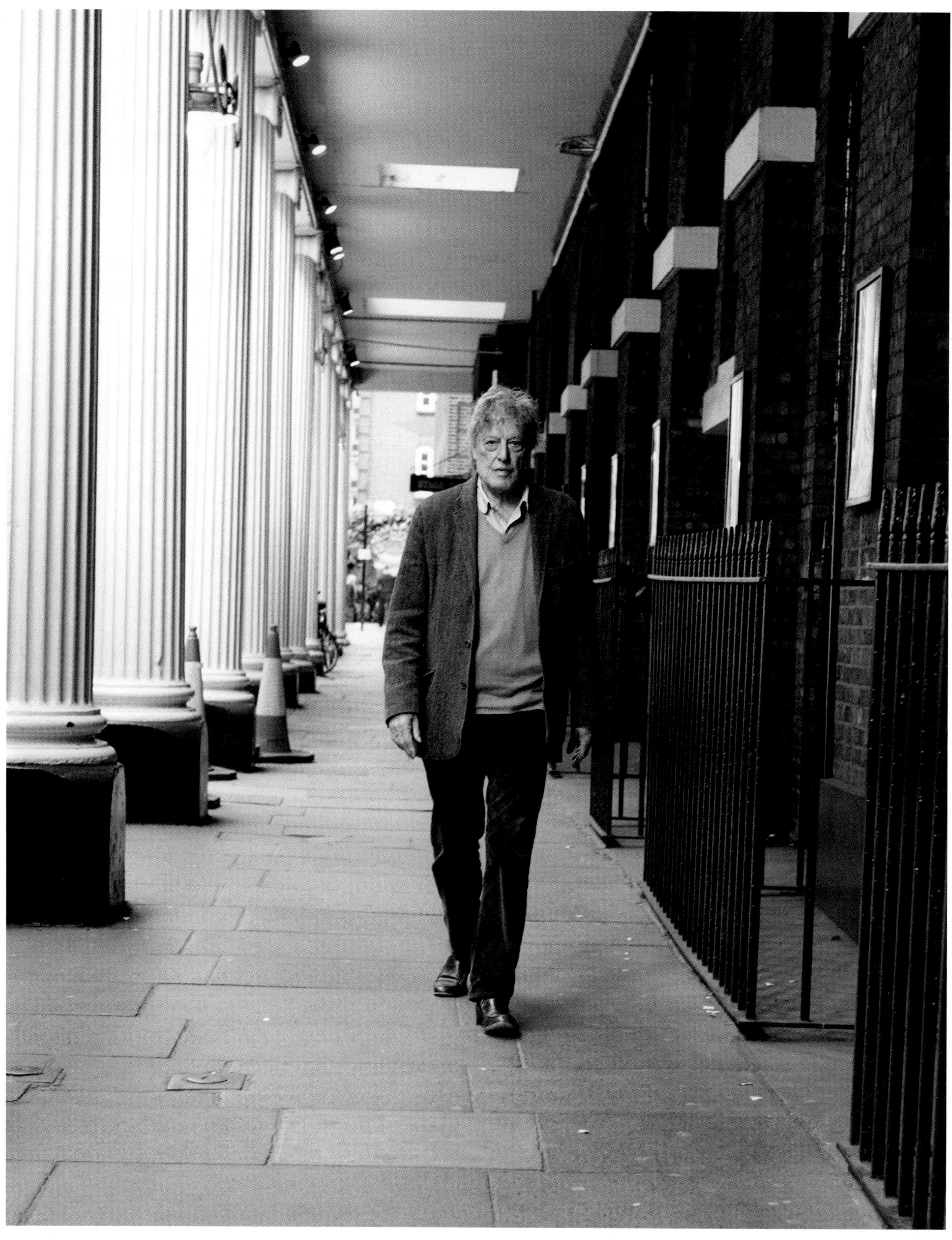

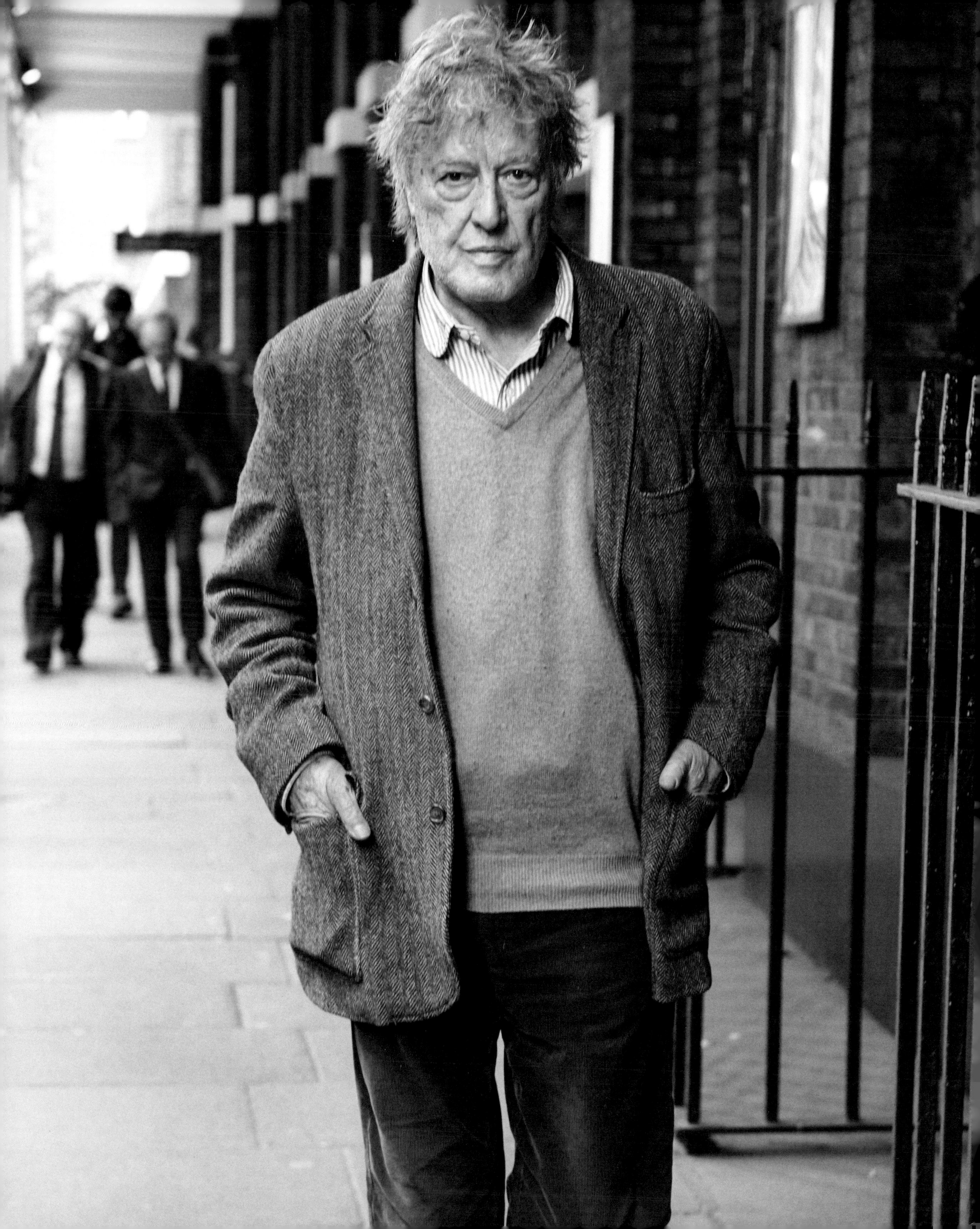

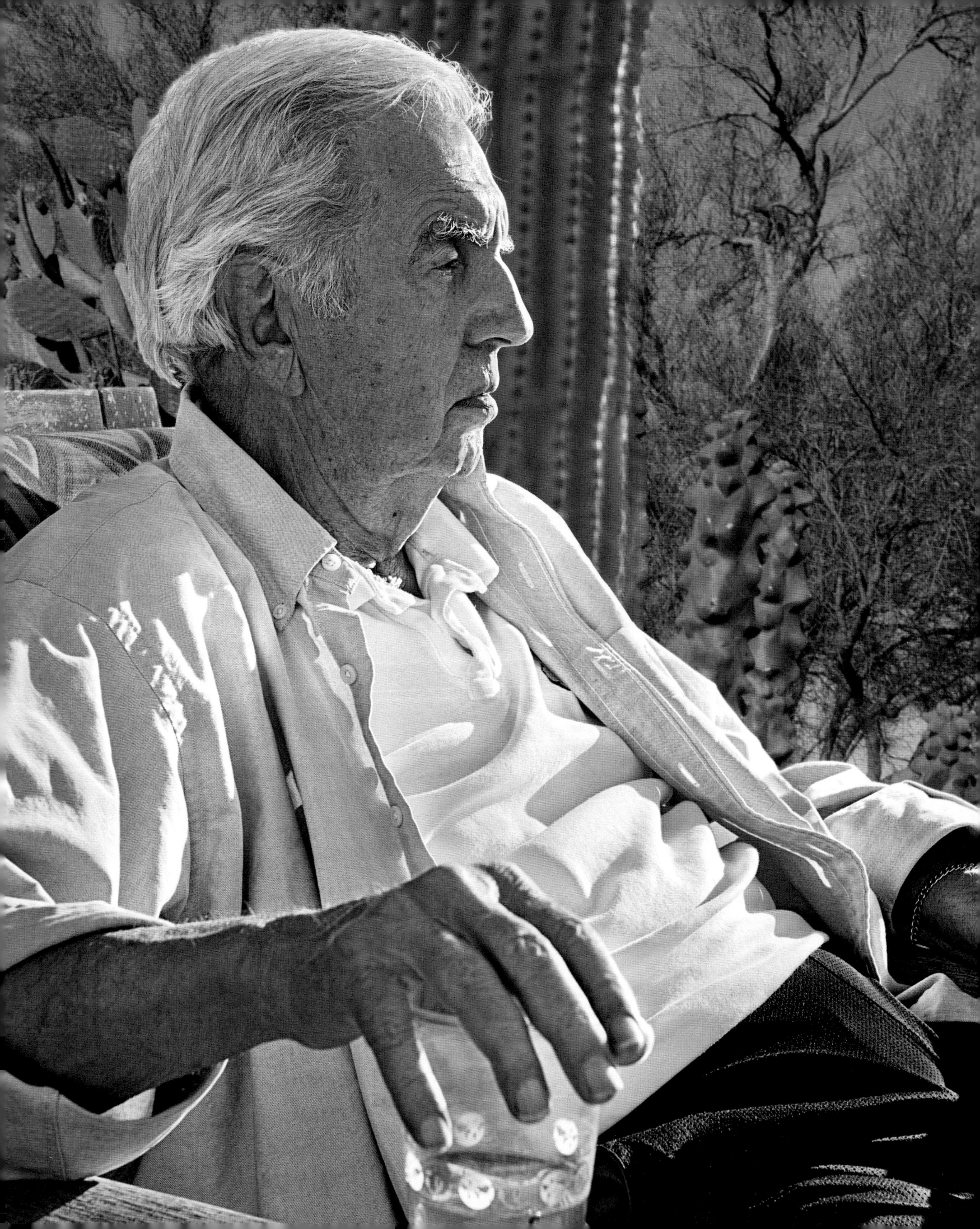

Larry McMurtry

American (1936–2021)

Photographed in Tucson, Arizona, May 2016

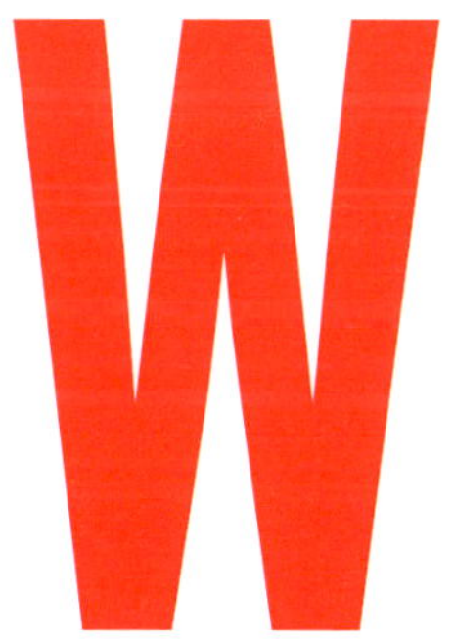

When I first wrote to Larry McMurtry to ask if I might photograph him for this book, he immediately wrote back:

> Dear Laura,
> I'm sorry to be disobliging but I don't want to be photographed. I'm afraid it's as simple as that.
> Best, L

As our paths crossed over the years, McMurtry's resistance began to weaken, until, at eighty, he agreed. I saw him in Tucson, where he lived at the time in a modest Territorial Style house owned by his longtime friend and writing partner, Diana Ossana.

In 2011, McMurtry married Norma Faye Kesey, the widow of his old friend Ken Kesey. And in an unusual arrangement, Larry and Faye moved in with Diana, her six dogs, and one rescue rabbit.

Amid the comfort and organized clutter of a busy house, they wrote, cooked meals, and entertained family and friends. The arid ground outside was landscaped with barrel cacti, native plants, and that ubiquitous symbol of the southwest, ceramic Mexicans resting after a hard day's work. These six sombreroed figures are descendants of drawings by Diego Rivera as an homage to Mexican laborers.

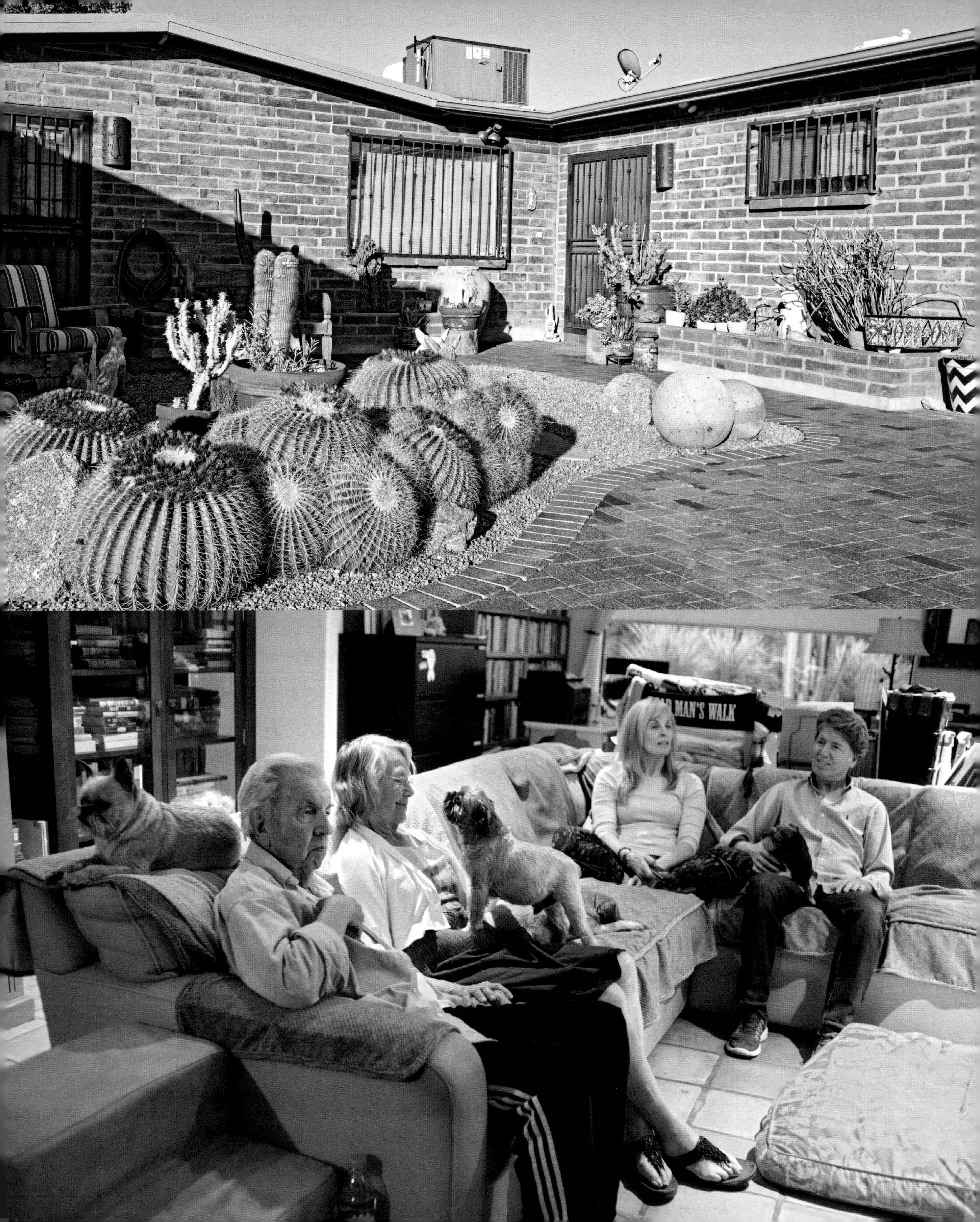

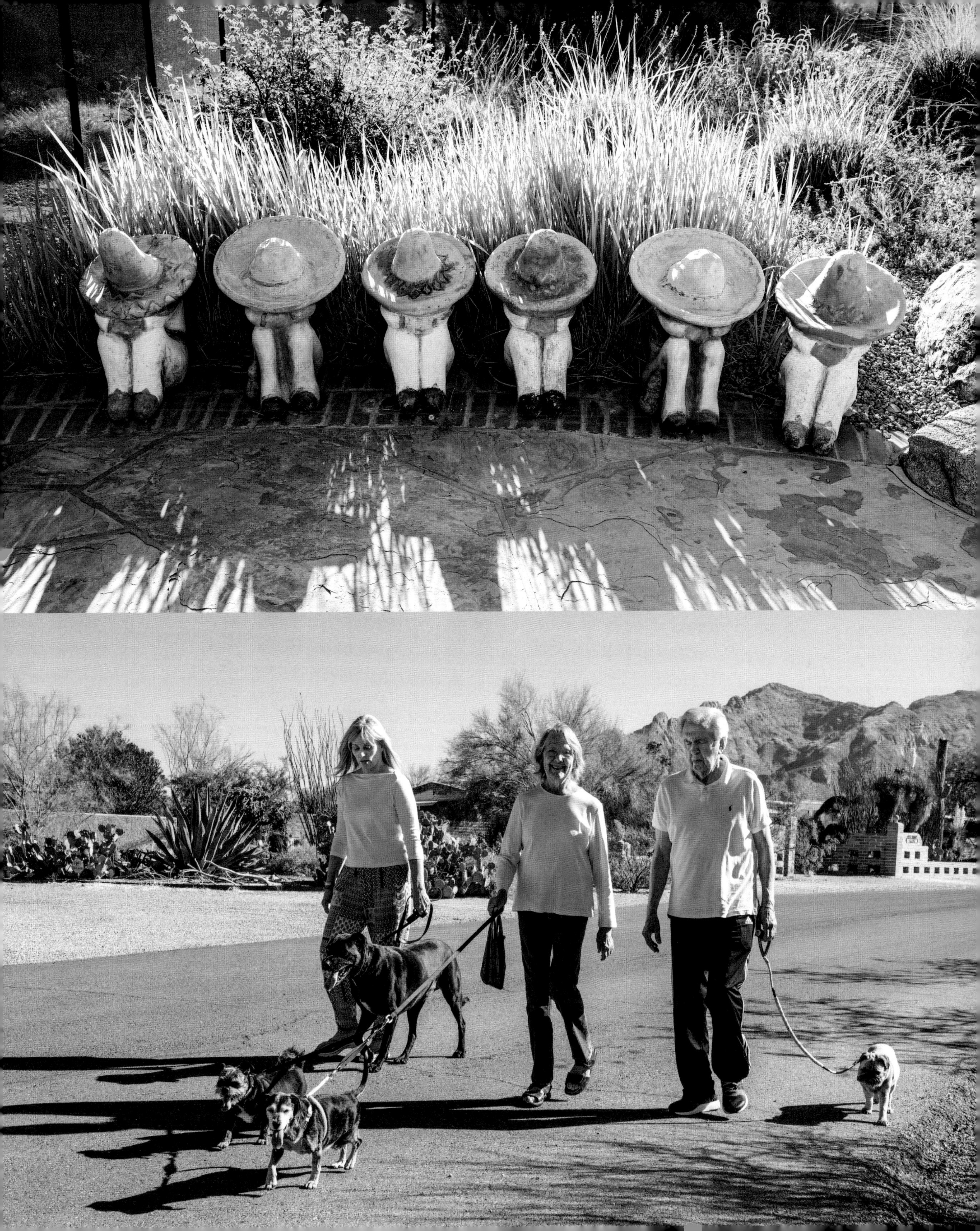

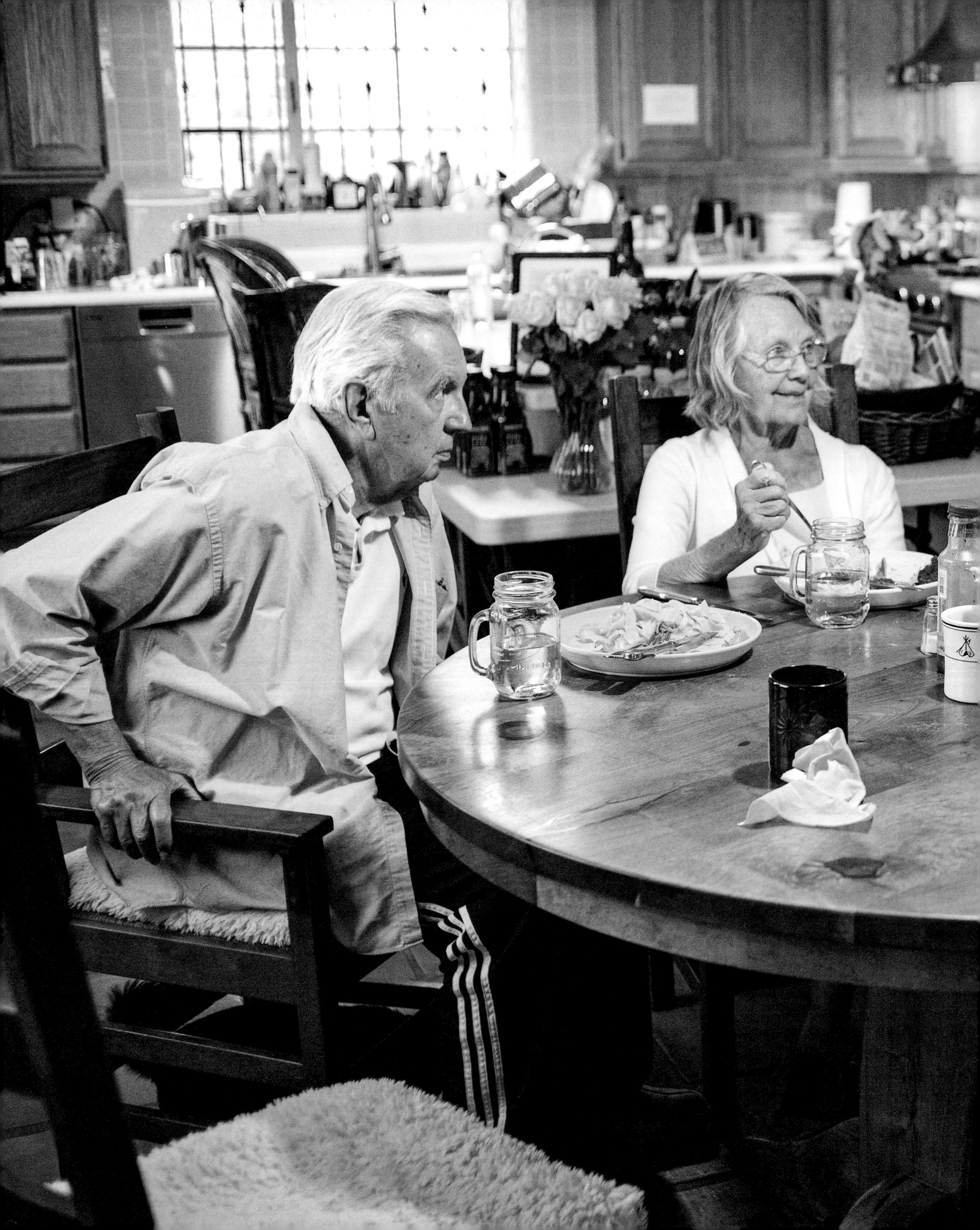

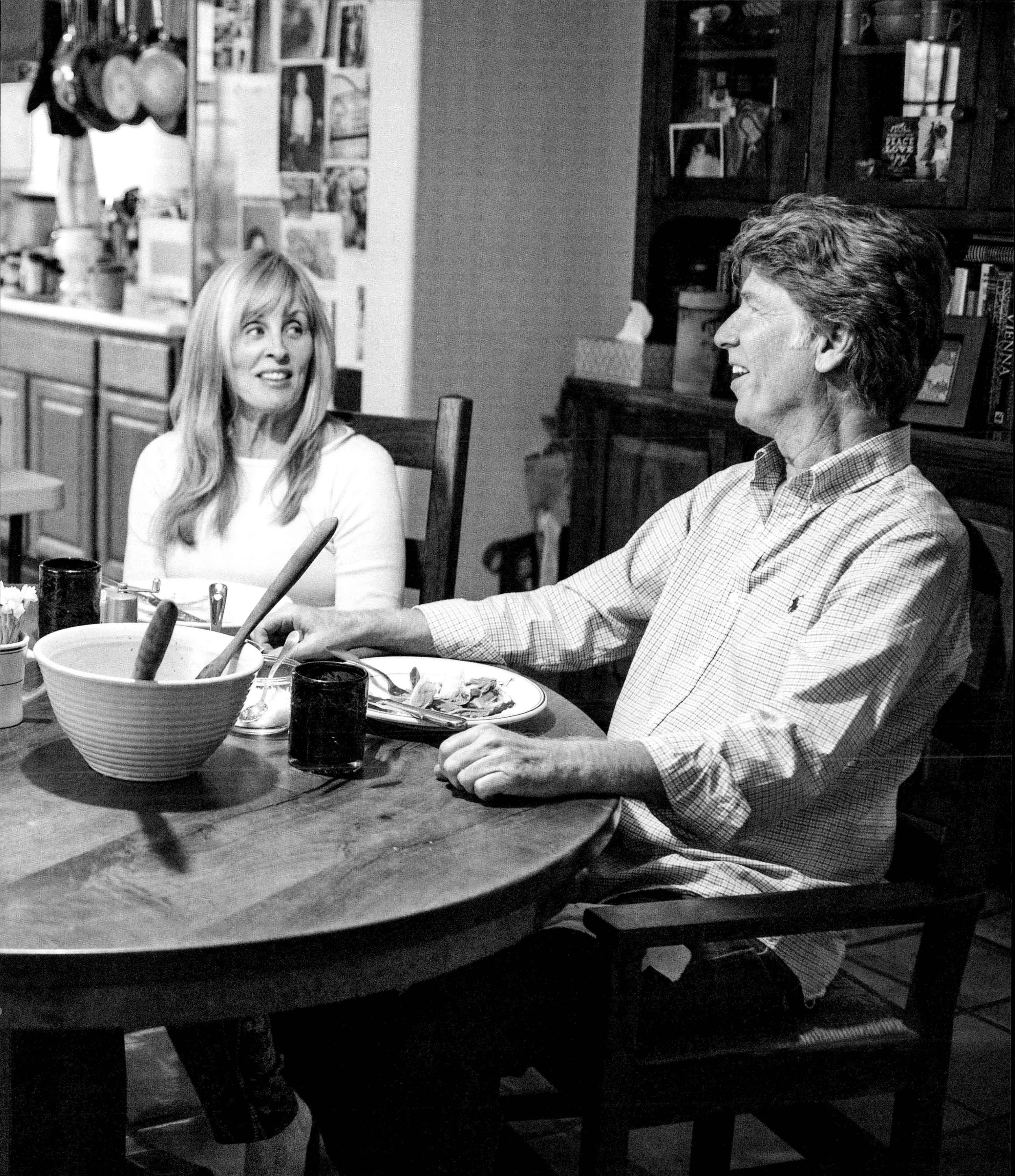

J. M. Coetzee

South African (b. 1940)

Photographed in Vienna, Austria, March 2019

As a teenager, the Nobel Prize–winning novelist J. M. Coetzee had been drawn to photography, as I was, by the work of Henri Cartier-Bresson and other *Life* magazine photographers. He set up a darkroom at his home in Cape Town, South Africa, and photographed the people around him—his mother, his father, farm workers, Rugby-playing schoolmates.

In planning a shoot with a writer, I always enjoyed the brief back-and-forth messages. Following a storm, I wrote to Coetzee, "I couldn't send an email because we were without power. A tornado came through." He replied: "The tornado in Dallas didn't feature on the international news. Maybe future extreme weather events will have to be extremely extreme before they will qualify."

When I first approached Coetzee, he said that "traveling thousands of miles to snap a photograph" was illogical to him. Several months later, when he learned he would be traveling from his home in Adelaide, Australia, to Europe for a literary get-together, he seemed relieved to write: "Vienna may be a more convenient locale for you than Adelaide."

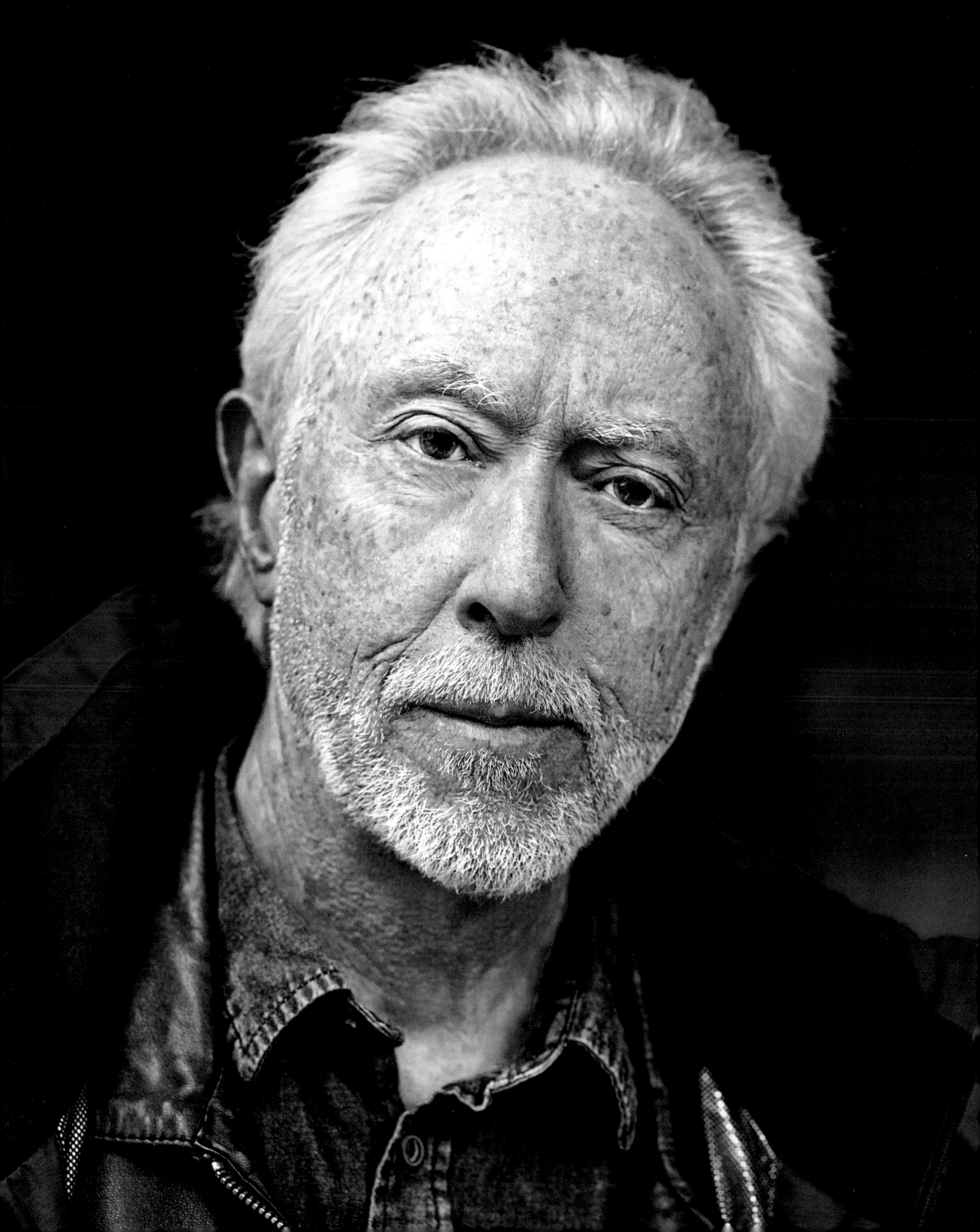

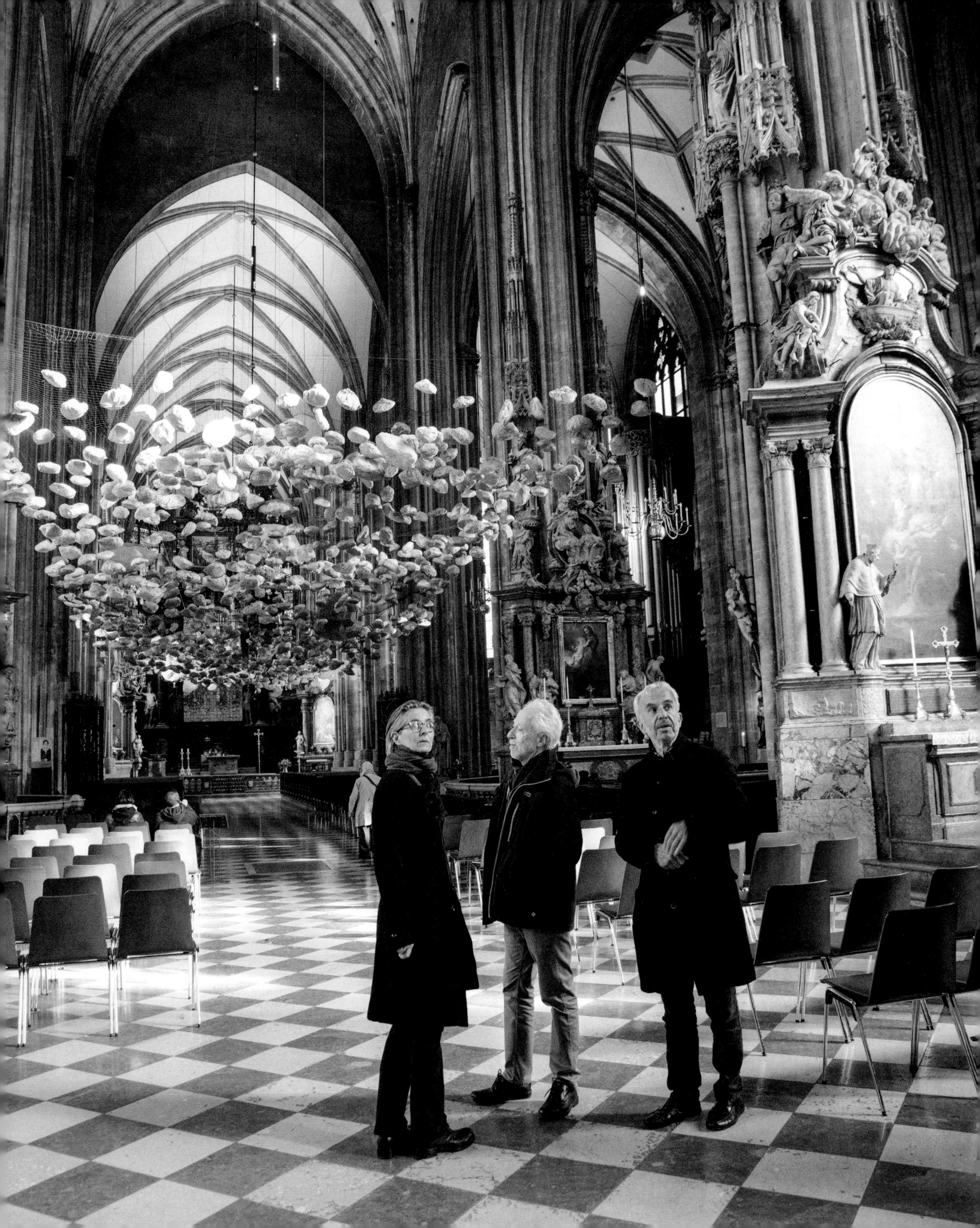

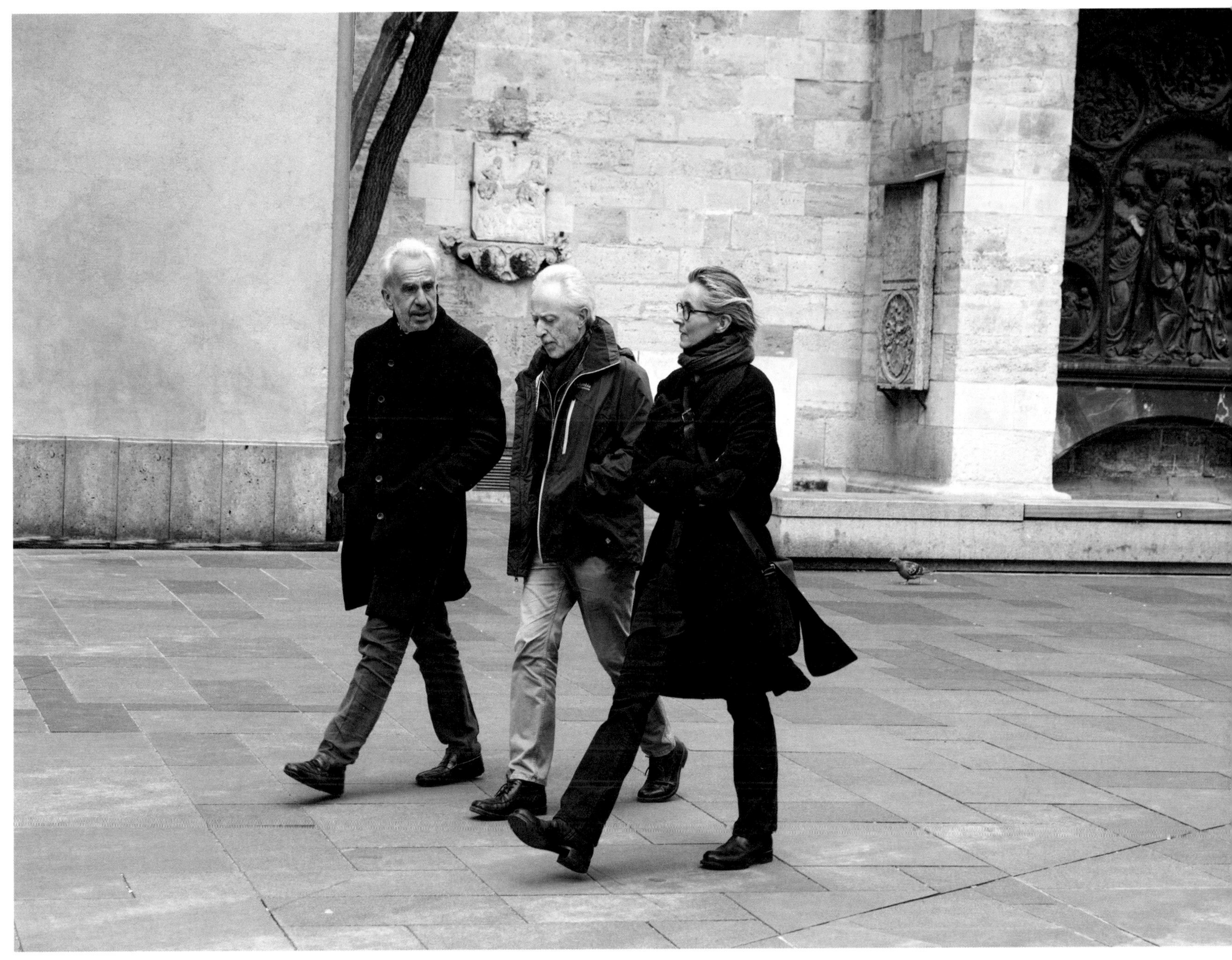

When we met, and found that we shared an early, persistent interest in photography, I realized what helped make Coetzee such a good subject. In front of the camera, he was cooperative, and without self-consciousness, positioning himself in crowded spaces in ways that allowed me easy access. He knew what I needed; he knew how to open his face or body ever so slightly for the camera. He has said that film and photography have profoundly influenced his fiction.

Christine and Rudolf Scholten, patrons of the Austrian literary event, welcomed Coetzee for two culturally packed days in Vienna. He was tireless, attentive to every painting and object in three museums, talking with various directors and curators anxious to open their buildings, the one day of the week they were closed, especially for him.

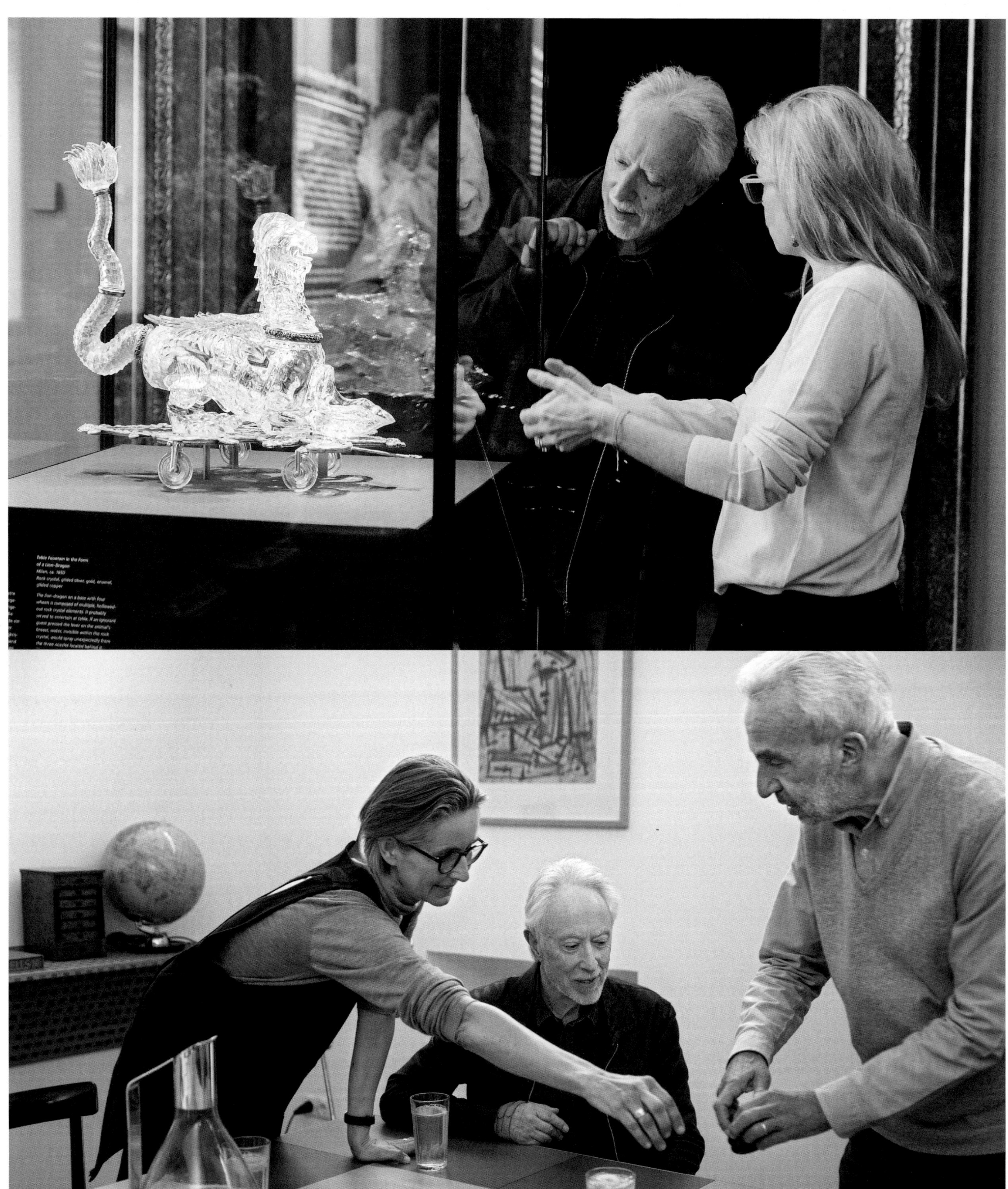
Table Fountain in the Form
of a Lion-Dragon
Milan, ca. 1650
Rock crystal, gilded silver, gold, enamel,
gilded copper

The lion-dragon on a base with four
wheels is composed of multiple, hollowed-
out rock crystal elements. It probably
served to entertain at table. If an ignorant
guest pressed the lever on the animal's
breast, water, invisible within the rock
crystal, would spray unexpectedly from
the three nozzles located behind it.

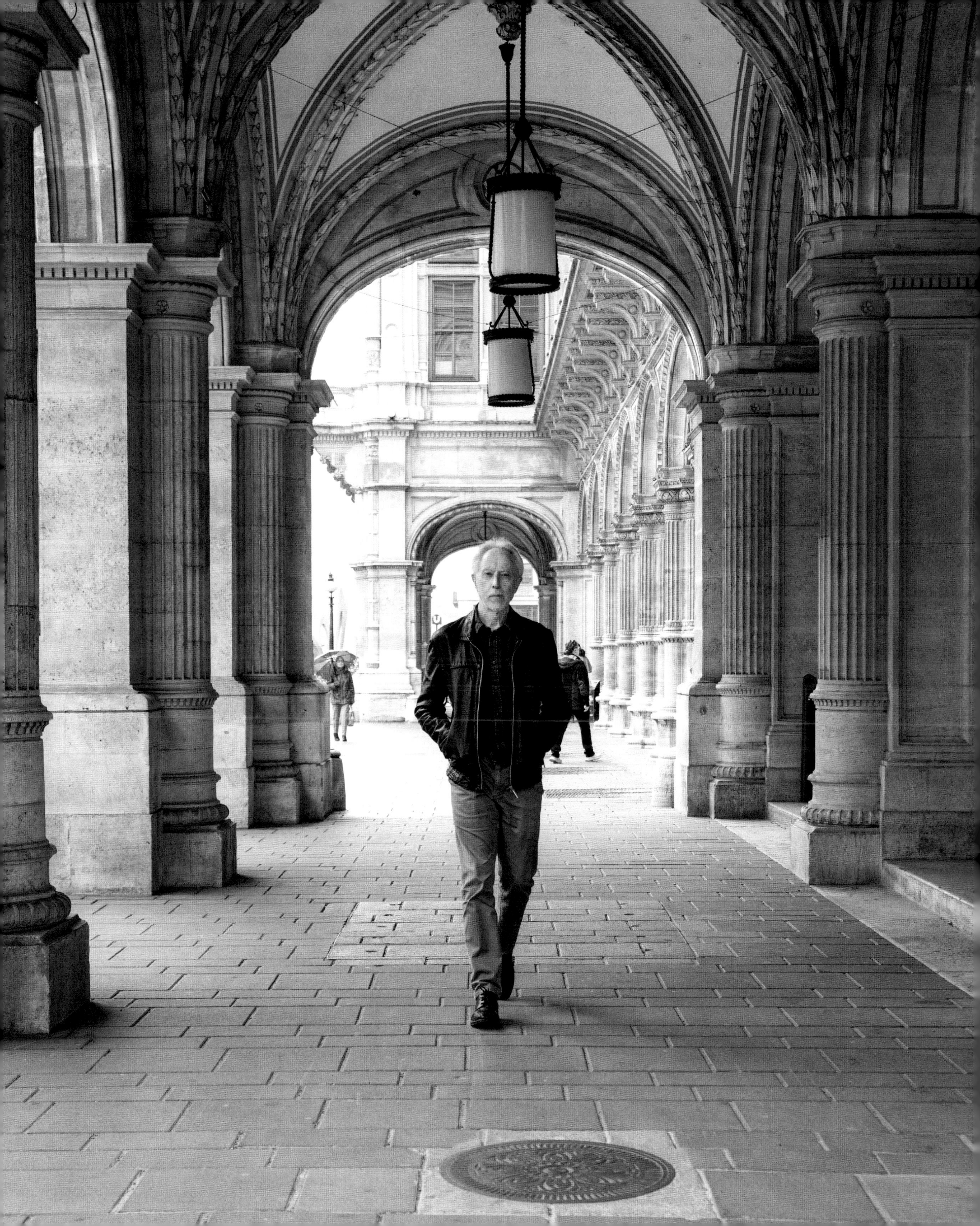

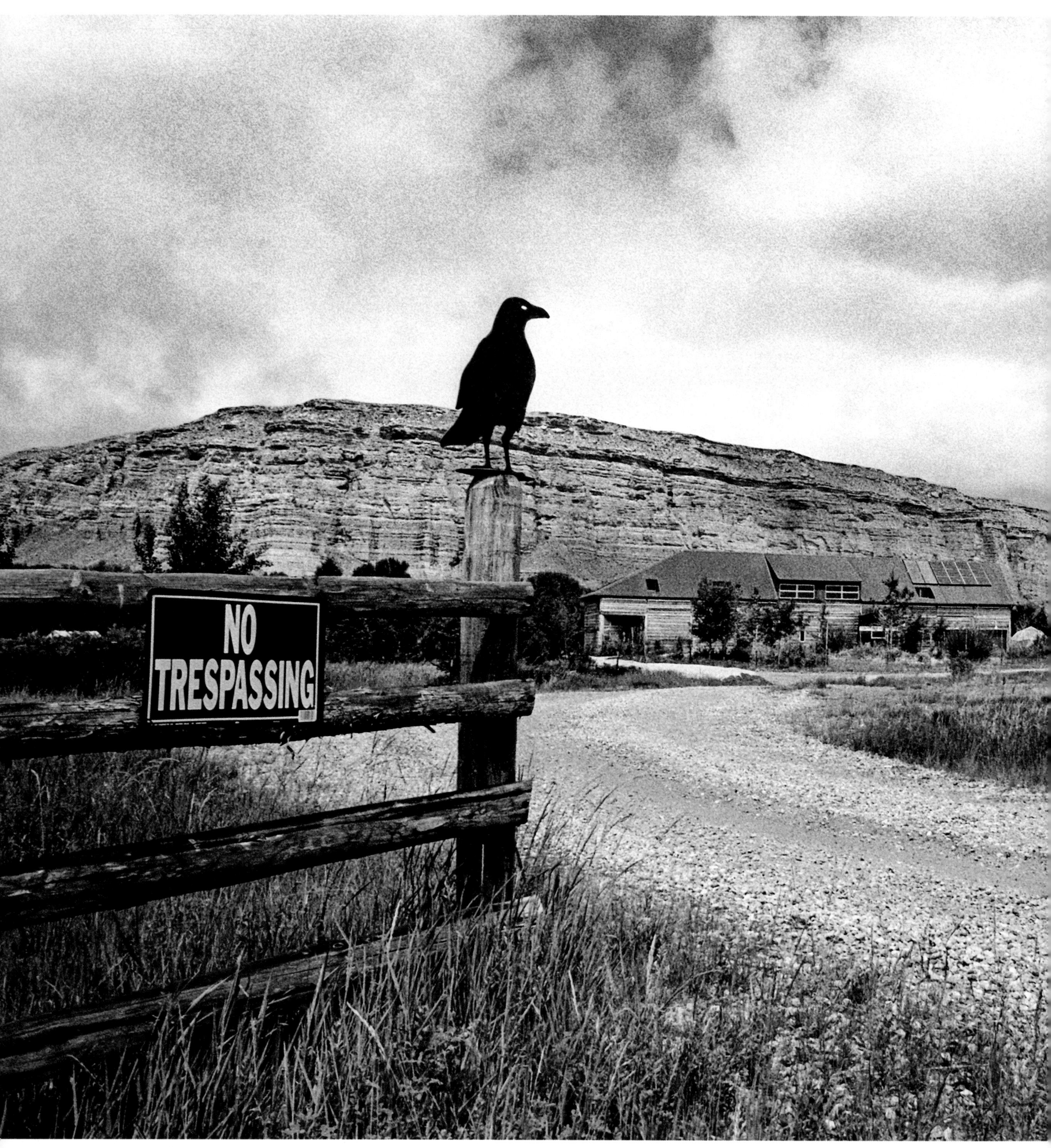

NO
TRESPASSING

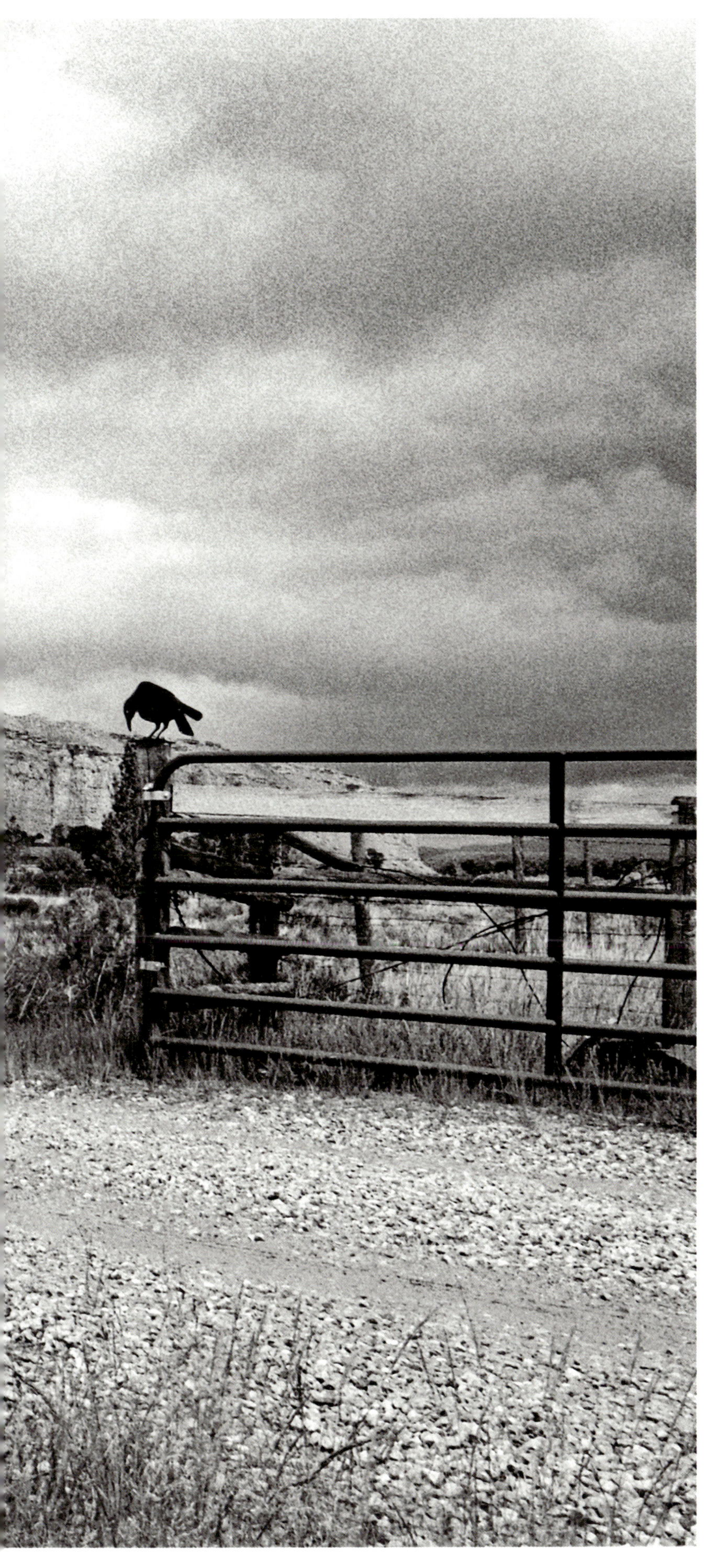

Annie Proulx

American (b. 1935)

Photographed in Saratoga, Wyoming, June 2011

Over several months, I received a series of urgent emails from Annie Proulx:

"There was a tremendous snowpack. We are currently under a scary flood watch."

"We are just coming out of a record-breaking flood."

"If flood waters threaten to cut off this house, I will not stay."

"The mosquitoes are vicious. Pools of water everywhere."

Then a last and more promising message: "However, if it's difficult, we can go up on top of the cliff or even into the snowfields of the Medicine Bows."

I drove from Montana with my old friend Ron Losee, a country doctor, through the Crow Reservation, south across the Wyoming border, past the Bighorns and onto high plains covered with sagebrush. We continued by the dry, alkaline Rattlesnake Hills, through Devil's Gate, a rock formation on the Sweetwater River that marked the Oregon and Mormon trails. All of Wyoming was behind us by the time we came to Bird Cloud, the 640-acre ranch owned by Annie Proulx. The large No Trespassing sign on the front gate was forbidding.

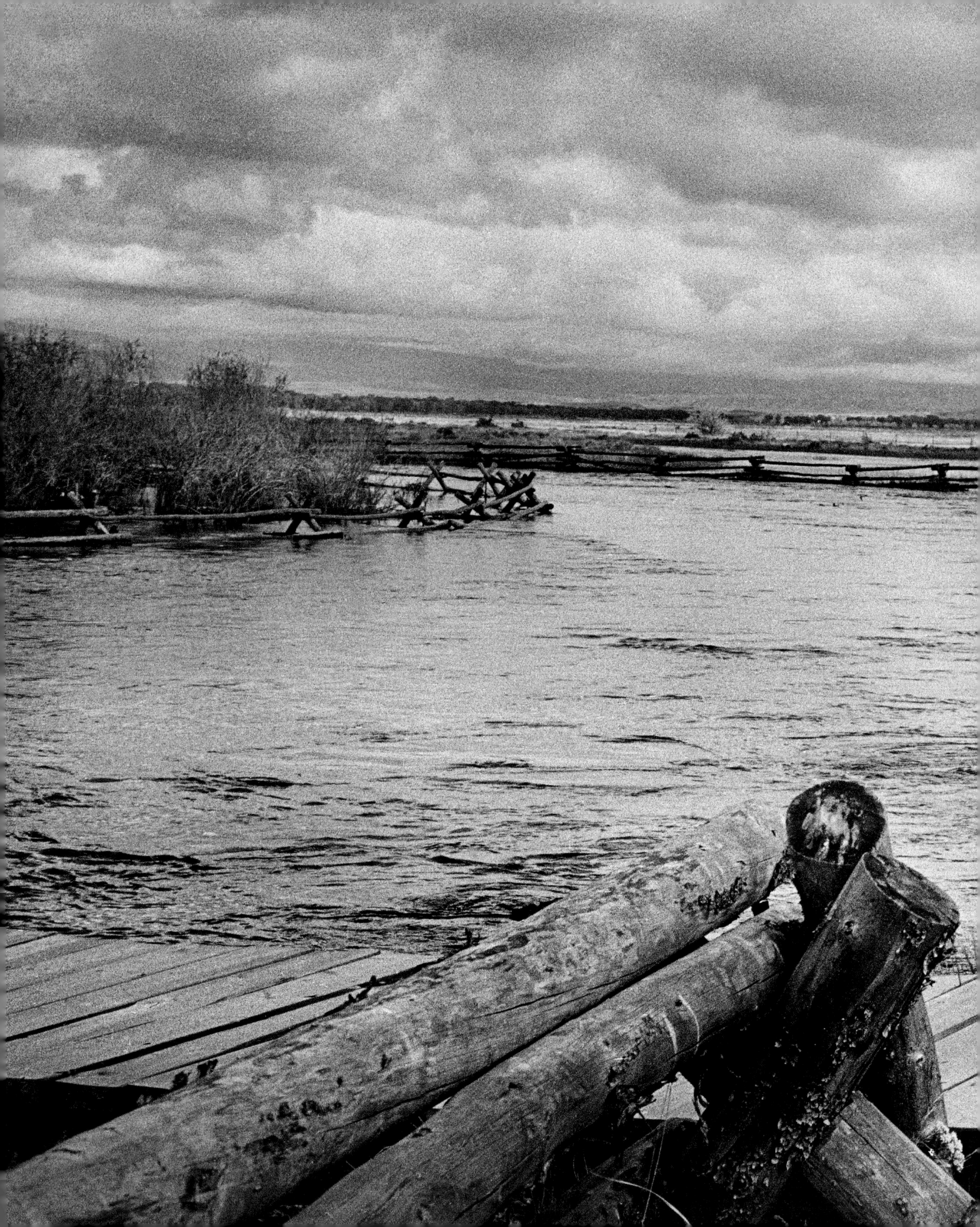

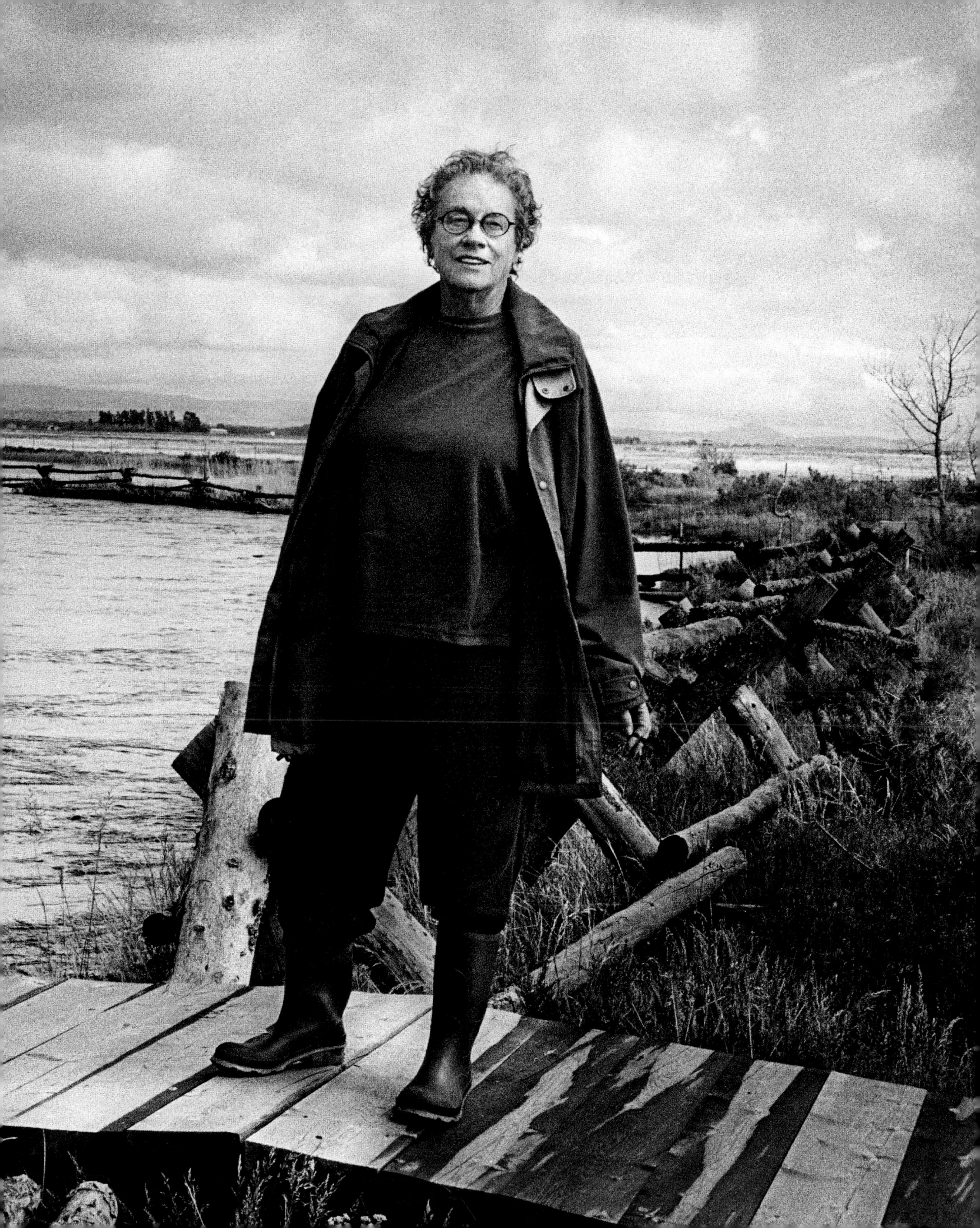

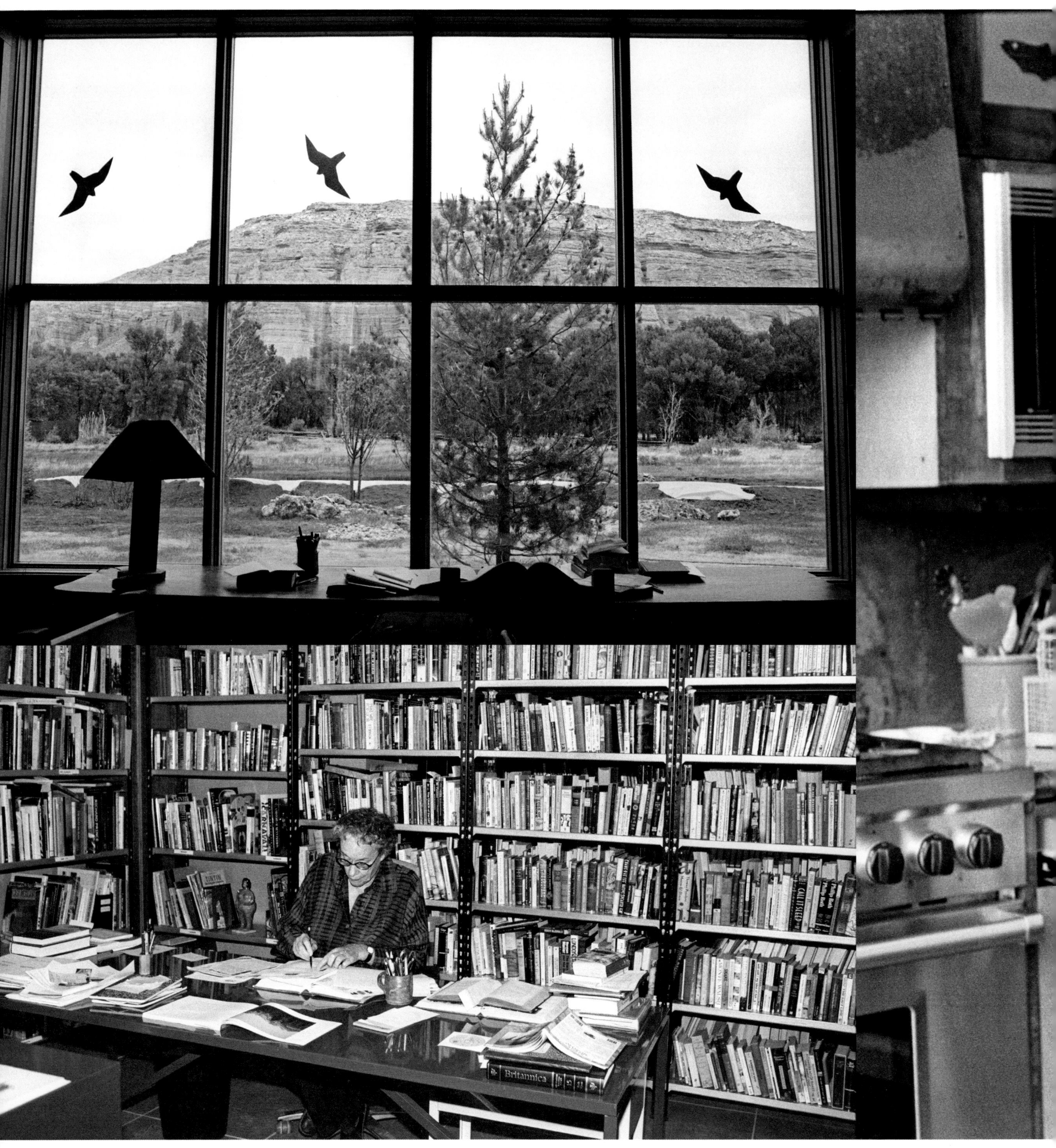

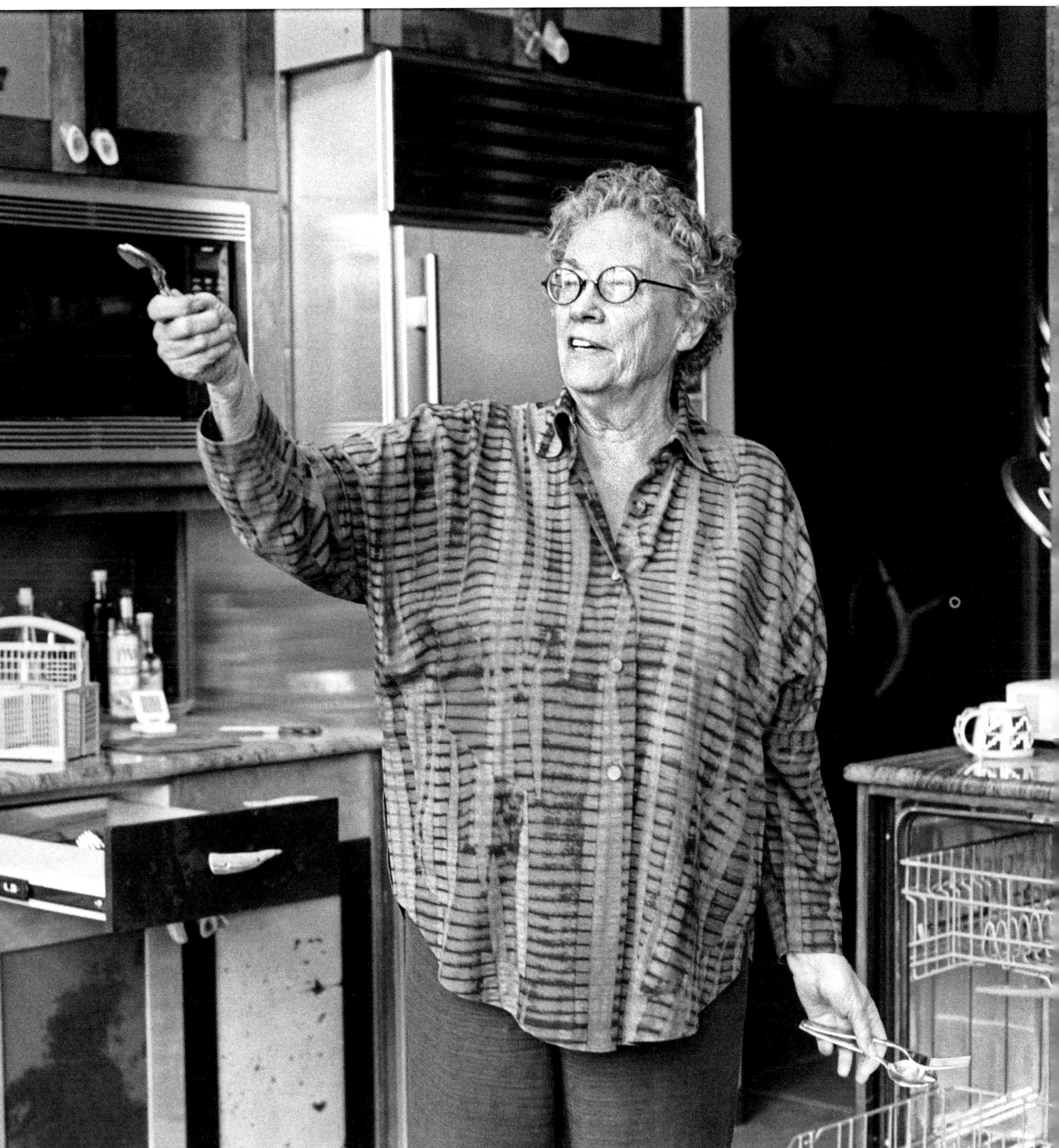

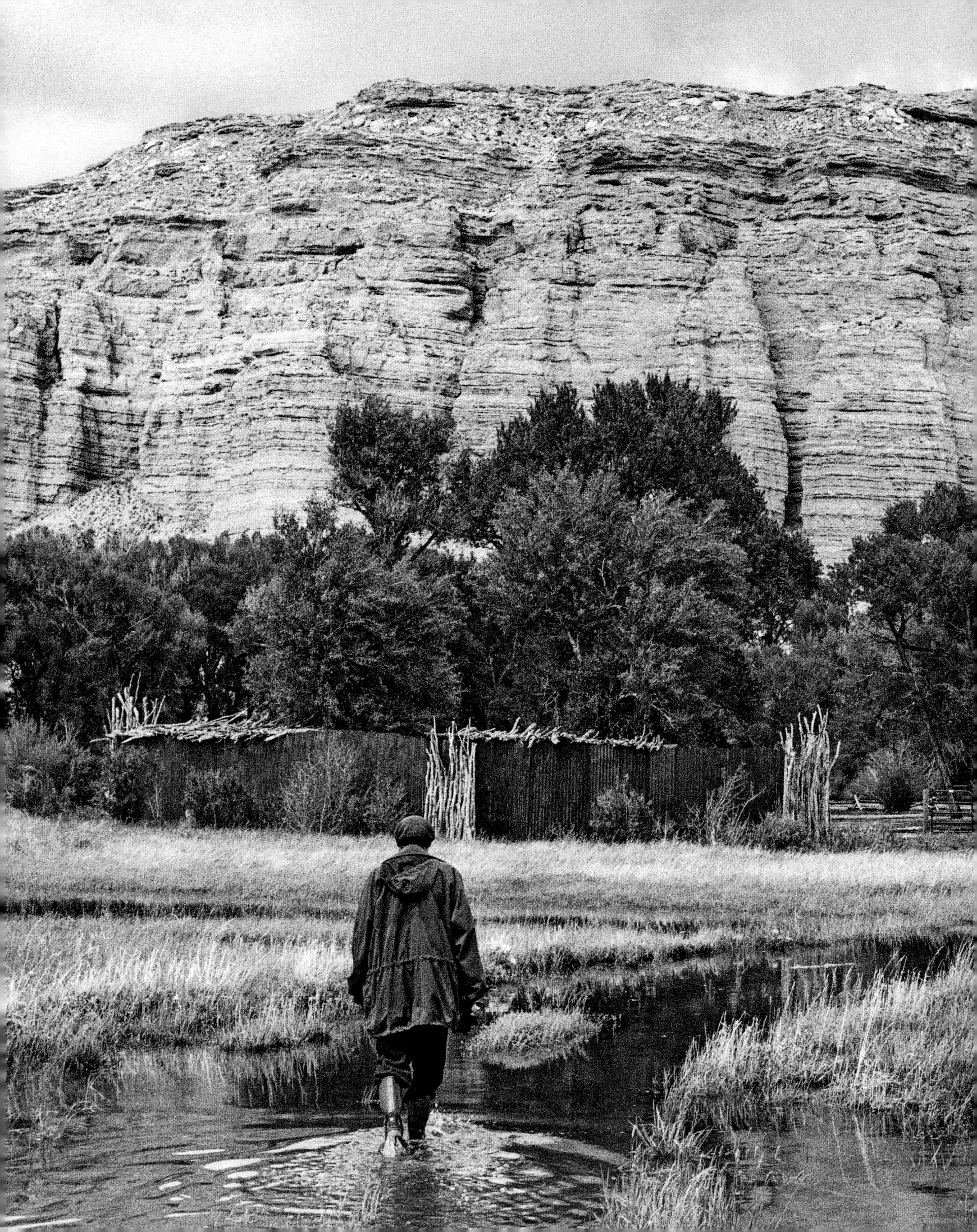

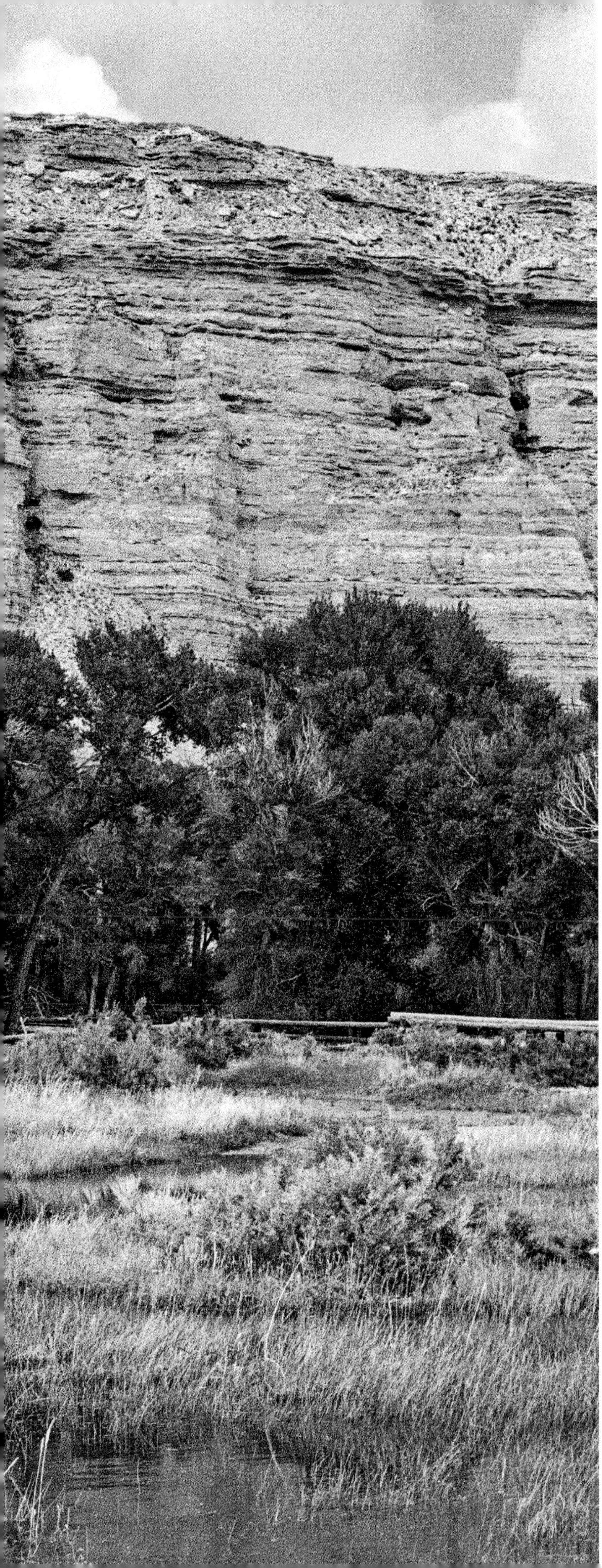

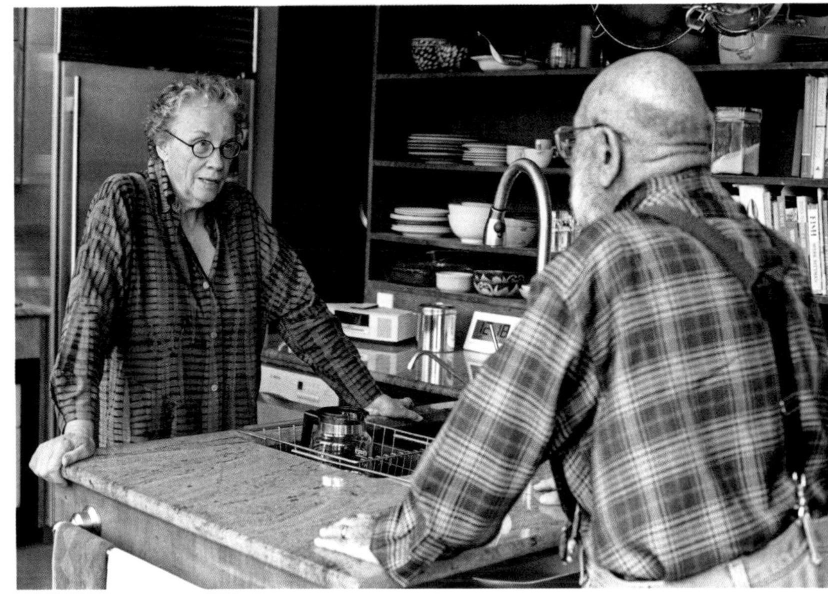

Both Losee and Proulx were independent, with a shrewd understanding of country people. I had thought they'd enjoy meeting, but they were wary of one another. It took several hours for her to warm up to us.

Proulx's messages had not been misleading. In that remote area of the state, the North Platte River had overflown its banks and flooded the surrounding meadows. She took us through her large, sensible house, with solar panels on the roof and a compact kitchen-living area looking out on a massive sandstone butte. Her knowledge of the natural world, and the history, geology, and archeology of the entire West, impressed Losee. We were both struck by the most unusual feature in her house: Proulx had designed an institutional-like library, forty-eight feet in length with shelves and shelves of books, six rows deep. We saw volume after volume dedicated to raptors and hawks, natural history, settler histories, geography, climbing adventures, and gardening.

Sam Shepard

American (1943–2017)

Photographed in Santa Fe, New Mexico, June 2012

For a writer whose work is often set in the American West, Sam Shepard had the good fortune, later in his life, to work at the Santa Fe Institute in the foothills of the Sangre de Cristo Mountains of northern New Mexico. There he was one of two writers living amid thirty physicists, mathematicians, and biologists—the idea behind the arrangement was that scientists might benefit from exposure to the creativity of first-rate writers.

My son Owen and I were in Santa Fe, ambling along one evening when we bumped into Shepard and his son, Walker. Sam invited us to lunch the next day at the Institute. Our lunch was lively, fueled by the wide-ranging curiosity of the scientists. Owen and I talked with the physicist Murray Gell-Mann, whose most famous discovery—the quark—was named for a word in James Joyce's *Finnegans Wake.*

The Institute provided financial support, a writing room, and a corner desk tucked into the library. When I arrived, I found Shepard at work on the last lines of his play *Heartless.* He was rereading notes, making adjustments, before he filled out a FedEx form and sent the play off to New York, where it went into production two months later.

Shepard was in good spirits, free for the afternoon to be photographed. We drove to his adobe house, about ten miles outside of town. The house was sparsely furnished, the place of someone on the move. Shepard was pleased to show me two typewriters, a Hermes 3000 and a gray-green Olympia, and an original pen-and-ink drawing by Will James. But he was most enthusiastic about a new acquisition, a titanium fly rod, which he cast about outside—here and there over the dry, dusty landscape. The lack of water seemed unimportant to him.

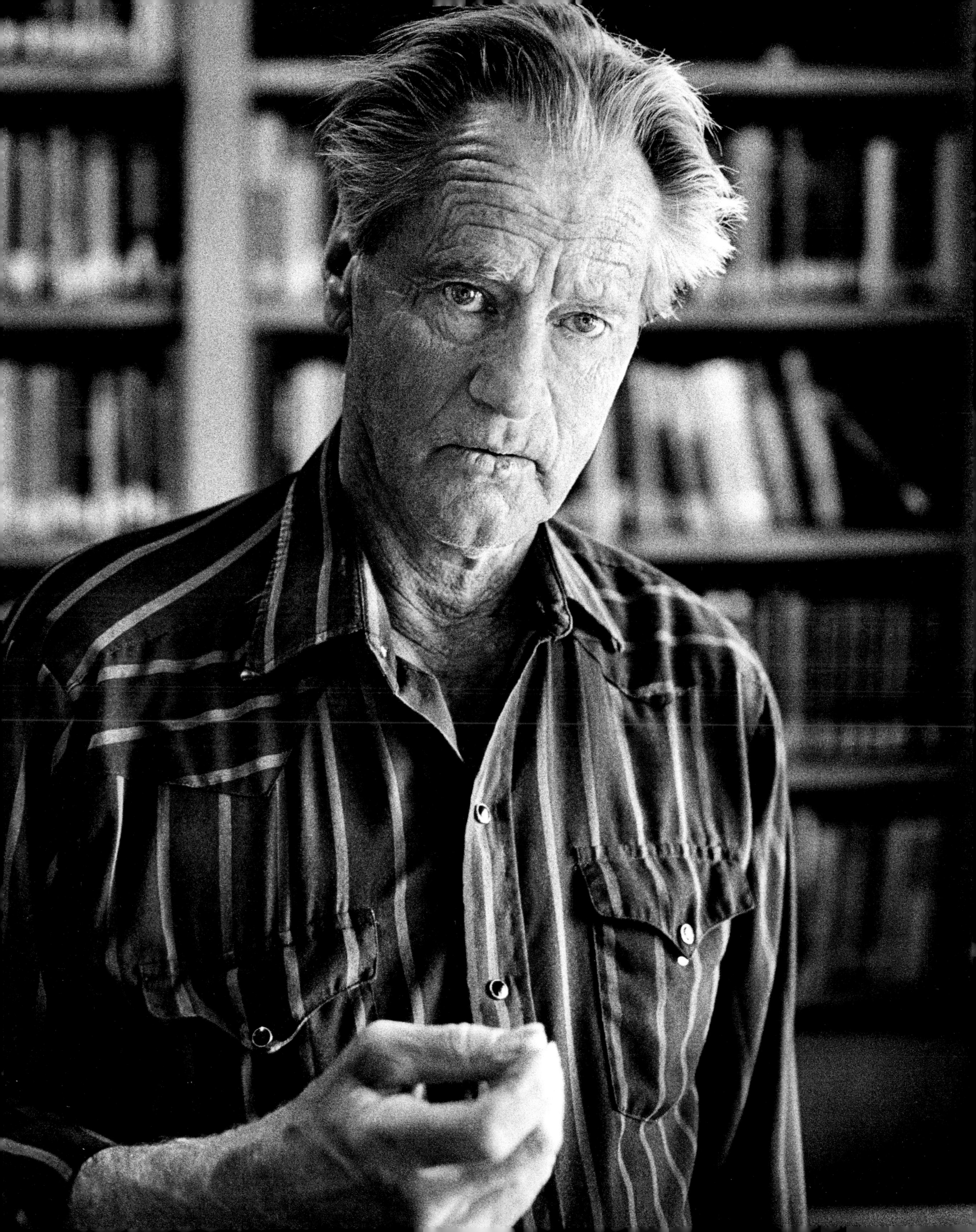

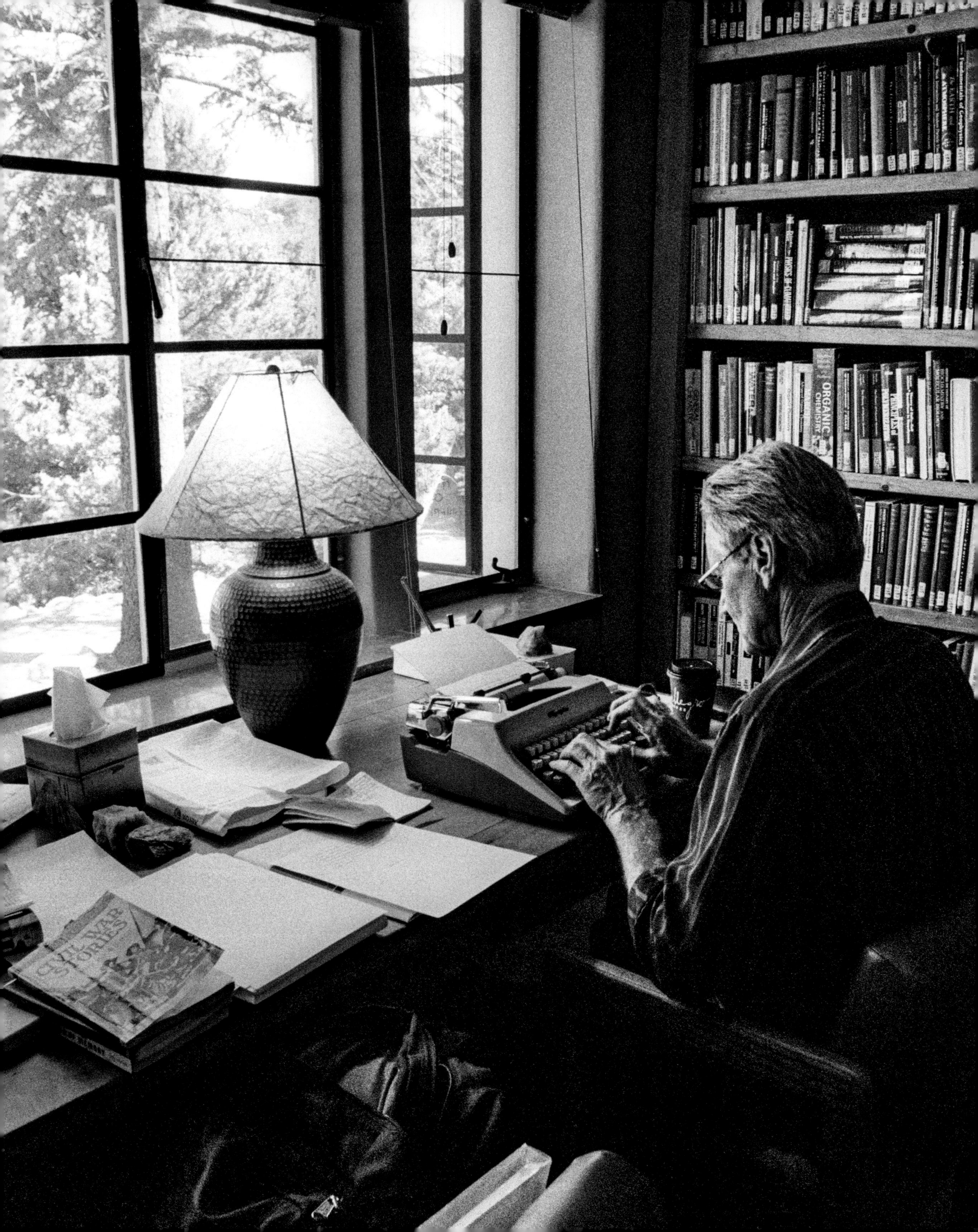

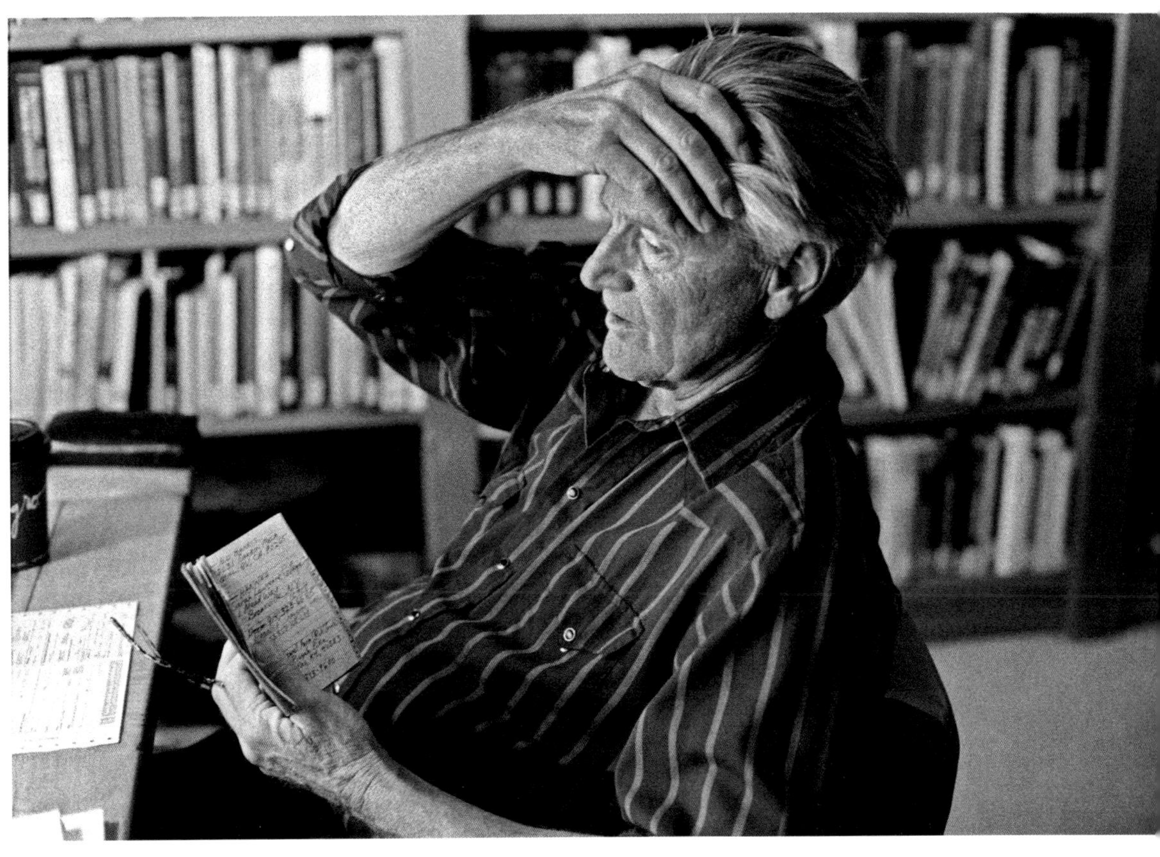

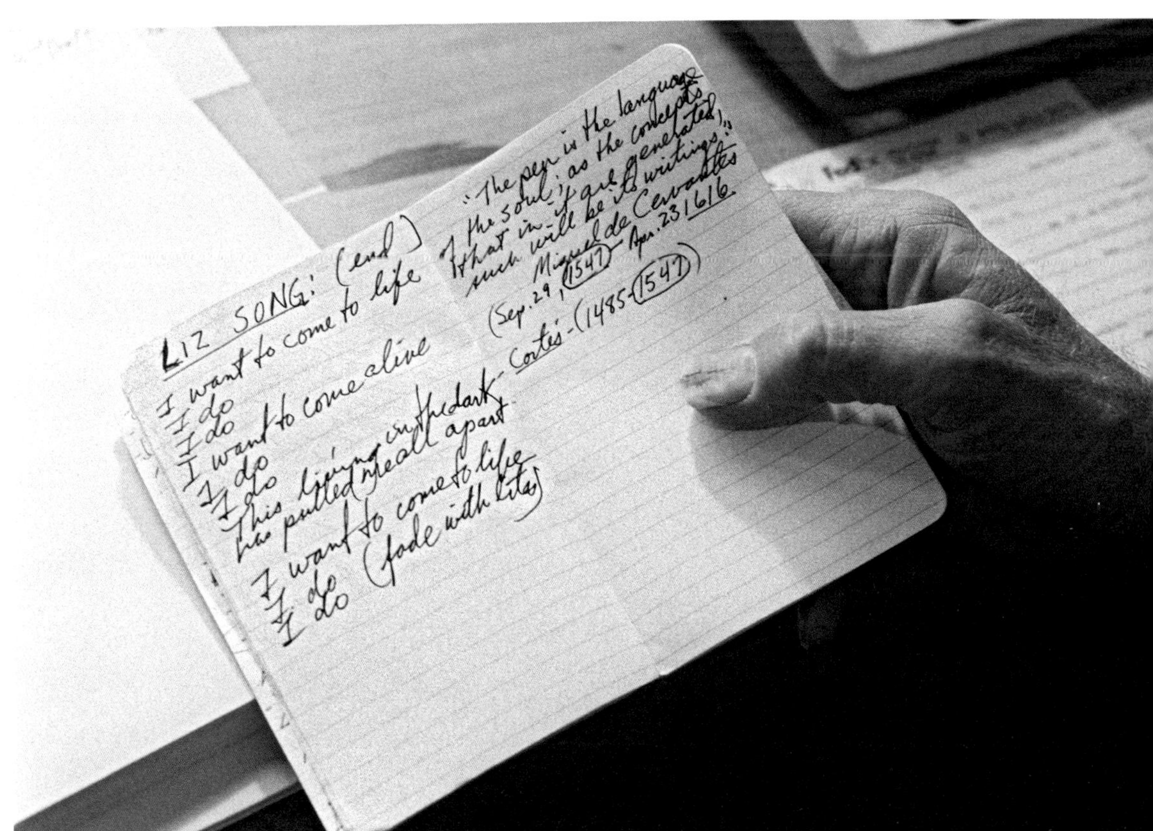
LIZ SONG: (end)
I want to come to life
I do
I want to come alive
I do
This living in the dark
has pulled me all apart
I want to come to life
I do (fade with Liz)
"The pen is the language
of the soul; as the concepts
that in it are generated,
such will be its writings."
Miguel de Cervantes
(Sep. 29, 1547 — Apr. 23 1616
Cortes - (1485 - 1547)

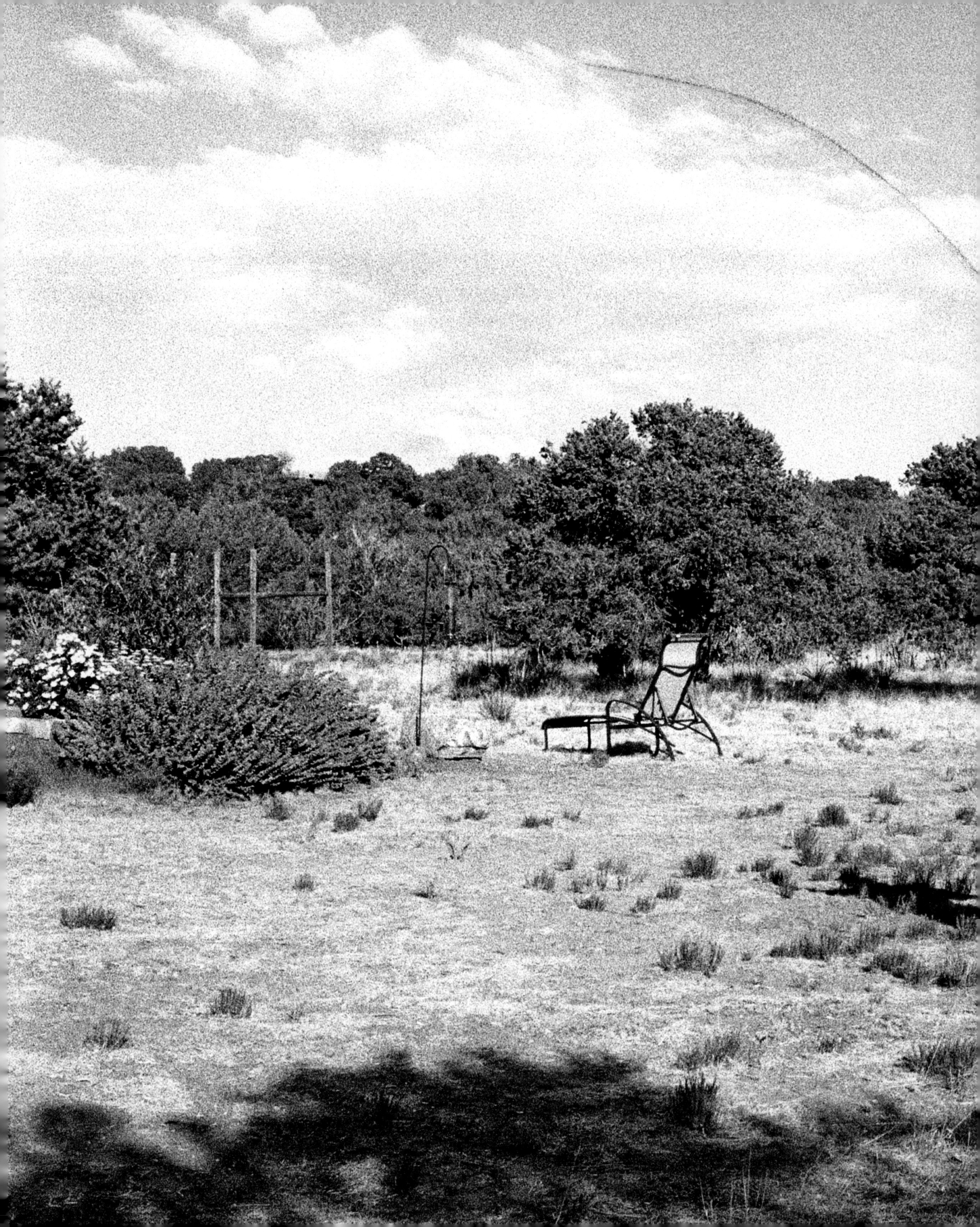

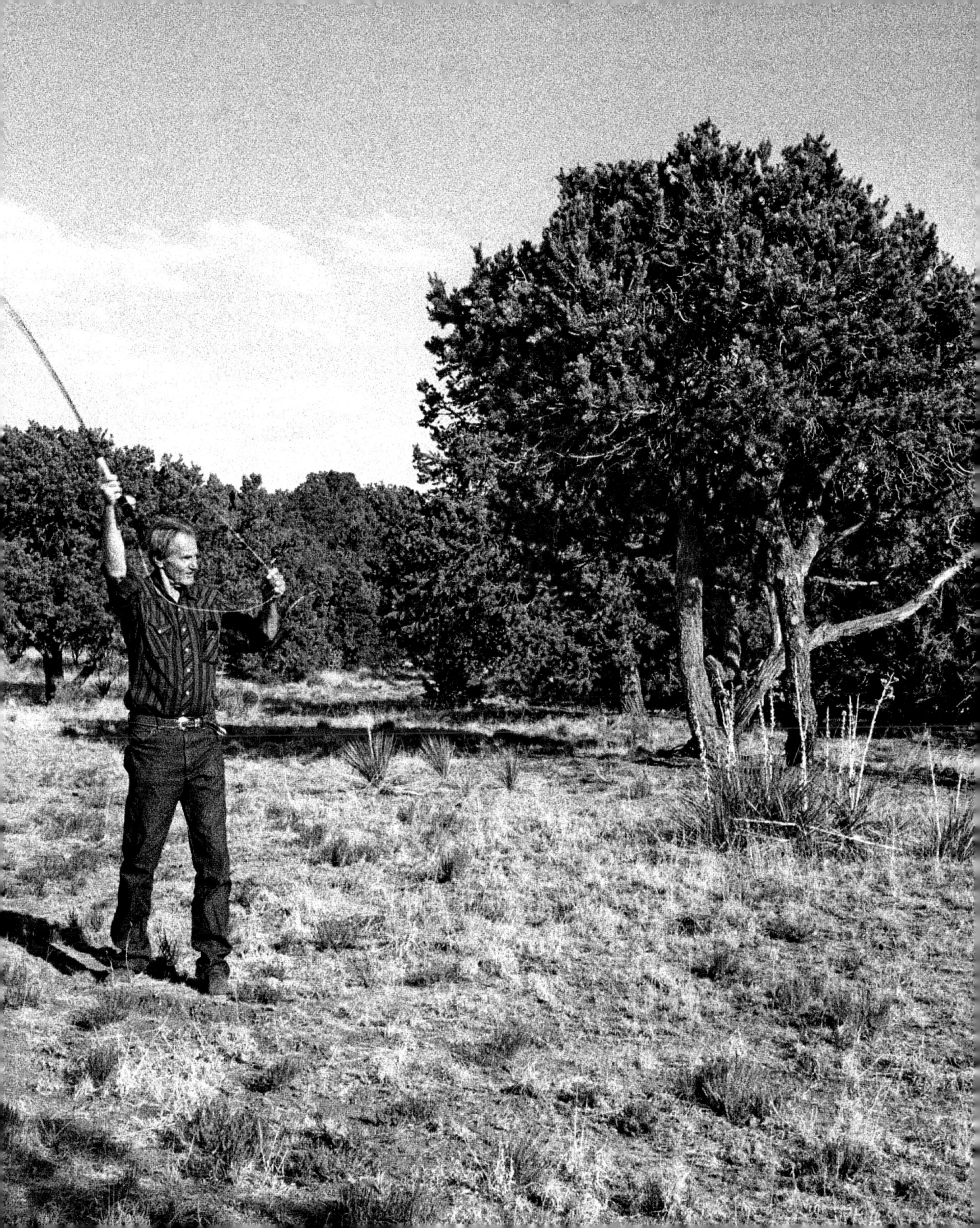

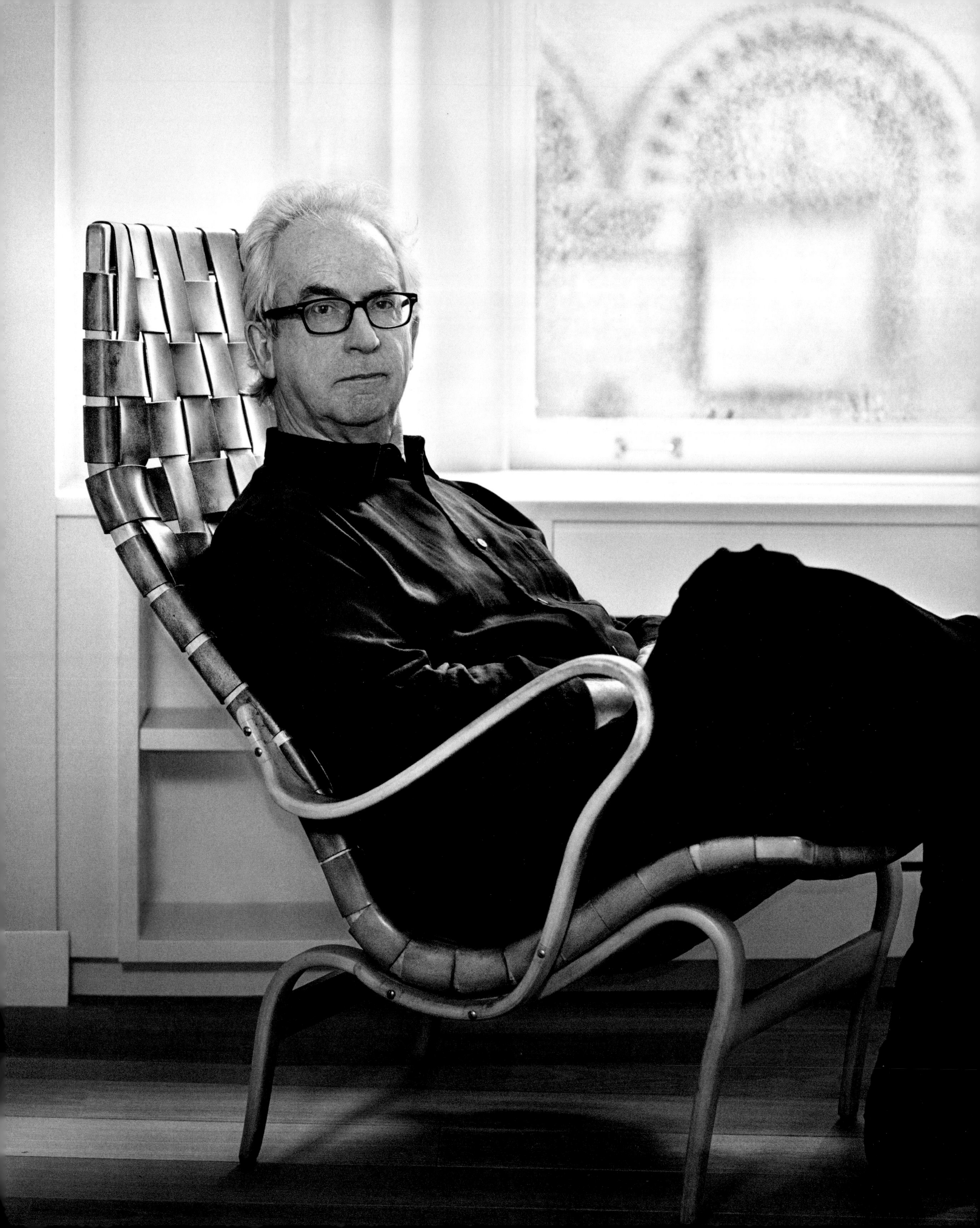

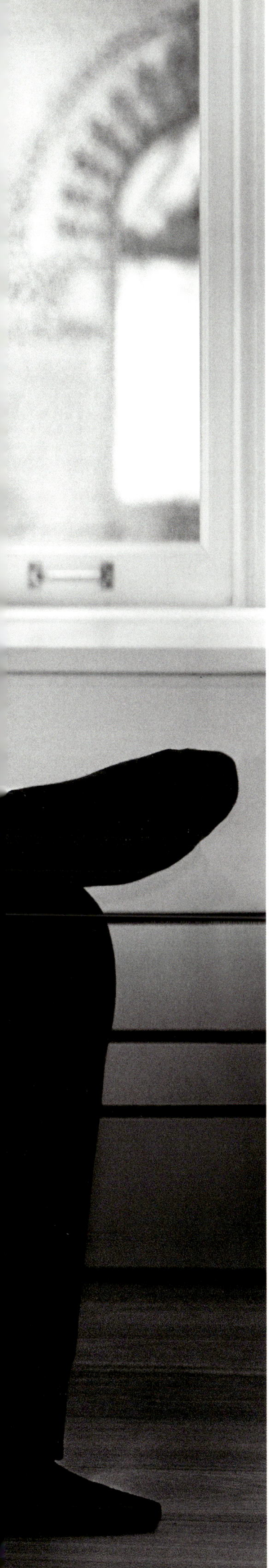

Peter Carey

Australian (b. 1943)

Photographed in New York, New York, November 2013

Peter Carey is Australian, irreverent and quick to laugh, but serious enough to be one of only five people writing in English to win the Man Booker Prize twice.

Three years before these pictures were taken, I had written to ask Carey if I might photograph him. He wrote back, saying that he had just returned from exhausting travels with "horrible bronchitis and a rather sour mood." He added: "And if the bronchitis has been any use at all, it is to convince me that I must spend my life as a writer, not as a travelling salesman and promoter of my work. I'm very sorry to say no."

But a year or two later, as you can see, he was generous and giving of his time.

When we met, Carey was working on a novel as well as teaching creative writing at Hunter College, but stopped long enough to let me follow along one afternoon and evening as he checked on some of his favorite neighborhood places. While selecting some wine, he introduced me to Eban, his wine merchant, whom he had known since Eban was a teenage puppeteer. Circling through City Hall Park, around the Jacob Wrey Mould Fountain, we moved on to an early dinner at a local restaurant, the Odeon. He talked about writing locations. As much as Carey likes New York, the city doesn't suit him more than any other as a place to work. "I have written in London," he told me. "And amongst hippies in a tropical rainforest, and on a desk shaken by the pile drivers between my nose and Sydney Harbour. When I write, I go to that same private place inside my head."

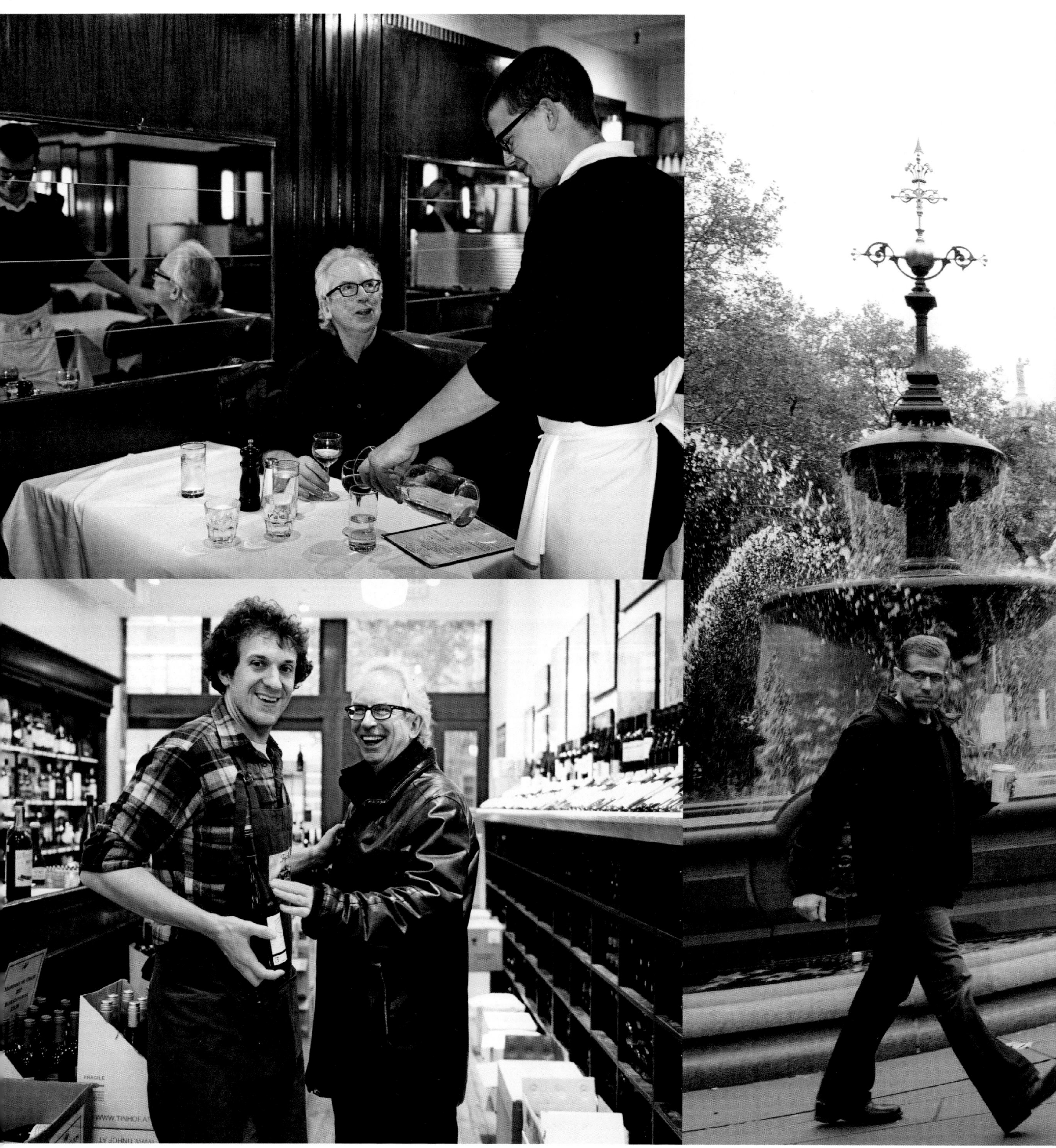

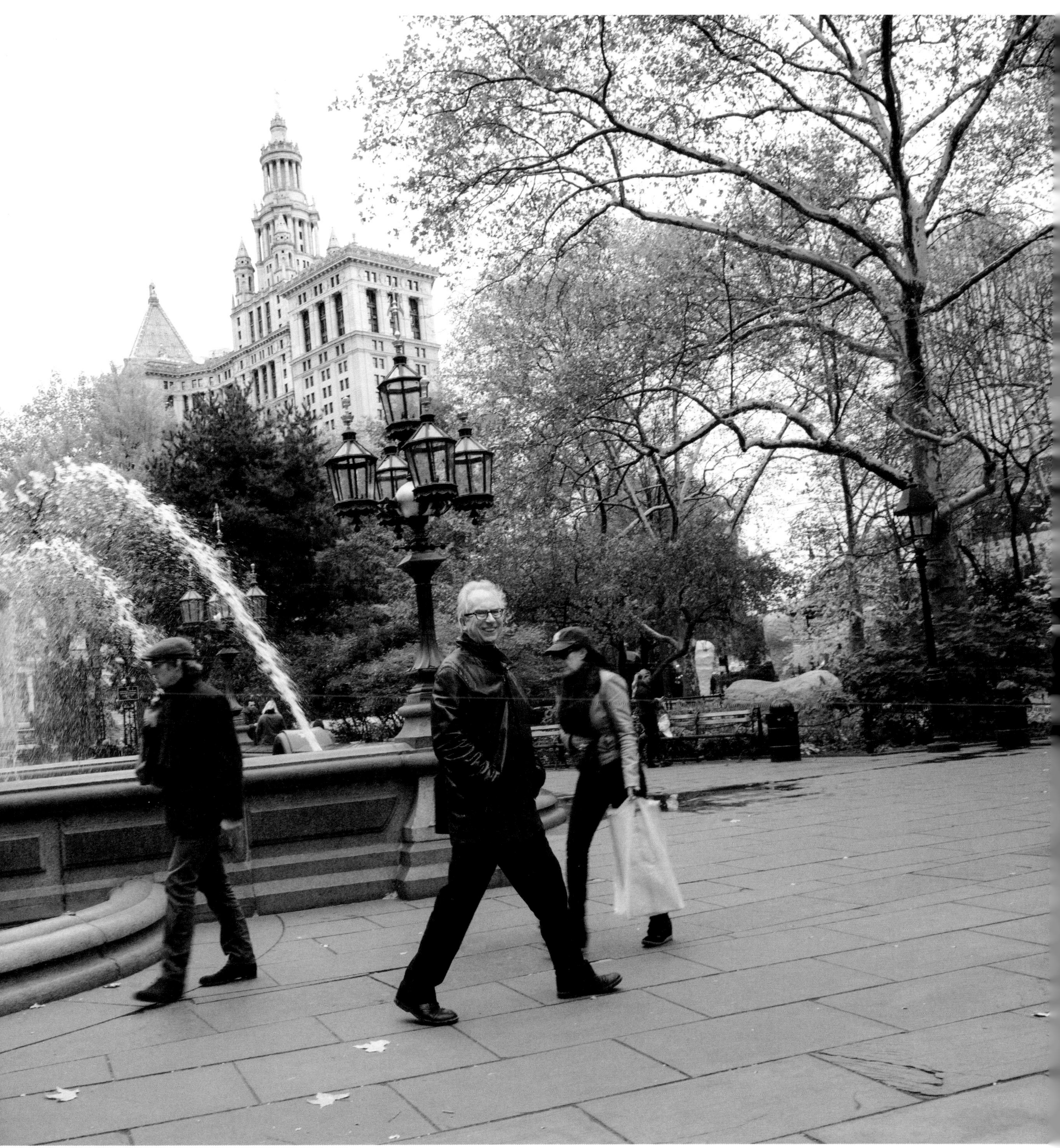

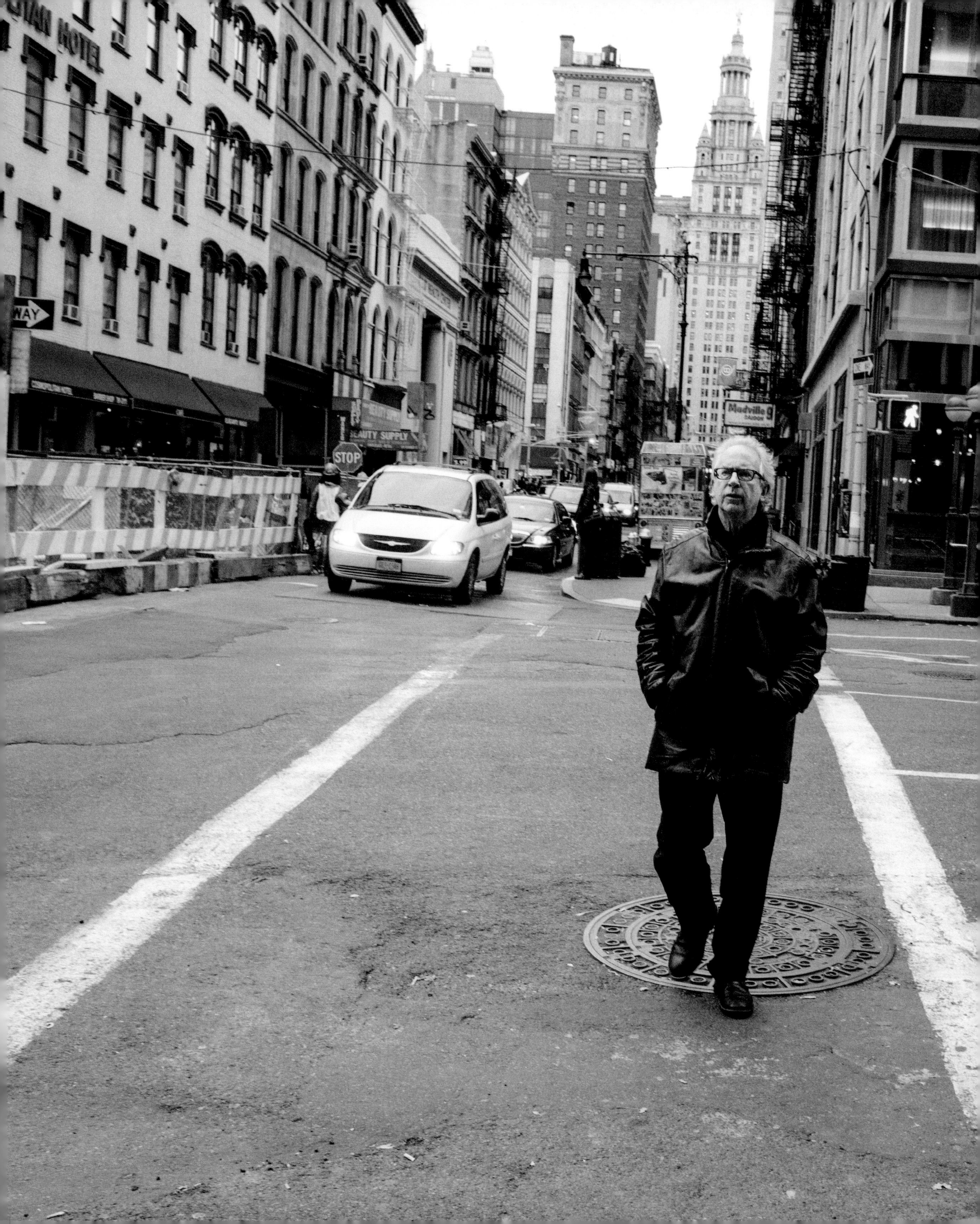

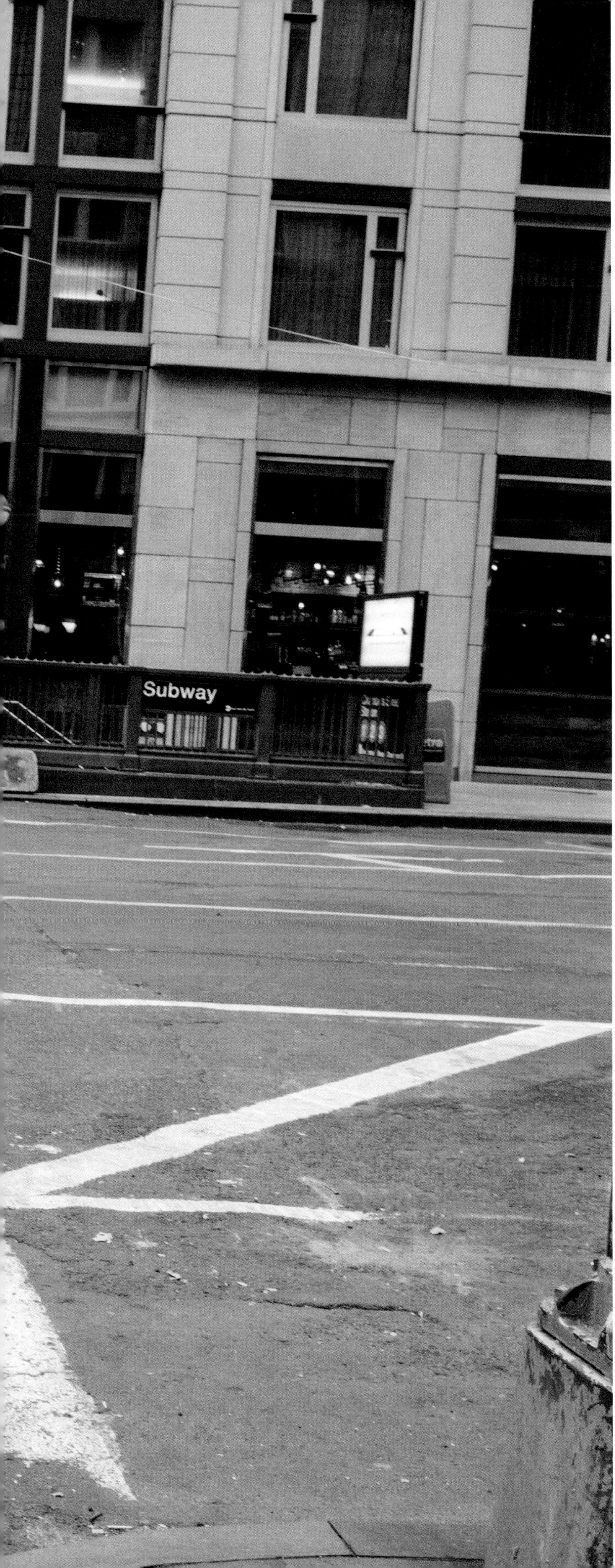

We spoke about writers of interest to him. He told me to read Kent Haruf. He admired his novels and liked him as a person. Haruf's concern with the lives of people in small towns on Colorado's plains could never be alien to someone like Carey who "grew up in my tiny hometown of Bacchus Marsh, whose dad sold cars to farmers, and who knew to expect itchy arms at harvest time from helping make stooks from sheaves of wheat."

To many people, myself included, Australians seem similar to Americans—informal, independent, a little brash. We both know, or should know, we are living on stolen land. But Carey pointed out the deep difference: "You need to swap your Mayflower pilgrims for our convict ships. Our histories are so very different. Generally speaking, you celebrate success. Generally speaking, we distrust it. Our great stories are about loss: Burke and Wills, Ned Kelly, Gallipoli."

A. S. Byatt

English (b. 1936)

Photographed in London, England, May 2015

had heard that A. S. Byatt was "fearsome." Yet when I knocked on her door in southwest London, she was welcoming and easily agreed to let us look anywhere in her house and garden for suitable locations. While patiently waiting to be photographed, Byatt returned to her living room television to watch a 10:00 A.M. snooker match.

We found a place to take her portrait in a doorway facing the garden. When we were all set, I reached for the roll of cello tape she had been fiddling with, but was quickly waved off. "No, no," she said. "I always hold it whenever I do an interview or T.V."

Normally, morning is Dame Antonia's best writing time. Her husband, Peter Duffy, is an economist who works at home as well. Married for fifty-two years, they seemed especially close. She dedicated *The Matisse Stories*:

> For Peter,
> Who taught me to look at things slowly
> With love

Their house, filled with books, and curious objects on shelves and tables and mantels, reflects their wide range of interests. The lamp and wallpaper are in a William Morris pattern, reminding visitors familiar with Byatt's work that she not only admires Morris but wrote a book about him and Mariano Fortuny, the Spanish textile designer.

On a shelf in their light-filled dining area, there is an unusual copy of her Booker Prize–winning novel *Possession*. This hardback edition with pages folded, not cut—a rare art—to create the number 25, was a gift from her UK publishers, Chatto and Windus, on the twenty-fifth anniversary of the publication.

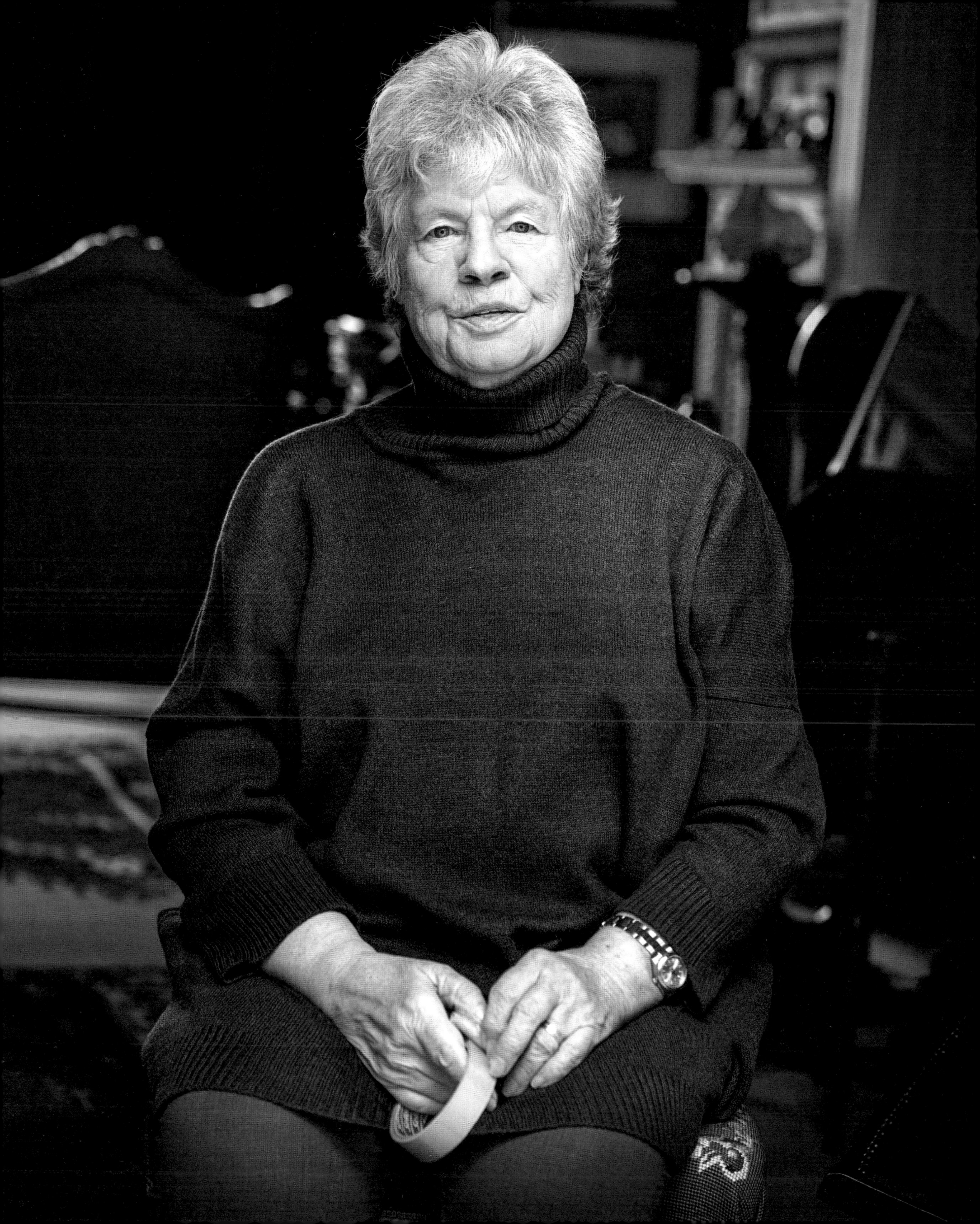

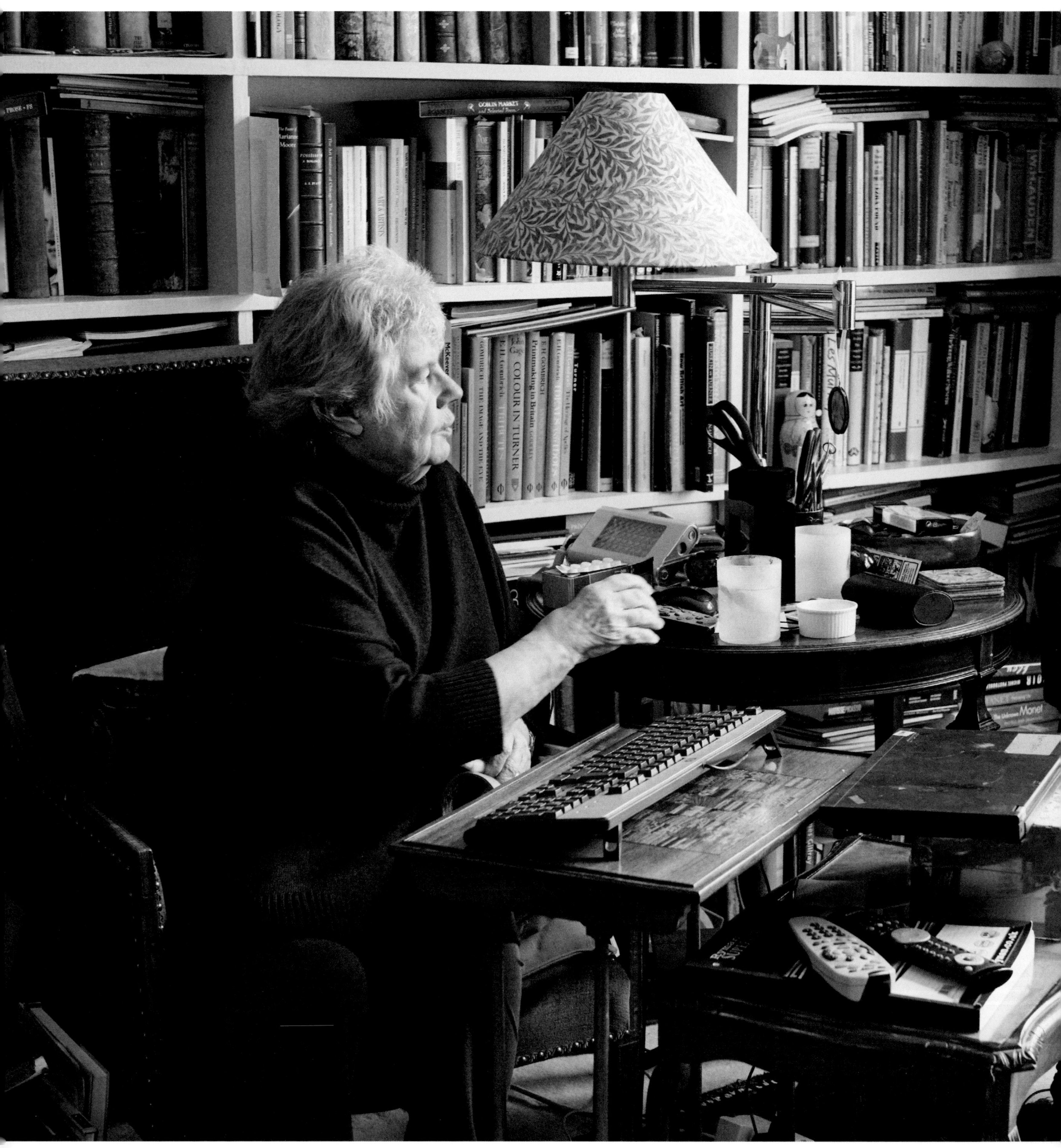

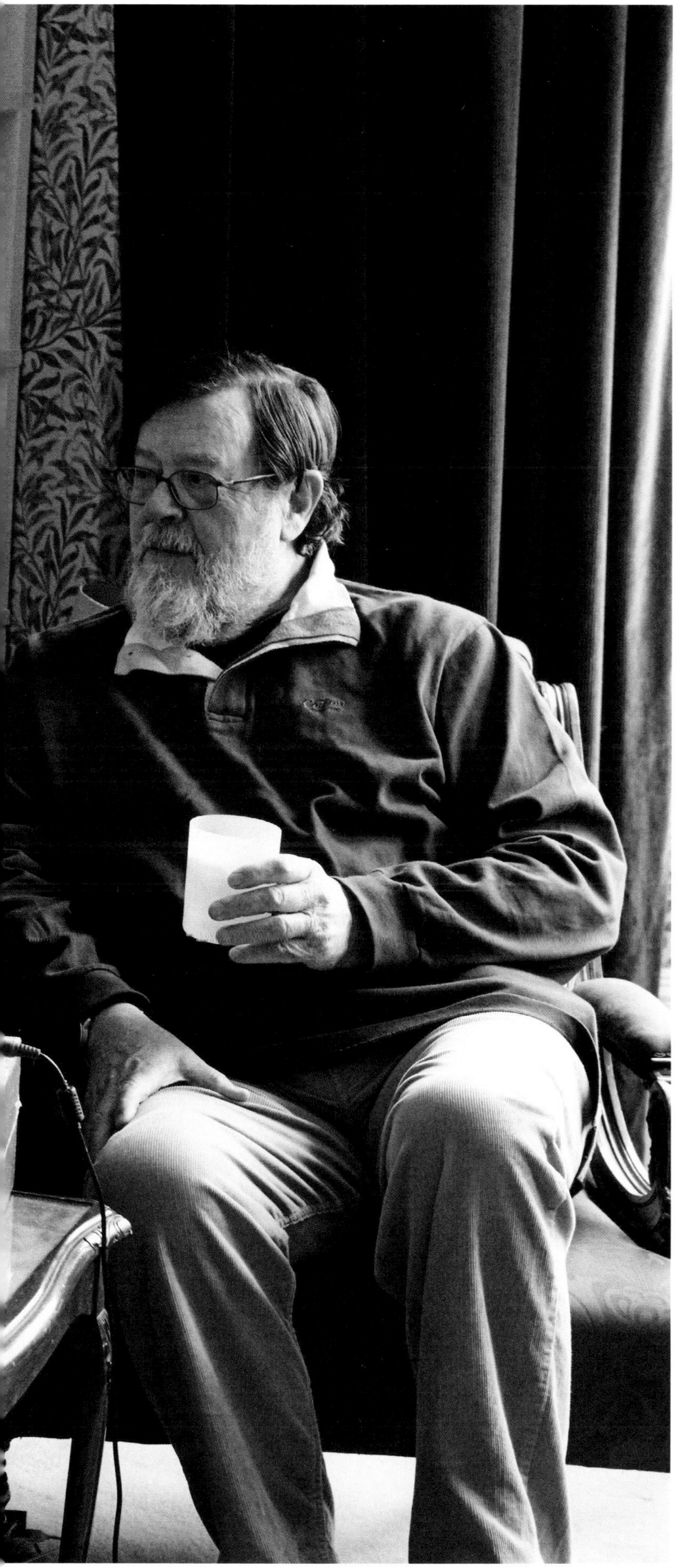

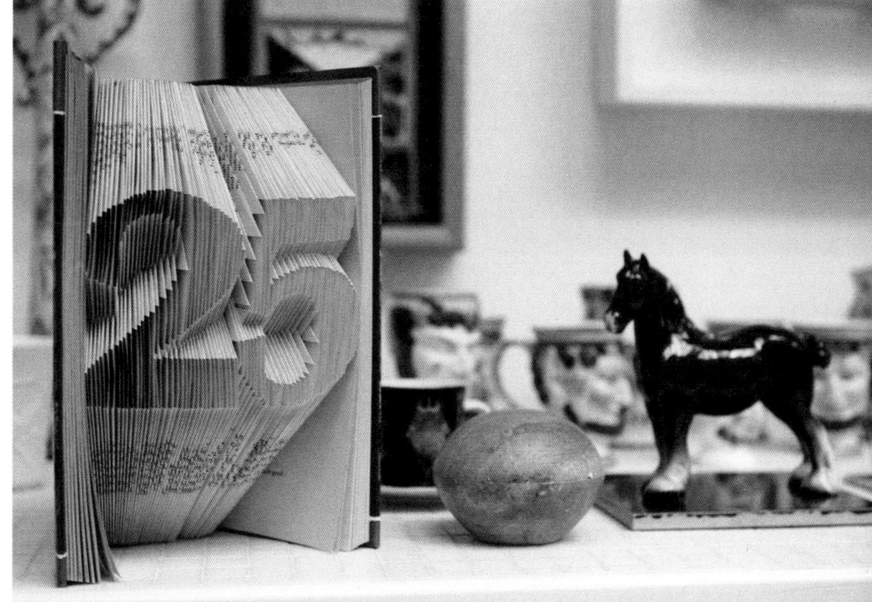

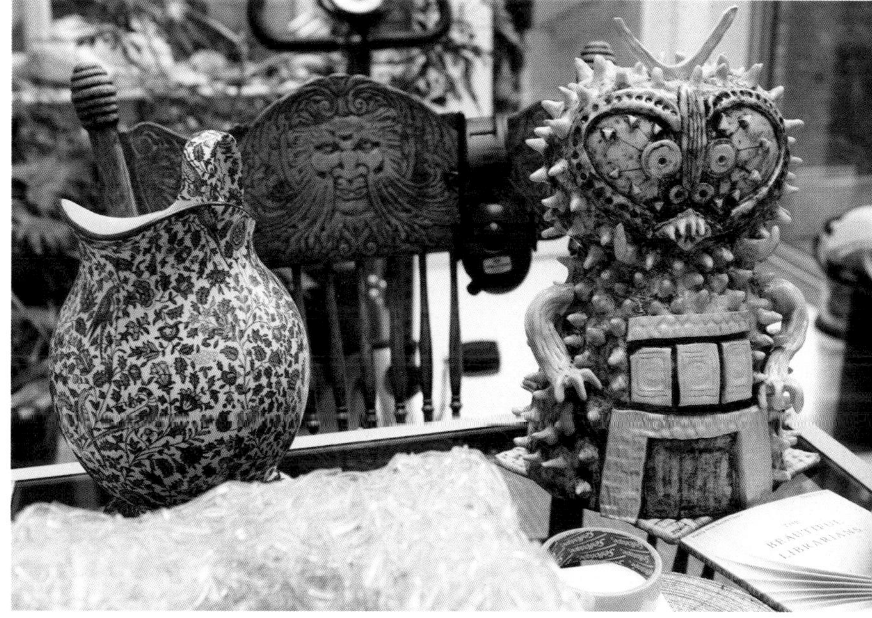

Byatt has said that writing and collecting are connected. Just as she collects Venetian glass balls and many varied art objects, she collects peoples' stories—their lives and ideas—and uses them to extend her exploration of human nature. She showed me a small sculpture, turning it this way and that in her hands. "I get great pleasure from my daughter Miranda Duffy's work as an artist in pottery. This piece is a monster called Lionel and was inspired by the work of Shinichi Sawada, the Japanese ceramicist."

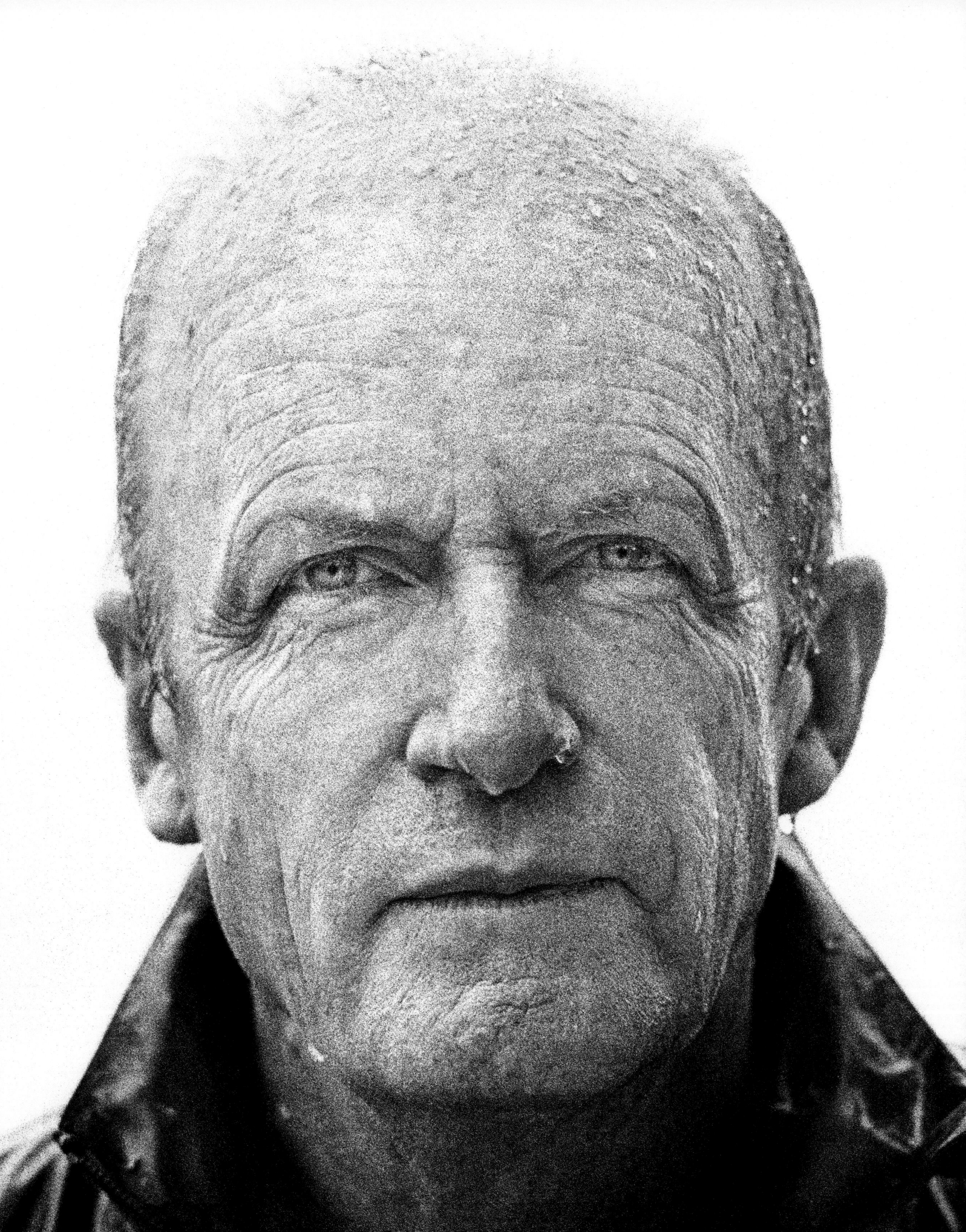

Jim Crace

English (b. 1946)

Photographed in Austin, Texas, October 2009

The novelist Jim Crace is known, among other things, for his interest in details of the mineral, bacterial, and gaseous worlds. He lives in Birmingham, England, but in 2009 was teaching in the Michener Center for Writers, at the University of Texas at Austin. I met him and his wife, Pam, there in a small house lent to them by the Center.

The day was rainy and dark; there was very little natural light inside, and I asked if we might do the portrait outside. Would he mind? "No, of course not," he said. "I'm English."

So we trudged up to the top of Mount Bonnell, where he patiently endured what a non-English person might consider to be cold, inhospitable weather.

The next day, Crace was animated during his three-hour graduate writing seminar, giving his students specific advice about the tough world of publishing. Later, at Zilker Park, in a huge mulching pile, he happily dug among the fallen logs and branches, looking for beetles and slugs and decomposed rodents.

Crace's archives are also in Austin, at the Harry Ransom Center, and he was amused one morning to come across his forgotten galley proof *Useless America*, a misprint of the intended title: *This Used to Be America*. His publisher, as a lark, printed seventy-five limited-edition blank copies of the novel to be used for a publicity contest.

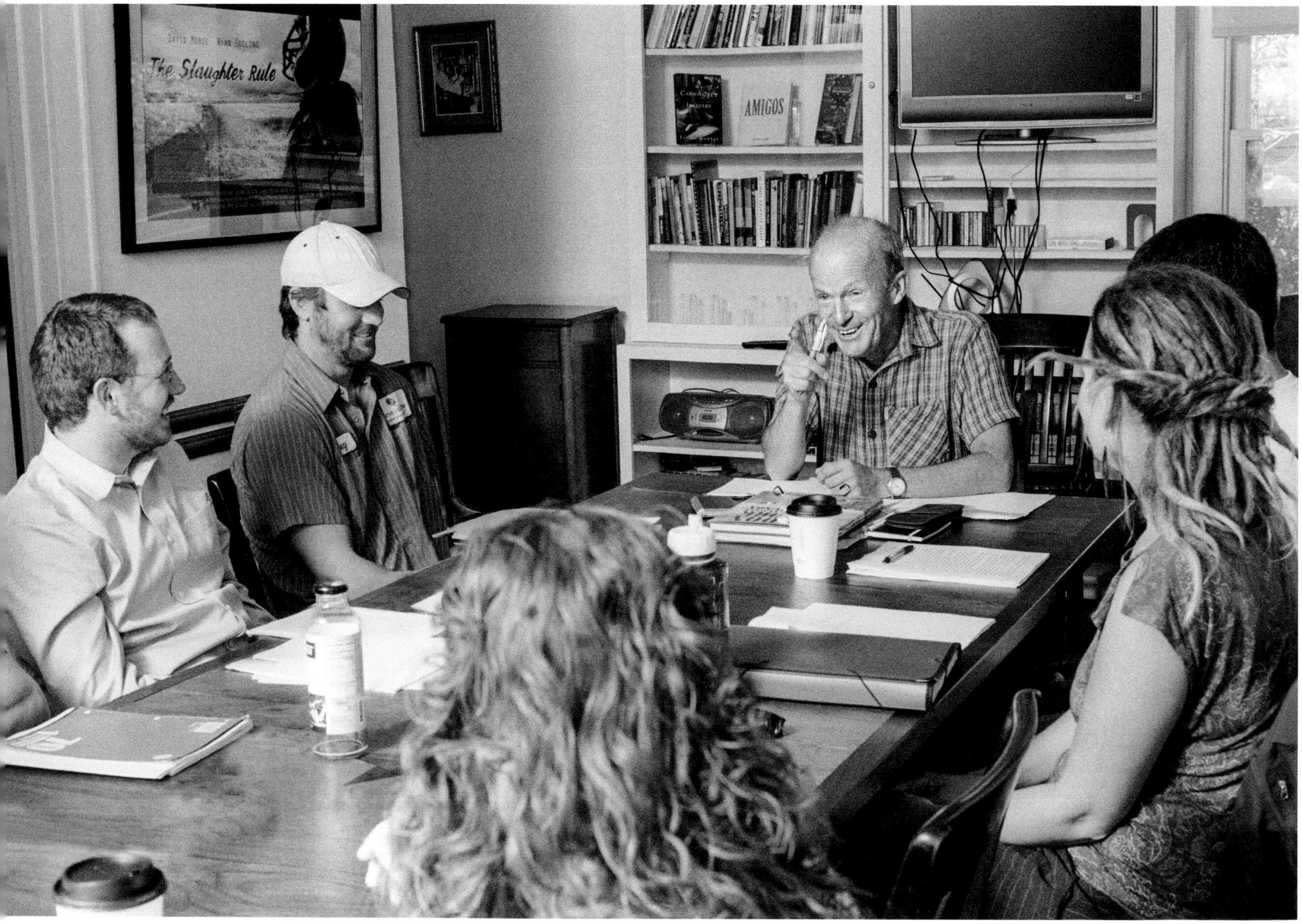

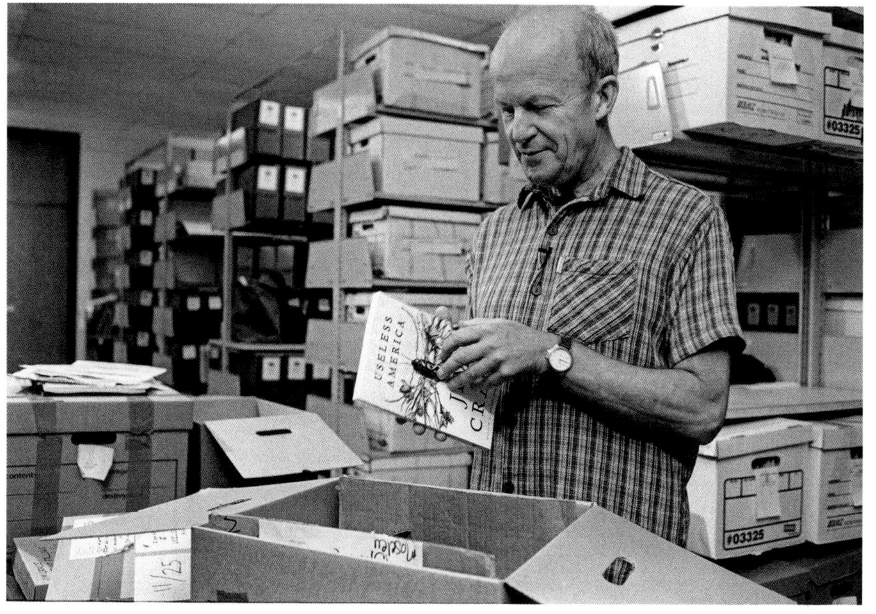

Crace was the first writer I photo-graphed for this project. My experience with him was such a happy, productive one, I asked if he could recommend any other writers. "I'm not very literary," he said, "I don't really know any writers. But good luck with your project. Don't let any of them get too grand. A bit of rain always does the trick."

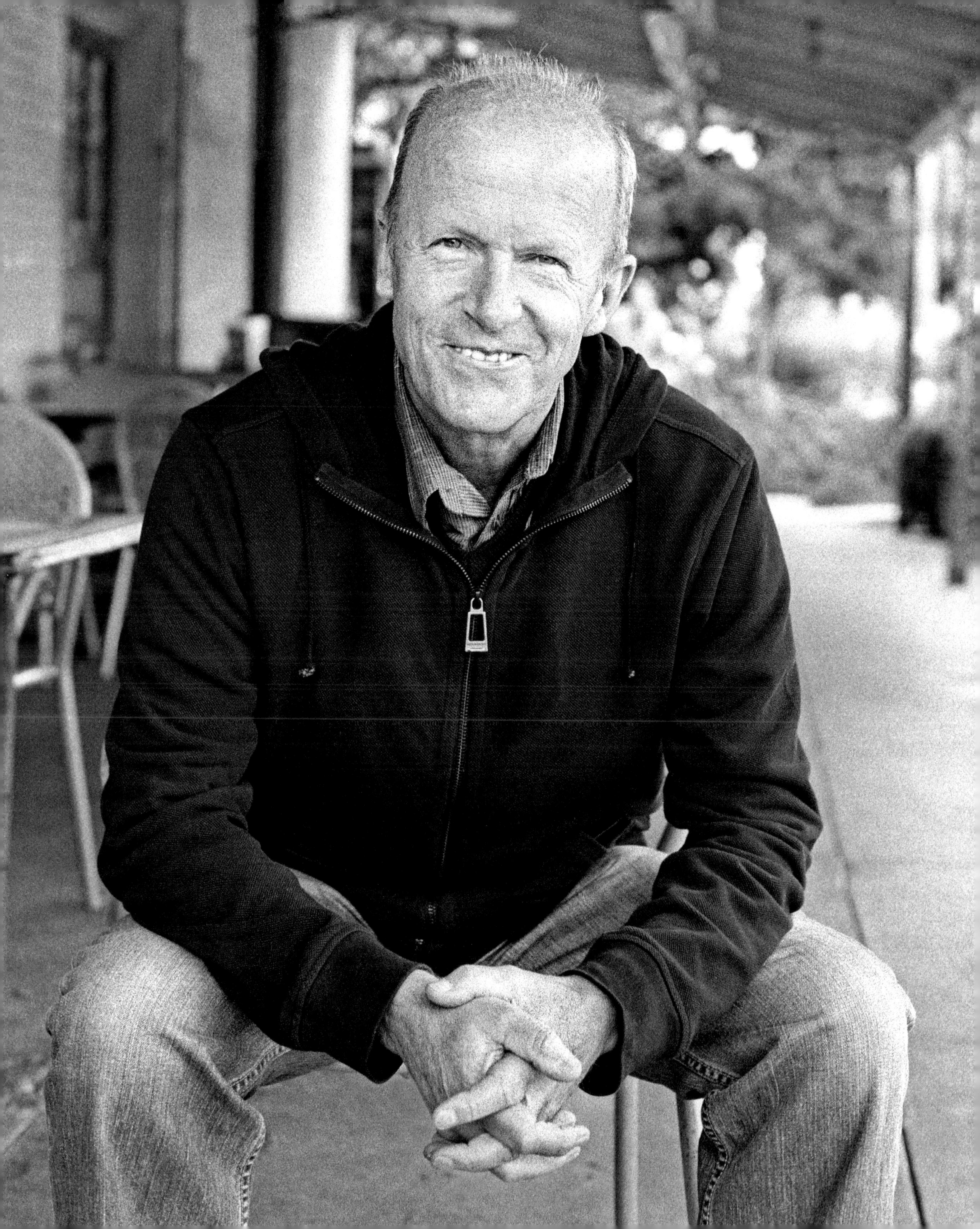

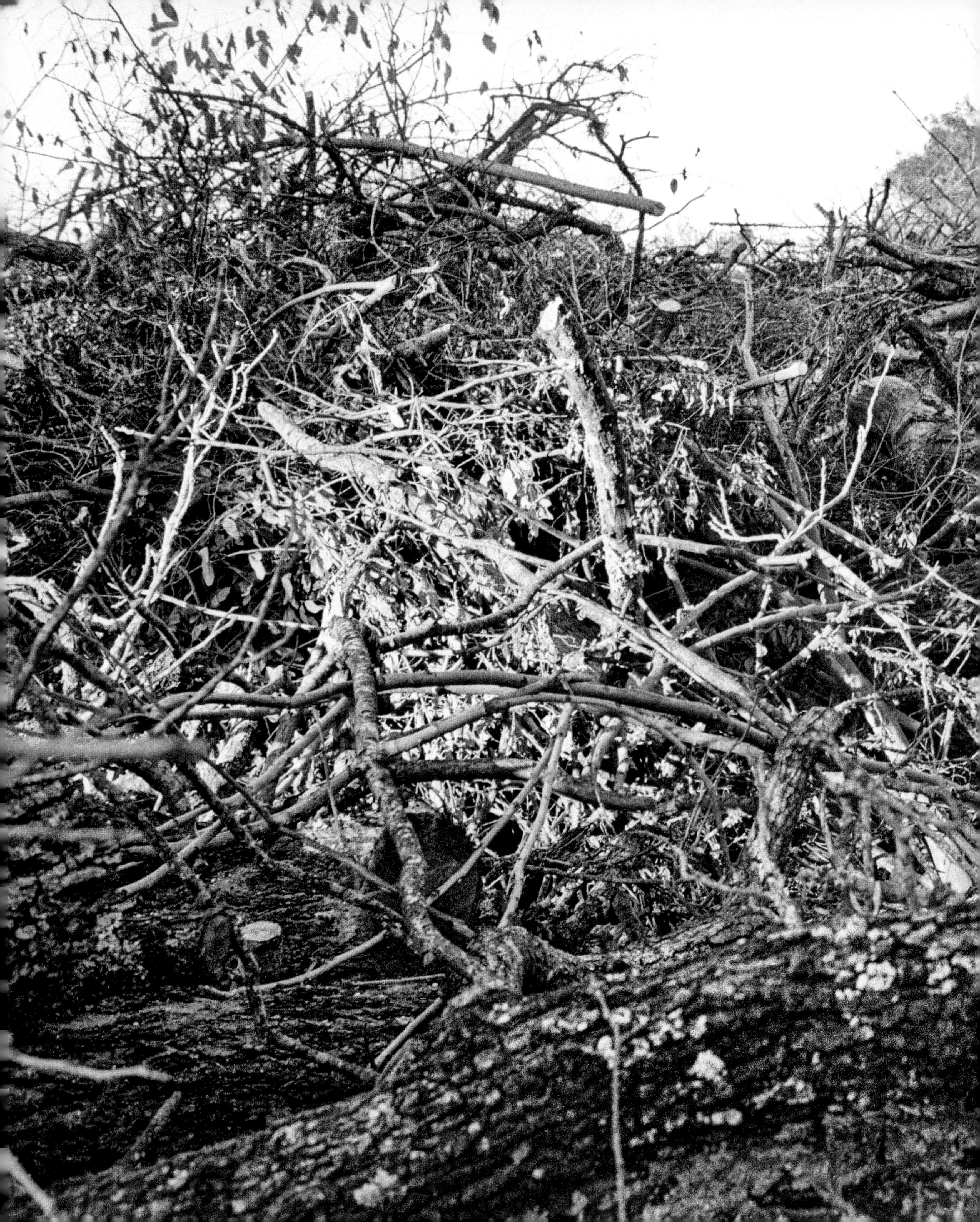

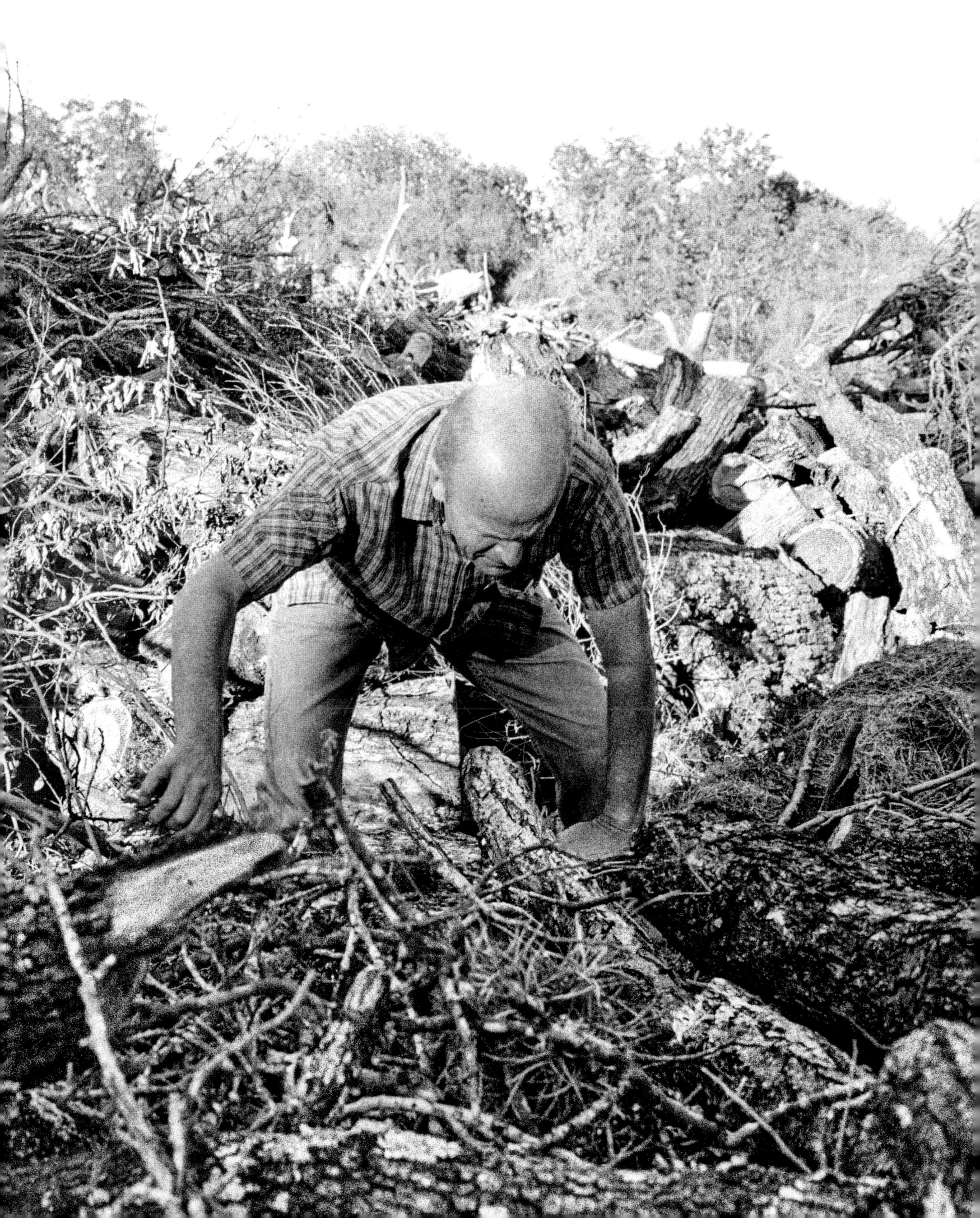

Russell Banks

American (b. 1940)

Photographed in Miami, Florida, February 2013

Russell Banks told me, "My romance with south Florida and Miami goes back to my adolescence and still sustains me, and still feeds my work—at least half of it." He dropped out of college in 1958, and fled from rural New England, where he grew up, to Florida with the hope of joining Fidel Castro in his armed revolt against Batista. But, as a skinny American teenager who knew no Spanish, he only got as far as Miami. The inspiration for the other half of his work is upstate rural New York in the Adirondacks, where Banks lives for six months of the year. The two locales are different in every possible way—socially, politically, racially, and economically. Banks said: "I seem to need access to both worlds in order to fill out the picture of America in the twenty-first century. Both places, taken together, connect to my past and provide me with a coherent lifelong narrative."

I photographed Banks in Miami, where he and his wife, Chase Twichell, live during the winter months in a stunning apartment with wide views overlooking the city's harbors. Twichell is a poet and writer herself, so she understands the demands of a writer's life. This is liberating for Banks, as he doesn't have to explain or make excuses. Twichell knows from her own experience the obsessional nature of writing.

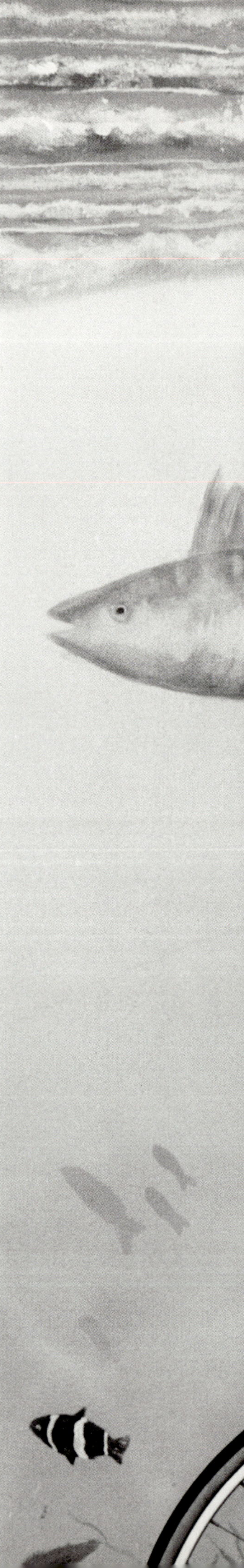

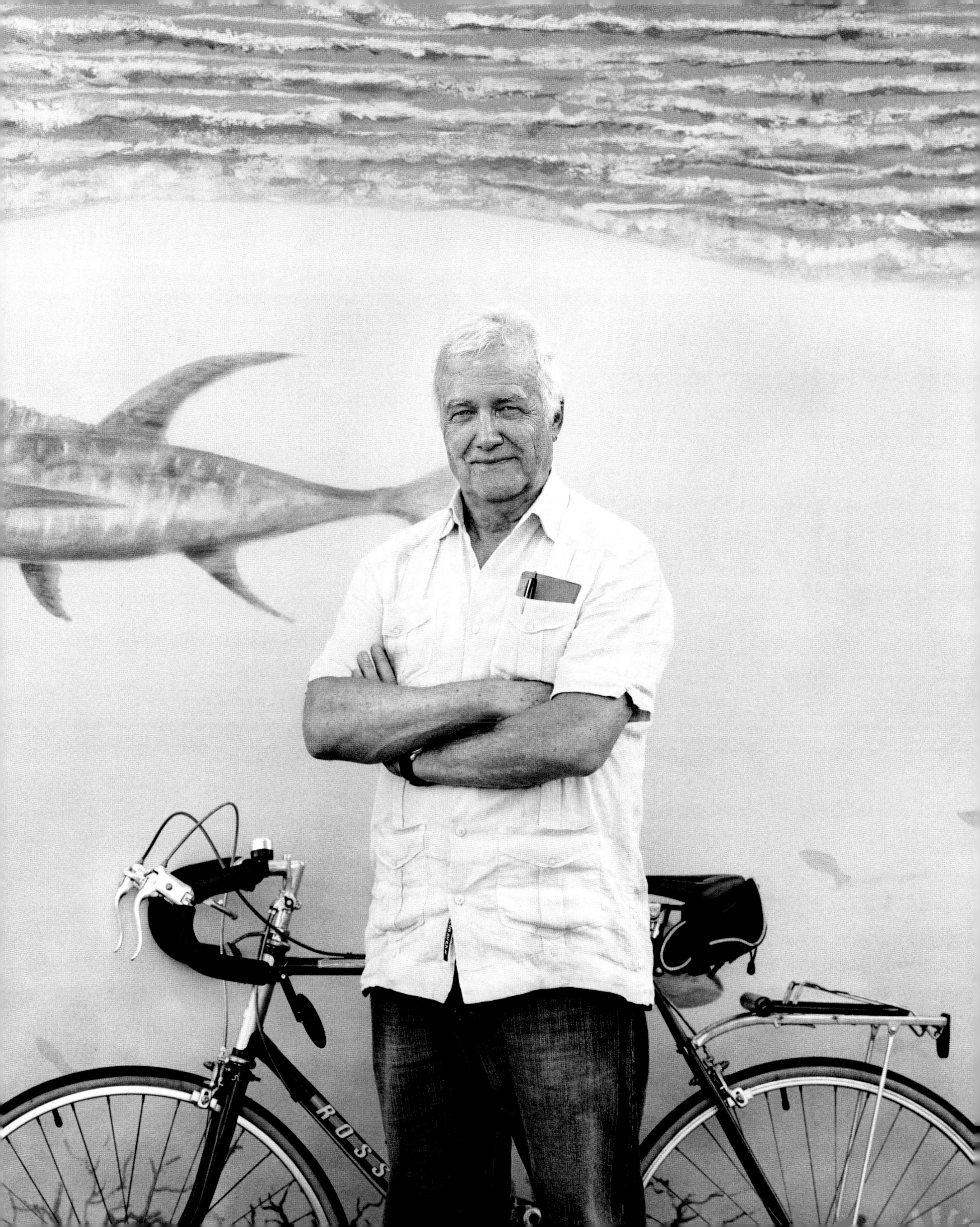

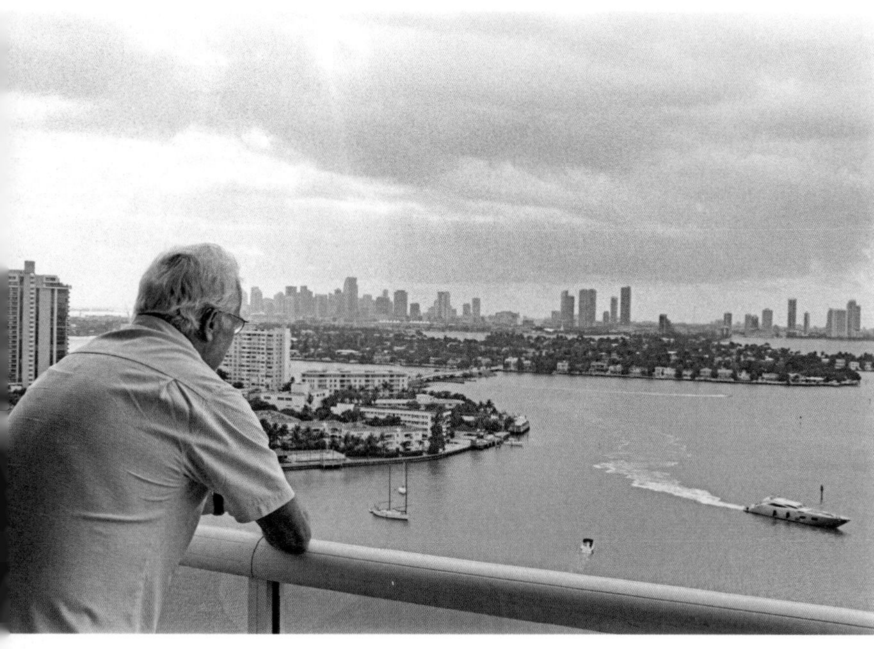

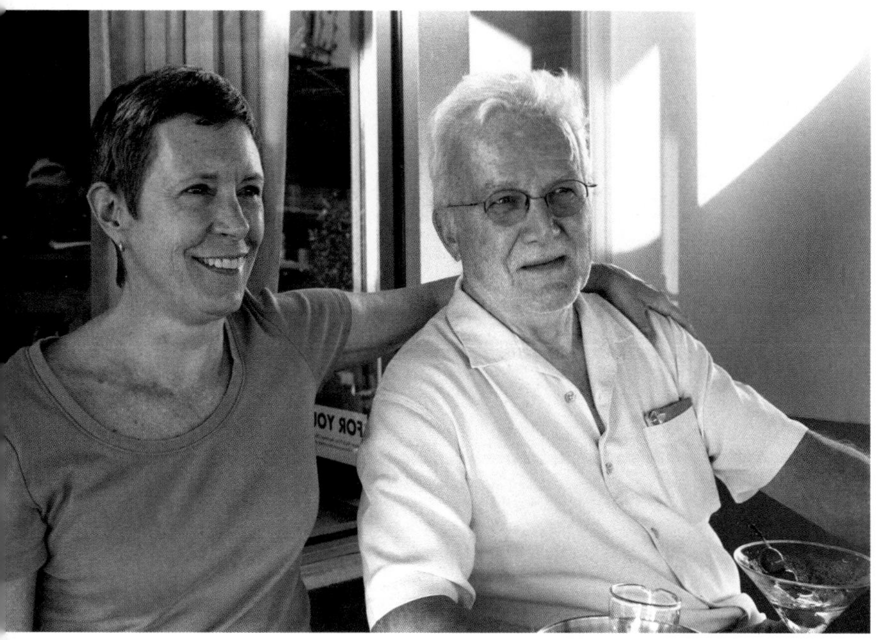

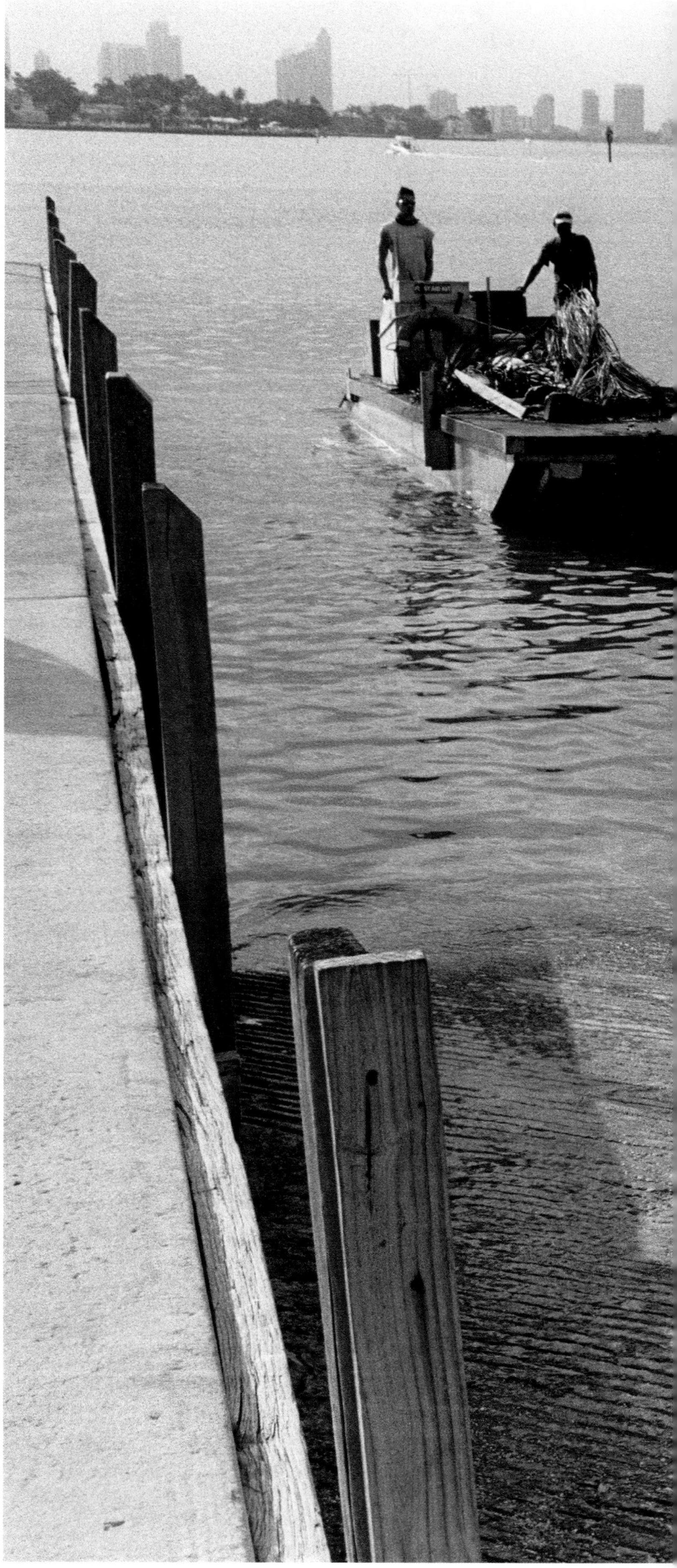

Banks likes to explore Miami on his bicycle. When
I asked what he looked for on his long leisurely rides,
he said: "Streets and alleys, buildings and houses,
yards and gardens and plantings that I could never
see from a car. Also faces and bodies, and the clothes
and decorations people adorn themselves with. Biking
gives me a deeper, more complex inner map of the city
than walking would or riding around in a car."

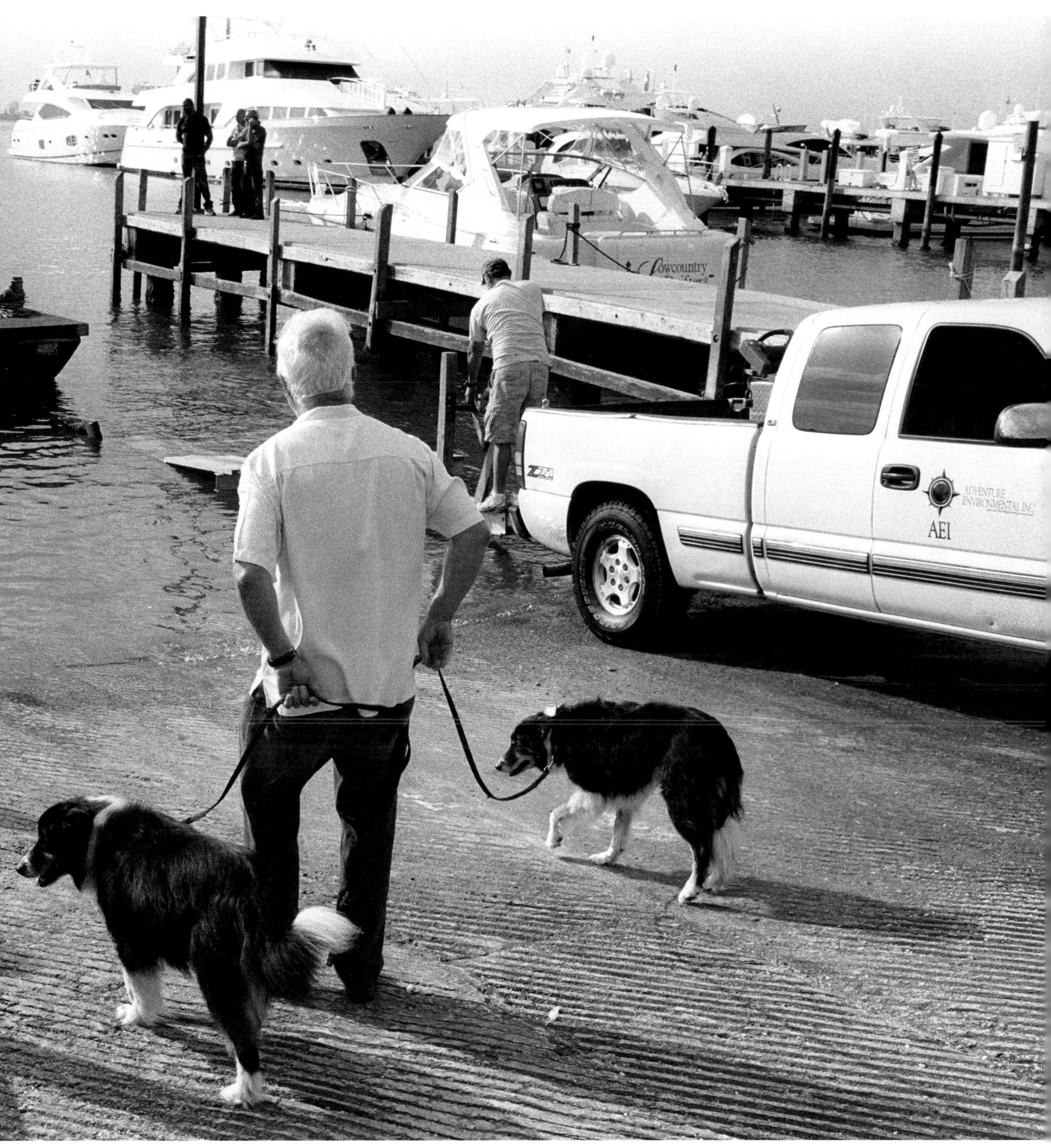

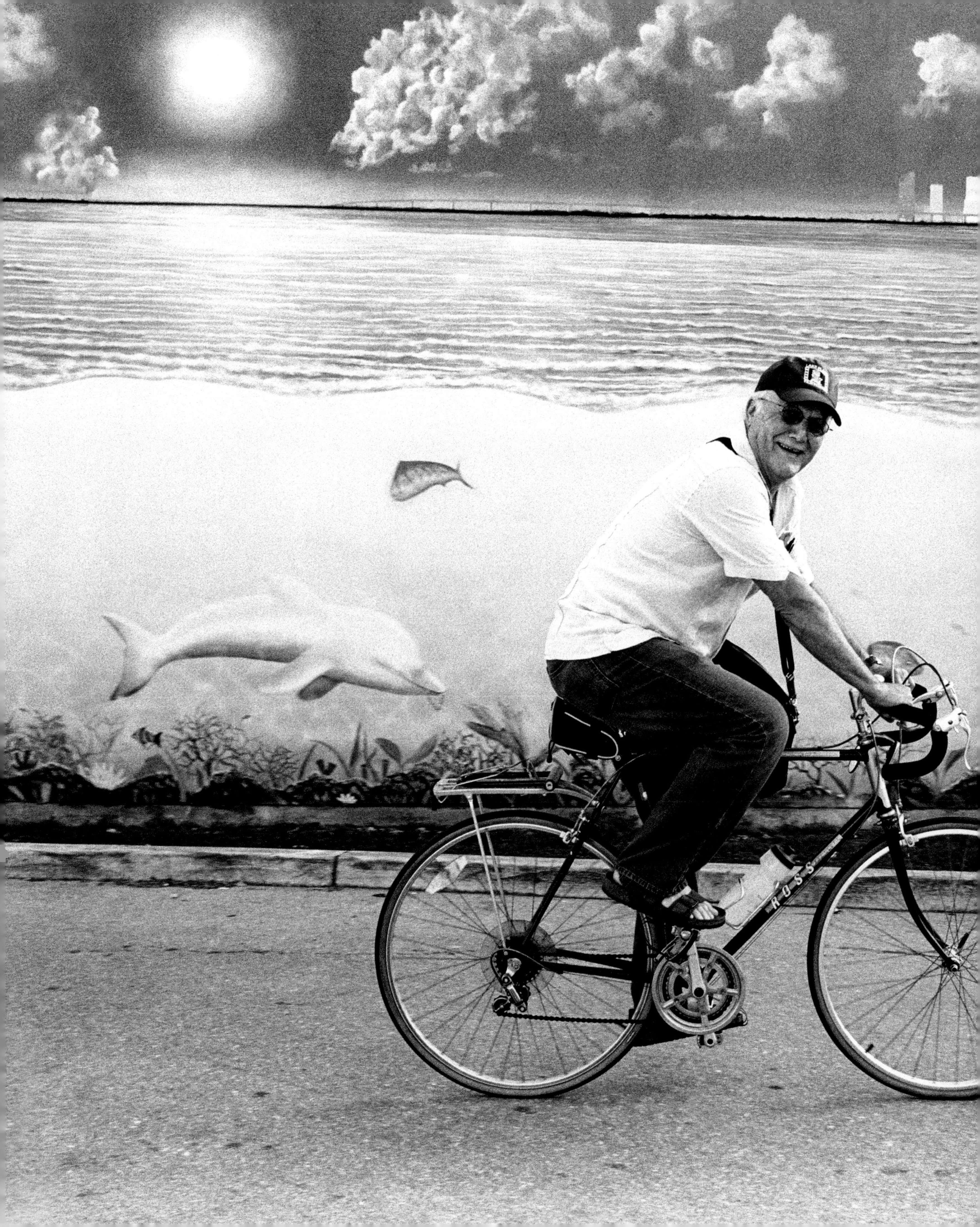

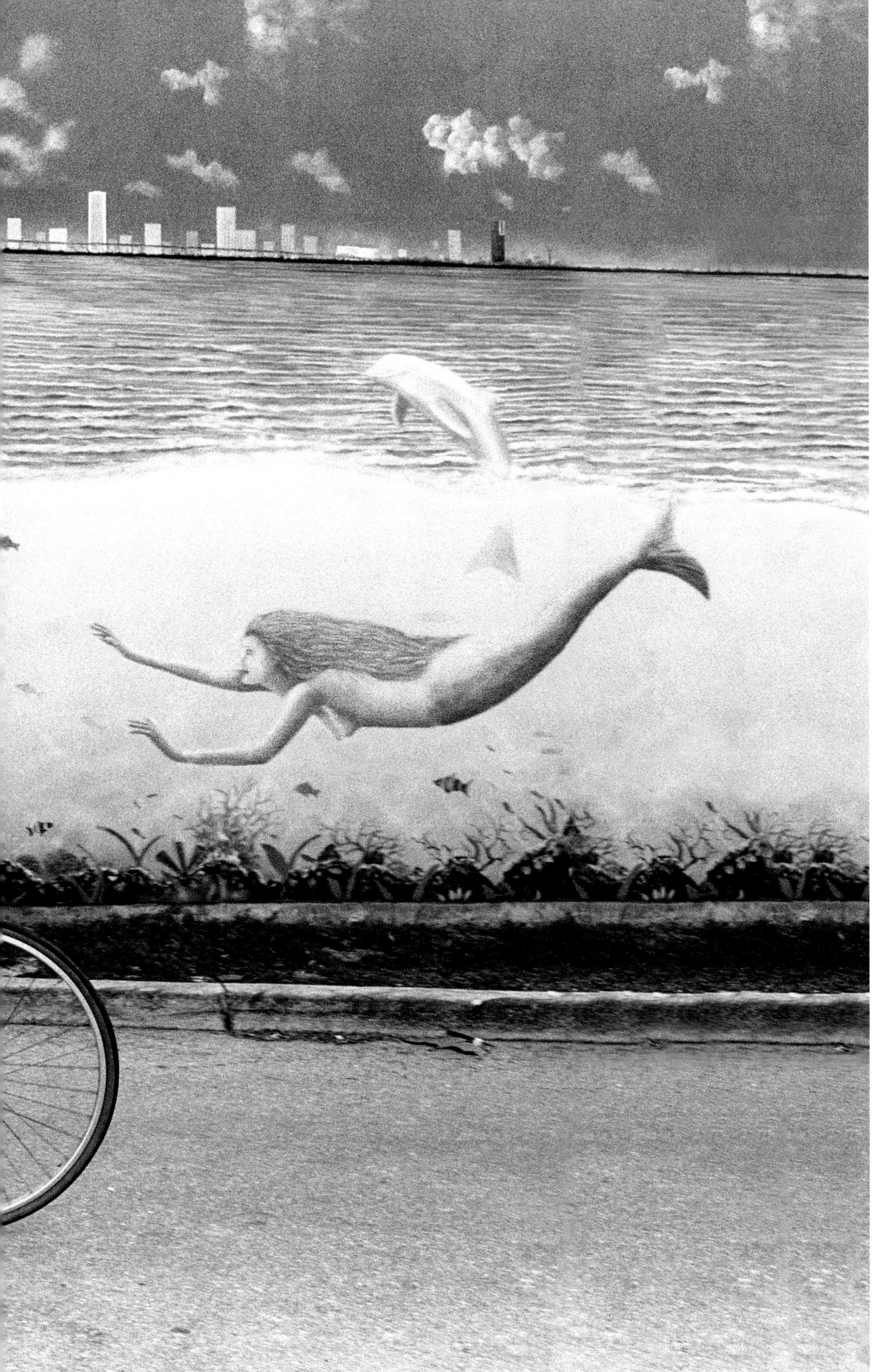

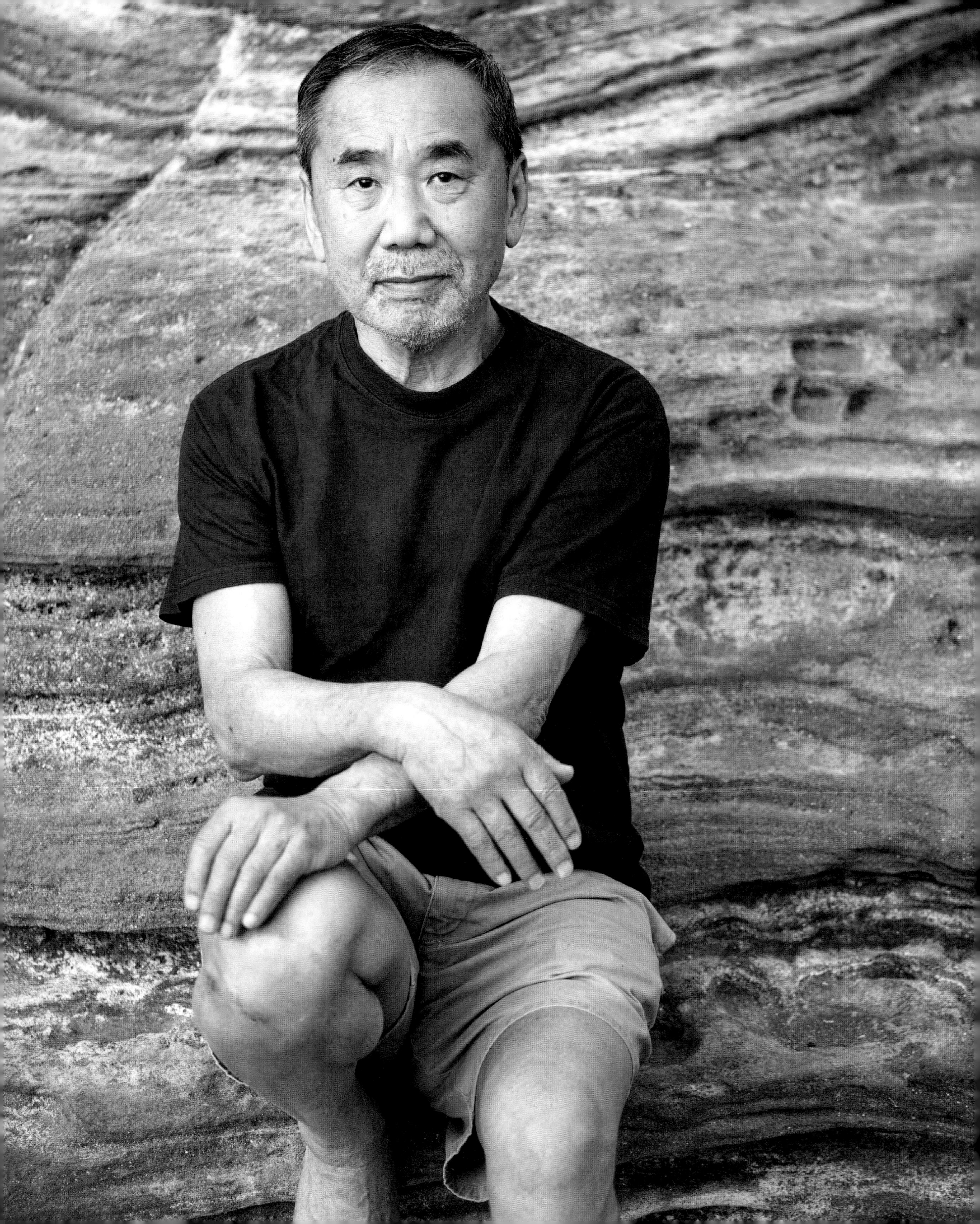

Haruki Murakami

Japanese (b. 1949)

Photographed on Oahu, Hawaii, February 2022

The moment Haruki Murakami rounded the corner of an apartment complex on Oahu, I knew who he was although I had never seen more than a postage-stamp-size photo of him. The curious, intent look in his eye and his boyish athleticism make him stand out.

Murakami gets up at 4 A.M. to write. "I like the hour to be early morning," he told me. "It's still dark outside. There are no sounds. I can concentrate." He writes in Japanese for two or three hours. "I just write what I want to write, when I want to write." He seems undaunted by writers' normal anxieties. "A story comes naturally to me. And I just write it down. I have to write. It's my work. When I'm tired, I quit and go for a run."

Murakami runs every day. It balances his mind. He has run a marathon a year, sometimes two, for a total of forty-three marathons. When he was younger, he tried to set new records for himself in each race, but not anymore. Now he just enjoys running. He takes a break from thinking when he runs. "I keep my mind vacant," he said. When it's raining or cold, he'll go to a gym or swimming pool to work out. In the afternoon he relaxes by reading or listening to his extensive record collection.

He is an active translator. Raymond Carver, Tim O'Brien, and F. Scott Fitzgerald have been converted by Murakami into Japanese. In 2006, he translated *The Great Gatsby*. "This is my favorite, my most favorite book," he told me. "If you want to write a good book, you have to read a good book. Translating helps me write the right way." Most successful writers, however, don't do translations. Murakami is the exception. "To write is my work," he said. "To translate is my hobby."

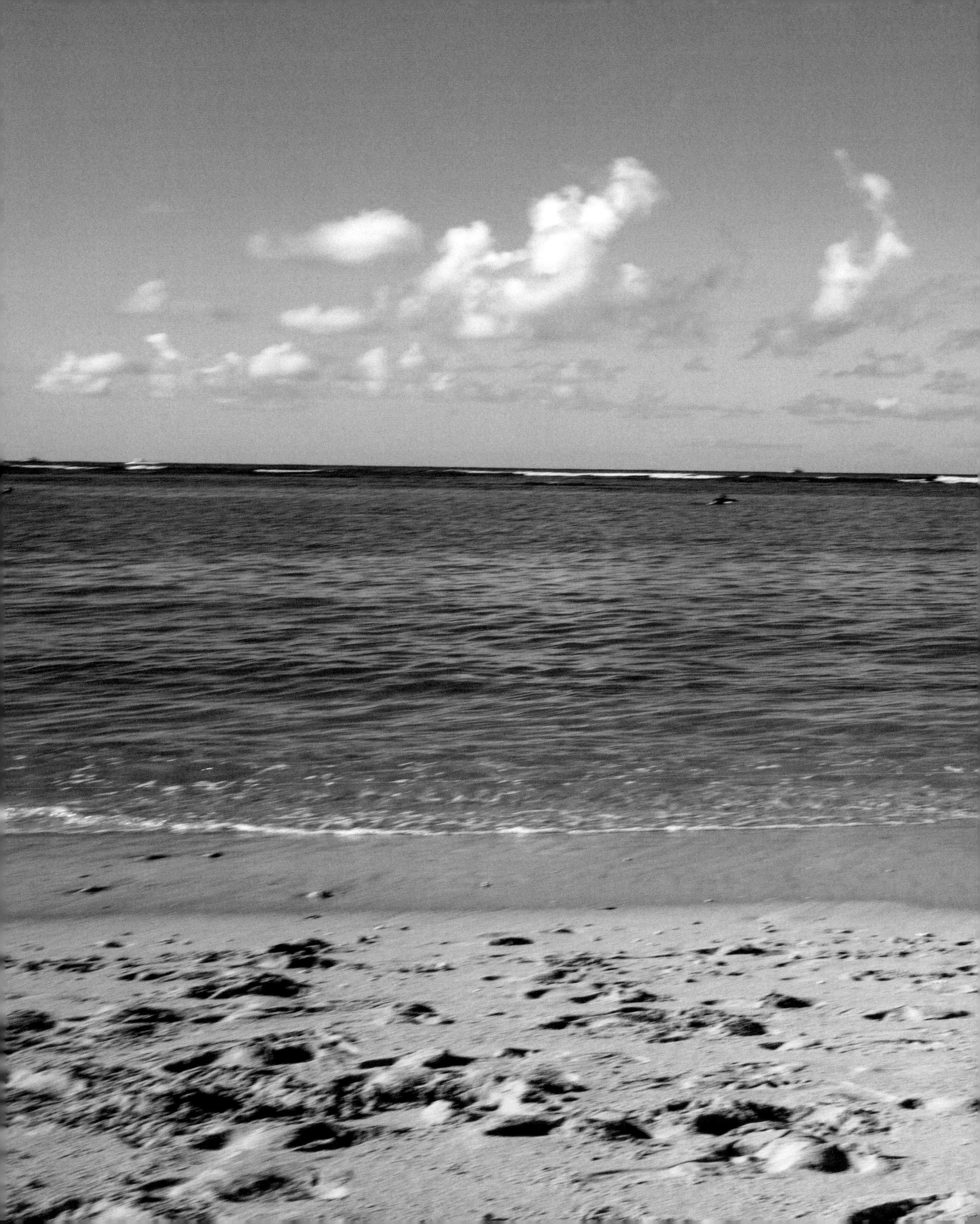

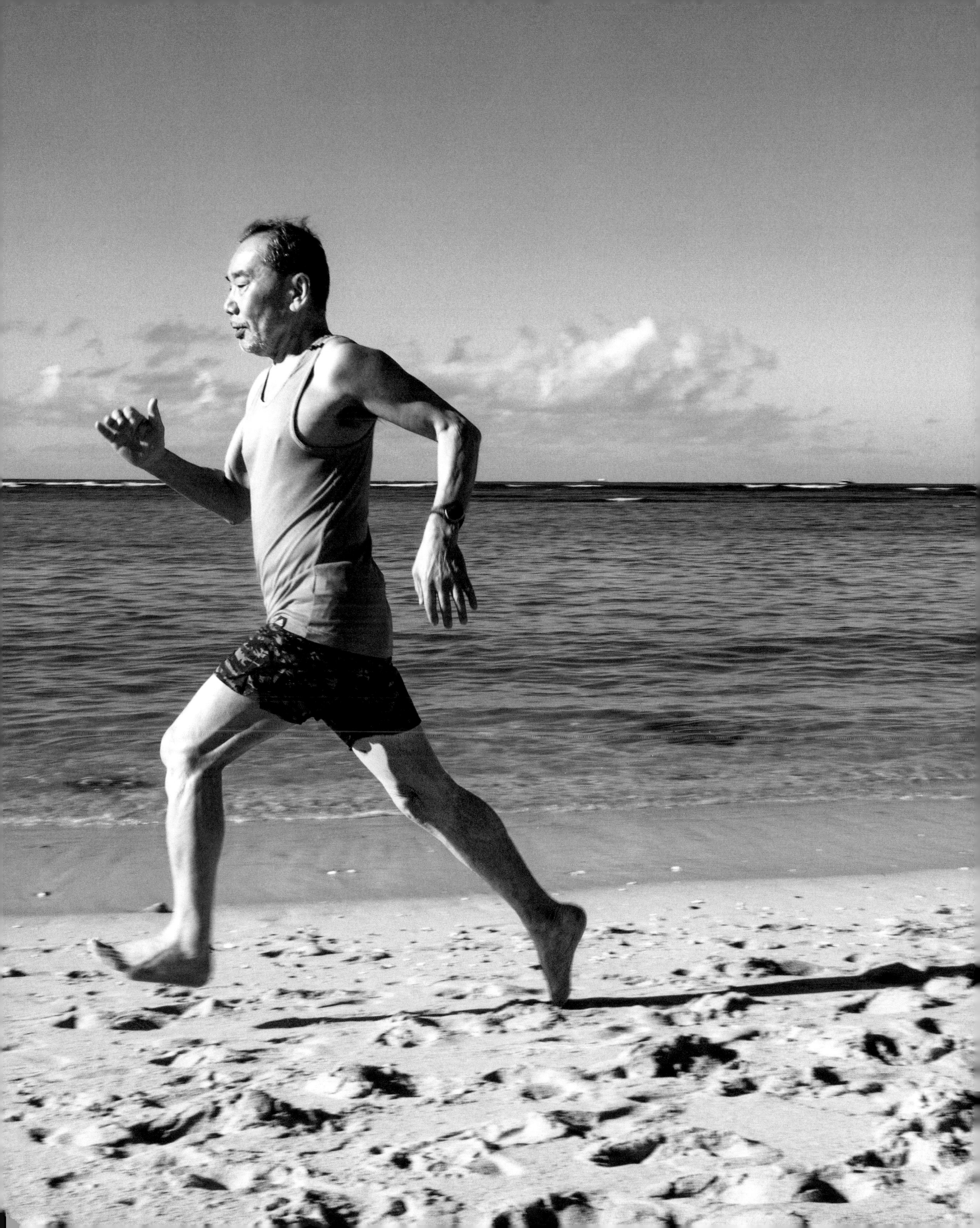

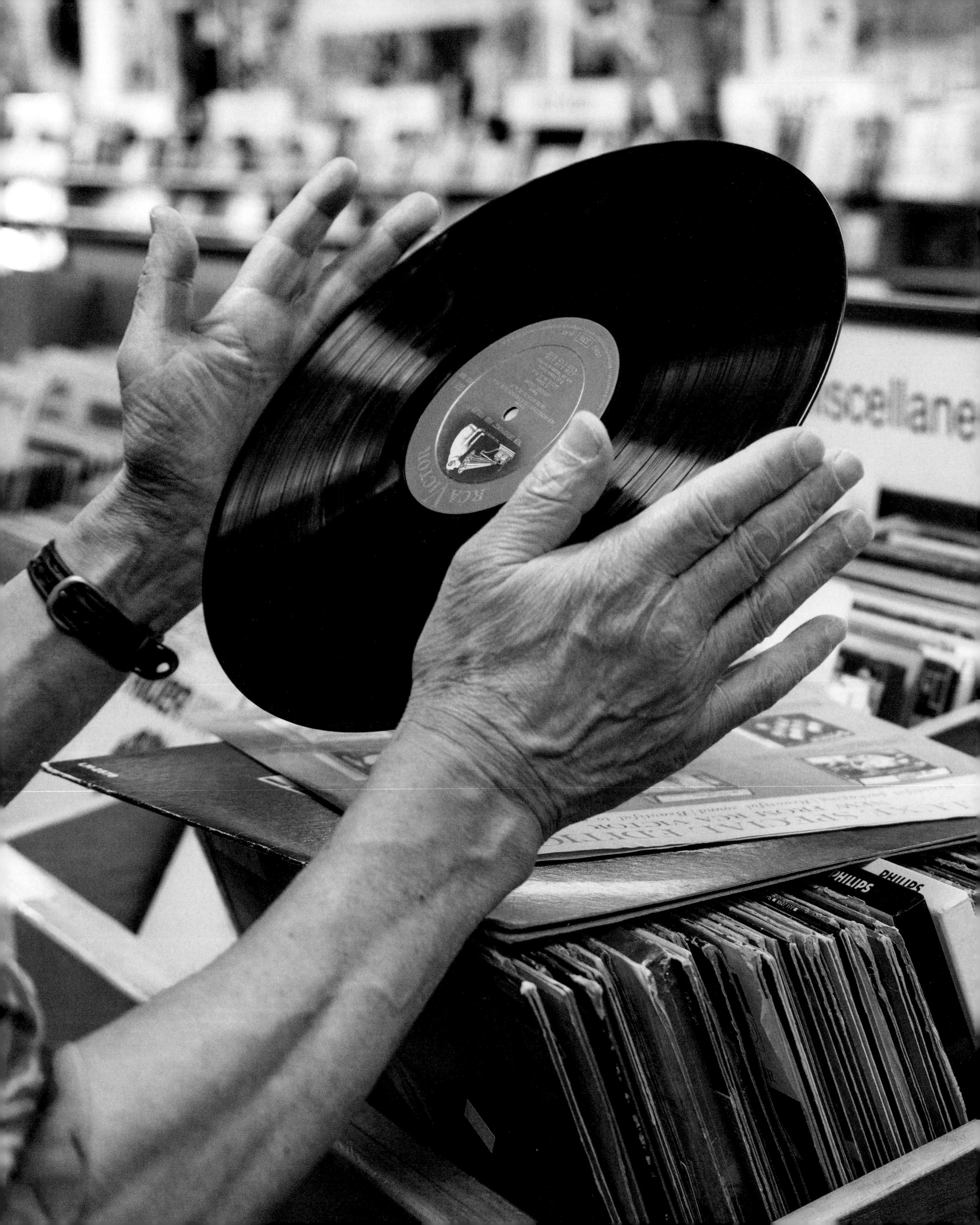

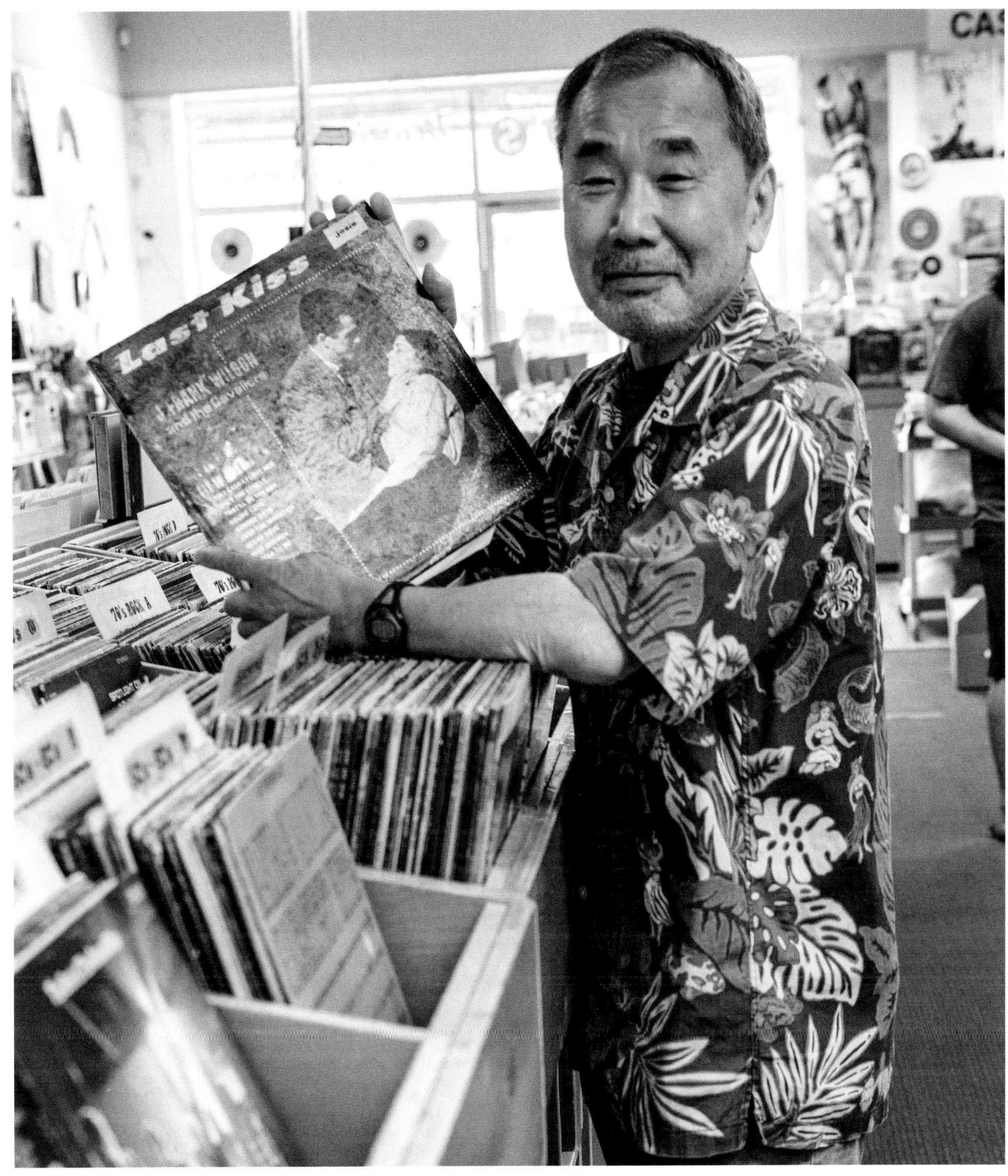

Wherever Murakami travels, he looks for vintage record shops. Some of the best ones are in Portland, Maine, and Copenhagen, Denmark. He buys and trades vinyl jazz and classical recordings. "I have learned so many things about writing from good music. Melody, rhythm, improvisation. Every time I write, I think of these three things. Stan Getz is my hero. I collect everything he played. The sound is beautiful and his improvisation is very imaginative. The first time I heard him, I was sixteen years old and I fell in love with his sound. I cannot explain why. And I'm still in love with those sounds." Murakami has interviewed musicians who played with Getz and realized not everyone liked him. "His personality was horrible," Murakami said. "I think he had his own demons. A very complex person like Charles Dickens. The work is everything. Personality is another thing."

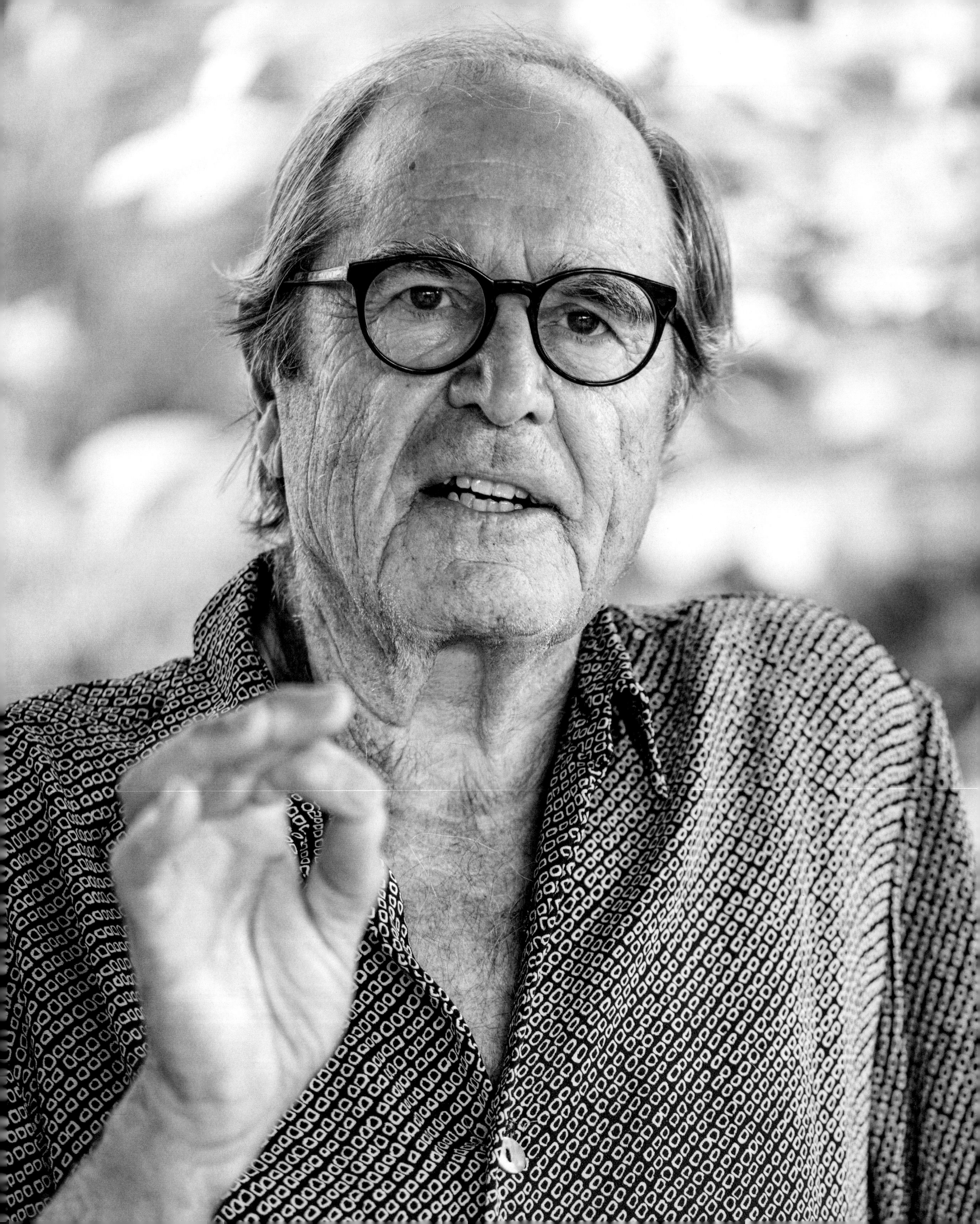

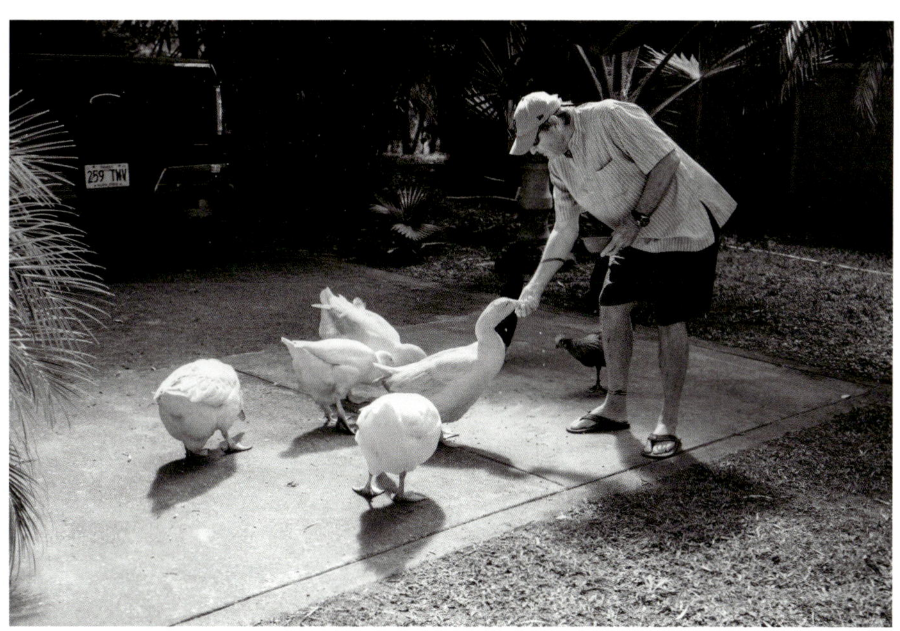

Paul
Theroux

American (b. 1941)

Photographed on Oahu, Hawaii, February 2022

The novelist and travel writer Paul Theroux lives high on a hill above the North Shore on the island of Oahu. His property is secluded among dense bamboo, tall palms, and avocado, mango, and lemon trees. But he can hop on his bike and ride less than a mile down the hill to swim in the Pacific Ocean. Or in the winter months, at the ocean's edge, he's in the catbird seat, watching the greatest surfers in the world compete at the Banzai Pipeline.

I had spent two days in Honolulu with Haruki Murakami and his wife, Yoko. On the third day, we decided to drive several hours along Oahu's coast to Hale'iwa to visit Theroux. In an attempt to warmly welcome the Murakamis, Theroux gathered his five unruly Emden geese; their obstreperous nature set the tone for a lively visit.

Even though we were the travelers, not he, I quickly saw how skillful Theroux was at gaining information. He was inquisitive, humorous, and self-deprecating, encouraging conversation and particularly pleased with an unexpected response.

Theroux found the courteous, shy Murakami a perfect foil, kindly teasing him about his fame and joking as they walked together through the house looking at indigenous objects from a lifetime of travels in Africa, India, Vanuatu, Tonga, and Samoa.

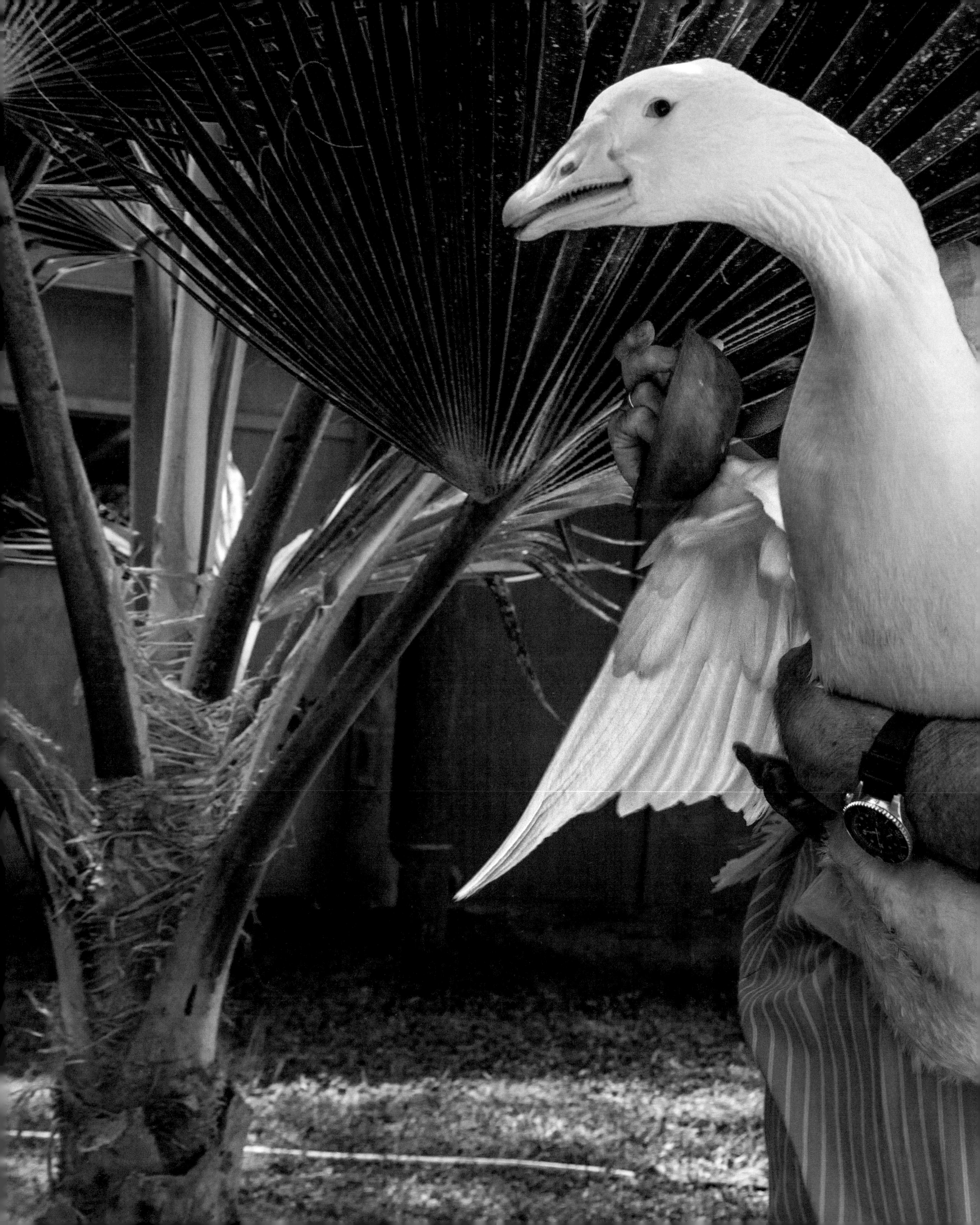

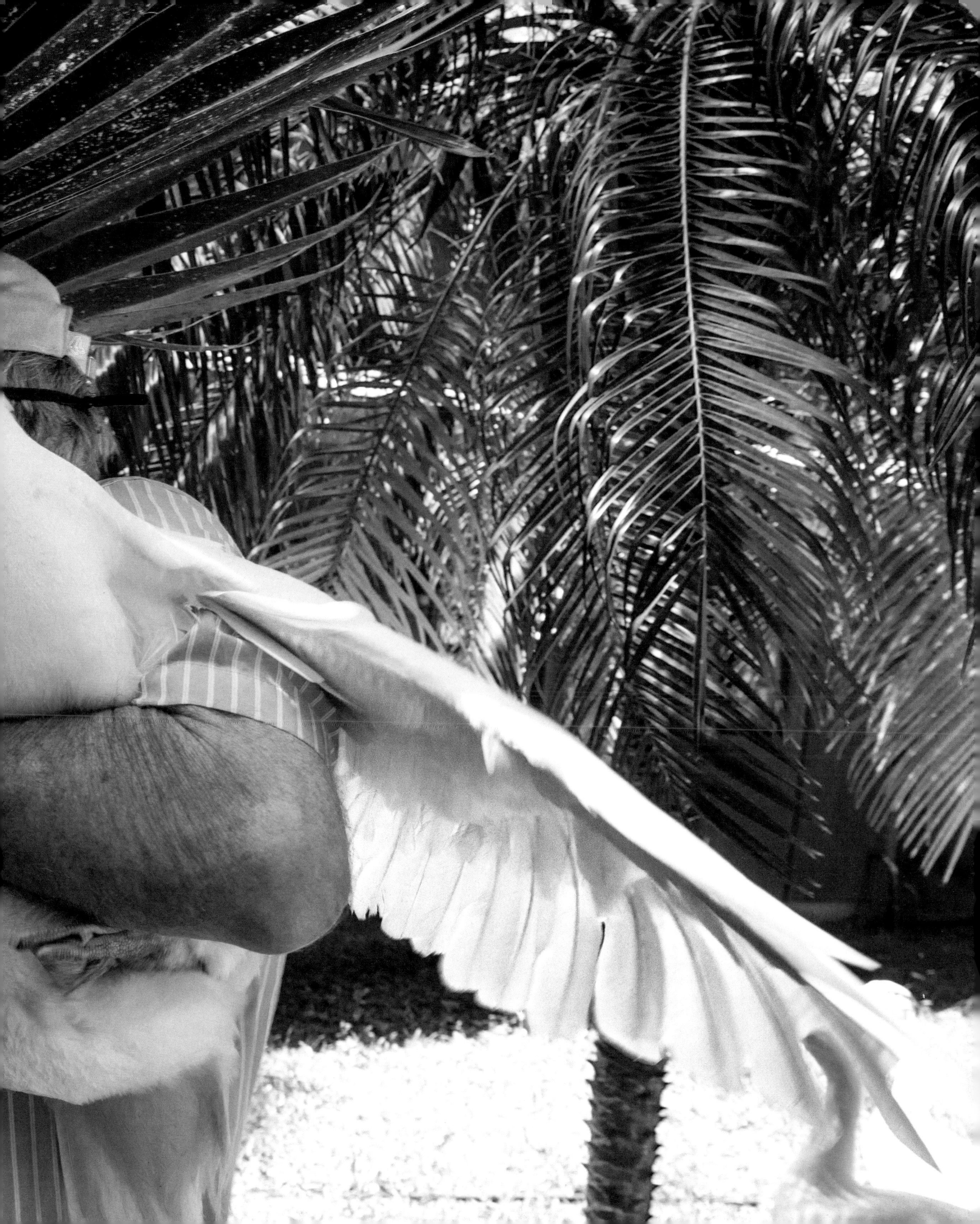

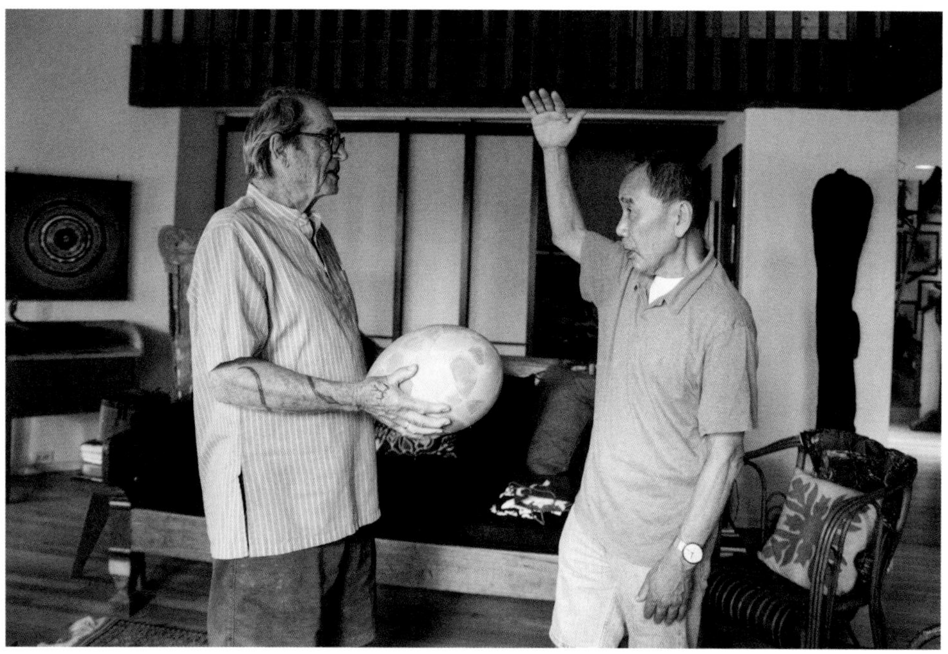

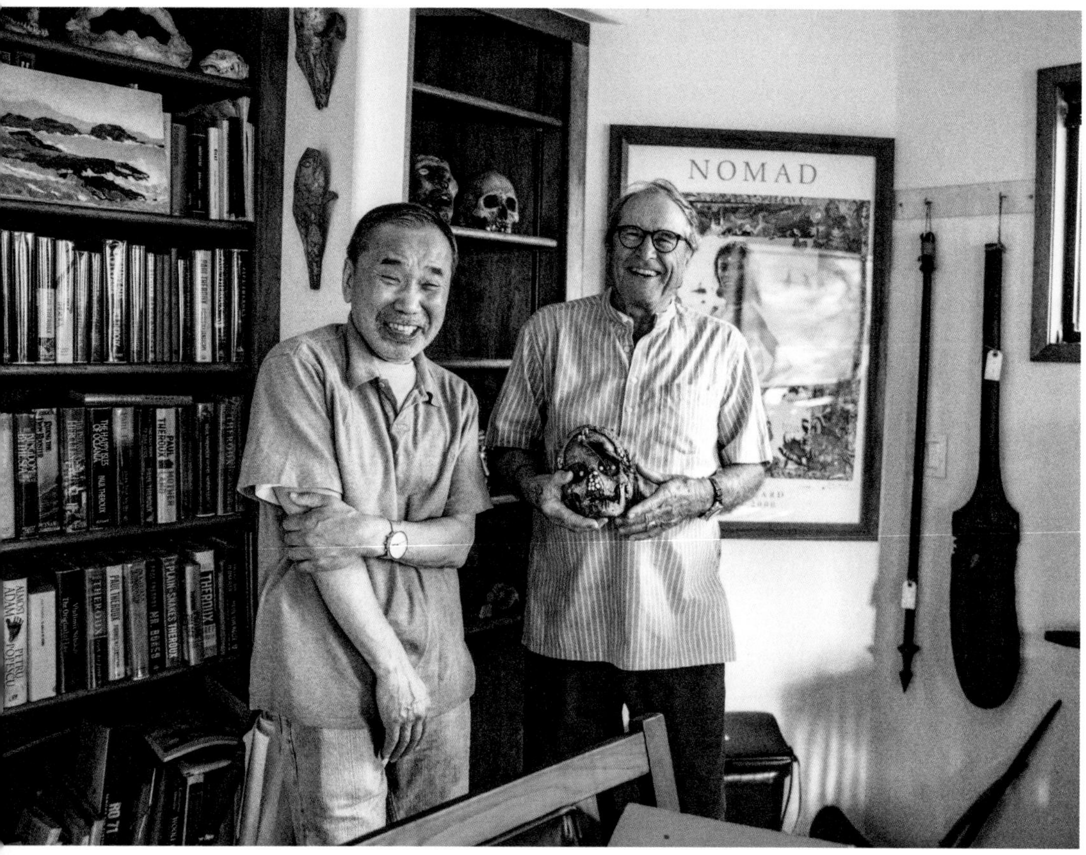

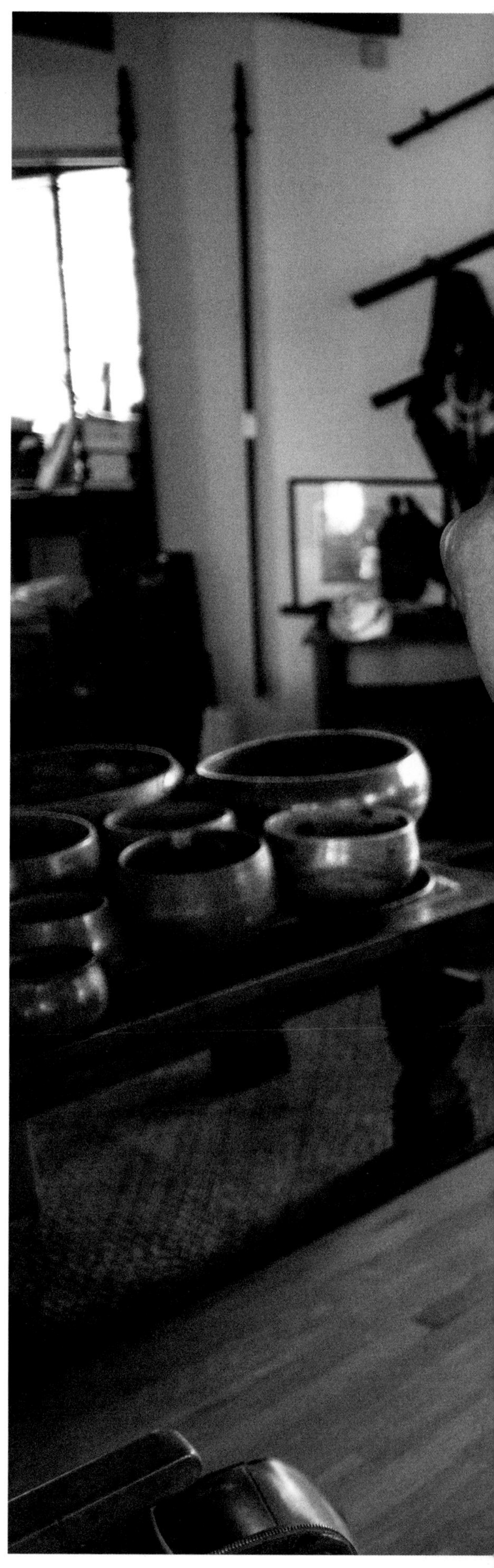

He inscribed his novel *Under the Wave at Waimea* to Haruki and Yoko, then urged Murakami to hold any of the human skulls he'd brought back from New Guinea, the Philippines, and Nepal. In the dark interior rooms, all the objects looked like treasures brought home by nineteenth-century sea captains from whaling voyages in the South Pacific.

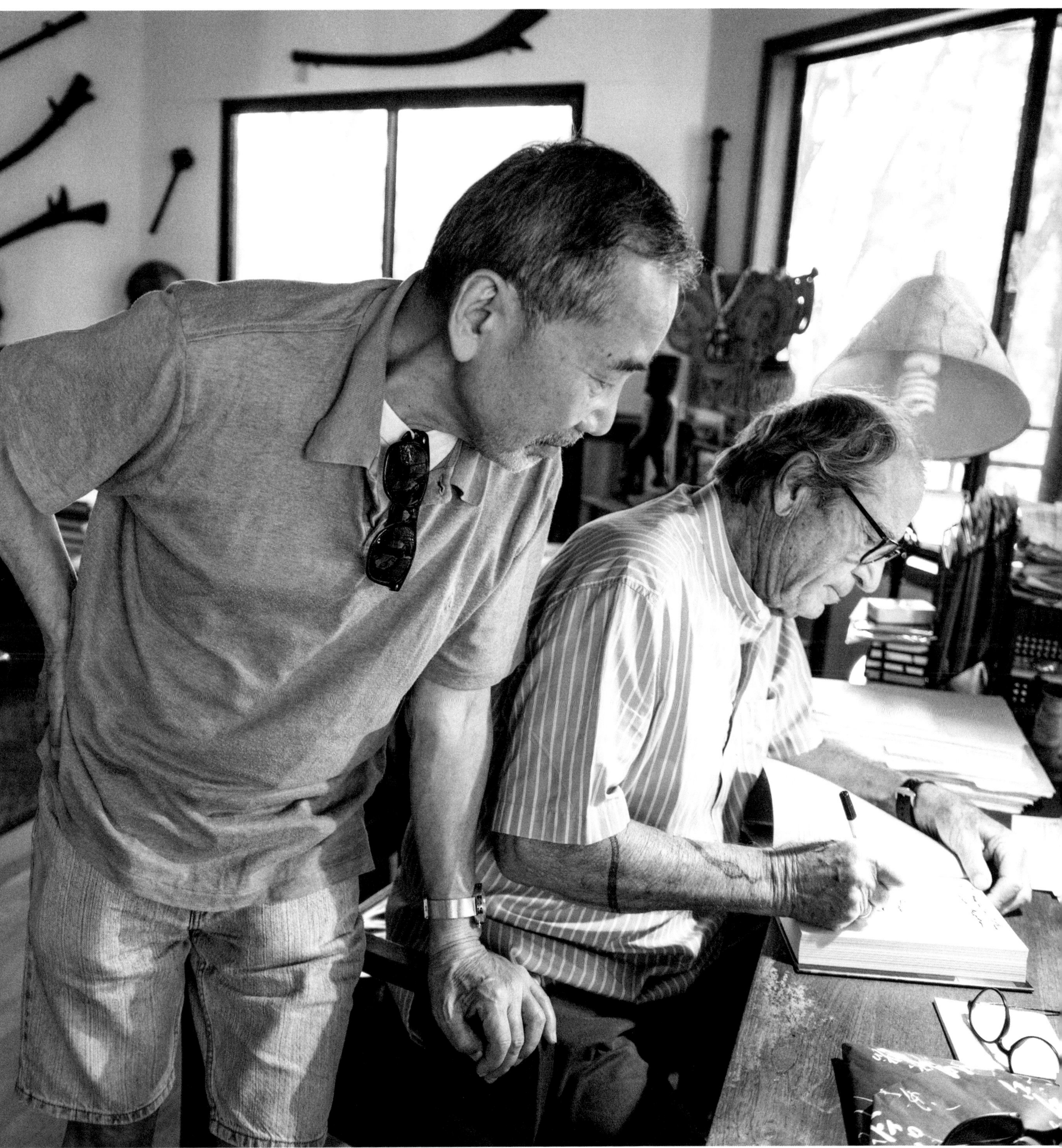

Edwidge Danticat

Haitian American (b. 1969)

Photographed in Miami, Florida, March 2019

Russell Banks first brought Edwidge Danticat to my attention in 2013. "She lives in Miami," he said, "and she's one of the country's best young writers." Born in Port-au-Prince, Haiti, where she was raised speaking French and Haitian Creole in her aunt and uncle's house, Danticat moved at twelve to be with her parents, who had immigrated earlier to New York. They lived in a Haitian American community in Brooklyn.

Now, with her husband and two young daughters, Danticat lives in Miami's Little Haiti neighborhood, where the warm, humid weather and vibrant culture form an elemental connection to the island of her childhood. She browses among the small businesses, visiting a clothes shop owner or a coconut vendor, and she enjoys the authentic Haitian food and getting a coffee at Tigeorges Kafé.

Danticat took me several times to the Libreri Mapou Bookstore, owned by her friend Jean-Marie Willer Denis. Jan Mapou, as he is known, has operated this Creole bookstore for more than thirty years, surviving economic downturns and, more recently, the pandemic. He checked on an order while Danticat and community activist Leonie Hermantin caught up on local news.

Colorful murals enliven the walls of public buildings in Little Haiti honoring the cultural and political history of Caribbean immigrants. For instance, there is one of Neg Mawon, the Black Maroon, a Haitian slave blowing on a conch shell, alerting people to the 1791–1804 revolt against France. There is even a mural paying tribute to Jan Mapou.

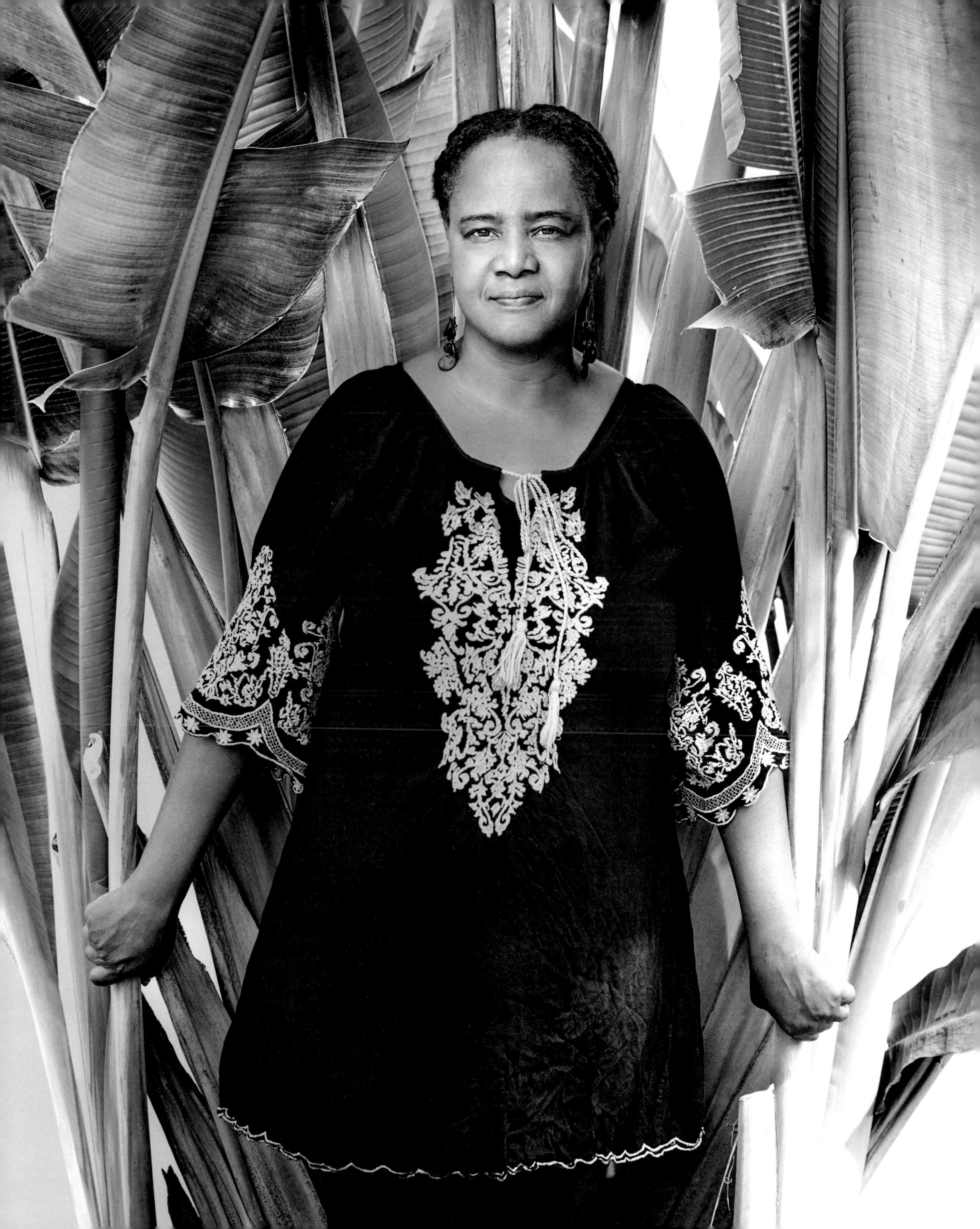

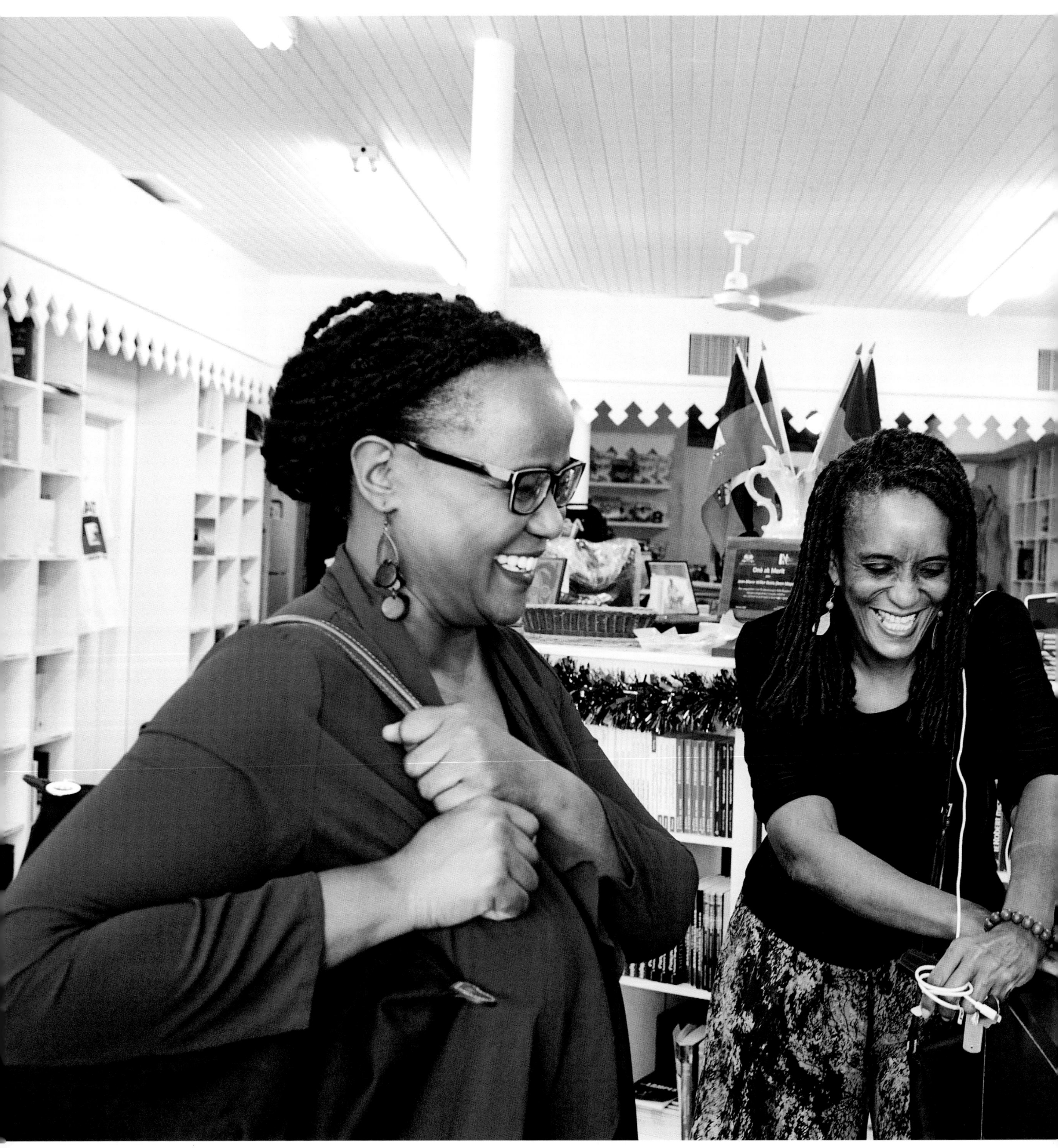

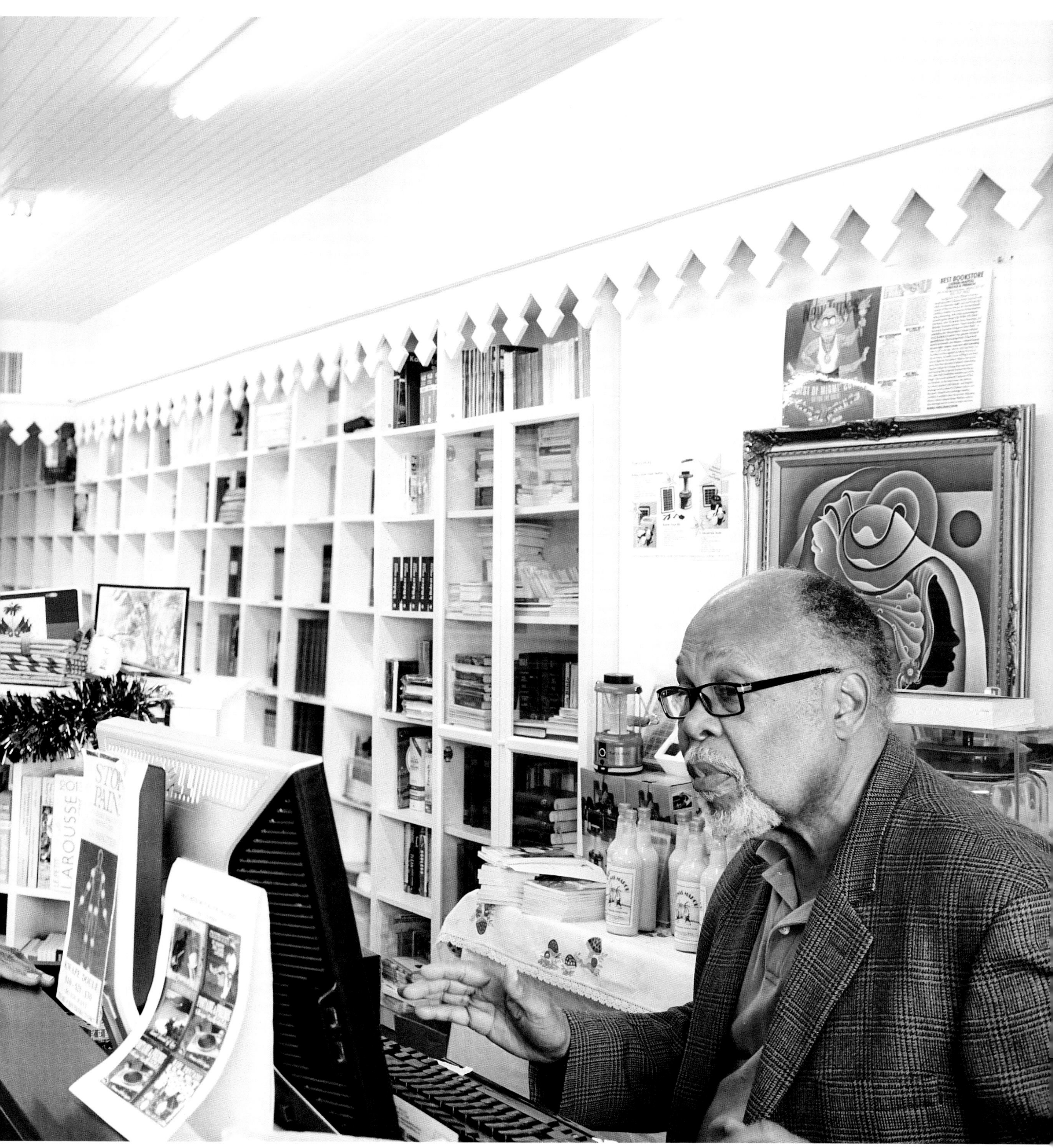

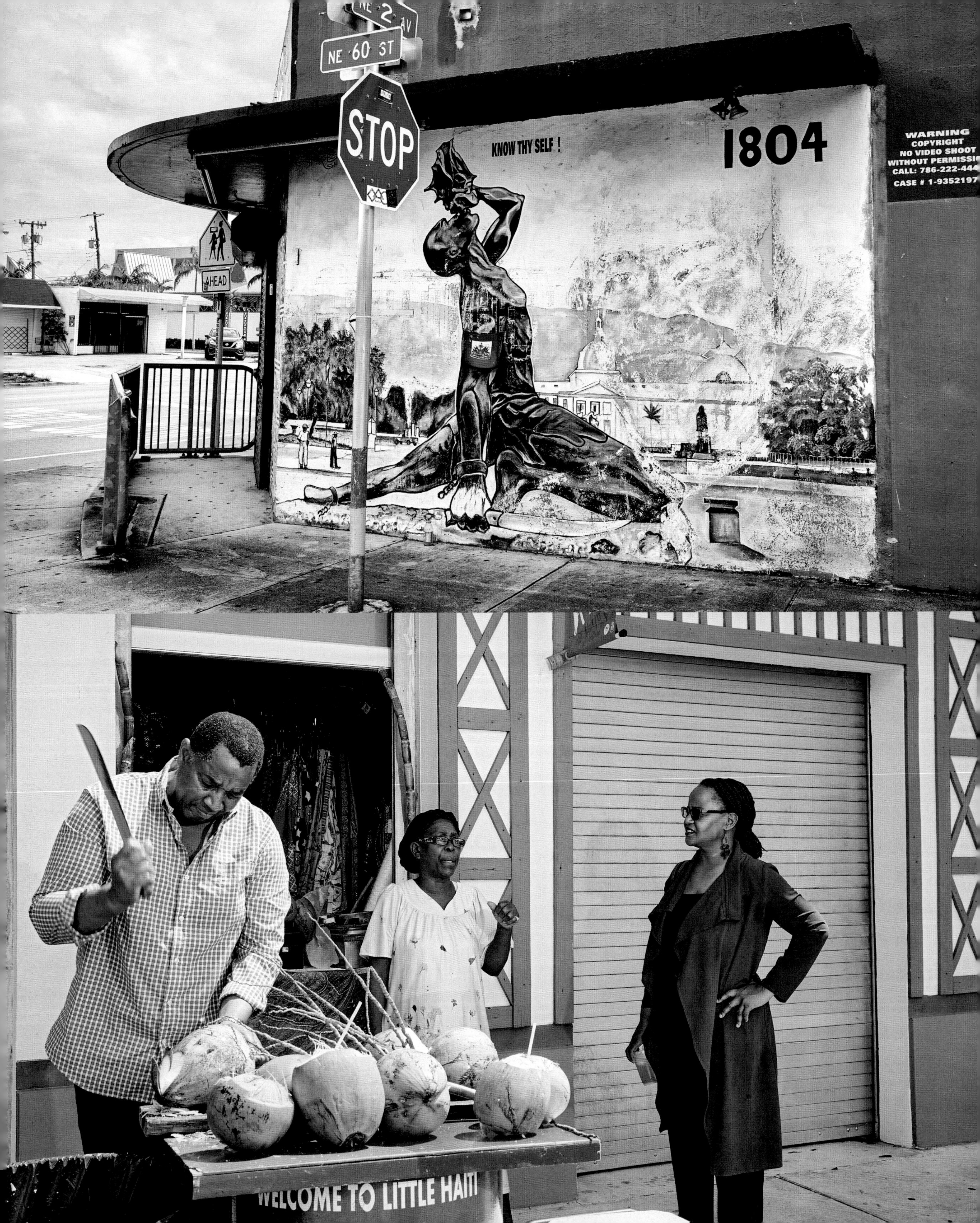

NE 2 AV
NE 60 ST
STOP
KNOW THY SELF !
1804
WARNING
COPYRIGHT
NO VIDEO SHOOT
WITHOUT PERMISSION
CALL: 786-222-444
CASE # 1-9352197
AHEAD
WELCOME TO LITTLE HAITI

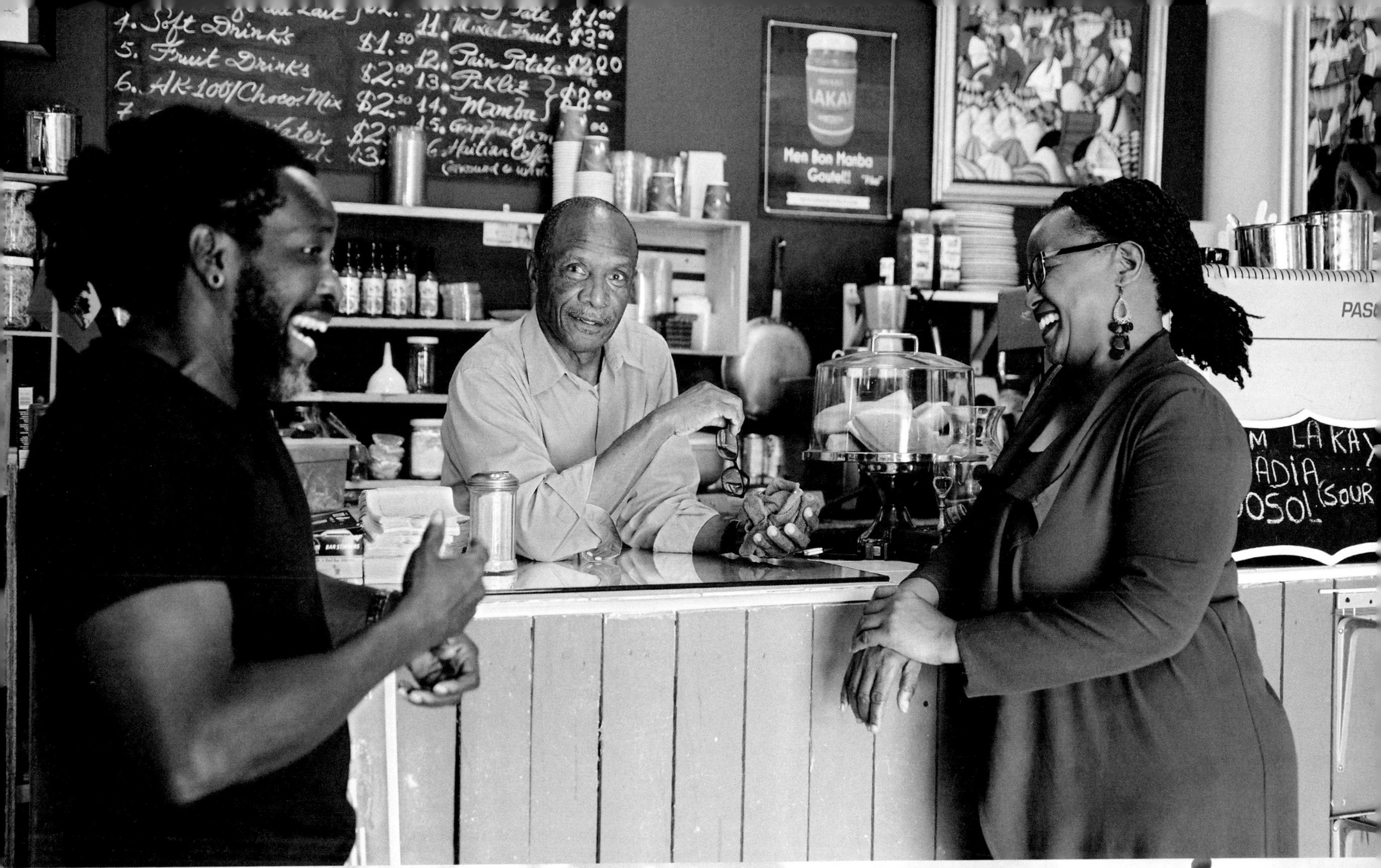

4. Soft Drinks
5. Fruit Drinks
6. AK-100/Choco. Mix
7. ...Water
11. Mixed Fruits
12. Pain Patate
13. Pikliz
14. Mamba
15. Grapefruit...
16. Haitian Coffee

LAKAY
Men Ban Manba
Goute! "Na"

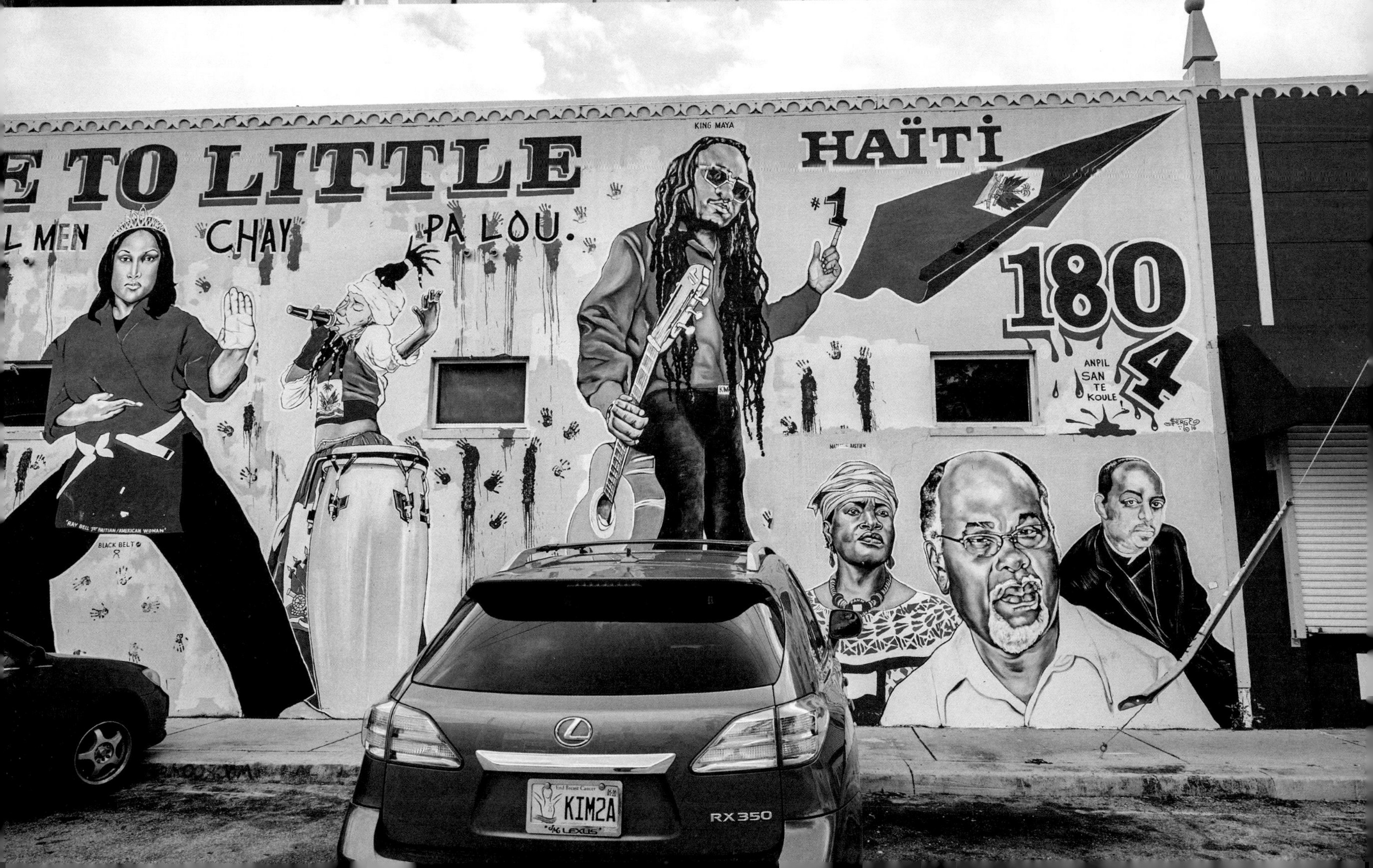

E TO LITTLE HAÏTI
CHAY PA LOU.
KING MAYA
#1
180 4
ANPIL SAN TE KOULE!

KIM2A
RX 350
LEXUS

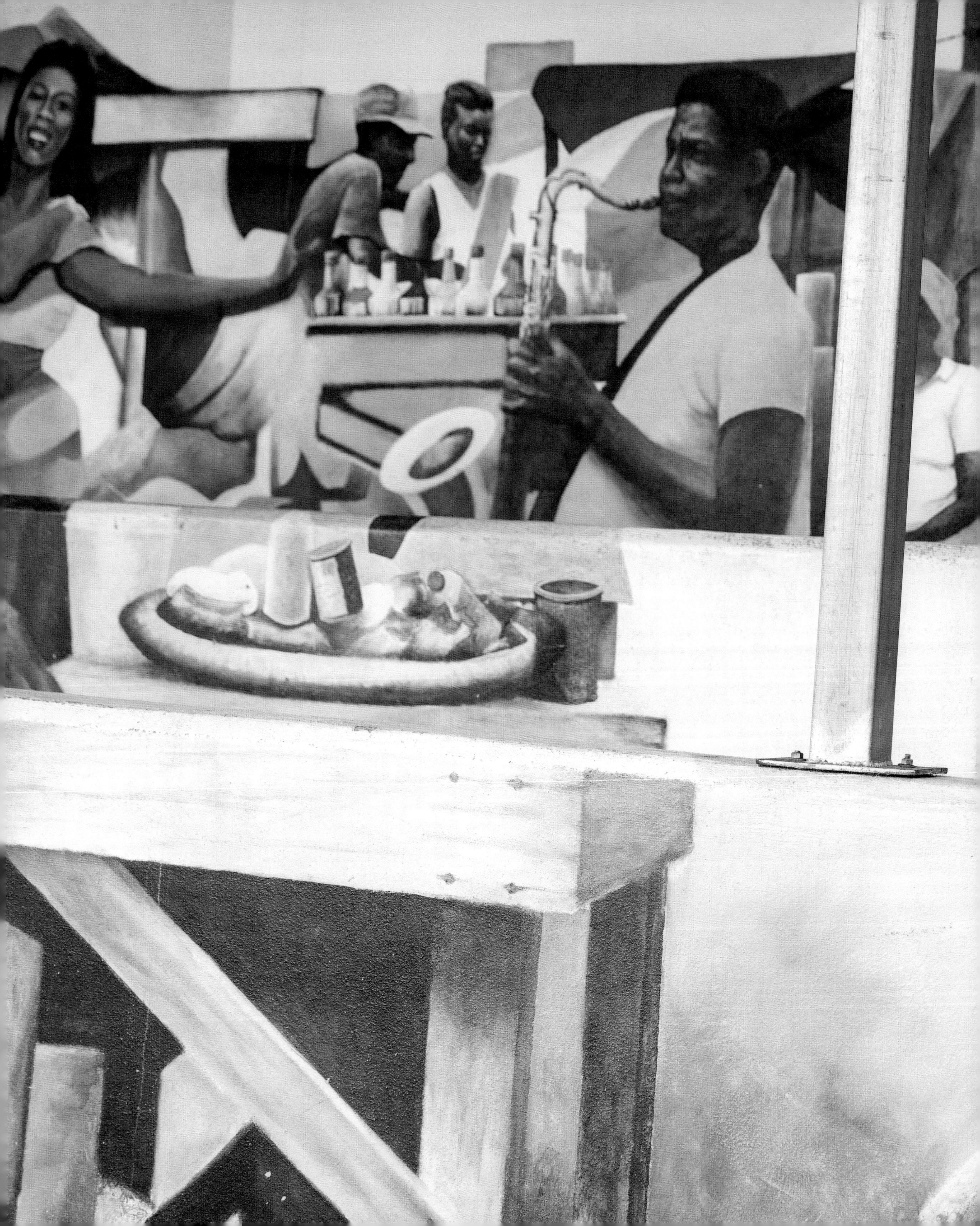

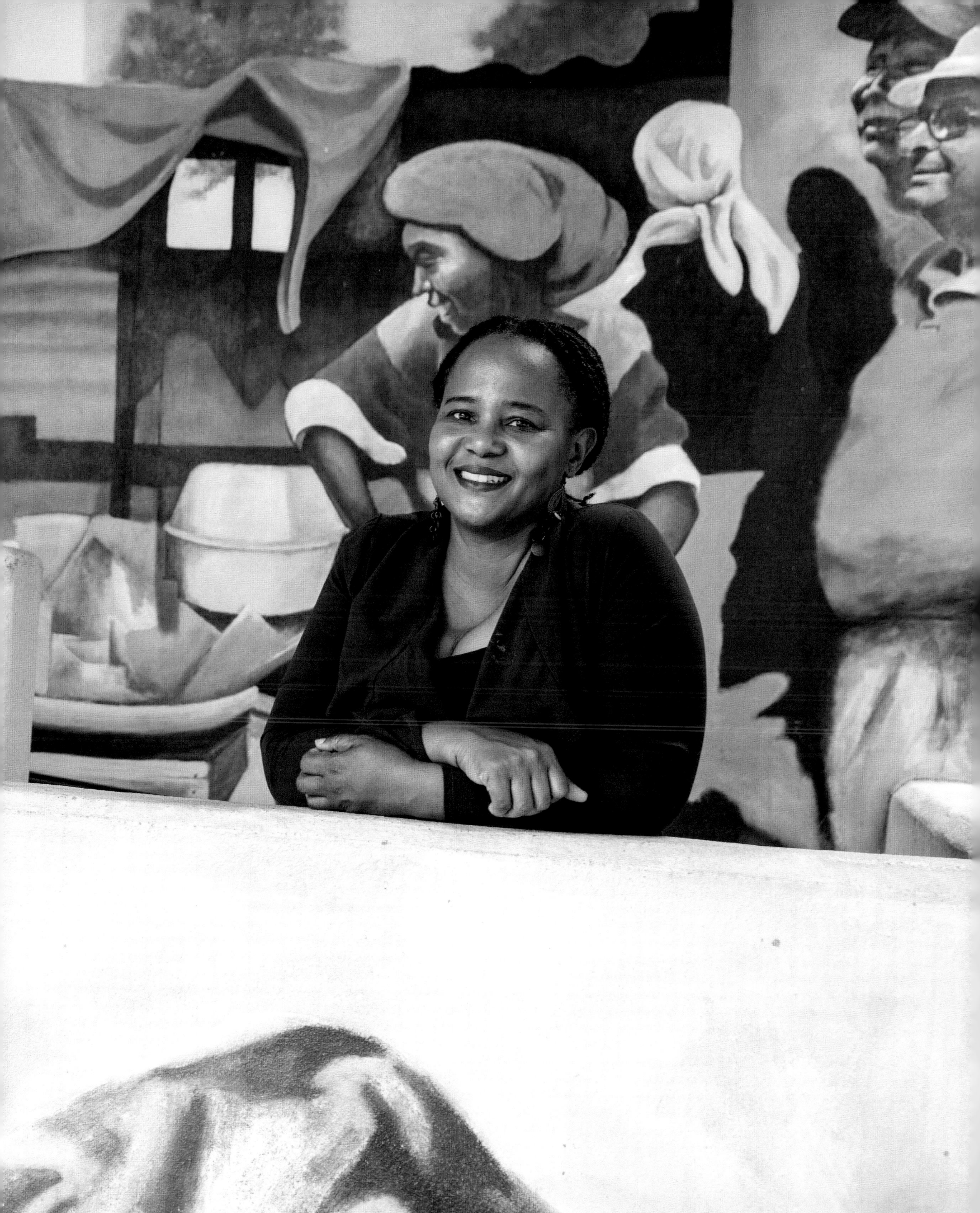

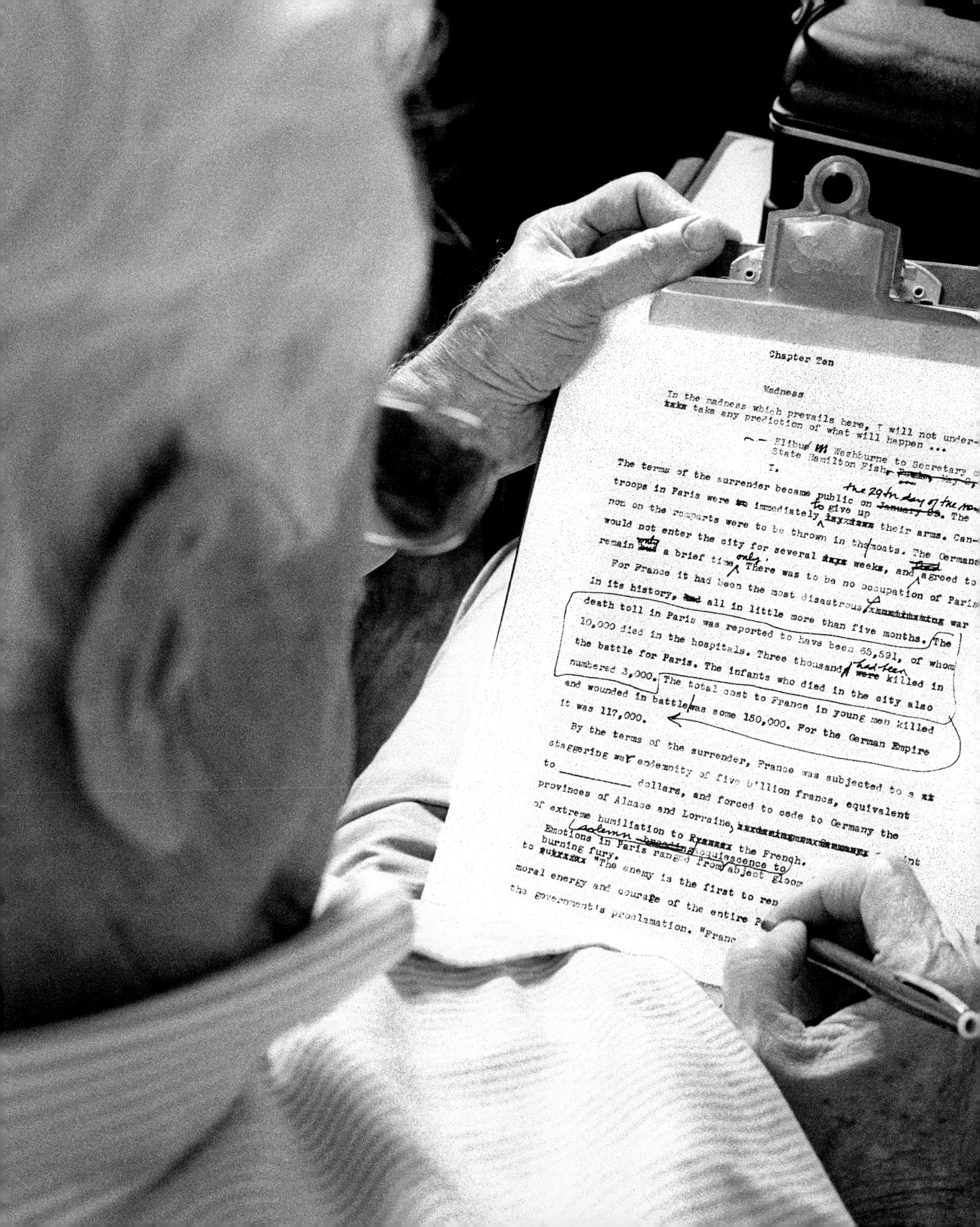

Chapter Ten

Madness

In the madness which prevails here, I will not under-
take take any prediction of what will happen ...
— Elihu M. Washburne to Secretary of
State Hamilton Fish,

I.
The terms of the surrender became public on the 29th day of the month. The
troops in Paris were immediately to give up their arms. Can-
non on the ramparts were to be thrown in the moats. The Germans
would not enter the city for several weeks, and agreed to
remain a brief time only. There was to be no occupation of Paris.
For France it had been the most disastrous war
in its history, and all in little more than five months. The
death toll in Paris was reported to have been 65,591, of whom
10,000 died in the hospitals. Three thousand had been were killed in
the battle for Paris. The infants who died in the city also
numbered 3,000. The total cost to France in young men killed
and wounded in battle was some 150,000. For the German Empire
it was 117,000.
By the terms of the surrender, France was subjected to a
staggering war indemnity of five billion francs, equivalent
to ____________ dollars, and forced to cede to Germany the
provinces of Alsace and Lorraine, the
of extreme humiliation to the French.
Emotions in Paris ranged from abject gloom solemn acquiescence to
burning fury. "The enemy is the first to
moral energy and courage of the entire Pa
the government's proclamation. "Franc

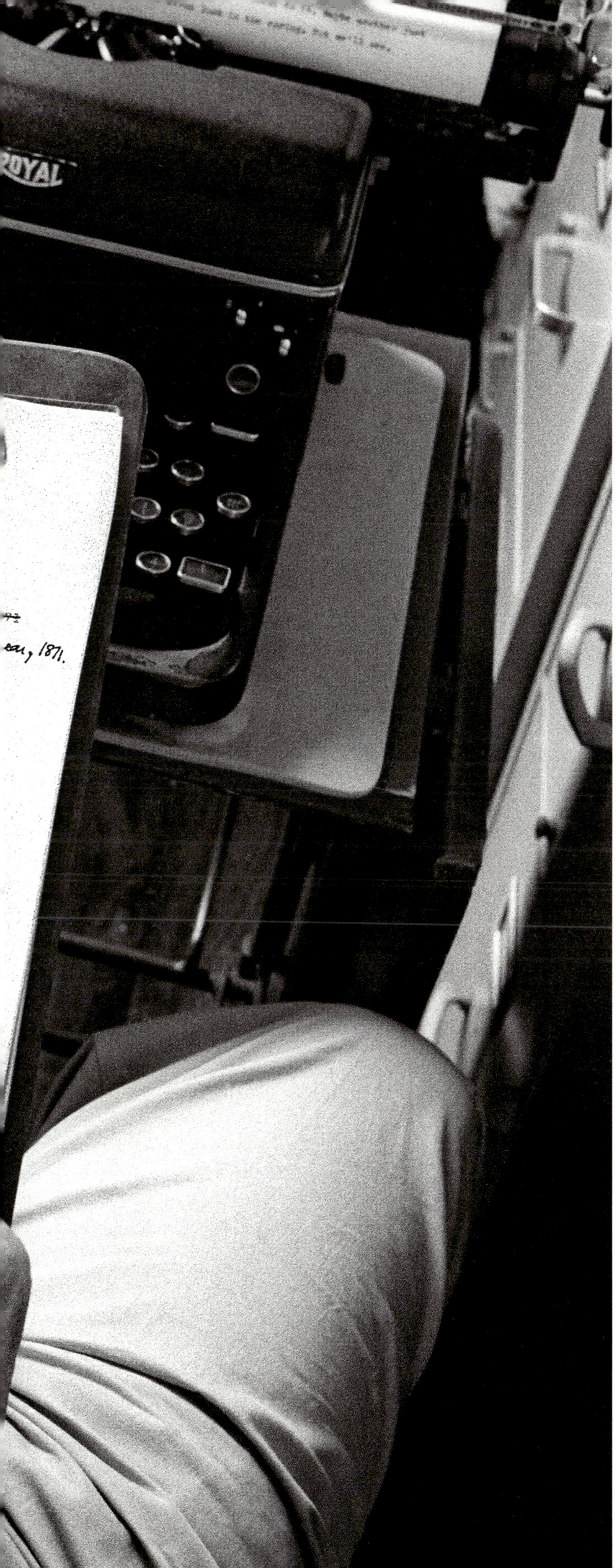

David McCullough

American (b. 1933)

Photographed in West Tisbury, Martha's Vineyard,
Massachusetts, July 2010

On this Royal typewriter, David McCullough wrote thirteen books, including two Pulitzer Prize winners and two National Book Award winners. He bought it secondhand in 1965. "It works perfectly every day," he said, "and always has. I like hitting the keys, changing the ribbon. I like working with my hands."

The freestanding building is only eight by twelve feet. McCullough has always called it his "office," although almost any New Englander would call it a shed. And one caretaker called it "The Book Shop." McCullough built the office in 1972, when he and his wife, Rosalee, moved full-time to Martha's Vineyard, an island off the coast of Massachusetts.

They bought one rectangular acre, with a house situated on the south end. The office was built on the north end as far away as possible from the house and the distractions of five children. The walk from the house, across the lawn and meadow to the office, took only a few minutes. None of the children were allowed past the stone wall separating the lawn from the meadow. There was no telephone and no computer.

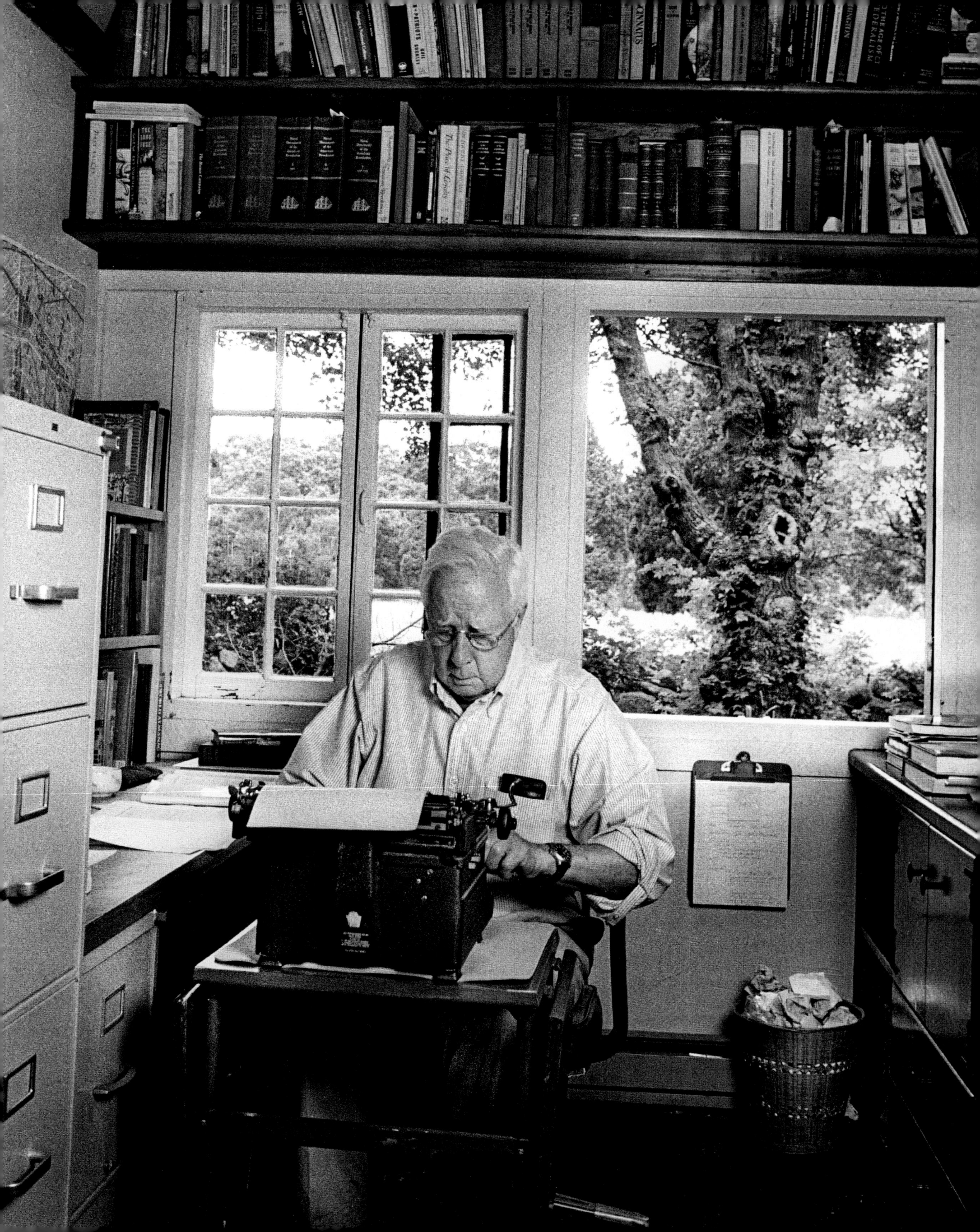

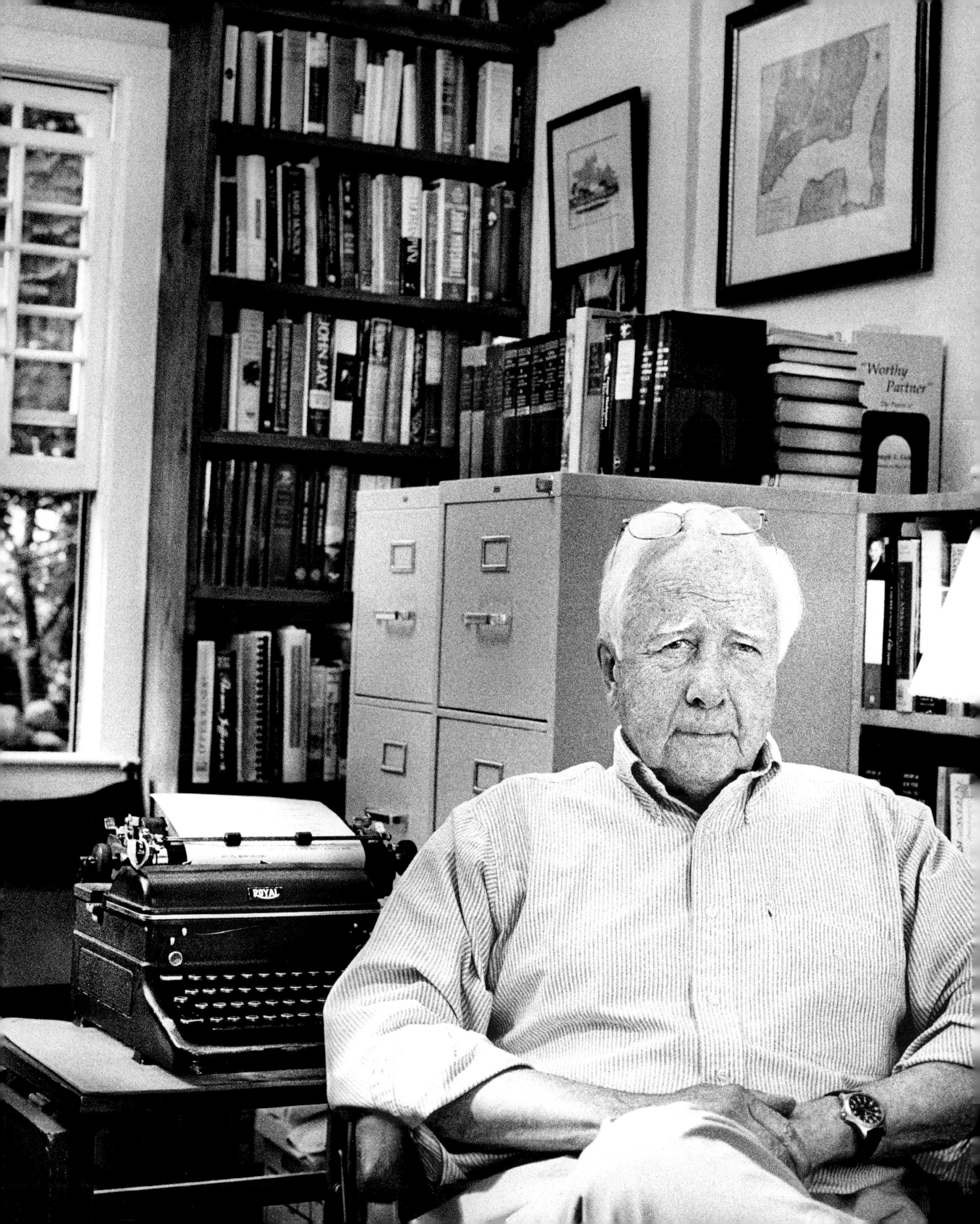

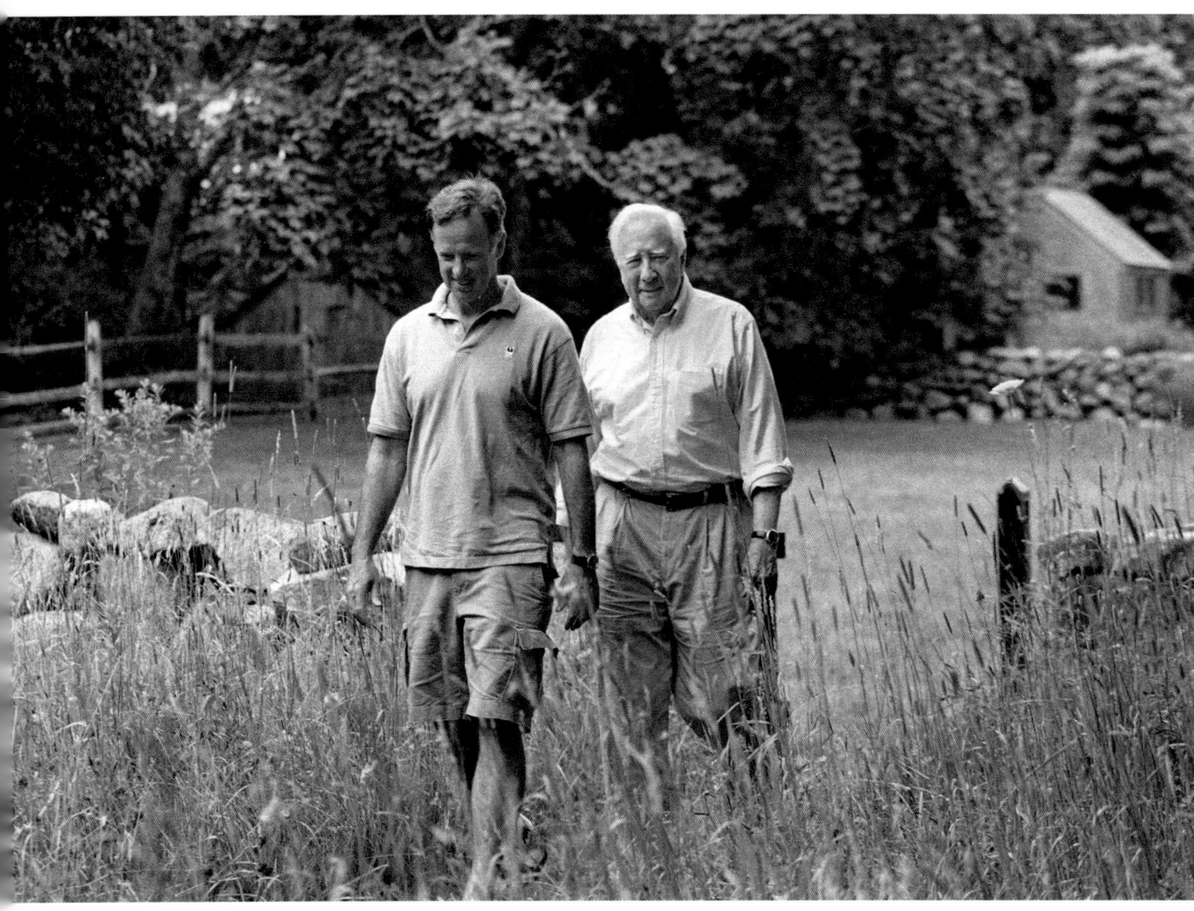

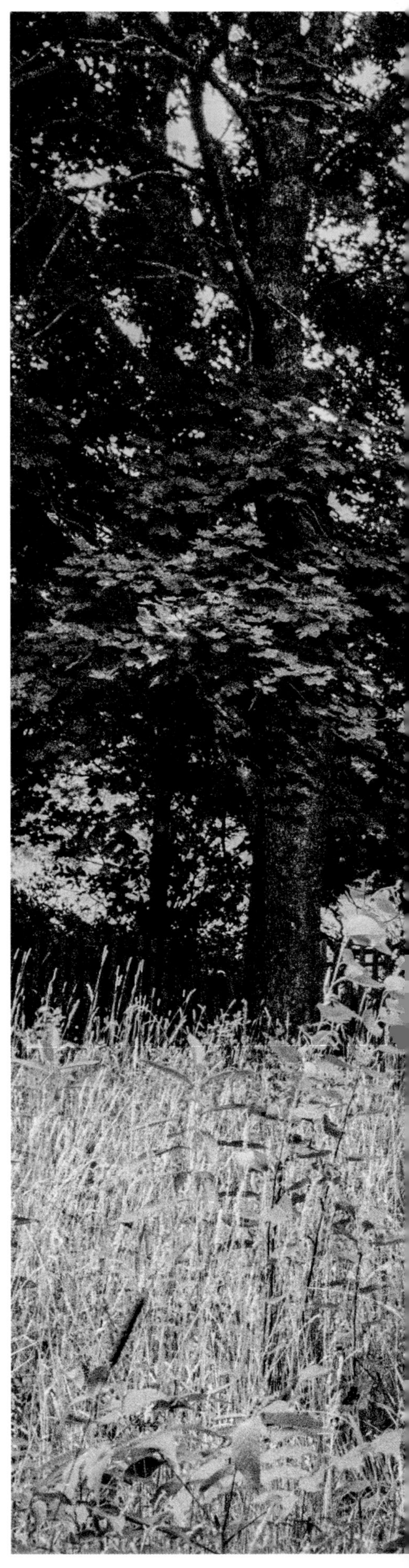

On mornings when their father hurried to "catch the train," the children steered clear. But later, for grandchildren, the rules loosened. A child shorter than the stone wall could go to the office anytime he or she pleased.

McCullough worked here winter and summer, but only books and files needed for the project at hand could fit inside. When writing, he faced south toward the house, when thinking he faced north to the meadow. The brief walk back and forth from the house was always a pleasure. He could feel the seasons, see the birds, and appreciate the shifts in weather.

ABOVE: David McCullough and his son, David McCullough Jr.

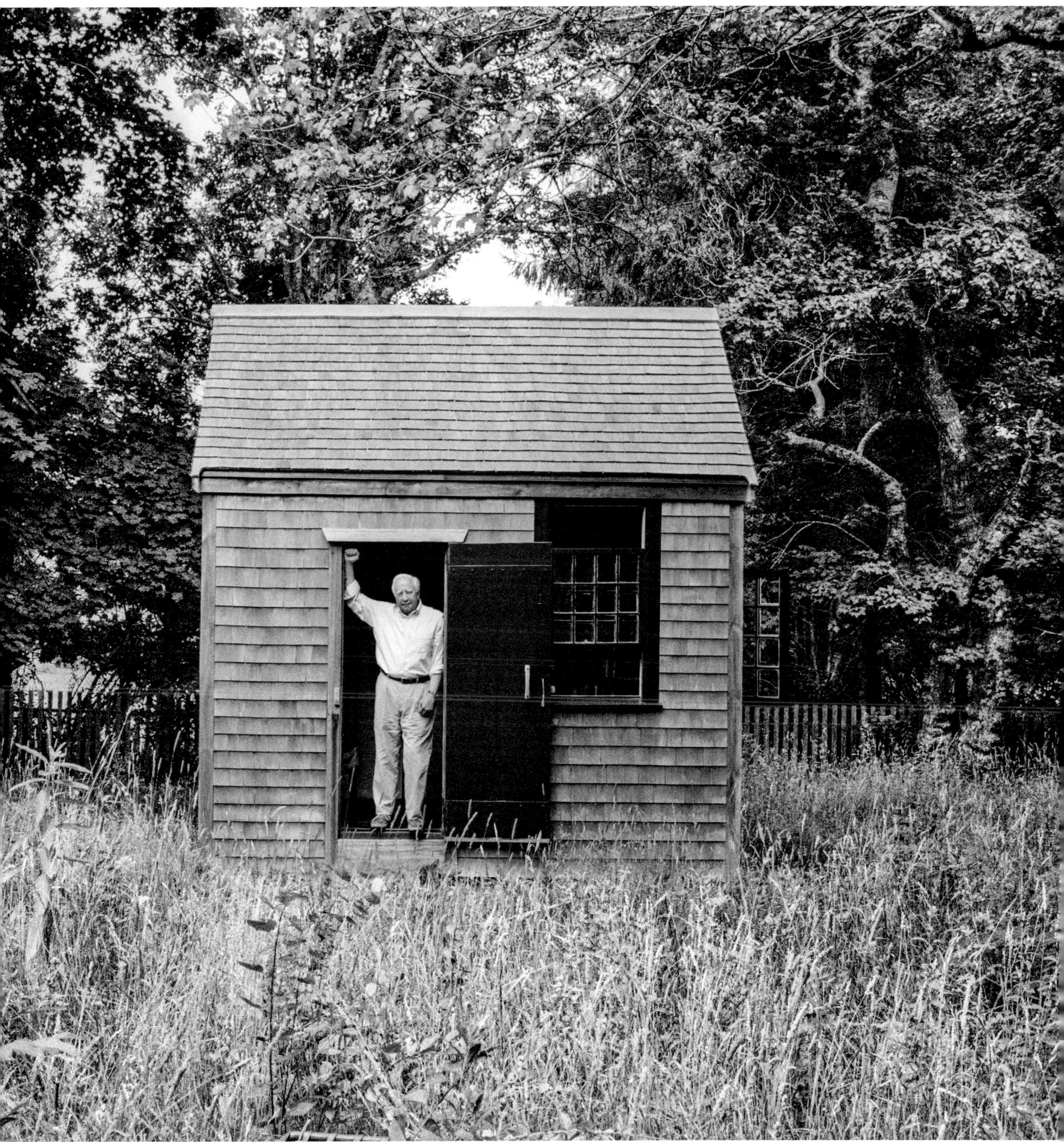

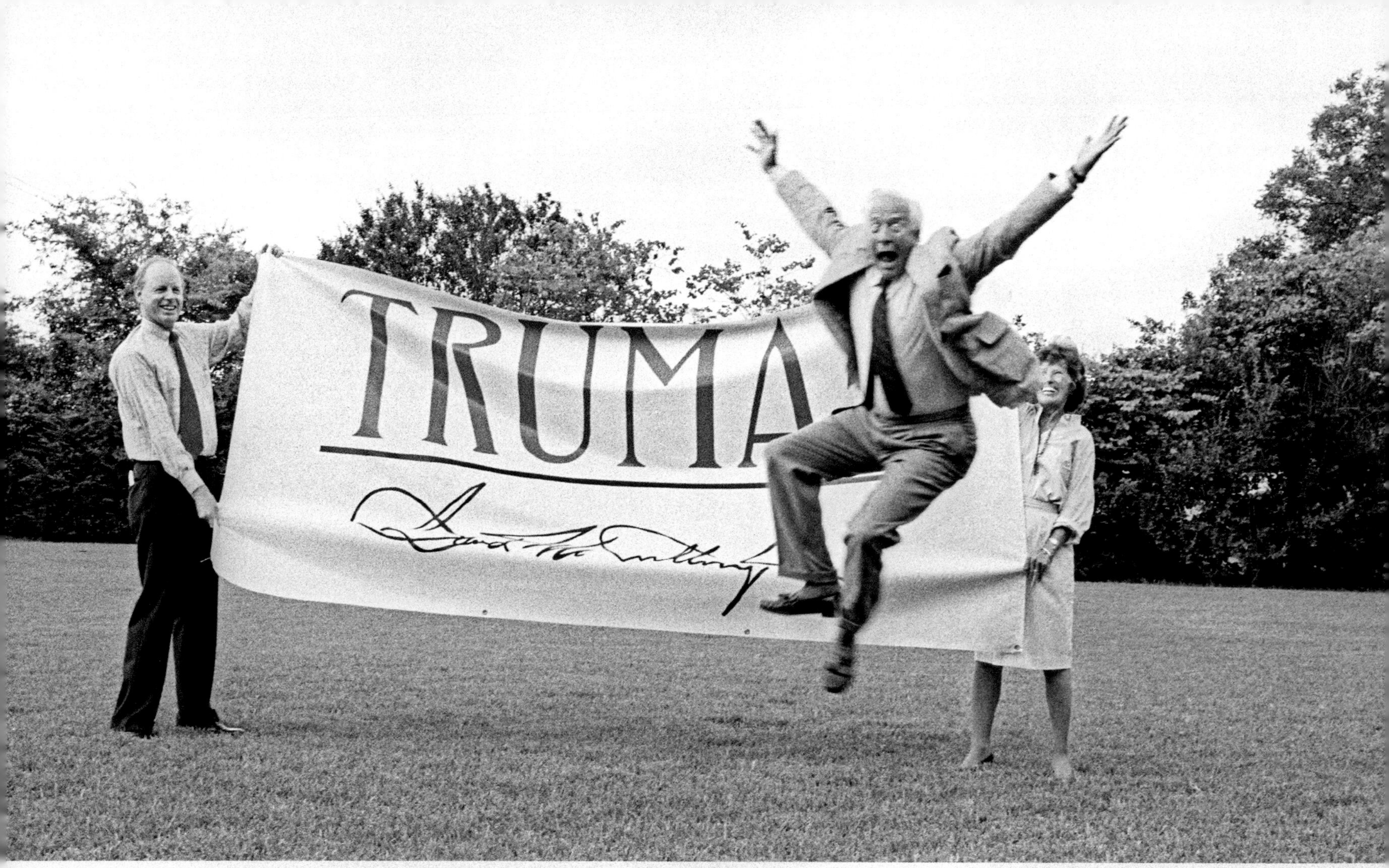

TRUMAN

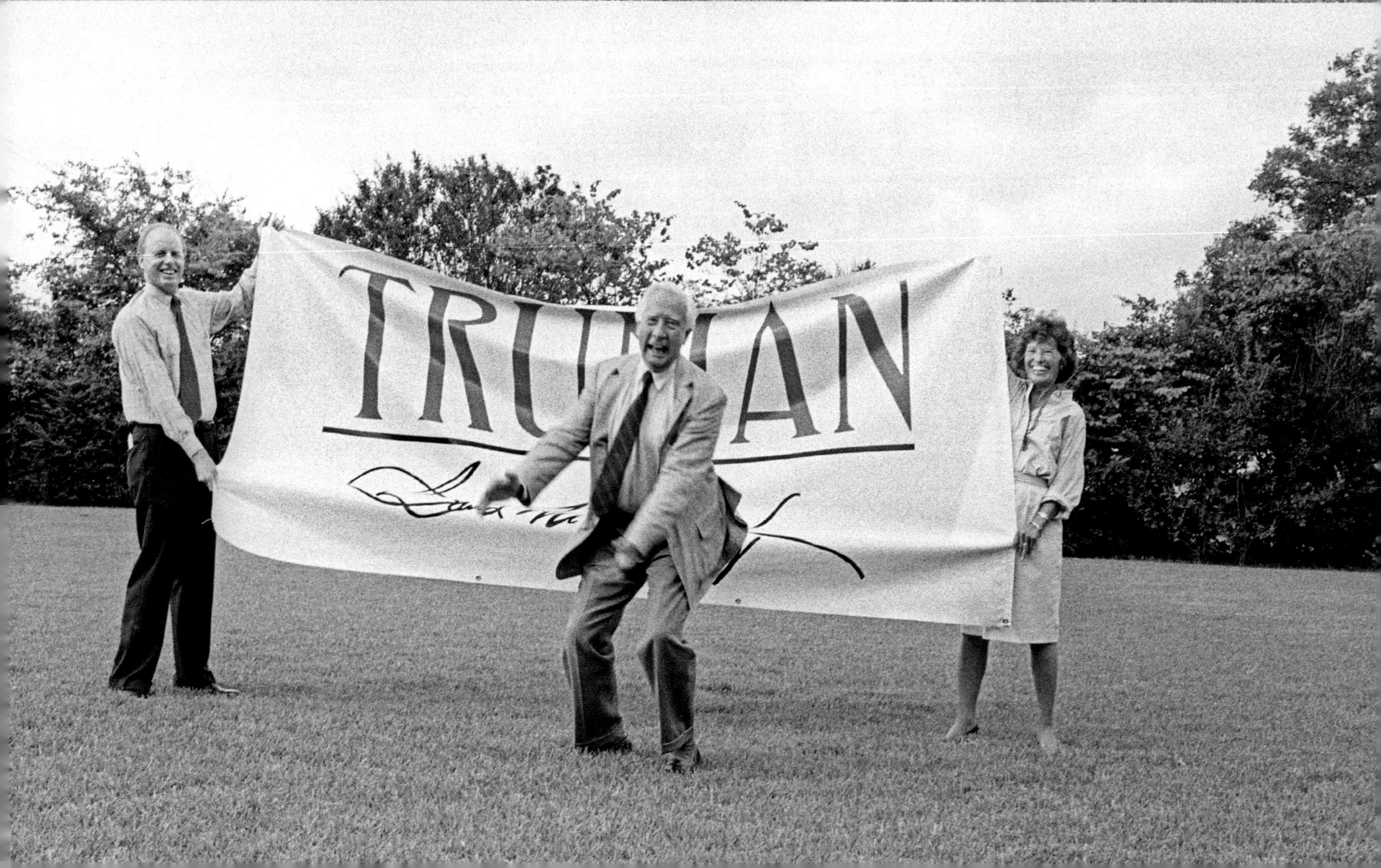

TRUMAN

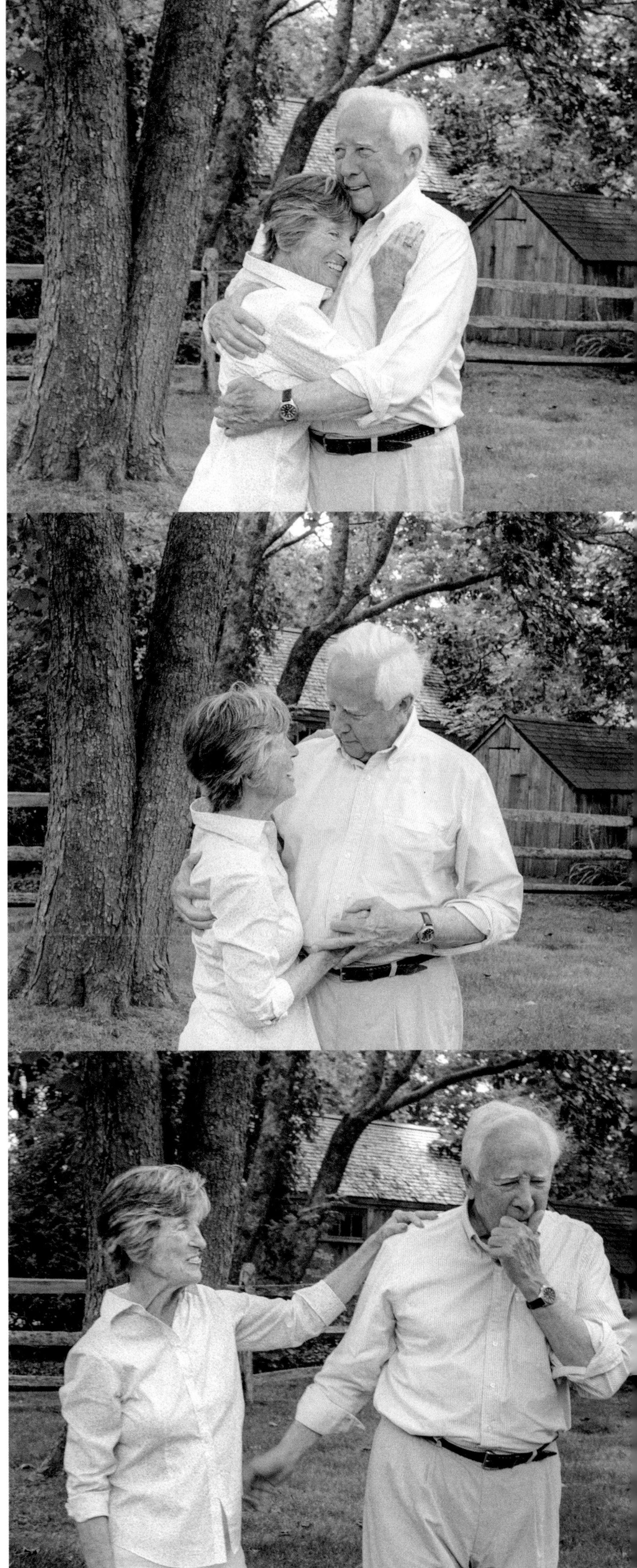

Of all the writers included in this book, David McCullough was the only person I knew. He and Rosalee were friends of my husband, Bob, and our family. When David's biography of Truman was published, we celebrated with a party at our house in Texas. Years later, back on the Vineyard, I photographed David and Rosalee as he set off for a televised interview. His disposition is not brooding or dark. He is optimistic and enthusiastic by nature, and fifty-eight years of a strong marriage have allowed him to flourish in his work.

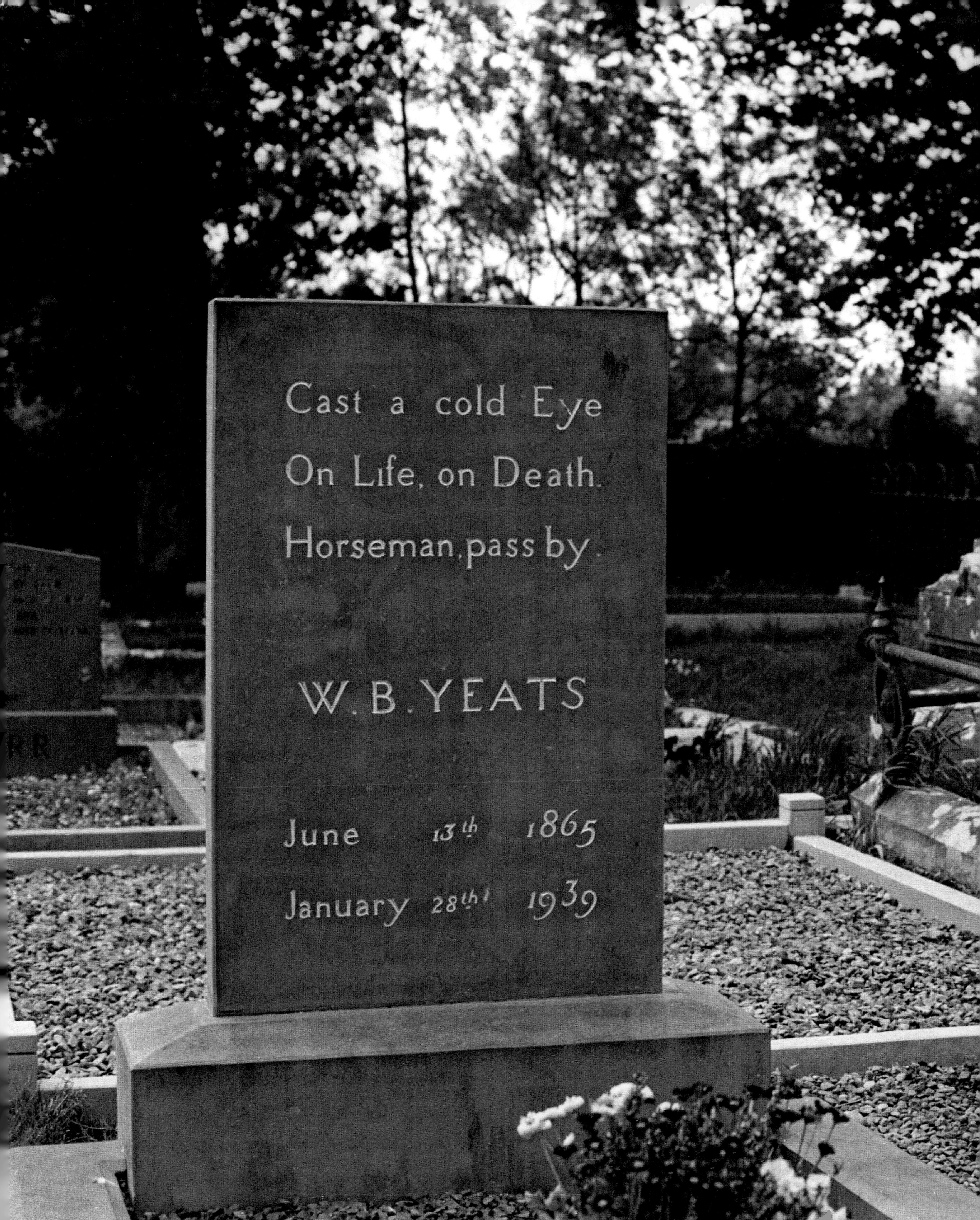

Cast a cold Eye
On Life, on Death.
Horseman, pass by.

W. B. YEATS

June   13th   1865
January   28th   1939

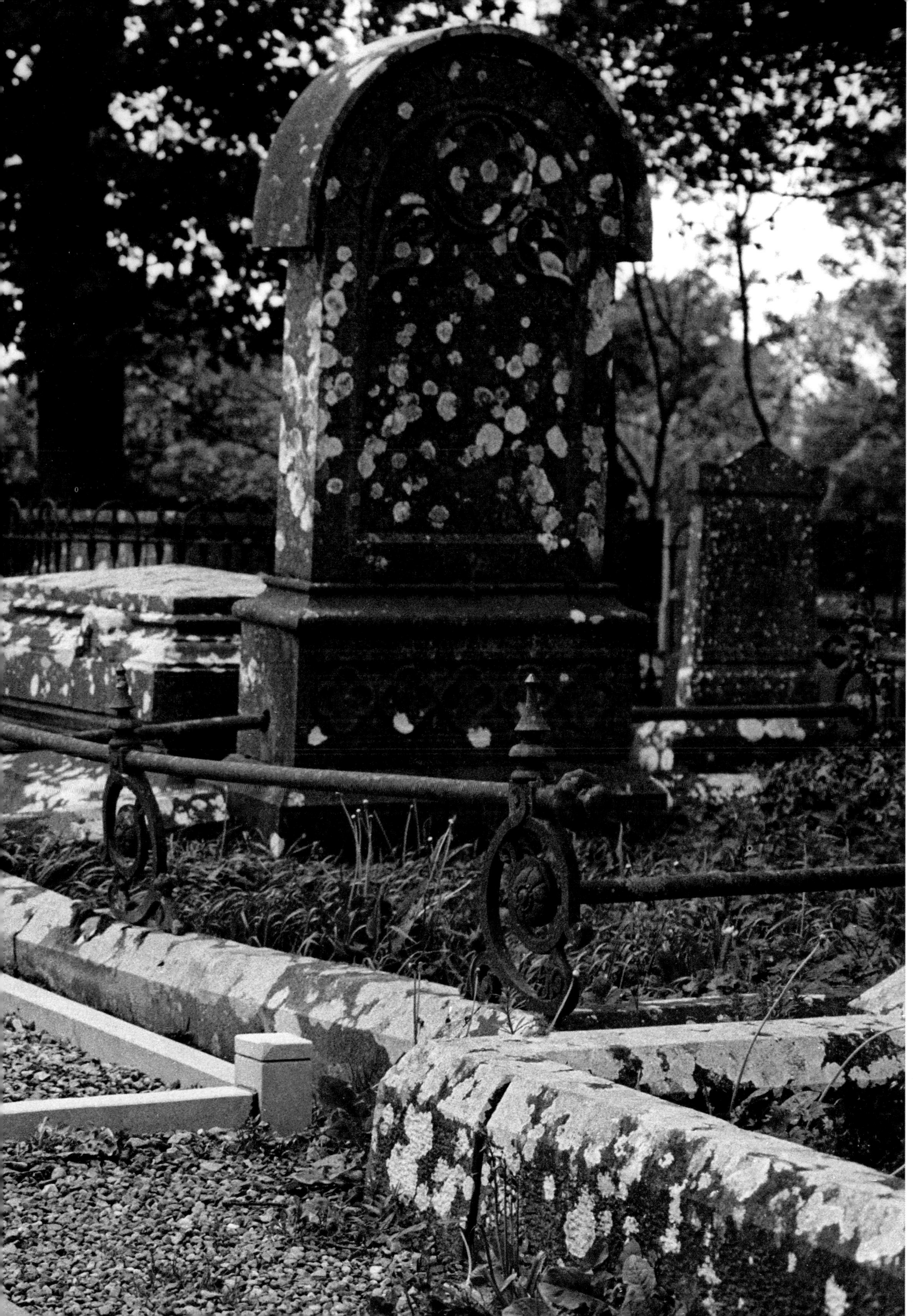

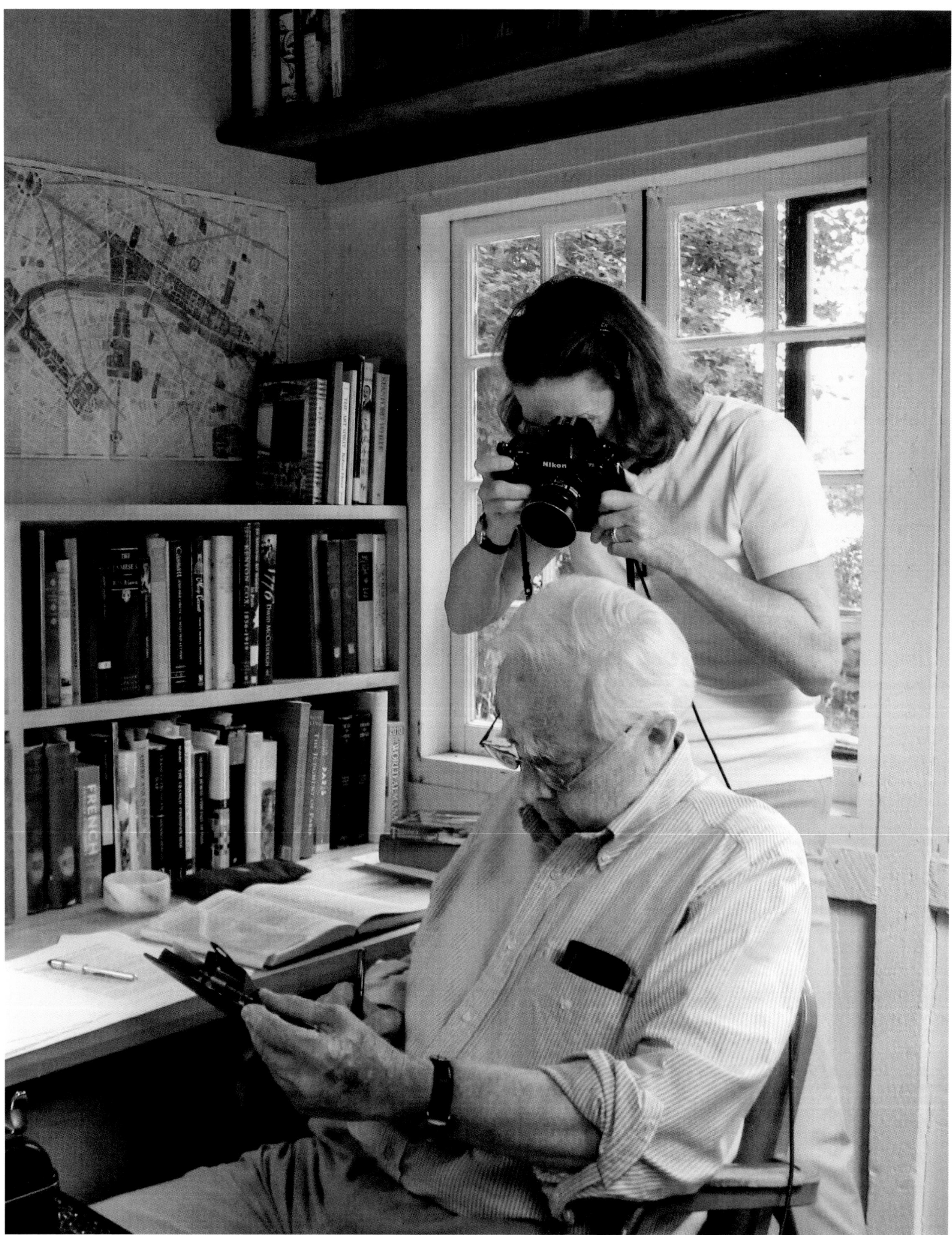

Epilogue

LAURA WILSON

In late fall of 2008, I met John Updike and liked him—and thought then I'd like to do a portrait of him. But I dithered around, and he died the following January before I had the chance. Earlier, I had seen some photographs taken by Dennis Stock of Updike in 1962 on the beach in Ipswich, Massachusetts. Updike, in street clothes, was at the edge of the waves, trying to get as close as possible without getting wet. The pictures were like stills from a home movie of a famous grown-up playing a children's game by the sea.

Updike's abrupt death prompted me to begin photographing writers in earnest. Over the course of twelve years, I was lucky enough to photograph some of the most influential writers of our time, women and men who will leave a lasting literary legacy.

We've all seen writers on the dust jackets of their books. These portraits, it seemed to me, generally failed to convey either character or personality. Writers deserve better. I wanted to make compelling pictures that would stick in the mind's eye. My own photographic style is informal, inspired by the classic photo-essays of Henri Cartier-Bresson and W. Eugene Smith in *Life* magazine in the 1940s and 1950s. So I set about taking candid shots, as well as more composed pictures.

I chose each person for the quality of their work. As often as not, I had never seen a particular writer before we met. But as I began to edit the film, I saw immediately that, no matter how each one appeared to me at first, when they came before the camera, they all appeared exceptional. Their faces were full of meaning.

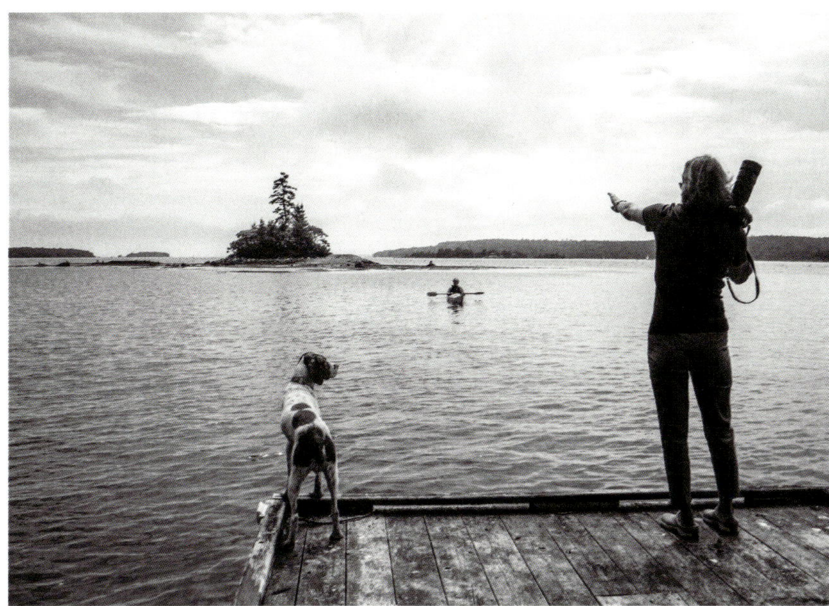

OPPOSITE: David McCullough, West Tisbury, Martha's Vineyard, Massachusetts, July 2010

RIGHT: Richard Ford, East Boothbay, Maine, July 2010

What is it that gives them such presence? How is it that writers, unlike any other group I've photographed, are so calmly centered, so seemingly free of anxiety? Don't most of us feel a certain level of discomfort when being photographed? But these writers seemed able to part the curtain of self-doubt. They were all highly accomplished and well aware of their reputations. Of course, having a portrait made takes little of the toll of writing. But what made these writers unusual, I believe, was their ability to go beyond the "picture face" that most of us present to the camera, to dig into themselves to reveal something of the human predicament. Tom Stoppard gave me fifteen minutes on a London sidewalk, when usually I would have had hours or days. We spent eight of those minutes searching for a quiet location in Covent Garden that would be suitable for the portrait. Once we found the spot, Stoppard looked directly into my camera, and in less than a minute, I knew I

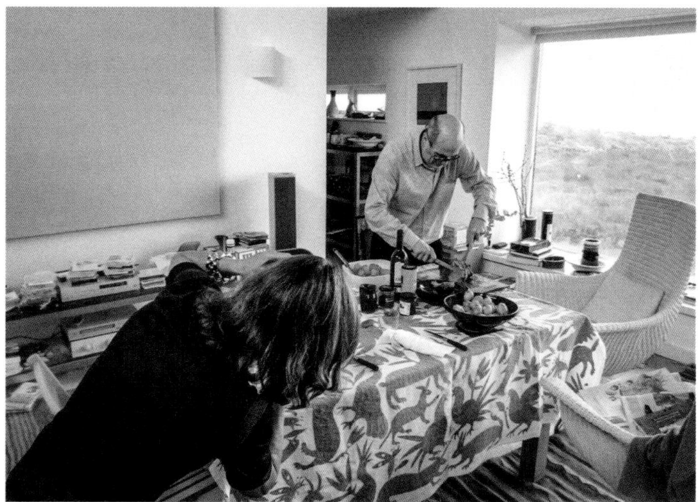

had the picture. The playwright had given me a gift—a look filled with emotion, heartbreaking and wonderful.

I made a portrait of each writer, then added photographic reportage to show where each person lived or worked or gathered with friends. Their private territories were full of objects and details that reflected their daily lives, those things that inspire and comfort them. By showing a combination of portraits and snapshots, I hoped to create a fresh series of pictures for each writer and provide insight into their singular personalities.

All the writers lived in interesting houses; some were uncommon, others were splendid, none were mundane. Their houses were in cities, in the countryside, by the sea, and even in remote borderlands. Not one of the writers seemed to have simply landed in a place by accident. Their locations were as specific as their writing styles. Upon visiting many of them at home, I found each to be visual in the extreme. And I was never disappointed, finding invariably a person of wide-ranging curiosity whose surroundings reflected a perceptive eye.

To give my subjects an idea of what I needed, I showed them a selection of photographs I'd taken of other writers for the book. Each of them seemed to enjoy looking at the pictures of the others, moving slowly through the entire batch. Holding one photo, Peter Carey noticed a tiny figure of Colm Tóibín, walking by the Irish Sea, barely recognizable in the far distance. "Oh, is that Colm?" Peter asked. Then, the next picture: Colm up close, sitting in a chair with his arms on top of his head, looking directly into the camera. "Ah, yes, you got it! Colm has such a good face."

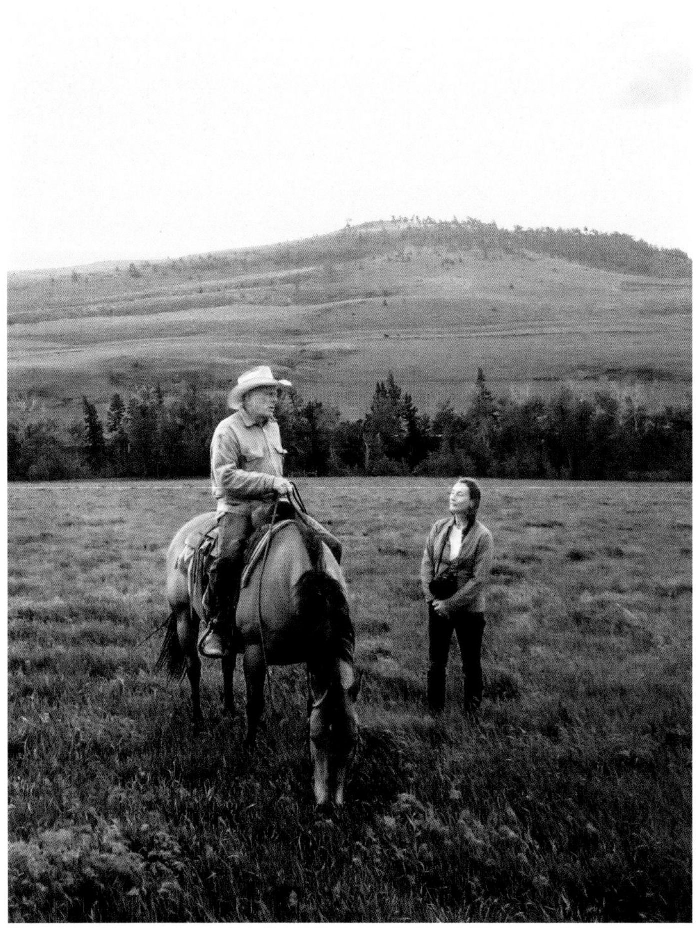

ABOVE: Thomas McGuane, McLeod, Montana, June 2011

TOP: Colm Tóibín, Cush Gap, County Wexford, Ireland, May 2011

OPPOSITE: Gabriel García Márquez, Mexico City, Mexico, April 2012

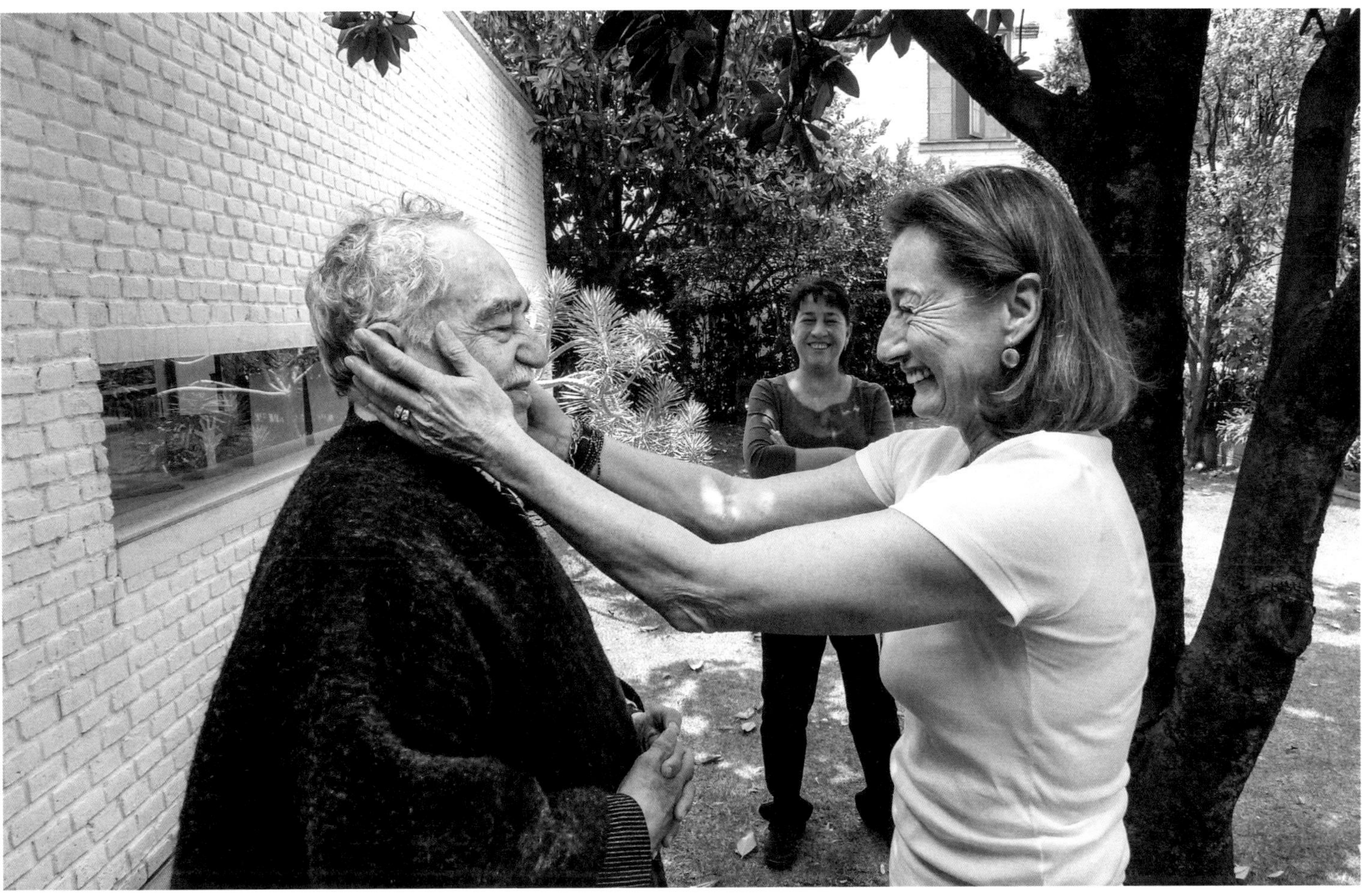

Sam Shepard asked, "May I keep this print?" when he looked at the photograph of Thomas McGuane on horseback. "He was really good to let me fish on his ranch."

Gabriel García Márquez looked through all the photographs without a word, finally holding up one of August Kleinzahler dancing a little jig down the aisle of Amoeba Music in San Francisco. With a quick shake of his hand, he let me know this particular shot surprised and amused him.

Carlos Fuentes said that throughout history people had been faceless until photography was invented. He used the word *revolution*. People had a face for the first time, an identity. As I watched the writers' reactions as they looked through my photographs, I sensed they felt as I do about photography—it's magic. Tim O'Brien even practices magic, entertaining his two sons with a magician's skill. O'Brien said that, for him, writing is another form of magic—invention, transformation, sleight of hand, all taking reality to another level—just like a photograph.

The rainy morning when I photographed Jim Crace on Mount Bonnell, seven hundred feet above the Colorado River in Austin, he was reciting to himself lines from a Philip Larkin poem about photography and memory and lacerations of the heart. Larkin wrote that "the impulse to preserve lies at the bottom of all art."

The writer takes up his pen, the artist his brush, the photographer his camera, each intent on halting the passage of time, the disappearance of memory. Pablo Picasso caught the brutality of the Spanish Civil War forever when he painted *Guernica*, just as Robert Capa, with his grainy, blurred images of the Invasion of Normandy, recorded for all time the pitiless slaughter of men at war.

For me, photography has always been a way to stave off loss . . . loss of family, loss of place, even loss of memory. We know life is finite. "Death is the great Maecenas," Carlos Fuentes said, "the great angel of writing." To work to record, to preserve what we saw and heard and felt, is the strongest impulse of the creative mind, a defiant gesture against time. The true artist is driven to take pictures, or arrange words, or draw lines. So much of life, of creativity, comes from the desire for permanence.

Acknowledgments

When Yale University Press became interested in my book, Amy Canonico became my editor. We have never met in person, but over two years by phone and email, her inspiration, good judgment, and sensitivity aided the development of this book. I am enormously grateful to Amy for her unwavering support.

Gregory Wakabayashi and I have worked together for twenty years. Greg has designed four books for me and redesigned two editions of my first book. He is a superb ally, as attentive to language as he is to photography. I rely on him now more than ever.

My gratitude to Charles McGrath has no limits. His positive response to my first photographs of writers reinforced my desire to move forward with a book. Throughout twelve years, he continued to advise me and share his contacts. In the end, his editorial contributions strengthened my text and helped bring the book to completion.

I am particularly indebted to Deb Garrison, who enthusiastically agreed to help expand this project by reaching out to writers she admired. As a poet herself, with many years of experience editing fiction and nonfiction, she suggested writers who added variety and strength to this book.

Amanda Urban kindly spoke on my behalf to one of the world's most important writers, which gave me the opportunity to photograph him and thereby improve this book.

Day after day, year after year, for seventeen years, Gail Bruno has assisted superbly and tirelessly in all aspects of my photographic work. She has carefully scanned, digitally organized, and then printed all the photographs for this book.

Matt Lankes, a gifted photographer, assisted at the beginning of this project. He helped when we photographed Jim Crace in the pouring rain in Austin, then continued in Mexico City and along the New England coast.

Andrew Mitchell, a top-notch photographic assistant, has cared about the quality and variety of these photographs as much as I have. He pays attention to every detail, never loses his focus—or patience—and worked on most sessions with the writers included here.

Lilly Albritton is my studio manager. She has contributed in essential ways to completing *Writers*, all the while tending to the responsibilities of an active studio.

From my first book in 1989, Ruedi Hofmann has offered continuous guidance and technical expertise. Our friendship over many years has reinforced my admiration for Ruedi, as well as for his creative approach to photography.

Donna Wilhelm and Greg Morse each supported the production costs of this book with large contributions, which allowed Yale to publish a book of the highest quality.

Kay and Elliot Cattarulla, lifelong supporters of good books, helped as well with publication costs.

I wish to thank Mike Ritchey, who made thoughtful edits to my early text, and Alison Hagge, who edited the final draft. I also thank Kate Zanzucchi, who oversaw the edits at Yale.

Sarah McGrath, Lyn Mattoon, Carolyn Bess, Carrie Kania, and Heather Brand each enthusiastically helped from her own special vantage point when I needed aid the most.

Stephen Enniss, Director of the Harry Ransom Center, right from the start showed me he cared deeply about this project and continued to keep it on course. The Ransom Center's exhibition team of director Cathy Henderson, Rob Hay, Wyndell Faulk, and Tom Sebulsky have carefully put forth a memorable installation for the benefit of a wide-ranging audience.

Scot Dykema and I married in the spring of 2020. His kindness and good judgment were a source of strength as I worked to complete this book.

And lastly, I am deeply grateful to my son Luke Wilson, who loves to read. Over twelve years he has followed the project with interest, often providing insights into writers' personalities and varied interests.

And to Andrew Wilson, my oldest son, who understands the challenges facing creative people and who wholeheartedly confirms their efforts in the most critical ways.

To my son Owen, to whom this book is dedicated, I owe the most by far. He supported, without question, the pursuit of all these writers on different continents over many years.

—Laura Wilson

yalebooks.com/art

Designed by Gregory Wakabayashi
Set in Bureau Grotesque and Minion
Printed in Italy by Graphicom S.p.A.

Library of Congress Control Number: 2022935143
ISBN 978-0-300-25778-6

A catalogue record for this book is available from the British Library.

The paper in this book meets the requirements of ANSI/NISO Z39.48-1992 (Permanence of Paper).

10 9 8 7 6 5 4 3 2 1

Photographs on pages 258–61 of Laura Wilson at work by Matt Lankes

Jacket illustrations: (front) Zadie Smith, New York, New York, November 2013; (back, from top, left to right) Thomas McGuane with his wife, Laurie Buffett, McLeod, Montana, June 2011; Louise Erdrich, Minneapolis, Minnesota, May 2018; Margaret Atwood, Toronto, Canada, April 2018; Seamus Heaney with his wife, Marie, Dublin, Ireland, May 2011; Gabriel García Márquez, Mexico City, Mexico, April 2012; Colm Tóibín, Cush Gap, County Wexford, Ireland, May 2011; Brit Bennett with her father, Duane, San Diego, California, December 2020